PORTRAIT OF A RACIST

PORTRAIT OF A RACIST

Byron De La Beckwith and the Assassination of Medgar Evers

WITH A NEW AFTERWORD

Reed Massengill

The University of Tennessee Press / Knoxville

Originally published in 1994 by St. Martin's Press under the title *Portrait of a Racist: The Man Who Killed Medgar Evers?*

Unless otherwise noted, the photographs are courtesy of the Betsey B. Creekmore Special Collections and University Archives, University of Tennessee, Knoxville.

Library of Congress Cataloging-in-Publication Data

Massengill, Reed.

Portrait of a racist : the real life of Byron De La Beckwith / Reed Massengill—1st ed. Portrait of a racist: Byron De La Beckwith and the assassination of Medgar Evers. With a new afterword / Reed Massengill—2024 ed.

p. cm.

ISBN 9781621908302 (paperback)
ISBN 9781621908555 (pdf)
ISBN 9781621908562 (kindle edition)

1. Evers, Medgar Wiley, 1925–1963—Assassination. 2. Beckwith, Byron de la. I. Title.
F349.J13M37 1993
364.1'524'092—dc20 93-7435
CIP

For Willie

The armour of falsehood is subtly wrought out of darkness,
and hides a man not only from others,
but from his own soul.

—E.M. Forster

Contents

Prologue

Portrait of a Racist

I distinctly remember the first time I asked who Byron De La Beckwith was. My ailing grandmother kept a family Bible in her bedside table, and she often allowed me to pull it out and sit on the floor by her bed and flip through it. At the age of eight or nine, I was as interested in the colorful pictures as I was in the scriptures or their meanings. What fascinated me most was the center section, listing the births and deaths and marriages of my grandmother's nine children, among whom my mother was the youngest. It was there, in the family Bible, that I first saw Beckwith's elegant name written in longhand. When I asked about him, my grandmother explained tersely—in a tone of voice I knew all too well—"He was your Aunt Mary's husband." I knew there would be no further discussion about him. Coming from a close-knit family in which aunts and uncles were numerous and affectionate, I was curious about this uncle that no one talked about. Several years later, I discovered why.

When my grandmother died in April of 1973—just a few months before my twelfth birthday—I asked my mother if I could have some clippings about Beckwith that were among my grandmother's papers. The ragged-edged newspaper cuttings, yellowed with age, were destined for the trash, along with a drawer full of old greeting cards and letters. With my allowance money, I later bought a small packet of file folders at Kent Drug Store, one of the few businesses within bike-riding distance of our house. I saved the Beckwith articles, taping them onto sheets of typing paper and placing them in a folder. On the outside, in the handwriting of a child attempting to write like an adult, I scrawled, "Byron De La Beckwith File." I liked writing his name. Its rich sound, its unusual fourth capital letter, and its inherent secrecy made me feel like a character in one of the Hardy Boys mysteries I loved to read.

Several months later, in September 1973, Beckwith was arrested while carrying a live bomb into Louisiana. For the first time, I clipped the articles from *The Knoxville News-Sentinel* myself. I was fascinated by this man, his mysterious relationship with my Aunt Mary, and his apparent estrangement from my family. Eighteen years later, on January 30, 1991, I carried that battered file folder full of yellowed clippings with me when I went to visit my former uncle, Byron De La Beckwith, in jail.

One month earlier, late on the afternoon of December 17, 1990, the Chattanooga police had arrived at Beckwith's modest home on nearby Signal Mountain with a warrant for his arrest. A Mississippi grand jury had indicted him on a charge of murder three days before. "Glad to see you boys," Beckwith said when he greeted the officers at his door, then asked if they wanted to check his pockets for bombs. He was not handcuffed, and rode quietly with them to the Hamilton County Jail in downtown Chattanooga. It was a cool evening, just a week before Christmas, and many of the homes along the circuitous route down Signal Mountain were decorated with colorful outdoor lights and inexpensive front-yard crèches for the holiday. Beckwith's neighbors on virtually all-white Signal Mountain were stunned when they picked up their newspapers the next day and read of his arrest. "The niggers," Beckwith reckoned, "have run out of something to do."[1] For the third time in nearly thirty years, Byron De La Beckwith was faced with the prospect of standing trial in Mississippi for the sniper slaying of civil rights leader Medgar Evers.

Before the assassinations of John F. Kennedy, Malcolm X, Dr. Martin Luther King, Jr., and Robert F. Kennedy numbed the nation, Medgar Evers's name was already etched in the public consciousness. Although many blacks had been lynched and shot in the rural South, Evers was the first prominent civil rights leader who was assassinated in a manner that was to become all too familiar during the 1960s. After struggling for nearly ten years in his native Mississippi as field secretary of the National Association for the Advancement of Colored People (NAACP)—spearheading voter registration drives, economic boycotts and sit-ins—Evers's funeral at Arlington National Cemetery commanded the cover of *LIFE* magazine. In the most oppressive state in the segregated South in the early 1960s, Evers was the natural target of the state's white supremacists. Just after midnight on June 12, 1963, returning home late from a rally at New Jerusalem Baptist Church in Jackson and a meeting with the NAACP's lawyer, Evers was shot in the back as he got out of his car. His crisp, white cotton shirt was pierced by a single bullet.

At that time, all the physical evidence uncovered during the murder investigation pointed to Byron De La Beckwith. He was tried twice in 1964, but two separate all-white, all-male juries deadlocked. During those trials, Beckwith faced the gas chamber if found guilty of murder. Although the death penalty has long since been abolished in Mississippi and the case against him was formally dropped in 1969, there is no statute of limitations on murder. Beckwith's arrest at his home on Signal Mountain was the culmination of a fourteen-month investigation during which new evidence in the murder case was uncovered after more than a quarter century of dormancy. Again, the evidence pointed to Beckwith as the probable assassin.

In more recent years, Beckwith had lived on Signal Mountain at the home of his second wife, Thelma Lindsay Neff, a sweet-faced, grandmotherly woman. He was sixty-two and she was seventy-four when they married in 1983, but they seemed well-suited. Thelma Beckwith, a retired nurse, was active in local politics and had many lifelong friends in the Chattanooga area, where she grew up and had at one time been a Miss Chattanooga contestant. White supremacist friends visiting the couple, and even reporters who frequently came calling, were given Beckwith's stock view of his new life there—"heaven on earth," he would say. Admittedly, a Jew or a black might move to Signal Mountain occasionally, but their houses would burn down and they'd move away. "Niggers are careless with their cigarettes," Beckwith was fond of explaining with a chuckle.[2]

A salesman of one sort or another all his life—tobacco, candy, liquid fertilizer, farm equipment, oil filters, wood stoves—Beckwith retired to Signal Mountain after his marriage in 1983 and immersed himself in his work with racist organizations. He ministered to the Ku Klux Klan and other hate groups, which held him in high esteem as a white hero, and he and his wife traveled to rallies held by the Klan and other organizations in neighboring states, often camping in a deluxe tent they bought to save on escalating motel bills. His new wife's home, although modest, was a haven for Beckwith. Prior to their marriage, his most recent home had been a ramshackle, unfurnished "retreat" in the sticks of Carroll County, Mississippi, where he had no electricity, no sewage system, no running water and no phone. It also had, he gleefully noted, "no niggers, no Jews and no sissies."[3] There, he had been intent on establishing a militant Christian camp, a hybrid Christian-survivalist retreat where visitors could learn the "truth" about Jews and blacks and enjoy firearms practice sessions at the same time. He named it the Rod of Iron Christian Mission, and his goal, he said in an open letter addressed "To White Christians All," was to fight, "to the death if necessary, our mutual and numerous satanic enemies."

Beckwith's only other recent residence of note had been the Louisiana State Penitentiary at Angola, where he had served nearly three years in solitary confinement for bringing a live bomb into the state without a permit. Tipped off by an FBI informant that Beckwith would be entering their parish with a bomb, allegedly targeting the home of a local B'nai B'rith leader, the New Orleans police had been given a description of his car. When Beckwith's blue 1968 Oldsmobile sedan approached them on the stretch of highway he was said to be traveling, they cautiously pulled him over.

Wearing a .45 caliber pistol in the waistband of his pants, Beckwith stepped from his car and approached the officers, who held a shotgun on him while he was frisked. His car, bearing stolen license plates, contained a hunting knife, a hatchet, a map showing the route to the Jewish leader's home, several rifles and rifle parts, a wide assortment of ammunition, and—in a black-painted plywood box sitting on the passenger-side floorboard—a bomb with a timing device made from a small windup Westclox alarm clock. Beckwith was tried and acquitted on federal charges in 1974, but was later convicted on separate state firearms charges in 1975. The state's jury, Beckwith told anyone who would listen, was comprised of "five nigger bitches." After a lengthy series of appeals had been exhausted, in 1977 he began serving his time at Angola, where the majority of the prison population was black. Beckwith was placed in solitary confinement because he was well known among the inmates as the man who had been tried twice for Medgar Evers's murder. There was a price on his head.

Now, thirteen years later, in the custody of the Chattanooga police and housed in a different jail cell, Beckwith was not the same man he had been earlier, when he was initially arrested for Evers's murder. Each of his jail terms—ten months during the two murder trials and three years at Angola—had only heightened Beckwith's racism. His theology was *markedly* different. Once a devout Episcopalian, then a fervent Independent Methodist, Beckwith had become an ordained minister in the Christian Identity Movement in 1977. According to experts who monitor extremist groups, the Christian Identity cult espouses the beliefs that Caucasians comprise the Lost Tribes of Israel; that Jews, blacks and others who they call "mud races" are the literal offspring of Satan, on the same spiritual plane as animals, without souls; and that "Christian" whites are divinely charged to rule over them.[4] The arrogant, impulsive Beckwith, who had basked in the glow of the limelight and publicity during the 1964 murder trials, no longer existed. In his place was a thoughtful, calculating man who realized that destroying his enemies meant operating, as Mississippi Klansmen used to say, like a submarine. Not a tank.

The revived murder case against Beckwith was, in large part, his own fault. In 1987, William Waller, the man who vigorously prosecuted Beckwith twice for murder and later served a term as governor, sought that office again. To muddy the political waters, Beckwith traveled to Mississippi to attend a political rally, hoping to publicly embarrass Waller and end his political career.[5] Beckwith knew that appearing friendly with Waller would alienate black voters against the former governor. The timing of Beckwith's visit was critical. Although Beckwith did not know it at the time, the state of Mississippi was a powder keg waiting to be lit. His appearance at the rally in 1987 provided the necessary spark. Newspapers across the state reported on the meeting of Waller and

Beckwith, and a prominent Mississippi attorney, Charles Ramberg, wrote a lengthy letter to the editor of the *Jackson Daily News*, suggesting that a twenty-fifth anniversary murder trial was in order.[6] Justice had never been served, Ramberg and numerous others believed.

The Evers family remained hopeful that the case would someday be reopened. Soon, city officials were also pressuring Ed Peters, the Hinds County District Attorney, who was reluctant to pursue a third trial. Not only would prosecution so long after the fact violate Beckwith's right to a speedy trial, Peters reasoned, but there were tougher obstacles to overcome. Transcripts of the first two trials, as well as the physical evidence used in the original case, were missing. Perhaps most problematic, if the case were reopened and a grand jury were to hand down a new indictment, Beckwith would have to be extradited from Tennessee to stand trial again—a process that could, and ultimately did, prove tedious, costly and time-consuming.

Secret documents that were leaked by an anonymous source to Jerry Mitchell, a young reporter at *The Clarion-Ledger* in Jackson, proved to be a turning point in the case. Mitchell had been aggressively reporting the numerous misdeeds of the state's defunct Sovereignty Commission, a spy agency created in the 1950s to preserve racial segregation. In October 1989, Mitchell uncovered documents that showed the commission had provided background information on prospective jurors to Beckwith's defense team prior to his second trial. Myrlie Evers, the victim's widow, believed that the intimation of jury tampering was compelling enough to warrant a new trial. The NAACP joined the call for a new investigation, and before the end of the month, the Jackson City Council passed a resolution asking the district attorney and the state attorney general to reopen the case. In the meantime, every reporter who called Beckwith's home in Signal Mountain got a similar story—Beckwith didn't worry himself with the restless natives in Mississippi who were screaming for his blood. In fact, in his spare time, he was writing a book that would name Evers's true killer.[7]

Reporters who came calling on Beckwith faced a series of obstacles. A young black reporter for a national television program, "Inside Edition," was run off Beckwith's property while the cameras rolled. A local Mississippi news reporter was treated to Beckwith's views on contemporary blacks who, Beckwith wildly asserted, still performed human sacrifices and practiced cannibalism. And a female reporter from one of Tennessee's most respected newspapers was asked to accompany Beckwith's wife to the bathroom and succumb to a strip search. Despite Beckwith's assurances that his wife was a registered nurse, the reporter declined.

Although the case was more than twenty-five years old, there was nothing standing in the way of a new indictment, assuming new and compelling evidence could be found. Assistant District Attorney Bobby DeLaughter spearheaded the vigorous and fruitful fourteen-month investigation which culminated in Beckwith's arrest in Tennessee. During the course of DeLaughter's investigation, *Klandestine*, a little-known biography of a former Mississippi Ku Klux Klan officer surfaced, and with it, a story about Beckwith's alleged appearance at a 1965 Klan rally. "Killing that nigger gave me no more inner discomfort than our wives endure when they give birth to our children," Beckwith allegedly confided to a group of Klansmen. "We ask them to do that much for us. We should do just as much. So, let's get in there and kill those enemies, including the president, from the top down!"[8] Only three thousand copies of the 1975 book were printed. One was placed in the hands of the district attorney.

One by one, the obstacles began to recede. When Myrlie Evers learned that no transcript of the trials were to be found in the court's files, she supplied a transcript of the first trial, which was later authenticated. The District Attorney's office succeeded in finding new witnesses who had failed to come forward during the first two trials, and who claimed to have seen Beckwith in Jackson the night of the murder, at a rally Evers led at New Jerusalem Baptist Church. And, although the District Attorney's office claimed the murder weapon disappeared after the second trial, it mysteriously reappeared in a closet at the home of the assistant district attorney's dead father-in-law, former Hinds County Circuit Judge Russel D. Moore III, a staunch segregationist and one of Beckwith's fiercest supporters during his two trials.[9]

From New York, I was monitoring the resulting media frenzy, and Beckwith sent me a copy of a *Clarion-Ledger* feature about the new investigation at its zenith. The article bore a large sketch of Medgar Evers, above which Beckwith had firmly written, "Who dat?" It was his flagrant way of denigrating Evers, as if his memory of Evers required prodding.

In short order, a Hinds County Grand Jury indicted Beckwith on a murder charge after two days of testimony from former and new witnesses. Upon his delivery to the Hamilton County Jail in Chattanooga, Beckwith made it clear he intended to fight extradition to Mississippi "tooth, nail and claw." The next day, at a hearing in Sessions Court, Beckwith entered the courtroom with his hands over his eyes, peering at the crowd. "How many Jews are among you? I see one Nigra man!" When he reached the defense table, he looked toward the judge and shouted, "The marines have landed!" His wife posted a $15,000 cash bail. "I didn't know I could have put up the house," she later commented in an interview, and Beckwith was temporarily freed. He was rearrested on the murder charge on December 31, 1990, on a warrant signed by the governors of both Mississippi and Tennessee, and was returned to jail in Chattanooga pending an extradition hearing.[10]

* * *

I had waited a full month after Beckwith's second arrest to visit him in jail. Although he and I had corresponded for five years and had spoken on the telephone many times, this was to be our first meeting, and I was nervous. The recent publicity about the renewed Evers murder investigation and Beckwith's indictment, coupled with our own tenuous relationship, made me anxious about meeting him face-to-face.

It would be kind to call Beckwith's marriage to my Aunt Mary stormy. The magnitude of their continual about-face love and hatred for each other manifested itself in three separate marriages and three bitter divorces, as well as numerous other separations during their twenty years together. Their mutual verbal and physical abuse was legendary in the small town of Greenwood, Mississippi. Through their only son, a seldom seen cousin of mine who had been estranged from his mother for a number of years, Beckwith got the word that I was the writer in the family. In 1986, I received my first letter from Beckwith, and I was immediately intrigued. In just two legal-size typewritten pages, he touched on almost every topic imaginable, from the White Knights of the Ku Klux Klan to the trials he had been through as a result of someone having "smote the darkie." In that first letter, he referred to his religious credo, Luke 19:27: "But those mine enemies, which would not that I should reign over them, bring hither, and slay them before me."[11]

For the next two years, we worked together locating background material for a book about his life. Beckwith's letters to me, often six or seven pages long, were full of rage and violence. He advocated total, uncompromising supremacy of the white race, a doctrine that extended to his theology. He had become deeply involved, he told me, in the Christian Identity Movement,[12] and wrote of his strong affiliations with the movement's leaders. He called me in January of 1987, after the Dr. Martin Luther King, Jr., holiday, and called the holiday "James Earl Ray Day" and referred to King as "Martin Lucifer Coon." Beckwith talked about a Ku Klux Klan celebration he and his wife had recently attended in Pulaski, Tennessee—the birthplace of the original Ku Klux Klan—where the anthem of the day was, "I'll Be Glad When You're Dead, You Rascal, You." He sang a few bars for me.

During my preliminary research, I unearthed copies of Beckwith's early letters to local newspapers, and the more layers I peeled back, the more clearly I saw the evolution of his racism. With each published letter, Beckwith's imagery grew darker and more menacing. To the *Jackson Daily News,* Beckwith wrote: "We must oust from our society any person or persons found guilty of advocating and supporting race mixing whether they be clergymen, politicians, corporations or private individuals. Those found guilty and purged shall not be called persecuted martyrs; instead they shall be known, to all men, as prosecuted criminals against humanity and treated as such." In 1956 in an open letter to President Eisenhower, published in *The Morning Star* in Greenwood, Beckwith crystallized his position on racial segregation: "We shall not be integrated and thereby mongrelized. We shall walk away from the field of honor avenged. Behind us shall lie the remains of all those responsible for the crime of promoting integration." The following year, in a letter to *The Commercial Appeal* in Memphis, Beckwith's mission was clear: "I believe in segregation just as I believe in God. I shall oppose any person, place or thing that opposes segregation. I shall combat the evils of integration and shall bend every effort to rid the United States of America of the integrationists, whoever and wherever they may be." Segregation-minded whites across the South read Beckwith's letter with interest. So did Medgar Evers, who had recently been named NAACP's field secretary in Mississippi, the home state he and Beckwith shared. One angry respondent wrote the newspaper, referred to Beckwith as a fool and said, "How can a man be so blind to life to believe there'll be a separation of people in Heaven?"

By 1958, Beckwith had drawn the parallels between race, religion and war that would guide his subsequent theological development: "The war to destroy the integration movement is a pure and holy fight resembling the crusades of the eleventh, twelfth and thirteenth centuries when men and women of deep Christian convictions gave their all in order to recover the Holy Land from the Moslems. No fighting man ever won a Congressional Medal of Honor by first going to his superior and requesting permission to perform some great act of valor! Don't waste a lot of time going around asking a lot of fool questions, and wondering: 'How are we going to get rid of the integration?' You must strike first."[13]

Several letters had come back to haunt Beckwith when used by the prosecutor in the original Evers murder trials, and Beckwith, in subsequent years, had stanched the flow of his diatribe. By the 1980s, his public letters had taken on a different tone. Believing that fluoride was being added to public water supplies to make Caucasians docile when the impending race war began, Beckwith wrote in 1986 to *The News-Free Press* in Chattanooga: "Sodium fluoride is also known to be a mind-bending chemical actually administered in measured doses to the more dangerous beasts in some public and private zoos to make the animals less dangerous to the keepers. So also does constant dosage work on the human mind to stifle normal resistance, to say, tyranny, and also, of course, to greatly diminish wholesome resourcefulness." He was slightly more concise in an open letter to Signal Mountain's water board. "Currently, all the queers/perverts, and even a few innocents with AIDS, die much faster drinking fluoridated water," Beckwith wrote. "So, there is a great scrambling/shifting of population to non-fluoridated water. Well, if fluoride kills AIDS-infected perverts, en masse, then that to me is great—God orders the same (using stones)—or have you read your Bible lately?"[14]

In his voluminous letters to me, not once did Beckwith deny murdering Evers, nor did he ever proclaim his innocence. Instead, he expounded on his Christian Identity theology and occasionally teased me with trivia that alluded to the Evers murder. For instance, his photograph had been enlarged, he said, and used for FBI target practice in Mississippi. And while he fancied himself an amateur long-distance shooter, a six-power scope "was always enough for me."[15] It was, in fact, a six-power Golden Hawk rifle scope that was mounted on the rifle used to murder Medgar Evers. The gun was traced to Beckwith, and the scope on it bore Beckwith's partial fingerprint.

The longer my personal correspondence with Beckwith continued, the more upset he became that I wasn't an active racist or eugenicist, and he constantly worried that I might be unduly influenced by the "Jewsmedia," as he referred to the national press. He began sending me racist pamphlets and flyers with almost every letter—"required reading," he called it—along with Identity tapes by Pastor Dan Gayman and others. He positioned himself as my mentor, hoping I would study racial activism at his knee. From Aryan Nations, he sent the Aryan Victory Prayer and a brochure on white racism that put forth the argument that militant racism is not based on hatred, but on love. From Crusade Against Corruption, Beckwith mailed me flyers proclaiming PRAISE GOD FOR AIDS, boldly asserting that "God is intervening in earthly affairs with AIDS to destroy His enemies and to rescue and preserve the White race." From a group called the Caucasian Empire, I received tracts pointing out the inevitability of conflict between the races, proposing that "Young White men who read this should get busy and establish a Caucasian Empire Colony in their community." It was Beckwith's hope that I would join him in the battle and become a leader of the next generation's fight.

He also sent me membership information on the American Pistol and Rifle Association, a militant survivalist group in Benton, Tennessee, where I could ostensibly hone my firearms skills. In 1981, this rural locale played host to future members of The Order, an extremist group which, during 1983 and 1984, committed armed robberies, counterfeiting, bombings and even murder. Randall Rader, Richard Scutari, Andrew Barnhill and Ardie McBrearty—all of whom were members of the self-proclaimed revolutionary movement that netted approximately four million dollars during its brief reign—first met on a three-day APRA survival hike at Benton, Tennessee, in 1981.[16] And from the Christian Patriot Crusader, Beckwith sent information about an important new survivalist camp under construction in the Arizona mountains near Flagstaff. I also received a revealing religious brochure entitled "Jews Are of Their Father, the Devil," that explained the Christian Identity thesis that Jews are literally Satan's offspring. And from the Southern National Party, with whom Beckwith had been affiliated for nearly thirty years, I received a newsletter claiming that the Confederacy never actually surrendered at Appomattox. "This is a popular misconception encouraged by liberal academics and the left-wing media, but it is in fact completely false," the newsletter noted.[17]

As the prospect of a new murder investigation loomed in Mississippi, Beckwith lashed out frequently in his letters to me, claiming the time was nigh when he would have to deal with his enemies, who were legion. He frequently positioned himself as a soldier at war with world Jewry, "the most evil force on earth," because he believed Jews plotted world domination and subjugation of the white race. His God Yahweh, he believed, had always been on his side, and Beckwith's other supporters were influential, as well. Among his staunchest allies were the upper echelon of America's violent racist underground. From cross-burning, old-school Klansmen to the baseball-bat-wielding neo-Nazi set, Beckwith's friends comprised the elite of the racist movement. Sam Bowers, the former Imperial Wizard of Mississippi's White Knights of the Ku Klux Klan, which the FBI credits with more than 300 acts of violence in the mid-1960s—including the famed triple murders of civil rights workers James Chaney, Andrew Goodman and Michael Schwerner—kept Beckwith on his personal Christmas card list.[18]

In his letters to me, Beckwith often included copies of fan mail he had recently received. Pastor Richard G. Butler, founder of the Aryan Nations, referred to Beckwith as a hero of the white race, signing "88," meaning "Heil Hitler," next to his name. Another constant presence in Beckwith's life was J.B. Stoner, a friend of thirty-odd years, who had helped support Beckwith both morally and financially during his darkest days in prison in Louisiana. Stoner's violently anti-Semitic National States Rights Party bore Hitler's famed "SS" symbol. Tom Metzger, the leader of White Aryan Resistance, a violent neo-Nazi group based in California, was an ally and ardent supporter. Even David Duke had once rallied to Beckwith's defense, calling him "one of the most selfless patriots in this nation." Through his Louisiana Klan, Duke once raised funds for Beckwith's legal expenses.[19]

Beckwith's least-known but most frightening affiliation, however, was with Richard Kelly Hoskins of Lynchburg, Virginia. Hoskins, an avid Christian Identity follower, was the self-appointed chronicler of the secret society called the Phineas Priesthood. Far more radical than the Klan, Aryan Nations or White Aryan Resistance, this secret society takes its name from an obscure character in the Bible. Numbers 25 chronicles the story of Phineas, who—acting alone but with the mind of God—stayed

God's plague on Israel by ramming a javelin through an Israelite man and a Midianite woman, killing them both. Their crime: race-mixing. God's reward to Phineas was the covenant of an everlasting priesthood. Today, an unknown number of individual warriors who call themselves Phineas Priests take what they perceive to be God's laws into their own hands. Their enemies include race-mixers, homosexuals, and others who have in any way compromised the purity of the Caucasian race. Beckwith's sanctioned biography, *Glory in Conflict*, states that he once turned down an opportunity to lead an unnamed group, "an organization with roots traceable to antiquity," but he declined, feeling that he was not qualified either "intellectually or spiritually."[20]

Although the Phineas Priesthood is revered as a secret society, Hoskins wrote a lengthy historical account of its activities, postulating that Robin Hood, Jesse James and John Wilkes Booth were secretly Phineas Priests acting on the laws of God. Although in an interview following Beckwith's arrest, Hoskins denied even knowing him, Beckwith's wife, Thelma, described their relationship as close, and said they often conferred on important religious issues. According to Thelma, Hoskins and his wife often sat with the Beckwiths at religious gatherings. Beckwith had even preached the story of Phineas at some of the racist gatherings where he was invited to speak. Hoskins's book, *Vigilantes of Christendom*, was an important tome in Beckwith's library, along with *White Power* by American Nazi Party founder George Lincoln Rockwell and *The Protocols of the Learned Elders of Zion*, a legendary anti-Semitic tract. Hoskins held Beckwith in such esteem that when Beckwith sent him a personal check in payment for *Vigilantes*, Hoskins returned it, uncashed.[21]

Among Beckwith's regular correspondents, I was not a known commodity in the white supremacist movement. On my end of our lengthy correspondence, I was sending Beckwith everything I could unearth about him from the national press, as well as obscure books and archived papers. The more I learned about his alliances within the Christian Identity, Klan, neo-Nazi and survivalist-right movements, the more deeply I investigated the backgrounds of his cronies and their racist affiliations. Although I was initially hesitant to discuss any of this with my aunt—who had legally changed her name and left Mississippi in 1965 following her final divorce from Beckwith—I felt compelled to ask whether she had been aware of his extremist activities, and whether I might be placing myself in danger. She and I had never talked about her marriages or divorces, and I had always been careful to let well enough alone. She was a recovering alcoholic and, by that time, had been proudly sober for ten years. During their marriages, however, her alcoholism and Beckwith's physical abuse not only fueled their hatred for each other, but undoubtedly created some attractions as well.

Although Beckwith was unaware of it, his former wife, during her many moves around the country, had held onto two small, flowered suitcases, which she pulled out of storage for me in late 1987, when I visited during the Christmas holidays. We sat on the living room floor in her apartment late one night, drinking coffee, as she talked of moving from city to city, leaving friends and possessions behind each time. Yet she had held on to these suitcases, she explained, and for nearly twenty-five years had kept them hidden. When she unzipped one of them and pushed it toward me—and I leaned down into a clutter of musty papers—I knew why. The suitcases contained nearly 400 letters Beckwith had written while jailed during his two murder trials in 1964, providing a daily account of his life behind bars. The letters also chronicled his visitors, both famous and mundane, his friendly relationships with the local law enforcement officers assigned to guard him, and the strategy his lawyers were going to use to attempt to get him acquitted. Most important, the letters offered a glimpse into Beckwith's mind.

"I don't really know why I kept them," my Aunt Mary said. "I guess I thought if I ever got hard up I might sell them." My aunt had never granted an interview to a reporter before, and although she was unwilling to discuss Beckwith even with me at first, she told me she wanted me to have the letters. "If you're determined to write a book about De La," she said, "these letters will help." She said she hoped they would also make me think twice about the danger of becoming involved with him. She had lived half her life in fear of him, and she did not want that constant fear to be her legacy to me.

I flew back to New York with the letters in my carry-on baggage, and spent several weeks organizing and reading them in chronological order. Meanwhile, Beckwith and I continued our own correspondence. While the prison letters provided me with a wealth of information about the ten months Beckwith spent in jail during the Evers trials, the real turning point proved to be a thirteen-pound parcel Beckwith sent me. The box, wrapped in brown paper, frightened me. When I cautiously opened it, the box held bound volumes of the FBI files Beckwith had obtained a decade earlier through the Freedom of Information Act. The voluminous files provided invaluable leads for further investigation, and confirmed dates, places and events I would otherwise never have been able to substantiate.

Beckwith later acknowledged that we were too far apart in age and background to produce a work that would satisfy him. I wanted to write an objective biography, and my research into his colorful past, and his even more colorful associates, didn't please him. I should have been content, in his mind, to take his story as he told it and sign the contract a Chattanooga lawyer had drawn up. When it was clear I was uneasy about his contract, and offered a number of points I wanted written into the document, he decided it was not in his best interest to collaborate with me further. His contract called for him to receive two-thirds of any royalties we might receive, and I asked for ownership of the book rights upon his death. Beckwith was incensed that I would try to profit unduly from his life story, and I reminded him that he had tried a number of times, unsuccessfully, to publish a book, and that I believed my ability to market the project would make it worth the trade-off. He wrote and told me to copy and return the materials he had sent me, which I promptly did. When the box was delivered to his door a few days later, he sent me a cordial thank-you note.

We continued to correspond, but after a time, he stopped including racist ephemera in his letters and instead wrote me with veiled, and not so veiled, threats. I could very easily become a target, he was quick to point out. What I was doing had its occupational hazards. He presumed I did know the risk, and would suffer if I betrayed a trust. At one point he said that "going to war with Russia in Siberia" would be safer than wrangling with him.[22] What Beckwith had wanted me to write was a book that would call attention to what he viewed as past legal injustices he had suffered at the hands of the Jews, "this chief most evil in our lands," as he referred to them. Additionally, while we would not write or say "anything incriminating," he wanted to use the book to fire the readers' imaginations and broaden and elevate the Beckwith myth.[23] Ultimately, a book that highlighted his personal trials and tribulations, and held him up as an example, would serve as a call to action for the White Race War he believed was imminent.

Beckwith sought out another collaborator, R.W. Scott—his fifth since 1964.[24] He must have suspected that I intended to continue working on my own, as well, because he subsequently mailed me a notarized letter informing me that Scott's book was the only "authorized and authentic" Byron De La Beckwith biography. Their collaboration, *Glory in Conflict*, was published by an Arkansas-based vanity press in 1990. With Beckwith pursuing his own book, in my free time, I pursued mine—thinking I would publish a comprehensive biography after his death. Using information and names from the racist propaganda Beckwith had frequently mailed me, I continued to research both the organizations and the individuals who influenced him. With pressure mounting for a new murder trial in Mississippi, I redoubled my efforts and began to conduct a series of lengthy interviews with my aunt, delving into the minutiae of her private life with Beckwith, their emotional and sexual dysfunctions, and the reasons behind their multiple marriages and divorces. Each time we talked, she stressed the danger of my project. Yet with each interview session, we also grew closer, and she disclosed increasingly frightening details of their tempestuous relationship.

When prosecutors reopened the Medgar Evers case, I knew no other reporter or writer would ever have access to the firsthand accounts of De La Beckwith's life to which I was already privy. Both of Beckwith's wives—my aunt and Thelma Beckwith, the two most important people in his life—had granted me numerous interviews, and at a time when most reporters were scrambling for background on Beckwith, I had already performed five years of research and possessed a voluminous dossier on Beckwith. Immediately following his arrest in Chattanooga in December 1990, I left my job of five years and began writing *Portrait of a Racist.*

On January 30, 1991, after driving through a cold, steady rain, I arrived unannounced at the Hamilton County Jail in downtown Chattanooga. The jail was housed in the Justice Building, a functional, austere monolith. It was a dark Wednesday morning, and while I knew it wasn't an official visiting day for Beckwith, I also knew I stood a better-than-average chance he would agree to see me. The older officer on duty, Lieutenant Sanders, with graying hair and a cautious demeanor, looked me over carefully when I told him I wanted to see Beckwith. He wrote on a small slip of paper the days and hours I would be allowed to visit. Tuesday at 2:45 P.M., which was the previous day, or Saturday at 1:45 P.M., still three days away. Standing on the other side of a glass wall, Sanders placed the piece of paper in a metal tray and slid it out to me on the other side.

"Can he see me if he wants to?" I asked. Lieutenant Sanders nodded behind his glass wall. "Then tell him his nephew flew in from New York, and that I'd like to see him today." Sanders made a brief phone call and told me Beckwith was just finishing his lunch. He asked me to wait in the hallway until someone came to get me. I sat down on a long oak bench—it looked like a pew rescued from an abandoned country church—and watched the rain through a glass door while I waited. After about twenty minutes, a young officer asked, "Are you here for Beckwith? They're bringing him down now. Come with me." I was escorted to a small room, no larger than a telephone booth, with a short stool and a thick glass wall showing an identical booth opposite me. I was not asked to sign in, nor was I searched. Through the open door on the other side, I could see an officer leading Beckwith in to see me. His feet were manacled.

At seventy, he was smaller and more frail than I had imagined he would be. His glasses were as thick as his hair was thin. He was wearing a white T-shirt under his grey prison jumpsuit, and had a Celtic cross dangling from a chain around his neck. As he was led into the room, his walk—perhaps because of the chains on his feet—seemed hesitant and uncertain. When he was seated across from me, he leaned forward to get a better look at me and said in his distinctive drawl, "I imagine that you are Reed Massengill. We have never met in your lifetime." He slowly placed the palm of his right hand against the glass, and I raised my left hand and pressed it against his, feeling only the coldness that separated us.

I was on assignment for *Vanity Fair*, having traveled to Chattanooga specifically to see if Beckwith would agree to an on-the-record interview for a magazine feature I was writing. When I pulled out my tape recorder, explaining that I intended to quote him accurately and in context, he chastised me. His manner was courtly, almost effusive, as he explained that he was asking $5,000 in exchange for any formal interview he granted. He made it clear that he was now sorry he had shared his personal materials with me and had encouraged me to keep copies of everything. He talked at length about the many national magazine articles about him, and complained that he had seen none of the proceeds from them. In his mind, it made perfect sense that if he was being written about, he should be making money from it. My renewed pursuit of a story made him edgy, especially as I pressed him to talk with me on the record. As our visit progressed, he made it clear that he and his many friends were highly distressed with me. Out of anger, or fear, he called up what he said was a quote from Omar Khayyam: "Let us make game of those who make as much of us." It was a threat he had used in his letters to me.[25]

What I confronted was quintessential Beckwith, a man of many words—most of them antagonistic, hateful and racist. He accused me, at one point, of abusing his trust, and I asked him to explain what he meant, since I hadn't yet written anything about him nor used any of the background materials he had provided me.

"Yet?" he asked, turning red. "*Y-E-T*?"

"Yes," I answered. Then I added, "*Y-E-S*."

He flew into a rage, and what fascinated me was the transforming power of his hatred. When we greeted each other initially, his brown eyes narrowed and locked my gaze; he struggled to see if I would look away, showing fear and giving him the upper hand. When I held his gaze, it made him angry. And although he had seemed frail at first, he gathered strength as he grew progressively more agitated with me and the prospect of a magazine article that might prove damaging to his battle against extradition to Mississippi. He called me a Jew—a heart-stopping epithet when hurled by a follower of the Christian Identity cult, as Jews are viewed as children of the devil, deserving of execution merely because of their existence.

His vitriolic attacks continued for about half an hour. Before he ended our visit and rose to leave, he was shouting at me. He accused me of recording him, although I had kept my recorder turned off, in plain sight during the entire visit. He told me not to bother his wife, Thelma, by calling or visiting her, apparently unaware that she had contacted me several times since his arrest and offered me an acre of land on Signal

Mountain if I could help him in any way.[26] And when he pointed his finger at me and said, "Now you be careful, and I mean *careful*," it was clear that I should keep a close watch over my shoulder, and that he was not being flippant.

"I have more power in jail than you have out there," Beckwith snarled. I looked at his forehead and saw the sign my aunt had earlier warned me about. "Before he's ready to hurt you," she once told me, "his face will turn red and a big vein will pop up in his forehead." As if on cue, an officer opened the door behind Beckwith and led him away. When Beckwith took his eyes from mine and walked through the door, I realized I was standing. Outside the jail, it was still raining and the wind was noticeably colder. In the car, I rested my head on the steering wheel for a few minutes.

When I later told my aunt about the encounter, she asked, "Were you scared?" I admitted that I was. "Good," she said simply. "You *should* be."

I

Tangled Branches

Fifty-five years after Lee's surrender at Appomattox, an only child, a son, was born to Susie Yerger Beckwith and her husband of eight years, Byron De La Beckwith. Although the year 1920 witnessed a surge of suffragette activity that mirrored the social unrest of the nation as a whole, there was no discussion about the child's name, no opportunity for the mother to cajole the father into considering her family's feelings in the matter. "His name will be Byron De La Beckwith, Jr.," the father told Dr. Drysdale, who had just delivered the baby.

At thirty-three, Susie Beckwith was much older than most of the other first-time mothers at Mater Misericordiae Hospital. The fifty-mile trip from the tiny northern California town of Colusa to the hospital in Sacramento had taken its toll on her, and this being her first child, labor and the delivery were difficult. Many mothers her age had already borne three children. Still, her joy was perhaps greater than any of the younger mothers', and she was determined her new son would have every advantage in life. That he was born in a hospital, delivered by a doctor, was an auspicious start. The Beckwiths' hometown newspaper, *The Sun*, announced the birth with a single sentence: "Born—Beckwith—In Sacramento, November 9, 1920, to the wife of Byron De La Beckwith of Colusa, a son, Byron De La Beckwith, Jr."

Susie Beckwith didn't argue with her husband about the child's name, never mind that it was a long-standing custom in her family—an expectation, really—to carry on the Yerger name.[1] Her son would have opportunities other children could only imagine. He was the beneficiary of a proud ancestry on both parents' sides. His father's wealth would buy him the best schooling, the finest clothes and the prettiest playthings, and his mother's Mississippi plantation upbringing would help the child cultivate a demeanor of sweeping courtesy and consideration. Their new son's true inheritance was his proud lineage, an attribute no amount of money could ever buy.

As for the father, he was overjoyed. At thirty-seven, he had finally produced an heir. From the moment of his birth, the child was called "Delay," a bastardization of the French particles in his name, *De La.* And although his birth certificate listed him as "Jr.," he was actually the third to bear the distinguished name.[2] His grandfather, B.D. Beckwith, had come to northern California from Ohio in 1861 as a young man, savoring frontier life in the wild, unsettled territory. For a while, he taught school just outside Stockton, being one of the few settlers with any college education. For several years he worked as a clerk in a general store in Woodbridge. When the Central Pacific Railroad came through the county, Beckwith moved to Lodi, another frontier town, and became its first permanent settler, hoping to make his fortune there. He built Lodi's first brick building, where he opened a drugstore in 1868. As the town grew, his business prospered. His establishment was the hub of Lodi's social activity, serving as a gathering place, post office and telegraph office. Beckwith was appointed the town's first postmaster,[3] and during the years he was in business there, he slowly accumulated and farmed 1,300 acres of land in San Joaquin County.

Nonetheless, B.D. Beckwith was not content as a postmaster or druggist. He was a visionary. Looking out across the vast stretches of California's Central Valley, he imagined hundreds and thousands of acres of land covered with crops, envisioning the bounty the soil would yield if properly irrigated. For nearly twenty years, he talked irrigation incessantly, causing some of his friends to question his sanity.[4] In late 1886, however, Beckwith used his earnings and influence to construct a canal in the nearby town of Woodbridge. He diverted water from the Mokelumne River through the canal, irrigating all the land from Newhope on the north, to Stockton on the south.

The irrigation project was an immense success, valued at more than $800,000 at its peak and adding millions of dollars worth of taxable property to the county. When the project was completed, Beckwith was both rich and surprised. As he had imagined, irrigation made the land and its crops flourish. Yet the real effect of irrigation, Beckwith found, was on the sheer dollar value of the real estate. What had previously been a plot of arid land worth five dollars could, once irrigated, sell for upward of $200. The exponential increase in the value of land was incredible, and entrepreneurs like Beckwith, who championed irrigation, helped establish agriculture as California's greatest industry.[5] Yet the greater his professional successes, the worse Beckwith's health became.

In his personal life, it is unlikely that B.D. Beckwith enjoyed the same good fortune that he experienced in his business dealings. The day after Valentine's Day in 1882, he married a young widow in Stockton, Mary Oliver Bray, who had two young sons, Elliott and Bert. Like Beckwith, Mary Bray was originally from Ohio. Two years after their marriage, in March of 1884, Mary gave birth to Beckwith's namesake and heir, Byron

D. Beckwith, in Newhope. Mary Beckwith died of consumption when her youngest son was only five years old.[6] Years later, with the Bray boys grown and away from home, B.D. and his son Byron frequently traveled farther north in California, and on one such trip in 1901, B.D. Beckwith had another vision. He would resurrect an abandoned irrigation project—the Central Irrigation District Canal—which had shut down prior to its completion more than a decade earlier. Although now in his sixties and in failing health, his earlier success with the Woodbridge Canal convinced him the same could be accomplished on an even grander scale. He devised a new scheme to divert water from the Sacramento River and began securing the local water and property rights.

In September of 1902, B.D. Beckwith entered into a contract with J.D. Schuyler, a prominent local engineer, and Willard M. Sheldon, a businessman, to form the Sacramento Canal Company, a corporation that was to be organized with $1,000,000 capital stock. Beckwith was to receive one-third of the total enterprise, as well as $50,000 for the water and property rights he had already procured, which were essential to the canal's success. Sheldon and Schuyler advanced Beckwith $400 against his third of the enterprise, and Beckwith deeded them the water rights and other property, which were to be conveyed to the corporation. When completed, the irrigation system would be the largest in California, commanding a territory of a million acres.

With the water and property rights in hand, Sheldon and Schuyler instead leased the Central Canal under Sheldon's name for a period of fifty years and attempted to bilk Beckwith out of his rightful share in the enterprise, as well as the money he had been guaranteed. He was in visibly poor health, and the partners apparently assumed Beckwith was so ill that he might die before he could bring action against them. Although Beckwith extended the deadline for payment several times to accommodate Sheldon and Schuyler, they simply refused to pay. Claiming that he was defrauded, and seeking to recover his property and water rights, Beckwith brought suit against them. He was represented by A. Van R. Paterson, a former Superior Court judge who later was appointed a justice of the Supreme Court of California. Beckwith's deposition in the case was taken just weeks before he died in May 1904, at the age of sixty-four, of typhoid fever. He left no will, and the value of his estate was limited to $300 cash and his rights to the irrigation project under litigation.

The local Colusa newspaper, *The Sun*, ran an account of his death on its front page. "This morning the hour of six was scarcely reached when Byron De La Beckwith's soul took its flight to that Better Land where sin and sorrow come not, and the spirit is at rest," the paper noted. *The Lodi Sentinel*, covering the Woodbridge area where Beckwith had seen his earliest successes, also gave his funeral lengthy front-page coverage, citing the pending litigation against Sheldon and Schuyler as a contributing factor in his death. "Mr. Beckwith's deposition was taken about two weeks ago, as he was in failing health, and since then he has worried over the case until there was a general breaking down of his system and he passed away." His son Byron, then twenty but still a student at Colusa High School, was not with him when he died. A nephew, Charles M. Beckwith, who had been like an adopted son to him, traveled from Sacramento when he got news of Beckwith's illness, and was with him when he drew his last breath. After a funeral service at the Presbyterian church in Colusa, Byron boarded a train with his father's body and, together with his cousin Charles, accompanied it to Woodbridge for another funeral service and burial beside his mother.[7]

Having inherited little more than his father's rights to the irrigation project, Byron D. Beckwith pursued the litigation for twelve and a half years until it was successfully concluded.[8] During the years between his father's death and the Supreme Court's judgement in his favor, Byron D. Beckwith became prominent in his own right in the small town of Colusa. When B.D. Beckwith's health began failing, Byron had busied himself with his father's business affairs, learning by doing. While life in turn-of-the-century northern California was never easy, the teenager was forced to accept the full responsibilities of his father at an early age. During the last years of B.D. Beckwith's life, when he traveled frequently to try to settle his affairs with Sheldon and Schuyler, Beckwith and his son lived in the Colusa home of Will and Sallie Green. Will Green was widely respected as one of the founding fathers of Colusa, having settled there with his uncle, Dr. Robert Semple, the town's first inhabitant.[9] Green had been appointed Surveyor-General of California by President Grover Cleveland. He met the elder Beckwith at the first Irrigation Congress in San Francisco. The two men, whose fervor for irrigation was almost zealous, became close friends. After his wife's death, B.D. Beckwith and his son Byron moved in with the Greens.

The Greens owned and managed the local newspaper, *The Sun*, and were surrogate parents to the teenaged Byron. They were educated, opinionated people, and they were not only widely respected, but genuinely well-liked in the small town. An early history of Colusa, published in 1918, called Will Green "California's first apostle of agriculture."[10] After Byron's mother's death, Sallie Green, who had no children of her own, took the teenager under her wing. She had been a spinster for years, and married her husband, Will, late in life. She was a large, affectionate woman with a pleasant, motherly disposition. B.D. Beckwith's death brought Byron totally into the Green family fold.[11]

Living with the Greens after his father's death was no great change for Byron, who had grown accustomed to the elderly couple's habits and idiosyncrasies. Will Green's chatter about irrigation was, to the young man, a comforting reminder of his father. With the Greens providing room and board, and a Sacramento friend of his father's, George W. Peltier, assisting him financially, Byron took the advice of his father's lawyers and continued the lawsuit against Sheldon and Schuyler. Advised that he would ultimately win the case if he persevered, the younger Beckwith resolved to see the lawsuit through to its conclusion. Sadly, just a year after B.D. Beckwith's death, Will Green died. Sallie Green waited a respectable amount of time mourning the loss of her husband, then set out on an around-the-world tour for a full year. Sailing from San Francisco on the steamship *Mongolia*, she crossed the Pacific and visited Hawaii, Japan, China, the Philippines, Egypt, Italy, France and England. Her lengthy letters about her travels were serialized in *The Sun*, and she wrote glowingly of her passage through the Suez Canal and the awe-inspiring magnificence of an erupting Mt. Vesuvius. She disembarked in New York almost exactly a year later, and crossed the country back to her adopted home, California. She was then seventy-five years old.

Byron continued to live in Sallie Green's home after she returned to Colusa and busied herself with the day-to-day operations of the newspaper, a business for which she had a natural gift.[12] Byron Beckwith, optimistically looking toward the day he might see a cash settlement in his father's irrigation case, set about establishing himself in business. He joined Company B of the National Guard of California and was named its captain. The excitement, however, was minimal. Although the unit had been called out to help calm a railroad strike in 1894, it saw no further service. The National Guard was called into the Spanish-American War four years later, but the company got only as far as Oakland before turning back. During his five years with Company B, the unit saw no action. It mustered out in 1910 from lack of interest, but Beckwith continued to carry the title of "captain." He began his career as an insurance salesman and moved into a boarding house on Market Street run by Thomas Vickers. In September of that same year, following in his father's footsteps, he was appointed Colusa's postmaster, a position he held until the spring of 1914.[13]

Back in Mississippi, Sallie Green had two favorite nieces, Mary Craig Kimbrough—called Craig throughout her life—and Susie Southworth Yerger. Their family tree had deep roots, with tangled branches that included the Yergers, the Kimbroughs, the Southworths and the Morgans. Together, they owned tens of thousands of acres of fertile cotton land in the Mississippi Delta, and before the Civil War had possessed vast slave holdings and wielded the influence and status accorded the landed gentry. Their progeny, an intricate web of intermarried cousins, became the community's lawyers, judges, educators and business leaders.

Craig and Susie were close in age, but quite different in disposition.

The Kimbroughs, who were wealthier and more influential, had educated Craig in New York, where she became something of a bohemian and was a peripheral member of literary circles in Greenwich Village. She questioned the tenets of her Southern upbringing and became a suffragette, returning to Mississippi espousing beliefs that were softly Socialistic. In Craig, Aunt Sallie undoubtedly saw the same willfulness she herself had possessed at an earlier age. The Yergers were less wealthy and less influential, but were still a powerful force in the Delta, having clung to thousands of acres of prime cotton land and the economic power that accompanied it. Susie Yerger was also well educated, but her nature was less gregarious. She was fragile, somewhat emotionally unstable, and seemed content with her station in life. Although her character was markedly different from her Aunt Sallie's, as she entered her twenties she was fast becoming a spinster, and her elderly aunt could easily identify with the quiet undercurrent of social ostracism that accompanied spinsterhood.

Both Craig's mother and Susie's mother, who were sisters, were involved in erecting the Confederate monument in Greenwood, through their local chapter of the United Daughters of the Confederacy (UDC). They named their chapter in honor of Varina Jefferson Davis, the widowed first lady of the Confederacy. After the Civil War's end and her husband's death in 1889, Varina Davis donated the president's Gulf Coast mansion, Beauvoir, as a home for aging Confederate veterans. It was at Beauvoir that Jefferson Davis, denied his right to United States citizenship by a Reconstruction Congress after the Civil War, wrote his volumes, *The Rise and Fall of the Confederate Government.* Through the Greenwood chapter's efforts to erect the monument, the Yergers became particularly friendly with Mrs. Davis, and she had bestowed upon Susan Yerger, Susie's mother, several small tokens of her friendship and affection over the years, including a copy of her limited-edition book, *The Grasshopper War*, and several pieces of willowware china from Beauvoir. The Yergers cherished these mementos, which they tucked away for safekeeping.[14]

Not long after Craig's return to Mississippi, her mother fell seriously ill. Mother and daughter Kimbrough traveled to the famed Kellogg Sanitarium in Battle Creek, Michigan, where young Susie Yerger had retired some time earlier to soothe her fragile nerves. There was always hushed talk among the family that Susie suffered from emotional problems or mental disorders, and her frequent respites at sanitariums, mineral springs and health spas fanned the rumors. During this particular visit, Susie met the writer Upton Sinclair, whose recent novel *The Jungle*, published in 1906, had been a huge success. He was visiting Dr. Kellogg, brother of the famous cereal company founder, to try his unusual milk diet. After Craig and her mother had settled in at the sanitarium, Susie introduced him to the Kimbroughs.[15]

Sinclair was a Socialist, and his political leanings were anathema to

Craig's Mississippi relatives and friends, who warned her against associating with him. When Craig later returned to New York, she sought Sinclair's advice on a book she had written. Recently divorced from his wife, who had been unfaithful, Sinclair began courting Craig. When it later became apparent the young couple planned to marry, regardless of her family's wishes, her father, a prominent Mississippi judge, took down Craig's portrait and placed it in the attic, facing the wall. The judge forever viewed him, Sinclair once said, as "the dreaded Socialist muckraker." The two were married in Virginia, with Craig's mother and Aunt Sallie in attendance. Craig's father, Judge Kimbrough, stayed home.[16]

Although Sallie Green did not need to promote Craig's determination to marry Sinclair, she was something of a Mississippi matchmaker. She had, in fact, facilitated Craig's parents' marriage decades earlier.[17] After her lengthy trip around the world and the opposed wedding of Craig and the future Pulitzer winner, it occurred to Sallie that another introduction might be in order. Her other favorite niece, Susie Yerger, was only four or five years younger than Byron Beckwith, who apparently had not given a great deal of thought to marriage in Colusa. He preferred to spend his time drinking and carousing with his lodge brothers. At twenty-eight, Beckwith was established in business and likely to win his father's court case; Sallie thought it appropriate that he and Susie should meet. Byron needed a wife to rein him in a bit, to stabilize his life, and Susie needed to marry and establish a family before it was entirely too late. Sallie invited her niece to visit California. She had plenty of room, and Colusa was full of friendly people and the climate would agree with her.

Yerger family legend held that Susie Southworth Yerger was one of the South's prettiest, most popular belles. Many years after her death, it would be supposed she had entertained as many as eight gentleman callers at one time, each of whom came bearing a box of candy.[18] As with most legends, however, this one may have been apocryphal. What seems likelier is that Susie Southworth Yerger, resplendent in her long gowns and taffeta crinolines, might have been a bit of a wallflower. Unlike her pretty cousin Craig, photographs of Susie show a wan, plain woman, hardly the fairest flower of the South. If she had, in fact, entertained so many young gentleman callers, none had seen fit—or been deemed fit by her family—to engage her in marriage. In fact, in an era when it was not only unusual but nearly unheard of to marry late, Susie had not only *not* produced several children by her twenty-fifth birthday, but had not yet even procured for herself a husband.

Since a woman's inheritance was, almost without exception, her dowry, each advancing year threatened Susie's due share of the Yerger plantation. The option of marrying an unattractive cousin would have been better than remaining single and becoming a burden to her brothers, who, according to tradition, would have supported her had she remained unmarried after her parents' deaths. The custom of marrying a cousin was a common practice in the antebellum South, and persisted even into the early twentieth century, when land was often the only tangible asset Southern families had left to impart to their heirs. Careers and marriages were enhanced through the concentration of wealth, and because such great stock was placed in the value of family and heritage, the practices of intermarriage and inbreeding were common. Marrying a cousin offered distinct advantages: foremost, that the extended family's property, contiguous land holdings, or money, would not be diluted through a union with an outsider.[19] Although there had been a number of marriages of this kind among the Yergers' extended clan, not even a cousinly union was forthcoming for Susie Yerger.

Perhaps, like many young women of her day, Susie was less concerned about romance than pragmatism. Although the Old South is often painted as a romantic land of moonlight and magnolias, which was indeed one aspect of its charm, marriage was very much a responsibility to one's family. Sex and childbirth were similarly thought of as duties to one's husband. Like her contemporaries, Susie may have been quite a pragmatist, desiring a husband with strength of character or business acumen. Like other girls her age, she may have ranked love a weak fourth on her list of attributes for a husband, caring less about his capacity for love and romance than his ability to support and sustain his family. Although love was certainly a plus, it was commonly held that "suitability" was the true foundation for marriage, and that affection grew between two people as their marriage blossomed.[20]

To Susie and her family, even a husband who was nothing more than suitable was preferable to spinsterhood, particularly in the clannish South, where spinsterhood was tantamount to social death. Even the woman whose husband drank and philandered could hold up her head in the community as a symbol of steadfastness. The spinster, on the other hand, could seldom rise above her station. With few viable options for employment, particularly among the upper classes, in which employment was contradictory to the very notion of feminine gentility, the spinster was consigned to become a financial burden to her family.[21]

Glen Oak Plantation, the Yerger family homestead, was situated in the fertile Mississippi Delta, and Greenwood—once called "a mosquito-infested mudhole in the country road"—was a small town steeped in tradition and rich in Southern gothic lore. Both Leflore County and Greenwood, the county seat, were named after a colorful local figure, Greenwood Leflore. The son of a French-Canadian trader and a Choctaw princess, Leflore became one of the South's wealthiest slave owners prior to the Civil War. He was granted a tract of Indian land by the United

States government, and to show his allegiance, he supported the Union throughout the Civil War. In 1854 he built a lavish plantation modeled after the Empress Josephine's palace, Malmaison. While his neighbors died on battlefields wearing the Confederate grey, Leflore died at his home, his grandchildren waving above him the Union flag in which he was wrapped for burial.[22]

After the war, just a few miles down the road from where Leflore had lived, a former member of Major General Nathan Bedford Forrest's Confederate Cavalry returned home. Lemuel Purnell Yerger, Susie's father, had joined the war effort at sixteen, like many young men. He suffered a leg wound as a member of Company D of the Cavalry's Twenty-Eighth Regiment, and walked with a pronounced limp the rest of his life. Yerger's regiment, under Colonel Joshua T. McBee, surrendered to Union forces at Citronelle, Alabama, on May 4, 1865, when Yerger and his unit were taken prisoners of war. When he proudly returned to Greenwood, he went into the practice of law. He was known to the townspeople as "Colonel Yerger," although, according to official records, he had never risen above the rank of private in the Cavalry. After his return from the Civil War, Yerger married Susan Fisher Southworth and started a family.[23]

To Southerners, Forrest was a war hero, and he also had a profound influence on young Yerger's life. Even in later years, the colonel was given to reminiscences of his former commander. While Lemuel Yerger was establishing a marginal law practice in Greenwood, Forrest became Grand Wizard of the original Ku Klux Klan, founded in Pulaski, Tennessee, in 1866. Although it was intended to be primarily a social club for a few bored Confederate veterans, the Klan, in the turbulent years of Reconstruction, quickly developed a virulent character of its own—intimidating, harassing and even murdering blacks. Within two years of its founding, the Klan had established itself as an organization with a whole new ideology:

No rations have we, but the flesh of man—
And love niggers best, the Ku Klux Klan;
We catch 'em alive and roast 'em whole,
Then hand 'em around with a sharpened pole.

Forrest, however, became so irate at the shift in the Klan's activities that he ordered it disbanded in 1869 after Tennessee Governor Parson Brownlow instituted martial law in some counties of the state to combat the Klan. Smaller clandestine groups, organized under a host of different names ranging from the Mississippi Society of the White Rose to the Knights of the Black Cross, sprang up in the Klan's place and continued a hateful program of harassment and murder of blacks in the years following the Klan's official dissolution.[24]

The Klan, as it was originally intended, might have been little more than an outlet for reminiscences of Confederate veterans. Like other prominent families of the Deep South after the deracination of the Civil War, the Yergers learned to emphasize not their ancient ancestry, which was English and French, but the family's status *prior* to the Civil War. They clung like many others to the material possessions and mementos of the antebellum era. It was not uncommon, in those years, for a family to become so immersed in the past that it failed to maintain its present role in the community. Such was the case with the Yergers and their extended family, the Kimbroughs and the Morgans and the Southworths. Their status rested on their glorious past, instead of on the rather commonplace present. What the Yergers aspired to was gentility, a rare combination of moral uprightness and high social standing. It was a common aspiration following the Civil War, when families wanted to regain the essence of what they lost—their pride.[25]

The Civil War and its outcome were constant sources of nostalgia for the Yergers. They failed to admit that the war had nearly destroyed their income. The Yergers simply clung to the past and would not allow it to die. Whether merely as a topic of conversation or as a pastime, the Civil War was constantly being resurrected at Glen Oak Plantation. The blacks who had been slaves continued to live on the property even after their official emancipation, serving in much the same capacity they had served before. They tended the cotton fields, under a sun that, in Mississippi, seemed as hot as Africa's.

After the family's original home on River Road burned, the Yergers built a rather simple, two-story frame house at 306 George Street in Greenwood proper, where Colonel Yerger conducted his law practice. Their daughter Susie returned from her extended stay in California in fine humor—she was betrothed. Although her parents had not been consulted before the fact, Aunt Sallie Green's long association with Byron Beckwith alleviated any of the Yergers' fears about him. When Colonel Yerger learned of the details of the lawsuit that Beckwith was still pursuing through the California courts, he felt sure Beckwith would win the judgment. He sensed that Beckwith was not a fortune-hunter, for he had shown pluck and perseverance, establishing himself in business and proving to be successful in his work. He would make a fine husband for Susie, especially given her advanced age.[26]

Beckwith planned a trip to Mississippi to spend some time with the Yergers and obtain their formal permission to marry Susie. Plans for the ceremony were quickly made, and the wedding was a strange little affair, perhaps designed not to call attention to the fact that the bride was twenty-five and her groom was nearly thirty. At a time when the prominent Greenwood newspaper, *The Commonwealth*, usually ran lengthy reports of local nuptials, the Yerger-Beckwith wedding garnered a scant paragraph, buried at the bottom of a page above an advisory about seed potatoes. The wedding was planned for the middle of the winter, and was held on Tuesday, January 30, 1912. Even more curious, it was held neither at the Church of the Nativity, which bore L.P. Yerger's name on its cornerstone as a founding member, nor at the relatively new Yerger home on George Street. Instead, the wedding was held at the home of a cousin who lived nearby.

The other local paper, *The Enterprise*, gave the wedding better placement and a lengthier article. "The house was filled with her relatives and a few intimate friends," it noted, adding that the bride's brother, Will, served as the groom's best man, and that Susie's little cousin, Fisher Morgan Southworth, was the ring bearer. At his daughter's request, Colonel Yerger wore his Confederate uniform to give her away. Word circulated through the small town that Colonel Yerger would be in uniform, and although the Civil War was by then decades past, a number of other men in attendance wore their musty uniforms, as well. The Reverend George B. Myers, Rector of the Church of the Nativity, officiated.[27]

The marriage was as much a business merger as a product of love, if love was even a factor. At twenty-nine, Byron Beckwith was weary of having no home and family of his own. Having a wife from a good family, with an appropriate dowry, would plant him firmly among the Colusa aristocracy. For Susie, Beckwith must have seemed an ideal mate. That he had been the town's postmaster showed his ability to handle public responsibility, and since he owned his own business he showed initiative. He would soon bring his father's lawsuit to a successful close and would inherit a large sum of money. Above all, however, he possessed the one attribute all of Susie Yerger's other suitors had lacked. He had asked her to marry him.

Susie's life in Colusa was quiet and comfortable. The town's first settlers had been from Kentucky, and Colusa seemed like a typical small Southern town to newcomers, strikingly similar in many ways to Susie Yerger's hometown, which made the difficult transition from Mississippi to California bearable. Both Colusa and Greenwood were primarily agrarian communities, although the crop of choice in Greenwood had been cotton and Colusa's staple crops were wheat and barley. Both towns drew their names from local Indians, Colusa having been built on the site of an ancient Indian village, Ko-ru, and Greenwood having been named for the great Choctaw. Even the architecture of Colusa's courthouse, with its columned facade, seemed familiar to Susie, and the smell of magnolias filled the air in the spring.

Colusa's early settlers went out of their way to build a town that was evocative of the ones they had left behind in Kentucky or Virginia. During the Civil War, Colusa held strong Confederate sympathies, and was sometimes called "The Little South."[28] The newlyweds moved in for a while with Sallie Green at her home at 220 Sixth Street. Nearby, there was the beautiful St. Stephen's Episcopal Church for Susie's worship, although Byron did not accompany her to services. The community even had an active chapter of the United Daughters of the Confederacy for social activity. Still, as similar as Colusa and Greenwood appeared, day-to-day life in California was different for Susie in some remarkable ways. The year was, after all, 1912, and there were, for example, no black servants to clean the house, serve her meals or mend her clothes.

The town had progressed considerably since the day in 1851 when Will Green had dragged a pile of brush across the plains to mark the outline for a road to haul lumber from Dogtown to Colusa. With a population of 7,732 by 1910, Colusa had its own Humane Society, a gun club, a movie theater, and even a league of baseball teams.[29] There was no dearth of social activities for the town's inhabitants. Byron Beckwith became active in a number of local groups, from the Independent Order of Odd Fellows, whose lodge was nearby on Fifth and Market Streets, to the Knights of Pythias and Native Sons of the Golden West. Byron and Susie Beckwith, like the rest of the townspeople, enjoyed the Colusa swimming craze of 1913, during which nearly everyone bought a bathing suit and walked each afternoon to the east side of the river.[30]

It was no secret in Colusa that Beckwith liked to drink, and the year following Byron and Susie's marriage, the town was embroiled in a bitter battle over whether to remain wet or go dry. Several shootings and stabbings had taken place in town—this was *still* the Wild West—and the county ultimately voted for prohibition while the city, under local option, remained wet until 1918. Even then, it was only a short ride to Orland, where alcohol changed hands legally, and many of the lodges to which Beckwith belonged were second homes to men who enjoyed spending their evenings drinking. Susie had always been frail emotionally, and her husband's drinking aggravated her fragile nerves. She knew alcoholism had taken its toll on her family in past generations, and also knew that the habit was capable of destroying homes and ruining families. Although she enjoyed having her husband's friends as visitors, their constant drinking and loud talk troubled her. She soothed her nerves with visits to a sanitarium in Tahoe, and at one point was even committed to a private mental institution in California.[31]

While Colusa was embroiled in a bitter wet-dry debate, Susie's mother, Susan Yerger, busied herself with plans for the Confederate Monument to be erected at the southeast corner of the courthouse in Greenwood. Although the war was a half century past, she relished every responsibility delegated to her. To Southerners, there were no more important cultural heroes than the Confederate dead, who imparted to their survivors the critical values of honor and courage. Susan Yerger had met with a group of Mississippi bankers in Greenwood in 1911 and urged them to provide funds for Confederate veterans at Beauvoir, as the home could not accommodate all the veterans who required shelter. She not only served on the monument committee, but also helped compose the florid inscriptions for the statue and even modeled for it. On one of the statue's facades, a kneeling woman—modeled after Susan—is shown comforting a fallen Confederate soldier and bringing a cup of water to his lips. When the monument was unveiled the following year, drawing the largest crowd in Greenwood history at that time, Colonel Lemuel Yerger, adjutant and past commander of the Hugh A. Reynolds Camp of the United Confederate Veterans, represented his group in accepting the monument to the Confederate dead, and gave a lengthy speech which was later chronicled in *Confederate Veteran* magazine.[32]

While many factions of the Sons of Confederate Veterans seemed disorganized, the United Daughters of the Confederacy enjoyed tremendous success in the early years of the twentieth century. By the time plans were laid for the Greenwood monument, the United Daughters had more than 800 chapters and 45,000 members around the country, double or possibly even triple the number of members of Sons of Confederate Veterans. While other women's groups around the country worked to further the suffragette movement, the UDC channeled its energies into monument planning and social events with similar passion. At about the same time children in Greenwood were unfurling Confederate flags about the new monument, Woodrow Wilson, born in Virginia, was being sworn in as President of the United States by a former Confederate Army officer, Chief Justice Edward Douglass White. Although it was purely coincidental, the symbolism was not lost on the South or even on residents of faraway Colusa, California. Wilson was the first Southern-born president since 1850, and his inauguration was notable for bursts of rebel yells and the spirited refrains of "Dixie."[33] For Byron and Susie Beckwith, life in Colusa was also exciting. The following December, at the age of thirty, Beckwith finally succeeded in bringing his father's lawsuit to a close and was awarded $50,000 in compensatory damages, $5,000 in punitive damages and his father's interest in the irrigation enterprise, its property and profits. It was a tremendous amount of money, given the times. The litigation, twelve years in reaching a conclusion, had finally wended its way through the California Supreme Court.[34]

In November 1917, flush with money, Byron and Susie Beckwith began planning a home of their own. Beckwith hired a local builder, L.S. Lewis, to build a bungalow on a corner lot at 341 Sixth Street at the intersection of Oak Avenue, situated near the Colusa County Courthouse. It was a prime location, just down the street from Aunt Sallie Green's home, and near Beckwith's office on Fifth Street. The house was a stylish, single-story structure with a gabled roof and clean, horizontal lines in the popular California Craftsman fashion. Seven steps led from the sidewalk to a spacious front porch under an overhanging eaves, supported by a number of simple Doric columns. The builder finished his work on March 20, 1918, and the Beckwiths moved in immediately.[35] From her front porch, Susie Yerger Beckwith could watch the goings-on at the courthouse and greet neighbors as they drove by or took their daily constitutionals.

The couple had also purchased a ranch of 740 acres, just eight miles north of Colusa, where they raised prunes, beans, corn and alfalfa. In addition to the abstract firm that bore his name, Byron Beckwith used part of his inheritance to purchase Senator J.W. Goad's abstract business as well, and became one of only five Colusa real estate dealers. As the town and the outlying area around Colusa grew, so did his businesses. He underwrote fire insurance and bought the Yuba County Abstract Company at nearby Marysville, expanding his holdings and thus, his local influence.[36] Between the several businesses he owned and the ranch, he spent a considerable amount of time away from home.

The Beckwiths moved in Colusa's most influential social circles. They counted among their friends not only Sallie Green and the Colusa establishment, but leaders of business as well, with whom Beckwith was associated through his enterprises and lodges. The couple seemed especially drawn to adventurers and writers, and among the most notable visitors to the house on Sixth Street and the Beckwith ranch were authors Zane Grey and Jack London. London and Susie Beckwith discovered they had an acquaintance in common, Upton Sinclair. Some years earlier, London had formed the Intercollegiate Socialist Society with Sinclair, long before Susie had introduced the writer to her cousin Mary Craig Kimbrough at the Kellogg Sanitarium. Jack London was also an alcoholic, which no doubt accounted for his visits to the Beckwith ranch, where the two men would sit around the campfire and share a bottle. Beckwith was an avid hunter and fancied himself an adventurer. The Beckwiths occasionally went camping, and Byron had encouraged his wife to learn to fish and target practice with him. He was a fine marksman, and was a firearms enthusiast with an enviable collection of antique weapons. At her husband's urging, Susie Beckwith had become quite a proficient shot herself, and target shooting was a common social activity for women in Colusa, which offered a number of local shooting clubs for both men and women.[37]

No matter what their local status, wealth or influential friends, the Beckwiths, like all residents of towns like Colusa, or Lodi or Stockton to the south, were viewed in nearby Sacramento or San Francisco as members of a yokel or even servant class. Whether out for a shopping expedition or a pleasure trip, the dust-covered visitors from the Valley were unfairly looked down on and could never shed the stigma of being clodhoppers of a sort,[38] even if they drove large automobiles, owned large holdings of land and had plenty of gold to spend. Nonetheless, Byron and Susie Beckwith prided themselves on their appearances, and shopped for their clothes in Sacramento or San Francisco rather than in Colusa.

The couple's early years together were a time of discovery and adjustment. There was, of course, the money Beckwith had inherited and all that could be done with it: building a home, buying additional farm acreage and new businesses, taking trips and enjoying the California wilderness with friends. The real exploration though, had been in learning about each other. Marrying late, both had become set in their ways enough to be somewhat selfish. As was the case with people of their social standing, status and appearances were critical. Colusa was steeped in Southern tradition, and much of the parochiality of a small Southern town held sway. Barrenness, for example, was a source of great shame and humiliation for a woman. Producing a child, preferably a male, and continuing the family line were paramount concerns.[39] It was also still thought that childlessness deprived a woman of her true power, which, even in the early 1920s, was rooted primarily in her ability to nurture her children and mold their moral character. To a husband, childlessness sometimes implied a lack of control over one's wife and diminished his masculinity.

The Beckwiths genuinely wanted an heir, not only for the sake of propriety, but because a child might bring them closer. They wanted a child to shower their affection on and who, eventually, would become the beneficiary of all they had been able to amass together. After nearly eight years of marriage, they both felt excitement when Susie became pregnant.

Following their son's birth, as Beckwith's stature within the community grew, Susie toiled at home, rearing their son. She was a proud, doting mother, taking the boy out in his perambulator and allowing her friends to tickle and coo at him. "Delay," as he was called, became a rambunctious child, full of energy and curiosity. In the fashion of the day, he resembled a little Buster Brown by the time he was three or four, his baby-blond hair long and curled, his breeches short. From the time he was able to walk, the outdoors became his playground.[40] When he was not on the front porch or in the backyard of the house on Sixth Street, he was playing in the dirt on the ranch north of the city, or out camping with his mother and father, poking around in the dirt with little sticks. During days in the city, when his father was working, the child would play in the yard while his mother watched from the porch, or she might take him walking along the sidewalks of town to window-shop or chat with neighbors. It seemed to be an idyllic existence.

Further down their street, elderly Aunt Sallie Green was quickly losing her physical mobility and clarity of mind. Susie would often roll the baby in his stroller down the sidewalk to Aunt Sallie's, where the women would sit inside in overstuffed chairs, or on the porch, where Susie could rock the baby to sleep. Aunt Sallie doted on De La, pulling him close to her smiling, wrinkled face. With Susie, Aunt Sallie could reminisce about days and people long gone. It was a particularly sad day for Susie when Aunt Sallie died at the age of ninety-two, in June of 1925,[41] because she had been such a comfort during Susie's first years in Colusa. She and Byron were shocked when, without any explanation, Sallie Green made no provision for them in her will. They had lived for a time in her home, and had kept her company and watched over her in her declining years. Susie Beckwith was stunned and deeply wounded. Perhaps as a protest to Byron Beckwith's drinking, Sallie Green made a gesture that would demonstrate to him that he would never drink *her* money away. She left half her fortune to her husband's children, and the other half she divided among three cherished nieces. Susie Beckwith was not among them.

A year later, in July 1926, Colusa attorney Thomas Rutledge, who served as executor of Sallie Green's estate, sued Byron D. Beckwith to recover $6,745.94 that Green's estate had paid on a promissory note she had cosigned for him in 1923. The terms of the note demanded payment in six months, but Beckwith did not repay the debt and Colusa County Bank began adding 8 percent interest against the personal loan, compounding it every six months.[42] That Rutledge believed legal action was required to recover the debt, which had been duly paid by Green's estate, worried Susie Beckwith. Rutledge had often served as her husband's attorney, as well, and it troubled her that he believed the debt would not be repaid.

Beckwith may have attempted to repay the 1923 debt, hoping to avoid embarrassment with his wife's Aunt Sallie Green. In July 1924, at Rutledge's urging, Beckwith filed suit to recover damages of $2,500 from the owners of a large herd of cattle that he claimed had trampled his crops at the ranch on numerous occasions. Beckwith filed the suit using fictitious names, as he did not know the identities of the herd's owners. The case dragged on for more than a year, but ultimately was dismissed.[43] Meanwhile, Beckwith—a poor money manager—continued to pay some of his debts by borrowing additional cash wherever possible, and on at least one occasion, was sued by an insolvent bank to recover a $1,500 loan, plus interest.

Beckwith's health, like his financial stability, was precarious, and had been deteriorating for quite some time. He had been treated with hot and cold sulphur baths at Wilbur Hot Sulphur Springs in Wilbur Springs,

California, and his personal physician in Colusa, Dr. W.T. Rathbun, had treated him thirty-six times between 1924 and his death in August 1926. Twenty-three of those visits were noted as house calls, some of which the doctor made late at night, according to documents Rathbun filed with Beckwith's estate when it was probated. Beckwith had also been seeing two doctors in San Francisco intermittently within the months preceding his death. He was treated eight times by Dr. Verlin C. Thomas in February, and visited Dr. Robert B. Williams at least as many times in April. Whether these office visits were to treat his alcoholism, or a separate medical condition, will never be known.[44]

From July 9 to August 10, 1926, Byron D. Beckwith was a patient at the Joslin Sanitarium in Lincoln, California. He had caught pneumonia and, perhaps aggravated by his alcoholism, he failed to recover. His condition was so serious that his wife stayed with him at the sanitarium from July 14 through July 28, and returned home to Colusa briefly to be with their five-year-old son. She returned to the sanitarium on August 3 and remained with her husband until his death at 6:00 A.M. on August 10. He was forty-two years old. She sent one telegram to her family in Greenwood, notifying them of her husband's death, and made four phone calls to her husband's business associates in Colusa to tell them the news.

At the sanitarium, Dr. F.E. McCullough attempted to complete the death certificate with Susie. Distraught, she was unable to offer the doctor accurate information to complete the form. Her husband's name was misspelled, the year of his birth was wrong, his age was incorrectly listed as forty-five, and the notation for his date of burial incorrectly read "August 10," which would indicate that he had already been buried. Dr. McCullough noted on the certificate that the official cause of death was pneumonia with "contributory alcoholism."[45] No coroner's report was filed and no autopsy was performed. A worker for Sullivan Brothers mortuary in Colusa drove to Lincoln to pick up the body, and returned it to Colusa for the funeral.

Word of Beckwith's death swept quickly through Colusa, and its repercussions were felt immediately. Articles in both local newspapers reported the facts as they were publicly known—that Beckwith had succumbed to pneumonia after a trip with his wife and son to Berry Creek in the Sierra Nevada mountains. It was the same story Susie Beckwith would later tell her young son when he asked how his father had died. Neither newspaper reported Beckwith's extended stay in the sanitarium, nor did they mention Beckwith's history of alcoholism. "The news," an anonymous writer reported with understatement in *The Sun,* "comes as a severe shock to not only Colusa people but to many throughout the state."[46]

Many of those shocked by Beckwith's demise were worried creditors.

Beckwith had written a will nearly three years earlier, and left it in the possession of one of his chosen executors, his business associates E.C. Barrell and H.C. Stovall. Susie had not even had time to think about her husband's will, and was surprised when her husband's employees began immediately worrying her with details of the estate and its disposition. First, she had a funeral to plan. Susie asked her rector, the Reverend Halsey M. Werlein, Jr., to conduct her husband's funeral service. Because her husband had not been a member of St. Stephen's Episcopal Church, and undoubtedly because Beckwith had a reputation as a drinker, the reverend agreed, but suggested they hold the funeral at the home rather than in the church. The service was held at 10:30 A.M. at the house on Sixth Street, and the body was taken for burial at Colusa Cemetery, where Susie Beckwith had purchased a single plot, apart from the other graves, for twenty-five dollars.[47]

Before Beckwith's name had been chiseled into his modest granite grave marker, his creditors were inquiring how they should go about filing claims against his estate. Beckwith's debts had been piling up—not just for weeks or months, but for years. Susie Beckwith had been blithely ordering groceries from M.P. Montgomery, the local grocer, unaware that her husband had not paid a grocery bill since 1923. Beckwith was meticulous with some of the smaller bills, like the utilities and the phone bill, although he had not even paid a phone bill for three months prior to his death. He had not paid the man who hauled walnuts from the ranch, nor had he paid for minor repairs to his lawn mower. Beckwith even neglected to pay Aunt Sallie Green's Colusa Sun Publishing Company during the past five years for letterhead and office supplies he ordered for his businesses. The children of a dead woodworker filed a claim against Beckwith's estate, claiming he had failed to pay their dead father ten dollars he was owed, and a hardware store in the nearby town of Williams had never been paid twenty dollars for a tricycle and a scooter Beckwith had purchased for his son.

Beckwith's debts were staggering.[48] At the time of his death, he had several outstanding personal loans of which his wife was unaware—some of which, she was horrified to discover, bore her name as cosigner. Beckwith had signed his wife's signature as her "attorney in fact." While the total net worth of his estate, when appraised, reached a value of more than $112,000, his debts far exceeded his worth. One debt, a 1923 mortgage on his 700-acre farm, totaled almost $57,000. In three years, he had paid none of the principal and only slightly more than $1,000 in interest. To some of his many creditors, Beckwith would write a brief note each year, acknowledging his indebtedness but making no payment against it. Susie Beckwith knew they had some significant outstanding obligations, but she had no idea her husband had mortgaged almost all his property. She was also shocked to find that her husband had a total of less than $300 in cash at the time of his death: just $22 in cash deposited in the Colusa County Bank, $150 in cash in the Bank of Williams, and $124 in cash in a safe at his office.

If she was devastated by the staggering debts her husband had accrued, Susie Beckwith was completely undone when his business associates came by the house with her husband's lawyer to explain the terms of his will. Beckwith had written the document by hand on July 9, 1923. The will was not witnessed, but it was clearly written in Beckwith's handwriting and had been left in the possession of his executors.[49] He bequeathed each of his half-brothers, Bert and Elliott Bray, residences unknown, the sum of one dollar, and instructed that a monument be erected to mark his father's grave at Woodbridge. In the twenty-two years since his father's death—even after the windfall of $50,000 at the conclusion of his litigation—Beckwith had not placed a marker on the grave.

To Stovall, who shared his passion for guns, Beckwith bequeathed all his antique firearms. Barrell was to inherit one-third of Beckwith's abstract companies. Then Susie Beckwith read an unfamiliar name, and went back to read provision nine again. To Ladye E. Cartmell, of Oakland, Beckwith had bequeathed a number of valuable shares of stock in his Yuba-Sutter Abstract & Title Company. Finally, Susie saw her son's name and her own. "I hereby bequeath to my only child, Byron De La Beckwith, Jr., and to my wife, Susie Y. Beckwith, all the rest and residue of my property, both real and personal, Share and Share alike."

Most disturbing, though, was the will's confirmation that her husband had turned his affections to another woman. Ladye E. Cartmell, Susie Beckwith remembered, was Edith Cartmell, a former stenographer of Beckwith's at his real estate office. His provision for her in his will might explain why he had drafted it without witnesses and placed it with his business partners, who undoubtedly knew of the liaison. For many years, Cartmell had remained single and lived in Colusa with her mother and stepfather, Fannie and Otho Mason, perhaps hoping Beckwith might leave his wife. Her hopes may have been dashed when the Beckwith's son was born in 1920, because she soon moved from Colusa to Oakland, where she lived with her younger sister, Loma, and obtained another stenography job. Any suspicions Susie Beckwith felt were supported by some of the bills that were submitted when her husband's estate was probated. From October 29 to November 20, 1923, her husband had lived in room 244 at Oakland's Hotel Sutter, near the Cartmell sisters' home. Beckwith's will was written in July 1923, just three months prior to his lengthy stay in Oakland. Also, Cartmell had loaned Beckwith several hundred dollars in 1922, which he never repaid. She submitted a copy of

Beckwith's promissory note when his estate was probated, and was promptly paid the $456.96 she was owed.[50]

Beckwith's executors, Barrell and Stovall, cautiously explained to Susie Beckwith that the only way they would be able to honor her husband's tremendous debts would be to liquidate his holdings. That meant giving up the ranch, the businesses, and the house in which Susie and her young son were living. As executors, it was their responsibility to see that Beckwith's debts were paid, but honoring them all was going to prove difficult. From the estate, they offered to pay her a monthly allowance of forty dollars. Thomas Rutledge, Beckwith's attorney and one of his pallbearers, stepped in to help Susie maintain her dignity and her home. He helped her petition the courts for an order exempting certain personal property from her husband's estate. "The widow is without estate of her own," the petition read, "and is entitled to an allowance out of the property of said estate, of a reasonable amount, for the maintenances of herself and the minor child of decedent, according to their circumstances and manner of living." The petition asked to the court to raise Susie's allowance to seventy-five dollars a month, nearly double the original figure. She was able to maintain the house on Sixth Street for a time, but the court denied the seventy-five dollars monthly allowance. Susie got forty dollars instead.[51]

Her life quickly began to unravel. Her emotional state, already fragile, was on the verge of collapse. She was pushed to the brink, left alone in California with a small child. Her Aunt Sallie Green was dead, and the many friends and mourners who came through the house on Sixth Street to offer their quiet condolences seemed like curious strangers to her, their eyes cast down toward the hardwood floor. Young De La's chattiness and energy were increasingly taking their toll on her. Although disciplining the child had primarily been her husband's task, more and more frequently she was locking her son in his nursery, unable or unwilling to deal with him. Susie Beckwith missed the comfort of her family, and the "mammy" her son would have if he were back in Greenwood instead of Colusa. She was forced to face mounting pressures and increasing loneliness, and became incapable of functioning. A baby-sitter was called into the house to watch after De La.[52]

Having never participated in her husband's businesses, the widow now watched as her husband's executors summarily disposed of them. Barrell bought the two-thirds of Beckwith's abstract company in Colusa which he had not been bequeathed, and later merged the company with J.B. DeJarnatt & Son to form the Colusa County Title Company. As fall crept into northern California, Susie's petition was resolved and the court issued a decree temporarily setting aside the house on Sixth Street for her use and keeping it from being subject to the administration of the estate. Her

October 26, 1926, homestead petition stated that "on the 29th day of May, 1926, the premises were and continued to be until the death of the deceased, the community property of Byron De La Beckwith and the petitioner, and that the same was acquired by them, by their joint effort, since the marriage of the petitioner and the deceased." As long as she remained in California, she fought to keep her home from being taken away from her to satisfy her husband's debts. Her struggle proved futile. The mortgage on her home was foreclosed, and the house was sold at public auction to pay the debt. Exempt from the administration of the estate were personal items of little use to Susie—her dead husband's clothes, the stovepipes, a typewriter, one shotgun, the decree stated. She gave away most of her husband's personal belongings to his close friends, a move that would deprive her son of many links to his father.[53]

In an order approved by the executors, the Beckwiths' 720-acre ranch by the Sacramento River was swapped for a bid of $57,204 and was transferred back to the man who held the mortgage on it. The paperwork on the transaction noted that it was "necessary to sell the same to pay the indebtedness of the deceased." Having stood by as she watched the disposition of her husband's holdings, Susie Beckwith prepared to move back to Greenwood. She had left her hometown a bride and was returning as an indigent widow. Her sister's son, Yerger Morehead, was summoned from Greenwood to assist her with the move.[54] Boxes and barrels were filled with the relics of her life in California—books, china, and other possessions. Susie carefully packed her clothing and her son's playthings, and with her nephew's help, began the lengthy journey back to Mississippi. On December 9, she wrote a check to Sullivan Brothers, the funeral parlor that had handled her husband's body and burial, in the amount of $489, paying in full the one bill her husband had not willingly charged. Then she left Colusa permanently.

Young De La Beckwith would never really know California, and he never returned to Colusa as an adult to see the house in which he had lived or to visit his father's grave.[55] He was five years old when his father died and his mother moved back to her family home in Greenwood. In later years, he would boast of his proud lineage or recount his ancestors' many noble deeds. His recollections of his father were scant—a particular facial expression his father would have before taking a razor strop to the boy's backside, or the seemingly giant trees that reached into the clouds on the family's ranch.

De La Beckwith's memories of the house on Sixth Street, even his memories of his father, really, were not his own. Instead, they were memories of his mother's later reminiscences. His mental images were formed not so much by having lived in California the first five years of his life, but by having heard so much about the place as he grew older.[56] California was a place of mystery, one of sadness. Susie Beckwith was always careful to keep certain truths from her son, and after their move back to Mississippi told him that their fortune, deposited in banks in California, had been lost in the stock market crash of 1929 when the banks became insolvent. She wanted De La to proudly carry his father's name into the world. Perhaps she hoped her son could make of himself the man his father never became.

2

Return to Glen Oak Plantation

Susie Yerger Beckwith had left her hometown fourteen years earlier, but the Mississippi she loved so dearly had changed little during her lengthy absence. World War I had not affected the face of the Delta, with its abrupt visual shifts between the antebellum homes and the shacks in which Greenwood's blacks lived. Perhaps because the South had been so poor since the Civil War, the abject poverty of the blacks—some homes having only dirt floors, without electricity or plumbing, and small children afflicted with worms or pellagra—seemed almost a comfort to Susie. It demonstrated how much more difficult her lot in life could be. It was a precarious time, the decades between the two world wars, and Mississippi was still a state in which both whites and blacks believed they exhibited a high degree of racial tolerance. Blacks in Greenwood *were* merely tolerated by whites, who still acted as though they were the masters they had been before the Civil War. Similarly, blacks tolerated the whites, seldom exhibiting any signs of discontent with their lot. What was lacking in Greenwood, and what would be lacking there and throughout Mississippi and the rest of the South for many years to come, was any manner of true racial appreciation, rather than simple tolerance.

Along with other families in Greenwood, the elder Yergers had lived for many years in genteel poverty. They had managed, after the Civil War, to maintain their house and a minimal number of servants, and tried to keep black tenants on the farm property to keep the crops viable. The section of town in which blacks lived was called "Niggertown," and no thought was given to the name or the subjugation inherent in it. Black men, regardless of their age, were still called "boy," and entered the Yerger home only through the back door. Jim Crow laws officially separated blacks from whites in public places such as restaurants, in rest rooms, and at drinking fountains, yet the laws, in Mississippi, were unnecessary. Blacks needed no written laws to keep them from mingling socially with the whites in whose homes they worked, in whose fields they tilled, or whose children they nursed. The racial ostracism had been so great, for so long—and lynching such an effective means on the part of whites to keep any potential problem in check—that every black man knew when he was splitting kindling or scuttling coal that the fire he was building would not long warm his own face, but would instead warm a white man's.

There was comfort, Susie Beckwith believed, in such order. It was a code of conduct with which she was intimately familiar, and to which she easily returned when she reestablished herself at her parents' home in Greenwood. Although there was certainly less stigma attached to widowhood than to spinsterhood, Susie Beckwith came back to Greenwood much as she had left it, a social misfit.[1] There was no welcoming fanfare in the local newspaper, nor was there a coterie of friends waiting to visit with her. She returned, in poor health and on the verge of emotional collapse, to a town that had in large part forgotten her during her years in Colusa. She retreated to her childhood bedroom, where she spent many of her days in solitude, having her meals brought up to her. It was a comfort to be back in the family fold, under the care of her parents again, but she knew that she and De La were going to be an additional burden to them in their declining years. At least, with her mother running the household and the servants to keep an eye on De La, Susie believed her boy would stay out of trouble.

Boxes and crates and barrels from the move East made fun playthings for the young De La Beckwith. He could build a fort from the huge piano crate alone, or roll one of the wooden-stave barrels through the back yard for fun. Many of the boxes from the house in California went directly into the attic, their contents uninspected and unremoved. The Yerger family's house at 306 George Street in Greenwood, near the vast stretches of cotton fields and the dark, muddy banks of the Yazoo River, was a new and unexplored place to De La, and he summoned up all the mischief a five-year-old could muster. Lemuel and Susan Yerger welcomed their grandson into their home, remembering how bright and busy it had seemed when their own children were still young. De La was a rambunctious child, and in Greenwood there were new family members to watch over him while his mother tried to recuperate and regain her fortitude.

When she was up to it, Susie would dress her son and attend services at the Church of the Nativity. She was glad to see her old friends. Occasionally, she and her bachelor brother, Will Yerger, who was also living at the George Street house, would "take the waters" at Allison Wells,[2] a prominent sulphur spa near Greenwood, hoping to find a remedy for whatever ailed them at the moment. In middle age, however, Susie never rallied back to complete health. She grieved and grew progressively more ill, both physically and emotionally. Grandmother Yerger ruled the George Street house like the Southern matriarch she was,[3] caring for Susie when it was called for, and leaving her alone when she seemed to need quiet and rest more than a mother's care. A fiery, strong-willed woman, Susan Yerger, even at her advanced age, was not about to let De La run rampant through her house as he had done in California. In her home, he would learn his place and take on some responsibilities. She decided De La was old enough to be delegated minor household chores, like bringing in kindling or coal, or emptying the ashes out of the fireplaces. The rather austere woman De La grew to love and respect, with her timeworn face and steely disposition, bore little resemblance to the gentle, caring woman who had modeled for the Confederate statue at the courthouse.

De La's cousin, Yerger Morehead, who traveled back from Colusa to Greenwood to assist Susie with the boy, quickly established the tenor of their relationship. Morehead, twenty years De La's senior, was held up as an example for the child. Morehead had recently finished law school and was entering the profession in Greenwood, as was expected of him. Morehead taunted his young cousin constantly, and for many years. It might have been his manner of showing affection, or he may have genuinely enjoyed teasing the child. He let De La sip beer, making him think it was root beer, or would send the boy off on a wild goose chase to find a left-handed wrench. Susie's brother, Will, took a genuine interest in his nephew, offering advice and constructive criticism on how to behave like a little Mississippi gentleman.[4] To the five-year-old De La, the house full of advisers seemed intent on spoiling his fun. In California, he had one boss: his mother, who was a docile one at that. Now, in this strange new Mississippi, he had five people telling him what to do.

Although there were many surface similarities between Greenwood and Colusa, there was one particularly curious difference, De La noticed: Mississippi had "mud people." In California he had never seen a black person, and now, with time to explore the plantation, he was interested in where blacks came from and why they were a different color. One evening at the dinner table, he asked about them. Morehead, again teasing De La, patiently explained that bad little white boys who asked too many questions were dipped in mud and hung on a fence to dry.[5] That's how they became picaninnies, or "mud people." The story so frightened De La that he stopped playing in the dirt. From then on, if he had any more questions, he went to his mother or Uncle Will.

In the fall of 1926, De La was enrolled in the first grade at Davis Elementary School in Greenwood, and for the first time he was around other children his own age. Unlike some of his young classmates, who seemed blithely ignorant of illness and suffering, death was a constant theme throughout De La's childhood. One relative after another seemed to die in rapid order after he moved to Mississippi with his mother, and their deaths somehow mirrored the disappearance of a bygone order. First, his grandfather Lemuel died, and was laid to rest in the Yerger family plot in Greenwood Cemetery, dressed in his Confederate uniform. Then his great aunt, Sallie Kimbrough, his grandmother's sister, died. Not long afterward, in 1932, grandmother Susan died, taking her rightful place beside her husband. Susie's parents' deaths took a tremendous emotional toll on her, and she fell into a deep depression from which she was never able to recover. Under her brother Will's careful guidance, the family had managed to hold onto its extensive properties, although the plantation remained heavily mortgaged throughout the Depression. Considering the property losses and abject humiliation Susie Beckwith suffered in California, there was little left of her husband's legacy except the memories she would recount to her son each night as she brushed her long hair before retiring to bed.[6]

De La was a precocious child, wanting terribly to belong to groups and clubs even as a boy. At an early age, he became a member of the local 4-H Club, reciting its "head, heart, hand, health" pledge and participating in club activities. He was elected secretary-treasurer, and, even though the club was very small, it was the first time he had been elected to anything. He liked the feeling. With a group of friends, he formed a backyard circus and charged admission to earn some spending money. He joined the Boy Scouts, a group Susie and her brother Will believed would be especially healthy for the boy, and De La enjoyed that group's camaraderie and outdoor activities. He was always roaming through the fields and woods on the Yerger spread, proud to know that he could walk until he was weary and still not get in trouble for being on some other planter's land.

As Susie's health grew progressively worse, De La's grades in school suffered. An early problem with spelling would plague him throughout his life; he would forever substitute "intrest" for "interest," "pluss" for "plus," "shure" for "sure," "loose" for "lose," "ammount" for "amount," "wounderful" for "wonderful," "stake" for "steak," "mirrow" for "mirror," and so on. To compensate for his inability to spell, he developed a flowery cursive handwriting in which he took great pride. He realized the distinction his name carried—he was no Henry or Joe or Ted, like other Greenwood boys with their pedestrian names. He also knew his name was his one unbreakable link with his father, who grew dimmer in his memory with every passing year. De La would write his name on his lined tablet, over and over. For the rest of his life, he took particular pride in his signature. He would not hesitate to sign a check or a letter with a flourish, then look down at his name, satisfied.

In addition to his problems with spelling, De La seemed unable concentrate on his school work. Although he did not consciously realize it, his mother was dying. He spent his days in school and his afternoons playing, so he saw little of her, and she often took her meals in her room upstairs instead of at the dining room table with her brother Will and her son.

Susie made arrangements to again visit the Kellogg Sanitarium in Battle Creek, where she felt her spirits might improve through better diet, extended rest, and the doctors' daily supervision. De La begged to go with her, and Susie relented. Their trip was a final blow to Susie's fragile health. The doctors at the sanitarium could do little for her but encourage her to rest and relax, as she appeared to be suffering from a cancerous growth. De La was placed in a school on the sanitarium grounds, and later recalled that when he told his mother there were three black children in attendance, she took him out of classes. It was the only time, he would later recall for friends, that he was "willingly integrated."[7]

When they returned to Greenwood, doctors from as far away as New Orleans and Memphis were called in to treat her, to no avail. In addition to her emotional problems, which had plagued her for years, Susie had developed inoperable cancer of the colon. De La began to see less and less of his mother as she spent all day in her room, in bed, and finally stopped coming downstairs altogether. He knew she was ill, but had no idea what was really wrong with her or how serious her illness was. Coming home from a Boy Scouts meeting one evening, his Uncle Will, looking gaunt, met De La outside the house. Seeing Susie wasting away with cancer had hurt her brother terribly, but nothing compared to the hurt he felt as he took De La by the shoulders and broke the news to the boy that his mother had just died. She was only forty-five years old, and starvation was listed on her death certificate as a contributing cause of death.[8]

Dressed in his Sunday best, twelve-year-old De La received visitors at the house with his Uncle Will and his cousin, Yerger Morehead. For the first time, he was forced to be a little man. He held his lips tightly shut so he wouldn't cry. Although he could not remember his father's death or funeral, he would certainly remember his mother's, for it was her death that orphaned him at a critical juncture in his adolescence. After the funeral service at the Church of the Nativity, Susie was buried in Greenwood with her mother and father, rather than in Colusa with her late husband. The distance that had existed between Byron and Susie Beckwith during their marriage was mirrored with finality by their burials, a thousand miles apart. De La was taken to the country by his aunt and uncle, Verdalee and Howard Morehead, Yerger's father and stepmother.[9] While De La rambled around the farm, mourning his mother's death and wondering what would happen next, his fate was being decided back in Greenwood.

De La's cousin and childhood nemesis, Yerger Morehead, was selected by the family to serve as the boy's legal guardian. First, De La's Uncle Will's emotional stability was questionable. Like his sister Susie, Will Yerger suffered several nervous breakdowns and was institutionalized at least once. Later in his life, when his nephew Yerger Morehead committed him to the state mental hospital, it was De La Beckwith who assumed responsibility for him and returned him to his rightful home on George Street. Additionally, Morehead was thought to be a suitable guardian for De La because he had a college education and might set a positive example for the boy to emulate, if only he would shift his attention from the outdoors to academics for a while. Although Yerger Morehead became De La's legal guardian, it was Uncle Will who always came to his aid as a youth, and who most strongly shaped and influenced De La during his adolescence. It was Uncle Will to whom the boy appealed when he wanted a particular favor, or when life under his guardian's thumb was disagreeable.

Will Yerger helped De La obtain his first summer job at Delta Steam Laundry as a teenager, and he also taught De La to hunt. It was also Uncle Will who kept the family estate together, eventually paid off its indebtedness, and gave each heir his part, debt-free. Death had thinned the Yerger ranks, but to De La, as long as his Uncle Will was alive, the Yerger reputation remained intact. In his youth, Will Yerger had attended the University of Mississippi, worked briefly in a bank, then assumed responsibility for the operation of Glen Oak Plantation and the family estate in his parents' declining years. A lifelong bachelor, he always wore a necktie, even when fishing on the lake, and he had a knack for gardening and arranging flowers.[10] Although the family placed a high priority on carrying on the Yerger name, Will apparently never gave serious thought to marriage, leading a fairly sedate social life. He was never known to date. He was active in the Church of the Nativity and saw to it that De La also attended church regularly while he was growing up. De La's Uncle Will seemed a harmless—if disoriented—old man. He often gave flowers to strangers on the street or, after a fishing expedition, stuffed the dead crappie into his dresser drawers at home, wrapped and rotting in newspapers. Although he never posed a danger to anyone, he was well-known in Greenwood as an eccentric.

Will Yerger rarely cursed, and De La, reminiscing later, remembered being shocked at hearing him say "Damn it!" when the porch roof on one of the black's cabins on the plantation collapsed while he was repairing it. He eschewed liquor, telling De La that the evils of whiskey had tarnished the grandeur of the Yerger name from time to time, and that he was determined to polish it back to respectability.[11] Not only had De La's father been an alcoholic, but there were apparently alcoholics on the Yerger side of the family as well. An avid hunter, Will Yerger shared De La's boyish enthusiasm about the outdoors, guns and fishing poles, and instilled in De La a love of nature that lasted throughout his lifetime. Uncle Will taught the boy to shoot, and target practice became one of De La's passions as a teenager, as he was small and group sports did not interest him.

After Susie's death, De La's great-uncle, Hunter Holmes Southworth, came to visit and took up residence at the George Street house. Uncle Holmes, as the boy called him, was grandmother Yerger's brother. He was an elegant, handsome man, a veteran of the Spanish-American War and a retired schoolteacher. He was also a lifelong bachelor who was fond of saying, "Why should I marry and make one woman miserable, when I can stay single and make so many happy?" In some ways, he was as eccentric as De La's Uncle Will. In later years, although he bathed regularly, Uncle Holmes seldom dressed. Instead, he would change his pajamas daily and wear them around the house. Together, Uncle Holmes and Uncle Will would talk politics, discuss the minutiae of planting and harvesting cotton, and reminisce about the old days, when the Yerger family still wielded tremendous influence throughout the Mississippi Delta. The bachelor uncles were De La's strongest influences as a child, and he grew up under their mutual care and guidance.

The next-door neighbors on George Street, the J.H. Freeman family, frequently entertained former Mississippi Governor James K. Vardaman, known as the "Great White Chief" during his reign at the turn of the century. It was always a major social affair when Vardaman came calling in Greenwood,[12] where he owned the newspaper, *The Commonwealth*. He carried tremendous influence with the cotton planters and plantation owners, and the tall, magnetic politician made a significant impression on De La, who later came to share some of his racial views.

Vardaman was an unparalleled demagogue in a state rife with demagogues. He loudly proclaimed that blacks were "physically, mentally, morally, racially and eternally the white man's inferior." He attempted to repeal the Fifteenth Amendment, ratified in 1870, which assured blacks the right to vote. He also wanted to modify the Fourteenth Amendment, which provided blacks, as citizens, full protection under the law. During one of his early campaigns for governor, when he learned President Theodore Roosevelt had had Booker T. Washington to lunch at the White House, Vardaman publicly denounced the President as a "bronco-busting nigger lover," and was elected handily by his Mississippi constituency. None of his political peers could match his ability to stir up the masses with racist rhetoric. Although, in the course of his lengthy career, he initiated some important social reforms, such as improved prison conditions, the abolition of convict leasing, and increased school appropriations, he relentlessly used blacks as a platform upon which to clean his bootheels. Over the years he referred to the Negro as "a lazy, lying, lustful animal," "a curse to the country," "a social scab," and "a political ulcer."[13] He had every intention of keeping them underfoot, as race was always a primary topic come election time. In Mississippi, the way to remain in office was to preach the gospel the white planters wanted to hear. King

Cotton dictated that blacks should toil in the fields, and local custom was that the white man would rule over them.

De La Beckwith had outgrown his curiosity about "mud people," just as he outgrew his cotton trousers, but even as an adolescent he believed intensely that there were inherent differences between the races that kept them apart. Politicians, newspaper editors and storekeepers all talked the same talk and walked the same walk in Mississippi. De La listened to the adults' conversations with rapt attention. During Beckwith's youth, the state's opinion leader was Senator Theodore G. Bilbo, a former state senator, lieutenant governor and twice the governor of Mississippi, who was the state's most vehement racist mouthpiece.[14] Talk of Bilbo was common among Beckwith's uncles, who were keenly interested in whether or not Senator Bilbo was watching out for their best interests in the Senate.

Bilbo was James K. Vardaman's heir apparent, and both politicians possessed great oratory skills. Although Bilbo lacked Vardaman's physical stature and eloquence, he had a down-home sense of humor that his constituents liked. Most Mississippians, as a rule, did not read books or newspapers, and the South's high illiteracy rate worked to Bilbo's advantage. When constituents gathered around the back of an oxcart or a makeshift platform to hear him speak, most had never read that the Mississippi State Senate, in a 25-1 vote, once resolved that Bilbo was "unfit to sit with honest, upright men in a respectable legislative body." He advocated total separation of the races and proposed a plan to send blacks back to Africa, at one point telling Eleanor Roosevelt—who looked disdainfully on his project—that he might entertain the idea of crowning her queen of Greater Liberia. He put forth his arguments about race, he said, after having studied race relations covering nearly 30,000 years. Just as De La as a child idolized Vardaman, as a teenager he revered Bilbo.[15]

When Bilbo talked about "the Negro problem," De La didn't have a frame of reference. There had been no blacks in his elementary school or junior high school. Blacks seldom came into Delta Steam Laundry at 409 Main Street, where De La worked part time, unless they were picking up laundry for their white employers. As the workers laundered, starched and pressed the clothing in the back, De La did much the same work out front that he knew blacks were accustomed to—waiting on customers, sweeping the floor, solicitously answering the phone and running deliveries. All the blacks De La knew were servants, like Mamie, who was both housekeeper and cook at the George Street house. She often brought Uncle Holmes, Uncle Will and De La their breakfasts in bed. After Susie Beckwith's death, Mamie firmly took control of the day-to-day maintenance of the Yerger household. She was the sole woman in a house full of bachelors, the only woman with whom De La had any daily contact, and the first black person he actually knew well.

Whether dealing with white customers in the dry cleaners or black servants on the plantation, De La demonstrated that he had grown into a polite young man. Under Uncle Will's tutelage, De La developed the manners for which he would be known throughout his life. He always used the emphatic, "Yes, *suh*" or "No, *ma'am*," and he was polite almost to the point of annoyance. He had also reached adolescence, a gawky stage for him. He was skinny, with a quick, sincere smile, proverbially as wide as his head. He had long, gangly arms and kept his dark hair close-cropped. He kept rapidly outgrowing his clothes, but his shirts were as faultlessly starched and his trousers as sharply creased as anyone else's in town. Most of Greenwood's white residents in the 1930s had their clothes done by black women who took in washing, but because of his job at the laundry, De La's clothes were cleaned free—a perk he greatly appreciated. With this job and the bit of money he made selling subscriptions to *Liberty* magazine, he had some spending money to do with as he saw fit, without regard to his guardian, who left day-to-day management of the boy to Uncle Will. The older and more independent De La became, however, the more of a handful he was for his uncles. The boy was willful, and was frequently intent on having his way or no way. He was also developing a temper.[16] As a child, his mother had been able to persuade him to behave, or to placate him into submission with a soft explanation or excuse. His uncles and his guardian, De La found, were more apt to just say "no" to his frequent requests, without explanation or recourse, which frustrated and irritated him.

Morehead watched De La spend several years meandering through the public schools with little success, and decided that the boy needed the discipline of a private school, where he might be more strongly encouraged to pay attention and show results. With his low grades and cavalier attitude, De La was an embarrassment to the family, which prided itself on its prominent planters, business leaders, educators and lawyers. Morehead had attended Chamberlain Hunt Academy, a fine school in Port Gibson, Mississippi, and he thought a private school would whip De La into shape academically. Standards were higher, and he might learn the value of an education. It would also keep De La out of Morehead's hair for a while.

The Webb School in Bell Buckle, Tennessee, seemed an ideal choice. The student body was small, indicating that students received a high degree of personal attention, and William R. Webb, Jr., the principal and son of the school's founder, Sawney Webb, was known to rule the school with a firm hand. His father, the school's patriarch, had served fittingly in the Confederate army and, in his later years, physically resembled

Robert E. Lee. Bell Buckle was little more than a whistle-stop situated between Nashville and Chattanooga, and the town comprised a few country stores, some nondescript homes and a church. The school campus was the highlight of the town, and there was little else that would have drawn a crowd of youngsters to Bell Buckle.[17]

The entrance formalities out of the way, thanks to Morehead's efficiency, Beckwith was enrolled in the ninth grade for the 1936–37 school year, just two months before his sixteenth birthday. De La was already behind in his class work, because he should have been enrolling as a junior. His grades in the public schools apparently were not high enough to get him classified as a junior. Morehead's incentive plan to get De La to read—offering him a dollar for every book he checked out of the library—had accomplished little except to empty Morehead's pockets and create a dusty stack of unread hardbacks in De La's bedroom. Henry Odom, D.S. Wheatley and several other Greenwood boys, friends of De La's from public school and church, were also enrolled at The Webb School that year.[18]

The boys quickly discovered that Webb was no ordinary school. The curriculum required four years of Latin and two years of Greek, as well as mathematics, history, English literature and composition. Students were not expected to become brilliant; they were expected to sharpen their abilities to think, and to develop character. An honor system, refined at The Webb School and later used as a model by Princeton University, ensured that students grew to value honesty and integrity above grades. Sawney Webb, debating the many ways he could invest the $12,000 he raised to start the school in 1886, decided to spend two-thirds of it on books. If it was any indication of Webb's success and its legacy, during its first fifty years The Webb School groomed more Rhodes scholars than any other secondary school in the United States.[19]

Students were expected to adhere to a strict set of rules. They were not allowed to stop on the way from one class to another, nor were students of one grade level allowed to walk onto the grounds where another grade's classes were held. A straight "A" student, however, was exempt from all the rules, and could do pretty much as he pleased. There were no uniforms or dress codes. In clear weather, students could hold classes outdoors if they wished, studying Ovid or Virgil under the beech trees that were plentiful on the campus.

Particularly in the South during the Depression, students who attended private schools represented an elite minority. That does not mean, however, that they were all from wealthy families. Many parents struggled financially to see that their children were able to remain at The Webb School, and although De La Beckwith had no parents, he did have uncles and cousins who fiercely wanted him to succeed. Yerger Morehead was watching over De La's inheritance from his mother, using part of the money to clothe and feed the boy and keep him in school. Even during the Depression, Morehead wanted to ensure the De La had a good education.

Professor Webb liked to point out that students who graduated in the top third of their class at The Webb School often went on to become world leaders, and they frequently did. De La knew by the beginning of his second year he would not be among them. One of his classmates, though, Logan Bostian, attended Princeton University and was named Phi Beta Kappa. As a research chemist under Dean Hugh S. Taylor, Bostian helped develop the atomic bomb. Beckwith, on the other hand, fared so poorly at The Webb School that he couldn't make it through his second year. Instead, he appealed to his Uncle Will to arrange for a transfer to Columbia Military Academy in Columbia, Tennessee, where he began classes in February 1938.[20]

The Webb School and Columbia Military Academy were as different as caviar and fried catfish. Each was exceptional in its own way, but each required a refined taste. De La was enrolled in time to complete the second half of the tenth grade, and his enthusiasm about the transfer was boundless. He was particularly drawn to the academy's snappy uniforms, which alternated grey wool slacks in the winter with white cotton ducks in the summer. If he thought he would fare better academically, however, he must have been sorely disappointed to find that Columbia's president, Colonel Clifford A. Ragsdale, was as much a taskmaster as Professor Webb had been.

Boys attending Columbia were carefully screened and only a limited number of applicants were accepted each year. Each prospective cadet had to offer former teachers and his local minister as references. Yerger Morehead undoubtedly had to pull some strings with Colonel Ragsdale to get De La enrolled, because by February, when De La started, half the academic year was already over. And Beckwith was already behind academically, which had contributed to his failure at The Webb School.

The cadets' rooms at Columbia were austere and utilitarian. Straight-backed chairs and a desk were the only furniture other than a metal bunk bed and a closet, and room inspections were held daily. Once each week, on Saturday, white-glove inspections were held. Each room housed two boys, and the students shared communal bathrooms. The majestic Main Barracks housed classes, and Columbia boasted one of the largest indoor drill halls in the country, which doubled as a gymnasium in the afternoons. From reveille at 6:30 A.M. until taps sounded lights-out at 10 P.M., the cadet's day was filled with class work and activities. The dining room, with its intricate honeycomb tile floor and the soft, soothing clatter of silverware against china, was perhaps the only place De La felt at ease and could relax.

Cadets were expected to apply themselves rigorously to their work, and the academy maintained strict guidelines regarding inappropriate behavior. A number of offenses warranted immediate expulsion. Hazing and fagging—"exacting personal service from fellow cadets,"—according to a CMA catalog from that era, were strictly forbidden. Gambling was also forbidden, and boys who were found with playing cards or dice were expelled. Indolence and idleness were dangerous habits that led to "moral turpitude," Colonel Ragsdale would say. Profanity, vulgarity and "immorality in sex life" brought immediate expulsion. Cadets leaving academy grounds for any reason were required to have a pass, and were to be checked out of the commandant's office. Any student found "absent without official leave" was immediately expelled. Students were expected to take turns serving guard duty at the academy's guard house overnight, and while the academy had several prison cells to house belligerent offenders, the cells were seldom used.

Columbia offered diplomas and certificates in the Academic Department, for students who were college-bound, and in the Commercial Department, for those who would enter the work world. Diplomas were awarded to candidates who scored 80 in all their subjects; those scoring between 70 and 80 were given certificates. Military science, English, tactics training and algebra were not De La Beckwith's idea of fun, and it did not take him long to see he was not going to succeed at Columbia. Perhaps most painful of all, study hall was held daily in the chapel of the main building for boys who were delinquent in their work, and they were required at night to work under the direct supervision of the faculty officer in charge. Grades were posted weekly, and cadets with demerits had to publicly and repeatedly walk the "bullring," a large circle on the school grounds about half the size of a football field.[21]

Despite the military discipline and the rigid academics, cadets at Columbia were a fairly content lot of boys. The motto on Columbia Military Academy's seal, "*Vincit qui se Vincit*"—"*He conquers who conquers himself*"—did not apply to De La Beckwith, who left the academy on May 31, 1938, after only four months, and never returned. He had been shipped from school to school in hopes of finding one where he would succeed. At each of them, he had failed. When fall came around, he enrolled at Greenwood High School as a junior. Neither he, nor his guardian Yerger Morehead, nor his uncle Will Yerger, ever asked to have his academic records forwarded from Columbia Military Academy.[22]

Implicit in De La's return to Greenwood's public high school was his failure at The Webb School and Columbia Military Academy. Not only was it an embarrassment for him and his uncles, but it also put him at an obvious disadvantage among his classmates. He was nearly two years older than most of them when he was enrolled as a junior at Greenwood High

School in September of 1938, just two months shy of his eighteenth birthday. Naturally, his attendance at the more prestigious schools, coupled with his age, gave him an aura of worldliness—the one upside to an uncomfortable situation for De La.[23] None of the high school's select clubs, however, encouraged him to join. He was small, and did not excel at sports. Neither did he play an instrument in the band, join the pep squad, try out for the school play, or earn election to the National Honor Society. Although from his childhood he had demonstrated a need to belong, his only extracurricular activity at Greenwood High School was the school's Study Club, for academically challenged students.[24]

For high school seniors graduating in 1940, the country was changing faster than they could change with it. The world was at war, and although the United States had not yet been drawn into its vortex, the boys and girls at Greenwood High School, and at virtually every other high school throughout the United States, were blithely living the last truly carefree days they would know, as the Great Depression of the 1930s came to a close. As an Indian summer crept through the Delta and the leaves began to rust, Greenwood High's football team, the Bulldogs, won seven games, lost two and tied two during the 1939–40 season. The school's band fared well in state competitions, wearing new purple and gold uniforms that had debuted earlier in the fall. Helen Sledge, a junior, won the ten-dollar prize awarded by the J.Z. George Chapter of the United Daughters of the Confederacy, as well as the state medal, for her essay "General Nathan Bedford Forrest's Campaign in Mississippi." And in the middle of the Mississippi Delta, America's most luscious cotton-growing land, classes were dismissed early on five consecutive school days in January because of a deep, unexpected snow.[25]

Beyond the serene campus, De La at eighteen became the youngest initiate in the history of Greenwood's chapter of the Knights of Pythias, a secret lodge. Because his father had belonged to the Colusa chapter, De La was a "legacy," warranting special consideration and assuring his selection for membership. He also became something of a hellion, using his earnings from his part-time job to keep himself and his friends stocked in beer. His tiny candid photograph in the Greenwood High School yearbook, in the "Campus Cut-Ups" section, is captioned "Beer-Guzzling Byron." His senior prophecy read, "De La Beckwith has turned reformer and missionary in the South Sea Islands," and suggested that he probably spent more time raising hell than raising his hand to answer questions in Mrs. Williford's senior English class.[26]

He was not unpopular, however, and many of his high school classmates remember him fondly. "He was just what we call a gentleman," said Jack Galey, who graduated with Beckwith in 1940. "Seems like everybody in school was his friend, as far as he was concerned. You know how in school you'll divide up into classes or cliques? Well, I believe that boy could have fit in any of them. He could get along with all of them." Galey's wife, the former Emma Day, also graduated with Beckwith and remembered him clearly. "He wore white shoes and a white hat and a white suit in the summertime. Just a Southern-type gentleman."

Another classmate, Eloise Duggins Johnson, had both English and history classes with Beckwith, and remembered his morning routine. "I always remember him coming up the walk to the school in the morning, just as jubilant as he could be, hollering at somebody or cutting up with somebody," she said. "He was a very happy-go-lucky boy, very congenial. He was always in the midst of a group, and I didn't know of anybody who disliked him. I never heard of him ever being in any trouble at all."

Two other classmates, who asked that their names be withheld, had less flattering recollections of the adolescent Beckwith. "He was kind of a joke," one man said. "People laughed at him and made fun of him behind his back—you know how cruel kids can be at that age. But De La was a laughingstock." A female classmate remembered that the local girls found him repulsive. "He was well known for his manners," one woman said. "But at dances at the Country Club, girls would congregate in the bathroom and scrub their hands after they'd danced with De La." She remembers that the Yergers had a reputation among the students as being "kind of weird," and said she could not recall a single girl from Greenwood who had ever dated De La. "Most of the girls here didn't want to have anything to do with him."

In February, when the members of the senior class voted for "Who's Who" winners in a number of categories, Beckwith tied for "Most Talkative Boy" with Minter Aldridge, the class salutatorian and yearbook editor. Beckwith also garnered enough votes to earn runner-up status in both the "Friendliest Boy" and "Wittiest Boy" categories, although he won no title outright.[27] He fared almost as well in the competition as some of the school's most popular boys. Jim Dulin, who was president of the senior class and was named "Mr. GHS," and who participated in a dozen extracurricular activities, led the pack with strong votes in seven different categories. Charles Parker, an attractive athlete with chiseled features that rivaled Jack Galey's, won by an upset in the "Glamour Boy" category and placed strongly in four others. Having ranked so well against the other boys at the school, Beckwith was apparently well-liked. Even today, most members of Greenwood High's senior class of 1940 have complimentary things to say about him, although none can remember the name of his best friend, nor that of any girl he dated in high school.

At the senior baccalaureate ceremony on May 26, 1940, Beckwith sat proudly among the members of his graduating class as Reverend Duncan Gray talked about the responsibilities of youth entering a complicated, troubled world. There was little in the address anyone could have taken issue with, and De La, like the rest of the seniors in his class, listened wistfully as the minister charged them with their obligations. Reverend Gray was the new rector of Church of the Nativity, having assumed spiritual leadership of the congregation in September 1939. In the coming two decades, it would be Gray, and his son, Duncan M. Gray, Jr., against whom De La would rail during the 1950s as the Episcopal church took a leading role in desegregation efforts in Mississippi and throughout the South.

At the commencement ceremonies on Friday evening, May 31, 1940, held in the high school auditorium, Beckwith accepted his diploma with a grin and went out into the world with a plan: He would go to college and become the latest success in the Yerger lineage. He spent the summer working at Delta Steam Laundry and saved some money for fall enrollment. He enrolled at The University of Alabama, and then immediately withdrew when he did not receive a bid from the fraternity he longed to join. He then enrolled as a freshman at Mississippi State College in Starkville.[28] Like the rest of the plebes, he wore a short-billed maroon cap over his shaved head and happily went through fraternity rush. Beckwith pledged Sigma Phi Epsilon, but fared so poorly in his classes that when midterm grades were posted, he was ousted from the fraternity and left campus to return to Greenwood.

Again, Beckwith retreated with his tail between his legs, much to Uncle Will's and Yerger Morehead's chagrin. Unable to excel at a private school, a military academy or the public schools, it was evident De La Beckwith was not cut out for college, either. Too old—or perhaps embarrassed—to sweep floors and make deliveries at Delta Steam Laundry, Beckwith took a job at the local Pepsi-Cola bottling plant, as an office boy. He worked for the company for about a year and a half, and after a time moved up to warehouse work and later, to a sales position marketing Orange Crush and other soft drinks throughout the Delta.[29] The house on George Street was beginning to suffer terribly, as the wallpaper downstairs began to chip and peel, and the house desperately needed painting and myriad minor repairs. Uncle Will, more concerned about paying off the Federal Land Bank mortgage on the house and property, allowed the home to fall into disrepair. Morehead's constant pleas to maintain the house, at least for the sake of the neighbors, went unheeded, as Uncle Will went about his daily routine, offering spare change and nosegays to children in the streets, and filling his bedroom with stacks of old newspapers and discarded cardboard boxes.

On December 7, 1941, the Japanese bombed Pearl Harbor. Like other young men in small towns throughout the country, De La Beckwith was determined to join the war effort and do his part to protect and defend the United States. After all, many of his illustrious ancestors had served their country since Revolutionary War times. There was little to keep him in Mississippi besides his affection for Uncle Will and Uncle Holmes. Aside from his mother's share of the land that comprised Glen Oak Plantation, which Uncle Will was farming for him, there was no reason for De La to stay in Mississippi. His job was mundane, and he was not dating anyone. So on January 5, 1942, almost exactly a month after the Pearl Harbor bombing, Beckwith drove to Jackson and enlisted for a four-year hitch in the U.S. Marine Corps.[30]

For a young man from a background of faded privilege, Beckwith was back at ground zero with the Marine Corps. His childhood, riddled with academic failures and marked by an intense desire to belong, was officially over. Had he applied himself at Columbia Military Academy, he would have been able to gain entry to any branch of the service as a commissioned officer. Instead, while many of his former fellow cadets from the Academy entered the armed forces with commissioned rank, De La Beckwith simply enlisted. From his very first day of boot camp in San Diego, De La Beckwith faced something new—complete, unquestioned authority; total discipline; and something he never experienced in school, the threat of losing his life if for any reason he failed.[31]

For a while, at least, he felt he belonged.

3

Identifying the Enemy

Boot camp at San Diego in 1942 was a turning point in De La Beckwith's life. This was no private school or military academy—this was Company A, Second Marine Division, U.S. Marine Corps. For Buck Private 337938, there was no possibility of calling the war to a halt on a whim and running back home to the safety of Greenwood. Gentility was an unnecessary virtue, and "Yes, *suh*" was no longer merely a polite reply. For the first time in Beckwith's life, he was expected to maintain a rigorous daily discipline that strengthened him both physically and mentally. He left high school a skinny young man, measuring in at five feet eight and a half inches, not quite 140 pounds, all grits and grins. Before long, though, he had put on ten pounds of hard muscle. The daily workouts at boot camp felt good. It was strangely satisfying to feel the dull pains of long-dormant muscles suddenly coming to life. At twenty-one, for the first time, Beckwith's abdomen rippled, his legs were taut and his shoulders broadened. He was becoming not just a man, but a marine. A leatherneck, he was proud to say.[1] He felt like he was finally living up to his potential.

From reveille until sundown, Beckwith and the rest of his platoon spent each day drilling, exercising and tumbling, running obstacle courses, carefully placing and then crawling under barbed wire—all under the tough, watchful eyes of Drill Sergeant Henry J. Kapica, who was determined to whip his scraggly bunch of recruits into a steely, indestructible fighting team. Men who never learned to swim as youngsters were taken to an indoor swimming pool and were ordered into the water, poked from the sidelines with a long stick to keep them from reaching for the safety of the pool's edge. For some of the marines, learning to swim was more frightening than fighting the Japanese, the faceless enemy they were being indoctrinated to despise and destroy. Kapica's men admired him, but it was an admiration deeply rooted in their fear of his authority, and of his power. The boots' days were highly structured, and Beckwith and the others were given explicit tasks to accomplish under tight time restrictions. Expectations were high, while the margin for error was nonexistent. There were no grades here, as at the several schools Beckwith had attended. In boot camp, he would either succeed or fail, and Beckwith was determined not to fail again.

After years of target shooting in the Mississippi Delta, Beckwith was already a fine shot when he enlisted, owning a small arsenal of firearms most young men his age would have envied. On his enlistment papers, he even named "weapons (collecting)" as his sole hobby.[2] At boot camp, though, he honed his skills with the Marine Corps' standard-issue rifles and pistols. He also learned hand-to-hand combat techniques—how to use his bayonet with confidence to "annihilate the enemy," according to *The Marine's Handbook*, or, when unarmed, to debilitate an enemy by pressing a thumb into his throat or pounding him in the kidney with a bent knee. So well indoctrinated were Sergeant Kapica's recruits that they came to believe they could take on the enemy with their bare hands, if necessary, and some of the more religious marines believed they were Christ's chosen warriors.[3]

Although Beckwith's Uncle Will had seen to it that his nephew attended church most of his young life, the boy was never particularly religious until he became a marine and faced his own mortality. He saw firsthand the results of war, as boys he knew from back home were reported dead or missing in action, and young troops from his own camp were regularly being killed overseas. When he left Greenwood, Beckwith packed his Bible and a book of poetry, the *Rubaiyat of Omar Khayyam.* He had never been an avid reader, but for the first time, during quiet moments in the barracks, he began reading his Bible regularly, finding comfort in it. Before boot camp was over, he knew the *Rubaiyat* by heart, often closing his eyes, book in hand, and murmuring the stanza, "Ah, love! Could thou and I with fate conspire/To grasp this sorry scheme of things entire/ Would not we shatter it to bits, and then/Re-mould it nearer to the heart's desire!" Even decades later, he could call it immediately to mind, reeling off whole sections of the epic poem on command,[4] just as he could quote lengthy passages from the Bible, citing chapter and verse.

There was no unresolved conflict in Beckwith's mind about killing the enemy. It fit his psyche. His ancestors had proudly killed the enemies of their young country, and he was proud to finally be among their illustrious company. His was a boy's pride, grounded in a sense of insecurity that made him want to prove himself worthy of his noble ancestry. He and his fellow soldiers were fighting a man's war, defending country and home and mother and liberty. Many of them, though, were still just boys, and Beckwith, in many ways, would always be a boy, possessing a man's body but a boy's immature rage.

Among the young men Beckwith got to know while at boot camp was another young Southerner, Private Norman Moïse, who was a New

Orleans native. The two met at the San Diego Boat Basin, and they quickly learned to side with each other against young men from the North or the Midwest. "Sometimes Beckwith would kid the other men," Moïse remembered. "He'd say, 'You boys don't know how to live—but Moïse and I do,' because we were both from the South." The two became casual friends, and later, before shipping out, had their photograph made together with a small group from their unit encircling the reigning Miss Laguna Beach, who was at a dance they attended. "Frankly, I liked Beckwith," Moïse said. "There were very few in our platoon that I didn't like, and he was a good marine."

Trained and ready for combat, and anxious to do his part in the war effort, Beckwith possessed a fierce sense of personal patriotism that was becoming increasingly intertwined with his religious beliefs. He knew that the fighting in the Pacific was a last resort, that the intention of his fighting was ultimately to bring peace. Protecting the United States, Mississippi, his own way of life—that was God's will.[5] And killing the enemy, at war, was not subject to the biblical commandment, "Thou shalt not kill." The Bible was full of war and bloodshed, and God smiled favorably upon His warriors, those men brave enough to do battle in His name. True Christians were a warrior people, Beckwith believed, and he was proud to count himself among them. He would later adopt a similar philosophy for other causes, as well.

Near the end of Beckwith's tenure at San Diego, Colonel Evans Fordyce Carlson visited the camp, looking for volunteers to join his Raiders Battalion, which was soon to earn a renegade reputation at Makin and Guadalcanal.[6] Carlson was looking for men with no close family ties, as his new commando group was viewed as a potential suicide mission. Along with several others, Beckwith stepped forward to volunteer, and he waited in the officers' quarters to meet with Carlson. The colonel interrogated him thoroughly, but ultimately, he was not selected. Embarrassed, Beckwith later blamed not making the cut on his height, claiming the colonel only selected the larger, stronger brutes to be Raiders.

The Second Marine Division, with Beckwith and his platoon in tow, shipped out for the Solomon Islands late in the summer of 1942 on the USS *Jackson*. The troops, traveling in Higgins boats and tank lighters, endured searing tropical weather as they crossed the Pacific from San Diego to the small group of islands that included Guadalcanal, Tulagi and Gavutu. The Second Division, with its amphibian tractor battalions testing their skills at amphibious assault, joined with the First Marines and took Guadalcanal from the Japanese with relatively few casualties on August 7, 1942. Having been groomed and motivated for combat, Guadalcanal was a decisive victory for the young marines. Beckwith's unit saw no combat, but was responsible for ferrying supplies back and forth to Guadalcanal, and when Henderson Field was captured and held, the U.S. saved 1,000 miles on essential convoy routes to Australia.[7]

Following Guadalcanal, the Second Division stopped for two weeks at Espiritu Santo, the largest island in the New Hebrides in the Southwest Pacific, to build a bivouac area. Then, after nearly sixty days at sea, the first land sighted was the small island of Tonga Tabu, a French possession. The men were allowed to swim ashore and explore the island for a couple of hours. Just as the movies portrayed the tropics, a tanned woman in a sarong appeared on the beach—sitting on a mat outside a native hut. Norman Moïse was with Beckwith when they went ashore. "It was an ugly little island, really," he remembered. "We rented a two-wheeled cart, pulled by a mule, and a lot of the fellows got in the cart and the mule flew off the ground," he said, laughing.

After a brief respite, the troops returned to the ship and later embarked for the brief eighteen-mile trip across the channel to Tulagi, where they were placed on standby for six weeks after the island was wrested from the Japanese. Like most of the men in his platoon, Beckwith soon contracted dengue fever. Severe joint pain and headaches made it difficult for the men to work, and the rash that accompanied the virus, coupled with the sheer heat, made it impossible to sleep at night. Rather than be crammed into an overcrowded sickbay area, however, many of the men continued to work, building a containment area on the island to house Japanese prisoners they expected to capture soon.

Confined to the island, some men pressed the juice from Tulagi's purple jungle berries, using it as ink to write lengthy letters home. Marines who were willing to trade cigarettes or other possessions to the natives left the island with several handmade tropical wood canes, beautifully carved and inlaid with mother-of-pearl.[8] When they recovered from the fever and finished the containment area on Tulagi, Beckwith and his platoon patrolled the nearby island of Gala. Later, they shipped off to Gavutu, another small island, where Beckwith received a letter from home telling him that one of his lifelong friends had been shot down over the English Channel by Germans. He brooded over the loss for days, angry and depressed.

Still, there were a few light moments. Norman Moïse remembered firing on the Japanese when he was situated at a machine gun emplacement near Beckwith. "Beckwith's sandbag emplacement was to the south on this little cove," Moïse said, "and a small Japanese plane came just around Gavutu. I was by my emplacement and Beckwith was on *top* of his, and all the time, he was cheering, 'Yea, State! Bite 'em in the ass! Bite 'em in the ass!' " It was apparently a football cheer Beckwith had learned at Mississippi State College during his brief stay there. Private First Class Charles Pruitt, a native of Greenville, Mississippi, remembered spending a great deal of time with Beckwith on Gavutu, where the two enjoyed swimming and fishing together. "We fished with hand grenades, just for devilment," Pruitt said. "We swam a lot, and there was a sunken boat near the dock, and we'd swim down to it and play like we were driving the boat. De La had a Japanese 13mm rifle, one of the captured guns, and he manned his post with that rifle. And I can't remember if it was Japanese skulls or teeth that he kept, but it was one or the other. That was one thing that was a little weird about him."

Thanksgiving came and went, then Christmas.[9] Beckwith and his platoon prepared to ship out of the Solomons for New Zealand at the end of January 1943. While most of the men in his battalion spent the holidays reminiscing about their mothers and girlfriends back home, and the meals they would be serving across fancy holiday tablecloths, Beckwith was thinking of Uncle Will and Uncle Holmes. They, too, would be celebrating with a holiday meal, two old bachelors sitting across the table from each other in a musty dining room with faded wallpaper. Mamie, the cook and housekeeper, would be serving them their supper, leaving her apron in the kitchen as she slipped out the back door to prepare a holiday dinner for her own family, miles away.

Having succeeded in capturing Guadalcanal and Tulagi, the Second Marine Division turned its attention to the Central Pacific with "Operation Galvanic," a battle to conquer Tarawa, Makin and Abemama atolls. Although there was initially a strong desire to take the Marshall Islands, lack of troops made the move too risky. Instead, the Allied forces had focused on a sixteen-island archipelago stretched along the equator, the Gilbert Islands. The United States was determined to strong-arm its way toward Japan, and capturing the Gilberts would pave the approach to the Marshalls, to the north.[10] Even at its inception, "Operation Galvanic" was critical; it would prove to be the turning point in the Pacific Theater of World War II.

Under the command of Major General Julian C. Smith, who inherited the division after its success at Guadalcanal, the Second Marine Division was assigned to conquer Tarawa. The U.S. Army's Twenty-Seventh Infantry Division would tackle Makin, and a separate landing party would scout the tiny island of Abemama. The problem, however, would be getting troops across the coral reef barriers that surrounded the tiny atolls. Unpredictable tides further complicated the problem, making it impossible to predict whether the small transport craft would be able to reach shore.[11] Some officers insisted the tide would be high enough for the troops to ride in over the reefs. Smith's operations officer, Major David M. Shoup, recommended landing the troops in amphibian tractors, commonly called amtracs. Shoup had seen the amtracs in action at Guadalcanal, carrying supplies from ship to shore, and believed they could also be used to transport troops across the reefs. Smith, concerned that his men would be stuck at the reefs and would have to wade ashore under enemy fire, later went to Hawaii to request a hundred additional amtracs for the upcoming operation. He did not know then how critically important they would become.[12]

The Second Division arrived at New Zealand on February 11, 1943, and were encamped in the small town of Petone, about thirty miles outside Wellington. They spent day after day in the water, learning to maneuver the amtracs, planning a direct frontal beach assault. The men were ostensibly on standby for the First Amphibian Tractor Battalion, then stationed in the Philippines. The amtracs, weighing nearly 22,000 pounds and moving at only about six miles per hour, were going to be used to carry groups of about twenty men from the transport ships onto enemy shore.

Smith obliquely recommended to Major Henry C. Drewes, commander of the Second Marine Division's amphibian tractor battalion, that he find some way to reinforce the amtracs before leaving for the assault. Drewes bought the only reinforcement material he could find on such short notice—some rusting nine-millimeter-thick steel—and the plating was cut and mounted on the amtracs, providing at least a little additional protection for the men who would travel behind it.[13] Beckwith, recently elevated to the rank of corporal, was trained as a machine gunner and crew chief, and was assigned to stand on a platform in the bow of his amtrac while firing at the enemy. Beckwith would go into battle at six miles per hour, with his body only partially hidden behind a nine-millimeter-thick shield of steel.

In New Zealand, Private First Class Edward J. Moore had almost daily contact with Beckwith, who lived in a four-man hut directly across the "street" from Moore. "We lived at a place called Hutt Park till November of 1943," Moore remembered. "Beckwith was a corporal by this time, and I can tell anyone who's interested in Beckwith's military background that he was one hell of a good marine," Moore said. "He made corporal exceedingly rapidly, in less than a year, and even in wartime that's fast. He always had a book in his hand, reading constantly." Private First Class Charles Pruitt shared Beckwith's hut, and the two Mississippi natives cemented their growing friendship. "De La was a very likeable person," Pruitt remembered. "He would go out on liberty by himself, and he would save up his money until he could afford to eat in the best restaurant, buy the best food, drink the best wine—he'd come back flat broke, but he'd be a happy marine. He was a guy you'd be proud to have at your side in combat, because you knew he'd never leave you."

The New Zealanders, who had sent so many of their own young men into battle in North Africa, were gracious hosts to the soldiers stationed there. As an indication of the good relations between the New Zealanders and the marines, Moore noted in his journal that the local newspapers carried the Second Marine Division casualty lists, just as they carried the casualty lists for their own native troops fighting in Africa. Although many of the men met and married local women, Beckwith did not date while he was stationed in New Zealand.

The Second Marine Division was comprised of young men, far away from home—most for the first and only time—engaged in a war that would cost a great many of them their lives. Friendships were erased, in a hail of gunfire or the solitary blast of a land mine, as quickly as they had been formed over a tray of grub in a mess hall. Religious services were held on deck frequently, and with few other places to go except overboard, most everyone was within earshot of the chaplain. "Religion was a personal thing, it wasn't discussed," said Ervin B. Jones, who like Beckwith was a corporal in the Second Amphibian Tractor Battalion. Although he and Beckwith were unaware of it, they shared a close mutual friend in Dewey Hobson Anderson III. "If anything," Jones said, "remember that these people had a certain amount of macho about them too, so religion was not something that came up. It was more a matter of camaraderie and closeness, and if that was a matter of having faith, you kind of gathered it from the rest of the group."

Private First Class Raymond L. DeJong, a devoutly religious amtrac driver, was also a member of Beckwith's battalion. He remembered clear delineations between his fellow marines with religious leanings and those without. "We had a group of guys in New Zealand that had Bible study every Wednesday or Thursday night, but it was only a group of about ten to twelve of us, out of about a hundred," DeJong said. "You had two different types of people—some that were Christians and some that weren't, some that were fearful and some that weren't." There were also those who, regardless of their religious beliefs, enjoyed drinking and carousing as a means of relieving stress. Norman Moïse remembered Beckwith as something of a rounder. "After Guadalcanal, we were trying to live it up every night that we got out," he said. "When it came to drinking, I didn't know any who were moderate. I know that Beckwith was just as wild as all of us, and we just drank too much, really." While Beckwith and his friends got into scuffles now and again on liberty, the lengthy periods of time he had spent aboard ship provided him with an opportunity to read his Bible. By the time he shipped out at New Zealand, he knew it backward and forward, and he took comfort in a renewed sense of faith he had not known as a youth. He faced the enemy knowing that his God would protect him and keep him safe. He thought about it and prayed about it, and knew he would survive whatever confronted him in the coming battle. For the rest of his life, Beckwith would be, as he saw it, a devout Christian. His sense of duty to God, his country and his family had been formed during wartime, and forever after, his unshakeable personal theology and strong sense of patriotism would be linked inextricably with war.

On November 1, 1943, on the deck of the USS *Lee*, rested and motivated after a lengthy stay in New Zealand, Beckwith joined his fellow marines in singing "Goodbye Mama, We're off to Yokohama," or, to the tune of the familiar "Caisson Song":

> *"Over sea, over foam*
> *Wish to Christ that we were home,*
> *But the transports keep sailing along."*[14]

Rear Admiral Keiji Shibasaki, commander of the Japanese Imperial Marines on Tarawa, had boasted that the Americans would not take the island with a million men in a hundred years. The Japanese had created an almost impenetrable fortress on the small island, fortifying it with nearly 5,000 Japanese Imperial Marines. Deep in the sand, they constructed garrisons covered with five feet of concrete and surrounded by ten-foot-thick walls of sand and coral.

En route to the Gilberts, the U.S. troops cleaned their rifles and sharpened their bayonets and knives, wondering how close to the Japanese they would be when they fired or lunged. Occasionally, a movie would be shown on deck to lift morale, or at least to pass the time. Many of the men spent their early evenings writing letters home, to girlfriends or parents in Texas or Arkansas or, in Beckwith's case, to uncles in Mississippi. Some played cards or read magazines, and those who were able, slept under the oppressive heat.

On November 15, ship commanders opened their sealed orders. They were to lead the first assault on the strongly defended atolls, the largest Pacific operation to date.[15] To conquer the Gilberts, two attack forces were assigned. From the north, six transports carrying 7,000 U.S. troops were to storm the island of Makin. A southern attack, comprised of transports carrying 18,000 marines, would capture Tarawa. The assault troops were reinforced by aircraft carriers, battleships, light and heavy cruisers, mine sweepers, destroyers and support craft.

Later that afternoon, Major General Julian Smith, aboard the *Maryland*, read a message to the officers and men of the Second Marine Division over a sound system that linked the ships. He referred to the initiative as ". . . the greatest combination of aerial bombardment and naval gunfire in the history of warfare." He wanted to keep morale high. "This division was specially chosen by the high command for the assault of Tarawa because of its battle experience and its combat efficiency. Their confidence in us will not be betrayed." His instructions to his men were clear and succinct: "You will quickly overrun the Japanese forces. You will decisively defeat and destroy the treacherous enemies of our country. Your success will add new laurels to the glorious traditions of our Corps." The words rang in Corporal Byron De La Beckwith's ears. This battle, he sensed, would be his moment of truth.[16]

November 20, 1943, was the designated landing day. "We got up fairly early in the morning," said Jones. "A lot of people didn't sleep, of course, the night before." Reveille was sounded in the middle of the night. It was so hot, most of the men who did sleep awoke in a sweat. The typical landing day breakfast, served this morning at 1:00 A.M., consisted of steak, eggs and fried potatoes. By 4:00 A.M.—some forty minutes later than scheduled—the marines were scrambling over the sides of the naval carriers and into the amtracs that were waiting to be manned and driven ashore.

Each amtrac plowed toward shore bearing twenty men, each man carrying—in addition to his rifle—a pack with rations, water, a toothbrush, a spoon, a shaving kit, a change of clothes and a blanket. Before the men were loaded in the outboard boats for the first assault on Tarawa, they were ordered to dress in clean clothing, to lower the chance of infection from wounds. Their targets were designated Red Beaches One, Two and Three. At 4:41 A.M., the Japanese sent up a flare, signaling to their troops that the attack was imminent. Then the Japanese opened fire.[17]

"We went in, really, not expecting too much on the island, because they'd been bombarding it and bombing it," said Jones, "so everything was fairly well relaxed, I think. There wasn't a great deal of anxiety. People were excited, but we weren't really expecting too much." The plan of attack was clear, although the commanding officers had told the enlisted men little about the heavy fortification on the island. The soldiers would move swiftly from mother ship to amtrac to shore, where each amtrac would unload the cargo of men and return to the ship to pick up another crew. "We had orders to hit the sea wall, and we were going to go over the sea wall and throw out grappling hooks and drag barbed wire with us, and carry the troops as far inland as we could before they disembarked," Jones said. Marines landing on the beach would storm the island and overtake it, rushing toward a relentless hail of enemy artillery, machine gun and rifle fire.

"Then, all hell broke loose," Jones said, "and it was just a scramble to get to the beach." Almost immediately, the leadership of the Second Amphibian Tractor Battalion was wiped out. The battalion's commander, Major Henry Drewes, was shot through the head, and his direct reports were dying with him. Beckwith was assigned to a unit moving out in the first wave assault; Jones was in the second wave. Both men were machine gunners and crew chiefs, standing partially exposed on the bows of their amtracs, facing enemy fire. The second wave amtracs, a later model nicknamed "buffalos," had been brought from Samoa to serve as backup vehicles. They moved slightly faster than the older "alligators" that Beckwith was on.

General Smith's demands for additional amtracs brought the total available for action at Tarawa to 125, but 95 went down in the battle. The amphibian tractor battalion, 500 men strong, saw 323 casualties.[18] In the first two hours of the naval bombardment, more than 3,000 tons of shells were hurled at the island, with little impact on the forts, while the amtracs rolled in, unloading troops. Those who were not killed, or whose amtracs were not disabled, either hit the shore or circled back for more troops.

While the Navy's guns fired overhead, Beckwith stood on the small platform in the starboard bow, manning his .50 caliber machine gun behind the thin plate of steel. His job, and that of the other machine gunners and crew chiefs, was to spray the enemy soldiers closest to shore with rapid fire so the amtracs could reach the beach, unload the men and circle back to pick up more men. Later, the amtracs would be used to ferry supplies and ammunition to shore, pick up the wounded and quickly evacuate them for removal to a hospital ship which was awaiting the casualties. Shell fire and small arms fire hit the amtracs loudly as they approached the shore, while enemy soldiers at the seawall threw grenades. From the coconut trees circling the island, individual Japanese snipers picked off the oncoming marines one at a time. Beckwith's "alligator" crept slowly, making it seem like an eternity to get from the ship to the shoreline, while relentless enemy fire whizzed past and cold water splashed over the side of the amtrac. Beckwith had never been more awake in his life.

He was 500 yards off Red Beach Two, which a few days later would become a cemetery for hundreds of his fellow soldiers. When his .50 caliber machine gun jammed about 400 yards from the beach, Beckwith instinctively tore the crippled gun off its base and grabbed a .30 caliber machine gun from the stern. He resumed his position at the amtrac's bow, crisscrossing the shoreline with gunfire, hoping his shots would keep the enemy down until the craft could unload its crew on shore. His upper body jutted above the platform, exposed, while the troops in the amtrac were behind him, hunkered down. Several men on Beckwith's deck were shot as the craft crept closer to shore. Enemy fire smashed his gun mount, jamming the machine gun's chamber and splattering Beckwith with hot lead. The action of his weapon was jammed with debris from the blast. Unable to fire again, Beckwith remained standing on the bow, facing the enemy and hoping they would see his raised gun and mistakenly believe he was firing on them. For a few seconds, while bullets and mortars screamed over the coral sands of the beachhead, Beckwith's machine gun was silent in his hands.

Still standing as the amtrac got within about fifty yards of the beach, he was hit. Hot lead ripped through his left thigh,[19] and the searing metal blast knocked him down on the deck of his amtrac. Blood gushed from his wound as his crewmates, now near the shoreline, jumped overboard and stormed the beach under a barrage of gunfire. Beckwith submerged, knowing his chances of survival were better underwater than on the surface, and in time, as he bled into the cool waters of the Pacific, a mobile medic unit swept through the area. A young Navy medic, moving quickly through the casualties trying to separate the living from the dead, slit Beckwith's pants open and applied a thick gauze compress on the large wound, binding it tightly and slamming a syringe of morphine into his thigh.[20] Beckwith fell unconscious, and later woke aboard a light tanker heading toward USS *Middleton*, a hospital evacuation ship bound for Navy Hospital 128 at Pearl Harbor. Edward J. Moore, who had also been injured, was aboard the same light tanker.

On Tarawa proper, the men who were successful in touching the sand had to pass through the bloody wreckage of their companions' bodies, strewn about like wreckage dropped carelessly from the sky. Dozens of troops died cruelly on enemy entanglements of barbed wire in the shallow waters between the coral reef and the beach. Others were burned alive as shells barraged their amtracs and lit them like roman candles. Grenades lobbed by the enemy nearest the shoreline exploded and ripped off a leg or an arm.

Out in the water, Dewey Hobson Anderson III saw his friend Beckwith's disabled amtrac, and rushed over to it to see if Beckwith was lying near it, dead. Anderson was also a small-town Mississippi boy, from a family of cattle ranchers in the tiny town of Okolona, in the northeastern part of the state. He and Beckwith had become friends at Hutt Park in New Zealand, but now, Beckwith was nowhere to be found. On board the amtrac, however, Anderson found Beckwith's pack. Certain that Beckwith was dead, Anderson slowly opened the pack and removed Beckwith's T-shirt. He took his combat knife and cut out Beckwith's name, printed inside the collar, and placed the swatch of cotton in his pocket. He carried it in his wallet for the next twenty years.[22]

Doctors on the USS *Middleton* performed surgery on Beckwith's thigh to remove the lead and clean the wound, and he was quickly stitched up. He was lucky, the doctors thought; slightly higher and to the right, and the Japs would have literally blown Corporal Beckwith's testicles away. Passing in and out of consciousness, Beckwith missed much of the daily routine of the other wounded men who were conscious; they confronted fresh corpses, wrapped in the stars and stripes, as they slid into the cold waters of the Pacific. The stench of death, emanating as much from the clothes of the survivors as from the dead themselves, clung to the ship and followed it, like a hovering cloud, to Pearl Harbor. On December 17, at Pearl Harbor, Beckwith, Moore and a contingent of wounded soldiers boarded USS *Solace*, the Navy hospital ship that would bring them stateside to San Diego, where they arrived on December 23, 1943. Employees representing *The Los Angeles Times* presented each of the wounded marines who were disembarking with an envelope containing a crisp ten dollar bill, as a goodwill gesture. Both Moore and Norman Moïse had visited briefly with Beckwith in the hospital in Hawaii, but lost track of him when he was admitted to Balboa Naval Hospital.

Beckwith never met the enemy on Tarawa, never got close enough to see the whites of their eyes, as he had hoped. He did, however, know a singular horror of battle that most of the other marines never knew—he had stood, completely vulnerable, and faced the Japanese with a machine gun that would not fire. He believed that God had spared his life this time, and Beckwith knew that because of the severity of his injuries, he had seen his last battle. He later received the Purple Heart for the injuries he sustained at Tarawa, the battle in which he never made it to shore. Later, he quietly and solemnly gave the medal to his Uncle Will.[21]

Fewer than twenty members of the Japanese garrison on Tarawa were captured alive. More than 4,800 of them died, killed in their bunkers by marines. Others chose to commit suicide by shooting themselves rather than surrender to U.S. forces. Many of the Japanese gracefully extended their rifles between their legs, barrel pointed at their faces, and pulled the triggers with their bare toes. In sheer numerical terms of lives lost, troops wounded, length of battle and amount of ground taken, Tarawa was the costliest battle the U.S. Marine Corps ever waged. More than 1,000 U.S. Marines and seamen were killed, and 2,296 were wounded.[23] But once the tiny island was taken, the path to the Marshall Islands was cleared. A valuable airstrip was captured, and the U.S. flag was raised on a coconut tree.

Circling over the carnage, Lt. Commander Robert A. McPherson, piloting a Kingfisher float plane from the *Maryland*, where Major General Julian Smith was anxiously monitoring the battle, radioed back a description of the tiny figures, rifles stretched overhead, slowly creeping toward shore. "I wanted to cry," he said.[24]

4

Misalliance

Beckwith heard her speak before he ever saw her. She sounded like a Southern version of Lauren Bacall, with a deep voice that was both sensuous and a little rough around the edges, like honey on gravel. To De La Beckwith, Mary Louise Williams, nicknamed Willie, was possibly the prettiest young woman he had ever seen. There were plenty of WAVES[1] at the Naval Air Station at Memphis—technically, the station was situated in a little Tennessee town called Millington, about eighteen miles from Memphis—but this twenty-one-year-old was a raven-haired beauty. Although he had been dating a young woman in Memphis, Willie immediately captivated him. As soon as they met, he knew there was something different about her, that she was not like the other young women on the base or in town. She had a fiery, rebellious personality and, like Beckwith, enjoyed drinking. Her captivating, cornflower-blue eyes could be alternately innocent and commanding. She looked not so much at him, as *within* him.

"I was in a little old partitioned-off place, giving out supplies like nuts and bolts and toilet paper," she recalled of their first meeting.[2] "I was a supply clerk, and we worked in the same airplane hangar. De La worked on airplane instruments." Beckwith had been shipped to the Naval Air Station in the spring of 1944 to work as a Marine aviation mechanic while he recovered from his wounds.[3] His thigh was not yet fully healed, but he was gradually gaining mobility and was getting around the base quite well by the time Willie arrived that September. Just a month before, she had enlisted in the Navy in her native Tennessee and attended the Naval Training Station in the Bronx, New York. Willie had dropped out of high school after the tenth grade. She had worked at Knoxville's Market House for a short time, and also waited tables at a local restaurant. Although she was anxious to join the service and thought it might be a way to see the world, her father would not sign papers for her enlistment, so she waited several months and enlisted when she turned twenty-one, against her parents' wishes. She was two and a half years younger than Beckwith.[4]

Beckwith was one of only a few enlisted men on the base at Millington, which housed mostly naval officers, and he and Willie became friendly before they became romantically involved. He would talk to her about the woman he was dating. "Sometimes, he'd want to buy her a gift, and I'd tell him something to buy her," Willie said. "At that time, he used to slip rum into the hangar, and we'd pour it in our coffee and drink it. That's how I first remember him."

It was not long before Beckwith stopped calling the young woman in town and was instead pestering Willie for a date. One afternoon, when Willie was returning to her barracks from picking up some dry cleaning, she ran into him. When he asked her for a date, Willie smiled broadly and told him she thought that would be fun. On impulse, Beckwith turned to her, a bundle of dry cleaning pressed between them, and kissed her for the first time. He particularly wanted their first evening together to be special, so to impress her he made reservations at the Peabody Hotel's Skyway lounge. The sleek, art deco Skyway was the most cosmopolitan gathering place in Memphis, and featured a circular dance floor covered by a low dome lit by concealed lights. The hotel was renowned throughout the South, and the centerpiece of the lobby was an imposing black and gold travertine fountain. A large flock of trained ducks swam in the fountain all day, and each evening a porter escorted the ducks by elevator to the rooftop, where they slept. Willie was duly impressed by the Peabody and the beauty of the Skyway, and on the dance floor she discovered that, for a man with a 30 percent disability from a gunshot wound to the thigh, Beckwith could cut a mean rug. "One thing about him, he wouldn't ask you to go into town with him, or have a date, unless he had money," Willie said. He fawned over her on their dates, lavishing drinks and attention and compliments, all intended to dazzle and beguile her.

Beckwith bragged endlessly about his plantation upbringing, romancing Willie with stories about life in the Mississippi Delta. He painted a romantic picture of women on wide verandas fanning themselves slowly and plantation owners in fine, white linen suits. Greenwood was the cotton capital of the world, according to Beckwith, with happy black field hands plucking the bolls of white gold and humming spirituals to pass the time. Willie was from a good family in Knoxville, but the Williamses had never been as wealthy as Beckwith made his clan sound. Willie's father was a small-time grocer with his own store, well-established and well-respected in his community, but the family was certainly not rich. Willie's background contrasted sharply with Beckwith's. He had been orphaned as a child and was reared in a large, drafty house by eccentric uncles. He had been given far greater rein than most children enjoy, tromping through the woods or pulling together a neighborhood carnival at his whim.[5] The household in which Willie had grown up was filled with loving parents and a passel of rambunctious brothers and sisters all of whom, as the oldest girl, she was expected to help rear. Beckwith's uncles always kept a black household servant and field hands to maintain the house and yard, and while his childhood was certainly not carefree, he had limited responsibilities. If he wanted something, he would get petulant and, in most cases, Uncle Will would weaken and give in to the boy's wishes. By the time Willie was sixteen, on the other hand, her own parents had borne nine children and sternly ruled their home. In the Williamses' home, petulance was rewarded with a firm spanking.

"My house was *too* full for me, growing up," Willie explained. Although her parents were loving and attentive, she was troubled at an early age by the expanding brood of children. "My childhood bothered me, as far as my mother having so many children, because I don't believe any woman wants that many children," she said. "But I always figured that she did it because that's what my *father* wanted, and I think it bothered her sometimes. It bothered *me*, because I used to wonder if my father really loved her as much as he said he did. Because having that many children was detrimental to her health. And when I was growing up, I resented the fact that he made us take care of the younger ones."

In the quiet old house on George Street, Beckwith may have wished he had brothers and sisters. Aside from the differences that marked their respective childhoods, however, Willie shared Beckwith's romantic view of the South and its traditions, which he instinctively sensed. He was gallant to a fault, opening doors for her, holding her arm to steady her in her high heels, pulling out her chair with a flourish before she sat down. She appreciated his fine manners and his courtesies. He was a gentleman, and he treated her like a lady.

Willie and Beckwith soon became the talk of the base at Millington. Their dates were never humdrum; they never merely went to a movie in town, or to a short-order restaurant for dinner. Instead, even if he had to travel to Greenwood to sell a rifle from his collection, or liquidate a pair of featherweight binoculars at a bargain basement price on the base, Beckwith insisted on the best for Willie and wanted to ensure their dates would never be common.[6] They made an attractive couple, and prided themselves on being the life of the party. On the dance floor, Beckwith's favorite song was "Rum and Coca-Cola." Willie's was the more romantic "Begin the Beguine." If another man cut in on him, or stopped at the table and asked Willie to dance, Beckwith asserted himself and quickly turned the man away. He became not just jealous, but livid, Willie remembered. "He acted, at that time, like he really owned me," she said, attributing at least some of the blame for his possessiveness to their mutual binge drinking. "We never went on a date that he didn't have a fifth of whiskey for him and a fifth for me," she said. "We never went anywhere then that we weren't drinking." Their dates always began and ended the same way;

he would come bearing liquor, and they would return to the base after he had vented his temper. It was the beginning of a spiral of alcoholism and violence that would plague the couple for the next twenty years.

She first became aware of his raging temper secondhand. Not long after she started dating him, Willie was supposed to meet Beckwith in Memphis for an evening out. At the last minute, she made other plans and asked another enlisted woman, who had a crush on him, to be a replacement date. "So she went, and he took a whole bottle of whiskey and just busted it on the table, all to pieces, in front of her." It was the first time Willie felt the power of his rage. She knew he had been put in the brig on occasion, and recalled that he frequently would try to find a reason to start an argument with other servicemen. "He had a bad temper, because when we'd go out on liberty, he was always wanting to fight with sailors or servicemen." She believed his constant belligerence was an attempt to overcompensate for his relatively small size, and that he tried to impress her with his fearlessness. "I never really thought too much about it then," she said, "because I just thought he was trying to show off all the time."

His violence, however, would be tempered by his incredible sweetness. He was incurably romantic and loving, and demonstrated it in quiet ways that appealed to Willie. He would keep his arm around her anytime they sat side by side, or would hold her hand when they walked through the city. Even his temper had a certain appeal. Although it surpassed acceptable gallantry, it demonstrated his passionate nature. By the time Beckwith got his orders to ship out to another base, he was very much in love with Willie. His idealized vision of Southern womanhood—beauty, virtue and honor—guided his behavior with Willie while they were dating, and although he had fallen deeply in love with her, he did not pressure her to have sex. Although Willie believed he had slept with other women before they met, she understood the common double standard which held that fast women were not the kind a well-bred Southern boy wanted to marry. Beckwith believed a bride should be a virgin on her wedding day. His sexual restraint was perhaps his way of showing his respect for Willie, his desire to keep her unsullied, but it caused her to question whether he was really all that deeply interested in her.

Occasionally, with a weekend pass, Beckwith and Willie would stay with Mrs. Willis Campbell, a cousin of his who lived in Memphis. Her husband had founded a prominent local dry cleaning company, and her Morningside Drive home was a local showplace. "It was just like a hotel," Willie said. "She had two or three maids and a chauffeur. The maids would come upstairs to see if you needed your clothes pressed, or needed a drink. And Mrs. Campbell took a liking to me and thought I was the girl for De La." Word got back to Uncle Will and Uncle Holmes in Greenwood that Willie seemed a suitable prospect for him, and Beckwith wrote glowing letters home about her.

Beckwith's Uncle Holmes traveled to Memphis one weekend to meet Willie, and took a comfortable room at the Gayoso Hotel. He took the couple on a shopping spree at Levy's, a fashionable department store on South Main Street, to buy them some civilian attire. Uncle Holmes fancied himself a snappy dresser—he often wore a tailored seersucker suit and always carried a walking stick with a silver handle—and wanted to ensure the couple had something besides their uniforms to wear. Some time later, Willie traveled with Beckwith to Greenwood to meet Uncle Will and see the Yerger family homestead, and she very nearly made up her mind not to marry him then and there, although he had begun asking her persistently to become his wife.

"I got a real big shock when we drove up," she said. "I just really couldn't believe it. Seemed like they lived in the past, all of them. They had the fine manners and everything, but they didn't have any money to back anything up." She was appalled at what she found in Greenwood. There was a vast difference between what Beckwith had described as a plantation, with a yacht on the river, and the small, flat farm she saw stretching ahead of her. The black tenant farmers lived in squalid shacks, and Beckwith's uncles lived not in a magnificent plantation home, but in the modest family homestead on George Street, a ramshackle house that desperately needed a coat of paint and a thorough cleaning.

In March 1945, Beckwith was shipped to another base at Cherry Point, North Carolina, to serve as Sergeant of the Guard with a Military Police battalion. Because of his deepening relationship with Willie, he was not particularly happy about the transfer, but there was little he could do but travel back to Memphis at every available opportunity. He had broached the subject of marriage with Willie before he shipped out, but she did not believe he was really serious and kept delaying things without giving him a firm answer. "When he left, I figured he was just somebody else shipping out, you know, and that would be the last I'd see of him," she said. "I tried not to even keep up with him when he went to Cherry Point, but he kept coming back and coming back. Every time he could get a leave, he'd come back to Memphis." He wrote her lengthy, florid love letters, proclaiming his passion for her and continually pressuring her to marry him.

He had earned his new staff sergeant stripe at Millington, and while stationed at Cherry Point, he applied to Officer Candidate School at Quantico. He had given some thought to a career in the Marine Corps. He was examined for Officer Candidate School on May 5, 1945, and told the examiner that both his parents were dead. In spite of the fact that his mother had suffered from emotional problems and had been institutionalized in California, and that his Uncle Will had endured several nervous breakdowns, Beckwith told the examiner there was "no mental disease in the family history,"[7] and in fact he may at that time have been unaware that they had spent time in mental institutions. His application, nonetheless, was rejected, but his flourishing romance with Willie softened the blow to his ego. He forfeited any serious thoughts of a Marine career, although his military interests would manifest themselves in other ways later on.

Beckwith's determination and persistence finally convinced Willie that he was serious about marriage. He was never hesitant to declare his love for her, and swore he would do everything in his power to make a good life for the two of them. To the alumni newsletter of The Webb School, which he had left in embarrassment, Beckwith wrote that he had finally found "the lady of my dreams."[8] He wrote a stilted letter to her father in Knoxville to ask his permission to marry her, and Willie's father—still angry over her move to join the WAVES against his will—tersely replied that she was old enough to make up her own mind about marrying him. Willie asked permission from her commanding officer at the base, who gave her blessing and wished the young couple well.

A quiet wedding ceremony was held in a small chapel in Hernando, Mississippi, on September 22, 1945. A local justice of the peace, H.F. Scott, officiated, as Byron De La Beckwith and Mary Louise Williams, wearing their uniforms, vowed to take each other as husband and wife, for better or for worse. None of the members of their immediate families attended. Mrs. Willis Campbell, De La's older cousin in Memphis, arranged for her chauffeur to take them to get married, then hosted a small reception in their honor at her lavish home. Uncle Will sent Beckwith $500 to have a proper honeymoon, but did not drive up for the ceremony. After the celebratory toasts were made and the cake was cut and served, Mrs. Campbell's chauffeur drove the newlyweds downtown to their final destination, the Peabody Hotel. After many dates at the hotel's Skyway lounge, drinking and dancing their evenings away, the couple had reserved a suite for a five-night honeymoon.[9]

Dressed in a delicately embroidered peignoir set that Uncle Holmes had bought her during his visit to Memphis, Willie Beckwith joined her husband in bed for the first time that evening. As Beckwith caressed and undressed her, his hands were warm and welcoming. Outside, Memphis was in the throes of a gentle Indian summer evening. The newlyweds explored each others' bodies for the first time, warmed by the drinks they had shared earlier. What Beckwith did not know, however—what he was *never* to know—was that his young bride had been married and divorced *twice* before.[10]

After their honeymoon at the Peabody, Willie returned to the Naval Air Station at Millington and Beckwith resumed duty on base at Cherry

Point. As soon as the war ended, Willie mustered out at the rank of Seaman Second Class, and she and several other WAVES, who were among the first to receive their final paychecks, were photographed for one of the Memphis newspapers. She took the bus to North Carolina to be with her new husband, and got a room at the Queen Anne Hotel in nearby New Bern, where they could be alone together off the base. "I stayed there until all our money ran out," she recalled. She traveled the short distance back home to Knoxville, where she settled in for a short time with her family.

On January 4, 1946, having fulfilled his four-year hitch, Beckwith was honorably discharged at the rank of Staff Sergeant. He joined Willie in Knoxville, where he met her family for the first time. "While we were in Knoxville, De La wrote me a beautiful letter," Willie said quietly. The letter described the symbolism of her wedding band and her husband's eternal love for her. "He said my diamond was to nature what his heart was toward me, the most perfect and indestructible of all things. They were probably the sweetest words he ever put on paper."

During their brief stay in Knoxville, Uncle Will called Beckwith from Greenwood to let him know he had arranged a job for him as operations manager for Chicago & Southern Airlines at the town's tiny airport. The arrangement suited Beckwith, as it removed the pressure of having to worry about an income, and he could return to Greenwood with his arrangements in place. Many young veterans were not so fortunate. Instead of the Marine Corps uniform to which he had grown accustomed, he would soon be wearing the double-breasted Chicago & Southern uniform and earning just under $2,000 per year.[11] When he and Willie began to pack for the move, it became apparent to Willie that Beckwith was not even considering the possibility of getting an apartment or house of their own. He took it for granted they would move into the big house on George Street, the only home he had ever known, to live with Uncle Will and Uncle Holmes.

At the Greyhound bus station on Main Street, Uncle Will waited with his truck to pick up the couple and drive them home. The old man chortled and slapped Beckwith on the shoulder and offered a warm embrace to the young bride who would be the new addition to their household. When he pulled the truck up next to the entrance, Uncle Will scurried out of the driver's seat to help Willie out of the passenger side. At the front door, he swept his arm graciously toward the parlor, as if welcoming the young couple to Versailles, and followed them into the house. Inside the dark house, Willie took a deep breath and thought, "Well, this won't be so bad for a little while."

To Willie, the aging bachelor uncles resembled the addled characters in a Frank Capra comedy. Uncle Holmes often bragged that in his younger days, he had gambled with some of the best of the famed riverboat gamblers who traveled the Mississippi and Yazoo Rivers. He left regularly on Saturdays to get his hair trimmed and have a meal and a few drinks in town. He had a keen sense of humor and a molasses drawl, and for comfort and convenience, was fond of wearing his pajamas in the house all day. He bothered to dress only when he was going out in public.

Uncle Will seemed truly out of touch with reality much of the time. He was a very religious man who unfailingly attended services at the Church of the Nativity, where his parents had been prominent members of the congregation. He still handled the day-to-day operation of the plantation, its accounts, the disposition of its cotton crops and management of the black field hands and tenant farmers, but by most accounts he was mentally incompetent.[12]

"He did crazy things all the time," Willie remembered. "For instance, he'd bring you something and set it down, you know, and then pick it up and carry it back with him. I always made him come into the house through the back door because it seemed like he was always dripping water." One family acquaintance recalled Uncle Will coming by her house one day with a present for her. "He brought some vegetables over, in a little paper tray, sort of, and had it in foil. One of each thing," she laughed. "One squash, one tomato, one cucumber, two or three beans." Whatever Uncle Will's mental condition, he had admirably fought through the Depression and the war to hold onto what was left of Glen Oak Plantation, and had successfully paid off the long-standing mortgage against the property while Beckwith was overseas.

Having met both the uncles before she moved into the George Street house, Willie knew she would have no problem getting along with them casually, but she was concerned about living in a house with two elderly men, day in and day out. The house, she soon discovered, was managed by neither Uncle Will nor Uncle Holmes, but by their maid, Mamie.[13] Agile and strong-willed, Mamie eyed Willie suspiciously for the first several weeks after her arrival. Other than Mamie, there had not been a woman in the house since 1933, when Beckwith's mother died. Each morning, Mamie slipped in the back door and started cooking breakfast, frying eggs and ham and bacon, and making a large pot of coffee. It had always been her custom to deliver breakfast on a tray to Uncle Will and Uncle Holmes, in their beds. Willie's first confrontation with Mamie came immediately after she and Beckwith moved into the house, when Willie refused to take her breakfast in bed, saying she would come downstairs and eat at the table "like folks are supposed to." Willie was not accustomed to having domestic help, and Mamie was not accustomed to having another strong-willed woman in the house, challenging her and wanting to change both the routine and decor.

Any efforts of Willie's to make the cluttered old house more cozy were met with skepticism and coolness. "They looked at that house like it was a mansion, but the wallpaper was falling off the walls," Willie remembered.

"They'd tried to paint over the wallpaper and do a few things like that, but it was halfhearted and the flowers on the wallpaper showed through." After some nudging, though, the uncles did paint the downstairs rooms, although they made no attempt to maintain the exterior of the house. Because of its decaying condition, the house became something of a local landmark as the years wore on. It was an eyesore. One Greenwood resident said the house was "the sort of place white people ought not to live in."[14] Uncle Will's energies went into the plantation and its waning cotton crop, rather than into a new roof or window screens. While his home improvement skills may have been overshadowed by more pressing matters, he and Uncle Holmes were unflaggingly well-mannered toward Willie.

"We all ate at the same time, no matter what," she said. "Uncle Will would cut the meat and serve, and we'd pass our plates around. But none of them ever sat down until I sat down. They were real courteous. And Mamie'd clean up everything, and reset the tables with the plates turned over for us to eat at night time. Uncle Will would put up the food, whatever was left, and she'd wash the dishes the next morning." Occasionally, a younger black woman named Annie came in to help Mamie with the chores, and over time she became another fixture in the household.

"Uncle Holmes had field hands, and called them 'his niggers,' " Willie remembered. "One morning I was coming down the steps to the kitchen and Uncle Holmes asked me whose nigger that was in the kitchen. And I said, 'Well, I think he's Annie's husband, because the baby calls him Daddy.' And she said, 'Miss Willie, that ain't none of my husband.' And I said, 'Well, the baby calls him Daddy. I just thought he was your husband.' She said, 'He's the baby's daddy, all right, but he ain't none of my husband!' And when I told De La about it that night, he said, 'All niggers are like that. She's not a bad nigger.' " For Beckwith, who had coexisted for many years with the local blacks, the issue of "good niggers" versus "bad niggers" was beginning to take shape. Many Southern black service members, having returned from the war, found themselves returning to a region of the country in which they could not enjoy many of the freedoms they had been fighting overseas to preserve. Those who "stirred up trouble," who contributed to a new awareness in the black communities when they returned home, were "bad niggers" to Beckwith, who had been fighting overseas to preserve the Southern status quo. Perhaps these blacks had "forgotten" their place in the stratum of Southern society, but De La Beckwith, for one, certainly had not.

Nor had a distant cousin of Beckwith's on the Southworth side of the family, Mississippi Senator James O. Eastland, forgotten the black man's position in the Southern landscape. When talk turned to politics, Beckwith was quick to boast of their familial ties, although he and Eastland had not yet met. Although the demagogues, Vardaman and Bilbo, had left their indelible marks on Mississippi, it was James Eastland who would help shape Beckwith's rapidly evolving views on race following the war. On the floor of the Senate, Eastland had stated flatly, "The Negro race is an inferior race." To support his thesis, he pointed to the combat record of blacks in Europe. "The Negro soldier was an utter and dismal failure in combat in Europe. When I make that statement, it is not from prejudice. I am not prejudiced against the Negro."[15] The *Congressional Record* noted that there was laughter in the galleries. There was no laughter in Greenwood, however, where white residents—the voters who kept Eastland and others like him in office—believed their senator was safeguarding their interests and protecting their way of life.

Willie and her husband seldom talked of politics or race. During the first few months in Greenwood, they spent their leisure time roaming the Mississippi Delta, target practicing and experimenting with antique black powder rifles, which were Beckwith's passion.[16] "He'd take an old muzzle-loading rifle and tie it onto a two-by-four, and use some wadding and stuff, and try to get it to shoot," she recalled. "And he'd tie a string to it and get around behind a building and try to make it shoot, to see what it would do." Beckwith was a good shot, and Willie gradually grew proficient both with his rifles and with a gun Uncle Will gave her to use—a Model 24D Savage .22 caliber rifle over a .410 bore shotgun. They both liked to fish, and Willie much preferred fishing to target shooting. One friend of the Beckwiths, who knew them during the early years of their marriage, remembers them as well-suited and convivial. "As a couple, I thought they seemed to get along real well, and things were kept on the light side." Having been separated by the war during the early months of their marriage, Beckwith and Willie began to learn about each other for the first time after they settled into the house on George Street.

Uncle Will often accompanied them on Saturday outings into the woods to fish or target shoot. "He'd take some chickens, and we'd stop at a nigger's house and they'd put a clean tablecloth on the table and cook for us, and we'd eat dinner," Willie remembered. "But they didn't sit with us. They'd eat after we left." Greenwood was a small town, and although there were activities for a young couple to enjoy—movie theaters, restaurants, dances at the Tack House and backyard barbecues—evenings out in the little town seemed stifling compared to Memphis. Their drinking was recreational, but seemed excessive to those possessed of a conservative, small-town mentality. In the midst of a ballroom full of other soldiers on liberty with their dates, Beckwith and Willie had fit in seamlessly. To Greenwood residents, however, the newlyweds clearly seemed to be hell-raisers.

The Beckwiths did not drink much in the house, but rather, like Uncle Holmes, went out to do their carousing. "We went mostly to parties, and we went to banquets and different things, like banquets for the Sons of the American Revolution," Willie said. "Things like that. But we always drank at them, and then we'd always fight afterwards, because De La would say I was drunk and he wasn't. I used to beg him not to drink so much when we went out, just drink a little, you know. But it would always wind up the same way, all those years," Willie said. Uncle Will also cautioned Beckwith strongly about his drinking, not in a chastising manner, but out of genuine concern. Although as a child, Beckwith probably had been protected from the truth about his father's alcoholism, Uncle Will undoubtedly knew it played a role in the elder Beckwith's early death. It was, after all, listed on his death certificate, and Susie Beckwith would have almost certainly shared her troubles with her beloved brother. There were also whispers about other members of the family on the Yerger side who had allowed liquor to get the better of them in years gone by. And although Beckwith delighted in regaling his friends with stories about his mother's many gentlemen callers or his father's National Guard activities, he gave little or no thought to the inherent weaknesses of his heredity—the potentially explosive combination of emotional problems and alcoholism.

Just after their first Christmas together in 1945, Willie became pregnant. Although she and Beckwith had not yet discussed the possibility of children, they were ecstatic over the news, and the uncles were overjoyed at the prospect of having a baby to bring some life into the house again. In March 1946, while looking for a better job, Beckwith applied for a government posting with the Federal Communications Commission in New Orleans. His fingerprints were taken along with his job application.[17] He did not get the job, but he continued to look for better-paying work. He clerked briefly in a sporting goods store, then served as a termite inspector for a pest control firm, and later bought chickens in Oxford, Mississippi, for a wholesale poultry house. He was restless, and had not yet found a job he considered worthy of his considerable talents. It never bothered him to rise early and work until dark, and he savored the opportunity to mingle with the public.

After the war, reacquainting himself with the townspeople he had not seen in four years, Beckwith reestablished his reputation for a distinct form of courtesy bordering on the outlandish. On the streets and in cafes, his deep-waisted bows and exaggerated flourishes occasionally elicited chuckles, of which he was blissfully unaware. "He amused me," said a longtime Greenwood resident. "It was as though he was trying to become a character back in the plantation days. I think he was trying to put history back in a time that was no more. . . . He *did* live with delusions of grandeur. And people, I think, more or less saw that." In all his jobs, Beckwith most enjoyed his contact with the public, regardless whether he was selling baseball gloves or spraying for termites. He thrived on his interaction with others, and became a well-known and colorful local figure. Everyone in Greenwood knew De La Beckwith.

Having been left alone at the big house with the uncles, Willie knew practically no one in Greenwood. Her only acquaintances were her husband's friends, and they never came calling during the day. Since there was no mother-in-law or aunt to assist Willie's segue into Greenwood's social circles, she was left at home, "like a lump on a log," she said. Beckwith would come home with stories about friends he ran into during the day, or how many houses he had called on and sprayed. Willie felt trapped and wanted to learn to drive, so she pressed him to teach her. They had no car of their own, and Beckwith always used either Uncle Holmes's truck or Uncle Will's truck to run errands or go out in the evenings. One Saturday afternoon, on the way from Greenwood to Itta Bena, Willie begged her husband to let her drive. She was skittish, but was making progress when the road curved toward a filling station that had two tall concrete pillars at its entrance. Trying to maneuver between them, Willie panicked and crashed into one. "I didn't try again after that for awhile," she said, "because I was about three months pregnant and I was afraid I'd kill myself and the baby."

At the house on George Street, living conditions were becoming increasingly complicated by Willie's advancing pregnancy and the sudden arrival of Beckwith's nemesis, cousin Yerger Morehead, who returned from the European Theater of the war. Morehead had advanced to the rank of Major in the Army. His work in the Army's legal department in England led Beckwith to refer to the "vicious war of words" Morehead had endured while *he* was absorbing shrapnel at Tarawa.[18] Morehead, who like the elderly uncles was still a bachelor, seemed genuinely to like Willie and treated her courteously. He quickly reverted to his old ways with his younger cousin, however, frequently denigrating Beckwith and making jokes at his expense. Morehead took up residence in the one unclaimed bedroom in the rickety house, and for an uncomfortable period of time both the uncles, Morehead, Beckwith and Willie all shared the house, the servants and the solitary upstairs bathroom.

As Willie entered the last few months of her pregnancy, embarrassed by her size and that she was living in a house full of bachelors, she sequestered herself in the house and seldom went out in public, even in the evenings. Both her bedroom and Uncle Holmes's bedroom exited onto a screened-in upstairs porch, and in the afternoons they sat outside or downstairs, where it was cooler. While he reminisced about the riverboat days, he taught her to play card games like cassino. "He taught me how to play, to pass away the time while I was pregnant," she recalled. "I spent a lot of time with him, and I just loved him to death." She eventually got so good at the game that she could beat him, which infuriated the old man, who would throw down his cards, muttering to himself. He would storm off, still wearing his pajamas.

When Willie went into labor and was rushed to Greenwood Leflore Hospital, Beckwith frantically paced back and forth in the hospital hallway. At one point, he drove home and paced around the kitchen, telling Mamie, "I think Willie's going to die!" On September 9, 1946, Willie gave birth to the couple's only child, a boy named Byron De La Beckwith, Jr.[19] They nicknamed him Little De La. When they brought the baby home from the hospital, Beckwith and Willie were as close as they would ever be during their marriage. Mrs. Lawrence Mallett, an older woman whose sons had been school friends of Beckwith's, stayed with Willie at the hospital and helped with the baby for the first few days. "I wanted her to be the baby's godmother," Willie said, but in one of their first violent arguments, Beckwith adamantly refused to allow the woman to be his son's godmother. She was Catholic, and although Beckwith had known her all his life and was fond of her, he ranted at Willie for even suggesting such a thing. Willie was crushed. "It was the first time I found out how he felt about Catholics," she recalled. In an attempt to make up for the argument, and to mark their first wedding anniversary which was approaching at the end of the month, Beckwith bought Willie an elegant white gold Hamilton watch with six small diamonds, and planned a trip to Memphis. They made reservations at the Peabody, and because Willie insisted they take the baby on the trip with them, they arranged for the hotel to provide a nurse while they celebrated at the Skyway lounge.

Beckwith wore his finest double-breasted suit, and Willie—who was nervous about not having something pretty to wear so soon after their child's birth—bought a simple black taffeta dress which she thought might conceal some the weight she had not yet lost. Downstairs, at the hotel's florist, Beckwith bought a gardenia for her to wear in her hair. They drank and danced as the sounds of the orchestra filled the ballroom. Their drinking led to an argument, however, which culminated back in the hotel room after they hastily dismissed the nurse. As Willie was undressing and taking off her jewelry, he swept the new watch off the dresser. "He threw it on the floor and crushed it with his heel," Willie remembered. "He broke it all to pieces." Willie later gathered up the pieces and put them in an envelope, and Beckwith took the watch back to Stein Jewelry in Greenwood, where he had just bought it. The sales clerk at the jewelry store, a longtime friend, kidded him and said, "De La, your drinking's getting the best of you!"

Although Beckwith was of course unaware of it, Willie had been emotionally and physically abused in both her prior marriages. She was still in high school when she met her first husband, an older man who persuaded her to quit school and run away to get married. Although their marriage lasted only five months, Willie lost thirty pounds. According to the divorce complaint, her husband literally starved her and eventually abandoned her. He threatened and harassed her when she returned to her parents' home and she initiated divorce proceedings against him. Later, she was forced to issue an injunction to keep him from calling her, accosting her on the street or molesting her in any way. Willie and her second husband were married a few days before Christmas 1942, when she was nineteen. An insanely jealous drinker, he traveled for a produce firm, hauling sweet potatoes and watermelons, and constantly accused his pretty young bride of being unfaithful to him while he was on the road. The divorce complaint claimed he "cursed and abused her unmercifully," and embarrassed and humiliated her by telling his friends that the reason he wanted her to drink with him was that he wanted to get her drunk and get her pregnant.[20] When the Beckwiths argued, and particularly when they *drank* and argued, the scenario was all too familiar and painful to Willie. Just a few months after their son was born, an argument in their bedroom upstairs at the big house turned particularly ugly and Beckwith, enraged, hit Willie for the first time.

"What you have to understand about De La is that he could be as *kind* as he was abusive," she said. "He could be good, and be real kind, and say he was really sorry—and have *tears* in his eyes—and then as soon as I disagreed with him, we'd be fighting again. We didn't always have to be drinking to fight, but it was worse when we were drinking." The couple's joy of having a newborn baby in the home was diminished by the tensions of both living in the increasingly crowded house and by their more frequent arguments. Willie pressed her husband more firmly to begin looking for a home or apartment for them, while their arguments escalated both in volume and in frequency. Living in close quarters, the uncles and Yerger Morehead were aware of the couple's arguments and Beckwith's occasional abuse, but they turned their backs to it.

Living conditions were not the only source of tension between the Beckwiths. Willie vehemently opposed having the black servant, Annie, helping out with the baby. Beckwith and his uncles, true to the manner in which they had been reared, wanted Willie free of any physical burden caring for the baby might create. "See, I didn't want Annie taking care of the baby, bathing him and everything," Willie said. "I wanted to do it myself. I remember, I was out in the backyard one time hanging diapers on the clothesline, and a neighbor, Mrs. Freeman, asked me—real indignant, like—what in the world I was doing out there hanging up clothes? And I said, 'Well, I'm hanging them out here to dry. Where I come from, that's the way people do.' And she said, 'Well, you ain't got no business hanging up clothes. Annie should do that.' "

The friction between Beckwith and Willie continued to escalate. "See, I wanted to get out and get in a house," she said, "because I knew I could function without a maid, and raise my son and have more to do with him, you know, instead of having someone else do it all. If Little De La cried, they called for Mamie or Annie to come get him, when I was the one that was supposed to be seeing about him. Things like that irritated me. I wanted to get a home and start a life of my own. I wanted to get out and live in a house, someplace where I wouldn't have to live with those older men and Yerger. De La was my husband, and it's what I expected of him." The situation became so dire that Willie repeatedly threatened to leave him and take the baby with her if he failed to provide them with a home of their own.

Although he was reluctant to broach the subject so soon after Uncle Will had paid off the mortgage on the property, Beckwith explained that Willie was unhappy and wanted to move. The two uncles, Yerger Morehead and Beckwith gathered one evening to discuss the matter. "They had a meeting in the living room, and De La decided to sell the share of the plantation his mother had left to him," Willie said. "He told them we were going to sell it and buy a house, and I knew after that we could keep going on De La's salary, which wasn't much. But at least we never had a mortgage we had to worry about." The roundtable meeting in the living room left a strong impression on Willie, who was amazed at the circuitous discussions that seemed necessary to allow Beckwith access to what was rightfully his. She finally understood the importance the Yergers placed on the tradition of inheritance. "Their goal in life, really, was to outlive the others," she surmises. Beckwith sold his parcel of land, which had been in the Yerger family for generations, to an outsider for approximately $13,000. It was enough money to buy them a house, furniture, and a new Ford convertible.

Beckwith bought a modest house at 331 West Monroe in Greenwood for a little more than $5,000. Willie remembered feeling euphoric when he closed the deal. "When he got it, he said, 'I'm going to buy you a house, like I told you I would, and put it in your name,' " she said. "And I can remember this lawyer asking him, 'Now, you don't want to do that, do you?' And De La said, 'Yes, sir, I promised her a house, and I'm going to give her one.' " He and Willie were particularly taken with the spacious backyard, which was perfect for barbecues and entertaining friends. There would be plenty of room for Little De La to play as he got older. Unlike the neighbors on George Street, who almost without exception were elderly and had lived in their homes for years, the neighbors on West Monroe were about the Beckwiths' ages and had small children of their own.

Willie finally had a home, and in her own name, no less. "For the first time we had something that was ours," she said. "I felt a little security. I didn't feel *any* when I was living in the big house." Beckwith insisted on moving his mother's antique living room suite with them, and Willie had expensive slipcovers made for the overstuffed sofa and chair. They selected new furnishings for the rest of the house at Greenwood Furniture Company, and Willie set about housekeeping with fervor. She was a good cook, but with Mamie and Annie to cook at the big house, she seldom had an opportunity to demonstrate her abilities. She was so meticulous a housekeeper that she dusted and vacuumed not once a week like most of the neighborhood wives, but daily. She washed her dishes in a certain order and arranged them in the dishrack to dry. When washing the laundry, she folded her family's clothes in a particular way, never varying her routine. She crisply ironed all her husband's shirts for work, "except the ones with French cuffs that he wore on Sundays," she remembered. Those she sent out to Delta Steam Laundry, so they would be blued and starched for her husband to wear to church. Even her obsessive cleanliness led to spats with her husband. "He would throw his suit on the bed after church," she said. "Because see, niggers had been picking up for him all his life."

On weekends, Beckwith went target shooting with his young gun buddies. He frequently traded guns or worked on them around the house, polishing the ornate wooden stocks of his rifles or melting lead to mold his own bullets. He slowly began to build a sizable collection of firearms, and often talked of getting federal and state firearms permits and setting up shop as a wholesaler of arms and ammunition.[21] But he never really hunted much, preferring instead to hone his skills as a marksman by shooting at targets. He also talked of setting up a local shooting range, hoping he would someday own his own business and turn his hobby into profit. With their home already paid for, the Beckwiths were getting by nicely on his salary and his monthly veteran's disability pension.[22]

As a young mother, Willie was warm yet overprotective, concerned about every new sound that emanated from her son. "I carried him to the baby doctor every time he coughed," she remembered, noting that her husband often thought she was silly to worry so much. Although their drinking fueled most of the couples' arguments, their child also caused rifts occasionally. Once, while changing the baby late at night, Beckwith left a restraining band off the baby in his crib. "I said, 'Well, that might cause something to happen to him,' because I was trying to do just what the doctors tell you to," Willie recalled. "And he said, 'This baby's supposed to bring happiness into the family, but he's just a damn nuisance.' And that made me furious and we had a big fight." Beckwith was detached, and showed little interest in the baby. He often jockeyed for Willie's attention and affection, trying to get her out of the house to dances and movies. He encouraged her to leave the child at home with Annie, who frequently came in to baby-sit. "He always seemed like he was jealous of Little De La," Willie said. "And he was jealous of the time

I spent with him. 'Cause we'd go to a movie and during the intermission, I'd go get on the telephone and call Annie to see if the baby was crying or something."

Annie was the only household help the Beckwiths ever had. "De La got along just fine with her," Willie remembered. "He'd come in and pay her for staying, and then take her home. Because see, she didn't have a car or anything, and we always stayed out late. It could be one or two or three o'clock in the morning when he'd take her home. But we always paid her extra to come and stay at night, and when he took her home, she'd ride up in the front with him." Willie often stood in the doorway of her son's bedroom, watching him sleep and waiting for her husband to return before she would undress and put on her nightgown. Frequently, if Beckwith and Willie had argued on the way home, they would resume the fight when he returned from taking Annie home. "De La told me one night I didn't love him as good as his mother did," Willie said, "and I told him I wasn't his mother. I was his wife. Little De La was too small to know it at the time, but when we'd argue or fight, he would cry and I'd have to go rock him."

The new parents understood that the arrival of their child would bring upheaval to their household, but Willie never expected that their newborn would have a dramatic impact on her sex life with her husband. "I'd say up until the baby was born, De La really enjoyed sex," Willie said, acknowledging that in the early days of their marriage, her husband had a healthy sexual appetite. But after their son's birth, their sex life became erratic. Two factors complicated sex. Beckwith was often afflicted with what he colorfully referred to as "the red ass," meaning things generally weren't going right and that he was in a foul mood. "And he had that most of the time," Willie chuckled. The other, more troubling problem, was that he began experiencing problems with his prostate and became impotent periodically. Willie believed that their mutual drinking played a major role in their sexual dysfunction, and said that she thought drinking might have been as responsible for his impotence as any prostate trouble he experienced. Willie also insisted that her husband always wear a condom when they did have sex. "We *always* used them—good humor, bad humor, whatever," she said.[23] "Because I didn't want to have any more children by him." Beckwith did not want another child, either. "It wasn't a problem. He said a son was what he wanted, and that's what he got," Willie said. They never considered having another child, and took the necessary precautions to ensure they wouldn't.

As their son grew to be a toddler and then a preschooler, the Beckwith household became a strange amalgam of religion, alcoholism and violence. Beckwith and Willie agreed they would take a more active role in the Church of the Nativity because they both wanted to rear their son within the Episcopal church. They also believed that taking a more active role in church affairs would put into perspective any marital problems they were experiencing. As with every other activity in which he participated, Beckwith became deeply immersed in church activities. After a time, he taught an adult Bible class and even played Santa Claus one year in the church's Christmas program. "We were real involved in church," Willie said. "We went to early communion on Sunday morning, and then we went out between Sunday School and church to have doughnuts and coffee."

Beckwith's escalating involvement in the church, combined with his slowly escalating verbal and physical abuse at home, created a contradiction that mystified Willie. "That's why I couldn't understand how De La could be so mean. Because he'd reach over in church and hold my hand. And then fight with me afterwards." Often his violence was mild and subtle. She remembered one incident when she disagreed with something Beckwith said as they were leaving someone's home after a cookout. "He was just as nice to the neighbors, as if nothing had ever happened. He opened the car door for me, in front of them, and then kicked me behind the door as I got in," she said. "What he'd do, he'd catch me off guard. It would be someplace or sometime when I didn't want to cause a confusion over it, because it was an embarrassment to me. I didn't want anybody to know it."

Another time, driving across the bridge that separates North Greenwood from the rest of the town after a formal dance, Beckwith remarked that the river was up. Willie gazed out the car's passenger window and, looking out on the dark river, said, "It doesn't look like it's up to me." He slapped her across the face with the back of his hand. "Things like that happened more times than I care to remember," she explained. "Sometimes, it would just come out of nowhere. He got meaner all the time, from when we were first married. Sometimes he'd throw stuff out the window, right through the window and break the glass," she said. "That was before he'd fight me so bad physically. One day he bent the steering wheel in the car—and I don't guess you believe it could be *bent*—but he did, in a fit of anger, and that's the truth." Her husband's behavior embarrassed her, and she was often ashamed to be married to him because of the looks he elicited on the street or the derisive manner in which others treated him.[24] She could see people were laughing behind his back. "It was his peculiar behavior," she said. "But we tried to go on as best we could, and do like everyone else we knew."

The Beckwiths tried to settle into much the same routine as other young families. As the 1950s began, the baby boom emerged and television was becoming the centerpiece of the living room. The Beckwiths appeared to be enjoying a distinctly middle-class existence. Willie was glad to be in a neighborhood with other young families, although her husband was cautious about becoming too friendly with the neighbors. He preferred to maintain a cool distance, and instead of inviting the neighbors over to socialize he would invite his gun buddies and their wives. Most of them, like the Beckwiths, had small children.

While the couple appeared to be a fairly typical Southern family, Beckwith felt he was different. "De La always acted bigger," Willie said. "He didn't fool with the neighbors or anything, and didn't really like for me to. And the neighbors didn't fool with us much." Two doors down from the Beckwiths lived a congenial family with several children, and Willie and the wife became close friends, much to Beckwith's chagrin. The woman was Italian and a Catholic, and he viewed her with disdain, remarking to Willie on a number of occasions that the family was beneath them. "De La thought everything he did was better than anyone else. I'll tell you the kind of fellow he was—if you had two guns, and you owned one and he owned one, and they were both just alike, and they both cost the same amount of money, and they were both brand new, his would be better than yours. He was that way about everything." Beckwith's feelings of superiority stemmed from his belief that his lineage was better than most of Greenwood's more common whites. On the Yerger side, his family tree had produced as many mental breakdowns as it had contributed lawyers and civic leaders to the community. And although he actually knew little of his father, he steadfastly held that the Beckwiths were Old World blue bloods, sidestepping the reality that his father had been—in the extreme—a debtor, a rounder and an alcoholic. Beckwith proudly spoke of his education at The Webb School and Columbia Military Academy, although he had left both schools in near disgrace before his lackluster finish at Greenwood's public high school and a false start at Mississippi State. Even the fine clothing he wore was, perhaps, a cut above his true station in life.

Appearances were everything to the Beckwiths. When they went out socially, they took great pains with their attire. "I had better clothes than other wives," Willie said. "He always bought me nice clothes." She had a growing collection of fine hats and gloves, and her dresses were reserved but stylish. Once, when he particularly liked a style of stiletto pumps on her, he ordered five pairs from the factory for Willie, in different colors. Beckwith never put a dollar limit on her clothing allowance, and took her shopping frequently, never questioning her taste or the apparel she selected for the family. He often remarked, both to Willie and to others, that he would never be able to dress himself well were it not for his wife. He was exceedingly proud of his family and took every opportunity to show off his handsome wife and son. He often bought Willie a corsage on Sundays or a flower for her hair, and maintained accounts at Greenwood's finest clothing stores—DeLoach's department store, Kantor's men's shop and Davis's ladies wear. His own eccentric taste in clothing was more apparent in the summer, when he and Little De La donned white father/son suits and distinctive string ties. Beckwith kept his white suede bucks chalked, and wore them often from Memorial Day through Labor Day, when he would put them aside for the season. "The way he kept me in nice clothes was with money he inherited from Uncle Holmes," Willie said. Beckwith's great-uncle died when Little De La was about five years old. "De La never did make but just a small salary, and you couldn't do anything but just eat and get by on it. Where he'd put it on your back, and show you off, I wanted to put it in the house."

She was lonely there. Still unable to drive, Willie began to feel increasingly isolated in the tightly knit community. After their son began attending North Greenwood Elementary School, her sense of isolation grew. "It kept me busy just looking after Little De La, because I'd just be getting finished with the house and cooking by the time he got home from school." Beckwith told his wife repeatedly that she did not need to drive, that it was his responsibility to take her wherever she needed to go. "He took me to the beauty parlor once a week, and to the grocery store to get groceries," she said. "Wherever I needed to go. Of course, we had a washing machine in the house where I'd wash clothes, then hang them out on the line, so I didn't need to go to a laundromat. I had a long, big backyard, with a clothesline running the length of it." Even for a woman who approached her housework compulsively, though, hers was a lonely existence.

"I didn't have any social life," she said. "The only place I went was with him." In hindsight, she believed her husband intentionally tried to isolate her to exert greater control over her and make her completely dependent on him. Although he was happy to show her off as an arm ornament at dances and other events, he seemed reluctant to allow her to get around town on her own. "He never seemed worried that I would run around on him with other men," she said. "I really think he just wanted me completely dependent on him. And then, the more violently we fought and argued as time went on, and the more we drank, I think he really got worried I might actually take the baby and leave him, if I was able to drive and get away." Her own drinking problem became more severe. Although when she and Beckwith first met, she primarily drank for fun when they were out with other couples, she found herself more and more often having her first drink earlier in the day, alone. She knew even then she was beginning a dangerous spiral, because she felt she needed a drink to face her husband and his frequent abuse. "You just couldn't live with him if you weren't drinking," she said. "You just couldn't."

Although Beckwith was aware that Willie's drinking heightened her anger toward him, she felt he was encouraging her to drink when they went out together socially. "Never one time in his life did he tell me, 'Don't drink,' and I don't really understand that, even now," she said. "I think he wanted me in a stupor part of the time, I really do." On her part, drinking masked her own pain. Willie grew to believe that her alcoholism was one of the few ways that Beckwith could exert almost total control over her. Although he had been initially attracted to her strong-willed personality during their courtship, he may have been disappointed to find that she was never going to be a docile housewife who nodded in agreement at everything he said. She questioned his ideas, told him when she thought he was doing something stupid—"like trying to raise worms for a living, my God"—and she refused to acquiesce to his opinions. "What he wanted was for me to agree with him on everything," she said. "He'd say, 'If I could just make your mind like mine, we'd always get along.' And I'd say, 'You'll never make my mind like yours,' because I've got a mind of my own."

Sex in the Beckwith bedroom became labored rather than loving. Occasionally, Willie's efforts to help Beckwith maintain an erection and achieve orgasm were successful, but just as often they were futile. "But I just more or less let it slide," she said, "and the longer we were married, the less I tried to help him. And of course, that just made him even madder." Willie believed her husband would have been violent toward her even if he had not been frequently impotent—that violence was simply part of his emotional and psychological makeup. "But I think his impotence aggravated the situation and made him *more* violent toward me," she said. His violent tendencies manifested themselves in bed occasionally, and although he never actually raped Willie, there were times when he very nearly did. "He'd try to force me to have sex," Willie said. "There was one time in particular I remember," she said, "because he wedged me between the washer and dryer in our washroom, and I had to bite him—so hard he had to go to the doctor—to get him off me.

"Sex was the one thing I denied him," she admitted, "because that's what he wanted most. I tried to hurt him in any way I could, and that was one of my ways of fighting back. I did it out of hate, really, pure *hate.*" With each passing year, Beckwith's impotence became a more significant problem. Even more worrisome, to Willie, was that his dominance and sense of power over her seemed inextricably linked to his level of sexual excitement. "If he got the best of you, it excited him," she said. "He thought he'd really conquered you then. I can remember that a lot of times after we would fight, then he'd want to make love—*always.* And I never would be in the mood my own self, and I wouldn't. It was like he was trying to make me his, and own me," Willie said.

Although Beckwith had skipped from job to job several times during the first few years of marriage, it wasn't until he took a job as a traveling salesman for New Deal Tobacco and Candy Company that he found his true calling. The job afforded him the luxury of a company car, and Beckwith quickly found that his innate politeness and gift for the gab made him a natural at sales. With a wide territory that included nearby Holmes, Montgomery and Carroll counties, he called on an array of small grocery and sundry stores, many of which were owned by black merchants who grew to know Beckwith and liked him. New Deal was owned by two Italian brothers, Vincent and Sammy Cascio, who were glad to find another crackerjack salesman for their sales force. By the time Beckwith's route was established, he was calling on more black merchants than any of New Deal's other salesmen—and making money for the company. Vincent Cascio spoke glowingly of Beckwith's sales performance, and said he was "a very good salesman, mixed well with people, and was friendly with customers." His brother, Sammy, also called Beckwith "a top-notch salesman."[25] It was a job Beckwith wildly enjoyed, and he was so good at sales that he later became the company's leading salesman for several years running. The single drawback to the job was that he frequently did not get home until after 10:00 P.M.

Rising early and coming home late meant Beckwith was able to spend little time with his growing son. Little De La was, at an early age, exhibiting some of his father's characteristics—he, too, was an only child, and became petulant if he did not get his way. And like his father and grandfather before him, the boy was fascinated by guns. In the large backyard on West Monroe, a menagerie of playground equipment began to appear—first a sandbox, then a swing set, then, as the child got older, a badminton net and a Ping-Pong table. He was frequently allowed to have friends over to camp out in his tent, and although his father worked long hours, his job with the tobacco and candy company did have some advantages.

"De La bought him all kinds of bubble gum and candy so he could have a little stand outside under a big tree," Willie said. "He would sell stuff to the other kids in the neighborhood, and that's the way he learned to count." In school, the boy's innate kinship to his father shone through. "He never did well in school," Willie explained. "We were all the time trying to get him to read more or study, and I used to bribe him, give him money or buy him something big, like a bicycle, if he'd make a good grade. But it never worked." Little De La had a short attention span and was a lackluster academic performer, as his father had been. Even in elementary school, he often suffered from migraine headaches, and the school nurse or his teacher would send him home.

At home, Beckwith showed little interest in his son until he was old enough to go fishing or target practicing. "For a long time, he didn't really have much to do with Little De La," Willie said. "He didn't read to him at night or tuck him into bed. The only thing he ever did, that I can remember real well, was take a bath with him once in awhile, because

Little De La was always so dirty from playing outside." Willie was constantly agitated by her son's inability to stay clean, and laid down the law with him nearly every day. There were plenty of other rules to be followed in the Beckwith household, as well. Willie admitted that she may have been too stern and overprotective and when the rules were broken, Beckwith acted as disciplinarian. Sometimes, instead of whipping his son, he would make Little De La run around in a big circle in the backyard, and he'd cry while he was running." This peculiar form of punishment may have harkened back to Beckwith's own punishments in military school, where boys who misbehaved were forced to walk the "bullring."

For all the changes in the Beckwith's life during those years—marriage, a child, acquiring a home, a stable job—nothing had alleviated his restlessness. The ten years following the war should have been the happiest of his life, and yet Beckwith had lost his focus; the acute sense of purpose he had felt while he was a marine. Two events in 1954 helped to restore that single-mindedness to De La Beckwith. First, on May 17, 1954, the U.S. Supreme Court handed down its rulings in the school segregation cases on appeal from Delaware, Kansas, South Carolina and Virginia. The unanimous decision of the court was that "separate educational facilities are inherently unequal." Segregationist Southerners would forever after refer to the date as "Black Monday."[26]

Second, but equally important to Beckwith, the Citizens' Council was formed a few months later in Indianola, Mississippi, to mobilize Mississippians against the Supreme Court's ruling.[27] Not since the assault on Tarawa during World War II had Beckwith felt so flushed with a sense of purpose, so completely focused on the role he felt he must play. With a small son preparing to enter the third grade, Beckwith knew he could never stand idly by and await the federally mandated desegregation of Mississippi's public schools. His segregated way of life was being threatened, and again, the enemy had myriad faces—the federal government, which was meddling in the affairs of the individual states; the NAACP, whose lawyers had effectively pursued the Supreme Court decision; the black activists who were now loudly voicing their demands for equality; and the moderate Southern whites who were quietly supportive of the desegregation decision as a first step toward social integration in the South. "That's when De La really went crazy," Willie said of the summer of 1954. "He just lost his damn mind."

The Supreme Court decision was not unexpected in the heart of old-world Mississippi. Mrs. Wilma Sledge, Sunflower County's representative in the Mississippi legislature, called a Sunday meeting of some of her influential constituents. She told them that she expected the Supreme Court ruling in the segregation cases to be "unfavorable," and that

Mississippians were going to have to accept the consequences—school integration at the rate of seven black children to every white child—when the Court ruled.[28]

A local farmer and former Mississippi State football star, Robert B. Patterson, had a daughter who would start school shortly, and as a parent he was concerned about the problems he thought the ruling would cause. Under no circumstances would he stand idly by and watch the federal government force her to share milk and cookies with black children. Patterson, whose nickname was "Tut," had served as a paratrooper during World War II and had been a football star at Mississippi State. He sat at his kitchen table one night and drafted an emotional letter, which he copied and circulated to newspapers, his congressman, and anyone else within handbill distance. In his letter, the foundation for the Citizens' Council was laid. Patterson advocated total white solidarity against the federal threat of integration, and asked that Southern whites "stand together forever firm against communism and mongrelization." He appealed on an emotional level to whites' prevailing racial sensibility. "If every Southerner who feels as I do, and they are in the vast majority, will make this vow, we will defeat this Communistic disease that is being thrust upon us. Of course, we must work out the details, but if we all stand together, this can be accomplished."[29]

Patterson and thirteen of his community's business leaders gathered and organized the Citizens' Council. The organization's doctrine was simple: there is strength in numbers. On its seal, which showed a Confederate flag crossing an American flag, the Citizens' Council legend read "States' Rights and Racial Integrity." The states' rights argument was well-known to Southerners, who had propounded it as the rallying cry for the Civil War. Although the states had willingly entered into this "more perfect union," they maintained their sovereignty and could, if necessary, defy the federal government and secede from the union. The doctrine was a thinly veiled protection of white supremacy, meant to maintain what segregation had continued after slavery was abolished. The states' rights argument was a major weapon in the Southern arsenal, and the states vigorously campaigned to protect their sectional interests, even as they became doomed to a minority position within the union.[30] By the time Governor Hugh Lawson White addressed the joint legislative session early in September 1954, seventeen counties in Mississippi already had organized local Citizens' Council chapters.

With its goal of ensuring the continued subservience of blacks by using any means to deny them social and political equality,[31] the Citizens' Council unified the white racist populations of both small towns and large cities. Its membership included farmers and plantation owners, leaders of Mississippi's business and professional communities, as well as local and state officials and congressmen, and even federal judges. As soon as the Citizens' Council was formed, De La Beckwith was eager to do his part to advance its cause. "He heard Tom Brady give a speech at a meeting one night," Willie explained, "and you never saw De La in such a froth." Mississippi Circuit Court Judge Tom P. Brady, who along with Patterson was one of the original architects of the Citizens' Council, spoke before the Greenwood Chapter of the Sons of the American Revolution (SAR), of which Beckwith was a member. The speech was full of vitriol and vinegar, likening blacks to chimpanzees, and Brady's oratory deeply stirred the angry crowd. "That speech changed De La overnight," a relative later told a reporter. "He became rabid on the race question. I do not say that lightly."[32] The Citizens' Council fulfilled two basic needs for Beckwith. It allowed him to feel as though he belonged, and it aligned him with the most powerful men in Greenwood's small business community.

In his "Black Monday" speech, as well as in a book of the same name, Tom Brady focused on racial differentiation, Communist influence, and ultimate mongrelization of the white race. "Let's get one thing unmistakably clear," Brady said. "There cannot be the slightest doubt that the leaders of the three million block-voting Negroes of the North and East and of California, together with segments of the Communist-front organizations of our population, have set as their goal the 'passing' of the Negro in these United States. Only the most stupid or gullible would dare to dispute this fact. These new deal, square deal, liberated, black qualified electors are determined to indoctrinate the Southern Negro with this ideal, and arouse him to follow them in their social program for amalgamation of the two races."[33] Like Bilbo earlier in the century, Brady advocated shipping blacks to a state of their own—perhaps California or Alaska—where they could govern themselves and "develop to the fullest extent" of their abilities. He backed up his emotional argument with a Bible verse from Matthew 18:8: "Wherefore if thy hand or thy foot offend thee, cut them off, and cast them from thee. It is better for thee to enter into life halt or maimed, rather than having two hands or two feet to be cast into everlasting fire."[34] The Citizens' Council launched its first project, the successful passage of an amendment to the Mississippi Constitution raising voter qualifications in the state. In this way, enraged whites could ensure that it would become even more difficult for blacks to register to vote.

Although Patterson became the Citizens' Council's figurehead—because of his widely circulated letter and his subsequent visibility—a Greenwood businessman was working behind the scenes, putting Patterson's concept into action and providing the financial support to get the fledgling group off the drawing board and into action. Ellett Lawrence, the owner of a successful printing and office supply company, was involved with Patterson from the inception of the Citizens' Council. It was his invisible hand guiding the Council's growth and activities, and he was one of its greatest initial financial supporters. He also reaped much of the profit, by printing all the Citizens' Council literature. Phillip Abbott Luce worked for a time as Patterson's secretary. In his 1960 M.A. thesis based on the Council, Luce referred to Ellett Lawrence as "the man who makes the decisions," and wrote that ". . . the real power in the Mississippi Council is not R.B. Patterson but rather Ellett Lawrence. The idea of creating a Citizens' Council actually originated with Lawrence, and Patterson only put the wheels into operation. All the money that was originally raised to support the Council came from Lawrence, and he is still the financial pillar of the group. Patterson spends at least two hours a day in conference with Lawrence and no decision is made without the permission of the owner of the Lawrence Printing Company."[35]

The literature of the Citizens' Council, which quickly increased in both quantity and frequency, served as its recruitment vehicle. Pamphlets quoted lofty passages from famous patriots, the Bible, and almost anyone else with any name recognition who spoke the segregation party line. Lawrence had a lock on the Council's printing business, and the constant stream of pamphlets and flyers was making him even richer. When journalist John Bartlow Martin visited Mississippi to write about the Citizens' Council for *The Saturday Evening Post*, he met briefly with Lawrence, whose demeanor was far less polished than Patterson's. Luce recounts the story of their meeting, and remembered Martin asking Lawrence if he didn't think it was a shame about the murder of Emmett Till, a fourteen-year-old black who had been found murdered nearby after allegedly wolf-whistling at a white woman in August 1955. Lawrence agreed that it *was* a shame—"a shame they didn't slit open his stomach so his body didn't rise in the river."[36]

Beckwith knew Lawrence and admired him. No one, though, had the effect on Beckwith that Bob Patterson had. "De La had kind of a worship thing about different people," Willie explained, "and he really looked up to him, like he was more than somebody, you know. De La just thought Bob Patterson was God. But I got the feeling from Bob sometimes that De La was going overboard." As an indication of Beckwith's regard for Patterson, Beckwith presented him with the gravy boat from the collection of Jefferson Davis willowware china the Yerger family had prized for generations. Willie did not share her husband's admiration for Patterson, and she never went to Citizens' Council meetings, which were attended almost exclusively by men. "But I went with him to a lot of other group meetings to sell that *Black Monday* book," she remembered. "De La wanted to put that book in everybody's hands."

After Beckwith became involved in the Citizens' Council, his troubles at home escalated. "He changed so much, so fast," Willie remembered. "It's like he was two different people. Like a set of scales—sometimes he could be so good that you'd think he was going to be all right, then he could be so bad—they never did balance." Although Beckwith maintained a steady job, Willie never felt she could depend on him. "I never knew if he was going to do some wild scheme like raise worms, or raise rabbits, or something like that. What I wanted him to do was have a job like ordinary people, and work and not fool with the Citizens' Council. Live like the rest of the people on the street lived instead of, you know, showing his butt all the time." With what little of his inheritance was left from his Uncle Holmes, Beckwith began buying himself friends. "He'd give like two hundred or three hundred dollars to somebody who was running for public office who was a segregationist, and buy all those *Black Monday* books to hand out to people on the street," Willie said. He grew closer to Bob Patterson, and spent a great deal of time selling Citizens' Council memberships. "He called it 'five dollars' worth of insurance,' " Willie remembered. "It caused a lot of arguments between us, because I was afraid his messing in the Citizens' Council and selling memberships would get him fired from his job. He was just too wrapped up in it, always going to meetings, always stirring up trouble. I argued with him about it constantly, and it became a real sore spot for us."

Their arguments over the Citizens' Council evolved from angry yelling matches to physically violent confrontations. Beckwith would often shout at his wife, "Stupid, say something!" It was his manner of egging her back into an argument when she finally had enough and turned her back on him to leave the room. Once, in a fit of rage, Beckwith swept his arm down hard across the top of their bedroom dresser and angrily thrashed her perfume bottles and jewelry box onto the hardwood floor. "I told De La it was going to be the Citizens' Council or me, because it caused that much trouble in our marriage," Willie said. "He would smooth things over for a while, but he couldn't stay away from it. I wish I'd known at the beginning just how much trouble it would cause."

5

Separate and Unequal Lives

Forty-five miles northwest of Greenwood, in Mound Bayou, another young traveling salesman was working his rounds in the Mississippi Delta, selling insurance policies for Magnolia Mutual Insurance Company. In 1952, just after graduation from Alcorn A&M College in tiny Lorman, Mississippi, Medgar Wylie Evers—a black World War II veteran who attended Alcorn on the GI Bill—had moved with his young bride, Myrlie, to the small community where he began his career. Dr. T.R.M. Howard, Magnolia Mutual's founder, had also founded a clinic in the tiny town, and was highly regarded as the county's wealthiest black businessman.[1]

At about the same time Susie Beckwith had packed up five-year-old De La to move him from California to her native Mississippi, Jessie Evers gave birth to her son, Medgar, in July 1925. Jim Evers, Medgar's father, was an impressive man, over six feet tall and weighing more than 200 pounds, who commanded respect from local blacks and whites alike. He was a sawmill worker, unable to read or write, who stacked lumber for a living. His wife, Jessie, was a small, stout woman who was part Native American, and whose paternal grandfather was white. Both Evers and his wife were dedicated workers. She took in laundry and worked for the white postmaster in the small town of Decatur, Mississippi, where the Evers family made its home. Jessie was a devout member of the local Church of God in Christ, and her husband, a Baptist, was a philanderer.[2]

As youths, had Medgar Evers been white or De La Beckwith been black, the two might have been fast friends, for there were some surprising similarities in their backgrounds. Both loved Mississippi with an almost religious zeal, and both were familiar with traditions that for generations had kept the black man subservient and the white man his oppressor. As boys, both had avidly enjoyed the outdoors, especially hunting and fishing. Each had changed schools frequently as a youth, although Evers was a far better student than Beckwith. Both had proudly served overseas during World War II, and each later became a traveling salesman who gradually moved into racial activism, dedicating himself to a cause.

Medgar Evers had witnessed events as a young man that illustrated all the hated inequities associated with his black skin. He and his brother, Charles, had often walked by the field where their father's friend, Willie Tingle, had been lynched, his bloody clothes left behind as a reminder. In adolescence, one of Medgar's childhood friends, a white boy, had called him "nigger" in front of a group of friends. The wound never healed. And after having served in France and Germany during the war, Evers returned to Mississippi, a state in which it was nearly impossible for him to register to vote. He pursued an education, but was unable to do so at any university except Alcorn; the doors of the University of Mississippi at Oxford and Mississippi State College at Starkville were closed to him.

At Alcorn, Evers blossomed, and it was there that he became the antithesis of De La Beckwith. He was a gifted athlete, a track star and a first-string halfback on the football team for four years. He grew increasingly self-assured, without a hint of the cockiness that Beckwith had shown as a student. Evers also earned the deep respect of his peers, who elected him president of his junior class. Beckwith's highest honor in high school was being named "most talkative" by his classmates. Perhaps most striking, Medgar was editor of the student newspaper, *The Alcorn Herald*, and cultivated an understanding of the power of the written word, learning, as Beckwith later did, that a carefully crafted piece of writing could strongly shape public opinion. It was also at Alcorn that Medgar Evers met young Myrlie Beasley, his future bride, while she was leaning against a fence on her first day of school. "He came over to me and said, 'Get off that post, you might get electrocuted,' " she remembered in an interview. "And I thought to myself, he has a lot of nerve."[3]

Evers did, indeed, have nerve. The more he matured, the more embittered he became over the endless Southern injustices against blacks. Nothing, however, made him consider leaving his native Mississippi. Rather than leave the state, like so many other educated, upwardly mobile blacks had done, he wanted to change the state from within, and he vowed that blacks would someday have a voice in Mississippi. While still at Alcorn, Evers and his brother, Charles, decided to register to vote, which caused a flurry of commotion at the county courthouse. The whole family was harassed and threatened continuously. Prior to the next election, in 1947, Theodore Bilbo—back in the Senate representing Mississippi—visited Decatur, and told the assembled crowd, "The best way to keep the nigger from the polls is to visit him the night before the election." Despite Bilbo's words, which inspired the threats and taunts of whites, the Evers brothers and four black friends went to vote on election day, but were met by a large mob of armed whites who turned them away. They returned later—armed—and again were turned away by a growing mob. "I was born in Decatur, was raised there," Evers said later, "but I never in my life was permitted to vote there."[4]

For a time, Evers planned to render vigilante justice by forming a band of blacks to wreak eye-for-an-eye violence upon Mississippi whites. After the war, he and his brother talked of forming a group like the Mau Mau of Kenya, who were reportedly led by Jomo Kenyatta in murderous uprisings against the British oppression. The Evers brothers considered assassinating unjust sheriffs and policemen throughout the South, and even talked about killing entire white families by having their maids poison them. It was no mere flight of fancy. The Evers brothers were serious, and they made a pact to name a son after the Mau Mau leader. Years later, when Medgar and Myrlie Evers's first child was born, he was named Darrell Kenyatta Evers.[5]

Evers's job selling insurance put him in daily contact with some of the Mississippi Delta's most impoverished black families. He often felt guilty trying to sell them insurance, because their living conditions and sheer level of poverty were appalling. They lived in overcrowded shacks, and their children often went without food to eat or shoes to wear. Most were sharecroppers who were, for all practical purposes, still slaves to their white landowners. Late in the summer of 1952, Evers began organizing chapters of the NAACP, convinced that the organization could help alleviate the plight of blacks and unify them to make their demands for justice heard.

By the end of the following year, the NAACP had twenty-one branches in Mississippi, with 1,600 members—in large part due to Evers's efforts. As he traveled, selling hospitalization and burial insurance for Magnolia Mutual, he tirelessly fought to elevate the lot of Mississippi blacks, wearing overalls and walking through the cotton fields to encourage blacks to register to vote. He also investigated the murder of fourteen-year-old Emmett Till, trying to turn up clues and evidence that might help convict the killers. "I can recall so well that Medgar cried when he found out that this had happened to Emmett Till," his wife later said, "cried out of the frustration and the anger of wanting to physically strike out, and hurt." Persuading blacks to testify against whites was an impossible task, even for Evers. He once had to hide a witness in a casket, in a hearse, to get him out of the state. Through his constant efforts to build a base of support for the NAACP in Mississippi, Evers was soon selected as the state's field secretary for the NAACP. Within months of becoming field secretary, he had also become the youngest man on a nine-man hit list circulated by local white supremacists.[6]

Just miles away, in Greenwood, De La Beckwith was tirelessly fighting to keep blacks out of white schools and off the voter rolls, wearing the respectable uniform of the Citizens' Council—a suit and tie. The popular sentiment among whites was articulated by an outspoken Citizens' Council member who said, "I'm not anti-black or anti-nigger. I work niggers. I still have five who have worked for me thirty-two years. But they're still niggers."[7] Beckwith was soon acting as an ex-officio membership chairman, trying to sell Citizens' Council memberships to everyone with whom he came in contact. "He called it five dollars' worth of insurance," Willie remembered. No matter where he went socially, Beckwith harangued people until they joined. "A lot of times, I think people gave him money just to get him to shut up," Willie said. In some ways, the Council offered a curriculum that must have seemed, to Beckwith, like the college classes he never attended. There was the constant flow of lectures by members of the Council's speakers bureau, whose roster read like a Mississippi "*Who's Who,*" including both a former and future governor, a host of prominent business leaders, influential ministers and local elected officials. The Council also circulated a reading list which included Bilbo's *Take Your Choice: Separation or Mongrelization*, Brady's *Black Monday*, and other racist literature that supported the group's segregation platform. Beckwith attended the lectures and read the literature voraciously.

If Evers and Beckwith shared any one defining moment, it was the U.S. Supreme Court's 1954 desegregation decision, which proved pivotal in both their lives. At the time the Court's decision was rendered, Evers's application to the law school at the University of Mississippi was pending. *The Jackson Daily News* picked up the story and shouted it throughout the state: NEGRO APPLIES TO ENTER OLE MISS. Evers was being advised by Thurgood Marshall, special counsel of the NAACP, and had been interviewed by Attorney General J.P. Coleman, later to become governor, and other school officials. In the wake of the Court's decision, Mississippi took swift legislative action to maintain segregation in its schools. State colleges and universities began to require applicants to submit recommendations from at least five alumni of the school, who lived in the home county of the applicant. Alumni were white, so that blacks seeking entrance were thwarted on yet another front, regardless of their academic qualifications. Evers, however, had approached one of his mother's white employers, Decatur's postmaster, Jim Tims, who provided a letter of recommendation. Even with a white man's recommendation, which took incredible courage on Tims's part, given the times, Evers's application was rejected.[8]

It would be tempting to imagine Medgar Evers and De La Beckwith in 1954, traveling the same dusty roads, jump-starting awkward conversations with strangers to sell them term-life policies or cigarettes, and then giving them the hard sell of the benefits of the NAACP or the Citizens' Council. Although the two men possessed a wealth of surface similarities, their differences formed a chasm that could never be bridged, for they lived in Mississippi, and one was black and the other was white. What the two men did not know—and could not know—is that they were traveling down different paths toward the same destination. The world would always wonder whether the juxtaposition of those two distinct and separate lives ultimately resulted in a one-sided confrontation on a sweltering summer night. In the silent seconds before a solitary shot was fired, did Medgar Evers feel De La Beckwith's presence behind him in a fragrant cluster of honeysuckle? If so, the price of their meeting was Evers's death—and the destruction of the very way of life Beckwith was so fervently trying to preserve.

"The Supreme Court of our land has decided that we Americans must become so mongrelized that we will produce human beings like the automobile manufacturers turn out cars; that is, in pastel shades," Beckwith read to Willie from a letter he was sending out to the local newspaper.[9] After hearing Judge Tom Brady speak in Greenwood, "mongrelization" became Beckwith's battle cry. "They are unwilling to try to evolve and develop through growth and struggle as has the white man," Brady said of blacks, while the crowd had applauded wildly. "Evolutionary advancement, the only way in which a substantial lasting contribution to their race and to this country can be made, is far too tedious and slow. Oh no—they desire a much faster detour, via the political tunnel, to get on the intermarriage turnpikes."[10] The root issue for Beckwith was not whether black children and white children should sit side by side in a schoolroom, but whether, given the opportunity, they might end up side by side in bed, with miscegenation the result. He began to use "Bradyspeak" at the breakfast table at home, and chatted up the merchants along his sales route with constant talk of segregation.

"All I heard was Citizens' Council and mongrelization," said Willie, who more often than not turned up the water in the kitchen sink to drown out her husband's incessant rambling. "I got so sick of hearing about the Citizens' Council that I just tuned it out, which made De La furious. He was always telling me I didn't understand 'the cause,' that I wasn't working to 'carry on the fight,' he called it. The Citizens' Council caused a lot of arguments between us, because I was constantly pressuring him to get his mind back on his job and stay out of all that stuff. All it did was get him riled up, and he'd be puffed up for days." Life in the Beckwith household was constantly tense, and Beckwith's growing involvement in the Citizens' Council only made matters worse. "We were both like rubber bands," Willie said, "and I just never could tell which of us was going to snap first, De La or me."

Beckwith's devotion to the Citizens' Council grew in direct proportion to its expanding influence in the white community. In December 1954, Mississippi voters, encouraged by Citizens' Council propaganda, ratified a constitutional amendment that would permit the legislature to abolish public schools in the state by a two-thirds vote or in a local school district by a majority vote, in hopes of establishing whites-only private schools.

Voters also authorized the legislature to liquidate real estate, school buildings, and other property through lease, sale or other means.[11] Other states adopted defiant resolutions, some calmly stating their protest of the Supreme Court decision and others proclaiming that it had no legal significance. The postures these states took, however, made it seem proper for a district judge or school board to ignore the Supreme Court's ruling.[12]

To legitimize their state legislatures' moves to maintain segregation, and because of mounting pressure from the Citizens' Council and their constituencies, a group of senators and representatives from eleven southern states in 1956 presented Congress with a statement criticizing the Supreme Court's decision. Their "Southern Manifesto" focused on what the group considered to be the federal government's usurpation of powers granted to the individual states by the Constitution. Beckwith's distant relative, Senator James O. Eastland, was among the signers, as was his representative, Congressman Frank E. Smith. They promised to use "all lawful means" to maintain segregation in their states. "We regard the decision of the Supreme Court in the school cases as a clear abuse of judicial power. It climaxes a trend in the Federal Judiciary undertaking to legislate, in derogation of the authority of Congress, and to encroach upon the reserved rights of the States and the people."[13]

President Eisenhower refused to enter the fracas. He lumped the NAACP and Citizens' Council together under the banner of extremism and said of Council members, "There are very strong emotions [among] people that see a picture of mongrelization of the race, they call it."[14] Eisenhower was fidgety using race-related words in his speeches, and pushed civil rights matters down to the cabinet level. All the while, the voice of the southern moderate—"any white Southerner who can prove he hasn't lynched any crippled old Negro grandmother during prayer-meeting hour," according to the journalist Carl Rowan—was a thin, clarion call above the segregationists' din. Famed *Delta Democrat-Times* editor Hodding Carter, winner of a Pulitzer Prize for his editorials in the small Greenville newspaper, called the Supreme Court decision "epochal," and wrote,"White Southerners cannot be forced to accept the Court decision. Until they want to do so, there will not be actual, full integration." Two years later, President Eisenhower eloquently echoed Carter's thoughts: "It is difficult through law and force," he said, "to change a man's heart."[15]

While the NAACP was using the judicial system to attempt to achieve equality for blacks, the Citizens' Council was refining the art of intimidation. As early as September 1955, the Council had declared war on the NAACP and had drawn a line in the Mississippi dust. The group was already working to destroy the NAACP petition movement to desegregate schools in five cities in the state. Black petition signers were listed in local newspaper ads, with a notice advising white readers to carefully check the lengthy list of names. Many black signers lost their jobs, were refused credit in stores or suffered similar reprisals. A black plumbing contractor, for example, was taken off construction jobs he already had underway and was refused plumbing supplies by a wholesale house when his name appeared on the published list. Within two months, nearly all the petition's signers had asked to have their names removed from it, and the Citizens' Council realized a significant victory. By the middle of 1955, the NAACP petition movement was dead.[16]

In his own way, gubernatorial candidate Paul Johnson, Jr., was doing his part to discredit the black organization. In one of his few campaign remarks directed to blacks—few of whom were voters—he encouraged them to ignore the recruiting efforts of the NAACP and similar organizations. "When these birds from the NAACP come around to collect a dollar or five dollars from you and say they're going to do something for you, don't believe them. You should see them in the nightclubs in Washington spending your money on whiskey and women."[17]

By the time the "Brown II" decision was rendered by the Supreme Court in 1955, directing that local school districts should act to end segregation "with all deliberate speed," the Citizens' Council momentum had grown, and the group had already implemented additional economic reprisals against blacks. A speaker at a Council rally in Selma, Alabama, said, "The white population in this county controls the money, and this is an advantage that the Council will use in a fight to legally maintain complete segregation of the races. We intend to make it difficult, if not impossible, for any Negro who advocates desegregation to find and hold a job, get credit or renew a mortgage."[18] Such tactics were common, and effective, Citizens' Council ploys. The group also mounted boycotts against major corporations they believed were guilty of encouraging equality for blacks, however obliquely.

Along with Falstaff Beer and Ford Motor Company, Philip Morris Incorporated was one of the first companies to be targeted, because its hiring and promotion policies encouraged black professionals to move into sales and management positions. The company was also alleged to have made sizable donations to the National Urban League and the NAACP, which riled the membership of the Council. The boycott blindsided Beckwith, because his employer, New Deal Tobacco and Candy Company, distributed the most popular Philip Morris cigarettes, such as Marlboro and Parliament. Like an acolyte caught sleeping during the sermon, Beckwith quickly sat bolt upright. In a letter dated July 3, 1956, he targeted wholesale distributors of Philip Morris products in Mississippi and throughout the South. He urged distributors to stop carrying the company's products because of its support of the National Urban League and the NAACP, who sought, according to Beckwith, "to put a Negro into your daughter's bedroom as master and ruler of a mulatto family."

Unfurling his banner against mongrelization, he continued: "Are you going to wait until your fair daughters, sisters, mothers or wives receive indecent proposals? Till some of them are led into marriage by the red and black demons who are literally tearing our civilization to shreds to satisfy their savage lusts and fiendish passions?"[19] A spokesman for Philip Morris later claimed that, even in the face of the boycott, the company's sales increased throughout the South and nationwide.[20]

Belonging to the Citizens' Council breathed new life into Beckwith. With a renewed sense of purpose, and—through the Council—access to some of Mississippi's leading businessmen, he began to gain a feeling self-importance. He spent as much time as possible in the company of Bob Patterson and Ellett Lawrence, assuring them of his commitment to the cause and his dedication to preserving segregation. He tenaciously wheedled people into buying memberships—so much so that he was asked to cool down a bit by local Council officials.[21] But Beckwith's participation in the Citizens' Council brought one of his long-dormant needs to the surface again. All of his life, he had ached to belong. Perhaps more than that, he now wanted to *lead.* The fight against integration was a battle with his name on it. To help spread the Citizens' Council gospel, as well as to fulfill his own need for acceptance, Beckwith began joining a number of other organizations.

Although he already belonged to the American Legion and Veterans of Foreign Wars (VFW), he vowed to become more active in their affairs. He joined the Moose Lodge, and was still affiliated with the local Knights of Pythias lodge. Willie's father and brothers were all Masons, and although there were none among the Yergers or the Beckwiths, Beckwith yearned to become a Mason as well, because many of the respected community leaders in Greenwood were members. He was initiated as Entered Apprentice in Greenwood Lodge No. 135, F.&A.M., on July 22, 1954, and by the end of the following September, had passed through the Degree of Fellow Craft and was raised to the Sublime Degree of Master Mason and followed the York Rite.[22] The secrecy, the vows and the pomp of the Masonic order strongly appealed to Beckwith.

An informal group in Greenwood labeled itself the Greenwood Historical Society, and he began attending meetings, offering to display historical artifacts his family had collected in the big house for generations. He steadfastly maintained his membership in the National Rifle Association (NRA), although there were no meetings to attend or rallies at which to cheer—just a membership card and the monthly magazine, *American Rifleman,* in his mailbox. Far more important to Beckwith were his memberships in the Sons of Confederate Veterans and Sons of the American Revolution; blue-blood organizations which validated his belief that his lineage was sterling.[23]

"He was trying to be something he was never going to be," Willie said. "He thought his name was better than anybody else's name in the whole world, and he joined everything that came along—anything that would take him," she noted. "He needed that kind of approval. And at that time, he wanted to get to mingle with all these important people in Greenwood." By broadening his sphere of influence in town, Beckwith believed he could rise into the upper echelons of some of these groups and thereby spread the Citizens' Council doctrine while enhancing his own reputation. For example, after he was elected sergeant at arms of the local chapter of the Sons of the American Revolution, he frequently introduced resolutions denouncing the Supreme Court and groups advocating desegregation. He once helped write a resolution entitled "False Philosophy of Equality," that was wordsmithed and passed by the National Society of the Sons of the American Revolution.[24]

"It got to where people hated to come to meetings for fear that De La would get the floor," Willie remembered. "They didn't seem real interested in what he had to say. Sometimes they'd get up early and leave, and the ones who stayed would just sit there glassy-eyed. But it made De La feel important, and he'd swell up for the next few days and be all proud. He never saw that the others were laughing at him behind his back. I remember one man shaking my hand one time at a dance or something, and he just held it and patted it, and I knew when I looked in his eyes that he felt sorry for me. It just humiliated me."

Beckwith decided that the most important place his influence could be felt was in the Church of the Nativity. He personally believed that separation of the races was biblically ordained by God—a thesis to which many segregationists subscribed—and he hoped to awaken the other members of his congregation. The church's rector, The Reverend Jones Hamilton, placated Beckwith as much as possible, but Beckwith felt that Hamilton was, at heart, also a segregationist. Beckwith also knew, however, that on the national level, the Episcopal Church was moving quickly toward a policy of integrating its congregations. He was determined to take on the national leadership of the church, as well as the Episcopal Diocese of Mississippi, and he became unbearably relentless on the issue of maintaining segregation in the church. Although Beckwith viewed himself as a leader of the congregation, others, including his wife, viewed him as a troublemaker. He badgered church leaders about the biblical position on racial separation, and questioned them about whether any of the Old Testament tribes were black. "If you talked about Noah and the Ark," one fellow churchgoer commented, "he'd want to know if there were any Negroes in the Ark."[25]

Black lips would never touch his communion chalice, Beckwith vowed, nor would blacks kneel with whites at his church's altar. In 1955, he mailed a report from the Christian Grass Roots League to several hundred people in Greenwood and the outlying area, many of whom were members of his congregation. The report set forth the thesis that the Episcopal Church was being infiltrated by Communists to stir up dissension, and that those individuals and groups promoting desegregation in the church were, in fact, Communist pawns. Beckwith accepted the document's arguments as fact. "He was just throwing good money away," Willie said, "because when he'd send this stuff out, people just threw it away as soon as they saw his name on it."

A short time later, when Bishop John Maury Allin was scheduled to speak at the Church of the Nativity, Beckwith began a one-man campaign to expose the bishop as an integrationist, but was unsuccessful at gathering enough supporters to confront him with the charge. After Allin spoke on the appointed Sunday, he entertained questions from the congregation. "Yes, sir!" Beckwith said, standing up from his pew, alone. "What do you, sir, as the Bishop of the Episcopal Diocese of Mississippi, plan to do to maintain absolute racial segregation in the church?" Bishop Allin handled the question with quiet aplomb. "I'm just like you," he replied. "I'm an Arkansas boy, and I saw the mess in Little Rock. This thing will work out as we pray over it." Beckwith remained standing. "Bishop, you have not answered my question." The bishop, taken aback, shifted his weight. "Bishop," Beckwith enunciated, tapping his fingers on the pew in front of him, "you have not answered my question. Shall I repeat it?" Bishop Allin held the edges of the lectern and said quietly, "Sir, I am going to do exactly what God tells me to do."[26]

De La Beckwith's dissatisfaction with the situation at church settled, finally, on the shoulders of the father-son team of Bishop Duncan M. Gray, who had been a peripheral figure in Beckwith's religious life for years, and his son, Duncan M. Gray, Jr., who was a young Episcopal minister. During Beckwith's youth, the elder Gray had served as rector of the Church of the Nativity, and had delivered Greenwood High School's baccalaureate sermon the spring Beckwith graduated. Unhappy that the bishop would not take a firm stand for segregation in the church, Beckwith assaulted him with a barrage of letters which demanded that he take his rightful place as the head of the church's clergy in Mississippi and stand firm against integration. In one letter, Beckwith chastised Gray for refusing to answer his questions about racial integration in the church. He noted that little De La was reaching confirmation age, and that only a staunchly segregationist bishop would "place his hands on my son's head and confirm him."[27]

Gray's own son, who later became the Bishop of the Episcopal Diocese of Mississippi, remembered Beckwith's attacks on his father, who died in 1966. "My impression was that when my dad would go to the Church of the Nativity for confirmations or Episcopal visitations," Gray recalled, "De La would badger him and heckle him, and try to get him off in a corner to talk to him. And Jonie Hamilton, the rector, would try to act as a buffer." Gray, who was only six years younger than Beckwith, had known him casually for years. "This is obviously just my judgment," said Gray, "but there was something a little different about De La. I mean, he was more extreme than most. I think Dad took him pretty much in stride, quite honestly. I mean, there were plenty of people who were segregationists who would have quarreled with their clergy and my father and anybody else, but not on the grounds, or in the manner, that De La did."

Having proven unsuccessful at goading the elder Gray into a direct confrontation regarding integration, Beckwith took up the gauntlet against him and his son through the open letters columns of Mississippi's newspapers. In one, Beckwith accused the bishop's son of believing he could "improve on God's laws of segregation by substituting the communist doctrine of a classless society." He ended his missive with a message for the bishop. "It shall be the painful duty of Rt. Rev. Duncan Gray to publicly rebuke his son (Junior) and all other priests in the Diocese of Mississippi preaching integration. These race-mixing promoters must be punished for their sinful conduct and be banished from the Diocese of Mississippi as Priests."[28] All the while, Beckwith continued to attend Sunday services at the Church of the Nativity.

The letters, like stones thrown into a pond, caused a momentary ripple and then disappeared. "Let's put it like this," the younger Gray said. "A letter to the editor criticizing my father was not going to hurt him very much. I mean, this was a real extremist who was talking. And I don't mean to say it was a joking matter, but it was something that my dad just sort of mentioned and passed off." Once, when the young minister spoke at a religious emphasis week at Mississippi State University, some of his remarks about segregation's incompatibility with the Christian gospel were widely published. "It was then that I started getting letters from De La myself," he said. "It didn't surprise me at all, and it didn't bother me, quite honestly. I would have expected it. De La was just making his views known, but he was saying some pretty intemperate things about the church and the clergy and this kind of thing—and *me* in particular. I think that was the first time, in the late fifties, that I remember hearing from him."

When the Bishops of the Lambeth Conference passed a resolution in the late 1950s condemning racial discrimination, it became increasingly difficult for Beckwith to reconcile himself to the ultimate integration of his own congregation. To make matters worse, The Episcopal Society for Cultural and Racial Unity was later organized to foster "acceptance and implementation of the principle that the Church is an inclusive fellowship which seeks out and welcomes all persons into the worship and parish life of any congregation without distinction as to race, color, national origin or class."[29] Beckwith's fears were unfounded. Greenwood's black families were not pounding down the doors of the church demanding entry, and the rest of the congregation at the Church of the Nativity, while certainly not as adamant about segregation as Beckwith, were still a very conservative group. Still, Beckwith's constant diatribes were divisive. "Anybody like that can create enough mischief to cause *some* trouble and dissension," said Gray in hindsight, "but at the same time, in terms of splitting the congregation down the middle and having them choosing sides between Beckwith and somebody else, I really don't think that could have happened. Because I don't think, quite honestly, that folks took De La that seriously."

Beckwith, however, took himself *very* seriously. He believed *his* was the lone voice of reason in the church, and took steps to ensure that no blacks would gain entry to his sacred sanctuary. "That's when he took to carrying a pistol to church," Willie said. "That's how determined he was that no niggers were going to come in. And I used to tell him that was awful, to go to church and carry a gun. But he thought it was all right, because he was going to keep them out, and he thought he was the only one that had any sense anyway." Beckwith made no bones about carrying a pistol, and proudly told other members of the congregation, including a local planter, that he intended to do his part to keep blacks out of the church, regardless whether the rector or the bishop did theirs.[30] The story eventually made its way to the Congressman Frank E. Smith, Greenwood's representative. "I didn't belong to the church," Smith explained in an interview, "but I heard the story about how a pistol had fallen out of Beckwith's pocket one day in church service, or while they were standing around after church." If Beckwith had not already convinced his townspeople he was their premier segregationist, his reputation as the pistol-packing Episcopalian cinched the title for him.

In his 1956 inaugural address to the state, Mississippi Governor J.P. Coleman said, "I know and you know that while there is no magic remedy for the Supreme Court decisions, there are multiple means and methods, all perfectly legal, by which we can and will defeat integration of the races in our state." On "Meet the Press," he later told more than forty million viewers that a newborn baby would never live to see a racially integrated public school in Mississippi,[31] and Coleman intended to make his prophecies truth. With Coleman's blessing, the state created the Sovereignty Commission, a legislative body specifically charged with preserving segregation in Mississippi. The Commission hired investigators to uncover inflammatory information about individuals involved in so-called subversive activities, and maintained files on individuals and groups favoring integration. Additionally, the state legislature passed a series of other measures meant to shore up the state's defenses against desegregation—in effect, creating a Mississippi KGB. School personnel were required to list organizations to which they belonged or to which they made financial contributions; the compulsory school attendance law was repealed; and common-law marriages were abolished, making children born to such unions, primarily blacks, "illegitimates." The Sovereignty Commission also clandestinely provided funding for the burgeoning Citizens' Council.[32]

Beckwith was ecstatic when he learned that the Commission was hiring investigators, and he pulled out his portable typewriter to peck out a note to the governor to let him know that if anyone was willing to give up a tobacco and candy sales route to save the state from integration, it was Byron De La Beckwith. In his application letter, Beckwith offered his services as an investigator, touting his expertise with guns and noting that he was "RABID ON THE SUBJECT OF SEGREGATION!"[33] The letter was written on stationery bearing Beckwith's address on West Monroe, and which identified him as a "wholesaler of arms and general merchandise." Although the stationery had spaces for federal and state permit numbers, none were noted, and Beckwith's hopes for being an arms wholesaler apparently were just another of his self-employment schemes that never got past the point of having stationery printed.

In the half-light of a spring evening, Willie Beckwith stood in the back door looking out into the backyard, a damp dishtowel in her hands. Her husband was working on one of his new inventions. In a pecan tree near the clothesline, he had strung up a stuffed dummy that resembled a scarecrow. Its legs fluttered just above ground level. "For target practice," he said, when she told him to come in and eat. If an investigative job came his way, his reflexes would have to be keen and his shooting skills would need to be polished. The week after his application letter was received, Beckwith received a form letter thanking him for his interest in the Sovereignty Commission.

Disappointed that Governor Coleman had not shown a personal interest in him, Beckwith channeled his energy into a serious letter-writing campaign that he thought might attract attention. Following the example of Bob Patterson's letter, which had been so successful at galvanizing whites in the formation of the Citizens' Council, Beckwith began spending his evenings and weekends writing letters to local newspapers, the hierarchy of the Episcopal Church, his elected officials, and even President Eisenhower. He was not concerned with the actual Supreme Court ruling anymore—he knew white Mississippians were resourceful enough to find a way to keep blacks from attending school with their children, and felt sure Governor Coleman and the Sovereignty Commission had that battle under control. What concerned Beckwith were the broader implications of the federal government's drive to make race mixing acceptable.

The previous year, in a letter published in the *Jackson Daily News*, Beckwith positioned himself as a warrior in a holy war against integration, and increasingly, this became his rationale. "We must oust from our society any person or persons found guilty of advocating and supporting race mixing," he wrote, singling out members of the clergy, private companies, politicians, and individuals. "Those found guilty and purged shall not be called persecuted martyrs; instead, they shall be known, to all men, as prosecuted criminals against humanity." In another letter submitted for publication, Beckwith wrote, "Believe it or not, the NAACP, under the direction of its leaders, is doing a first class job of getting itself in a position to be exterminated."[34]

The Beckwith-as-warrior concept was entwined with manifest destiny in a letter he submitted to the Memphis *Press-Scimitar*. He likened "the war to destroy the integration movement" to the Crusades, saying that soldiers don't win their medals by asking superior officers permission to act heroically. "Don't waste a lot of time going around asking a lot of fool questions, and wondering: 'How are we going to get rid of the integration?' You must strike first."[35]

When word began to circulate that the new eleven million dollar Veteran's Administration hospital in Jackson would be integrated—because it was federally funded—the Citizens' Council passed a resolution asking Congress to allow it to remain segregated, stating that integration caused "deep psychological reactions on physically helpless war veterans which could greatly injure their health and well-being in a way likely to never be undone."[36] Beckwith, spurred on by the Council's example but not content to let the resolution do his talking for him, took his personal argument all the way to the White House. In 1956, he crafted a lengthy letter to Eisenhower, then took it to Congressman Frank E. Smith's Greenwood office to ask him to deliver it to the president. During an interview, Smith remembered the encounter, and called Beckwith's letter "abusive" and "illiterate." Recalling that particular visit, Smith said, "I knew that De La was a racial nut. He was an extremist, and he wasn't rational at all." Smith recommended to Beckwith that he soft-pedal the letter a bit, and suggested that he cut some of the more directly critical passages.[37] Beckwith, incensed that Smith found the letter unfit to deliver to the president, decided to try another approach. He submitted it to the local newspapers as an open letter. Only Greenwood's *Morning Star* printed it in its entirety—misspellings and all.

The four column diatribe[38] called the Citizens' Council "the greatest power in our state," and stated unequivocally, "We shall not be integrated and thereby mongrelized. We shall walk away from the field of honor avenged. Behind us shall lie the remains of all those responsible for the crime of promoting integration." Plank by plank, Beckwith built his platform. "Please notice," he directed, "that segregation has been practiced with great dignity, throughout all ages by all men, for the mutual benefit of all men. Mongrelization has produced mules and mulattos." Speaking for his fellow Mississippians, he said, "We have all had an overdose of the NAACP and all its affiliates and their fiendish associates," and he predicted that "the crushing blow will descend upon the heads of foul individuals who defy the laws of God and man by promoting race mixing." His battle cry shouted: "Arise with us to unite and destroy the madmen who sow the seeds of mongrelization, for they are rapidly delivering us into the hands of those whose sole purpose is to enslave us all." Finally, Beckwith cryptically predicted that integration would "inevitably lead to the loss of life itself."[39] Beckwith began filling a manila file folder with clippings of his published letters and replies he had received from prominent individuals to whom he had written. Willie was embarrassed by his letter-writing campaign and belittled him constantly about venting his spleen in public. "That's all he did when he was home, was write letters," she said. "I raised hell constantly about him pecking on the typewriter, when the grass needed cutting." She remembered thinking at the time that he was only providing more ammunition to those who laughed at him. "I knew he'd never accomplish anything with his letters, but he felt like he was doing something constructive. And he *loved* publicity, *loved* getting his name in the paper—just *loved* having everybody know him. He wanted to be just as well-known as he could be, and that's one reason he wrote to the newspapers so much. It got to the point where they'd print a letter of his, and he'd write them a thank-you note just to get his name in there again."

Throughout the spring and summer of 1957, Beckwith suffered from a variety of maladies, perhaps physical manifestations of his psychic pain. In early fall, he typed a one-page, single-spaced letter to his physician, Dr. H. Reed Carroll, listing his symptoms in great detail. He complained of aches and pains from his elbows to his wrists, with numbness in his hands and fingers, and noted that he was losing the full use of his hands occasionally and had suffered from occasional numbness and coldness in his arms. He felt partially deaf in his left ear, and occasionally felt numb and swollen on the left side of his face. Often, he had headaches which started at the base of his skull and moved toward the left side of his head, during which he would experience a strange sensation in his left eye. He boasted that he continued to work long days on his sales route for New Deal, and that not only had he quit smoking the previous March, but he had quit drinking the prior December, as well.[40]

If his physician found evidence of any neurological or circulatory problems it is unknown, but the letter is significant for several reasons.

First, Beckwith was so bothered by these recurring ailments that he put them on paper. Second, the letter represents one of the few times Beckwith acknowledged in writing that his drinking was detrimental enough for him to attempt to quit. Finally, it substantiates the time frame during which his physical health began to deteriorate, and although it is purely speculation, it might also mark the beginning of his emotional unraveling. Willie remembered that he suffered from other physical problems, as well. "He'd wake up sometimes strangling on his own saliva," she said, "and he'd tell me part of his tongue and mouth would get numb, and it caused him to strangle. And his hands began to shake all the time."

Willie was not the blushing picture of health, either. By 1957, her alcoholism was so chronic that for the first time, she was hospitalized for it.[41] She was admitted to Greenwood Leflore Hospital on January 2, 1957—just after the New Year's holiday—and would be hospitalized twelve more times during the course of her marriages to Beckwith. Four of those stays were attributed solely to "acute alcoholism," according to hospital records. "Drinking became more and more of an escape for me," she explained. "De La never admitted he was an alcoholic,[42] but I knew even then that I was, because I depended on it too heavily. It was the only thing that made my life bearable, you know, made it possible to keep living with him all those years that he was abusing me. I never did drink day in and day out," she remembered. "I was a periodic drinker. And I didn't drink for fun, because believe me, being married to De La Beckwith was *not* fun. I really drank to escape, pure and simple."

The physical pain and emotional cruelty Beckwith inflicted on his wife remained vivid, and her personal recollections are critically important because they show the most private side of a man whose capacity for violence has been repeatedly called into question. Willie Beckwith knew the humiliation of appearing in public with black eyes. She was kicked in the kidneys—as Beckwith had been taught to do in boot camp—by the man who promised to love and cherish her, a man who later restrained her and held a lit cigarette against her flesh. On more than one occasion, drunk and angry, Beckwith held knives at her throat and threatened to kill her. To quiet her during an argument once, he hit her in the head with the butt end of a pistol. The wedding-ring finger Beckwith once broke in a fit of anger—trying to forcibly remove her wedding band—jutted out, gnarled and healed at a thirty-degree angle, a constant reminder of his abuses.

"I never really knew him," she said. "The whole time I was married to him, I never really knew him. I never could tell what he was going to do or how he was going to react to anything I might say. He got meaner all the time, and I got more nervous and drank more. Of course, I'm guilty of fighting with him, because I *had* to fight to live."

The Beckwiths' brawls were frequent and much discussed by their neighbors and the rest of the townspeople. Beckwith's own cousin, a local judge named Orman Kimbrough, once fined him for a domestic disturbance the couple had created one night. On another occasion, at a dance, two Greenwood police officers watched the Beckwiths embrace at their table, and one of them nodded toward the couple and remarked to his companion, "There'll be trouble at home tonight." Late that evening or early the next morning, Beckwith showed up at the police station and asked the police to come arrest his wife for threatening him, but they refused when he declined to sign an affidavit that could be used to issue a warrant for her arrest. It was common knowledge among Greenwood policemen and the Beckwiths' neighbors that they had drawn guns on each other at times and fired through their house. Both were good shots and apparently never meant to hit their targets. A story was frequently passed around in cafes that Willie had, in fact, made Beckwith "dance with the bullets" and shot him in the toe with a .22 caliber rifle.[43]

Willie Beckwith always knew when a physical confrontation was imminent, because the warning signs seldom varied. "De La would fly into a rage over the slightest thing, and get wild with his hands and look wild in his eyes," she remembered. "He'd get mad quick, at the drop of a pin. I'd fight back with him, but I always got the worst of it. Sometimes he'd take his knee and kick me in the back, or he'd use pressure on my throat, you know. He'd try to use Marine Corps tactics. I had many black eyes, and then, I had to go out and it would show, you know, and it was humiliating." Often, her black eyes were so pronounced that she was unable to disguise them with makeup, and she sometimes stayed in the house for two or three days until they abated.

Finally, their teenage son's health brought the couple to an impasse. "Little De La was in the hospital really, really sick, and they couldn't find out what was wrong with him," Willie recalled. "They finally opened his hip and took bone marrow samples to see if he had leukemia. When they didn't find what they wanted, they cut a gland in his throat and decided he had mononucleosis and histoplasmosis, and it didn't look good at all. The doctor said the histoplasmosis could be fatal, and said it was a fungus in his lungs or something. They were afraid it would spread to his liver, and they ran blood tests all the time and gave him medicine.

"While he was in the hospital I stayed with him, because he was so sick he didn't want me to leave him," she said. "He was a big boy then, maybe about fifteen. And De La told me he wanted me to come home instead of staying at the hospital on and on, but I wouldn't leave. We argued about that, and he said, 'Well, he's going to die. He's not going to live—you just don't know it. The doctor said he's *that* sick.' And so he grabbed me and said, 'You might as well go on home with me, because it's just going to be me and you again.' It was as cruel as anything he ever did to me, physically, to tell me I was going to have to give up my child.

I think that hurt me more than all the beatings, because I knew then that he just wasn't human, if he could bear the thought of losing our son."

By 1960, the abuse had continued for fifteen years, since the beginning of the marriage. Beckwith was apologetic about his temper and violence, but he never seemed genuinely remorseful. And although their son recovered and the Beckwiths smoothed over their arguments again, it was clear nothing was ever going to change. "When somebody just keeps doing something over and over again," Willie said quietly, "you finally get to where you just don't believe anything they say. I mean, it got to the point where the only reason I was staying was Little De La. I threatened to leave De La lots of times, but I couldn't drive and I hadn't even finished high school, and I was afraid I couldn't make a living for me and Little De La. And then De La would bring me flowers and sweet-talk me, and tell me he'd never, never hurt me again, and we'd go along all right for a while."

Willie Beckwith graphically recalled one incident that occurred on June 21, 1960. "When we came home one night, we got into an argument over something—I can't remember what—but he threw me down and tied me up with an electrical cord, an extension cord," she said. "He tied my feet and hands together, and ran the cord up my back so I couldn't get loose, and then left me that way, on the bed. And the way he had me hog-tied, the more I pulled to get loose, the more I hurt myself. Little De La came home and found me that way, and I begged him to let me loose, but he just stood there and cried. He said he couldn't, that he was afraid to, and I really couldn't blame him."

The following day, fed up with her husband's chronic abuses and filled with self-loathing because of her own inability to stop drinking, Willie separated from Beckwith and filed for divorce. The divorce was never granted. Willie dropped the suit when her husband repeatedly threatened to kill her if she went through with it. He said he would not be able to live without her, and that he would rather see her dead than divorced from him.[44] For several months, she placated him, but finally realized there was no way she could stay in the marriage. Although she was terrified of him, she again filed for divorce in September 1960, just two weeks before their fifteenth wedding anniversary. Willie was named their son's legal guardian and assumed custody of her son, who had been enrolled at Chamberlain Hunt Academy, a military school in Port Gibson, Mississippi.[45]

One Sunday afternoon that month, as Beckwith prepared to move out of the house on West Monroe, he sat at his typewriter and wrote a painful parting letter to his wife and son. With Little De La safely tucked away in military school, and the house in her name, Willie decided to sell the house and live off the proceeds as long as possible. A neighbor, James L. Howard, helped her find a buyer for the house, and she gave him $500 for his assistance. "I intended to keep the money," she said, "because it gave me some security. I paid for the divorce out of it, and lived on it and took care of Little De La on it." She sold the contents of the West Monroe house, including Beckwith's mother's overstuffed living room suite. "De La didn't care, he didn't take anything because he didn't want the problem of fooling with anything. He just wanted his papers and books and guns, and he packed them up and left."

He pleaded with Willie for a reconciliation, fervently promising he had changed his ways and would not fight with her anymore. "He promised to do better, and had tears in his eyes," she remembered. "He said we were a family, and that his rightful place was at the head of it, and that he would never hurt me again." Four months after their divorce was finalized, they were remarried. "When I went back with De La, I wasn't having sex with him," Willie said. "I was waiting for the bishop to give our priest permission to remarry us, and I told De La that I wasn't going to go through with it unless we were married in the church, with the church's blessing. I thought that might make him realize the seriousness of it, and I really believed then that he would do better." After filing a Declaration of Intention in Holy Matrimony with their rector, Jones Hamilton, the Beckwiths were quietly remarried in the Church of the Nativity on Valentine's Day evening in 1961.[46] Willie had sold the house on West Monroe, and she tried to convince Beckwith to move away from Greenwood and take a job in another city, where they could make a fresh start and put the painful memories of Greenwood behind them. "I thought if he got away from some of those guys who were talking race and segregation and Citizens' Council all the time, then he might settle down a little," she said. He began to make inquiries around town, and within a few weeks, he had accepted a job with Carr-Williams Tobacco Company in Natchez. He joined the company in March, and he and Willie excitedly moved into unit 131-B at River Oaks Apartments there. To celebrate the move, and their renewed marriage vows, Beckwith went to Butts & Yoste Jewelers and bought Willie a simple silver bracelet with a single sterling charm: a four-leaf clover, for good luck. On the back of the charm, he asked the jeweler to engrave the simple message, "De La, Natchez, '61."

For all their good intentions, the Beckwiths did not seem destined to begin a new life together in Natchez. On May 16, Will Yerger died at age seventy-six, and his death dealt Beckwith a devastating blow. "He really loved Uncle Will," Willie said, "because Uncle Will was the only person who thought De La wasn't a disappointment to the family." Beckwith and Willie returned to Greenwood for the funeral, and although he continued to work for Carr-Williams in Natchez until August,[47] they agreed to move back to Greenwood to settle the estate and clean out the old house on George Street. The Beckwiths lived briefly in an apartment at the home of one of his cousins, F.M. Southworth, and ate at a nearby boarding house while they sorted through sixty years of clutter at the big house. In the meantime, Willie bought a red Impala and made her teenage son teach her how to drive.

Still living on the money from the sale of their home on West Monroe, the Beckwiths spent their days going through each room of the musty old Yerger home, sorting through boxes of books and ephemera. For four months after leaving Carr-Williams, Beckwith did not work. He approached the University of Mississippi with an offer to sell the collection of books and ledgers to its library. Strangely, although the papers had been packed up in the Yerger home for decades, and had primarily belonged to his grandfather, Beckwith insisted it be called the Beckwith Collection. It was described in the Ole Miss student newspaper as "a very large and valuable collection of manuscripts relating to the history of Mississippi," and was said to include more than 2,000 "letters, as well as ledgers and other records, dating from the late 1700s to the early 1900s." The acquisition was managed by Dr. J.H. Moore of the university's history department, and Sigma Phi Epsilon fraternity provided the funds to purchase the collection.[48]

Back in his hometown, with time to socialize with his friends in the Citizens' Council again, Beckwith quickly reassumed his mantle as Greenwood's most ardent segregationist. He and Willie bought a new home at 103 Montgomery Street, in the middle of a neatly manicured, middle-class neighborhood. Riding his motorcycle through town one day during his summer break from Chamberlain Hunt, Little De La saw the house and later took his parents by to look at it. "He came home all excited and said, 'Mama, I've found a house like you're always talking about,' " Willie remembered. "Sure enough, the house on Montgomery Street was under construction, and we all loved it. I took it as a good sign, and thought maybe this time things were really going to work out for us all." With the money she had left from the sale of the house on West Monroe, and a substantial sum bequeathed to Beckwith by his Uncle Will,[49] they paid almost $18,000 for the house on Montgomery Street, and again, the house was purchased in Willie's name. Convinced their lives were taking a turn for the better, Willie set to work planting redbuds and mimosas in the yard.

The Beckwiths settled back into a day-to-day routine, and even got a pet—a small black dog Beckwith insisted on naming "Smut." Their son returned to Chamberlain Hunt Academy to begin the tenth grade, while the Beckwiths again began attending services at the Church of the Nativity. But Beckwith's heart, however, had hardened against the church. Although he would go to church intermittently, he put more time and energy into writing about the downfall of the church than attending services there. "It got to where he started going target practicing on

Sundays instead of going to church," Willie remembered. Just before Christmas, the Greenwood *Commonwealth* ran a photo of the Beckwiths taken at their new home, surrounded by historical artifacts unearthed at the big house on George Street.[50] The smiling couple, back in Greenwood, looked happily at the camera. It was the last smiling picture the Beckwiths would ever have made together, because their marriage was entering its darkest phase.

The following nine months found Beckwith at his most brutally violent at home, while Willie's alcoholism reached its apex. No sooner was their son back in school than the physical abuse began in earnest. This time Beckwith attacked with a hatred unlike any Willie had witnessed during the first fifteen years of their marriage. She recalled a fight during which her husband attempted to rip her wedding ring off her finger. "He twisted my hand back some way, and broke my finger." On another occasion, he took her swimming at the VFW lodge. "He said, 'Oh, come on. I've got a key.' And this was late night, black night," she remembered. "We got up there, and he turned on the floodlights and we got in the pool and puttered around a little. We were the only people there, and I was afraid, because I couldn't really swim well. I was really scared of him that night, because something came up, we got into an argument, and he got wild and tried to hold me under the water. I really wrestled him around and struggled until I got away from him, but I really believe he would have drowned me if he hadn't just come to all of a sudden."

On August 1, 1962, Willie forced her husband to move out of their home and placed him under a peace bond to keep him from threatening and harassing her. In September, she again filed for divorce. "One night he came over to get the lawn mower to mow the grass at the big house on George Street—that's where he'd moved to—and I told him he couldn't have it. He was still under a peace bond, and he wasn't even supposed to be on the street. Little De La and some friends of his were playing cards at the table when I went to get my rifle, and I shot through the door at De La, and he left." Beckwith's threats against his wife's life increased dramatically. On numerous occasions, he said he would kill her if she reported his violent attacks, or if she left him. In Beckwith's reply to her divorce suit, he denied threatening or beating her, and claimed he had only used force to disarm her and to keep her from killing him. He also said that her alcoholism contributed to her "mean and quarrelsome disposition," and that he had, on several occasions, called the police and had his wife taken into custody.[51] The Beckwiths' second divorce was granted on October 9, 1962. On October 30, the Beckwiths were married for the third time in Rossville, Georgia.[52]

"It all happened so fast, a lot of people didn't even realize we'd divorced and remarried again," Willie said. "I agreed to go back with De La on the condition that he would see a psychiatrist and try to straighten himself out." Their physician, Dr. Carroll, had recommended that they go together to see a respected psychiatrist, Dr. Roland Toms,[53] at the University of Mississippi Medical Center in Jackson. Willie remembered the first visit with Dr. Toms clearly. "We drove to Jackson to see him, and he talked to De La a little while, then to me—not together, but separately. He had us look on the front of a *Reader's Digest* and asked, if you just picked it up, which articles would you read first. And then he asked some questions, nothing I thought was really important." Willie asserted that the psychiatrist diagnosed her husband as schizophrenic with paranoid tendencies. "I remember it clearly," she said, "because he told De La that, and De La told me himself. It scared me. It scared me to death."

Willie Beckwith did not mention to the psychiatrist that she and her husband had a history of sexual problems, nor that they were verbally and physically abusive toward each other, nor that they had problems with alcoholism. She feels sure Beckwith did not mention their domestic problems, either. "I remember, the doctor asked me if I loved De La, and I told him, 'Well, I've lived with him this long, and I really don't know if I love him or not, but we're trying to make things work, and that's one of the reasons we're here to see you.' " She said her husband saw the psychiatrist more than once, and that she knew he had been evaluated by other psychiatrists during their marriage, as well. She did not know what their clinical diagnoses were.

When they left Dr. Toms's office, Beckwith asked his wife what the doctor said. "Well, he just talked to me," Willie said. "What'd he say to you?" Beckwith did not respond. In the parking lot, he stopped to open her car door. "You look like this is the saddest day of your life," he told her. "Well," she said, "It may be."

Between the Beckwiths' separation in the summer and their remarriage in the fall, Mississippi experienced one of its defining moments. Under federal force, the University of Mississippi enrolled the first black student, James Meredith, at its bucolic campus in Oxford. Meredith arrived on campus on September 20, 1962, flanked by agents of the Kennedy administration, but he was denied entry three separate times. The crisis reached a climax on September 30 when, on the fourth occurrence, the Justice Department got a federal court order to enforce Meredith's admission. President Kennedy federalized the Mississippi National Guard, added deputy U.S. marshals and laid the groundwork for Meredith's enrollment at the Oxford campus. To the segregationist faction in Mississippi, almost all of whom were states' rights advocates, the federal intercession was a direct parallel to the horrors of Reconstruction. That evening, several thousand students and rioters—many of whom had traveled the breadth of the state to take their stands at Ole Miss—spearheaded an armed riot.

Inspired by the possibility of an armed confrontation at the campus, Beckwith piled his pickup truck full of weapons and drove toward Oxford. He was intercepted by local policemen, who were expecting him. They asked him to turn back and just go home, and after some discussion he relented.[54] "He was always loading a lot of guns in his truck," Willie admitted, "but I just thought he was going off to show them to somebody, to trade them. He was doing that all the time." The rioters in Oxford, however, went on about their work without Beckwith's assistance. As darkness slowly fell over the lush campus, taunts and violence began to escalate. Just before 8:00 P.M., federal marshals were ordered to use tear gas to disperse the rioters. A small portion of the mob dissipated, but others, the diehards, saw the tear-gassing as a catalyst to real violence.

Even as the riot was reaching its peak, President Kennedy was on television telling the nation that the orders of the court in the Meredith case were being carried out without incident, and that Meredith was safely installed on the campus. More than 5,000 troops were required to quell the rioting, and in the ensuing gunfire, two people were killed and hundreds more were injured. Former Major General Edwin A. Walker was arrested and held on $100,000 bond, charged with insurrection. He was prepared to lead the armed locals in a battle against the federal troops. As dawn broke the next morning, October 1, charred hulks of burned-out cars continued to smoke quietly, while broken glass, rocks and lengths of pipe were strewn over the campus. Even as the white rioters were hurling bricks and bottles at federal marshals, Meredith was escorted through a rear entrance to his dormitory, Baxter Hall. He was placed in a two-room suite. The other room, for a time, remained occupied by a federal agent. The following day, Governor Ross Barnett ordered that the state's flags would fly at half mast.[55]

Meredith received both letters of support and hate mail. One person sent him a length of burned rope, and another mailed him a poem which read, "Roses are red/Violets are blue/I've killed one nigger/And might as well make it two." Along with his fellow SAR member, C.E. Holmes, Beckwith later wrote a resolution protesting Meredith's enrollment and the federal government's continued interference in state affairs, and Meredith later claimed that the FBI had investigated a report that Beckwith planned a "mission" to kill him at the university.[56]

Just as Thurgood Marshall had offered advice and encouragement to him when he applied to Ole Miss nearly a decade earlier, Medgar Evers advised James Meredith prior to his enrollment. "That's really about the time I began to hear De La talk about Medgar Evers," Willie remembered. "He called him 'that bad nigger' or 'the NAACP nigger' or 'the head nigger.' One time he said, 'He's a bad nigger. He's got to go,' " Willie remembered. Demonstrations throughout Mississippi—but especially those that made headlines in Jackson, and in Greenwood, which Beckwith was personally witnessing—captured his imagination. He began riding through Greenwood with a group of friends, heckling the demonstrators and taking pictures to distinguish between the local troublemakers, "outside agitators," and suspected federal agents. Beckwith made quite a show of slowing down in front of clusters of blacks and pointing his camera at them, snapping pictures. He also liked to photograph men he suspected to be FBI agents. He and his buddies "had a lot of fun showing them to their friends," one informant told the FBI later.[57] "If he rode around heckling the demonstrators, I didn't know it," Willie said. "But he could have and probably did, because every time somebody called him and told him the niggers were going to the park or the playground, he'd say, 'We're going over there and run 'em out,' meaning him and his buddies. They always took things upon themselves."

True to form, when Beckwith heard that the white waiting room at the Greyhound bus terminal in Greenwood had been desegregated, he went down and resegregated it himself, claiming that he was going to have to keep an eye on it. He had also taken to driving through the black section of town at night, and had been admonished by a few of his friends on the police force who were afraid he was stirring up trouble. One of the leaders of the Student Nonviolent Coordinating Committee (SNCC), who set up a voter registration drive in Greenwood, later told of calling Beckwith and asking him to come down to the office to meet. One of the organization's workers had recognized him riding through the black section of town, and perhaps naively thought if they talked to him, he might stop. Beckwith declined the invitation to SNCC headquarters, and said, "If I'm ever in nigger town, I'm merely passing through heading for the highway."[58] Beckwith had also taken up target shooting at a police rifle range behind the Golden Age Nursing Home in Greenwood, where some of his friends on the police force—who had occasionally taken his wife into custody, at his request—honed their sharpshooting skills.[59]

Beckwith had a history of good relations with the local police. His cousin and former guardian, Yerger Morehead, once discussed Beckwith's abuses at home with FBI agents and mentioned that the police had been called several times to conduct investigations, although Beckwith had never been arrested or charged with domestic violence. Willie also knew that her husband had numerous friends on the local police force, and she believed that they intentionally refused to investigate his constant wife abuse. Having been held in their jail several times, she was skeptical about the relationship her husband had with members of the force. "I thought the policemen in Greenwood *all* were his friends," she said. "They never would come and get him when I'd try to have him arrested after a bad fight." Outside Greenwood, Beckwith's influence with the police was minimal, as evidenced by an incident in Arkansas in early 1963.

"We were going to take a little trip, just an outing, to Hot Springs, Arkansas," Willie remembered. "And we were all dressed up in our finest clothes—we were going out dancing. He was also going to see somebody while we were there. But we got to drinking, and we got into an argument while he was driving the car. It turned real nasty, and he took his arm and hit me two or three times hard, and then he took his lit cigarette butt and pressed it into my side. He burned through the dress and burned me, too. I never will forget it, because I was at an age when I was, you know—I was really pretty then. And this was a beautiful navy blue knit dress. And so we were fighting and arguing, and the police happened to come up—just happened to drive by. They questioned us, and I guess they could tell we'd been drinking, and of course we looked like we'd been fighting. So they locked him up in jail that night, and I went and stayed in a motel, and they let him out the next morning, and we just went back to Greenwood. We never got to wherever we were going."

By the beginning of 1963, racial tensions in Mississippi had flared not only in Jackson, the state capitol, or in Oxford, home of the University of Mississippi. Even smaller towns like Clarksville, Ruleville and Tylertown had experienced race-related hate crimes. On February 20, 1963, four black businesses in Greenwood burned—Jackson's Garage, George's Cafe, Porter's Pressing Shop and the Esquire Club. The pressing shop was located next door to SNCC headquarters, and the fire was believed to be arson meant to destroy the civil rights group's headquarters. In late 1962, SNCC had focused its efforts on Leflore County, where 64 percent of the population was black, and the group's concerted voter registration drives had finally begun to show results. Nancy Brand, a worker in the SNCC office, had received an anonymous phone call at home, asking if she ever went to the office. When she replied that she did, the man on the line said, "You won't be going down there anymore. That's been taken care of." After SNCC Field Secretary Sam Block made a public announcement suggesting that the fire had been deliberately set, he was arrested and charged with making a statement designed to disturb the peace. At his trial in late February, officials offered to free him if he would leave Mississippi. He refused and was given a six-month sentence.[60]

Although black workers were automatically targeted for harassment, white civil rights workers faced harsher treatment because they were viewed as "nigger lovers" or even Communists. White civil rights worker Pete Stoner, who was helping in Greenwood with voter registration, was harassed by police, who angrily told him, "You're a disgrace to your race." One black civil rights worker told a researcher that winter, "The average

Negro here in Greenwood, if you're trying to talk to them about going out to try to fight for their freedom, they'll say, 'I don't want to get involved in this mess, because I might get shot.' But the way it's been going so far, Negroes have been getting shot for doing nothing. I'd rather get out and do something and get shot than to do *nothing* and get shot."

Black youths in Beckwith's hometown became so discouraged they often sang a new set of lyrics to the most popular freedom song of all time, "We Shall Overcome," which became, "We shall keep the nigger down/We shall keep the nigger down/We shall keep the nigger down always. . . ." Even the lyrics to "Jesus Loves Me" were changed by civil rights workers, who called the altered hymn a Citizens' Council anthem:

"Jesus loves me 'cause I'm white
Lynch me a nigger every night,
Hate the Jews and hate the Pope
Jesus loves me and my robe.

Yes, Jesus loves me,
Yes, Jesus loves me,
Yes, Jesus loves me,
The Citizens' Council told me so."[61]

The persistent black voter registration efforts in Leflore County startled local whites, who believed they could successfully intimidate civil rights workers by merely driving through town menacingly, or by showing up at the courthouse and lingering in the hallways. SNCC worker Bob Moses focused his efforts in Greenwood, and said, "The large numbers of Negroes congregating in the street in front of the courthouse frightened the white people, and the inevitable reaction was to turn to violence." Along with other SNCC workers, Moses was targeted for harassment by local police. "The police began trailing us every night," Moses said. "There's not a night passes that they don't trail us, even now. There's a great amount of fear there." Comedian Dick Gregory, who rallied to the side of Greenwood workers that winter, chastised the federal government's lack of action in the face of local lawlessness. "They say that it's real silly to send in federal marshalls when the local police is doing such a good job," Gregory remarked facetiously. "They're doing a good job, all right. That's one thing you can be guaranteed of—they'll fire that warning shot right in the back of your head."[62]

Both Moses's fears and Gregory's cynicism were justified. On February 28, Moses and two voter registration workers—Randolph Blackwell and Jimmy Travis—were traveling on Highway 82 in Greenwood when a 1962 Buick pulled alongside their car. Travis was shot in the head and shoulder and nearly died in surgery before a .45 caliber slug was removed from an area near his spine. When it was examined later, the car in which the civil rights workers had been traveling was riddled with eleven bullet holes. Mayor Charles Sampson and Commissioner "Buff" Hammond, both friends of Beckwith's, issued a statement placing the blame for the shooting on "individuals and organizations from other areas who, activated by motives other than the welfare of our people, are dedicated to creating disunity and discord among us." The shooting caused voter registration efforts in Greenwood to be redoubled. "We brought in all of our staff in the wake of the violence," Moses said, "in an effort to make an example out of Greenwood, to try and tell the world that it wasn't possible any longer to shoot a Negro to scare him out, to run him out of town, to try to break up any kind of drive for civil rights."[63]

The following week, on March 6, four SNCC workers parked in front of the headquarters building and their windshield was shot out. No one was seriously injured. The second week of March, a twelve-year-old black girl was pelted with eggs by a passing truckload of white teenagers. Later in the month, the interior of a voter registration office at 115 E. McLaurin Street in Greenwood was partially destroyed by fire, rendering the office unusable. Two white men were seen fleeing the scene shortly before the fire was discovered. Finally, on March 27, SNCC Executive Secretary James Forman sent a telegram to President John F. Kennedy asking that he send National Guard troops into Greenwood to maintain order. In what SNCC had hoped would be a show of force, more than a hundred blacks staged a march to the Leflore County Courthouse to register to vote, and Greenwood police unleashed police dogs on them. Bob Moses announced plans to supplement local efforts by bringing in civil rights workers from outside the state to redouble the demonstration efforts.[64]

The Justice Department went into federal court on March 31 with a petition for a restraining order against Greenwood officials, demanding that they release eight movement organizers from prison, refrain from further interference with the registration campaign, and "permit Negroes to exercise their constitutional right to assemble for peaceful protest demonstrations and protect them from whites who might object." Less than a week later, the Justice Department withdrew the petition in return for the release of the prisoners and a hollow promise from officials not to inhibit further registration attempts.

Blacks planned a mass meeting in Greenwood to discuss the developments. Reverend Theodore L. Tucker, the local black minister of Turner's Chapel, recounted having a police dog released on him the following week. The dog's bites were healing, but Turner pointed out that the wounds would remain. He implored other church leaders, who remained reluctant to offer their support or their facilities to the movement, to look into their hearts. "We have a charge to keep," Turner said. "We have a job to do in Greenwood, Mississippi. If you are true—a good shepherd—I ask that you go back to your church, and ask that your people stand up, and go down to the courthouse and put their names on the book." Dick Gregory, speaking after Tucker, limited his remarks. After a brief talk, he said simply, "Heaven is here now, or hell will be forever."[65]

By the spring of 1963, with racial tensions flaring in Greenwood and throughout Mississippi, Beckwith and Willie had again settled in at the big house on George Street, where they had spent the earliest years of their tumultuous marriage. Mississippi had become a battleground, and so had the Beckwith household, in which their familiar spiral of drinking and fighting had been renewed. When they drank together, Beckwith had learned to stop at a certain point to maintain control over Willie. Her own drinking was, she admitted, uncontrollable. "One night he shot at me," she remembered. "He was downstairs and I was upstairs, and I got my gun and shot back at him. This was after we'd come back from Natchez. At the time, we were both drunk and mad, and I was trying to keep [him] off me." During the blistering argument, while they screamed and threatened each other, Beckwith broke out a window and threw her jewelry box, shoes and clothes out onto the front yard. "Get out!" he shouted, his face red and his body shaking violently. "Just get out and don't ever come back!"

"I told him, 'I'm not going to put up with this,' and I just left. I had a red Impala then, and Little De La had taught me how to drive. He was still away at school, because this was around the beginning of May." She gathered up as many of her belongings as she could get in the car, then drove to the Greenwood Leflore Hotel, where, with money she had saved from the sale of their last home, she checked in for the night. The following day, she rented Apartment 16 at a complex at 210 West President Street. She later returned to the big house to get her son's belongings, as he was soon to return home from Chamberlain Hunt Academy for the summer and she expected him to live in the apartment with her. When friends and neighbors asked Beckwith about his wife, he told them she had moved into the apartment because of the "fearful condition" of the old house.[66]

To entice her son, Willie promised him a new car—a ploy his father had successfully used just months before. On June 10, Willie and her son traded in the 1963 red Ford Falcon his father had bought him and purchased a stripped-down 1963 white Chevrolet Biscayne.[67] She knew how upset Little De La was that she and his father had separated again, and wanted to do her best to keep him away from her husband, partly out of concern that he eat well and have clean clothes to wear to school, and partly out of sheer selfishness.

In the midst of the civil rights turmoil in Greenwood, Beckwith was settling into the routine of a new job. He left New Deal Tobacco and

Candy Company in February 1963 and took a new job selling custom-mix liquid fertilizer for Delta Liquid Plant Food Company, headquartered in Greenville. This would prove to be a good career move, he thought, because now instead of calling on small-time grocers and merchants, he would be selling to influential farmers and wealthy plantation owners. Just as he had aspired to align himself with the local leadership of the Citizens' Council over the past decade, Beckwith now hoped to build close contacts among the plantation elite. These men, he believed, were more similar to him in breeding and ideology than many of the small retailers he had previously been calling on. And of course, none of the Delta's prominent planters were black.

Although Beckwith saw no apparent connections between his new job and the tense racial situation in Mississippi, companies like Delta Liquid were exacerbating the economic problems for blacks. Weed-killing chemicals and crop fertilizers—along with mechanical cotton pickers and other automated equipment—were displacing black workers and deepening their level of poverty. Beckwith liked his new work, however, and the job's perks were impressive as well. Not only did he rank a company car, generally a white Valiant, but it came equipped with a two-way radio for communicating with the office. If he tinkered with changing the frequency, he could also pick up the local police or other citizens band communications. Beckwith's new employer C. Dewitt Walcott, Jr., traveled the 200-odd mile route with him during his first few days of work, and described him as "polite to a point of being ridiculous," and said Beckwith's personal mannerisms made him nervous.[68] Beckwith was assigned to work with other salesmen who knew the route, including John Book, and he stayed up nights reading the company's literature to learn about the liquid fertilizer business. He enjoyed working the fields, meeting new people. Occasionally, while touting the virtues of liquid fertilizer or talking about the Citizens' Council, he would meet someone he found particularly intriguing.

Betty Carter, whose husband Hodding's editorials had been the frequent target of Beckwith's public pontificating, recalled wondering whether Beckwith might have been interested in planning an attack on their home. She remembered a local high school boy, John Keating, who stayed with them part of the summer of 1963 while his parents were away. Beckwith ran into Keating at Delta Liquid, where the boy was working for the summer, and heard that he was staying with the Carters and knew them well. Beckwith pulled the boy aside and inquired about the layout of the house. "How is that house put together, that big house?" Beckwith asked. "Oh, I don't know," Keating hedged. "You know, there's a living room, dining room, kitchen, like any house." Keating cut the conversation short and went on about his work. "But John thought he was trying to find out for a reason," Mrs. Carter said in an interview. Beckwith's interest in the Carters was more than casual. His employer, Dewitt Walcott, once overheard Beckwith talking about Hodding Carter. "If I get my chance," Beckwith said, "I'll kill him."[69]

As the civil rights campaign in Greenwood became more turbulent, Beckwith's public messages became more vitriolic and his attacks, more specific. He continued to rail against the Church of the Nativity and the clergy. His mimeographed flyers, distributed publicly and mailed to members of the church's congregation, took on an overtly sexual tone. "Anglo-Saxon poet Lord Byron referred to those 'ebony beauties,' " Beckwith wrote in one leaflet, "and it is noted throughout history that the master of the house, his sons (and, yes, even his daughters) consorted with slaves. Even present-day white women have been found guilty of enjoying a wide variety of carnal entertainment provided by black menservants."

Even when criticizing the church, Beckwith used interracial sex as a theme to heighten fear and cause alarm. Another of his flyers boldly asserted, "The race mixing in our church has got to stop now. The black race in America must not be permitted to enter the white bedchamber through the open doors of the integrated church." He pointed to the "renegade Christians" advocating integration, and proposed using "physical force, if necessary, to halt further spread."[70]

Along with his growing references to sex between the races, Beckwith's published writings also became filled with images of death and destruction. One of his flyers, delineating between segregation and integration, said, "The two ideologies are now engaged in mortal conflict and only one can survive. They cannot be fused any more than day can exist in night. The twilight of this great white nation would certainly follow. There is no middle ground." Another stated: "We are saying to each other that we will slay the monster as soon as he sets his black foot on the sacred soil of Mississippi. This courageous talk is a poor substitute for preventive measures to keep the beast off the backs of our BROTHERS who now actually SUFFER with the real live virus of integration, elsewhere." Beckwith then held himself up as a man who possessed the right, the courage and the strength to "lead you in the attack on our enemies."[71] He then set forth a number of charges against the presiding bishops, whom he accused of promoting integration. "God willing," he wrote, "I will assist in their prosecution and punishment."

In his final flyer, issued just three months prior to Medgar Evers's murder in Jackson, Beckwith's enemy had been clearly targeted. "The foul, contemptible, selfish person who continually tells the Negro that America is equally his—that he's as good as anybody—that he has the right to govern this land—should be ashamed to lie like that," Beckwith wrote. "Believing such a lie has put many a darkie in the river late at night; some at the end of a rope, stirring others of their race to unrest.

The Negro in our country is as helpful as a boll weevil is to cotton. Some of the weevils are puny little runts and can't create the volume of damage that others can. Some are powerful, becoming mad monsters snapping and snarling and biting the cotton. They must be destroyed, with their wretched remains burned, lest the pure white cotton bolls be destroyed."[72]

6

The Rising Tide of Discontent

In Jackson, ninety miles from Greenwood, Medgar Evers was having another hectic day. Even as the movement was reaching its inevitable boiling point during the spring and summer of 1963, Evers had grown disillusioned. He knew the movement in Jackson had accelerated beyond the comfort level for NAACP Executive Director Roy Wilkins, who had only recently seen a Mississippi jail cell from the inside—something hundreds of black citizens in Jackson had already experienced. Evers was married to the movement, and to progress—not to the NAACP. The previous August, as part of a group of black parents, Evers had placed a petition before the Jackson school board requesting reorganization of "the entire school system into a unitary nonracial system." The petition was ignored. The NAACP's lawyers later filed suit on behalf of ten black children, pressing for the desegregation of Jackson's public schools, as mandated by the Supreme Court decision nearly ten years earlier. It was the first such suit introduced in Mississippi's courts, and was still pending as the summer's demonstrations and boycotts escalated.[1]

Early that spring, Evers had firmly cautioned Governor Barnett, Jackson Mayor Allen C. Thompson, and the city's Chamber of Commerce that "the NAACP is determined to put an end to all forms of racial discrimination in Jackson." He noted that the organization would use "all legal means of protest—picketing, marches, mass meetings, litigation."[2]

As students prepared to demonstrate, one youth stood at the front of a church congregation and said, "To our parents we say, we wish you'd come along with us, but if you won't, at least don't try to stop us." Evers wanted to open a dialogue with the mayor, but Thompson would not be swayed. On May 12, in a televised address targeted specifically to Jackson's blacks, Thompson asked them not to cooperate with the NAACP's demonstrations and described Jackson in such glowing terms that many of the blacks listening thought he must have been talking about a different city. He referred to Jackson's civil rights groups as "outside agitators" and vowed he would never meet with their leaders, saying that once the state's agitation subsided, "Jackson will still be prosperous, people will still be happy, and the races will live side by side in peace and harmony."[3]

On May 20, 1963, in an equal-time reply to the mayor broadcast over white television stations WJDX and WJBT, Evers outlined how the average Negro in Jackson viewed the city. "He sees a city where Negro citizens are refused admittance to the city auditorium and the coliseum; his wife and children refused service in a downtown store where they trade; students refused the use of the main library, parks and other tax-supported recreational facilities." His voice was controlled and assertive. "The mayor spoke of twenty-four-hour police protection we have," Evers continued. "There are questions in the minds of many Negroes whether we have twenty-four hours of protection or twenty-four hours of harassment." He again urged the mayor to appoint a biracial committee to oversee the integration efforts, as other cities had done. "History has reached a turning point, here and over the world," Evers said, his voice firm. "Here in Jackson, we can recognize the situation and make an honest effort to bring fresh ideas and new methods to bear, or we can have what Mayor Thompson calls 'turbulent times.' "[4] Evers's appeal was simple and eloquent, and for the first time, many white Mississippians had an opportunity to hear him explain the rationale behind the boycotts and sit-ins he had been leading, which they had been tensely watching.

When Mayor Thompson turned a deaf ear to Evers's protests, the NAACP began a series of sit-ins at a downtown Woolworth's store on May 28. White onlookers threw pepper in the participants' eyes and splattered demonstrators with paint, attracting national television coverage. Mayor Thompson began negotiations with a group of local black ministers, hoping to ease the demonstrations. Evers watched as Jackson policemen brusquely snatched flags out of children's hands on the picket lines, and saw students beaten and spat on during the lunch counter sit-ins. Having seen blacks held in stockades, singing spirituals despite being corralled like cattle, Evers felt sure the movement's economic boycott of white businesses would work. The sit-ins would work. He was determined to propel the movement forward in Jackson, even if it meant leaving the often reluctant NAACP and spearheading a movement of his own.

John Salter, one of the Jackson movement's chief organizers—and later, its most provocative chronicler—believed Evers was ready to form an alliance with Dr. Martin Luther King, Jr.'s Southern Christian Leadership Conference (SCLC) and SNCC—organizations that were not reluctant to take direct action. Evers pushed to keep the pressure on, while the national leadership of the NAACP encouraged restraint, and the threats on his own life increased. He constantly received harassing phone calls both at work and at home, and hate literature had been distributed on his street. On the evening of May 28, after a torturous day during which

Mayor Thompson had both agreed to some concessions and reneged on them because of pressure from leaders of the Citizens' Council, someone threw a Molotov cocktail on the Evers's carport, where it exploded into flames. Myrlie Evers rushed out of the house to douse it with the garden hose.[5]

Three days later, on May 31, students at a local high school sang freedom songs on the school lawn during their lunch break, and were joined in song by hundreds of others. Police with attack dogs attempted to quell the crowd by beating the students with billy clubs, but the violence could have been worse. One Jackson policeman told a reporter, "There are a lot of young, hot-headed Negroes here who are willing to die for what they believe in. And we've got a lot of white men who are ready to kill them." Later the same week other demonstrators were clubbed, while conducting a protest march. They were arrested and taken to the nearby fairgrounds, which had been converted into an open-air jail for the occasion. More than 500 demonstrators were arrested. NAACP Executive Director Roy Wilkins flew to Jackson to speak that evening.[6] Evers hoped to respond to the mass arrests by mounting massive protest demonstrations, but Wilkins made it clear that the board of directors of the NAACP felt that their supply of funds was not inexhaustible, and that they were more comfortable pursuing lawsuits than bailing Mississippi demonstrators out of jail. Evers was strongly encouraged by Wilkins to shift his focus from the demonstrations to voter registration drives, which were less confrontational. Frustrated, Evers decided to try to raise money on his own, through rallies and concerts. Singer Lena Horne agreed to fly to Jackson to give a benefit performance.[7]

The threats against his life now mounted daily. "The whole mood there of white Mississippi was to eliminate Medgar Evers and the problem would have been solved," his wife remembered in an interview. "Our home was firebombed, we received threats on almost an hourly basis at home, he received threats through the mail. It was a life of never knowing when that bullet was going to hit." Still, Evers moved ahead, both aware of the danger and in spite of it. Almost every night of that first week in June, a rally was held somewhere in Jackson. In addition to the mass meetings, there were boycotts, marches, pickets and prayer vigils. In the two weeks during the peak of the activity, Evers and more than 600 demonstrators had been arrested and jailed.[8]

Lena Horne's appearance at the June 7 rally at the Masonic Temple was one of the Jackson movement's highlights. "It was a turning point in my life," she said in an interview. She went to Mississippi to witness firsthand what the conditions were, and to place her support behind the city's demonstrators. "I didn't feel Medgar was making progress," Horne said. "But he was trying against all odds to make progress." While she was aware of the unique form of Mississippi "justice," she still was not prepared for what she found when she arrived. "I never expected the downright cruelty. I had seen all the subtle forms of it, but this was very open and blatant, and it made me more angry."

John Herbers, a former UPI bureau chief and reporter for *The New York Times*, who covered the civil rights movement in Mississippi, remembered the obstacles Evers faced during those tortured months. "Medgar was almost an angelic type," Herbers said. "He was so quiet and restrained, and his values were so pure. Of all the civil rights leaders that I knew back in those years, there was none as exemplary as he was, as sincere and as dedicated to what he was doing. And at the same time, Evers was courageous, because he knew he was going into the maelstrom of very bad things and very bad people. He was treated in the most abysmal way by all of the important people in Mississippi at the time. Treated like trash."[9]

By 10:00 A.M., temperatures were already climbing in the sweltering Mississippi Delta, but with the windows rolled down, traveling at a quick clip, De La Beckwith could work up a pretty good breeze. He had long before reconciled himself to the pros and cons of a company car, which he had almost always been fortunate enough to have. New Deal had always supplied him with a car to work his rounds, and now, with Delta Liquid, he was generally driving a white 1962 Valiant. The car had its faults—white was certainly not the color Beckwith would have selected for traveling the dirt roads of the Delta, and the speedometer and odometer were broken,[10] making it impossible for him to track his mileage for the daily work reports he was required to submit to the head office in Greenville. Still, he could gas up, take off and drive all day, and it would not cost him a penny. That was one good thing about sales, no capital outlay was required. And he was allowed to drive the car for his personal use, as well, which was a perk, since Willie had taken her car when she moved out of the big house. He actually preferred the company car to his own station wagon.

After more than a decade of selling tobacco and candy for New Deal, then later for Carr-Williams when he and Willie lived briefly in Natchez, Beckwith knew sales was his true calling. He had a gift for gab, and could press the flesh with the best of them. His mother's early efforts to teach him manners and courtesy had not been futile; he had long ago learned that the art of careful listening was as persuasive as fast talking. Selling to people in the Delta, he knew, was best accomplished by building relationships over time, particularly with the plantation owners and planters to whom he was now selling. High-pressure tactics and hard selling just would not work. It was hard enough to convince his prospects that customized liquid mix fertilizer was the wave of the future, and could be formulated specifically for *their* soil, for *their* crops, without complicating matters by offending them with a hard sell. If he was lucky or persuasive enough to convince a planter to submit to a tissue test or soil sample, all Beckwith had to do was pick up the two-way radio and tell his boss to wait at the office, because he was bringing in a lab sample.

In the three and a half months he had worked for Delta Liquid Plant Food, Beckwith had already established a reputation of sorts. His boss, Dewitt Walcott, heard about him from a mutual friend in Greenwood, Jim Pegues. Walcott had an opening and Beckwith knew the Delta and came highly recommended as a salesman. His job interview at Delta Liquid was informal, and Walcott didn't even ask Beckwith to fill out an application. He did, however, conduct a cursory background search, talking to one of his former employers and calling his bank. When Beckwith was hired in late February 1963, Walcott personally worked the sales rounds with him during his first couple of days on the job. He later said working with Beckwith made him nervous, and that his personal mannerisms were annoying.

In terms of his work, however, Beckwith was an ideal salesman. He was meticulous at everything he did, got on well with farmers in the area, and "went to extremes to see that everything that he had promised to the farmers was done on their behalf," Walcott said. He knew Beckwith was a gun trader, and had accompanied him on his rounds one day when Beckwith sold a pistol to someone at a minnow shop in Tchula. He had also heard that Beckwith was a "self-appointed committee" to keep blacks out of the Episcopal church in Greenwood, and knew from their discussions that he was an ardent segregationist. Walcott had seen him interact with blacks on his rounds, and said he was quite friendly toward older blacks on the plantations, but had little use "for the younger breed." One of Beckwith's co-workers, John Book, who also worked with him occasionally, said he talked segregation constantly. It was "difficult for him to keep his mind on his business," Book said.[11]

On Tuesday, June 11, 1963, one of Beckwith's first prospective customers was Doyle Wood, a planter in the little town of Sidon. While trying to convince Wood to test his products, Beckwith impressed on him the importance of customizing his fertilizer mix to his soil and crops, and left him with some sales literature. He also called on several other farmers in Sidon, two of whom were distant cousins. One, Mack Kimbrough, had purchased some of Delta's liquid fertilizer and was seeing good results. Beckwith noted in his work report that Kimbrough's prettiest cotton was on the section of the field where they had tested the fertilizer.

By midday, with the scorching June sun high overhead, Beckwith's white cotton shirt was sticking to his back. He stopped to have the car's brakes adjusted and added brake fluid, noting it in his work report.[12] It was Beckwith's custom to save a late sales call in Greenwood so he wouldn't have an extended drive at the end of the day. Late that afternoon, he met for two hours with Hugh Warren, the owner of the Refuge Plantation, who kept telling Beckwith, "Hell, I know how to raise cotton!" After explaining how Delta Liquid's products worked, Beckwith harangued Warren until he consented to a tissue test, agreeing that a fertilizer mix was the best way to get a prize crop, but unsure that liquid fertilizer was the way to go. Beckwith finished his work day at 7:00 P.M., according to the work report, and he headed home to the big house for the evening. It would be hot when he got home, he knew, because the house had been closed up all day and was not air-conditioned.

Beckwith could not have been both making sales calls all day in the Delta and in the NAACP offices in Jackson on the afternoon of June 11, but that is exactly where several witnesses placed him. NAACP Southeastern Regional Director Ruby Hurley later recalled seeing Beckwith in the organization's offices on the second floor of the Masonic Temple building on June 11, and she also remembered him from a rally at the Masonic Temple on June 7, when Lena Horne and Dick Gregory appeared. Hurley's story was especially compelling, because she remembered that at the rally at the Masonic Temple, Evers had slipped her a note asking her to tell one of the white men to quit smoking. From the right side of the stage, Evers rose to address the audience. His topic was "Where Do We Go from Here," and in his closing remarks, he said, "We're going to keep up the fight to end discrimination, regardless what our opponents do." Two NAACP employees later questioned by the FBI recalled that, at one point, Evers had pointed to Beckwith and the men with him and said facetiously, "And I will tell our *friends* that this fight *will* continue."

Hurley later told FBI agents that one of the white men at the June 7 rally was a Jackson policeman, whom she recognized, and that Beckwith was definitely one of the two others. The Jackson police officer was memorable owing to his frequent attendance at NAACP meetings and rallies, and because he usually sat with members of the press and took copious notes. After Evers's murder, the policeman never attended another meeting. Another civil rights worker gave FBI agents a similar story about the three white men, and explained quite calmly that she knew they were not affiliated with the NAACP, or she would have known them. She was also quite certain they were not affiliated in any way with the press, because they remained at the back of the auditorium and did not mingle with the other press representatives. They took no notes during the proceedings, she said, and they could not have been press photographers because they had no cameras with them.[13]

After Evers's murder, several witnesses, including Evers's secretary, Lillian Louie, reported that on at least two occasions they had seen Beckwith lingering around the NAACP offices. One woman later told FBI agents she was sure the man was Beckwith, and that he once came into the office and stayed for about two minutes. When she asked if she could help him, he said no, and left. She said she had seen him outside about an hour before, standing across the street from the office, talking to a policeman. Three other witnesses who were in the office at the time corroborated her story. Another civil rights worker questioned by the FBI said that the week before Evers's murder, she had seen a white car with a long antenna double-parked across the street from the NAACP office. She remembered noticing the men in the car—four men in street clothes—because they stared for some time at the activity in the office.[14]

Beckwith's daily work report did not contain sufficient detail to establish conclusively his whereabouts on June 11. First, Beckwith wrote a combined report for June 10 and June 11, on the front and back of a single daily report form, while other work reports for that period are filled out individually, on separate sheets. Second, he noted that his brakes were down, and that he took time out to service them and add brake fluid. No receipts for service were ever produced, nor was any accounting made of the time involved to service the car. Third, he wrote that he made sales calls to seven planters on June 11. Three were in Sidon, a small town just outside Greenwood, and two others were his cousins. The sixth planter was not available, but Beckwith left "fresh literature" for him. The last planter he reportedly called on that day, Hugh Warren, later testified that Beckwith had indeed spent about two hours on his plantation that week, but he could not remember which day. Finally, with his car's speedometer and odometer broken, Beckwith could have called on the planters he claims to have visited that day, and still driven to Jackson and back without raising any eyebrows. There were no speedometer or odometer readings to give him away, no tissue samples to turn in at headquarters before day's end, and no wife waiting at home for his return.[15]

In Washington that evening, President Kennedy's staffers were scrambling to cut and paste a draft of a speech he was to deliver on national television within the hour. Earlier in the day, Kennedy unexpectedly told his advisors he wanted to announce new civil rights legislation on television that night. White House speech writer Ted Sorensen was given little more than two hours to come up with a text, and while Kennedy found the initial draft a little stiff, the message was there. Kennedy began dictating to his secretary, Evelyn Lincoln, putting his personal stamp on what would become one of his most famous addresses.[16]

Kennedy was seizing the moment. Just a few months before, the Southern Regional Council had issued a report chronicling crimes against Southern blacks since 1961, offering a day-by-day listing of attacks, mutilations, killings and injustices in the Southern courts. The atrocities had continued, and Kennedy was impelled to act by recent events in Birmingham, where widespread demonstrations and police violence had shaken the city. Police Commissioner Eugene "Bull" Connor had turned the city's police dogs and high-pressure water hoses on demonstrators to disperse them. In the wake of the violence in Birmingham, other cities across the country were experiencing violence and disruption. Dr. Martin Luther King, Jr., powerfully argued in *The New York Times* that the president would have to put his "total weight" behind proposed civil rights legislation, and urged him to address the race crisis in moral terms.

Complicating matters in Alabama was the state's staunchly segregationist governor, George Wallace. Earlier in the day, Wallace had defied U.S. Deputy Attorney General Nicholas Katzenbach, who was sent to Alabama to personally enforce the court-ordered admission of two black students to the University of Alabama, the last state-supported university to cling to racial segregation. Wallace stood in Katzenbach's path as he approached the entry of the university's administration building. Katzenbach, looking around at the crowd that had assembled and the podium erected on the concrete landing, told Wallace he was there to enforce a court order. He asked for the governor's unequivocal assurance that he would not bar entry to the students who wished to enroll, and that he would do his duty as governor to see that they were admitted, as the court had ordered.

"As governor and chief magistrate of the state of Alabama," Wallace told him, posturing, "I stand before you today in place of thousands of Alabamians whose presence would have confronted you, had I been derelict and neglected to fulfill the responsibilities of my office. It is a right of every citizen, however humble he may be, through his chosen officers of representative government, to stand courageously against whatever he believed to be the exercise of power beyond the Constitutional rights conferred upon our federal government. It is this right which I assert for the people of Alabama by my presence here today . . . Now, therefore, I, George C. Wallace, as governor of the state of Alabama, do hereby denounce and forbid this illegal and unwarranted action by the central government."[17] Wallace saw his political future stretched before him, in the angry faces of his white voters. They—not Katzenbach nor Kennedy—would determine his political future.

After President Kennedy federalized the state's National Guard later in the day, Wallace stepped aside and allowed Vivian Malone and James Hood to enroll. With federal force, but without the violence or rioting many spectators had anticipated, the University of Alabama finally admitted its first black students. In a televised statement that evening, Wallace acknowledged to his public that it was "a bitter pill to swallow." While Wallace had conceded to federal pressure, he had assumed a stance that allowed him to save face with voters. The University of Alabama had been integrated, and it had been accomplished without the rioting, violence and killing that had accompanied the previous fall's integration at the University of Mississippi.

* * *

At 8:00 P.M. on June 11, President Kennedy went before the nation, using a patched-up and pieced-together draft of a script. The worries of the day's events were etched in the lines on his face as he talked about the nation's "rising tide of discontent" and addressed, head-on, the racial tensions that were ripping the country at its seams. He said he would seek a law to open places of public accommodation to all; a law to accelerate the pace of school desegregation; and a law to protect the right to vote, noting however, that "law alone cannot make men see right." The speech was a landmark, not only because it broke new ground in the nation's struggle to right past injustices, but because of Kennedy's passionate and heartfelt conclusion, which he delivered without referring to his notes.[18] "We preach freedom around the world," Kennedy said, "and we mean it. And we cherish our freedom here at home. . . . But are we to say to the world—and much more importantly, to each other—that this is the land of the free, except for Negroes; that we have no second-class citizens, except for Negroes; that we have no class or caste system, no ghettos, no master race, except with respect to Negroes?

"Now the time has come for this nation to fulfill its promise. The events in Birmingham and elsewhere have so increased the cries for equality that no city or state or legislative body can prudently choose to ignore them. . . . We face, therefore, a moral crisis as a country and a people. . . . A great change is at hand, and our task, our obligation, is to make that revolution, that change, peaceful and constructive for all." He spoke of the impending civil rights legislation, and asked Congress "to make a commitment it has not fully made in this century, to the proposition that race has no place in American life or law."

Near the conclusion of his speech, the president paid tribute to those citizens, "North and South, who have been working in their communities to make life better for all. They are acting not out of a sense of legal duty," Kennedy said, "but out of a sense of human decency. Like our soldiers and sailors in all parts of the world, they are meeting freedom's challenge on the firing line, and I salute them for their honor and their courage." He spoke directly to the plight of blacks. "This is one country. It has become one country because all of us and all the people who came here had an equal chance to develop their talents. We cannot say to ten percent of the population that you can't have that right; that your children can't have the chance to develop whatever talents they have; that the only way they are going to get their rights is to go into the streets and demonstrate. I think we owe them, and we owe ourselves, a better country than that."[19]

At her home in northwest Jackson, Myrlie Evers reclined on her bed, all three children in tow, and listened to the president's speech. After putting the youngest, Van, to sleep, she allowed Darrell and Rena, ages nine and eight, to stay up late and wait for their father to come home.[20] The past several weeks had afforded Medgar Evers scant time with his children; his time was consumed by directing the Jackson movement. President Kennedy's speech was an unexpected development in Evers's already crowded day. He called home several times throughout the day and spoke to his wife and children, which was unusual. At a meeting that night at the Masonic Temple, Evers and Clarksdale, Mississippi, NAACP leader Aaron Henry ran through their testimony for a House Judiciary Committee meeting scheduled for June 14. Later, Evers drove Gloster Current, NAACP's director of branches, to a rally at New Jerusalem Baptist Church. Reverend R.L.T. Smith had made his church available for that evening's rally, which, after the President's impassioned speech, seemed both lengthy and disappointing. Smith, a prominent black minister, served as chairman of the *Mississippi Free Press*—the Jackson movement's newspaper—and was like a surrogate father to both Medgar Evers and his brother Charles.[21]

Two witnesses claim Beckwith was lingering at the rear of the church sanctuary that evening, with one foot propped up against the wall, gazing over the crowd watching Medgar Evers. Reverend Smith and one of the church's deacons, Willie Osborne, both of whom kept silent for nearly thirty years, in 1990 claimed the all-white juries and fear of reprisals kept them from coming forward after the murder. Smith remembered Beckwith clearly. "There was something about him," Smith said. "I felt like he beared watching." The reason he did not come forward during the first trial, he explained, was that, " If I had testified, the jury would have cleared him before I finished testifying." Osborne, too, feared for his life. "I was afraid I would have been killed," he said. However, John Salter, who was also present at the meeting, refuted the two men's assertions and claimed the man they believed was Beckwith was, in fact, a plainclothes Jackson policeman named Jim Black, who resembled Beckwith.[22]

Since Reverend Smith had been a close friend of Evers's, and because of his long involvement in the Jackson civil rights movement, there are many, like Salter, who question whether time, and the state's intense desire for justice in the Evers murder case, may have influenced these witnesses' memories. "He's a good man," former Mississippi Congressman Frank E. Smith said of Smith. "I just don't know whether he can be led into believing he saw something that he didn't." Late that evening, after the rally at New Jerusalem broke up, Medgar Evers drove Current to attorney Jack Young's house to spend the night. "Everywhere I go lately," Evers told Current wearily, "somebody has been following me." He wanted to get home to his family, he said, and he lingered as he shook his friend's hand and held it.[23]

* * *

Just after midnight on June 12, Evers pulled into his driveway at 2332 Guynes Street. As he stepped out of his powder blue 1962 Oldsmobile, a thundering shot from a high-powered rifle pierced the darkness and ripped through the back of his white cotton shirt, exiting through his chest. It was so late, and he was so tired, that he had forgotten the house rule—turn off the car lights and get out on the passenger side, nearest the door of the house. He taught his wife and children to follow the drill, just as he taught them to drop to the floor when they heard a strange noise. In his car, Evers carried a .45 automatic pistol. "I slept with a small revolver next to me on the night stand," his wife remembered, "and he slept with a rifle next to him. We had one in the hall, we had one in the front room. He had one with him the night he was killed, and we often talked about that. He said, 'Yes, I will use it if it's necessary to protect myself, to protect my family, to protect my friends. However, Myrlie, one may never know if one will be able to get to the gun in time.' And the night that he was killed, it was right there next to him." At the age of thirty-seven, Medgar Evers lay facedown in his carport, the culmination of his life's work emblazoned across the front of the fund-raising sweatshirts he dropped in a pool of his own blood. The shirts read simply, "Jim Crow Must Go."[24]

Darrell and Rena hit the floor when they heard the blast, and Myrlie Evers rushed through the house and out the backdoor to find her husband stretched out in front of her. "When I got to the door," she said later, "I turned on the light and opened the door at the same time, and I saw my husband, where he had fallen facedown, and I saw the trail of blood that he had left behind him, and I saw the keys in his hand. He had dropped everything but his keys."[25] Evers was killed by a single shot. The bullet entered his back, passed through his body and then through a living room window. It clipped a venetian blind and traveled through a living room wall into the kitchen, where it glanced off the door of the refrigerator at a forty-five-degree angle and came to rest on the kitchen sink counter, after shattering a small glass coffee pot. It landed next to a watermelon.[26]

The Evers's next-door neighbor, Houston Wells, heard the shot and grabbed his .38 caliber pistol. He ran outside and fired the gun in the air while his wife called the police. Rushing next door, he found Myrlie Evers crouched over her husband, screaming and hysterical. "I ran into the house and got a mattress," Wells said. Another neighbor, Willie Quinn, arrived to help. Wells said, "I rolled him over onto the mattress and pushed the mattress. I ran back and got my station wagon and I pushed him into the back of my station wagon. By that time the policemen were there, and they escorted him to the hospital."[27] In the station wagon on the way to the hospital, Wells heard Evers say, "Let me go, let me go."

He died less than an hour later at University Hospital, a white hospital, where his black doctor was not allowed to attend to him.

In Greenwood, just minutes after Evers's murder and prior to any news bulletin about his death, an anonymous male called an official of the Leflore County chapter of the NAACP in Greenwood and said, "We have just killed Medgar, and you are next."[28] At the murder scene, police found blood and remnants of Evers's flesh splattered on the hood and windshield of his car. His chest had been blown apart by one extremely powerful bullet. Detective Sergeant John Chamblee of the Jackson Police Department described a trail of blood from Evers's car door to the steps of his house, where Evers had crawled after being shot, and added, "it wasn't like a little tiny stream," but instead looked like it was "poured out of a bucket along the side of the car." As soon as she heard about the shooting, Ruby Hurley rushed to the murder scene. Later, when Myrlie Evers started to get some rags to clean up the blood, neighbors took her back inside and Hurley cleaned up the blood on the carport and on Evers's car.[29]

Dr. Forrest Bratley, a Jackson pathologist who performed autopsies in criminal cases, was awakened at 2:15 A.M. and called to University Hospital to attend to Evers's corpse. The body was still warm when Bratley arrived. The bullet that killed Evers entered his back just below his right shoulder, shattered his eighth and ninth ribs, and had blown a hole in the lining of his chest cavity that measured seventy millimeters by forty-five millimeters, slightly larger than a half dollar.[30] The bullet then burst the right lower lobe of Evers's lung, fractured his fifth rib and tore through the front of his chest just above his right nipple. The bullet passed through his body, causing the hemorrhage which was ruled the official cause of death.

At 3:05 A.M., Jackson attorney Jack Young called Assistant Attorney General Burke Marshall in Washington to give him the news of Evers's murder. Marshall called FBI Assistant Director Alex Rosen and asked him to get confirmation. New Orleans Special Agent in Charge, Harry Maynor, who was in Jackson at the time working on another case,[31] confirmed the murder and supplied Rosen with the details, adding that he personally offered the local police the facilities of the FBI Laboratory and Identification Divisions to cover out-of-state leads. Rosen duly dictated a memorandum elaborating on the details of the murder to FBI Assistant Director Alan Belmont. A last-minute addendum read simply, "Upon being furnished the information on the morning of 6/12/63, Mr. Marshall advised that he desired no further action by the FBI."[32]

In the outlying neighborhood, near Evers's house, Jackson policemen and FBI agents surfaced two witnesses who earlier in the evening saw a late model white Valiant with a long radio antenna parked at a nearby drive-in restaurant. Police also interrogated two taxi drivers who said a white male had inquired about Evers's address the prior Sunday, at the bus station. Several neighbors reported that a white-top cab had been seen in the neighborhood the night of the murder, and another neighbor remembered that the day before, another taxi had been seen slowly driving through the neighborhood. The driver slowed down and asked one of the neighbors where Evers lived, explaining that he had a telegram to deliver. Later in the evening, concerned about the incident, a neighbor called the Evers home. No telegram had been delivered. In the police department's quest to comb the neighborhood, more than a hundred people were interviewed before daybreak.[33]

Charles Evers flew to Jackson from Chicago as soon as he received the news of his brother's death. "Mama used to always tell us that God will take away the thing closest to you," he said in an interview. "And somehow, when he took Medgar, something just hit me. I had been wrong. I had made money, and I had taken care of him real good. That's the one thing I feel real good on. I hadn't let him worry about nothing. I just sent him this, you know, high pay, and he said, 'Charles, why do you send us this money?' And I said, 'Just take it, don't you worry about it. You just take it.' And I just took care of him—I bought him everything I thought he wanted. He had new cars, and I helped him buy his house. I bought him all his furniture, and—well, he was all I had." At the morgue, before his brother's body had been taken to the funeral home for preparation, Charles Evers asked to see him. "So I went in there," he said, "and stayed about an hour with him, back in the back. He was lying on the table—hadn't even been embalmed. And, well, I don't know. I just haven't been the same since. Well, I wanted to die, really."[34]

7

The Lone Suspect

In the sweltering heat that precedes the onslaught of summer, Jackson erupted on the morning of June 12, 1963. In the early morning hours following the announcement of Evers's murder, students at Tougaloo College and Jackson State College began rallying supporters and demonstrators and arranged a mass meeting at the Masonic Temple. Local ministers met at the Pearl Street African Methodist Episcopal Church to decide what course of action they should take. The Jackson movement, which had experienced some frustrating starts and stops in the months prior to the assassination, coalesced briefly after Medgar Evers's death. At the church later that morning, thirteen of the ministers decided to demonstrate, aware that they would be jailed. They walked with determination from the church, in pairs, and were immediately arrested and jailed by policemen dressed in riot gear. Inside the Masonic Temple, the crowd slowly grew. James Salter and Ed King, leaders of the student movement, along with the workers at the NAACP offices upstairs, were determined to demonstrate.[1] Although Evers himself had acquiesced to his national organization's pleas for restraint, in the wake of his death, his friends wanted to show their solidarity with their fallen leader. They were determined that the movement would continue. Several hundred people had gathered by that time in the auditorium of the temple and waited for some word of the group's plans.

Anne Moody, who had long been active in the Jackson movement, and Dorie Ladner, a worker from SNCC, spent the morning gathering a group of demonstrators at Jackson State. They roamed through the hallways, opening classroom doors and asking for marchers. As they passed President Jacob Reddix's office, he came out and told them to leave, saying that they could not make announcements without his consent. His apparent apathy for Evers's murder appalled them. "I didn't say anything to him," Moody said. "If I had I would have called him every kind of fucking Tom I could think of." Although Reddix appeared unmoved, President John F. Kennedy, who was informed about the murder by an aide at 7:00 A.M., issued a brief statement which said he was "appalled by the barbarity of this act." He dictated a brief letter to Mrs. Evers, which read in part, "Although comforting thoughts are difficult at a time like this, surely there can be some solace in the realization of the justice of the cause for which your husband gave his life." The president's brother, Attorney General Robert F. Kennedy, said he was "saddened and shocked," and immediately offered the assistance of the FBI to authorities in Mississippi. Speaker of the House John W. McCormack called Evers's killing "not only disgraceful, but vicious."[2]

While news of Evers's murder hit the newspapers and television, local police continued their investigation at the murder scene and the surrounding area. On the "Today" show, Lena Horne and Roy Wilkins were already eulogizing Evers.[3] Outside Evers's home, in a honeysuckle thicket 150 feet away, Detective O.M. Luke found the murder weapon, resting about a foot above the ground and concealed in a clump of vines. "It was well hidden and wasn't even touching the ground," he said.[4] Jackson Police Captain Ralph Hargrove, who had been called the previous night to photograph the murder scene and Evers's wounds at University Hospital, was again called to photograph the removal of the rifle from the honeysuckle vines. The gun, a 1916 Enfield 30.06 army surplus rifle bearing the serial number 1052682, had a six-power Golden Hawk telescopic sight mounted on it. The rifle was common enough—about two million had been produced during World War I and had been sold and traded by sportsmen ever since. It was an inexpensive rifle, easy to obtain. It was a particularly fine rifle for deer hunting.

Back at headquarters, Hargrove, the Jackson Police Department's identification expert, carefully dusted the gun with gray powder for prints. Although the stock and barrel of the rifle were smeared, a near-perfect right index fingerprint surfaced on the telescopic sight. Hargrove photographed the fingerprint, then lifted it with fingerprint tape. Because of the perspiration present in the print when he photographed and lifted it, Hargrove estimated it to be less than twelve hours old. After the fingerprinting, when Detective Luke had an opportunity to examine the rifle closely, he pulled back the breech. "It threw an empty hull out," he said, "and a fresh round of ammunition came up to go into the chamber. I fished them out and there were six live rounds in the magazine underneath the chamber. One had been fired. It had not been ejected."[5] The murderer, prepared to fire seven rounds, hit his target with a single shot.

At FBI Headquarters, Assistant Director Alex Rosen noted in a memorandum that the FBI had offered its Laboratory and Identification Division, as well as coverage of out-of-state leads, to Jackson police. He noted that Assistant Attorney General Burke Marshall "indicated he desired no further action be taken by the FBI," but continued, "nevertheless, in view of the nature of this case and in view of the momentum that obviously will be generated because of the Evers killing . . . we are instructing all pertinent offices in the South to immediately alert racial informants and other sources to our interest in this matter, and if these offices obtain any information which might have a bearing on the Evers killing, we want to be immediately advised." FBI Director J. Edgar Hoover wrote on the memo simply, "OK," Burke Marshall and the Kennedy boys be damned.[6]

Mississippi Governor Ross Barnett called the murder "a dastardly act," although he had clearly loathed the civil rights leader. "As Governor of Mississippi, I shall cooperate in every way to apprehend the guilty party," Barnett said the morning of the murder. In an attempt to force the governor to accept at least part of the moral responsibility for Evers's murder, civil rights workers later launched a chain letter requesting that individual checks for one dollar be sent directly to "Ross Barnett, Trustee of Memorial Fund of Family of Medgar Evers." Barnett was livid when checks began pouring in and he became *ex officio* guardian of the Evers's family's well-being.[7]

James Meredith issued a more emotional statement to the press, later retracting two important sentences at the behest of Ole Miss history professor James Silver: "If I were charged with the responsibility of finding Medgar Evers's killer, I would look first and last among the ranks of law officers of this state. The chances are at least one hundred to one that the killer is to be found there."[8] It was a bold assertion, but one that had crossed many people's minds when they heard the news of the murder. It was widely known among people in the Jackson movement that the police, and sometimes just ordinary thugs, had taken to following Evers home. For blacks in Jackson, particularly those involved in the civil rights upheaval, either prospect was frightening. But strangely, no one—police or otherwise—had followed Evers home the night he was killed.[9]

In Jackson, several hundred demonstrators left the Masonic Temple and headed for the downtown business district, down Lynch Street, singing freedom songs in the one-hundred-degree heat. They were met along their route by police and state highway patrolmen with loaded rifles and idling paddy wagons. More than 150 people were arrested and carried off to stockades at the fairgrounds, where they were penned in a makeshift jail where the annual cattle auctions were held. Even in their imprisonment, the demonstrators were segregated. Hundreds more demonstrators remained on the sidewalks and in front yards along Jackson's streets, singing and chanting, while their friends were carried away.

Leaders of the movement regrouped at the Masonic Temple to plan their strategy. They scheduled a mass meeting to be held that evening at the Pearl Street African Methodist Episcopal Church, after which they wanted to march downtown. John Salter returned to the Tougaloo campus to rally students for the evening's activities, while workers at NAACP headquarters mimeographed flyers to be distributed throughout the city. By the time Salter returned to the Masonic Temple, plans for the evening's march had been cancelled by NAACP leaders, who believed the danger was too great. They also believed Evers's widow was going to address the church rally that night, and they did not want to further upset her with a massive march. Instead, they began planning a series of daytime demonstrations and focused their energy on a march they wanted to hold the day of Evers's funeral, for which no date had yet been set.

With her husband's murder less than twenty-four hours past, Myrlie Evers, clad in a pale green dress, made her first public appearance that night at the Pearl Street African Methodist Episcopal Church. In the stifling sanctuary, a huge congregation sat fanning themselves with paper fans. Several introductory speakers made remarks, and their words were more moving, and more militant, than ever before. As the Reverend R.L.T. Smith introduced the widow, who entered from the rear of the church, the crowd fell silent. "I come here with a broken heart, but I come because it is my duty," she said. Tears fell softly down her cheek as she spoke. She pleaded passionately for those in the audience to continue to support the movement, so that her husband's death might not be in vain. She appealed for direct action. "I ask you for united action in this effort, in memory of my husband," she said. "Nothing can bring Medgar back, but the cause can live on."[10] Moved by her speech, people throughout the church wept silently.

A short time later, nearly forty teenagers, in small groups of two and four, stood in the downtown streets with small American flags. Although it was Flag Day, the students were arrested and charged with parading without a permit. A "demonstration of sorrow" was announced for later in the week. Mourners planned to march silently after Evers's funeral, which had been set for the next day. All the women in attendance at the rally were asked to wear black, and the march was scheduled to go from the Masonic Temple—where Evers's funeral service would be held—across Capitol Street through the heart of the downtown business district, onto Farish Street, where many black businesses were located.[11]

In Washington, as word of Evers's death spread throughout the Capitol, Southern Senators vowed, in a special caucus, to block upcoming civil rights legislation. Separately, Berl Bernhard, staff director of the Commission on Civil Rights, called FBI Liaison Agent D.J. Brennan to stress the potential violence that might erupt in the wake of Evers's death, and said, "the shooting of Evers could be the spark that will set off the biggest and most violent racial demonstration this country has known."[12] In New York, while attending a Gandhi Society fund-raiser, Dr. Martin Luther King, Jr. was blindsided by the news of Evers's death. King and one of his mentors, Mordecai Johnson, discussed an idea that had filtered up from one of their colleagues in Jackson. Later that day, after their luncheon, they announced the Gandhi Society's Medgar Evers Memorial Bail Fund to honor the slain martyr. Roy Wilkins's chagrin was evident when not only the Gandhi Society fund, but other Evers funds, began to spring up, independent of the NAACP, where Evers had channeled his energy and efforts. Wilkins quickly had his local Jackson aides approach Myrlie Evers to obtain her agreement that funds in her husband's honor should be controlled by the NAACP. While this task posed little difficulty, getting Mrs. Evers to agree to bury her husband at Arlington National Cemetery, rather than in his native Mississippi, proved slightly more daunting. She and her husband owned adjacent funeral plots in a black cemetery in Jackson, where they had agreed they wanted to be buried, and she initially declined the offer of burial at Arlington. She later relented.[13]

Wilkins said Evers's death "demonstrates anew the the blind and murderous hatred which obsesses too many Mississippians. In their ignorance they believe that by killing a brave, dedicated and resourceful leader of the civil rights struggle, they can kill the movement for human rights." The NAACP announced a $10,000 reward for information leading to the arrest of the murderer. In Jackson, Gloster Current, director of branches for the NAACP, who had been one of the last people to see Evers alive,challenged city officials to match the organization's reward offer.[14] In a short time, $27,000 in reward money was being offered for information leading to the arrest of Medgar Evers's killer.

At her home in Jackson, Eudora Welty sat down and wrote a now famous short story, "Where Is the Voice Coming From?" She wrote of a murder like Evers's, spinning the tale from the perspective of the killer. Welty had lived in Mississippi all her life, and like most Mississippians, even if she did not know the killer's name, she knew him just the same. He could have been almost any white segregationist in Mississippi. "He was down," Welty's murderer thought to himself after pulling the trigger, "and a ton of bricks on his back wouldn't have laid any heavier. There on his paved driveway, yes sir."[15] The short story was published in *The New Yorker* just three weeks after Evers's murder, and just a week and a half after the apprehension of a suspect in the case.

While Mississippi scrambled to make sense of Evers's murder, De La Beckwith was back in the fields of the parched Delta, trying to sell his company's fertilizer. He started his day on Wednesday, June 12 at 6:45 A.M., according to his work report, and may have picked up the morning newspaper at the Crystal Grill or Lackey's Cafe; wherever he stopped that morning for breakfast. The old house was in such disrepair, and he was such a poor cook, that he no longer even tried to fry an egg or make toast at home. That day's *Commonwealth* ran an editorial entitled "Black and

White" on its front page, adjacent to coverage of the Evers murder. "We detested what Medgar Evers was doing to Mississippi," it began. "We were aware he was a reverently hated man, that his name was an epithet on thousands of lips. But we would have argued until doomsday that what happened to the NAACP leader early this morning couldn't have." The writer denounced the murder and the culprit who committed it, although, he noted, "Negro leadership have invited just such action as this." Beckwith clipped the *Commonwealth* articles and saved them.[16]

He went on about his work for the day, spending most of his day in Money, Mississippi, where young Emmett Till had been abducted and murdered in 1955. Beckwith met with several farmers, including Harold Terry, who farmed 500 acres of cotton. Terry said he might be persuaded to have a tissue test done on his plants and would consider using a side dress of liquid fertilizer, but he would have to think about it. Beckwith then headed toward Itta Bena, just a few miles outside of Greenwood. He left a lot of literature with the local planters, but did not make any sales. He noted on his work report that he had a flat tire out in the country and could not get the trunk open—he had to take out the back seat to get to the spare tire. Then he had to take the tire from Money to Greenwood, his report said, as no one in Money could repair it. He spent a dollar and a half having the tire patched, and his speedometer, he noted again on his report, was broken.[17]

News of the fingerprint found on the murder weapon made the national wire services later in the day on June 12. A memo from Assistant Director Alex Rosen to Assistant Director Alan Belmont, circulating through FBI headquarters in Washington, summarized the local excitement over the print in Mississippi. Apparently, the print was found by the local police almost by mistake. "While looking at the gun, the police were anxious to determine whether the telescopic sight was a professional job and mounted on the rifle by a gunsmith," Rosen noted. "In doing this they had to remove the sight and consequently, in order to preserve and not mutilate any fingerprints, they called in their ident[ification] man to process the gun for fingerprints." Hoover wrote on the memo, in his stiff scrawl, "Well at least they are not using our facilities," and initialed it. Rosen also suggested in the memo that if evidence was turned over to the FBI, they might want to personally alert Attorney General Robert F. Kennedy, "as this may be the subject of news comment." Hoover wrote simply, "No" on the memo, and initialed it.[18]

That night, Jackson Police Chief W.D. Rayfield and Chief of Detectives M.B. Pierce, who in 1961 had arrested nine black students who refused to leave the public library,[19] began drafting a document formally asking the FBI's help in the Evers case. The next morning, they sent an urgent letter to Hoover, explaining their findings and requesting assistance from the FBI Laboratory. They forwarded by hand the bullet, the murder weapon with its telescopic sight, the lift of the latent fingerprint, a photograph of the latent print, the six live rounds of ammunition found in the rifle and the empty shell casing. Rayfield and Pierce requested that the lab search its extensive fingerprint files, check the rifle through the National Stolen Property File, perform ballistic examinations on the rifle, and conduct "any other logical examination deemed advisable." The evidence was delivered by Special Agent Samuel E. Virden II, who took Eastern Airlines flight 526 to Dulles Airport and delivered it directly to the FBI Laboratory.[20]

Hoover replied to Rayfield and Pierce—in an urgent, collect telegram—that the bullet from the Evers home was a .30 caliber slug of the same type as the bullets in the live cartridges found in the weapon, and that "this bullet could have been fired from submitted Enfield rifle, but due to condition of bullet, cannot be specifically identified with this gun to the exclusion of all other weapons." Hoover also noted that the fingerprint search was underway. What he did not tell Jackson Police was that he had already ordered special agents in Boston and New Orleans to begin checking the records of the Springfield arsenals in an attempt to trace the murder weapon, *before* the Jackson police asked for the Bureau's assistance in the case.[21]

A photograph of the murder weapon was widely published in the nation's newspapers on June 13. The fingerprint Hargrove lifted was already being researched in the FBI's fingerprint files, and, unfortunately, by the time photographs of the weapon hit the newsstands, the FBI had already determined that no record of the murder weapon existed in the National Stolen Property File. That evening, at the police offices in Jackson, Captain Hargrove received a phone call from a farmer from Itta Bena, Mississippi, a tiny town about eight miles west of Greenwood. Innes Thornton McIntyre, a twenty-six-year-old who called himself "Thorn," asked for a description of the rifle he had seen in the paper—it looked awfully familiar. Except for the telescopic sight mounted on it, the gun looked exactly like one he had owned a few years back. Hargrove described the murder weapon in detail, and McIntyre said that it was possible that the gun the police had found was the same one he had bought by mail and later traded to a salesman from Greenwood who was a "segregation fanatic."[22]

"His name," McIntyre told Hargrove, "is De La Beckwith." It was the first time anyone connected Beckwith to Medgar Evers's murder.

If the Jackson Police Department believed it had the first hot lead in the case, the investigators kept that information to themselves. Captain Hargrove had duly taken down Thorn McIntyre's name and number when he had called from Itta Bena about trading rifles with De La Beckwith, but neither Hargrove, Chief Rayfield nor Chief Detective Pierce told the FBI agents working with them that they had received the tip. Before word could leak that Jackson Police had the name of a suspect, Hoover sent an urgent, fifteen-word telegram to Chief Rayfield, collect:

> LATENT FINGERPRINT FROM TELESCOPIC SIGHT OF RIFLE NOT IDENTIFIED IN OUR SINGLE FINGERPRINT FILE.
>
> HOOVER[23]

Although the FBI would later take credit for having matched the latent fingerprint on the murder weapon with Beckwith's Marine Corps fingerprints in the Bureau's files—which the Bureau eventually did—the initial search had turned up nothing of value. Jackson police, however, for whom Evers had created so much work with his marches and boycotts and demonstrations, already had the name of a possible suspect. They did not share that name with the FBI. Across the state of Mississippi, Klan blacklist leaflets soon began to appear. Photographs of Medgar Evers, James Meredith, John Salter, Bob Moses, Emmett Till, Reverend R.L.T. Smith and others were printed on the flyer. Medgar Evers's photograph, like Emmett Till's, had a bold "X" marked through it.[24]

On Saturday, June 15, Medgar Evers's funeral service was held at 11:00 A.M. at the Masonic Temple. Dressed in a gray suit, a white shirt and a gray tie, Evers lay in state, wearing a white Masonic apron around his waist. The building was so packed with people that more than 1,000 gathered outside under the hot midday sun, unable to enter the auditorium to hear the service. Most stayed, however, knowing Mayor Thompson had temporarily lifted a parade ban to allow a silent march when the funeral concluded. Dr. Martin Luther King, Jr., flew to Jackson for the service, and the local police, fearing an attempt might also be made on his life, escorted him directly to the Masonic Temple.

Roy Wilkins offered a eulogy in which he blamed the Southern political system for Evers's death. "The killer must have felt that he had, if not an immunity, then certainly a protection for whatever he chose to do, no matter how dastardly it might be," Wilkins said. Wilkins described Evers just as the Citizens' Council, the Klan and even Byron De La Beckwith had characterized him—as an enemy of segregation. "Medgar was more than just an opponent," Wilkins said. "In life, he was a constant threat to the system that murdered him, particularly in his great voter registration work. In the manner of his death he was the victor over that system. The bullet that tore away his life four days ago, tore away at the system and helped to signal it in." Dr. Ralph Bunche, Under Secretary of the United Nations, sat on a stage above the flag-draped casket with Wilkins, looking out toward the victim's widow, who was seated in the front row.[25]

Evers's simple, gray metal casket was carried out of the building after the service and was placed in a hearse, which proceeded slowly toward Collins Funeral Home on North Farish Street, with thousands of people following it on foot. The police had agreed to allow the cortege, with the understanding the marchers would walk in strict silence. Several Jackson ministers led the group, followed by officials of the NAACP and other civil rights groups. More than 5,000 people, most with tears and perspiration streaming down their faces, walked silently behind them.[26]

After Evers's pallbearers had carried his body into the funeral home, most of the crowd dispersed. About 1,000 mourners remained, and one smaller group of marchers started walking toward Capitol Street, the site of Evers's boycotts. They were angry, and their anger was compounded by the sorrow that they felt for their assassinated leader. Just as the demonstrators began to turn onto the main thoroughfare, where their presence had been forbidden, the police reacted swiftly. Approximately 250 officers—Jackson police, state highway patrolmen and Hinds County sheriff's deputies—met the marchers. Armed with pistols and riot guns, and with billy clubs and attack dogs at the ready, the officers tried to push the marchers back toward Farish street. "We want the killer! We want the killer!" the crowd screamed. Fire trucks were positioned close to the demonstrators along the street, to hose down the rioters if necessary. The crowd, even angrier now that they were being resisted, pelted the policemen with rocks and bottles. Police started grabbing individual protesters, dragging them to waiting paddy wagons or garbage trucks, sealing most of the others in a one-block area.[27]

Immediately, a white man stepped between police and the rioters, the sleeves of his white cotton dress shirt rolled up. John Doar, a Justice Department attorney who had worked with the civil rights activists, placed himself in the middle of the crowd. "A black kid had come out of the crowd and thrown a bottle, and it bounced in front of this line of police," Doar remembered, "and the glass kind of skidded into them, or a rock had come out, or a brick had come out, and it hit the street in front of them, and skidded into them. I was just afraid that if this kept going on, somebody was really going to get hurt, because I didn't have any confidence in the discipline of those county officers. So I walked through the line of police and walked out and persuaded everybody to stop."

Doar's appearance failed to ease the tension. Dave Dennis, a Congress of Racial Equality staff member, saw a black man pull a rifle on Doar, but quickly pulled him away. "I said, 'Come on Dave, help me. Let's get this thing stopped,'" Doar remembered. "In my judgment, the kids had gotten so frustrated with their inability to seize the system . . . they had gotten totally disillusioned. And [they] were willing to turn to more violent behavior." Doar was able to quiet the rioters on the front lines, explaining who he was. He cautioned that if the violence escalated, someone would be killed. In a few minutes, the crowd calmed down and slowly began to disperse. Nearly thirty people were arrested, a woman was bitten by a police dog, and a man was hit in the face with the butt of a shotgun. Myrlie Evers, already back at home with her children, learned of the riot later.[28]

Four days later, on Wednesday, June 19, another funeral service was held at Arlington National Cemetery. The American Veterans Committee and NAACP leaders had pressed Myrlie Evers to bury her husband at Arlington, and after sharing him with the world for the duration of their marriage, she agreed to his burial at Arlington. Evers's body was sent by rail to Union Station, where more than 1,000 mourners met the train in silence. During the march from the station to the funeral home, handbills with Evers's photo and the legend, "He sacrificed his life for you" were circulated among the crowd. As more than a hundred policemen watched, the marchers silently followed the hearse on foot to McGuire Funeral Home, twenty-five blocks from the train station. About 2,000 people waited outside the funeral home until Evers's body was carried inside. Clarence Mitchell, Washington director of the NAACP, said that he expected no trouble in Washington like that experienced after Evers's funeral in Jackson. "The only trouble here," Mitchell said, "will be troubled consciences." The next day at 3:00 P.M., Myrlie Evers and her two older children arrived at Washington National Airport. Her husband's body lay in state at John Wesley African Methodist Episcopal Zion Church until it was escorted to Arlington for burial at 10:00 A.M. the next day.[29]

Attorney General Robert F. Kennedy and a number of government officials attended the graveside services at Arlington, near Sheridan Gate. In his second eulogy for Evers, Roy Wilkins said, "Medgar Evers believed in his country. It now remains to be seen whether his country believed in him." A lone bugler sounded "Taps." A photographer for *LIFE* magazine, covering the funeral, shot a poignant photograph of the widow leaning down with her arms around her crying son, Darrell, comforting him. The photograph was printed on the magazine's cover the following week. Six white soldiers folded the flag atop Evers's casket and handed it to the young widow.[30]

President John F. Kennedy broke from his schedule and invited the Evers family to visit the White House before returning to Mississippi. In the Oval Office, awaiting the president, his secretary told the children there was a story that if you sat in the president's chair and made a wish, it would come true. Darrell said he wished his father had not died in vain.[31] Kennedy was sympathetic and warm, offering condolences to the widow and PT-boat souvenirs to the children. Later, on a private tour of the White House, Myrlie Evers stood in the window of the Lincoln

Bedroom and watched Kennedy board a helicopter as his son John-John stood and waved goodbye.[32]

In Greenwood, De La Beckwith drove by Dr. H. Reed Carroll's house and saw him puttering in the front yard. Beckwith stopped and talked with his physician a long while, the doctor later recalled, primarily about his hopes of a reconciliation with Willie. He had heard that she had been admitted to the hospital a couple of days earlier, and wanted to talk to Carroll personally to find out what was wrong with her and how she was getting along. A short time later, inside Room 313 of Greenwood Leflore Hospital, Willie Beckwith heard her estranged husband in the hallway, saying hello to someone. She closed her eyes and her entire body tensed. Dr. Carroll had admitted her to the hospital on June 17, with acute cystitis and secondary pyelitis, and this was the first opportunity Beckwith had had to visit her.[33] Hoping to warm her up for a visit, he had stopped at Mary Bell's Flowers on West Claiborne Street the day before and picked out a bouquet to be delivered to the hospital. He and Willie had been separated for more than a month now, but Beckwith was hoping a reconciliation would be in the offing. He made small talk for a few minutes, asking how she felt, then stretched out across the bottom half of her hospital bed to discuss her recent purchase of a new car for Little De La.

"He looked like he was tired, exhausted, completely worn out," Willie recalled. "I remember it just like it was yesterday. It was hot, hotter than hell that month. He laid back across my hospital bed." When he reclined, she noticed the half-moon cut over his right eye, and she asked how he got it. "Target practicing," he said.

On June 20, a full week after Thorn McIntyre called the Jackson Police Department, J. Edgar Hoover was still telling Attorney General Robert F. Kennedy that "no logical suspect has been developed as of the present time." According to Hoover, the Jackson Police Department had compared the latent fingerprint from the telescopic sight with the fingerprints of more than 300 possible suspects in Mississippi. De La Beckwith was not among them. Another day passed. "The only leads to date that appear to have potential," the Special Agent in Charge in New Orleans noted in a decoded radiogram, "are leads to trace instant telescopic sight."[34]

The immediate question was an obvious one: Why did Jackson police safeguard the one clue that might have led to Beckwith's questioning? The best-case scenario was that the local police department hoped to solve the murder on its own. If that were the case, though, the Jackson police would have been reluctant to turn over the murder weapon to the FBI Laboratory. The worst-case scenario, and one which many blacks in

Jackson found credible, was that Jackson police wanted to ignore any evidence linking Beckwith to the murder. It later came to light that Beckwith had attended at least one NAACP rally with a Jackson policeman, fueling speculation that he might have had friends on the Jackson force, just as he had close friends on the Greenwood police force. The Jackson Police Department's record of conducting thorough investigations in racially motivated crimes had been appalling, and for that reason, blacks were naturally reluctant to place their trust in the police.[35]

Although the Citizens' Council had been the most vocal opponent of integration in Mississippi, its economic reprisals—firing household help, denying credit to blacks—became less and less effective as tensions mounted and blacks began to assert themselves through demonstrations and boycotts. Various fringe groups, less respectable and more forceful, sprang up throughout the South that summer, and the long-dormant Ku Klux Klan burgeoned. In the three years following the Supreme Court's desegregation ruling in 1954, more than 100,000 Klansmen took their oaths. Social instability bred an instant form of reactionary behavior, creating a renewed feeling that the survival of the white, segregationist South could only be achieved through repressive means.

While there is no evidence that the leadership of the Citizens' Councils and the Klans worked in tandem, their methods seemed to complement each other. The Council hoped to deprive blacks of their rights through all legal means, while the Klan worked outside legal channels to thwart black progress. Although occasionally, individual Council members may have carried out acts of vigilantism, even murder and bombings, the Council organization *per se* was never directly linked to such acts.[36] It is likely, however, that there was a significant overlap in membership of the Council and the Ku Klux Klan. Many Council members wanted to take a stronger stand, however, and joined the Klan. One prominent Citizens' Council figure, John Kasper, said at a Council rally in Birmingham that he was "deeply honored" by the presence of robed Klansmen. "We need all the rabble rousers we can get," he told the crowd. Like many other Council leaders, concerned that their "legal" efforts were not working, Kasper advocated using any means possible to stop integration. "We want trouble and we want it everywhere we can get it," Kasper said.[37]

That summer, the state of Mississippi grew rife with conspiracy theories. It was common knowledge that Evers, along with a number of other civil rights movement leaders in the state, was on a Ku Klux Klan hit list, even though the Klan had not yet formally organized in Mississippi. Delmar Dennis joined the Klan after Evers's murder. He later came to believe Evers's murder may have been sanctioned by the Klan's Imperial Wizard, Sam Holloway Bowers, Jr. Klansman Billy Buckles later discussed an upcoming "job" which he said would make Evers's death "look sick."

The Clarion-Ledger, Jackson's rabidly racist newspaper, set forth the theory that "a paid assassin might have done the job. There are rumors that the man was expendable."[38]

James Meredith, along with many of Mississippi's blacks, believed members of the Jackson Police Department were involved in the conspiracy to murder Evers. John Herbers, a reporter for *The New York Times* who covered events in Mississippi, also believed police were involved. "I would have bet, from what I knew at the time and what I found out later, that the Jackson police—or at least a large number of them—were in cahoots with Beckwith," Herbers asserted. Even NAACP Executive Secretary Roy Wilkins alluded to the implicit guilt of the Jackson police in Evers's murder: "If the State of Mississippi cannot find and punish the killer, then it will be hard to erase the thought that the State of Mississippi, through its authorities, is responsible for that killing." Henry Kirksey, who later became a state legislator, once even went so far as to say he believed employees of the Sovereignty Commission ordained Evers's assassination, and possibly other murders.[39]

Another natural suspicion was that members of the Citizens' Council conspired to murder Evers. Their businesses, after all, had been hurt by Evers's economic boycotts. One FBI informant, who did not know Beckwith's name until his photograph was widely published following the arrest, came forward with information that implicated Beckwith and other Citizens' Council members in the Evers murder. The informant told FBI agents he believed members of the Council in Greenwood met after hours at an unnamed local gathering place. He recounted overhearing part of a conversation between Beckwith and some other men "approximately three or four days before Evers was shot," in which "they were talking about shooting someone," according to FBI files. A memo recounting the witness's report had Beckwith saying, "I'll do whatever has to be done. I do not mind killing the S.O.B."[40]

The men continued to talk, and the witness overheard another man volunteer to drive the car. "If someone can do the shooting," the unnamed man reportedly said, "I'll do the driving." Beckwith continued to talk about the "goddamned niggers," and the informant recalled that the man who offered to drive said he would not use his own car. After taking his report, FBI agents noted that the witness refused to furnish a signed statement, refused to testify at any trial or hearing in Mississippi, and believed he would be killed if the information was disseminated to anyone outside the FBI.[41]

One iffy theory, kept strictly within FBI circles, was that agents working in Mississippi pinpointed a Jackson Citizens' Council member who was rumored to have played a role in planning Evers's assassination. A small-time burglar named "Julio" (reputedly an alleged mobster named Gregory

Scarpa) was said to have been approached by FBI agents in New York, who offered him a deal: If he would perform some dirty work the agents themselves couldn't risk, and pinpoint the triggerman in the Evers case, they would make sure he was released in an upcoming interstate flight case. Scarpa allegedly flew south to Miami with his girlfriend, where he staged an alibi for himself in case it was later necessary. He drove to Jackson and, through an elaborate ploy, allegedly abducted the Citizens' Council member. An FBI agent reportedly drove the pair to an isolated house across the state line in Louisiana, deep in the bayou. There, Scarpa allegedly threatened and pistol-whipped the man until he made a statement.

While FBI agents posted themselves outside, under the windows, Scarpa pressed the man until he got several versions of the Evers murder story. Finally, the third time around, with a pistol shoved in his mouth, the man named Evers's killer: Byron De La Beckwith. Scarpa allegedly took a signed statement from the man before taking him back to Jackson and depositing him there. Scarpa did, in fact, walk on the interstate flight charge. Anthony Villano, an undercover FBI agent who infiltrated the Mafia and later recounted the story to his co-author, Gerald Astor, helped Scarpa obtain a $1,500 reimbursement from the Bureau. Scarpa reportedly signed a receipt for the payment, and that was that. The Bureau had the name of a suspect, and when the partial fingerprint on the murder weapon was compared, it checked out.[42]

There is, of course, no documentation for the story, and it is likely that if the incident did occur, the agents who elicited Scarpa's help wanted it kept silent for fear of reprisal from J. Edgar Hoover. His agents' reputations would have been tarnished by such behavior, and no agent was willing to incur Hoover's wrath. It would be much better, and safer, if Hoover believed his agents had identified Beckwith by tracing the Golden Hawk sight, or that the FBI Laboratory had later identified the partial print lifted from the murder weapon after failing the first time. Gregory Scarpa declined repeated interview requests to confirm or deny the story. Regardless, all the evidence pointed to Beckwith.[43]

A second and more credible scenario is that FBI agents did, in fact, trace the serial numbers 69431 on the six-power Golden Hawk Riflescope mounted on the murder weapon. The Japanese scope was mounted on the American rifle using counterclockwise British screws. The FBI discovered Beckwith through a tedious process of elimination. On June 15, while the Jackson police were still not disclosing McIntyre's call of two days earlier, FBI agents in Chicago were checking the shipping records of United Binoculars Company, the sole U.S. importer of the Golden Hawk rifle scopes, which were manufactured in Japan. Their search was not difficult. The particular type of scope found on the murder weapon had only been sold for a few years, and while 15,000 sights had been sold to 200 dealers across the country, only sixty had been shipped to the Southeast. Agents quickly located shipping orders documenting the sale of one six-power scope, two four-power scopes, one WP riflescope and one rifle mount to "Duck" Goza at Duck's Tackle Shop in Grenada, Mississippi, near Greenwood.[44]

On June 21, Special Agents Sam H. Allen and Walser Prospere visited Goza at his shop in Grenada. They read him his rights and interrogated him thoroughly about the telescopic sights he had ordered from United Binocular Company in Chicago. Goza, a stocky, hairy man with heavily tattooed arms, told the agents that he had sold or traded all the sights, but that only one of them had been a six-power scope. He acknowledged that he realized he was being questioned concerning the killing of a black man in Jackson. The agents visited Goza three separate times, each time toughening their stance and digging deeper. Later in the questioning, according to a report Allen and Prospere filed, Goza said, "Wait a minute, I'll tell you what I think you want to know."[45]

Goza said that he was almost certain that in May or June, he had bartered one of the scopes to a gun collector named De La Beckwith, a friend who traded with him frequently. He recalled that Beckwith had offered two .45 caliber pistols and some shotgun shells for it. He described Beckwith as a friend, and said he didn't want to get him into trouble, but that he thought the scope he sold Beckwith might be the one found on the murder rifle. According to the FBI report, Goza then said he had "a terrific headache, that he wanted a drink, and that he'd rather not discuss the matter anymore." As the agents were leaving, Goza said, "I think you have what you're looking for."[46]

That afternoon, Allen and Prospere got Beckwith's address from a directory at a nearby phone booth and staked out the big house at 306 George Street in Greenwood. Several hours later, at 7:45 P.M., Beckwith pulled into his driveway in a 1962 Plymouth Valiant. They made a note of the long whip antenna that was affixed to the rear of the car, remembering that one of the women questioned in Evers's neighborhood after the murder had mentioned a white car with a long antenna on it. Beckwith saw the men sitting in their car, wearing their dark business suits and ties in spite of the sweltering heat, and recognized them as agents he and a friend had photographed at a large integration rally a few months before. He strolled over to the agents' car, leaned in the driver's window, and asked them to leave. Allen and Prospere identified themselves as special agents of the FBI and asked if he was Byron De La Beckwith. "Yes, but I have no comment to make," he said. "We'd like to talk to you about a rather serious matter," Prospere said, and De La again replied, "No comment." The agents then asked Beckwith if he had in his possession, or had in the past possessed, a rifle scope which he had purchased from Duck's Tackle Shop. Beckwith turned and walked into his house.[47]

Other members of the FBI's team in Jackson were also being fed information about Beckwith from additional sources. Tom Van Riper, a special agent of the FBI working in Jackson at the time of Evers's murder, remembered that Klan informants and Citizens' Council informants had circulated Beckwith's name as the probable assassin. "I remember when De La Beckwith's name came up as a possible suspect," Van Riper said in an interview, "and then I heard that there was some informant information available that he had bragged that he killed 'that nigger.' Beckwith's bragging came back to us, to me and to other agents, through a number of informants. He was saying things like, 'It was no different killing Medgar Evers than shooting a mad dog,' and just letting people know that he was very proud of his accomplishment."

Van Riper had personally spoken to Evers a number of times when the civil rights leader called the FBI to report threats and harassment. "Given the tenor of the times," Van Riper said, "Medgar Evers was a dead man walking around. That was the consensus. And there was nothing we could do—short of putting him in a cage, or a metal box—to protect him. He was either a very brave man—and maybe he didn't even think about his bravery, if he *was* brave—or he was a very stupid man. Because he definitely was a marked man. And I think if Byron De La Beckwith hadn't murdered him, he would have been murdered in any case, by someone else." Still, Van Riper felt certain Beckwith was the killer, and believed his fellow FBI agents felt that they had found the murderer. "There is no question in my mind that Byron De La Beckwith murdered Medgar Evers. No question in my mind," Van Riper said. "From everything we know, and what our informants have told us. You know, informants—like everyone else—have motives. But for that many to have had the same information, that consistently, there is no question. And then, there was all the physical evidence."

At 2:20 A.M. on June 22, an FBI fingerprint examiner in Washington advised that a fingerprint of Byron De La Beckwith, taken January 5, 1942, Marine serial number 337948, was positively identified with the latent fingerprint developed on the telescopic sight on the murder weapon. The agent's identification was then verified by Latent Fingerprint Examiner George Goodreau. The Special Agent in Charge in St. Louis was ordered to check with military records housed there, to obtain Beckwith's service file and any photographs in it, and have an agency courier fly with the files to Memphis immediately.[48] Later that morning, FBI officials in Memphis got their first look at Beckwith, who glared back at them from his official Marine Corps photo, taken twenty-one years before. The

Identification Division of the FBI quickly searched the entire civil print file to locate additional information about him. They found a Federal Communications Commission job application and fingerprint record Beckwith had filed on March 18, 1946, at New Orleans. The prints were identical to those on the Marine Corps files.[49] The FBI immediately changed its method of recording information about the "unknown subject" they were seeking in the murder of Medgar Evers. After June 22, "UNSUB" became "Byron De La Beckwith."

Saturday morning, June 22, 1963, was an uncharacteristically busy morning at FBI headquarters in Washington. At 8:00 A.M., staffers at the FBI and the Justice Department were discussing ways to obtain a complaint charging Beckwith with a federal violation in the Evers murder. FBI Assistant Director Alex Rosen called Assistant Attorney General Burke Marshall first thing that morning, hoping to catch him for a brief talk. Marshall was already meeting with Dr. Martin Luther King, Jr., and passed the call on to John Doar. Doar, who had quelled the riot in Jackson the day of Evers's funeral, went directly to Marshall's office. Doar and Marshall discussed the possibility of proceeding against Beckwith under Section 241, Title 18—charging that he "conspired with unknown persons to injure, oppress and intimidate Medgar Evers in the free exercise of his rights"—but argued over the weaknesses of the federal statute. No co-conspirators had been identified, and "the question of clearly establishing a right guaranteed under the Constitution was difficult," Rosen noted in a memo for the record.[50] The matter became so heated that Marshall was called out of a meeting with the president at the White House to take a phone call on the matter from Rosen.

John Murphy of the Civil Rights Division was called in, and spent Saturday afternoon drafting a complaint. U.S. Attorney Robert Hauberg of Jackson questioned the complaint, as he believed it was defective. Probable cause, he felt, was not clearly demonstrated. Attorney General Robert F. Kennedy was contacted at home in McLean, Virginia, and spent a half hour on the phone with Rosen discussing the fine points of the complaint. Rosen noted, in his lengthy account of the conversation, that Kennedy "continued to express concern over the weakness of the case" and that "somewhere along the line the government might be tested if we had to go to trial. He understood there were no co-conspirators identified," which weakened the government's position. Rosen stressed repeatedly that "if the government didn't precipitate some affirmative action at this time, chances are nothing would be done." Rosen tried to get Kennedy to make a decision about moving forward with the complaint, but Kennedy insisted that the Bureau make its own decision in the matter.

J. Edgar Hoover and his closest associate, Clyde Tolson, were consulted. It is telling that Rosen attempted to resolve the situation with Kennedy before disturbing Hoover and Tolson on a Saturday. Burke Marshall was consulted, and Marshall made the final decision to proceed with the federal complaint against Beckwith.[51] This course of action would allow the FBI to arrest Beckwith and deliver him to Jackson, where he could be arraigned and turned over to local police once they filed the more serious charge of murder. Marshall asked FBI Assistant Director Alan Belmont to notify Attorney General Robert F. Kennedy when the warrant was issued, so the attorney general could personally phone the mayor of Jackson before the arrest was made. It would be Kennedy's attempt to show the highest level of federal cooperation with local authorities. Belmont argued that such a call would not be possible; once the warrant was issued, agents would have to immediately take Beckwith into custody. Awaiting a telephone call at Kennedy's convenience might mean "chasing [Beckwith] over the countryside at one hundred miles an hour," Belmont said. He agreed to notify Kennedy as soon as Beckwith was in custody; then the attorney general could take whatever action he deemed appropriate. It was a power-play that would be demonstrated time and again in the next few years, as J. Edgar Hoover and Robert F. Kennedy sought control over each other.[52]

At 4:45 P.M., in a complaint prepared by the Civil Rights Division, Beckwith was charged with violation of Section 241, Title 18, United States Code. The complaint was filed before U.S. Commissioner Margaret Estes at Hattiesburg, Mississippi, and the hunt for Beckwith began.

Beckwith had risen early on June 22 to make his Saturday rounds. He made some of his best sales calls on Saturday, when planters who were busy on weekdays were often home. Beckwith was out of Greenwood by 6:30 A.M., trying to put a good stretch of dirt road behind him before the day heated up. Had he left Greenwood even an hour later, he would have been met by a swarm of FBI agents. All possible means of exiting the city—the municipal airport, the local bus station, the railroad station and all the highways surrounding Greenwood and Leflore County—were being searched by agents. Greenwood Leflore Hospital, where Willie was still hospitalized, was also staked out in case he tried to slip in to see her. Agents also skimmed the local cafes, motels and the entire downtown business district thinking they might run across him while he was getting a haircut or having a cup of coffee. Afraid the local police were sympathetic to Beckwith and might tip him off, giving him a head start out of the state, the agents were instructed not to use their two-way radios, which the police might be monitoring. Instead, they were to use the telephone to ensure that information about the hunt for Beckwith was not leaked.[53]

After a long day in the field, Beckwith called Delta Liquid Plant Food's head office in Greenville on his two-way radio to ask his boss, Dewitt

Walcott, to wait for him to return with some tissue and soil samples one of the planters wanted processed right away. While he was at the office, Beckwith took a call from a hysterical neighbor, Mrs. J.H. Freeman, who told him his yard had been crawling with FBI men all day. Beckwith immediately called Hardy Lott, the city attorney and a former Citizens' Council president, and related the neighbor's story. Lott advised Beckwith to come to his office, where they could discuss the matter privately. About an hour later, Beckwith's cousin and former guardian,Yerger Morehead, called two FBI agents he knew, Bon McElreath and Orville Johnson, to tell them that Beckwith was aware the FBI was looking for him, and that he was currently conferring with his attorney. Morehead said he did not know what Beckwith planned to do, but that he had indicated he might give himself up to local police or the local sheriff. McElreath, knowing Beckwith was on friendly terms with the local police, advised Morehead that a *federal* warrant had been issued for Beckwith's arrest, and asked him to to try to get Beckwith to turn himself in to the FBI.[54]

Morehead called again a short time later and asked the agents to accompany him to Beckwith's house to get some clean clothes. Beckwith did not want to be arrested in the same sweaty clothes he had worn in the fields all day. In the meantime, Beckwith and Lott had gone to Lott's home to discuss the situation, and Beckwith showered and shaved there. Special Agents Prospere and Thomas Hopkins arrived at Lott's office to take Beckwith into custody, and spoke briefly with Lott, whom they knew. Beckwith dressed in a dark suit with a jaunty pocket square, placed his Shriners pin in his tie, and laced up his Stacey-Adams white bucks. Lott introduced the agents to Beckwith, who shook their hands, and then they explained to him that a complaint had been filed charging him with violation of Section 241, Title 18, U.S. Code, and that a warrant had been issued and turned over to the U.S. Marshal. Lott read the section to Beckwith in the presence of the agents. He then called U.S. Attorney Robert Hauberg at Jackson and discussed the specifics of the complaint.

At 10:35 P.M., Beckwith was handcuffed and taken into custody. The agents left Greenwood with him at 11:00 P.M., with three unmarked government cars following the one in which Beckwith rode. Every precaution was taken to ensure that he did not attempt to escape, and the Bureau provided sufficient manpower to keep a vigilante band from whisking the suspect away. Although Beckwith was quiet for most of the ride to Jackson, shortly after leaving Greenwood he proudly told the agents in his car that he had attended The Webb School in Bell Buckle, Tennessee, where he had studied Latin. He offered to recite some Latin poetry for the agents, but they declined. Near Lexington, Beckwith slept for a few minutes, but on rousing, Hopkins heard him mumble, "Niggers, niggers."[55]

* * *

While the convoy proceeded to Jackson, Beckwith was moved from car to car several times, and he remained quiet for most of the trip. At one point, near Yazoo City, one of the agents offered to get him a sandwich. Shortly before passing through the small town of Canton, Beckwith jokingly told the agents he was being taken to Jackson at the taxpayers' expense, and wondered aloud if the government would defray the cost of his return trip to Greenwood. As they drove into Jackson, Beckwith thanked the agents for the courtesy they'd shown him during the trip. The cars pulled into the police station at 1:40 A.M. Mayor Allen Thompson had been awakened from a sound sleep by the ringing of the telephone on his bedside table just a few minutes earlier. FBI Assistant Director Courtney Evans told Thompson that a suspect in the Evers murder, Byron De La Beckwith, had been arrested and was in FBI custody en route to Jackson, and that after his arraignment, he would be immediately available to the local authorities on the state's more serious murder charge. Evans stressed to Thompson that he had the attorney general's assurance that the FBI would continue to cooperate with the local police, and the Bureau promised to make available any agent whose testimony might be needed to help prosecute Beckwith. Then Chief Rayfield was put on alert, awaiting the convoy's arrival.[56]

A group of local reporters and photographers were also awaiting the suspect's arrival, having been tipped off that someone had been arrested and was being brought to the jail at Jackson. Once inside the jail, Beckwith was asked if he would like to make a statement. He declined. His pockets were emptied and with a small blackboard hung around his neck, Beckwith posed for his mugshots. He was fingerprinted by Captain Ralph Hargrove, the same man who only ten days earlier had discovered the latent fingerprint on the rifle used to murder Medgar Evers, and who had heard Beckwith's name a week and a half earlier, when Thorn McIntyre called. When Hargrove compared Beckwith's fresh fingerprints with the latent print found on the Enfield rifle, he found fourteen points of comparison.

Beckwith was arraigned at 1:45 A.M. on Sunday, June 23, before U.S. Commissioner John R. Countiss III. He was remanded to the custody of the U.S. Marshal, awaiting a preliminary hearing. He was then placed in a police lineup with his bold monogram glaring at the observers from the breast pocket of his shirt. Special Agent Joseph Peggs was present during the lineup, which was conducted by Jackson Police Detective Fred Sanders. Two of the men in the lineup with Beckwith were FBI agents, and three others were Jackson residents. Leroy Pittman, owner of a grocery store near Evers's home, said he was "pretty sure" Beckwith was the same man he had observed near the store the weekend prior to the murder.

Hubert Speight, a Jackson taxi driver, also selected Beckwith from the lineup and said he was "quite certain" Beckwith was the same man who had stopped him at the Jackson Trailways station a few days before the murder and asked about Evers's address. Although a carhop at Joe's Drive-In, near the murder scene, was unable to identify Beckwith in a police lineup, she later identified his Valiant as the car she had seen parked in Joe's back lot the night of Evers's murder.[57]

In Greenwood later that morning, two FBI agents returned to 306 George Street to photograph the house. On the right door frame, they noticed a Citizens' Council sticker. A Masonic emblem was also nailed on the doorway. The agents described the house as "obviously in need of painting and other repair." The back lawn was littered with debris and two rusting refrigerators, and the front windows had cardboard over them because the screens had rotted away. Meanwhile, at the jail in Jackson, a pathologist examined the semicircular scar above Beckwith's right eye, which was still puffy and slightly swollen at the time of his arrest. The doctor estimated the wound was no more than seventeen days old, a time frame that encompassed the night of the murder. The doctor projected the curved scar into a full circle and concluded that the measurement of the scar approximated the circumference of the eyepiece of the sight on the murder weapon. Front and profile close-up photos were taken, with an officer holding a ruler against Beckwith's head.[58]

District Attorney William A. Waller filed local murder charges against Beckwith and a hearing was scheduled for two days hence. Waller asked the FBI fingerprint expert and the FBI laboratory expert, who had examined the rifle, to appear at the hearing. Waller, Chief Rayfield and Assistant Chief Pierce also requested continued assistance from the FBI in the investigation. They specifically asked for an investigation in and around Greenwood to determine who mounted the scope on the murder weapon for Beckwith, and to determine if Beckwith had purchased 30.06 caliber cartridges or was known to have any in his possession. They also requested background information on Beckwith, including interviews with his wife, neighbors and business associates.[59]

Later that Sunday, police seized the company car, of which Beckwith had been so proud. The white Valiant bore Mississippi license plate WB2458, and had a long whip antenna for a two-way radio. The car was brought to Jackson, where a thorough investigation failed to turn up any evidence of value. Investigators did note, however, that the odometer was broken, making it impossible to determine Beckwith's exact mileage at any particular time.[60] Jackson police officer R.Q. Turner traveled to Greenwood and obtained a warrant to search Beckwith's residence. At 10:30 P.M., Turner began his search, which he completed at half past midnight. Three guns were found—and left—on the premises: a Stevens model 311 double-barrel shotgun, a Remington model 03-3A rifle, and a Galesi Italian automatic .25 caliber pistol. He noticed a large amount of loose ammunition which he did not take from the premises.

Turner also found a check made out to a local sporting goods store, dated May 11, and noticed a Peters Sporting Ammunition booklet containing underlined references to 30.06 Springfield ammunition, the caliber fired from the murder weapon, although none of the three guns found on the premises was a 30.06. Turner also found a twelve-inch wood rasp; a pair of tan leather work gloves; a December 29, 1962, letter to Beckwith from Dr. Roland E. Toms, the psychiatrist at the University of Mississippi Medical Center, in Jackson; and a manila file folder containing Beckwith's published letters-to-editors, along with correspondence from congressmen, senators and officials at the White House, acknowledging his ardent views on segregation.

At 2:15 P.M. on June 24, Countiss released Beckwith on the federal charge, which was later dropped. He was immediately taken into custody by Jackson police on the state's murder charge, which stated that Beckwith did "willfully and unlawfully, feloniously and of his malice aforethought kill and murder Medgar Evers, a human being, against the peace and dignity of the state of Mississippi." The press picked up the story immediately, but it was unfortunate that the FBI arrest had not occurred earlier in the day; Sunday morning papers were already printed and loaded on trucks, ready for early delivery. The broadcast media and Sunday late editions picked up the slack. "Starting at 1:30 A.M. Sunday and continuing throughout the day, it was the top news story," noted a memo circulated up the rungs of the FBI ladder by Crime Records chief Cartha "Deke" DeLoach.[61] "In all instances we received full credit for the arrest." Although Hoover had personally sent a collect telegram to Jackson police stating that his men had been unable to identify Beckwith's partial fingerprint in the Bureau's print files, he wanted to ensure his men received credit for the investigation and arrest.

Most important to Hoover, though, was the reaction of the black press. Charles Sumner Stone, editor of the *Afro-American* (who had been photographed with the Director the previous Friday afternoon) was contacted personally about the arrest. "After I related the facts to Mr. Stone, in a voice quavering with emotion, he responded, 'Thank God for the FBI.' I think this best typifies the reaction responsible Negro elements throughout the country will have as a result of our work in this matter." Hoover wrote, at the bottom of the memo, "A job well handled." On the bottom of a clipping from another newspaper, headlined "Evers' Brother, Wife Praise FBI," Hoover noted, "Send copy to A.G."—Attorney General Robert F. Kennedy.[62]

The following afternoon, on June 25, Hoover sent a memo, marked with the precise time, 1:01 P.M. to Tolson, Belmont, Rosen and DeLoach, recounting a discussion he and Kennedy had just held concerning Beckwith. Hoover told the attorney general it was obvious "the defense is going to be insanity." Kennedy said he was glad to know the right person had been apprehended, and Hoover "assured him this was true." As far as Hoover and Kennedy were concerned, Medgar Evers's murderer had been successfully apprehended.[63]

It wasn't until the following day, however, that FBI Assistant Director Rosen dictated a critical memo to the FBI hierarchy: "We have been able to come up with what appears to be a most important bit of evidence," he stated. "Our investigation . . . disclosed that an individual named Innes McIntyre of Itta Bena, Mississippi, traded a rifle of similar description to Subject Beckwith." FBI agents interviewed McIntyre and scrambled to locate the mail-order house from which he had purchased the rifle. When McIntyre pointed out a similar advertisement in the back of a sporting magazine, agents had the name of a firm to query. The firm's records were checked, and the company still had on file the shipping order for McIntyre's rifle. "The serial number and make of the gun are identical with the gun which was picked up near Evers's home," Rosen concluded.[64]

It had taken the FBI only ten days to discover what Jackson police knew the day after Evers's murder.

8

"Such Is the Fate of a Patriot"

The day after Beckwith's arrest, he was the sudden subject of discussion on television's popular "Meet the Press." The guest for June 23, 1963, was Attorney General Robert F. Kennedy, who was to discuss the issue of President Kennedy's sweeping civil rights legislation. Instead, during the program, the panel of newsmen asked about the arrest. Although Kennedy was reluctant to discuss the details of the case, he acknowledged there was more evidence than the partial fingerprint. "It was the Jackson Police Department that uncovered the fingerprint," Kennedy acknowledged. "I think that they are very sincere in the efforts they have brought to bear."[1]

Throughout the Mississippi Delta, Beckwith's acquaintances expressed their incredulity at his arrest by the FBI and the state's subsequent indictment for murder. A lifelong Greenwood resident who had been a high school classmate of his said, "I can't believe he'd sneak around and shoot somebody." Some, like Greenwood Mayor Charles Sampson, softly took Beckwith's part and perpetuated the myth of Beckwith's breeding and gentility. "I don't think he's the type," Sampson told a reporter following his arrest. "He would always greet you with a smile," as if this were a fail-safe declaration of innocence. Others saw the murder as a patriotic act. One of Greenwood's business leaders said, "If De La pulled the trigger that night, he must have felt he was doing it for the South and the state," leaving open the possibility, especially in towns like Greenwood, that Beckwith might have committed the murder, for *honorable* reasons. Another friend of Beckwith's sent a postcard to the jail reassuring him that, "You are most highly thought of, and sincere sympathy is expressed for you in the severe punishment that you are having to undergo for all of us who feel just as you do."[2]

To those who had tangled with Beckwith on the race issue in the past, however, it was no great leap of imagination that he might have shot Medgar Evers in cold blood. "If you had come up to me and said somebody from Greenwood was involved in this, well, he's the first one I would have suggested," said Beckwith's former congressman, Frank

Smith. And Beckwith's Episcopalian nemesis, Duncan M. Gray, Jr., said he clearly remembered when he first heard the news of Beckwith's arrest for Medgar Evers's murder. "I thought, 'Well, that's plausible. He probably did it.' I'm not talking about evidence," Gray explained. "I'm talking about an inner feeling, a *conviction*. Gut instinct."

Regardless of the nature of the speculation, Greenwood was consumed by gossip and rumor. The white townspeople rallied to the aid of their most infamous resident by establishing a fund on his behalf. Tom Barrentine and J.T. Thomas were quickly named co-directors of the White Citizens Legal Fund, ironically patterned after the NAACP's own legal defense fund. Within forty-eight hours after Beckwith's arrest, the fund had been established, a board of directors named, a post office box procured, thousands of flyers printed, letters mailed to all of Greenwood's townspeople, and articles placed in Southern newspapers. Greenwood's three bank presidents were named acting financial advisors for the fund. "When one considers the awesome array of power against him, which includes the full force of the federal government, the FBI, the Jackson Police Department, and $27,000 in reward money, it staggers the imagination," the fund's first solicitation letter said. A city commissioner provided envelopes prepared on an Addressograph™ machine, and each solicitation included a blank counter check for a quick contribution. Ellett Lawrence's printing company provided the paper and printing for a series of flyers and letters, and Lawrence's son was named to the fund's board.[3]

The fund was created to pay Beckwith's legal expenses, with excess assets to be used to establish a permanent fund for "future defense of white peoples' rights." The spokesman announcing the fund said, "We do not condone the murder of Medgar Evers and, of course, we have no idea of the guilt or innocence of the accused."[4] Money quickly started pouring in from all over the South, sometimes in increments of one dollar and two dollars and occasionally by the hundreds of dollars. Patriotic groups like the Sons of the American Revolution and the Veterans of Foreign Wars began taking up collections and forwarding the proceeds to the fund. Some of Beckwith's former customers on the New Deal route—even black store owners—placed collection jars next to their cash registers and turned over their customers' spare change to the fund. Bridge clubs, ladies' auxiliaries and local lodges sent checks along with cards offering their best wishes. The Memphis local of the International Union of Electrical Workers donated the considerable amount of $500. Three of the group's members drove ninety miles to Greenwood to deliver the check. The union's international president, James Carey, demanded that the local's president and financial secretary recover the money or resign their offices.[5]

Meanwhile, in the state capitol in Jackson, Mississippi, Governor Ross Barnett was deluged with chain letters bearing one-dollar and two-dollar checks, each made payable, in miniscule print, to "Ross Barnett, Trustee of the Memorial Fund of Family of Medgar Evers." Enraged, Barnett returned hundreds of checks to people who sought to make him the Evers fund's trustee. When the letters bore no return address, checks were returned to the banks on which they were drawn. The contributions flowed in so swiftly that Barnett petitioned Chancellor E.W. Stennett of Hinds County to appoint a local banker as trustee. The governor later joked about it, and said he did not mind outsiders' money flowing into Mississippi. "The more they send the better," Barnett said. "Money will help our economy. Let them send truckloads of it."[6]

Other funds reflecting concern for the Evers family, however, also took root. Within two months after the murder, the NAACP's Medgar Evers Memorial Fund for the Evers children's educations passed the $40,000 mark, and grew to nearly $60,000 at its peak. When Myrlie Evers finally received the proceeds of the fund Barnett had declined to administer, she received only $10,000 of a total of $17,000 mailed in by concerned citizens. The difference had been whittled away by "administrative" and "legal" fees. The Gandhi Society, encouraged by Dr. Martin Luther King, Jr. and Mordecai Johnson, established the Medgar Evers Memorial Bail Fund the day the civil rights leader's murder occurred, much to the dismay and displeasure of the NAACP, the rival organization for whom Evers had worked. The *Chicago Daily Defender* started a Medgar Evers Memorial Fund, which quickly swelled to $2,000 after the *Defender* ran a front-page appeal. The Anti-Defamation League of B'nai B'rith and the National Council of Churches donated $1,000 and $2,000 respectively to the NAACP fund, and the directors of the National Baptist Convention also adopted a resolution and started an Evers fund of its own.[7]

While Governor Barnett was deflecting any responsibility—moral *or* financial—for any kind of Evers fund, his law partner, Hugh Cunningham, agreed to join Beckwith's Greenwood attorneys in mounting the segregationist's defense. While checks for the Evers fund piled up in a large box in the governor's office, Barnett was personally delivering contributions to Beckwith's defense fund, even as the state was mounting a murder case against him. One out-of-state contributor who sent Barnett fifty dollars for Beckwith received a cordial note of thanks on the governor's letterhead. Beckwith's attorney, Hardy Lott, followed up with a second letter of thanks, and encouraged the contributor to ask his friends to send donations to the White Citizens' Legal Fund.[8]

In his cell at the Hinds County Jail, Beckwith was virtually delirious when he heard news of the White Citizens' Legal Fund's growth. Not only were the tremendous expenses of his defense certain to be covered; the fund was a sure sign his Citizens' Council cronies weren't going to desert him in his hour of need. When the initial shock of his arrest wore off, Beckwith wrote cautiously worded letters to his teenaged son and his estranged wife, Willie. If there were any public doubt about where the sympathies of the Jackson police rested, their loyalties were well-known to Beckwith. "The law anywhere down here will help you," Beckwith wrote his son, adding that the police would assist him if necessary, and that the sheriff's deputies would help him even more. To his wife, he wrote as though he were a man on vacation. "As you know, this is the first rest I've had in twenty years," he wrote. "I could take all of us to Europe and to Mexico for what all this will cost—such is the fate of a patriot."[9]

In the custody of Hinds County Sheriff J.R. Gilfoy, Beckwith was afforded any number of visitors, and in their presence, he acted more like a monarch holding court than a prisoner charged with murder. His friends, Bob Patterson, Tom Barrentine, J.T. Thomas, came down from Greenwood to visit occasionally and updated him on the legal fund's steady growth. Patterson and Ellett Lawrence later sent Beckwith a parcel of sporting magazines and books, including a novel entitled *Uhuru* by Robert Ruark, which Beckwith described as the story of "a white hunter who killed a real bad nigger." He wrote Willie that the book drew the "closest parallel to the actual situation I ever saw." Barrentine, visiting Beckwith on another occasion, reassured him that the legal fund would cover all the costs of the trial, and that if for any reason it didn't, he would provide the balance from his own pocket.[10]

Beckwith's fan mail piled up at a rapid rate, and many letters to jail from friends and well-wishers included cash contributions and checks which Beckwith used for his family's bills and personal expenses. Sheriff Gilfoy often provided official envelopes for Beckwith's personal use, so he could write—true to the tradition of his gentlemanly upbringing—polite replies to those who sent money or notes of encouragement. One of his best friends from the Marine Corps, Dewey Hobson Anderson III, flew into Jackson from Albuquerque to hand deliver $100. A woman from the small town of Durant, Mississippi, groping for just the right thing to say, wrote on National Good Will Committee of the American Contract Bridge League stationery, "We have had much cooler days and that's nice on the cotton pickers." A local member of the Daughters of the American Revolution visited the jail and gave Beckwith twenty dollars, then went to the nearby home of a state senator and, with the senator's wife, made Beckwith a platter of stuffed celery and sent it back to the jail. Greenwood Commissioner Buff Hammond wrote Beckwith, "I can appreciate your state of anxiety, but knowing the feeling of the white people, it is hard for me to imagine any justification for your fears." Even former Major General Edwin A. Walker, in Jackson to speak to a Citizens' Council rally, stopped by the jail to visit with Beckwith and encourage him. Walker told reporters he found Beckwith in "good spirits and very courageous."[11]

When Beckwith made it known he needed a portable typewriter, the Meridian Citizens' Council bought him one and delivered it to the jail personally. Former co-workers from New Deal kept him supplied with cigars and candy, and one Jackson policeman dropped by his cell occasionally with bunches of white grapes to lift his spirits. Meanwhile, Beckwith contacted a cafe in Jackson to start a collection for a portable radio, and tried the same tactic to get a department store to supply him with a television set. He wrote a group in Memphis asking its members to pay for his lifetime membership in the NRA (the members declined) and a local hardware store sent over a portable Iso-Kit Exerciser for him to use in his cell.[12]

It took Beckwith only a short time to realize that, whether out of support or out of fear, people would rally to his aid with useful gifts or small amounts of cash. From his cell, he furiously wrote letters, some in his tortuous longhand and others on his newly acquired typewriter. Most were solicitations for money to support either the "cause" of the White Citizens' Legal Fund or to fatten his personal fund. The rest were letters thanking people who had already sent personal contributions. He wrote Mayor Sampson in Greenwood, along with several of the town's prominent businessmen, asking them to help find a job for Willie, and he mailed more than thirty forceful form letters to scattered chapters of the Sons of the American Revolution demanding "personal financial assistance." One of Beckwith's defense attorneys, Stanny Sanders, had a sister who was Commander of the WAVES, in which Willie had served during the War. Without his attorney's knowledge, Beckwith wrote the woman and asked her to anonymously circulate fund flyers throughout the armed services on his behalf. To newspapers and television stations, Beckwith mailed wallet-size photographs of himself in hopes that they would stop using the wire service photographs of him in handcuffs, which he loathed. A Jackson newspaper published his photo submission with the caption, "Beckwith's Favorite Photo of Beckwith."[13]

Whether writing to close friends or distant organizations, Beckwith mastered the fund-raising ploy and used it to great financial advantage. Finally, his incessant need to join appeared to be paying off—many of the organizations he had joined over the years pitched in to send contributions. To the dismay of the FBI and District Attorney William Waller, Beckwith began enclosing fund solicitations with his regular credit card payments. An employee of American Oil Company, finding one of Beckwith's flyers with a handwritten note included with his late payment for May 1963, immediately turned it over to FBI agents.[14]

For a man awaiting trial for murder, Beckwith adopted an insouciant tone in his letters. From jail, he wrote Intercontinental Arms requesting information on the company's .45 Maverick, describing himself as "somewhat of a gun nut." Company officials were so disturbed, they turned the letter over to the FBI, thinking it might be of evidentiary value in the trial.[15] Beckwith also wrote the Minox Camera Company, manufacturers of miniature cameras customarily advertised in the classified sections of magazines, along with sea monkeys and the Charles Atlas weight-training course. Beckwith wrote in his furious cursive about the "many actual threats" he received and noted that he might need several miniature cameras. "I find that I am going to have to photograph FBI agents and keep a file on them," he wrote.[16]

Beckwith's suspicions about the FBI were well-founded. Ever since his name had surfaced as the lone suspect in the Evers case, agents had been interrogating everyone with any known links to him. Many of the prosecution's big breaks in the case came directly from the FBI, which was aggressively pursuing leads that would help strengthen the state's murder case after federal civil rights charges against Beckwith were dropped. A *Washington Post* reporter tipped off the Bureau that Beckwith had written a letter to the NRA—another indication that his own letters, written from jail, might prove useful to the prosecution. Robert C. Joerg III, Director of Public Affairs for the NRA, searched through his files and released to the FBI two letters he had received from Beckwith. One, written in January 1963, requested information about setting up a public shooting range for Greenwood whites. Beckwith's rationale was as follows: "For the next fifteen years, we here in Mississippi are going to have to do a lot of shooting to protect our wives and children from bad niggers and sorry white folks." The second letter, eight pages long and written from jail, strongly cautioned Joerg against revealing the contents of his letter or disseminating it to the media, and included White Citizens' Legal Fund flyers which Beckwith hoped Joerg would distribute on his behalf. Both were in Beckwith's unmistakable handwriting.[17]

Beckwith's letter-writing and fund-raising campaigns received discreet assistance from a number of people. Ellett Lawrence's printing firm donated paper and printing for his fund flyers; Dewitt Walcott, Beckwith's boss at Delta Liquid Plant Food Company, mimeographed at least one of his form letters, in quantities of 200 or 300; and Sheriffs Gilfoy and Pickett in Hinds County gave Beckwith their official envelopes from time to time, when the prisoner's personal supply dwindled. All that Beckwith had to worry about, really, was postage money. At a time when a dollar would mail twenty first-class letters, one good donation from a patriot would buy at least a month's supply of stamps.

Beckwith was also eating well in jail. The other prisoners looked on enviously as well-wishers, visiting around lunch or dinner time, often brought Beckwith steaks, fresh Gulf Coast shrimp or rich desserts, and local cafes frequently sent food to the jail for him. "While he was in jail, he ate better than Little De La and I did," Willie remembered. "He had his hand out constantly, and he was always mailing me cash and checks people had given him, to deposit in the bank and pay bills with. And with us separated. It was crazy."

A Greenwood resident, who at the time was a close friend of Beckwith's, recalled receiving a number of letters from him, which—out of fear that the police or FBI agents might discover them—were burned. "His letters were incriminating," said the former friend, who agreed to be interviewed at length on tape, but who—afraid of retribution—wished to remain anonymous. "He never said, 'I'm glad I did this,' or 'I pulled the trigger,' or 'This was my plan,' but he alluded to it. It was even more than he alluded to it—he would speak as though this plan had been carried out exactly as it should have been, and speak of himself in the plan. I'll tell you one thing I got from his letters—he was almost in a state of glee over this whole situation. And that he was going to come out on top, and 'that nigger' was dead, you know? That's the way he would write it, 'that nigger.' I really expected the police to come ask me some questions, but they never did."[18]

Occasionally, without referring to Evers by name, Beckwith would make frightening allusions to the civil rights leader in his letters. To his brother-in-law, Beckwith referred to himself as the accused slayer of a "civil rights integration monger," and a month later referred to a passage from Omar Khayyam's *Rubaiyat*: "Why, all the Saints and Sages who discuss'd/Of the Two Worlds so learnedly, are thrust/Like foolish Prophets forth; their Words to Scorn/Are scatter'd, and their Mouths are Stopt with Dust." Beckwith spoke of his struggle against the integrationists and said, "some of them have already stopped talking—ha ha ha." To his son, away at school at the Chamberlain Hunt Academy in Port Gibson, Mississippi, Beckwith wryly sent an article he'd ripped out of a sporting magazine. Its title: "Why Targets Dodge."[19]

Strangely, in none of his letters did Beckwith proclaim his innocence in the Evers slaying. He occasionally referred to the sacrifices he was making, and frequently called his predicament "the cause."

On July 15, 1963, District Attorney William Waller filed a "Suggestion of Insanity" which stated that information gathered following Beckwith's arrest and during the ensuing investigation placed his sanity in question. Waller asked the court to select a competent psychiatrist to examine Beckwith to determine his mental state at the time of the murder and to assess his ability to make a defense. The defense team countered with two motions of their own—the defendant's response to the sanity motion, and a motion to strike the suggestion of insanity. To support his motion for a mental examination, Waller called four witnesses to testify at a sanity hearing on July 18.

Dr. Roland Toms confirmed that he had treated Beckwith on referral from a physician. "I arrived at a diagnostic conclusion," Toms said, but did not elaborate when he was swiftly interrupted by the objections of Beckwith's attorney, Hardy Lott, who wanted no shadow cast on his client's sanity. Toms had earlier been questioned by Assistant Chief of Police M.B. Pierce on June 27, and told Pierce that Beckwith was "an extremist," but he would not comment further or offer a clinical diagnosis. Beckwith's cousin and former guardian, Yerger Morehead, testified that he had reared Beckwith since the age of five, and that his mental condition had changed after he returned from World War II. Morehead also said that he believed Beckwith was competent to prepare his defense adequately, and that he did not believe him capable of a crime of violence. Morehead did volunteer, however, that their uncle, Will Yerger, had been committed to the state mental hospital.[20]

A Delta planter, Hugh Warren, told of Beckwith's lengthy sales visit just before the Evers murder, and recounted their conversation. Warren said Beckwith had told him that he carried a pistol to church to keep blacks from attending services. The final witness, *Commonwealth* reporter Jane Biggers, was unable to testify when Beckwith's attorneys objected to entering an article of Biggers's into evidence, claiming it was hearsay. Waller then offered as evidence files of three divorce suits filed by Willie Beckwith. The first suit was inadmissible, because no decree had been rendered by the court, but the other two files were admitted as evidence since the decrees in each case found Beckwith guilty of acts of violence against his wife. Waller also entered as evidence a Peace Bond that found Beckwith guilty of threatening Willie during one of their many separations.[21] The only evidence offered by the defense was the testimony of defense attorney Stanny Sanders of Greenwood, who said Beckwith was competent to make rational decisions. After closing arguments were made, Circuit Judge Leon Hendrick ruled that Beckwith should be examined by Dr. W.L. Jaquith, director of the Mississippi State Hospital at Whitfield.

At the sanity hearing, Yerger Morehead's testimony was brief in contrast to the wealth of incendiary information he had provided FBI agents, who had questioned him just two days earlier. Morehead had previously told federal agents that Beckwith had "a definite psychotic disturbance." He provided details about Beckwith's violence at home, and said the police had been called several times to conduct investigations, although Beckwith had never been arrested on any of these occasions—perhaps in some instances an indication that he was on friendly terms with local police. Morehead also told agents he believed Beckwith's violence was triggered by his drinking. Perhaps most interesting of all, Morehead told agents Beckwith was "psychotic" on the racial question, and that it would not surprise him if Beckwith would "take credit for something he did not do, such as the shooting of Medgar Evers." He also pointed out that Beckwith would fiercely protect anyone involved in the shooting.[22] The questions posed to Morehead at the sanity hearing were highly focused, and thus none of these more frightening and germane details made their way into the public record.

On July 26, Beckwith was transferred from the Hinds County Jail to Mississippi State Hospital at Whitfield, Mississippi, about ten miles east of Jackson. It was the same hospital—often simply called "Whitfield"—where his Uncle Will had earlier been committed. En route to the hospital, Beckwith was "smiling, wisecracking and posing readily for news photographers," according to an Associated Press report. Watching on television as Beckwith was transferred to the hospital, Myrlie Evers was convinced he was the man who had murdered her husband. "He was all smiles, bowing and gracious to the crowd, and the police smiled at him, patted him on the back, and treated him with respect," she recalled in her book, *For Us, The Living.* "He was being accorded the status of a savior of white Mississippi, and that, I felt, meant he must be the man."[23]

Sheriff Gilfoy led Beckwith from the jail at Jackson and escorted him to the maximum security unit of the hospital. The admitting clerk pulled out her customary paperwork and asked Beckwith a number of questions prior to his admission. After the cursory name, address, age, and Social Security number questions, she asked, "Are you happily married?" Beckwith smiled broadly. "Yes, ma'am, and no, ma'am." When the clerk became impatient, Beckwith told her he was not trying to be disagreeable. "You see," he said, "I've got fifteen thousand dollars' worth of lawyers advising me to answer questions with discretion."[24]

Even as Byron De La Beckwith was being admitted to Mississippi State Hospital as patient number 39193, his estranged wife was settling into Room 57 at Gartly-Ramsay Hospital on Jackson Avenue in Memphis to dry out after a violent alcoholic binge that had lasted several days. Beckwith's arrest, the tremendous publicity surrounding it, and the harassing phone calls and letters she began receiving in Greenwood after she was released from Greenwood Leflore Hospital were too much for Willie to bear. Beckwith's own letters, sometimes just a single page and sometimes upwards of thirty pages in length, arrived daily in her mailbox, constant reminders that she was still married to a man accused of murder. He floridly professed his love for her and casually assumed a reconciliation had taken place concurrent with his arrest. He was constantly needing errands run or supplies sent to the jail. The requests were frequent: Pay the gas and phone bills at the big house; retain his GL3-3110 phone number; please try to find some thin clear plastic like this sliver; when you come to visit, bring real chocolate fudge, not the cake kind; bring some Welch's grape juice—"your favorite, I know." Willie began to drink heavily, and sequestered herself in her apartment, afraid to venture outside. When she did go out, people either crossed to the other side of the street to avoid her or stopped to sympathetically and loudly ask about "De La." Were they treating him all right in jail? How terribly, terribly awful it was that such a thing should happen. How in the world was she holding up under all the pressure, with all the stories in the newspaper every day?

The manager of the apartment complex on President Street called two of Willie's close friends, asking that they come check on her. She had been drinking for several days and had scared some of her neighbors by firing a gun in her apartment. "It had poured rain that day," one friend remembered, "and we waded in water nearly up to our knees. We had to park our car out in the street. Willie said she was going to shoot any son of a bitch that came through there, and that she had five guns or something like that in the apartment with her." After a lengthy attempt to persuade Willie to let them in, she relented. "The apartment was in *bad* shape, and there were holes—she had literally shot holes through the walls. And it was so unlike Willie—she had been drinking for several days." Her friends got her sobered up, and after a long discussion, she agreed to go to Gartly-Ramsay Hospital for treatment. In quick order, her friends made arrangements to get Little De La enrolled at Chamberlain Hunt for the fall, and moved all of Willie's furniture out of the apartment into the big house on George Street, which had sat vacant since Beckwith's arrest.

At Gartly-Ramsay, Willie talked at length with a psychiatrist, walked the quiet grounds and played Ping-Pong to pass the time. She wrote one of her brothers from the hospital, "By the time I leave here I will know who is a nut—me or Beck!" Unaware that Willie was hospitalized, Beckwith kept sending letters to her apartment on President Street, which were forwarded to her at the hospital in Memphis. He described the other patients as though he were an outsider looking in, and claimed he was given "literally rags" to wear and had to share a shaving mug and brush with other patients. One of the doctors gave Beckwith a prostate massage, causing him to wonder "if a finger in my rectum and a sharp pain in my ass won't—in a day or two—straighten out a frown on my face." He also discovered while at Whitfield that another patient in his ward was accused of severely beating a woman he and Willie had known. When Beckwith heard that the woman had required a hundred stitches for her head wounds and that her arm had been broken in three places, he threatened the man in front of some of the other patients. "You'll never make it to the jail," Beckwith told the man, his face flushed and his rage barely contained, "but you might make it into the river." Ironically, for a man with a documented history of wife abuse, such violence against a woman was to him infinitely worse than murdering a black man with a gun.[25]

The last thing Beckwith's lawyers wanted was for their client to submit to a series of mental examinations, so they filed a Writ of Habeas Corpus to have the examinations stopped. "It was just like De La," Willie said of her former husband. "He'd rather be accused of murder than have anybody question his sanity. That alone shows he was crazy." On August 1, 1963, Rankin County Circuit Judge O.H. Barnett—a cousin of Governor Ross Barnett's—ordered that Beckwith's mental examinations be halted on the grounds that subjecting him to tests to which he objected was "evidence by compulsion." Ruling that his detention at Mississippi State Hospital was illegal, Judge Barnett ordered Beckwith removed from Whitfield and remanded him to the custody of Rankin County Sheriff Jonathan H. Edwards. Beckwith was moved to the county jail at Brandon, Mississippi, to await the prosecution's appeal to the Mississippi Supreme Court. Three months later, in a six to three vote, the state's highest court upheld Judge Barnett's ruling to halt Beckwith's mental tests, writing that "the state's evidence in support of its motion was weak and limited in scope." While detained at the jail in Brandon, Beckwith missed two hearings to determine his trial date. Both were aborted when the defendant was absent from court.[26]

Rankin County Jail was an oasis for Beckwith, who wrote that he was being treated like a soldier who "just took a Jap admiral alive." It was clear to Beckwith that, at least in this jail, he would be treated with respect and consideration. "I hope you never get in jail," he wrote Willie, "but if you do, be sure it's for what I'm accused of—ha! ha!"[27] A local bootlegger brought Beckwith $200 and told him, "I've killed a hundred niggers and they ain't never done anything to me yet."[28] Beckwith became especially friendly with the jailer, who occasionally took Beckwith out of his cell for a quiet walk through the courthouse to peek in offices and look around. When Sheriff Edwards was out of the office, the jailer would sometimes take Beckwith into town for a haircut, or to pick up supplies at the drug store and have a bite at a cafe. He also afforded Beckwith "red-carpet treatment," waiting on him "hand and foot," Beckwith wrote. The jailer may have enjoyed his own momentary celebrity, walking through town with a prisoner of such notoriety, but District Attorney Waller would have been seriously alarmed to discover that the man he was prosecuting for murder was walking around loose in Brandon—without handcuffs, having coffee with his jailer. On at least one occasion, by Beckwith's own admission, Sheriff Edwards allowed him to leave the jail on his own recognizance, although he was sternly warned to "get back by four o'clock."[29]

Shortly after Beckwith was removed from Whitfield, Willie returned to Greenwood from Gartly-Ramsay Hospital. She had not yet seen her husband in jail, and she refused to live in the George Street house, where her furniture and belongings had been stored. Instead, she made arrangements to live at the Hotel Greenwood Leflore, a comfortable but slightly faded resident hotel. "That night, she was drinking again," said a close friend. At the hotel, her calls were screened by the switchboard and anyone placed on her floor was carefully checked by the manager. The desk clerk, John Roland, wrote Beckwith occasionally to let him know Willie was being watched and protected. When she called down to the desk to have beer or liquor brought up to the room, which she did with alarming frequency as the trial drew nearer, Roland made sure she got whatever she wanted.

"I lived in constant fear," Willie said of her months at the hotel. "I was afraid outside, and I was afraid inside." For two or three days, she would try not to drink, but then one of Beckwith's daily letters might set her off, or a segment on the evening news, which she tried to watch each night in the hotel lobby. "I lived a lonely life," she said. "*I* was in jail, really. Staying in one little hotel room? With just a bed and a desk?" She often sat alone in her room and drank until she could fall asleep.

Beckwith's letters to her, generally disjointed, were full of grandiose plans. He fully expected to be acquitted, but seemed mystified that his lawyers spent little time briefing him on the case or discussing their plans for the trial. They had visited him once at Whitfield, but seldom visited him in jail. When they did call in person, they drilled him with questions and helped shape his answers to make him a more responsive witness. Beckwith continued his fervent letter writing, and often told Willie of his business plans for the future. "He was still scheming," she said. "Always coming up with some crazy business he wanted to try." Although he often fell back on his fertilizer sales job, and made it clear he was happy that the people at Delta Liquid were holding his place for him until he returned—the company continued to pay his hospitalization insurance while he was in jail—Beckwith showed them little of the same loyalty. A book, *Turning Concrete into Gold*, piqued his interest about the ornamental concrete business, and he entertained thoughts of starting his own company. Through a Marine Corps buddy who had a successful business of his own, Beckwith learned about marketing surgical supplies and began to investigate that as another potential opportunity for him.[30] He still hoped to someday open a public shooting range and also toyed with the idea of marketing a line of plastic fish bait, thinking it would be a money-maker.

Most of all, Beckwith wanted become an author. His endless letters to editors had only whetted his appetite. He used his incarceration to begin writing a book about his life and experiences, so that all the world could share his passion for "the cause," the total segregation of the races. He began writing letters to stir up book interest among right-wing publishers such as The Devin-Adair Company.[31] Beckwith had also begun a letter-writing campaign that he hoped would pull in several thousand dollars for his defense fund and, possibly, help his lawyers get his trial moved outside Hinds County. He penned a carefully crafted letter, and submitted it to the *Jackson Daily News* and other newspapers. "I am forced to go beyond the scope of my family and friends and let people who do not know me, except by reputation, also do something in our behalf, financially that is," Beckwith wrote in the letter, published November 13, 1963. He thanked those who had held him in custody "for their kind and considerate treatment." He made it clear that he was making a sacrifice for the cause, and said he was anxious to serve in any way he could—"even if it takes my life or my liberty to do it."[32]

Beckwith's plan, which had been quietly sanctioned by his lawyers, was to "muddy the waters" with a direct appeal to the whites of Jackson. They hoped to make it impossible to select a jury in Hinds County, and believed such a move might help get his trial moved to another county. The plan backfired, and Hardy Lott called Sheriff Gilfoy with a message for Beckwith to take it easy, and not to write any more letters until they were able to meet and talk about it.[33] Beckwith was disappointed. Not only had the published letter been edited to about half its original length; it did not create the desired effect and his lawyers were now in a stew over it, as well.

Although he and Willie were still legally separated, she began visiting her husband in jail at Brandon, trying to stop drinking for several days before making the ninety-mile trip. Always meticulous about her appearance, she planned her outfits and matched her earrings and jewelry before getting dressed for the trip. When she arrived, Beckwith would cling to her and tell her his plans for their lives once the trial was over. "He talked about 'the cause' constantly, and it was always tied up with the Citizens' Council and the work they were doing," Willie said. "He acted like being in jail was just the best thing in the world, and called it his 'involvement.' He was always telling me he was making sacrifices, and that even though he was making sacrifices on his own time and at his own risk, people with money were carrying the ball." More than ever, she believed it was the Citizens' Council that had gotten him into trouble. "He told me once this 'involvement' was like a long trip," Willie said, "and that it was carefully planned and cautiously made, and that now we just had to end up at the right destination." She feared that several members of the Citizens' Council might have encouraged Beckwith to take action they themselves could not have risked, and her worries intensified when her husband began to talk about another shadowy group, the Ku Klux Klan.

By late September 1963—five months before the official formation of the White Knights of the Ku Klux Klan of Mississippi—Beckwith was boasting to his correspondents that the Klan was active again in Mississippi, and that he had already been invited to join.[34] That fall, while Beckwith was jailed, approximately 300 Mississippians were recruited into the Original Knights of the Ku Klux Klan of Louisiana, which was one of the many Klan groups that blossomed after the U.S. Supreme Court's 1954 school desegregation ruling. Internal strife and accusations of funds mismanagement caused a splintering of the Louisiana group, and by February 1964, the White Knights had been established in Mississippi under the aegis of Imperial Wizard Sam Holloway Bowers, Jr. Unlike many other Klan organizations, Bowers's White Knights moved with stealth, and in near total secrecy. None of its members admitted their affiliations with the group publicly, and the White Knights eschewed public rallies and cross burnings, which the other groups used to gain publicity, acceptance and new members. The Mississippi group's methods were far more serious, as the nation was to discover in 1964 with the brutal murders of Andrew Goodman, Michael Schwerner and James Chaney, three civil rights workers who were shot and buried in an earthen dam in Mississippi's rural Neshoba County.[35]

Medgar Evers's murder may have marked the Klan's unofficial launch in Mississippi. Delmar Dennis, a former Titan in the White Knights of the Ku Klux Klan of Mississippi, joined the Klan and worked in its ranks for three years as an informant for the FBI. During those years, Dennis met Beckwith on several occasions following the Evers murder trials and heard him speak at a Klan rally. Dennis knew Beckwith to be a Klansman, and he was also present at the Klan meeting at which it was announced that Beckwith had been appointed a Kleagle, or recruiter.

"Beckwith was a recruiting man," Dennis said in an interview. "He was out getting members all over the state." Dennis believes that because of Beckwith's notoriety as Medgar Evers's accused assassin, he was handpicked by Imperial Wizard Sam Bowers to bring new members into the White Knights fold. "Beckwith would not have been an officer in the Klan or a recruiter for the Klan if he had not been on good terms with Sam," Dennis said.[36] During Dennis's rise through the Klan hierarchy, he worked closely with Bowers and came to know him well. Dennis thought it was possible that Bowers originally sanctioned the Evers murder, and recalled that at the first Klan meeting he attended, Edgar Ray Killen, the Klansman in charge of the proceedings, referred to actions already approved by Bowers.

"Somebody brought up the name of Goatee, which was Michael Schwerner, and said, 'I think we ought to vote on what to do about him, whether or not we just eliminate the S.O.B.,' " Dennis remembered. "And Killen said, 'No, you don't have to vote on that. That's already been approved by the state.'

"Later, when Schwerner was killed, I remembered that and said, 'Ooooh. These guys are playing for keeps, and what he said was true.' It *had* been approved, and they were just waiting for the right time to do it. The other statement Killen made was that the Klan was responsible for the death of Medgar Evers, and I thought, aw, come on. The Klan's just now getting organized, and this happened last year sometime. So I totally discounted that as just bragging on his part. So now I look back and I say, 'Well, he *said* the Klan had approved Michael Schwerner's death, and this was *before* Michael died, and they *did* kill him—so maybe he knew what he was talking about. Maybe it was true."

Independent of Beckwith's Klan membership, Willie knew that about the time he took his job with Delta Liquid Plant Food Company, he had gotten friendly with men who, a few years earlier, he would have looked at disdainfully. Although the Delta Liquid job gave him entree with rich planters, Willie believes some of his new friends were significantly farther down on the continuum of Mississippi's white social stratum. "They just weren't the kind of people he would have associated with ten years before, when he wanted to be accepted by the SARs and the Sons of Confederate Veterans," she said. One such friend, Gordon Lackey, spent most of his time behind his parents' small cafe in Greenwood, working on motorcycles. He surrounded himself with a group of teenage motorcycle enthusiasts. Another was David Short, whose father owned Short Tire & Oil Company in Greenwood, where Delta Liquid Plant Food maintained its gas and oil account. He became a close friend of Beckwith's, and sometimes signed his notes as "Herr Short," which was Beckwith's nickname for him. John Ashcraft, a friend of David Short's, flew a small, single-engine airplane and became a friend of Beckwith's. Ashcraft was also related by marriage to Thorn McIntyre, the young farmer from whom Beckwith acquired the 30.06 caliber rifle with which he was accused of murdering Evers. "De La was always trying to get me to relay messages to these guys," Willie remembered. "He would write me, 'When you see Gordon, tell him all is well and not to become disturbed,' like Gordon was tied up in all this and was worried over it."

It was Lackey who reportedly recruited Beckwith into the White Knights of the Ku Klux Klan of Mississippi.[37] By the time Beckwith was officially initiated in Lackey's trailer in 1964—"naturalized," in Klanguage—he had, he said, already been asked to provide his services to the Klan. From jail, he wrote, "When the KKK needs me enough, then I will be happy to serve them—they've asked me and I haven't said no." Although the Citizens' Council had long been Beckwith's primary hope of maintaining segregation, many right-wing Mississippians turned to the Ku Klux Klan for more direct action than the Citizens' Council could safely tolerate. Beckwith was among them, because the Coucil's economic sanctions, while effective, had not halted black efforts to register to vote or lobby for other civil rights.

In one of his essays, written while he was jailed awaiting trial, Beckwith wrote about his favorable view of the Ku Klux Klan and the rationale for the group's white robes, noting that "the only way a fellow can hunt A CROW IN THE SNOW is in a snow white outfit, for you must surely blend with the background." He referred to himself as a "varmint hunter" and wrote of hunting a "coon neath the moon," explaining that the prey would likely be found "with a bright light shining in his face and all he knows is that there is something after him—probably a white man."[38] Beckwith's imagery—a "coon" being hunted under the moon, with a bright light on him, by a white man blending into his background—chillingly paralleled the true scenario of Medgar Evers's murder.

"De La always said his enemies were trying to destroy him, but I never knew who his enemies were," Willie said. "They seemed to change all the time. You know, there were the blacks, the ones he thought didn't know their place. Then Bishop Gray would be his enemy, or Hodding Carter, or the civil rights workers who came to Greenwood. You just never could tell. Most of the time he treated *me* like I was his enemy."

Another of Beckwith's perceived enemies was President John F. Kennedy, whose proposed civil rights legislation—announced the night of Evers's murder that June—infuriated him. On November 22, 1963, Beckwith was visiting with his boss from Delta Liquid Plant Food Company, Dewitt Walcott. Walcott was still at the jail when news of the president's assassination flashed across Beckwith's portable television. While the rest of the country sat in their living rooms watching the news coverage in stunned silence as the day grew darker, Beckwith was busy writing letters again. To Willie, he wrote of the possibility that the country might get straightened out now that "Adolph Kennedy" was dead, and said that he would never again be without a TV as there was "always something good on." Of Kennedy's as-yet-unknown assassin, Beckwith wrote, "That fellow sho' done some fancy shooting didn't he HAW HAW HAW. I'll bet Medgar Evers said I thought you'd get down here pretty soon boss. HA HA HA." When he caught a bad cold a few days later, he wrote that "mourning for Kennedy gave it to me—HA HA HA."[39]

President Kennedy's assassination thrilled Beckwith for several reasons. First, he believed the country's politics would inevitably take a turn for what he believed would be the better, as he had never liked Catholics in general and President Kennedy, with his civil rights stance, in particular. Second, Beckwith thought the assassination might be a sign to those pressing for the Civil Rights Bill's passage that white Americans would not tolerate such folderol. Although the March on Washington in August 1963 had taken place several months earlier, culminating in Dr. Martin Luther King, Jr.'s famed "I Have a Dream" speech, Beckwith never mentioned it or referred to it in his letters. King had referred specifically to Mississippi in the aftermath of the Evers murder, calling it "a state sweltering with the heat of injustice." Beckwith was probably incensed that the president would allow such a march to occur in the first place, much less that King should be allowed to discuss his own home state in such unfavorable terms. Ultimately, though, Beckwith believed the Kennedy assassination would take some of the pressure off him and deflect attention from the Evers case.

"When the Kennedy half-dollars came out later," Willie said, "he wanted to flush them down the commode. That's how he felt about Kennedy." Most telling, perhaps, is that in his letters, Beckwith referred to the Kennedy assassination as "the act of a patriot."[40] It was the word he used most frequently, and with great pride, to describe himself. He was fond of saying that a patriot could live and fight on little more than free air and honor. Many more reactionary Southerners viewed Beckwith as a patriotic hero, just as some of the South's more twisted minds began to view Lee Harvey Oswald after President Kennedy's assassination. A man from Etlel, Louisiana, wrote Beckwith that he had asked some high school students to select the "greatest man" of the era. Two named Beckwith, while three selected Lee Harvey Oswald.[41]

Late in November, as the time drew near for Beckwith to be moved back to Hinds County to await his trial, Sheriff J.R. Gilfoy told a Jackson *Clarion-Ledger* reporter that Beckwith had written him a letter, asking that he be allowed to bring his television set and gun collection with him from the Rankin County Jail at Brandon. Gilfoy laughingly said he had refused Beckwith's request, and that "no exceptions to the jail rules would be made in this case."[42] The story was partially true; Beckwith had written to ask whether he could bring the contents of his cell with him to Hinds County. Beckwith had become spoiled at Brandon, where he was treated with respect and made to feel like a local hero, but he was *not* so well-treated that he was allowed to have guns in his cell. A close friend of Beckwith's had left an old pistol for him in Sheriff Edwards's office, wrapped in a box, but Beckwith did not have access to it and no one knew the box contained a pistol.[43] Beckwith laughed the articles off, and wrote Willie that Sheriff Gilfoy was just trying to get a little publicity for himself and would have to be accountable for his remarks. Still, the story made good copy and was circulated by a number of newspapers.

When he was moved back to the Hinds County Jail on November 25, Beckwith took only his clothing, a portable typewriter and his isometric exerciser.[44] Sheriff Gilfoy refused to allow him to bring his television set, since none of the other prisoners were allowed entertainment in their cells. Beckwith was placed alone in a cell with a small window, located on the fourth floor above the courthouse in which he would be tried. Having been returned to Jackson, where he believed visitors would call in greater numbers, he often sat pathetically in his cell dressed in a suit and tie, awaiting their arrival. When they did not come, he began a daily program to work his way through the Bible, which he called "hard, dull reading," and when he did have visitors, he was as animated as if he were on a sales call.[45]

When Willie visited the jail, her estranged husband often wanted to have sex. His new cell was more private than the cell at Brandon, and Beckwith thought the added privacy might help persuade her to enjoy the possibility of conjugal visits. Sometimes she begged off, saying she was menstruating, but on at least three occasions, she consented. She visited the jail as infrequently as possible, and grew more resentful with each visit. "I hated to even see him," she said. "To him, it was nothing to be in jail for what he was in for." Inside his cell, with a piece of cardboard taped over the cell door's small window, she fretted over what people at the jail were saying about her visits. "I felt real low-class, because I just knew how men were, and what they were thinking and saying outside. It always humiliated me."

Compounding the problem of sex in jail was the unavailability of condoms—Willie still would not have sex with her husband without them—and also his recurring impotence. "Same problems as always," she said with resignation. Beckwith proposed writing his Greenwood pharmacist, Jimmy Hogue, to have him mail condoms to the jail.[46] As for his impotence, there was no quick remedy, and several sexual encounters were aborted when he proved unable to respond. Willie was frustrated and embarrassed, but to some degree, relieved.

"We fought even when he was in jail," she remembered. "He'd ask me to bring him liquor when I came, and I'd just say, 'What do you think I am, a fool?' " Although they would argue, Beckwith was never physically violent toward her in jail—much to her relief. "He couldn't have been," she reasoned. "There were people who would have heard us, and our divorces had already been brought up at his sanity hearings. The other thing was, he wanted to stay on good terms with me," she asserted. "I believe he knew it was to his advantage to keep me on his side, even though we were separated, because he knew the FBI had questioned me, and I think in the back of his mind he didn't know what I might have told them. Or what I *might* tell them, if he made me mad or hurt me."

Hinds County's new sheriff, Fred Pickett, took office in January 1964. Beckwith knew immediately he was going to get on better with Pickett, because the sheriff came by to see Beckwith with a few visitors, one of whom was Judge Tom Brady's brother from Brookhaven, Mississippi.[47]

He also took it as a good sign that the trial had been delayed beyond Governor Ross Barnett's final months in office. He hoped that Barnett—who had made it clear he was a Beckwith fan—might make a well-publicized splash by joining his law partner, Hugh Cunningham, in leading the Beckwith defense team to victory.[48] Beckwith told his friends and visitors that his "drill team" was shaping up, and that he hoped the "captain" would be none other than Ross Barnett. After nearly eight months, the nation's most celebrated civil rights murder case was ready for trial. His dress clothes neatly pressed and his memoirs well underway, Byron De La Beckwith was prepared for a quick acquittal.

9

"My Ass, Your Goat and the Republic"

"Do you believe it's a crime for a white man to kill a nigger in Mississippi?" The young District Attorney, William Waller, approached the venireman, W.E. Greer, and awaited an answer. The potential juror hesitated. "How did he answer?" asked the white-haired judge, Leon Hendrick, leaning forward. "He's thinking it over," Waller replied.

"Well," said Greer thoughtfully, "I *do* believe it's a crime for a white man to kill a nigger. I'll try to put the race issue out of my mind for the present time."

"Not for the present time," said Judge Hendrick. "It's for all time." Greer was dismissed as a prospective juror in the Beckwith murder trial.[1]

Jury selection began at 9:00 A.M. on Monday, January 27, 1964, seven months after the murder. A prayer group assembled on the steps of the courthouse, but quietly dispersed after the proceedings began. Spectators were carefully searched before entering the courtroom, and reporters were allowed only notepads and pencils—no cameras or tape recorders. Civil rights groups had threatened to demonstrate on the opening day of the trial, but they failed to materialize.[2] Aaron Henry, Medgar Evers's close friend and the head of the NAACP in Mississippi, was one of about thirty blacks who sat in the half-filled courtroom during the first day of jury selection. Beckwith glared at him as he entered the courtroom. "His eyes followed me to my seat," Henry told a reporter. "I wouldn't have that, so I guess we kept it up for about five minutes before he turned away and fiddled with that peaked handkerchief in his coat pocket."[3] To the dismay of many whites who later came to sit through the proceedings, blacks were allowed to sit anywhere they wanted, on the judge's orders, and were allowed to use the "Whites Only" restrooms down the hall. By the beginning of 1964, segregation was beginning to break down, and this was just one example.

District Attorney William Waller demonstrated his own ingrained racial prejudices. He, too, was from a prominent Mississippi family, and he addressed the white veniremen as "mister" while calling the black veniremen by their first names only, yet he seemed determined to cull an impartial jury from the venire. "If you go into the jury room and somebody says, 'I can't convict a white man for killing a Negro, let's go home,' would you agree?" Waller pressed the prospective jurors. "Even if Evers's work was obnoxious to you, can you put it out of your mind in this case? Would you be influenced by the fact that one of Mr. Beckwith's attorneys, Mr. Cunningham, is in law practice with former Governor Barnett?"

Waller worked every angle: "Have you, or any of your friends, contributed money to Beckwith's defense fund? Did you hear that the niggers might want Mr. Beckwith acquitted so they can go North and raise more money [to fund civil rights activities]? That they could use his acquittal to get that pending civil rights bill passed?" Waller stretched his arm out toward the spectators sitting in the courtroom and watched a venireman's facial expression change as he asked, "Day after day you may sit here and see this room jammed with nothing but niggers. Would that influence you in your deliberations? Would you hesitate to reach a just verdict, just because you felt it would be unpopular with your friends or customers? Are you strong enough to stand up to somebody on this jury who might try to change your honest opinion by asking if you'd convict that white man for killing that nigger?" To a Jackson banker, Waller even asked, "Would the fact that I owe some money to your bank influence you?[4]

The venire was comprised of 109 people, included seven blacks. Another hundred veniremen, on standby, were not present during the initial questioning. The first black prospective juror, a barber named J.E. Conic, Jr., was excused because his father was killed in a robbery ambush in 1948; the second, Clifford Holloway, because he allegedly took the day off from work the morning Evers was killed, reportedly saying "I lost the best friend I ever had. I'm sick. I can't work." Beckwith watched the jury selection with interest and occasional amusement, jotting notes in a looseleaf binder and leaning in to confer with his attorneys from time to time. One morning while questioning a prospective juror, defense attorney Stanny Sanders said, "You realize before the trial begins that Mr. Beckwith is presumed guilty—I mean, innocent!" The defendant, looking up from his notebook at Sanders, grinned.[5] Special night sessions were called by Judge Hendrick, but it still took four days and the interrogation of ninety-three veniremen before the final jury, including an alternate juror, was selected and sworn in at 5:40 P.M. on January 30.[6] Even after careful questioning by attorneys for both the prosecution and the defense, it seemed unlikely that a truly impartial jury had been seated. One juror's brother was a Jackson police officer, and another juror's labor union had contributed to Beckwith's defense fund.[7]

John Herbers, a reporter for *The New York Times* who covered the trial, remembered Waller's unorthodox queries of the veniremen, as well as Beckwith's demeanor in the courtroom. "He was just so cocky,"

Herbers said of the defendant. "I didn't have any expectations *at all* of him being convicted. I never even assumed there would be a hung jury." Beckwith shot his cuffs frequently to show off his cuff links, and turned his seat at a three-quarter angle so a sketch artist in the balcony could get a better likeness of him.[8] Wearing a dark suit set off by red socks and a red tie, Beckwith told one reporter, "My tie has not been the color of my politics."[9] Herbers had seen Mississippi justice firsthand; the first celebrated murder trial he covered was that of Roy Bryant and J.W. Milam, the men accused of murdering fourteen-year-old Emmett Till in 1955.[10] A native of Tennessee, his coverage of the trial for the *Times* was remarkable for two reasons. First, Herbers began his career in journalism in Beckwith's hometown at Greenwood's *Morning Star*, and had worked for United Press International, for a decade, as Jackson bureau chief. He knew the temperament and mind-set of the Mississippians who comprised the jury. He also had a unique perspective shared by few other national journalists. "I knew Evers very well," he said. "I had written about him extensively and met with him extensively. He and Myrlie were both extraordinary, not in any way self-serving."

To launch the trial proceedings, Waller first called Detective Sergeant Bennett D. Harrell, Jr., of the Jackson Police Department to the stand. Harrell took the initial call about the murder, at police headquarters, and Waller established that the first call came in at 12:45 A.M. on June 12. Harrell sent two officers, Sergeants John A. Chamblee and Fred Sanders to the crime scene and called for backup. Beckwith's defense attorneys had no questions for Harrell, and he was asked to step down.

"The State calls Myrlie Evers," Waller said, and his second witness walked toward the front of the courtroom to take the witness stand. Wearing a simple aqua dress and settling into her seat, Myrlie Evers exhibited none of the animosity she had felt for the district attorney during the past several months. Prior to the trial, she and Waller had a confrontation when he tried to give her instruction on how to act in court. He told her to act with humility, not to chew gum, or cross her legs "enticingly," and intimated that she would be called by her first name rather than be addressed as "Mrs.," as any married white woman would have been addressed. She protested, and Waller finally broke the impasse by simply not addressing her by name at all. A similar situation occurred just months earlier. In a separate case in Alabama the previous June, a black woman was held in contempt of court, fined fifty dollars and sentenced to five days in jail when she refused to answer questions unless she was addressed with the courtesy title "Miss." The Supreme Court of Alabama later upheld her conviction and stated, "The record conclusively shows that the petitioner's name is Mary Hamilton, not Miss Mary

Hamilton." The U.S. Supreme Court reversed the ruling, finding Hamilton's conviction appallingly unconstitutional.[11]

Mrs. Evers succinctly explained her husband's background as she was led through her rote questioning by Waller. She gave the dates of their marriage and their move to Jackson, and then explained the events of the night of her husband's murder. "When we heard him pull in the driveway I sat up, so I was already in an erect position," she testified.[12] "And the moment I heard the blast I ran to the door. My children automatically fell to the floor as we had taught them to do."

"What did you see when you went to the door?" Waller asked.

"When I got to the door I turned on the light and opened the door at the same time, and I saw my husband where he had fallen face-down, and I saw the trail of blood that he had left behind him, and I saw the keys in his hand. He had dropped everything but his keys. That was what I found."

During his cross-examination, Lott deftly baited Mrs. Evers—wasn't her husband "very active" in the integration movement? Wasn't he "the first person, as a matter of fact, who attempted integration of the University of Mississippi?" At the time he was shot, hadn't he filed "a suit to integrate the white public schools" of Jackson? Lott was building a broad motive for Evers's killing, hoping the jury would see that almost anyone who saw integration as a threat saw Medgar Evers at the heart of the Mississippi movement.

"Now," Lott asked, "I believe one of your children who you stated was present that night is Thomas Kenyatta Evers?"

"No, that is not correct," she answered firmly.

"What is his name?" Lott asked.

"Darrell, D-A-R-R-E-L-L, Kenyatta, K-E-N-Y-A-T-T-A, Evers, E-V-E-R-S," she replied, spelling each name slowly. When Lott started to ask after whom the child was named, Waller objected. "This is a deliberate attempt to poison the minds of the jury about some child's name," and Judge Hendrick sustained. Any of the white men on the jury who read the newspapers regularly assumed the Evers's son was named after the reputed leader of the Mau Mau uprising in Kenya. His point made, Lott said he had no further questions, and Myrlie Evers stepped down.

The next witness, Evers's next-door neighbor, Houston Wells, testified that when he heard the shot that killed Evers, he ran outside and fired his .38 caliber pistol into the air while his wife called the police. When he ran across the yard, Evers was still alive and had crawled about ten feet toward the front door, where Myrlie Evers found her husband when she ran outside. When Wells arrived, she was by her husband's side, screaming. "Did you do assist then in doing anything in the way of emergency aid for Medgar Evers?" Waller asked Wells.

"Yes, sir," Wells replied, "I ran into the house and got a mattress. By that time some more help had gotten there. And I rolled him over on the mattress and pushed the mattress. I ran back and got my station wagon and I pushed him into the back of my station wagon. By that time the policemen were there and they escorted him to the hospital." Wells testified that while Evers was lying in the back of the automobile, he said quietly, "Let me go, let me go."[13]

Waller's witnesses continued to build the scenario at the murder scene, explaining for the jury the chronology of events. The attending police officers described what they found on their arrival at the murder scene. Dr. Forrest Bratley, who performed the autopsy, described in grisly detail the wound that shattered Evers's ribs, burst his lung and tore apart the front of his chest just above his right nipple.

"There was a lot of blood, like someone had butchered a hog," testified Detective Sergeant John Chamblee, describing the trail of blood from Evers's car door to the steps of his house, where the victim had crawled after being shot. Mrs. Evers was "incoherent and almost in a state of shock" when he and his partner, Detective Sergeant Fred Sanders, arrived on the scene. Chamblee testified that they had also found blood and particles of flesh on the windshield of Evers's powder blue Oldsmobile. Waller introduced his first physical evidence, a series of enlarged photographs of the crime scene. Chamblee pointed out splatterings of blood and flesh across the car's windshield, as well as the pool of blood that had been smeared on the carport. "There was a tremendous amount of blood," Chamblee testified. "It wasn't like a little tiny stream or pencil stream of blood. Looks like it was poured out of a bucket along the side of the car." Medgar Evers, Chamblee surmised, had been killed by a blast from a high-powered weapon. The bullet entered Evers's back and passed through his body and through a window of the living room, where it clipped a venetian blind and traveled through a wall into the kitchen. It ricocheted off the door of the refrigerator, glanced at a forty-five-degree angle and came to rest on the kitchen sink counter, after it shattered a small glass coffee pot. The bullet fell next to a watermelon on a kitchen counter.[14] "Even then," Myrlie Evers said later, "I wondered what the white policemen had said to each other when they saw the watermelon."[15]

During the proceedings, Beckwith closely watched each witness and occasionally scribbled notes in his notebook, adding fodder for the memoirs he was writing in his cell. Most of the time, he seemed unconcerned with the testimony being presented against him, and if he had any inkling the jury of white men might find him guilty of murder, it did not show in his face. He smiled broadly at the whites in the packed courtroom, and once, during a break, strolled toward the jury box to chat. A bailiff yanked him away.[16]

Beckwith also launched a plan to unsettle his prosecutor. Each day, before being led from his cell to the courtroom, he stashed a few cigars in the breast pocket of his jacket. On several occasions, when he could get within arm's length of Waller, Beckwith patted Waller on the back and quickly slipped the cigars into his suit jacket.[17] Waller finally protested and Beckwith's attorneys asked him to cease and desist. This incident raised a chuckle in the courtroom, and Beckwith told the story for decades to illustrate his carefree demeanor in court and to demonstrate his disdain for Waller.

Beckwith seemed confident to the point of arrogance. Once, walking with a court officer during a break in the trial, Beckwith made it clear he believed he would be acquitted. One reporter overheard him remark to some acquaintances, "Well, fellows, we're up the hill and we're going down the other side, right out the door."[18]

His wife, sitting in the courtroom, began to feel less confident about his case. When the district attorney introduced photographs of the Evers home and the murder scene, she became uncomfortable. She remembered that after their appointment in Jackson with Dr. Roland Toms, the psychiatrist she and Beckwith had consulted, they had taken a different route back to Greenwood. They drove off the highway, into a modest neighborhood comprised of clean, cookie-cutter houses. The photographs of the Evers home looked vaguely familiar, and she wondered whether her husband had not been looking for Evers's house on their way back home. "It wasn't the same way we drove down," she said later, in an interview, "but I never really did think much about it at the time. It dawned on me later that he could have done something," she hedged, cautious with her words, "and I wondered in my mind. But I couldn't say for sure."

Betty Coley and Kenneth Adcock, Coley's daughter's former boyfriend, each testified that they had been taking a walk together down Missouri Street near the murder scene when they heard the first shot fired.[19] "We were positive that the shot had been fired at us," Coley testified, and said she had heard someone running away immediately afterward. As the two made their way back to Coley's house, they heard a pistol shot and then a shotgun blast. The first shot, Coley said, had sounded just behind them, near a clump of bushes, and that it sounded "very close, too close for comfort." Adcock also testified that the first shot had come "out of the clump of trees" and that he then heard someone running "toward Joe's Drive-In."

Afterward, Detective Sergeant O.M. Luke recounted the police investigation of the area near the murder. Approximately ten to fifteen policemen were on-site, searching for evidence. In a clump of trees, Luke discovered what appeared to be the sniper's nest. The underbrush had been trampled down, and a small clearing in the surrounding vines had been made about five and one-half feet off the ground. Looking through the clearing in the vines, the Evers house was clearly visible. One sweet gum tree, Luke testified, had an abrasion where something apparently had struck it.[20] The detective then told of crawling around, looking closely for an empty cartridge hull, when he saw something peculiar. Looking more closely, he recognized the butt of a rifle barely visible through a clump of honeysuckle vines. The rifle was suspended about a foot off the ground. "The gun was not dropped," Luke asserted. "It was well hidden and wasn't even touching the ground."

Captain Ralph Hargrove photographed the scene as Luke used a stick to dislodge the rifle from the honeysuckle vines. Luke used his handkerchief to lift the rifle by its trigger guard and placed it on the back seat of a police car. He stayed with the gun until it was delivered to Hargrove's office at police headquarters for a fingerprint examination. "No one had touched the gun from the time I found the gun until Captain Hargrove examined it in his office," Luke testified. After Hargrove checked the gun for fingerprints, Luke testified he had pulled back the breech and it threw out an empty cartridge. Six live rounds were in the magazine underneath the chamber. The assassin had hit his target with a single shot.

Having set the stage, Waller brought out the heavy artillery. Wearing dark green sunglasses, Innes Thornton McIntyre III, the twenty-six-year-old farmer and gun collector from Itta Bena known by the nickname "Thorn," testified that he had ordered a 30.06 caliber Enfield from International Firearms Company in 1959.[21] McIntyre was noticeably ill at ease and must have known that his testimony against Beckwith was going to make him a highly unpopular figure in his hometown and in nearby Greenwood.

Waller established that when a photograph of the murder weapon appeared in local newspapers, McIntyre voluntarily contacted the Jackson police to inquire about it. McIntyre might have been afraid the murder weapon was the same rifle he had ordered by mail—and that it might be traced to him through a paper trail. Jackson police officials allowed him to examine the weapon shortly after the murder, and he told them then that the weapon was virtually identical to the rifle he traded to a man from Greenwood. McIntyre noted, however, that his rifle had been equipped with only standard iron sights at the time he traded it. It had no mountings for telescopic sights.[22]

Waller brought McIntyre to the stand to establish the rifle's purchase and the trade, but skimmed over important dates that might have implicated the Jackson police in a cover-up. McIntyre testified that he had called the police the day after the murder, told them that the rifle looked like one he had owned, and had given them Beckwith's name. As was previously shown, Jackson police did not provide McIntyre's name or the valuable information he had given them to the FBI, who would have been able to quickly check Beckwith's fingerprints through his military records.[23]

On the witness stand, McIntyre examined the murder weapon and said, "In my opinion, it is the same gun," acknowledging that he had traded it about January of 1960. "Who did you trade guns with?" Waller asked. "A man from Greenwood named De La Beckwith," McIntyre replied, pointing to the defendant.

Over Hardy Lott's boisterous objections, Waller brought out a copy of an invoice from International Firearms Company, as well as a receipt from Railway Express, the shipping agent which had handled delivery of the rifle to McIntyre. Since McIntyre could not remember the invoice, Judge Hendrick refused to allow it into evidence, although he did allow McIntyre to confirm the information written on it.[24] McIntyre also testified that he had turned over to FBI agents fifty-three spent cartridges which had been fired from the rifle. He also acknowledged that after seeing a photograph of the weapon in the newspaper, he had called Captain Hargrove at the Jackson Police Department and had asked for a description of the rifle. The following day, he spoke to Hargrove again. "Did you give him a name the next day?" Waller asked.

"Yes, sir," McIntyre replied.

"And what was that name?" Waller pressed.

"Byron De La Beckwith," McIntyre said.

On cross-examination, Lott highlighted the differences between the weapon McIntyre had traded to Beckwith and the rifle in question. He had traded only the "action" of the rifle, not the wooden stock, and therefore, he admitted, he could only identify the rifle by the barrel. It was the barrel, however, which bore the rifle's serial number that had been traced. Lott also made the point, for the jury's benefit, that more than two million rifles of that type had been manufactured and had likely passed hands many times.

At the conclusion of McIntyre's testimony on Friday afternoon, Judge Hendrick called a special Saturday session because of the length of time it had taken to select a jury. Special Agent Francis Finley, a twenty-two-year veteran of the FBI, was Waller's first witness Saturday morning. Finley testified that he had questioned Thorn McIntyre on June 24, 1963, almost two weeks after Evers's murder, and had obtained fifty-three individual 30.06 caliber cartridges McIntyre believed to have been fired by the rifle he had traded to Beckwith. Richard Poppleton, an FBI firearms specialist, said he had microscopically compared McIntyre's spent cartridges with eight others he had personally fired from the murder weapon, and that thirty of them conclusively matched the fresh rounds fired by the murder weapon. Poppleton could not, however, state conclusively that the battered slug which was determined to have killed Evers was fired from the murder rifle, to the exclusion of all other rifles. He testified, however, that it could only have been fired from an Enfield.[25]

John W. "Duck" Goza, the owner of a sporting goods store in Grenada, Mississippi, took the stand. Stocky and heavily tattooed, Goza testified that he had been friendly with Beckwith for a dozen or so years, and that Beckwith had frequently come to his shop to trade guns. He recalled trading a six-power telescopic sight to Beckwith on May 12, which was twenty-nine days prior to Medgar Evers's murder. Beckwith may have traded for the scope, rather than purchased it outright, so that there would be no receipt on it. Still, there was a paper trail linking Beckwith to the scope. Assistant District Attorney John H. Fox III produced a paid invoice from United Binocular Company in Chicago, the vendor that sold the scope to Goza. The FBI had traced the scope from its manufacturer to Goza's shop.

Interestingly, police who searched Beckwith's house after his arrest found a canceled check dated May 11, the day prior to Beckwith's visit to Goza, in payment for a pair of field glasses. If Beckwith was planning to murder Evers and went to Goza's specifically to obtain a telescopic sight, as the prosecution suggested, Beckwith might also have purchased the field glasses to scout the murder scene and the neighborhood. During the search, police also found a Peters Sporting Ammunition booklet containing highlighted references to 30.06 Springfield ammunition, although none of the three guns found in Beckwith's home fired 30.06 ammunition. The murder weapon, however, did.

Goza was a critical link in the prosecutor's chain of evidence. Waller knew that Goza had been questioned at length on a number of occasions, both by the Jackson police and by FBI agents. It was Goza's recollection of his trade with Beckwith, the FBI claimed, *not* the fact that McIntyre had given his name to the Jackson police, that led to Beckwith being considered a suspect in the case. FBI party line was that Goza provided the name and then the FBI Identification Division instituted another search of its fingerprint files.[26] The prosecutors were unaware, however, that since Beckwith had been jailed, Goza, a witness for the prosecution, had mailed money to him in jail to show his support.[27]

"Did you trade or did Mr. Beckwith buy anything else from you that night?" Assistant District Attorney John H. Fox III asked.[28] "No," Goza replied. "I was trying to run him out. I wanted to go home. He said, 'I've got one more trade to make—what will you give me for this .45 automatic?' And I wanted to go home. I just noticed the scope laying there in the showcase, and I told him I'd trade him even."

The final witness called to testify on February 1 was Lloyd M. Price, a Jackson gunsmith who examined the weapon and said that someone with a minimum of knowledge had attached the telescopic sight to the rifle. Judge Hendrick adjourned the proceedings until 9:00 A.M. the following Monday, February 3.

On Monday, Captain Ralph Hargrove, head of the Jackson Police Department's identification division, testified that at approximately 1:30 A.M. on the morning of the murder, he had been called to University Hospital to photograph the wounds on Medgar Evers's body. He then photographed the crime scene extensively and returned later in the morning to photograph the position of the cars in Evers's driveway and the removal of the murder weapon from the honeysuckle thicket. Back at headquarters, Hargrove dusted the murder weapon for fingerprints. On the telescopic sight, he found a clue worthy of a real-life whodunit: a near perfect print of a right index finger.[29] Waller offered the original lift of the fingerprint into evidence as State's Exhibit 34, and Hargrove explained that in his opinion, because of the amount of perspiration present when the print was lifted from the rifle's scope, it could not have been more than twelve hours old.

"When, if ever, did you personally identify whose fingerprint that was?" Waller asked.

"On June 23, 1963, I fingerprinted Mr. Byron De La Beckwith," Hargrove said. "After fingerprinting Mr. Beckwith I compared the fingerprint—the latent fingerprint against his fingerprints." Waller introduced a card bearing Beckwith's right index fingerprint, which Beckwith had signed when his prints were taken on June 23, into evidence. Hargrove testified that when he compared the two prints, he had found fourteen points of comparison. After a lengthy demonstration, during which Hargrove pointed out each of the areas of comparison between the two prints, Waller asked, "Is that comparison definite or indefinite?"

"Positive," Hargrove replied. "The latent fingerprint was made by Mr. Beckwith's right index finger."

In his cross-examination, Lott pressed Hargrove on a number of points, intent on giving the jurors some hint of reasonable doubt. He asked Hargrove to confirm that his education at the Institute of Applied Science was a correspondence course, "to show you didn't have a science degree or a medical degree or some other kind," Lott said. He also challenged Hargrove's expertise in dating a fingerprint as specifically as he had, reading passages from the FBI fingerprint manual and a medical reference on perspiration glands to get Hargrove to concede his lack of knowledge in certain areas. Finally, in an attempt to get Hargrove to contradict himself, Lott offered into evidence a partial transcript from another trial in which Hargrove had testified that there was no way to tell how long a fingerprint had been on a gun. Lott hoped to shatter Hargrove's credibility in the minds of the jurors.

In his redirect examination, Waller asked Hargrove about the other case. "Is your testimony in this case in any way inconsistent with your testimony then?"

"It's quite different . . . inasmuch as the revolver was found inside the room," Hargrove said. "It was not on the outside in the grass and the weeds and coming in contact with honeysuckle vines or the many elements that would destroy a print." Hargrove's testimony, and Lott's tedious cross-examination, took nearly the entire morning.

To further verify the fingerprint testimony, Waller called George Goodreau, an FBI fingerprint expert. Goodreau testified that on June 14, 1963, he received the original fingerprint lifted from the murder weapon by Captain Hargrove. Eight days later, in the early morning hours of June 22, he was awakened from a sound sleep to come to the Bureau's Identification Division. He was asked to compare the original latent print found on the murder weapon with the Marine Corps fingerprint card for Byron De La Beckwith of Greenwood, Mississippi, filed in January of 1942. Goodreau testified that when he compared the prints, Beckwith's right index fingerprint matched the latent partial print found on the telescopic sight. It could belong, he said, to "no one else in the world."[30]

Although Waller did not surface the issue during the trial—the information might have placed reasonable doubt in the minds of the jurors—the FBI Laboratory had performed a cursory search of its single fingerprint files just days after the murder, when the Bureau initially received the original partial fingerprint. The FBI's experts were unable to identify it. In J. Edgar Hoover's telegram to Jackson's police chief, dated June 14, 1963, the FBI director acknowledged that the Bureau's search of its files had been unsuccessful. In a later FBI memorandum, Hoover even belittled his laboratory for its poor performance in the case. "There was certainly good *investigative* work done in this case by our Agts.," Hoover wrote in his tight cursive, "but at the same time our Laboratory runs true to form in being *inconclusive* on matters checked by it."[31]

Having tied Beckwith to the murder weapon, the sight and the fingerprint, Waller called witnesses who established that Beckwith had an unusual interest in Evers and the location of his home. A Jackson cab driver, Herbert Speight, testified that the Saturday before Evers was murdered, Beckwith approached him at the Trailways bus station in Jackson and asked whether he knew where Evers lived. Speight said he remembered Beckwith because he went into the bus station several times to consult the phone book, and returned to the cab three times to ask about addresses, all of which were in white sections of town. On cross-examination, Lott asked about a visit the defense attorneys had made to Speight's boarding house to question him about his knowledge of the case.

"We told you that we had seen where you had been subpoenaed and that we wanted to know what, if anything, you knew about this matter, did we not?"[32] Speight acknowledged his earlier conversations with Lott, and the defense attorney was able to persuade Speight to admit he had told one story to him and another to the prosecutor. Lott further attempted to discredit Speight's testimony by asking whether, when he identified Beckwith in a police line-up, all the other men were wearing suits, while Beckwith, without his belt or suit jacket, was wearing a boldly monogrammed shirt. A second Jackson cab driver, Lee Swilley, bolstered Speight's testimony and recounted the same story about Beckwith asking them questions about where Medgar Evers lived. According to Swilley, who had been carrying on a conversation with Speight when Beckwith approached them, Beckwith said of Evers, "I got to find out where he lives in a couple of days."[33]

To positively identify Beckwith's vehicle, his employer at Delta Liquid Plant Food Company, Dewitt Walcott, testified that Beckwith normally drove a company car, a white Plymouth Valiant with a whip antenna for a two-way radio. On cross-examination, defense attorney Stanny Sanders questioned Walcott about the half-moon cut over Beckwith's eye, and Walcott remembered that Beckwith had "a fresh cut" on the Monday prior to the murder. Walcott also testified that Beckwith had come to work that Monday morning and shown some high school boys a target at which he'd been shooting the day before.

Several prosecution witnesses recalled seeing the white Valiant with the whip antenna in the Evers neighborhood the night of the murder. Martha Jean O'Brien, a seventeen-year-old carhop at Joe's Drive-In, a restaurant whose parking lot was about 200 yards from the sniper's nest, testified that she was working the night of the murder and saw the same car parked in the back lot late that evening. Another witness, Ronald Jones, spent the night with a friend near the Evers home on the night of the murder, and testified he saw the Valiant driving slowly along Delta Drive earlier in the evening and, because of the long antenna, thought it was a police car. Ronald Mark Acy, sixteen, testified that the Saturday before the murder, he had seen the same car parked in front of a small grocery store near the Evers home. He remembered the car because of the antenna, and because it had a Shriners emblem hanging from the rearview mirror.

Barbara Anne Holder, a former employee at Joe's Drive-In who had dropped by to talk to O'Brien, said she also saw the car in the parking lot that night. Holder said she stayed at the drive-in until it closed, shortly before midnight, and noted that the car was still there. At one point in the evening, she saw a slim, dark-haired man get out and go to the rest room, but did not get a close enough look at the man to identify him.

She said she especially remembered the car because of its long antenna, and said she thought it was a police car. Both O'Brien and Holder looked at photographs of the Valiant Beckwith was driving at the time and identified it as the same one parked at Joe's the night of the murder.[34]

FBI agents Sam H. Allen, Jr. and Walser Prospere testified about their initial attempt to question Beckwith about the rifle scope that had been traced to Duck's Tackle Shop. Dr. Forrest Bratley—the same pathologist who performed Evers's autopsy—testified he had examined Beckwith on June 23, immediately after his arrest, and asked about the scar over his right eye.[35]

"I asked the defendant what this was," Bratley testified, "and what that mark was, and he said, 'It looks like a scar.' I asked him further how long it had been there, and quoting the defendant, he said, 'You, an expert, should be able to tell.' " Bratley said he estimated the scar to be at least ten days old but not more than thirty days old when he examined Beckwith, a time period which would have included the night of the murder. He further testified that in size and shape, the scar was consistent with that which might be inflicted by the recoil of a telescopic sight. When Bratley's brief cross-examination was completed, Waller rested the state's case, having called his thirty-sixth witness. Judge Hendrick excused the jury, and Beckwith's attorneys moved for a direct acquittal on the grounds that the state had failed to prove the defendant guilty, and that no evidence introduced by the state could leave the jurors without a reasonable doubt as to Beckwith's guilt. Judge Hendrick rejected the motion.

The first witness for the defense, a neighbor of Evers's named Willie Mae Patterson, testified that she heard the first shot and ran from her dining room to her front door. She looked across to the Evers house and watched as Medgar Evers fell toward his doorstep.[36] "What else did you see?" asked Hardy Lott. "Well," Patterson said, "everything was still for a few minutes before some boys—there were three boys took off in front of my house right following the shot." She further testified that the three were not boys—"I could tell they were men," she said, but said that she did not recognize them. On cross-examination, Waller asked whether or not Patterson could identify Kenneth Adcock as one of the men, or whether—if she was wearing slacks—Betty Jean Coley might have been mistaken for one of the men. "I couldn't tell," Patterson replied.

Lee Cockrell, owner of the drive-in at which several witnesses had placed Beckwith's car, testified for the defense that when he arrived at work at 11:30 P.M. on the night Evers was shot, he saw no white Valiant in the parking lot. He also testified that after his black cook called his attention to the shots, he went outside the restaurant, and that he had heard no one running, nor any cars driving away, after the shots were fired. Cockrell also stated that Martha Jean O'Brien, the carhop who testified that she had seen Beckwith's car on the lot between 8:30 P.M. and 10:00 P.M., had already left work when the shooting occurred. On cross-examination, Waller nudged Cockrell until he conceded that some drunks inside the drive-in were occupying his attention, and that a car could have slipped out of his parking lot without him seeing it leave.[37]

Doris Sumrall, who worked part time at the drive-in, also testified for the defense that Martha Jean O'Brien was not present when the shooting occurred. She also stated that while she was outside after the shots were fired, she neither saw nor heard a car leave the parking lot. On cross-examination, Sumrall's memory proved faulty on several questions Waller asked, such as whether she had heard three or *four* shots, and whether Cockrell had preceded her to the back of the drive-in. To the jury, her responses may have undermined her credibility. Ansie Lee Haven, another drive-in employee, who had worked an eighteen-hour day on June 11, recalled that when she left the drive-in at approximately 11:00 P.M., she passed a white or cream-colored Dodge—not a Plymouth Valiant—parked off by itself in the corner of the lot. "I walked almost to the back of my car to take a look," she testified. "I did not see anyone near or around the car and I saw that it was a Dodge."

"Did it have an aerial on it?" Lott asked. "I did not notice any aerial at all," Haven said. She testified that when the police had later brought by a car for her to identify—the Valiant Beckwith had been driving—she told them "it was definitely not the car I saw out there that night." On cross-examination, Waller read back to Haven a statement she had given police, in which she described the car as "a light-colored Dodge or a Plymouth."[38] The defense then called two witnesses who were in a police line-up with Beckwith; both recalled that Beckwith was wearing a monogrammed shirt. Another witness, Fred Conner, recalled having dinner with Beckwith at the Crystal Grill in Greenwood between 6:00 P.M. and 7:00 P.M. on the night of the murder.[39]

Hardy Lott called C.D. Brooks as an expert witness regarding fingerprints, hoping he would raise questions in the minds of the jurors about whether or not the length of time a latent fingerprint had been on an object could be determined. Judge Hendrick ruled that Brooks was not, in fact, an expert. He allowed the consultant from Birmingham to testify, but left it to the jury to determine his credibility.[40] When asked about his qualifications, Brooks admitted that he was a "self-taught" fingerprint expert, that he had done no fingerprint work during the past six years, and that the only time he testified in court regarding fingerprints was in 1940 or 1941.[41]

Three of Beckwith's co-workers at Delta Liquid Plant Food, John

Book, James McCoy and his son, James McCoy, Jr., all testified for the defense that they had seen the half-moon cut over Beckwith's eye on Monday, June 10, two days prior to the murder.[42]

A Greenwood auxiliary policeman, Roy Jones, was the first of three surprise witnesses called by the defense to provide an alibi for Beckwith. Jones testified that he had seen Beckwith in his white Valiant at 11:45 P.M. the night of the murder, in an alley by Billups service station at the junction of Highways 82 and 49 in Greenwood. After work, he had stopped at Short's Cafe, about a half block from the service station, to get a sandwich before he went home, and saw Beckwith in his car, about to pull out of the alley. Two additional police officers who were patrolling together that night, Hollis Cresswell and James Holley, also claimed to have seen Beckwith at a Shell service station in Greenwood—ninety miles from the Evers home in Jackson—at approximately the same time the murder occurred. Although the Billups station and the Shell station were adjacent to each other, Cresswell and Holley testified that they had seen Beckwith at approximately 1:05 A.M.—almost an hour and a half after Jones testified he had seen Beckwith.[43]

Cresswell and Holly each testified that he had spoken to several other Greenwood officers and to Beckwith's attorneys. Holly added that one of Beckwith's attorneys "asked me not to discuss it any further unless some authorized person, in other words, law enforcement officers, asked." Neither officer volunteered his information to the Jackson police nor to the prosecutor. Under cross-examination, Waller asked each of the three alibi witnesses why he had waited eight months—months Beckwith had spent behind bars—to speak to Jackson police on the defendant's behalf, particularly since they were lawmen who knew the information they were withholding was material. Beckwith had been hauled into court with much fanfare on three separate occasions, in June, July and August of 1963, and at no time did any of the three witnesses come forward with their stories. Wasn't it odd, Waller wondered aloud to each of the men, that officers of the law should withhold material evidence which might exonerate Beckwith?

"Who did you see at 1:10 on the morning of June 12?" Waller asked Holley.

"I don't know, sir," Holley replied.

"Who did you see at 1:15?"

"I don't recall seeing anyone."

"Who did you see at 2:00?"

"I don't recall."

"Who did you see at midnight?"

"I wouldn't know."

"Do you know of anybody you saw that whole night on that whole shift?" Waller pressed. "Not specifically, no, sir."

"That's all," Waller said firmly, striding back to the prosecutor's table.

From her seat in the courtroom, Willie Beckwith watched each of the Greenwood policemen who testified, and tried to remember if she had seen them with her husband socially. She believed they may have come to his aid by providing him with an alibi. "He was tight with them—he had to be," she claimed. "When policemen stood up for him at the trial, I thought they were lying to protect him, but I had no way to prove it. We were living apart then, and I didn't know for a fact where he was that night. But in my own heart, I believed they were lying. And I still believe that."

Even if two of the Greenwood policemen did see Beckwith around 1:00 A.M. following the murder, it would not preclude his having committed the act. Although Waller did not pursue the possibility, any farmer attending the trial recognized that Beckwith could have both committed the murder and returned quickly to Greenwood, simply by flying in a small plane, like a crop duster. Beckwith's earlier work at the Greenwood airport had put him in contact with many local men who flew. Years later, arguing that Lee Harvey Oswald murdered Evers, Beckwith suggested that Oswald may have used a private plane. "Private planes were commonplace in Hinds County . . . and there were numerous private landing strips for small craft."[44]

Beckwith was soon given a chance to tell his own story. At 3:25 P.M., many spectators in the packed courtroom gasped when Byron De La Beckwith was called to testify on his own behalf. Even Waller and his Assistant District Attorney, John H. Fox III, appeared surprised as Beckwith took the witness stand, because they had speculated that his defense attorneys might try to keep him off the stand—to avoid their cross-examination.[45] Gazing out at the faces of the curious onlookers, Beckwith reveled in the attention, enjoying the opportunity to deny the charges against him. He testified for two and a half hours, punctuating each of his answers with "Yes, suh" and "No, suh."

"Now, Mr. Beckwith, did you shoot Medgar Evers?" Lott asked, after some cursory questions about background, family and military record.[46]

"No, suh," Beckwith said emphatically.

"Were you in Jackson, Mississippi, when Medgar Evers was shot?"

"No, suh."

Beckwith testified that he never had a conversation with the cab drivers at the bus station in Jackson, and denied he had ever even seen them, much less talked to them. He stated firmly that he had not parked his car in the drive-in parking lot in Jackson the night of the murder, and said if the car was in Jackson, he "had no knowledge of it." He explained the scar above his eye as being a wound he received—"before this Evers business came up"—while target practicing at a police shooting range behind a nursing home in Greenwood. "I got my right eye up in that scope," Beckwith said, "and I got it up a little close and I squeezed that trigger and that heavy recoil came back and cut a hole—cut a gap in my head." Beckwith admitted obtaining a telescopic sight in a trade with "Duck" Goza, and further admitted to owning a 30.06 Enfield rifle which he got through a trade with Thorn McIntyre. "Did you have the scope put on the rifle?" Lott asked.

"Yes, sir," Beckwith replied, "after a time I did, because I saw I wasn't going to trade the scope by itself and so, I thought maybe I can trade the rifle and the scope." Goza had previously testified that he traded the scope to Beckwith in late May or early June, which meant Beckwith had mounted the scope on the rifle in the week or two prior to Evers's murder. Lott handed Beckwith State Exhibit 21, the murder weapon, and asked him to examine it. Beckwith pulled the butt of the rifle to his shoulder and automatically brought the scope up to his scarred right eye. He sighted it eerily over the heads of the jurors.[47]

"There is much similarity between this weapon and the weapons—several weapons that I possess," Beckwith testified. "Much similarity between them."

"Do you know whether or not that is the rifle and scope that you had that you have just testified about?" Lott asked. "No, sir, I don't know that," Beckwith replied. "No, sir, I don't know that it's my rifle or one that I have ever had, but it is similar to it." Beckwith said he never kept a record of his guns' serial numbers, and that his rifle had a military sling on it—the murder weapon bore marks where a sling had once been mounted on it. He testified that after shooting at the rifle range, he took the gun home, cleaned it and stored it in his bathroom closet.

"What happened to the rifle that you testified you had the scope mounted on?" Lott asked. "The rifle disappeared," Beckwith said. "It left my possession."

Lott needed to establish that the house on George Street could easily have been broken into, and asked Beckwith a series of questions germane to that argument. "Now," Lott asked, "going back to your house that you were living in then, who else was living in that house with you in June 1963?" Sitting in the front row, in a section reserved for officers of the court, Willie Beckwith began to get uneasy. "At that time, I was the only occupant of the house," Beckwith said. "What about your wife?" Lott asked. "My wife and son, they—have you ever seen a picture of that old house?" Beckwith hedged. "Don't ask questions, Mr. Beckwith," Lott said. "They were in an apartment because the house was in such a fearful state of repairs, it wasn't hardly fit to live in. So they got a nice apartment and were in this apartment, and it was air-conditioned. They were very comfortable there, but I had my phone connected up there, and I kept all my company equipment out there in the big yard."

"You were living in the house by yourself?" Lott asked. "Yes," Beckwith said. "That's right. And I would just go and come."

"Were you and your wife separated at the time?" Lott asked. "Only by geography," Beckwith lied. His wife had moved out of the George Street house more than a month before the Evers murder, after Beckwith had thrown her possessions through the front window onto the yard.[48]

When asked why he refused to answer questions when FBI agents approached him after the Evers murder, Beckwith referred to an article in the Greenwood *Commonwealth,* which reported that a citizen had the legal right to refuse to answer any question not asked in a court proceeding. Lott introduced the clipping as an exhibit for the defense.

Beckwith's mood—initially jovial—turned dark when Waller stunned the defendant and his attorneys by producing several letters Beckwith had written in his private war against integration. To a local newspaper, Beckwith wrote, "I believe in segregation just like I believe in God. I shall oppose any person, place or thing that opposes segregation. I shall combat the evils of integration and shall bend every effort to rid the United States of America of the integrationists, whoever and wherever they may be."[49]

"And you mean any force—when you say any force, you mean . . ."

"Within reason," Beckwith interrupted. "You understand reason. And moderation. I won't say moderation. I say within reason, civilized reason. Reason within civilized and organized society." Beckwith, wearing matching tie and socks, with his Shriners pin on his lapel, shifted uncomfortably in his seat. Waller produced another letter, to the NRA, in which Beckwith allegedly wrote, "For the next fifteen years, we here in Mississippi are going to have to do a lot of shooting to protect our wives, our children and ourselves from bad Negroes."[50]

"After you talk about killing bad Negroes, I ask you whether or not you asked for advice on setting up a shooting range at Greenwood where white folks could train to shoot weapons?" Waller asked. "Mr. Waller," Beckwith replied, "I have been interested for years in setting up a shooting range for white folks to use, a rifle and pistol range and run an arsenal range along with it as a way to make a living, because I am interested in those things and I think people should know how to use them—have arms and use them." Again, Waller pulled one of Beckwith's letters out of a manila folder. This one, a query letter written just a week and a half earlier, offered to the editor of *Outdoor Life*[51] an article Beckwith had written about "shooting at night in the summertime for varmints." One of the titles Beckwith was considering for the piece was "After Sundown."

Waller turned to Beckwith. "Would you say an integration leader is a varmint?" he asked, clearly implying that Beckwith saw Evers as someone worthy of extermination, much as one would kill a possum or a raccoon. "Oh, that's a human being," Beckwith replied almost sarcastically, "but we're talking about varmints. I'm talking about crows and things like that."

The article, which Beckwith was still writing and which Waller did not have in his possession at the time, and thus could not offer into evidence, contained chilling allusions to the Evers killing. Beckwith's stated weapon of choice: "I prefer a 30.06." Of the quarry: "I don't believe in letting anything suffer from a wound or take a chance on an evil thing escaping to do still more damage." Beckwith described the varmints (large, predatory fish called gars) as growing "six feet or longer . . . well over 150 pounds." Medgar Evers was more than six feet tall and weighed about 180 pounds. Of shooting technique, Beckwith wrote: "I hate to waste ammunition on a still target when—for the defense of home, honor and country—we will hardly be shooting at a still target from a prone position with the light just right." And finally, about marksmanship: "If you get two shots, consider yourself lucky." Evers's killer had fired a single shot.[52] Beckwith had even included a White Citizens' Legal Fund flyer and a wallet-size photo of himself in his query letters to *Outdoor Life* and *Field & Stream*, hoping to stir up financial support.

"Now, in four months' time and one hundred and fifty letters,[53] I'll ask you whether or not you have frequently referred to the fact that you are making sacrifices for the cause?" Waller asked Beckwith. "This is a cause, yes, sir," Beckwith said. "All right. Now, I'll ask you further if you have not referred to the fact that you have written a book about the subject matter of which you are being tried now, you have given it a title, and you have offered it to publishers to print, is that not so?" Beckwith fidgeted and explained that he had compiled some information for a book, and had perhaps misrepresented it as a book when it was not. After a series of objections by Lott, Waller asked Beckwith if the title of his proposed book was *My Ass, Your Goat and the Republic.*

"Would you explain that to us?" Waller asked. "It is thus explained," Beckwith said, growing red-faced, "by the left-wing forces riding my donkey. They intend to aggravate the public and continue on with their method of destroying states' rights, constitutional government and racial integrity." The jurors, reporters and onlookers were watching a man suddenly crazed. For the first time during the trial, Beckwith appeared to be losing his composure.

Stanny Sanders jumped up. "If the court please, we are not here to discuss philosophy!" Beckwith regained his composure and redirected his attention to the prosecutor, but his answers to Waller's questions became curt and acidic.

"I believe the subject matter we have talked about here began in 1957," Waller said, alluding to Beckwith's published letters. "Your philosophy and using force, your sacrifices for the cause, and the statements that you have made in all these matters that we've brought out here before the jury, indicates, Mr. Beckwith—yes or no—that you are going to do whatever is necessary and use whatever force you deem best to stop integration or the forces of integration?"

"No, sir, I am not going to go that far. I won't go that far."

"How far will you go?"

"To do whatever is morally, legally and spiritually right to preserve the wholesome forces in this nation and in this republic. To do whatever I can in a small way with a pen. I am a writer."

Waller turned to the subject of Beckwith's skill with a rifle. "You are accurate at two hundred feet with a .30-06 Enfield rifle with a six-power scope, too, aren't you?"

"At two hundred feet?"

"Yes, sir."

"I should do better than that," Beckwith bragged, shifting in his seat. "I ought to hit something at a range better than two hundred feet, sir."

Following Beckwith's lengthy appearance on the stand, one final witness, E.H. Hawkins, testified briefly that he had seen Beckwith the morning before Evers was murdered, and that Beckwith had a noticeable cut over his eye. Neither the defense nor the prosecution had asked Beckwith to pinpoint his whereabouts at the time of the murder. Nor was Beckwith asked whether he knew of others who might have been involved in a conspiracy to murder Evers. The defense team's scant physical evidence—a signed statement from a witness for the prosecution who varied her story about the make of car she had seen in the drive-in parking lot, and a single clipping from the Greenwood *Commonwealth*—was meager in contrast to the prosecution's sixty items of evidence, which included the murder weapon, the partial fingerprint lifted from the weapon, numerous fingerprint records, enlarged photographs of the murder scene and such.[54]

Assistant District Attorney John H. Fox III then led the impassioned closing arguments for the prosecution. "You take the conscience of the state of Mississippi into the jury room," Fox told the jurors, noting that Beckwith "sat in that witness chair as if he were on a throne of glory—and he reveled in it. He proudly demonstrated to you that he is a crack shot. He wanted the world to know that. Is it possible that he also wanted all the world to know that he killed Medgar Evers—but he didn't want it spelled out so plain you'd have to find him guilty?" Fox called Beckwith "a fanatic, pure and simple. He had not only the capacity and the capability and the power to kill, he also had the deep compelling motive. And as calmly as he would kill a turtle on a log, as coolly as he would shoot a crow out of a tree, he did execute Medgar Evers, a human being—shot him like a varmint, in the driveway of his home, in the night time, in the summertime, in 1963."[55]

District Attorney Waller walked through his ten-point argument that Beckwith had murdered Medgar Evers, having clearly possessed a motive, the ability to plan the crime, and both the ability and capacity to commit the murder. Waller's argument included physical evidence such as the telescopic sight traced through Duck Goza, the murder weapon traded to Beckwith by Thorn McIntyre, Beckwith's partial fingerprint on the scope of the rifle, and the cut over his eye. Waller finished his argument, reiterating the facts presented by witnesses who identified Beckwith's car in the immediate vicinity of the crime, his presence in Jackson, and his activities since his arrest. "What's going to really kill me," Waller told the jurors, "is to pick up *The Saturday Evening Post* a few weeks from now, if Beckwith is acquitted, and read 'My True Story'—and he's already written it!

"This was not a crime of passion or revenge," Waller asserted, calling the murder a "heinous execution." Instead, Waller said, "Beckwith came down here to kill a cause. He wanted to get the number one man, the leader of the cause. He wanted to be a martyr, a big man." Waller described Beckwith as a murderer who lived out "one man's short-lived hold on destiny."[56]

Stanny Sanders, leading the defense team in its closing arguments, implored the jury not to come back with a guilty verdict just "to satisfy the attorney general of the United States and the liberal national press." He claimed Beckwith had been cleared of the crime through the testimony of the police officers who testified they had seen Beckwith in Greenwood at approximately the time the murder occurred. Hardy Lott told jurors, "The state has failed to put on a single witness who could place Mr. Beckwith in Jackson on the night of the crime." And, Lott told them, "If you are going to bring up everybody in Mississippi that believes in segregation when somebody gets shot, I had better move."[57]

From the audience, Hinds County Judge Russel Moore listened intently to the closing arguments. During the jury selection and trial, he had been a mainstay in the courtroom. Moore was a well-known segregationist and racial extremist, but, said John Herbers, who covered the trial for *The New York Times,* "Moore was not your usual Mississippi redneck. He was a man of some intelligence and background."[58] Moore was an icon among segregationists in Jackson because of the firm stand he had taken during the earliest Freedom Rides and voter registration drives which divided Mississippi. It was Moore who, just a year earlier, had been confronted by civil rights veteran Diane Nash, who had been convicted of "contributing to the delinquency of minors" after holding direct action workshops for Jackson teenagers who were preparing to join the Freedom Rides. In April 1962, Nash—while under appeal—made a dramatic move. Noticeably pregnant, Nash presented herself in Judge Moore's court to begin serving her two-year sentence. In a statement to reporters, Nash said, "Some people have asked me how I can do this when I am expecting my first child, but this will be a black child born in Mississippi and thus wherever he is born he will be in prison." Judge Moore asked Nash to continue her appeal, but she refused. He angrily cited her in contempt of court for standing on the white side of the courtroom and sentenced her to ten days in lockup.[59]

Nor was Moore the only prominent visitor to the courtroom. After the jurors retired to a dormitory one floor above Beckwith's cell in the Hinds County Courthouse to deliberate the evidence, the monotony of Beckwith's wait for a verdict was interrupted by another courtroom visit. Former Mississippi Governor Ross Barnett arrived, shaking hands with Beckwith and greeting him warmly. Barnett's public show of support for Beckwith spoke volumes. Herbers remembered the former governor's visit clearly. "You could just feel the chemistry of the thing move through the courtroom," he said in an interview, acknowledging that Barnett's interest in the case and his pro-Beckwith position were clear. Major General Edwin A. Walker also visited Beckwith briefly the following morning, while the jury was entering its final hours of deliberation. University of Mississippi history professor James Silver later called their visits "as public as daylight."[60]

Although one onlooker at the trial had predicted the jury would quickly acquit Beckwith,[61] almost everyone following the trial was surprised when the jury was unable to reach a verdict on the first day of deliberations. At 9:21 P.M. on February 6, 1964, Judge Hendrick called for the jury to be brought back into the courtroom. With their shirt sleeves rolled up and their ties loosened, the jurors said they had not yet been able to reach a verdict. Although by late evening most of the local spectators had left the courtroom, those present knew the longer the jury deliberated, the less likely the chances of a direct acquittal. Under heavy guard, the jury was sequestered for the night and resumed their deliberations the following morning. Just after noon on February 7, after taking twenty ballots, the jurors filed solemnly back into the courtroom. Beckwith sat in rapt attention with his hands clasped tightly in his lap as the jurors were polled individually. One juror told Judge Hendrick, "We are hopelessly deadlocked." Five white jurors steadfastly held out for Beckwith's conviction. "In the light of Mississippi's history, and of the fears and hatreds which still haunt that troubled land," Harold H. Martin later wrote in *The Saturday Evening Post*, "the fact that six [sic] white men held out for a conviction was in itself a victory for the law."[62]

Judge Hendrick declared a mistrial and forbade the jurors to discuss their deliberations. Beckwith was remanded to the custody of Sheriff Pickett to await a second trial. One juror later said that emotions were volatile in the jury room. "We got so mad we would all have to stop talking fifteen or twenty minutes and simmer down," he said. "We knew it would never change."[63] The *SCLC Newsletter*, the publication of Dr. Martin Luther King Jr.'s Southern Christian Leadership Conference, called the verdict a "pretense at justice," and said it told Beckwith, in essence, "just be patient and you soon will be free to go on about your fertilizer business."[64]

Myrlie Evers was stunned by the mistrial, and although she had prepared a statement in the event of an acquittal, she was taken completely aback by the hung jury. In Greenwood, Beckwith's friends, who expected his acquittal, were forced to cancel plans for a celebratory dinner in his honor. In Jackson later that night, SNCC Field Secretary Bob Moses led blacks in a rally at an overflowing Methodist church. "Some think we have won a victory because of the mistrial," he told the congregation, "but remember—Ross Barnett shook Beckwith's hand."[65] The former governor, talking to reporters after the trial's conclusion, added his own perspective and assumed a casual air. "You can't be surprised what a jury does," Barnett said cavalierly, "or who a woman will marry."[66]

Beckwith's father's grave in Colusa, California. (Raymond Cushing)

Byron De La Beckwith as pictured in the 1940 Greenwood High School yearbook.

"A" Company, Second Amphibian Tractor Battalion, Second Marine Division, photographed in Hutt Park, Wellington, New Zealand, in the spring of 1943. Beckwith is in the third row, third from the right. (Edward Moore Collection)

Members of Beckwith's Marine Battalion surround the reigning Miss Laguna Beach before shipping out for the Pacific. From left to right: Beckwith, Norman Moïse, Joe Burton, Ralph Peters, Willie Reader, Jack Probasco, Bill Sparks, and Thomas "Willie" Handlon. (Norman Moïse Collection)

Mary Louise Williams as she looked when she met Byron De La Beckwith.

Beckwith with one of his favorite black-powder rifles.

Byron De La Beckwith in his U.S. Marine Corps uniform, before he sustained serious injuries at the battle of Tarawa.

Willie and De La Beckwith celebrating their first anniversary at the Peabody Hotel in Memphis in 1946.

The Beckwith family in November 1946.

Beckwith and son in the bathtub at their home on West Monroe.

Willie and De La Beckwith at a formal dance in December 1955.

De La Beckwith—holding one of his favorite rifles—with his son.

Beckwith in the Church of the Nativity, where he was known to carry a pistol to Sunday services.

Dressed for church, Beckwith and son display their sartorial flair with new neckties.

Byron De La Beckwith plays Santa Claus as his young son (at left) watches.

The Beckwiths in the kitchen of their home on West Monroe in Greenwood.

De La Beckwith and Willie Beckwith in studio portraits taken in 1961, when they were 41 and 38 years old.

The Beckwiths in 1961, surrounded by some of the Jefferson Davis items inherited from Beckwith's uncle, Will Yerger. (Courtesy of *The Commonwealth*)

The Yerger home at 306 George Street as it looked in the early 1960s after years of neglect.

For several years in the early 1970s, Beckwith was on a one-man mission to circulate copies of the notoriously anti-Semitic book *None Dare Call It Conspiracy*.

Mary Louise Williams (Willie) at age 50 in 1973, dressed for a formal party celebrating her entry into an alcoholic rehabilitation program. (Robbie Massengill Collection)

Thelma and Byron De La Beckwith photographed by a friend at a Ku Klux Klan rally. Photo mailed to the author by Beckwith.

Thelma Beckwith in the front yard of her Signal Mountain home. (Reed Massengill)

"Let The High Praise Of God Be In Their Mouth, And A Twoedged Sword In Their Hand" Ps. 149:6

ARYAN NATIONS

Church of Jesus Christ Christian

Rt. 3, Box 167
Hayden Lake, Idaho 83835

November 20, 1980

Byron De La Beckwith
Rt #1, Box 109
Cruger, MS 38924

Greetings, Kinsman,

Dear Byron,

We have your November 1st letter telling of your financial problems which I am sorry to hear about.

However, I want you to know, Byron, that in no way do we here at Aryan Nations require your donation to remain on our mailing and tape list. You are an honorary member from now on, so don't worry about matters of a money nature as far as we are concerned.

Your faithful application of time, sustenance, and energy in the past and in the present is of unending value for our Faith, Race, and Nation and we thank our Father for those faithful kinsmen who fight on for His assured victory.

Hail His Victory!

RG Butler
Pastor R. G. Butler

A hero of our race is forever *ours* to Honor, you stand among the finest in our eyes.

RGB

In a handwritten postscript to a letter telling Beckwith not to worry about paying his Aryan Nations dues, founder Richard Butler wrote, "A hero of our race is forever *ours* to honor, you stand among the finest in our eyes."

WHITE KNIGHTS OF THE KU KLUX KLAN-WKKKK

VOLUME: 4-91
NUMBER: Apr-May

WHITE KNIGHTS NATIONAL OFFICE
P.O. Box 14220
KANSAS CITY, MO 64152
Hotline- 816-254-0038

WHITE BERET PUBLISHING OFFICE
P.O. Box 434
Catoosa, Ok 74015
918-834-1042

"White Beret Editor
-D.W. Mahon

The White Knights are a Division of the CONFEDERATE KNIGHTS of AMERICA, P.O. Box 602, Huntersville, N.C. 28078. Imperial Wizard Terry Boyce

Subscription rate: 1 year-$15, 6 months-$8. Send Money Order payable to D.W. Mahon

SUPPORT WHITE AMERICA'S

TOM METZGER

BYRON DE LA BECKWITH

LATEST TRUE HEROS

The New World Dictionary defines the word Hero as a man of great strength and courage- any man admired for his courage, nobility, or exploits- any man admired for his qualities or achievements and regarded as an ideal or model. Your editor would like to add his own definition to what a hero is. A man who knowingly stands for his ideals inspite of enormous persecution or oppression; and is willing to lose his wealth, family, and his very life to bring his ideals to successful reality.

By these definitions, then, the word hero is being used very loosely by ZOG's media

The cover of the White Knights of the Ku Klux Klan's April–May 1991 newsletter pictured Beckwith alongside Tom Metzger, leader of the violent neo-Nazi White Aryan Resistance, under the all-caps headline, "SUPPORT WHITE AMERICA'S LATEST TRUE HEROS."

VI

that up on the wall where I can
read it EVERY day — No Foolin.

I am getting intrested in Klan
activities again — as you know
Im supposed to be in the Super
Secret White Knights of the Ku Klux
Klan so says the Jews-media, or is
that the news media ha! ha! any
way this is an open non-secret
group and I think Ill drive down
to hear what they have on their
minds this Saturday night. about 300 miles round trip

I know Robert Shelton slightly
and I know Durell Fordham very
closely but Im not excited by
public Klan meetings at all — but
havent been to one since I ran for
Lt Gov — So — Im Curious!

On page 6 of a lengthy letter to Willie dated May 13, 1973, Beckwith wrote, "I am getting interested in Klan activities again—as you know I'm supposed to be in the Super Secret White Knights of the Ku Klux Klan so says the Jews-media or is that the news media ha! ha!"

Byron De La Beckwith
Manufacturers Representative
Route 1 Box 105 A
Cruger, Mississippi 38924

know what it all means. But as i've been told before [it dont matter anymore.]
So when you think of me you see a man
deep in debt — facing 5 years in prison —
living like a niger and as far in global [not state or county]
Klan work as a 56 year old man can to
be in and Happy at it. If you are woman enough to
get in the middle of all this — catching up
on all background and live in a state
of perpetual war with the forces of evil in
the world then you let me know!
I never have found you interested or
anxious for that way of life or willing to
make those real sacrifices for our Lord, our
Republic and our People nor for your family — you have not changed a top!
If you are Playing with me then Please
stop it — I have no time to play except
with those who have a long history of actual
assults against the forces of organized Jewery and
then those peoples company I seek during the
—over—

On page 5 of another letter to Willie dated November 16, 1976, Beckwith wrote, "So when you think of me you see a man deep in debt—facing five years in prison—living like a niger [*sic*] and as far in global not state or county Klan work as a 56 year old man can to [*sic*] be in and Happy at it." It's worth noting that in grand jury testimony, under oath, Beckwith swore he'd never been affiliated with the Ku Klux Klan.

(2)

shied away from him & then and now me too! He was always viewed with suspicion among pure patriots.

He & his wife divorced and it seems that it was convenient to him for this to transpire while he & his spouse were in & out of Thelma's home — a real good size piece of white trash!

I just threw the snotty nosed, 6'4", yellow skinned, mongrel, damned by God & stinking son of a bitch jew out of my comfortable chamber 7/18/92 as he crept in with a long time true friend of mine here. He's been writing on anti-DLB, anti-White, anti-Christian, anti-Dixie books — one a mother defiler, Adam Nossiter who months ago had the gall to ask me to release my F.I.A., FBI file to him! All of which is awful for a jew and all who associate with jews — for jews pleasures are worse than the jews — so says Jesus! Who is Very God dontcha know! You call jew shabbas goys proselytes —. Jesus is on their ass & me too.

He slithered in Thelma's home — Home and that could be the end of a happy marriage — my wife letting a God Damned obvious jew in to her home where we live!!!
Shit. Shit Shit

YOUR jew Buddy shucks!

I've had a file on him for several yrs —

On page 2 of a letter to the author dated July 21, 1992, Beckwith wrote from jail that he had recently thrown journalist Adam Nossiter out of his cell, using a lengthy string of invective. "He slithered in Thelma's home and that could be the end of a happy marriage—my wife letting a God Damned obvious jew in to her home where we live!!! Shit shit shit."

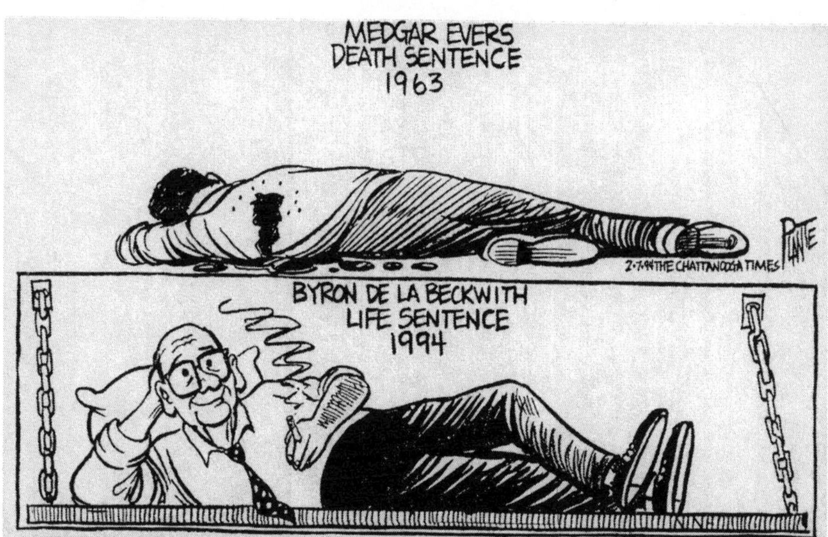

Of the many editorial cartoons that ran when Beckwith was convicted, Bruce Plante's succinct commentary from the *Chattanooga Times* on February 7, 1994, was the most powerful. (By permission of Bruce Plante/Planteink.com)

Medgar Evers at work at his desk at NAACP headquarters, Jackson, Mississippi. (Author's collection)

Former Ku Klux Klan Titan Delmar Dennis, who served as an informant to the FBI during the 1960s and who testified during Beckwith's 1994 trial. (Reed Massengill)

Beckwith's attorney Jim Kitchens, left, questions the author during the final days of testimony in the third murder trial. (Courtesy of the artist, Sanders McNeal)

The author in 1993 at Beckwith's father's grave in Colusa, California, which Beckwith had never visited. (Raymond Cushing)

The author in 2023 at Beckwith's grave in Chattanooga, Tennessee. (Judy Valliant)

10

And Ten Crosses Burned

Escorted out of the courthouse by her brother, Willie Beckwith, wearing a conservative Bobbie Brooks dress with a double strand of pearls, looked down into the throng of reporters who were waiting for her. They engulfed her as she came through the door, asking for a statement about her husband's mistrial. "I planned to take him home tonight," she said, moving steadily ahead. "Will you be at his next trial every day?" a reporter asked, his pen poised on his notepad. "Yes, sir," she lied, knowing she would not attend a second trial. "I'm just like he is. I'm an arch-segregationist."[1] While the reporters scrambled to get the quote, Willie slipped away from them, into her brother's waiting car.

When she made her initial appearance at her husband's trial on January 31, 1964, Willie had missed only the first few days of jury selection. She entered the courtroom wearing a red dress and a fur stole. The wire services and local reporters noted her presence, her attire, and that Beckwith seemed surprised to see her. Throughout the testimony, Willie sat near her husband's defense table at the front of the courtroom in a section reserved for officers of the court. Her older brother, Jesse Williams, Jr., had driven from Knoxville to attend the trial with her. When court adjourned at the end of each day's testimony, Willie and Jesse returned to their adjacent rooms on the second floor of the nearby Heidelberg Hotel. After the closing arguments, when the judge gave his charge to the members of the jury, and they left to weigh the evidence against her husband, Willie left the courtroom, too. She had seen the same evidence and heard the same testimony, and when she got to the hotel and stretched out facedown on her bed, she was firmly convinced of her husband's guilt.

"I didn't know a lot that was going on until I sat at that trial, the first trial," she said in retrospect. "I learned a lot just sitting there, listening, that I didn't know. But I began to put two and two together, and I thought he wouldn't get out of it, the way the trial was going." Willie, along with Myrlie Evers, was stunned by the mistrial. Both had married men who were consumed by racial passions and who were equally committed to their respective causes. Although no white man had yet been convicted of murdering a black in Mississippi, Willie found it difficult to believe the jury had been unable to reach a conclusion about her husband's guilt. "I didn't think it'd be a hung jury, based on what I had heard," she said. "I believed, based on the evidence, that he'd be convicted."

As the trial progressed, Willie kept weighing the information the witnesses were offering against things *only* she knew. The jurors never heard about Beckwith's violent tendencies or his history of wife abuse. She had heard her husband refer to Medgar Evers as "the big nigger" or "the head nigger," and she knew that Evers was a target of Beckwith's venomous hatred. And although District Attorney William Waller had unearthed several of Beckwith's incriminating letters, Willie knew there were dozens more her husband had sent out over the years, likening the war against integration to the Holy Crusades and himself to a crusading warrior. She agreed with Waller's characterization of her husband as "a man at war." She had lived under the same roof with him long enough to know it was a war he would wage alone, if necessary.

What troubled Willie most, though, was her firm belief that her husband was capable of murder. "I just couldn't think of him doing a thing like that until I went to the trial," she reflected. As the jurors filed out of the courtroom to debate her husband's fate—and to determine whether he would face the gas chamber—Willie steeled herself for the worst. "All I know for sure, all I could swear to in a court of law, is what he did to me," she said quietly. "But in my heart, no matter what anybody says, based on the evidence, I believe De La's the only one capable of killing Medgar Evers."

Back in his cell, awaiting word from his lawyers about his retrial, Beckwith got his first good news in months. His hometown newspaper, *The Commonwealth*, ran a cover story about five local property owners whose land had been purchased by the General Services Administration to build a $1.1 million post office in Greenwood. His house on George Street, along with several neighbors' houses and their adjoining land, had been approved for purchase. The news elated Beckwith, buoying him somewhat from the emotional low into which he had descended after the trial. He had known for almost two years the property was under consideration—that was one reason he refused to do any cleanup work on the old house—but the *Commonwealth* article was the first official word that the deal was being closed.

When the transaction was completed, Beckwith became $25,630 richer, but publicity about the government's purchase brought down the wrath of the NAACP. Unaware that the site had been selected prior to Beckwith's arrest, Charles Evers sent telegrams to President Lyndon Johnson, Attorney General Robert Kennedy and other government officials complaining that it was "insensitive and irresponsible" to give public money to the man accused of his brother's murder. Evers called the purchase "a reward," and urged the government to rescind payment.The controversy quickly made its way into the FBI's files. The General Services Administration queried the FBI about the date Beckwith was indicted for murder, then entered for the record that the purchase of his land was agreed on prior to his indictment.[2] When the deal appeared in the headlines of Drew Pearson's popular syndicated newspaper column, Beckwith was ecstatic. Even from jail, he was able to stir Charles Evers and the NAACP to a froth.

The post office transaction proved to be just one more incident during which Beckwith's attorneys were unable to keeping the press away from stories unfavorable to their client. During the first trial, when Lott, Sanders and Cunningham should have been able to concentrate exclusively on Beckwith's defense, they were constantly being blindsided by his foolishness. His letter-writing, his fund-raising pleas and his arrogance in the courtroom had collectively worked against him. With a hung jury to drive their point home, the attorneys chastised Beckwith and told him he would have to humble himself to convince a jury of his innocence. He wrote Willie that he had made only "a passing grade" during the first trial, and that his lawyers stressed that he would have to improve his score next time. Beckwith had also been told that the jury's initial ballot had been 2-10 in his favor, and he subsequently blamed the mistrial on the irrationality of a quarreling jury.[3]

As evidence of shifting public opinion, visitors to the jail—and personal donations to both Beckwith and to the White Citizens' Legal Defense Fund—dropped dramatically after the mistrial. Beckwith's demeanor changed, as well. He was not as well-treated at the Hinds County Jail. For the first time, his mail and newspapers piled up for days at a time before they were brought to him, and the relative freedom he enjoyed earlier was curtailed without explanation. He grew increasingly suspicious, afraid his letters were being intercepted and copied for the prosecution. He was also concerned that the district attorney was out finding additional witnesses who would offer evidence against him in the upcoming retrial.

In his cell, which had been freshly painted for him in early March, Beckwith pored over the transcript of the first trial. His attorneys told him to "memorize" his earlier testimony,[4] and Beckwith agonized over each page, realizing that he could face execution if he was convicted in the coming trial. Although Beckwith placed the blame for the mistrial squarely on the shoulders of an irrational jury, his attorneys felt the unrelenting strength of the ballots against their client. In a case that offered no eyewitnesses to the crime, white Mississippi jurors had held out for conviction because they believed the prosecution had proven Beckwith's guilt beyond a reasonable doubt. What they needed, Beckwith's attorneys believed, was a more favorable jury.

Defense attorney Stanny Sanders enlisted the help of A.L. Hopkins, an investigator for the Mississippi Sovereignty Commission. The group was notorious for financing the Citizens' Council and harassing and infiltrating civil rights groups, and Hopkins secretly provided information to Sanders about prospective jurors' backgrounds, affiliations and racial beliefs. Jurors who might have proven sympathetic to Beckwith made the final cut.[5] Those even remotely likely to be sympathetic to integration were not selected.

Infighting among the defense attorneys also weakened Beckwith's case. Ross Barnett's law partner, Hugh Cunningham, maintained a low profile during the first trial; Beckwith told his wife that Cunningham did not perform at all, and confided that Lott and Sanders were not planning to pay him his full fee. During jury selection for the second trial, however, Cunningham took a leading role in questioning the veniremen, while Lott and Sanders took a more aggressive stance than they had during the first trial, when they apparently believed their client would benefit from a quick acquittal.[6] Sanders approached a Sovereignty Commission investigator to inquire about potential jurors on the defense team's behalf.[7] Although Beckwith criticized Cunningham's work during the first trial, he still believed the jurors would react favorably to him because of his affiliation with Barnett. Cunningham's increased visibility was only one of several changes in the new trial. Beckwith's bright socks and ties were gone, along with his jovial demeanor and self-assuredness. Gone, too, was Willie Beckwith. After hearing the evidence presented against her husband during the first trial, she did not resume her place at his side during the second murder trial.

Jury selection for the new trial began on April 6, 1964, with a venire of 310 men. Because jury selection had proven so tedious and time-consuming during the first trial, Judge Hendrick automatically slated evening sessions to speed the process. By the end of the first evening, the state had approved eleven jurors, although they had not yet been questioned by defense lawyers. Acknowledging that the state would be presenting essentially the same case, District Attorney William Waller told a reporter for *The New York Times*, "Let's face it, a fingerprint is a fingerprint and a gun is a gun. We have done the best we could, and we will try all the harder this time."[8]

No new witnesses came forward with additional evidence implicating Beckwith, although District Attorney Waller had unearthed a few more of Beckwith's incendiary letters to add to his private arsenal. The same prosecution witnesses took the stand to build the state's ten-point case against Beckwith. Only one witness changed his testimony. White taxi driver Herbert Speight, who during the first trial positively identified Beckwith as the man who approached him at the bus station asking for directions to Medgar Evers's house, now said he was "almost positive" the man was Beckwith. "Have you been threatened in any way?" Judge Hendrick asked the witness. "Yes," Speight replied meekly.[9] Speight was beaten after he testified against Beckwith in the first trial, and some believed he was attacked by Klansmen in retaliation for his testimony.

A strange amalgam of Mississippi's white supremacist factions attended Beckwith's second trial. Some were incensed that the first jury had not reached a quick acquittal. Some wanted to hear for themselves whatever evidence could possibly have swayed white Mississippi jurors to vote for Beckwith's conviction. Klansmen, Citizens' Council members and other white segregationists eyed Speight and the other witnesses suspiciously, their presence no doubt intimidating the witnesses. During the new trial, they filled the courtroom as quickly as possible each day to keep out the growing numbers of black spectators. One such attempt resulted in a violent confrontation between a young black woman and an elderly white man. Norma Stamps, a secretary at Jackson State College, was standing in a crowded line to enter the courtroom when she was pushed from behind into an elderly man, who told her to stop shoving. When she explained that the man behind her had pushed her into him, the octogenarian ahead of her said, "Stop lying," and slapped her. She slapped him back and was arrested and charged with assault. The arresting officers reportedly hit her and twisted her arm dragging her away from the scene.[10]

The mood was equally tense in the courtroom, where the once jovial Beckwith now seemed sullen and edgy. No longer did he twist around in his chair so the courtroom artists could capture a more flattering likeness of him. Instead of the fine cigars he slipped in the district attorney's pocket during the first trial, all that passed between them now were cold, resolute glances. After the evidence was once again presented against Beckwith—his fingerprint, his rifle, his scope, and the testimony of those who claimed to have seen him or his car in Evers's neighborhood prior to the murder—the state rested on April 13, after four days of testimony. Beckwith took the stand the following day and was questioned for an hour by his attorney, Hardy Lott. His replies were curt and to the point; noticeably different from the rambling explanations he offered while on the stand during the first trial.

Lott also produced an important additional defense witness, James L. Hobby. Hobby testified that he lived in Jackson at the time of the murder, but had since been moved to Memphis by his company, Gordon Transports Inc. He claimed he parked his 1960 Valiant in front of Joe's Drive-In the night Evers was shot, bolstering the defense argument that the car identified as Beckwith's actually belonged to someone else. Barbara

Holder, a prosecution witness had previously identified Beckwith's car in the parking lot and testified that she saw the driver enter the rest room, although she had been unable to identify him.

After having Hobby describe his car and his visit to the drive-in on the night of Evers's murder, Lott asked, "Do you recall whether you went into the rest room?"

"Yes sir, I did," Hobby replied.[11]

Although during the first trial, Beckwith had never directly been asked his whereabouts on the night of the murder, his case again hinged on the testimony of two Greenwood policemen and an auxiliary policeman. Again, twelve white male jurors listened intently as all three witnesses recounted their earlier testimony, each witness claiming to have seen Beckwith in Greenwood at approximately the same time the murder occurred in Jackson. The prosecution had again failed to unearth any new witnesses who could place Beckwith at the scene of the crime or even in Jackson that night.

In his closing arguments for the second trial, defense attorney Stanny Sanders employed some tactical changes. During the first trial, the defense, through Beckwith's claim that he could not positively identify the murder weapon as his own, tried to introduce reasonable doubt about the weapon's provenance. During the second trial, Sanders instead tried to convince the jury that the gun had been planted at the scene of the crime to implicate Beckwith. "Does it make sense to you that a man who had a car parked twenty-eight feet away would take the time to hide a gun when he could have gotten in his car and driven out of Jackson?" Sanders asked the jurors. "Does that make sense? Whoever put that gun there was bound to have known the police would find it. It suggests to me the gun was planted there." Lott called the state's case "conjecture, guess and suspicion," and said, referring to Beckwith's assertion that his gun had been stolen, "Mr. Beckwith was a sitting duck for anybody, white or colored, who wanted to get a gun to shoot someone."[12]

District Attorney Waller, in his own closing arguments, again characterized Beckwith as a man obsessed with killing the cause of integration. "Mr. Beckwith by his own demeanor is guilty. He planned the crime and he had a motive. He came down here to kill the leader of the forces of integration in Mississippi. How can we live with honor . . . if we don't honor the law?" he asked the jurors. "What kind of example are we showing . . . to the man who would hide in some other clump of trees and whose finger might be black instead of white, and aim a gun at another who might be white instead of black?"[13]

The case went to the jury at 12:53 P.M. on April 16. When Judge Hendrick brought the jury in before retiring it for the night, juror J.T. Reynolds was told that his aunt had died. He was sequestered and remained with the group, which had deliberated for seven hours. The following day, when Judge Hendrick polled the jurors after three more hours of deliberation, it was clear that they were unable to reach a verdict. "I think it would be an endurance contest if we went back," juror John J. Offenhiser told the judge. The final ballot reportedly stood at eight to four for acquittal,[14] indicating that the Sovereignty Commission's input regarding the jurors' backgrounds may have helped garner more votes for acquittal, or that Beckwith's defense team mounted a more persuasive case the second time around. After declaring a second mistrial, Judge Hendrick released Beckwith into the custody of the Hinds County Sheriff, awaiting payment of a $10,000 bond.

Beckwith returned to his cell and quickly gathered his clothes, papers, and typewriter. After ten tedious months in jail, he was again a free man. He conferred with his lawyers, who advised him that even though he would be free on bond, he would remain under indictment for murder and that the district attorney could pursue a third trial if he could locate additional witnesses or unearth new evidence. While a swarm of newsmen and onlookers gathered at the main entrance of the courthouse, Beckwith was swept out the side door, where he crouched on the rear floorboard of an unmarked car as the sheriff and a deputy sped him back home to Greenwood. Although the sheriff and his deputy were in front, Beckwith had some company in the back seat—a .30 caliber carbine Beckwith had been given, in case there was any violence.[15] News of the mistrial aired on the car radio as the trio passed through Tchula, and Beckwith was stunned to see a sign that read, "Welcome Home De La." Another welcome banner hung from an overpass on the outskirts of Greenwood. "It brought tears to my eyes," Beckwith told a reporter.[16]

At 3:15 P.M., Beckwith was delivered to the Leflore County Courthouse in Greenwood, where G. Hite McLean met with Sheriff Pickett to pay Beckwith's bond from the White Citizens' Legal Defense Fund. Additionally, the fund paid the fees for defense attorneys Hardy Lott, Stanny Sanders and Hugh Cunningham, which, Beckwith later told his wife, amounted to an additional $70,000.[17] A bevy of local newspaper reporters and photographers descended on the courthouse to record the historic moment. From the courthouse, Beckwith called Willie at the Hotel Greenwood Leflore. "I'll be over there in just a minute," he told her. "We have to tend to this bond business and sign a few papers, and I'll be right along." Beckwith's friends planned an impromptu celebration dinner in his honor that evening at one of Greenwood's finest restaurants. Willie was excluded from the event.[18]

"His real friends, the Citizens' Council people, didn't know whose side I was on," she said. She believed she was not invited to the celebration because the organizers sensed her ambivalence. "I didn't even know he was coming back that day," she said. "I stayed in my hotel room until he came. They called me from downstairs and told me he was down there, and he came up to the room." Beckwith made at least one important stop on the way to the hotel. "When he came back that day," Willie said, "he had already bought a new car for Little De La." It was a new Pontiac GTO with a chrome engine, purchased on the way home.

Beckwith had big ideas about all he was going to be able to accomplish with money coming in from contributors. From jail, he had frequently written Willie with ideas about business ventures he wanted to explore and places he wanted to go. He had promised his family a trip when he was "acquitted"—perhaps to the Bahamas or Mexico or Europe, using leftover funds. When the acquittal did not materialize, neither did the foreign trip.[19] Instead, one of Beckwith's most ardent supporters offered to pay for a brief vacation in Biloxi on the Gulf Coast, so that he and Willie could spend some time together before he returned to work at Delta Liquid Plant Food. Willie remembered the trip vividly.

"We left Little De La at the hotel and went on to Biloxi," she said. "We drank and fought all the time we were down there. He was real hard to get along with when he came out of jail. Just the least little thing set him off." Their earliest arguments centered around Willie's drinking, Beckwith's continued violence and the home he had promised to buy her. "I had told him that I was going to leave him," she said. "I wasn't even going to go through another divorce—I was just going to move away. But he said he'd paid his dues, and that he was going to buy me another home and we could start over."

Within the first few days of his return, he acquired a fifty-two-foot trailer—an "instant villa," he called it—and bought lot number six in Rebel Court Trailer Park on West Park Avenue in Greenwood. "It was degrading to me, to live in a trailer," Willie said, acknowledging that it was indicative of a dramatic change in her husband. "He would never have thought of living in a trailer, had he not come down to that level. He always thought he was too good for it." Willie believes the trailer cost about $5,000, but said she was never certain whether her husband paid for it with contributions or from the sale of the house on George Street. It is also possible that the trailer was a gift from Klansman Bernard Akin, a friend of Beckwith's who owned Akin's Mobile Homes on Highway 80 just outside Meridian, which was a well-known gathering place for Klansmen.[20] Although the Beckwiths were settled into their new home by the second week of May, Willie grew increasingly resentful, and her alcohol abuse escalated.

Beckwith's renewed friendships in Greenwood also troubled Willie, who saw her husband sliding down the small town's social ladder. Especially troubling to Willie was her husband's friendship with Gordon Lackey. During the ten months Beckwith was incarcerated, Lackey's mother frequently fed Little De La at her cafe in Greenwood, and Lackey had visited Beckwith in jail on several occasions.[21] Willie particularly disliked Lackey, and he may have sensed her hatred. He once told Beckwith, "Why don't you kill that woman? She's just a damn drunk."[22]

It also still bothered Willie that Beckwith always seemed to have his hand out, as though the people of Mississippi owed him something for the time he spent behind bars. "He was still taking contributions, and sometimes people would just give him money and presents," Willie said. "It always embarrassed me, just like it embarrassed me to live in a trailer after I'd had nice homes. And it embarrassed me when we used to go out after that and people wanted to buy us drinks at the Travelodge. After the trials, we went there lots, and people in the bar would send over drinks for him and me both." Sometimes, well-wishers offered more than just drinks or cash. "One time, a man came up to me on the street and said, 'Honey, you tell De La if he needs another rifle, I'll personally go out and buy him one.' "

As Beckwith began traveling the Delta again, selling fertilizer for Delta Liquid Plant Food Company, civil rights activists expressed their bitter disappointment with the outcome of his second trial. At a speaking engagement in Indiana, James Meredith characterized the two trials as "phony," and said they were merely efforts by the state to "get back some of its image." He predicted that a black would probably assassinate Beckwith within six months. "How long can a nation survive with a dual system of justice?" Meredith asked. "No white man in the history of the United States has ever been punished justly for killing a Negro in Mississippi."[23] In Jackson, Charles Evers applauded the jurors who held out for conviction and made a personal appeal to both blacks and whites. "Please do not resort to violence in any form against Beckwith or anyone else, because Medgar nor I would want you to do so, but instead keep moving in a nonviolent way for justice and equality for all Mississippians regardless to race, creed, or color without malice or hatred in our hearts."[24]

Charles Evers's statement belied his true feelings, which were more in line with Meredith's prediction that Beckwith would face vigilante justice at the hands of angry blacks. Evers was so embittered over his brother's death and Beckwith's subsequent mistrials that at one point he would have murdered Beckwith if their paths had crossed. "Just like that. I would have broke his dirty, slimy neck," Evers told *Playboy* interviewer Eric Norden. Even three decades later, Charles Evers remembered his all-consuming hatred for Beckwith, asserting "I would have killed him. Point blank." For a time he reconsidered the idea of forming a Mississippi Mau Mau such as he and Medgar had earlier envisioned, and he even began storing arms and ammunition toward that end. His plan was to shoot, stab and poison the most rabid racists in each Mississippi county, one at a time. So overwhelming was his hunger for "white folks' blood," he said, that "just killing the man who murdered Medgar wouldn't have been enough."[25]

If Charles Evers loathed Beckwith, the feeling was mutual. On a copy of a news article about Evers, Beckwith wrote, ". . . it seems somebody killed de wrong nigger! Ha!"[26] Both De La Beckwith and Charles Evers clung to their bitterness. Evers passionately told a crowd in New Jersey two years after Beckwith's second mistrial, "It's time to start killing." Citing thirty-two unsolved civil rights deaths in Mississippi following his brother's murder, Evers said the FBI and the Justice Department had "no intention of bringing justice" to his brother's murderers. He called for black violence to counter the ongoing vigilantism against blacks in the South. "I will do all I have to do so that Medgar is avenged," he told a captive audience. "We'll have to lay and wait for them at night, and fight with them all day. No Negroes are free until all Negroes are free. No one can free us but ourselves."[27] Evers's call for violence was a descant to the crescendo of Klan violence that was spreading throughout Mississippi like a cancerous growth.

In Gordon Lackey's cramped trailer, just a few doors down from Beckwith's shiny new "instant villa," a robed Klansman stood stoically before Beckwith. "I will require from you at this point a solemn promise, upon your word of honor, that regardless whether or not you decide to join this order at this time, you will hold all of the information and facts and circumstances that you learn here absolutely secret and *never* reveal them to anyone, at any time, in any way."[28] Lackey's familiar voice emanated from beneath the white hood as he read the words of the initiation ceremony of the White Knights of the Ku Klux Klan of Mississippi, bound in a blue folder.

Beckwith took his vow. Although for ten years he had devoted his energy to the Citizens' Council and its work, when it became clear the Council's machinations and economic sanctions were not forceful enough to halt black progress, he turned to the Ku Klux Klan for more direct action than the Council would tolerate. Three months before the formal organization of the White Knights of the Ku Klux Klan in February of 1964, Beckwith boasted to his correspondents, from jail, that the Klan was active again in Mississippi and that he had already been invited to join.[29] Now Beckwith was making his affiliation with the White Knights of the Ku Klux Klan official. Lackey explained the tenets of the organization: secrecy and Christian militancy. "We do not accept Papists," Lackey said, "because they confess and bow to a Roman dictator in violation of the First Commandment, and the American spirit of liberty. We do not accept Jews, because they reject Christ, and are actually at the root center of what we call Communism. We do not accept Negroes, Orientals and people of other races foreign to the Anglo-Saxon culture, and we do not deign to explain that." Beckwith nodded. He understood. He was asked a series of questions, to which he responded with an emphatic, "Yes, sir."

Finally, with his right hand raised and his left hand solemnly placed over his heart, Beckwith repeated the Oath of Allegiance to the White Knights of the Ku Klux Klan of Mississippi. "I, Byron De La Beckwith, consciously, willingly and soberly, standing in the presence of Almighty God and these mysterious Klansmen, do hereby pledge, swear and dedicate my mind, my heart and my body to the Holy Cause of preserving Christian Civilization, the Dignity and Integrity of the Holy Writ, and the Constitution of the United States of America as originally written. I swear that I will preserve, protect and defend the Constitution of the White Knights of the Ku Klux Klan of Mississippi and obey the laws enacted thereunder, and the lawful orders of the Officers of the Klan.

"I swear that I will wholeheartedly embrace the spirit of Christian Militancy which is the basic philosophy of this Order, and I swear that I will pray for daily guidance to help me determine my proper balance between the humble and the militant approach to my problems, in order that my arms shall always remain as Instruments of Justice in the Hands of Almighty God, and not become tools of my own vengeance. I swear that I will constantly and continuously prepare myself physically, morally, mentally and spiritually, in order that I may become an increasingly useful instrument in the hands of Almighty God, and that His will be done through me, as a part of His divine purpose. I swear that I will remain constantly alert to the satanic force of evil, which is and shall remain my eternal enemy, and I swear that I will oppose and expose this force at every opportunity, in Klonclave and in life. I swear that I will offer the utmost of both my physical courage and my moral courage, which may require the sacrifice both of bodily comfort in combat with the enemy, and also the sacrifice of my ego and prestige in daily life.

"I hereby dedicate my being not only to combat Satan, but, God willing, to the triumph over his malignant forces and agents here on earth. Not only will I die in order to preserve Christian Civilization, but I will live and labor mightily to live for the spirit of Christ in all men. I swear that I will cleave to my brethren in this Order, and their families above all others, and will defend and protect them against all of our enemies, both foreign and domestic. I swear that I will never be the cause of a breach of secrecy, or any other act which may be detrimental to the integrity of The White Knights of the Ku Klux Klan of Mississippi. All of these things I do swear to do, and I will daily beseech God, my Creator and Savior, that I may be granted the strength, the ability and the grace that I may be eminently successful in my performance of this sacred obligation. I do hereby bind myself to this oath unto my grave, so help me Almighty God."[30]

Kneeling on his right knee, Beckwith looked up at Lackey, who lightly anointed him four times with dedication fluid, signifying body, mind, spirit and life. After a brief prayer, the small group of men in the trailer unmasked themselves and welcomed Beckwith to their order. According to custom, his Klan application was destroyed after he was formally initiated—"naturalized," in "Klanguage"—and paid his ten-dollar "Klectoken" fee. With the formal ceremony completed, Beckwith must have felt slightly disappointed. There was no fiery cross and no throng of Klansmen to welcome him into their midst, and the ceremony itself had been notable for its lack of pomp. Even so, Byron De La Beckwith, the perpetual joiner, finally found an organization worthy of his time, talents and energy.

For a decade, Citizens' Council leaders in Mississippi had credited themselves with keeping the Ku Klux Klan out of the state by providing a more legitimate vehicle through which to fight integration. With blacks in Mississippi demonstrating, marching and holding sit-ins with increasing frequency, however, in late 1963 and early 1964, a Louisiana Klan—the Original Knights of the Ku Klux Klan—began recruiting members in Mississippi. In February 1964, 200 former members of the Mississippi realm of the Original Knights of Louisiana founded a splinter group, the White Knights of the Ku Klux Klan of Mississippi. By April, the White Knights were operating under the aegis of Imperial Wizard Sam Holloway Bowers, Jr. of Laurel, Mississippi.[31]

Like Beckwith, Bowers was also a World War II veteran. He briefly attended Tulane University and the University of Southern California, and later returned to his hometown of Laurel, Mississippi, and became a partner in Sambo Amusement Company, a wryly named jukebox and vending machine company. Bowers had a swastika fetish and was an avid collector of firearms and explosives. Although many who knew him have described him as intelligent, articulate and charismatic, he was also a man with unusual proclivities. He was once seen giving a clipped Nazi salute to his dog. Robert Larson, whom Bowers met at USC, was both his roommate and partner in Sambo Amusement.[32]

One of Bowers's first Klan initiatives was an eerie show of solidarity with Beckwith during his second trial. At about 11:00 P.M. on April 10, while local police were changing shifts, ten crosses burned in and around Jackson. The next morning, as testimony in the trial began, approximately seventy-five burly white men, some of whom were suspected Klansmen, filled the courtroom early to keep blacks out. Beckwith was touched by the show of Klan support, noting in a letter to Willie that the men stood in his honor as he entered the courtroom and remained standing until he had taken his place at the defense table.[33] He was deeply moved by the gesture, and commented that his lawyers had told him it was without precedent.

As another sign of solidarity with Beckwith, the Klan sanctioned a statewide cross-burning to celebrate his second mistrial later that month. Bowers's grandiose plan was to burn a cross on every county courthouse lawn in Mississippi. His men succeeded in sixty-four of Mississippi's eighty-two counties, and blacks and whites alike shuddered at the Klan's apparent strength in the state.[34] Although his friends in the Citizens' Council had come to his financial rescue by founding the defense fund immediately after his arrest, Beckwith increasingly saw that the Klan was placing its support squarely behind him. The White Knights were willing to take whatever steps were necessary to maintain segregation, and Beckwith recognized the group's collective willingness to get its hands dirty. The Citizens' Council, in his estimation, accomplished too little, too late.

Sam Bowers initially recruited his Klansmen from Laurel and the surrounding area, and they were traditionally at the bottom of the social ladder in the community. Most were uneducated, with poor-paying blue-collar jobs, not the kind of folk Beckwith had previously felt were of his family's stature.[35] The gas station attendant, the logger who cut pulpwood, the tenant farmer—these were the men who comprised the rank and file of Bowers's White Knights of the Ku Klux Klan of Mississippi. Word of the group's militant stance quickly spread into other Mississippi counties, however, and many Mississippians were pleased to find that the White Knights were no mere "bedsheet brotherhood," like other Klan organizations that held public public cross-burnings as a recruiting tool or launched women's auxiliaries to hold fund-raising bake sales. The White Knights organization differed strongly from other Klans. The White Knights' constitution restricted the group to the state of Mississippi, while other Klans hoped to develop into national organizations. With two parliamentary bodies, a "Klanburgess" and a "Klonvocation," the White Knights assumed the posture of a democratic organization even though it was operated in a military manner with Bowers all-powerful at its helm. And while other Klans adopted the rituals and language of the original Ku Klux Klan founded in Pulaski, Tennessee, the White Knights established its own nomenclature and ritual, designed to make it truly mysterious to "aliens," or outsiders.

The White Knights bore Bowers's strong religious imprimatur. He fashioned the group as a "Christian militant" organization. "As Christians," Bowers wrote, "we are disposed to kindness, generosity, affection and humility in our dealings with others. As militants, we are disposed to the use of physical force against our enemies." Different factions of the Klan had, in the preceding century, proven their anti-black and anti-Catholic bents. Bowers's White Knights brought a strong anti-Semitism to the fore. "We do not accept Jews," a recruiting brochure explained, "because they reject Christ, and, through the machinations of their International Banking Cartel, are at the root-center of what we call 'communism' today. We do not accept Papists, because they bow to a Roman dictator, in direct violation of the First Commandment, and the true American Spirit of Responsible, Individual Liberty."[36] Bowers also propounded the teachings of Dr. Wesley Swift, a California minister whose written and taped sermons were Beckwith's introduction to the theology of the Christian Identity Movement. The Christian Identity doctrine teaches that whites comprise the Lost Tribes of Israel, and that blacks and Jews are the literal offspring of Satan.

While all Klansmen affiliated with the White Knights subscribed to Bowers's "Militant Christianity," very few possessed the religious fervor Beckwith exhibited. He immersed himself in Swift's tapes, and referred frequently to the minister's printed sermons for guidance. For the first time since his falling out with the Episcopal church, Beckwith felt he had a sense of divine purpose, and the Klan's use of religious argument to justify white supremacy aligned perfectly with Beckwith's own thinking.[37] Other racist groups also began to gravitate toward the Christian Identity movement in the mid-1960s. The National States' Rights Party, another fanatically anti-Semitic group, also subscribed to Swift's theology.

Bowers believed in 1964 that a race war was imminent. He urged his followers to prepare for the battle by burying half their arms and ammunition to protect against confiscation by the authorities when the race war began. Each Klan unit drew detailed road maps of its area, which were frequently employed when acts of violence were committed by volunteer Klansmen from another county, or "province." Not only were weapons and ammunition to be accumulated and stored—squads were to be drilled; counterattack maps, plans and information were to be studied and learned; and radio and other communications were to be established.[38] Bowers wanted to take no chances that his men would be caught off guard, and his writings were essentially manuals for Klan terrorism.

He also taught his White Knights collectively to threaten their enemies socially, economically and physically. He explained that, when used effectively, propaganda alone could disturb the enemy even more than murder. "This is our sacred task," he wrote. "If our enemies can be humiliated and driven out of the community by propaganda, well enough. If they continue to resist, they must be physically destroyed before they can damage our Christian Civilization further, and destroy us." Occasionally, on his own publication masthead for *The Klan-Ledger*, Bowers shrewdly used the same type font as Mississippi's staunchly segregationist newspaper, *The Clarion-Ledger*. Such subtle touches were indicative of Bowers's attention to detail and the high value he placed on his organization's subversive materials. If an enemy could not be destroyed socially or economically, the next course of action was to destroy him physically. While propaganda and intimidation could be handled at the local "Klavern" level, more serious acts, such as "exterminations," had to be personally approved by the Imperial Wizard.[39]

With Bowers's Christian militance concept firmly taking root among his followers, Klansmen were pressed to read guerilla warfare manuals such as Virgil Ney's *Notes on Guerilla Warfare*, and were trained to build booby traps, bombs, Molotov cocktails and other incendiary devices. Klan terrorists were as well armed as any legitimate fighting force, with arsenals that included automatic rifles, hand grenades, Thompson submachine guns, mortars, bazookas, rifles and shotguns, dynamite and other explosives, and large quantities of ammunition. Bombings were a favorite ploy of Bowers's because when properly carried out, a well-made bomb would destroy itself and leave no traceable evidence.[40] Individually, the White Knights were instructed in judo and karate, and they practiced their firearms skills with rifle and pistol practice sessions. They were encouraged to volunteer to serve as deputies on their local law enforcement agencies, although they were frequently reminded that their Klan oath took precedence over any other oath they might take to uphold the law.[41] Infiltrating police departments, county sheriff's offices and the highway patrol was Bowers's insurance policy that his Klansmen would be able to maintain some level of "legitimate" control over outside civil rights activists and their local collaborators.

Bowers encouraged his most devoted followers to form secondary groups to take "extremely swift and violent" action when necessary. The men comprising these "hit and run" groups were to act for not more than an hour, and were directed to travel as far away from the scene of conflict as possible within two hours after their attack. "The action of this secondary group must be very swift and very forceful with no holds barred," one of Bowers's Imperial Executive Orders directed.[42]

Bowers's most powerful weapon, however, was secrecy. Unlike many other Klan organizations, none of the White Knights admitted their membership—under penalty of death for identifying another Klansman or revealing Klan secrets—and the White Knights eschewed the public rallies and cross-burnings other Klan organizations used to grandstand and recruit members. If a Klansman breached his vow of secrecy, he faced not only expulsion but death. One Klansman who had broken from the group and was believed to be an informant to local law enforcement agencies was found dead close to his home near Meadville, Mississippi, in 1965. His cause of death was listed as heart failure, but an examination of the body showed welts from the top of his head to the bottoms of his feet. A gash in his face was so deep that the roof of his mouth was exposed, and his head had been bashed in.[43] The White Knights, writer Nicholas Von Hoffman noted, were "truly secret and truly dangerous," and even the group's leaders denied their links to the organization.[44] Bowers's Klansmen occasionally planned cross-burnings merely as a show of their strength throughout the state—as they had with Beckwith's second mistrial. Their ends, however, were far more serious, as the nation was to discover with the 1964 murders of Andrew Goodman, Michael Schwerner and James Chaney, three civil rights workers who were shot and buried in an earthen dam in Neshoba County. The White Knights intended to stop the integration movement and were willing to kill to do it.[45]

Shrewdly, Bowers ordered his Klansmen to follow the "Need to Know" rule, which he outlined in one of his most revealing documents.[46] He was so concerned about breaches of security that he told his men, ". . . no officer nor member should have any information that he does not absolutely have to have in order to perform his duty. No member should feel 'left out' because he is denied such information. Instead, every member should strive to avoid knowing anything that he does not need to know. Modern techniques of drugs, hypnotism and brain manipulation have made it impossible for any man to withhold information under capture. Our only defense against this is that a man cannot tell what he does not know." Bowers also provided directions for carrying out individual attacks against civil rights leaders. "Any personal attacks on the enemy should be carefully planned to include *only* the leaders and prime white collaborators of the enemy forces. These attacks against these selected, individual targets should, of course, be as severe as circumstances and conditions will permit."[47]

At its zenith in 1964, the White Knights boasted a total of 6,000 active, and violent, members. During Bowers's three-year reign of terror in Mississippi, he authorized more than 300 acts of violence, including bombings and burnings of homes and churches, kidnappings, assaults and murders.[48] If Beckwith respected Citizens' Council founder Bob Patterson for his idealism, he truly found a new hero in Sam Bowers, who proved more than willing to take action against the perceived enemies of Mississippi. Beckwith had long since grown restless with the Citizens' Council's ruminations over the integration problem—sanctions and reprisals that sounded good on the surface but ultimately proved ineffective. Beckwith craved action, and he had already proven his willingness to pay the price with his personal freedom.

As Beckwith saw it, with Medgar Evers safely in his grave at Arlington National Cemetery and his own freedom finally restored, he could focus on the Klan's aggressive methods of exacerbating Mississippi's racial ills. If Beckwith murdered Evers in a vain attempt to stop integration, as District Attorney William Waller had asserted, he both succeeded and failed. The bullet that ended Evers's life halted the Jackson movement temporarily, but it also made Evers far more famous and powerful in death than he had been while alive, and created a national symbol for the civil rights movement.[49] Although the Jackson movement had lost its most vocal proponent—and its impetus—Medgar Evers's murder created a martyr, foreshadowing the effect that Dr. Martin Luther King, Jr.'s assassination would have five years later.

Delmar Dennis, a former Klan "Titan" who reported directly to Imperial Wizard Bowers while working for the FBI as an informant, acknowledged that it would have been characteristic of Bowers to launch his Klan with an act such as the "extermination" of Medgar Evers. Klan killings were seldom random or ill-planned. "In the case of the White Knights, it was more likely that they would focus on an individual and decide in their minds that they were justified in taking his life," Dennis said in an interview. "They would identify him as the enemy, think of themselves as being soldiers in a war, and therefore, it was all right to kill him."[50] Through his letters and activities, Beckwith had long positioned himself as a soldier in the war against integration, and now, with additional troops in the form of the White Knights, he was no longer waging war alone. If Beckwith carried out Medgar Evers's execution with the Klan leadership's approval, it was a textbook murder: "carefully planned" and "as severe as circumstances and conditions" would permit. Mississippi's most powerful proponent of integration was felled by a single sniper shot, there were no witnesses, and the killer had not been convicted. From the perspective of the Klan's Imperial Wizard, it was a flawless execution.

Beckwith's participation in Klan activities came at a critical time. During the ten months he was in jail, violence against blacks and white moderates, throughout Mississippi and the South, had grown in direct proportion to increases in voter registration activities, boycotts and civil rights demonstrations. Some groups, such as the Citizens' Council, continued to use economic leverage to intimidate blacks and white moderates. "Whites have been driven out of town, subjected to cross-burnings, and destroyed economically, for any show of sympathy to the Negro cause," civil rights worker Bill Hodes wrote his parents from Greenwood. "It is just as dangerous for the Southern white, maybe more dangerous, to show sympathy for the Negro cause as it is for Northern whites to come down here and work with the Negroes."[51]

Local Mississippi politicians were equally unyielding, and wielded even greater power. In Greenville, the Washington County Board of Supervisors refused government surplus commodities because, in the words of one newspaper, "the program would probably benefit primarily Negroes, and landowners are said to feel they would have more difficulty in getting spring labor if commodities were not cut off in March."[52] Still, by the spring of 1964, civil rights workers and blacks in Mississippi seemed more hopeful. The largest civil rights project to date, Freedom Summer,[53] was planned for the coming months, and with its sizeable black population and lengthy history of resistance, Leflore County would prove pivotal to the success of the program.

As with other white supremacists in Greenwood, Beckwith was not about to allow his hometown to succumb to integration during Freedom Summer without a fight. He was horrified by the toehold civil rights workers had made there during his ten months in jail. The phrase "Freedom Summer" quickly became an epithet on the lips of Mississippi's segregationists, and the White Knights of the Ku Klux Klan redoubled its recruitment and propaganda efforts. Cross-burnings—although never commonplace, even in Mississippi—became more frequent, the crosses glowing like a necklace of hate that stretched across the state. In the spring, three crosses were burned on the lawn of the Leflore County Courthouse the night before a major black voter registration effort was to begin. The following day, more than 200 blacks tried to register, but were thwarted by noxious vapors from a chemical substance that had been placed on radiators throughout the building. The fumes halted the day's efforts, and only sixty blacks took the required registration test. The tests were notorious among blacks throughout Mississippi, overtly designed to keep blacks from registering. "There are no right answers for people of the wrong color," Nicholas Von Hoffman wrote that summer.[54]

The state legislature was also doing its part to create legal barriers to the summer program, introducing more than three dozen bills to thwart the efforts of the volunteers, who were viewed as "outside agitators." An anti-leafleting law, a curfew law, an anti-summer project bill designed to prohibit entry into the state, and a bill allowing the courts to treat juveniles arrested in civil rights cases as adults were all introduced. Legislators also tried unsuccessfully to revoke the charter of Tougaloo College and yank its accreditation. Lieutenant Governor Carroll Gartin called the black college "a cancerous growth," and said it was a haven for "queers, quirks, political agitators and possibly some communists."[55]

To test the anti-picketing ordinance passed by the legislature, civil rights workers in Greenwood declared Freedom Day on July 16, 1964. The workers assembled a large group of blacks and marched to the Leflore County Courthouse in an attempt to register to vote. The workers carried picket signs denouncing interference with voter registration, and fully expected to face repercussions. Approximately one hundred young people were arrested that day, and most stayed in jail until the following Monday.[56]

Meanwhile, Beckwith had brought his own macabre humor to the streets of Greenwood. He frequently rode through the black section of town at night in a police car as an auxiliary policeman. Armed with his own billy club and pistol, he flaunted his association with the local police force, and how friends on the force had provided his alibi in the Evers murder. The Greenwood Police Department's implicit support of Beckwith was not unusual. Throughout the state, as racial tension and violence grew at an alarming rate, local police were frequently implicated in encouraging or participating in the violence.[57]

Many of the summer volunteers in Greenwood harbored a personal resentment against Beckwith—living and struggling, as they were, under his watchful gaze. It was ironic that even as Beckwith tried to harass and intimidate them, he owed them a debt of gratitude. Their very presence in Mississippi helped postpone a potential third murder trial which would have been called on Monday, July 13, 1964. The FBI's Special Agent in Charge of the New Orleans office advised J. Edgar Hoover that the prosecution would not attempt to try Beckwith again until at least October 1964. "Due to the reported influx of college students into Mississippi in connection with racial matters during coming summer," the agent wrote Hoover, "they do not feel it is advisable to try the case during summer, as these college students in attendance at [the] trial might create difficulties in Jackson."[58]

FBI agents in Greenwood, who were already overworked because of the growing number of young volunteers, also scrambled to keep tabs on Beckwith's travels and his growing firearms collection. Less than a month after his second mistrial, he had approached several gun traders attempting to acquire used .45 caliber pistols, which he described as "throwaways." By early June, he had also acquired a 7mm Mauser rifle and a .38 caliber revolver, and was trying to trade for an inexpensive .22 caliber rifle. At least one of the men with whom Beckwith traded guns later met with FBI agents and told them of Beckwith's specific firearms needs, on the condition that his identity be protected. When notified of Beckwith's growing storehouse of arms, J. Edgar Hoover shot back an Airtel communication to the heads of both the Memphis and New Orleans offices, instructing them to notify Greenwood police, who probably laughed the information off, as well as the Jackson Police Department and other state authorities. Ironically, Hoover's behest to his men was dated June 12, 1964—exactly a year after Medgar Evers's murder. He further instructed his men to report any future Beckwith firearms purchases to the NAACP—perhaps fearing Beckwith might target another of the organization's leaders for assassination.[59]

Freedom Summer signaled a critical shift in black attitudes about their rights under the law. Volunteers, most of whom were students from northern college campuses, spent the summer in Mississippi trying to persuade blacks to register to vote and teaching them the basic skills necessary to pass the voter examinations.[60] At the program's root were three efforts: Freedom Schools, through which blacks learned basic literacy skills as well as their constitutional rights; Freedom Vote, a mock election through which blacks learned the election process and cast mock ballots; and the Mississippi Freedom Democratic Party, a move designed to show that blacks desired to participate in the political process. The new party ultimately created a stir at the Democratic National Convention held in Atlantic City that August, when it attempted to unseat Mississippi's all-white delegation.

National attention focused on Mississippi that summer not only because Freedom Summer volunteers were pouring into the state to lead voter registration drives and teach at freedom schools, but because three young civil rights workers disappeared in June. Mississippi Highway Patrolmen, FBI agents and more than 400 sailors from a nearby Naval air station searched the murky waters of the Bogue Chitto swamp under a sweltering sun, hoping to find the bodies. U.S. Assistant Attorney General Burke Marshall traveled to Mississippi during the first week in June, and was stunned by the blatant increase in Klan activity and by the FBI's relative inability to counter it. The day after Marshall returned to Washington, Attorney General Robert F. Kennedy wrote President Johnson, "I told you in our meeting yesterday that I considered the situation in Mississippi to be very dangerous. Nothing in the reports I have seen since then changes my view on that point."[61]

In the search for the missing workers, several mutilated bodies were found in a nearby river, but proved to be none of the three who were officially missing. The bodies of James Chaney, Andrew Goodman and Michael Schwerner were found buried in an earthen dam in August 1964, a month and a half after their disappearance. The workers were victims of a triple murder planned and executed by members of the White Knights of the Ku Klux Klan of Mississippi. Delmar Dennis remembered Imperial Wizard Sam Bowers's reaction to the murders: "He was gleeful," Dennis said in an interview. "He said it was the first time that Christians had planned and carried out the execution of a Jew." Both Goodman and Schwerner were Jewish.

Although the FBI had not had an official presence in Jackson since World War II, J. Edgar Hoover quickly laid the groundwork for a new field office there to meet the growing need. On July 10 and 11, he visited the state capitol to meet with public officials and, with considerable fanfare and publicity, opened the new Jackson FBI office. The opening was critically important, and Hoover positioned himself in the most favorable light. He sent an eight-page "briefing" to President Johnson immediately following his visit, along with a healthy swatch of press clippings. Mississippi Governor Paul Johnson seemed cooperative, asking Hoover's permission to train five additional officials of the Highway Patrol at the FBI National Academy. Hoover, pleased with the governor's apparent willingness to cooperate, offered to place the prospective trainees in the upcoming August class. "Governor Johnson was most outspoken in deploring the violence which had occurred in his state," Hoover informed the president.

"He emphasized that as long as he sat in the Governor's chair, ignorance, hatred and prejudice would not take over in his state."[62]

Hoover then agreed to meet for thirty minutes with Charles Evers. "Mr. Evers stated he sometimes becomes discouraged, particularly because of the constant threats on his life," Hoover wrote. "I told him that while I could understand his feelings, he must expect some degree of personal danger—particularly in view of his position of leadership during an era of turbulent social upheaval. I mentioned the numerous threats to my life over the years, mostly from the lunatic fringe. I again suggested to Mr. Evers the necessity of keeping in constant contact with local law enforcement authorities and told him that now the FBI has opened a field office in Jackson to keep in touch with Special Agent in Charge Roy K. Moore."

Evers complained to Hoover that neither Jackson Mayor Allen Thompson nor Mississippi Governor Paul Johnson would meet with him, and Hoover suggested he continue his attempts and that he also get in touch with former Florida Governor LeRoy Collins, who was appointed by President Johnson to spearhead the new federal Community Relations Service. "I told Mr. Evers that along with his position of aggressive leadership went a responsibility for the truth and observance of all laws," Hoover wrote the President. "I specifically made the point that the FBI had solved the murder of his brother at great cost and sacrifice, yet we had never hesitated in our quest for solution. I added that despite this hard-earned success, a number of Mr. Evers's followers, both before and after the solution of the murder, had unjustly criticized the FBI. I told him that such tactics are divisive and do nothing to resolve the troublesome issues confronting the American people today. Mr. Evers denied that he or Mrs. Medgar Evers had ever criticized the FBI."[63] Despite a new and fully staffed Jackson field office of the FBI, complete with Hoover's fanfare, the state's tally sheet on violence looked worse than ever the following fall. By October, fifteen additional murders, four woundings, thirty-seven church bombings or burnings, and more than a thousand arrests were recorded.[64]

With Freedom Summer underway, one of Greenwood's local black youths was inciting riot in the small town by integrating the Leflore Theater, a local movie house. Silas McGhee, a lanky twenty-one-year-old, spent much of the month of July trying to see movies at the previously "whites only" theater. Because of President Johnson's recently passed Civil Rights Act, McGhee knew he should be allowed to enter and sit where he wanted. On his first visit on July 5, McGhee was repeatedly harassed by whites in the theater, and after he protested to the theater manager and returned to his seat, he was beaten and kicked by a large group of whites in the auditorium. When McGhee reported the incident to police, they asked, "Who put you up to this?" McGhee replied, "I only wanted to see a movie." The same week, he went to the Leflore County Courthouse to try to register to vote. "Three men in a pickup truck got me and took me to a garage and beat me up," McGhee said. The men, armed with a length of pipe and a thick plank, abducted McGhee at gunpoint and beat him badly. Beckwith took a position outside the theater, determined to do his part to keep it segregated by picketing and shining his flashlight in patrons' eyes as they left the darkened theater.[65]

To make McGhee a singular example to local blacks, as well as to the Freedom Summer volunteers, his family's home was fired on. Violence against him escalated dramatically in August. The week after a freedom school play, based on the life and death of Medgar Evers, was performed in Meridian, McGhee was shot in the face by a white man in a passing car outside Lulu's Restaurant on H Street in Greenwood. A bullet entered through the left side of his face, near his temple, and lodged near the left side of his throat. He was rushed to University Hospital in Jackson in critical condition. Two SNCC workers were refused into the hospital with McGhee because they were shirtless; they had used their shirts to try to stop his profuse bleeding.

Several hundred blacks gathered at Friendship Baptist Church in Greenwood to protest the shooting. Greenwood policemen, wearing full riot gear and armed with tear gas, blocked the street housing the SNCC headquarters until the crowd dispersed. McGhee's family also suffered violent retribution. Three days after the shooting, his younger brother Jake was arrested for a traffic violation, and when his mother, Laura, went to pay his fine she was hit in the chest by a police officer. She struck back at the officer, who pulled his gun on her. Jake McGhee was fined and a warrant was issued for his mother's arrest for assaulting an officer.[66] The threats and attacks lasted more than a year. Employing a common Klan tactic, the perpetrators later tossed eleven crudely constructed bombs at the McGhee house in an attempt to burn it to the ground. The bombs, made from quart beer bottles filled with gasoline, were lit by rag wicks and then hurled at the house.[67]

The more aggressively Freedom Summer volunteers fought to register black voters and teach in freedom schools in Greenwood, the more Beckwith distanced himself from his family. "He got to staying out," Willie remembered, "and he'd tell me they were going to have some kind of meeting and he wouldn't be back for awhile. I never thought about the Klan at that time. All I thought about was maybe it was the Citizens' Council." She began to worry more frequently about Beckwith's friends, as well. "He was running with hoodlums and everything. Low-class people," she said. "But he would say, well, they had a cause."

Although she suspected he was involved with the Ku Klux Klan, she never saw any proof of his association with the White Knights. She seldom even questioned his whereabouts. "When he was out working, I never knew where he was," she said. "He was all over the Delta." She knew, however, that he was still attending meetings, but assumed they were Citizens' Council gatherings. "De La never told me he belonged to the Klan while we were married," Willie said, although she acknowledged that he later admitted his Klan membership in letters to her.[68] Beckwith's violence at home abated for a brief time after he and Willie reconciled and moved into the trailer. It wasn't long, however, before his sexual frustrations again led to wife abuse. Two months after Beckwith's release from jail, Willie underwent an anterior-posterior vaginal repair operation at Greenwood Leflore Hospital.[69] Willie had complained to her husband that sex was painful, but he seemed to believe she was just withholding sex from him, as she sometimes had in the past. Willie recalled that Beckwith went so far as to accompany her to the doctor's office. "He told Dr. Carroll, 'If you've got to keep working on her, just go ahead and take everything out,' and he wanted the doctor to give me a hysterectomy. And Dr. Carroll said, 'De La, you just don't take everything out of people who have a little problem. This is just a normal thing that happens sometimes.' "

Although he was placated temporarily, his impotence also resurfaced when he and Willie resumed having sex. "It just infuriated him," Willie said. "It made him mad at himself and mad at me, because there was just nothing I could do, no amount of persuasion, that would help him. When he began to beat me again, I knew I was leaving for good." Psychologists point out that physical abuse is not uncommon with some men when impotency occurs, as if the act of the beating serves as a poor substitute for sex itself. Both Beckwith and Willie had quickly reneged on their mutual agreement to start a new life. Beckwith's violence at home escalated in direct proportion to his increased Klan activity, and although he often tried to take his frustrations out on the dog instead of hitting Willie (he once flung the dog out the door of the trailer and broke its leg) he continued to abuse her verbally and physically. Willie had promised to stop drinking, yet her alcoholism became uncontrollable after she moved into the trailer with her husband. She said things when she was drunk that she would never have said to her husband while she was sober.

"I called him a murderer to his face," she said. "He just grinned at me." She was convinced after the first trial that her husband was Medgar Evers's killer. "Until the trial, I really thought that maybe they were just blaming this on him, because of all of his letters to the papers and everything," she said. "I'd think, how could he treat us like he does, and say he loves us, and do something like this, knowing how it would affect us? But after the trial, I was convinced." In drunken fits of rage, Willie taunted her husband, asking, "Did you kill him? Did you?" She used the question as a weapon. "He'd just scream at me, 'He's *dead,* ain't he?' I can't understand why he didn't just kill me then. But I know it crossed his mind, and it crossed mine, too. Toward the last, when he'd abused me so badly and I couldn't see my way clear, I thought about waiting until he went to sleep and hitting him in the head with a hammer. Those thoughts went through my mind."

By the fall of 1964, the Beckwith name was again making headlines, but this time it was Byron De La Beckwith, Jr., who was in the news. Little De La and three of his teenage friends, Joe Boolos, Jr., his brother James Boolos and Frank Caperton, Jr., were arrested for stealing and killing a hog for a pig roast. Willie explained how differently her husband reacted to the incident when someone on the street mentioned the incident.

"De La was sort of like, 'Oh, boys will be boys, and we've taken care of everything.' " But at home, Beckwith was furious with his son. "I remember him yelling at Little De La, 'If you're going to kill something, kill something important,' " Willie recalled. He was angrier to see the Beckwith name in the newspapers under another dark cloud, she said, than he was that his son had broken the law. According to the Cattle and Theft Bureau of the Mississippi Highway Patrol, a witness saw the four teenagers kill the hog at a farm outside Greenwood. They were arrested and charged with grand larceny, but the case was resolved quietly when the boys' parents agreed to provide restitution to the hog's owner.[70]

At home, Little De La grew more protective of his mother. "I remember once, De La and I had been fighting," Willie said, "and Little De La came into the trailer and told his father, 'If I come home again and find her crying, and you tell me you haven't done anything to her, I'll take you outside and deal with you myself.' " It was no idle threat. By his senior year in high school, Little De La was an inch taller than his father and carried an additional twenty pounds on a broader frame. With several years at Chamberlain Hunt Academy behind him, he was entertaining thoughts of enlisting in the Marine Corps. Even with her son's temporary intervention, Willie still feared her husband. "I've always been scared of him, really and truly," she said. "I'm scared of him now. Right today. I've often wondered why something didn't happen to me, why I didn't just turn up dead somewhere."

On August 8, 1965, Beckwith was appointed "Kleagle," or organizer, in the White Knights of the Ku Klux Klan of Mississippi. All Kleagles were appointed by Imperial Wizard Sam Bowers, according to the doctrine set forth in the Klan's constitution, and their responsibilities included helping expand the Klan in Mississippi. According to Section Six of the Constitution of the White Knights of the Sovereign Realm of Mississippi, "No Kleagle, Officer or Klansman in any capacity shall ever attempt to recruit an alien for membership into the Klan who is a Negro, Jew or papist, nor shall any alien who is cohabiting with or married to, by common law or pagan ways, a Negro, Jew or Papist ever be allowed membership in the Klan." The Klan also refused membership to non-U.S. citizens and professed atheists. Section Nine stated that Kleagles would scout into new areas and "contact prospective Christian militant aliens [non-Klansmen] for membership in a careful and judicious manner using maximum possible secrecy, after being commissioned for this work by the Imperial Wizard."[71]

During his three years working within the Klan for the FBI, Klan Titan Delmar Dennis met Beckwith on several occasions and heard him address Klan rallies as the featured speaker.[72] Dennis was also present at the August Klan meeting near the Pearl River at which Beckwith was appointed a Klan officer. "Beckwith was a recruiting man," Dennis said. "He was out getting members all over the state." Dennis believed that because of Beckwith's fame as Medgar Evers's accused assassin, he was handpicked by Bowers to bring new members into the White Knights fold.

"It was at a time when Klansmen were being trained in bombing techniques and how to burn churches and that kind of thing," Dennis said. "And he was the hero of the hour, because the Klan *believed* that he had killed Evers—that's not to say that he did, but they surely *thought* that he did. So he came in as inspirational or motivational speaker for the group, and it was at that time that he talked about the need to kill the enemy from the top down." In the book *Klandestine*, which recounts Dennis's years within the Klan, Beckwith is quoted as telling his audience, "Killing that nigger gave me no more inner discomfort than our wives endure when they give birth to our children. We ask them to do that for us. We should do just as much. So, let's get in there and kill those enemies, including the President, from the top down!"[73]

Although Beckwith had not mentioned Evers by name when he talked about "killing that nigger," Dennis knew it was an important admission. "He said, 'I've not been through any more problems or suffered any more pain than your wives do to have babies for you,' which we took to mean, 'Hey, I haven't suffered very much for what I did.' But he never said 'I killed Medgar Evers.' We *assumed* that, because that's why he was the speaker. There was not a Klansman in Mississippi who did not believe that he killed Medgar Evers." After the meeting, he approached Beckwith, who was surrounded by Klansmen, and asked for his autograph. "Certainly," Beckwith replied, signing a slip of paper with a flourish and handing it back to him. Dennis noted the date on the slip of paper and showed it to his FBI contacts when he filed his report about the meeting.

The August 8 meeting was not, however, the first time an FBI informant came forward with information that Beckwith had admitted committing Evers's murder.

Tom Van Riper, then a special agent of the FBI, was one of Dennis's two initial primary contacts. He remembered Dennis's report of the August 8 meeting and Beckwith's appointment as Kleagle, and said that additional informants within the Klan came forward with corroborating stories about that evening's events and Beckwith's remarks. "Beckwith really looked up to Bowers," Van Riper said. "Bowers was very big on having a covey of people like Beckwith that he could depend on—that was very important to him. And in turn, I think it was very important to satisfy Beckwith's ego to curry favor with Bowers. I don't know whether Beckwith emulated Bowers with the intent of being recognized by Bowers, or possibly with the idea in mind of eventually taking over from him. But we had gotten reports that Beckwith was bragging about killing Evers within days after the murder occurred. He seemed to like to talk about it."

Beckwith's own FBI files reveal that several different sources who attended the August 8 meeting filed slightly different reports, although each noted Beckwith's remarks to the assembled Klansmen and recounted his advocacy of violence. A separate informant reported that during his talk, Beckwith had advocated Klan infiltration of youth groups, labor unions and civil rights groups. At the same meeting, a bill was introduced to allow youths under twenty-one years of age into the White Knights to assist in infiltration, but the proposal was defeated. The informant also reported that Beckwith spoke earlier that day at a meeting of the "upper house" of the White Knights, and described Beckwith as "very nervous and a very poor speaker. He did not have any subject and spoke briefly on his war record. He did not talk about anyone but himself." Beckwith also spoke to sixty-four Klansmen at a guarded province meeting held in a rural area in Leflore County later that month.[74]

By the end of the summer in 1965, Willie Beckwith had moved out of the trailer she had shared with her husband and son for slightly more than a year. Beckwith had grown increasingly secretive and abusive, and he frequently attended night meetings after he made his daily sales calls. His unexplained time away from home contributed to her drinking problem. Willie took her clothes and stayed for several months with a friend, Pauline Woods, a secretary at Delta Liquid Plant Food Company. "I never intended to get another divorce," Willie said. "I just intended to leave and get as far as I could get, even though De La and I were still married." Once, in Greenwood to visit Little De La, who was working in a gas station, a man approached Willie and said, "Ma'am, I'm sorry to do this, but . . ." When it dawned on Willie that the man was serving divorce papers on her, she touched his arm lightly and said, "Mister, if I'd known you had these, I'd have come looking for *you.*" That Beckwith was suing her for divorce had a temporary calming effect on her. "I figured if he finally got a divorce himself, maybe he'd finally be satisfied that our marriage was through, and maybe he'd finally quit coming after me to remarry him."

Beckwith's divorce complaint stated, "That during recent years, the defendant has begun to drink intoxicating liquor to excess; that she has drunk more and more heavily as the months have passed, and is now so addicted to alcohol that she becomes drunk with great frequency; that when she becomes intoxicated, she stays in a drunken state for prolonged periods, frequently requiring hospitalization to return her to sobriety; that when she is intoxicated, she is unreasonable, inconsiderate, and reckless in her conduct, and is entirely incapable of performing any of her marital obligations to complainant; that when she is under the influence of intoxicants, she gets profane and obscene and curses complainant in front of their son and others."[75] The complaint then pointed out that Willie had shot at her husband, and that in the months prior to the divorce, she had become so violent "that defendant and others have had on many occasions to confine her in jail until her reason was restored."

Willie did not contest the divorce. She told her husband that he would have to move out of the trailer, as she intended to sell it and use the money to leave Mississippi. In September 1965, the Beckwiths were divorced for the third and final time. "He tried to divorce me on the grounds of habitual drunkenness and habitual cruel and inhuman treatment," Willie said, "but my lawyer, Norman Brewer, told De La that either his lawyers would strike it from the record or we would bring up his violence against me." Since Beckwith's wife abuse had constituted Willie's grounds for the two prior divorces, the phrase "on the grounds of habitual drunkenness and habitual cruel and inhuman treatment" was stricken from the official record. Even as the divorce he initiated was being finalized, Beckwith lost control in the courtroom. "He went crazy and jumped up at the hearing," Willie remembered, "and he screamed, 'I don't care what anybody says, she'll be my wife no matter what! She's still my wife!' "

Their teenaged son was given the option of remaining with his father in Greenwood or leaving with his mother. He chose to stay with his father rather than uproot himself and leave his friends behind. It was a decision that deeply hurt Willie Beckwith. Because Little De La was still a minor, however, Willie was named his legal guardian, and oversaw a guardianship of almost $10,000 for him until his twenty-first birthday.[76] When the guardianship was resolved and her son received the money, Willie was officially discharged as his legal guardian.

Willie moved the trailer to Monticello, Arkansas, where her friends

Doug and Mildred Merck had a home and some land. She lived alone in the trailer briefly while she tried to find a buyer for it, but much of the time she stayed in the trailer drunk, refusing to come out. Taking the trailer, her red Impala, her clothes and her dog, Willie left behind her wrecked marriage and her eighteen-year-old son. The Mercks tried to help Willie as much as possible, but her drinking placed a tremendous strain on them. After a particularly debilitating binge of Willie's, Mildred Merck had to be hospitalized for several days.[77] Suffering from exhaustion, she was forced by her doctor to rest after she cleaned Willie's car and trailer of dog droppings and whiskey bottles, and washed, dried, folded and ironed nine loads of Willie's dirty laundry.

When a buyer for the trailer materialized, Willie pulled herself together. "He offered me three thousand dollars," Willie said, "and I made him give it to me in cash. I wouldn't even take a cashier's check." The buyer did not know the trailer had been Byron De La Beckwith's, but Willie took him through it again to point out a few idiosyncrasies. "There was a little vent over the stove that had a chain on it, like a bathtub stopper chain," Willie remembered. "It kept slipping through there, and I made De La fix it. So he put an empty shell casing on to hold it, and when I took the man through the trailer, I told him that was one of De La Beckwith's shells, and that it was a little something extra that came with the trailer. He was mortified." With cash in hand, Willie headed north.

"When De La divorced me, I washed my hands of everything," she said, if one can ever "wash one's hands" of such a significant relationship. "I went as far as I could go, and worked as long as I could, and all that time I was hoping nobody would ever know who I was, or that I'd been married to De La." She legally changed her name before leaving Mississippi, reclaiming her maiden name, Mary Louise Williams.[78] It was her way of having the last word—a final retort to Byron De La Beckwith. It was also an affirmation of her new self. "It's really bothered him more than anything for me to change my name," she said. "It's hurt his ego. But I'm not married to him, so I refuse to carry his name. The Beckwith name was always an embarrassment to me."

Although in each of her three marriages to Beckwith she had worn the same wedding rings, when she went through Knoxville to visit her family, she sold her diamonds, her mountings and her wedding band. "It hurt me to move away," she said. "It's hurt me all my life to be moving from place to place and really have no home." Willie believed—perhaps naively, that she could leave her husband and the scars of their failed marriages behind her in Mississippi. Yet even decades later, she was resentful. "De La won," she contended. "Because what he wanted to do was keep Little De La from me, he hated me so much. So he's the winner, not me. Because he's got the family. Not me."

11

A Period of Self-Delusion

Family—or more accurately, the trappings of family, such as the fancy surname, the bold coat of arms, the distinguished bloodline—were all important to Byron De La Beckwith. His ancestry, or at least his presumed ancestry, was always his greatest source of pride. Never mind that his father was a drunkard and a debtor; the Beckwiths were reportedly descended from a lineage that stretched back through history to the Norman conquest. His mother was an emotionally unstable widow, but she was a Yerger, the daughter of a proud Confederate cavalry private. It was precisely this heritage Beckwith fought to protect for his descendants. Nonetheless, during his decade-long war against integration, Beckwith lost sight of his flesh-and-blood family. He embarrassed them with his public rantings, and he tried unsuccessfully, on repeated occasions, to beat his wife into submission. His true legacy—violence and abuse—resonated louder than the chiseled inscriptions on his family's crumbling tombstones.

For a short time after their final divorce, Beckwith thought that he and Willie would reunite, as invariably they had in the past. She was weak, he believed. Her drinking was a sure sign of it, as was her past willingness to reconcile with him after their tempers had cooled. Inevitably, his florid apologies and cajoling and promises of new homes, new lives, would win her back. This divorce proved otherwise.

Even before Beckwith fully realized that he had driven the final wedge between himself and Willie, their son was making plans of his own. Perhaps frustrated at his parents' inability to resolve their marital differences, or just plain fed up with their mutual mistreatment of each other, Little De La enlisted in the U.S. Marine Corps just three weeks after his parents' third divorce became final.

Like his father before him, Little De La's military school background was undistinguished, and when he shipped off to boot camp at Camp Lejeune, North Carolina, his enlisted rank was private. His military career was short-lived. He served only six months of active duty, winning a Rifle

Sharpshooter Badge before returning to Mississippi to fulfill his enlistment obligation in the U.S. Marine Corps Reserve.[1] Unlike his father, who had been shot off his amtrac at Tarawa, Little De La saw no foreign soil and performed no heroic feats.

For Beckwith, the months between the divorce and Little De La's return home from Camp Lejeune were wearying ones. When Willie sold the trailer, he moved to 1206 Magnolia Street in Greenwood and set up housekeeping as a bachelor.[2] With Little De La gone and Uncle Will dead, it was the first time he had truly lived alone. He had never cooked for himself, or kept house, or washed his own clothes. Mamie or the Marine Corps or Willie had always taken care of such tasks. That fall, at a time when most families come together to celebrate the blessings they share, Beckwith faced a bleak Thanksgiving season. He had little for which to be thankful. His marriage had disintegrated, his only son had joined the armed services, and he was left alone in an unfamiliar new apartment. To add to his misery, the FBI was trailing him closely, investigating a report that he had torn up a voter registration sign in the Greenwood post office early in the month.

During the afternoon of November 6, 1965, the Federal Voting Registrar on duty in the Federal Examiners Office in Greenwood was interviewing two potential female voter applicants. A sign taped outside the basement-level office said, "Voting Office Opened Saturday Only," written in red ink on white poster board. A civil rights worker with the Mississippi Freedom Democratic Party, who was standing at the top of the stairway near the office, later told an FBI agent he heard a man's voice coming from a doorway downstairs. According to the worker, one man said, "What is that sign doing there? They shouldn't be putting signs on public property!" Beckwith was identified by two people who claimed they saw him holding, then dropping, the pieces of the torn sign. Neither witness actually saw Beckwith rip the sign, although a black post office employee was standing near Beckwith at the time of the incident and undoubtedly saw what happened. When he was interviewed by the FBI, the worker refused to furnish any information, perhaps out of fear of retribution.[3]

The allegation, although seemingly petty, was a serious one—President Lyndon Johnson had signed into law the Voting Rights Act of 1965 on August 6, exactly three months before. The act authorized federal examiners to supersede blatantly racist regulations and local registrars in counties such as Leflore, where less than half the adults voted in the 1964 presidential election, and where biased tests were routinely administered to blacks attempting to register to vote. Bypassing local FBI agents stationed in Greenwood, someone notified the Civil Service Commission, and a worker there called the U.S. Justice Department's Civil Rights Division to report the incident. Almost immediately, J. Edgar Hoover sent an

Airtel communication to Special Agent in Charge Roy K. Moore in Jackson, whose nickname was "The Smiling Assassin." Hoover asked for a complete investigation and noted that it had been requested specifically by Assistant Attorney General John Doar of the Justice Department's Civil Rights Division. Hoover wanted the pieces of the sign immediately forwarded to the Bureau's Latent Fingerprint Section for an examination. If any latent prints surfaced, he specifically wanted them compared to Beckwith's fingerprints, FBI file number 541216E. Hoover also asked his agents to ensure the Federal Examiners Office in Greenwood was under federal jurisdiction. Hoover hoped to nail Beckwith not only on charges of violating the Voting Rights Act, but also on charges of Crime Against Government Reservation and Destruction of Government Property. Beckwith was Hoover's only suspect.[4]

Although a number of people in both Greenwood and Jackson had handled the five pieces of the torn sign, no latent fingerprints were developed. Hoover demanded an investigation and pressed Moore on the issue, sending him three separate Airtels asking that he quickly submit a full report. When an FBI agent approached Beckwith in the street and inquired about the torn sign, he refused to talk.[5] A separate report was filed with the Bureau on January 10, although no new evidence against him had been uncovered.[6] Although he was still under indictment for murder, and the new charges against him would have been serious federal charges, Beckwith shrugged off the investigation. The FBI's "harassment" was a new constant in his life, something to which he grudgingly became accustomed.

Far more unnerving to Beckwith was a subpoena served him on November 19, requiring his appearance at the January 1966 hearings of the House Committee on Un-American Activities. In the aftermath of the Chaney, Goodman and Schwerner murders in Neshoba County and the national attention that focused on Klan vigilantism throughout the South, the Committee launched a full-scale investigation of the many Ku Klux Klan organizations in the United States.[7] Even though most people involved in the civil rights movement felt a federal investigation of criminal violence in the South was long overdue, some organizations and individuals adamantly believed the House Committee was the wrong agency to conduct the investigation. Claiming the Committee had, throughout its history, "centered its attack on the very same people the Klan has attacked—people working to bring about justice and implementation of our democracy," the Southern Conference Education Fund (SCEF) mounted a futile attack on the Committee. "It is very difficult for us to believe that a group with this history can possibly conduct an investigation that will go beyond the surface of violence, which will probe to the depths and uncover all of those responsible for the acts of terror in the South, and which will reveal such findings without fear or favor," a Fund press announcement reported. The leaders of SCEF—along with leaders of other organizations—believed partisan politics would sway the Committee's findings. They called on President Johnson to appoint a special commission, comparable to the Warren Commission, which investigated President Kennedy's assassination, to conduct the Klan investigation.[8]

Beckwith's growing involvement with the White Knights and his close relationships with the group's leaders gave him a significantly higher profile than most Klan members enjoyed, and he was known to have spoken before secret Klan gatherings on a number of occasions since his second murder trial. He had also recently acquired a one-tenth interest in *The Southern Review*,[9] a newspaper front for the White Knights. The *Review* was organized by men who comprised the "maximum-effort faction of the white Christian right," as Beckwith referred to his fellow Klansmen, and the publication mirrored the Klan party line.[10] Elmore D. Greaves, the *Review*'s founder and editor, also served as Chairman of the White Christian Protective and Legal Defense Fund, which was also a front organization created and controlled by the White Knights. The fund, ostensibly established to provide defense money for the men accused of the Neshoba triple murders, instead financed the operations of the White Knights of the Ku Klux Klan.[11] Greaves was a close associate of Imperial Wizard Sam Bowers, and it is likely that Bowers encouraged Beckwith to become active with the *Review* as a way to both expand his sphere of influence and, as a Kleagle, help recruit new Klansmen. Bowers encouraged others close to him, including Delmar Dennis, to participate in the *Review* and the fund. Dennis wrote for the paper on occasion and was named to the Board of Directors of the fund, a role he accepted at the Imperial Wizard's urging.

Naturally, Beckwith was flattered to be associated with anything that allowed him to rub shoulders with Bowers and, in a characteristically contorted way, he was also flattered to have been called to testify before the House Committee. First, it publicly cemented his place among the leadership of the White Knights, and second, he believed he had a message for the Committee. For years, he had considered himself something of a free-lance investigator of "subversive" activities—following and photographing FBI agents, civil rights activists and local blacks who were participating in demonstrations—and he believed he could shed new light on the "alien forces" which were destroying the country. He claimed to have been engaged in "political investigation" for several years preceding the House Committee's hearings, and felt he had an inside perspective to share with its members. The bitter irony, as Beckwith saw it, was that there existed no more patriotic organization than the White Knights of the Ku Klux Klan of Mississippi. One of the tenets of the group was that it be a pro-American organization that oppose "any thing, person or place that is Un-American."[12] In the collective consciousness of the Klan, it was performing the highest calling of patriotism—ridding the United States of what it perceived to be Communist-inspired civil rights activity and activists.

Beckwith immediately began working on a report he intended to present when called to testify. "The Secret Report," as Beckwith titled it, never saw daylight. Although he worked on it furiously for more than a month, creating a single-spaced, typed document nearly thirty pages in length, he closely guarded its secrecy. His intention was to present the report in its entirety before the Committee, but he discovered there was a rule of procedure requiring him to submit in advance any presentation he planned to make. Curiously, an investigator for the Committee, John Sullivan—a friend of Beckwith's who was also an active Citizens' Council member in Vicksburg, Mississippi—acted as his intermediary and tried to get the rule waived. When members of the House Committee refused, Beckwith interpreted the move as an act of suppression, and he balked. Under no circumstances would he submit it prior to his appearance.

It was an unfortunate turn of events. As the House Committee on Un-American Activities was to learn, almost without exception, the White Knights who were called to testify pled the Fifth Amendment and shed little light on their secret society. In an ironic twist, all the Mississippi Klansmen claimed protection against self-incrimination under the provisions of the Fifth, First, Fourteenth and other amendments to the Constitution—hiding behind the very amendments they refused to acknowledge when they took their Klan oath to uphold the U.S. Constitution "as originally written." During the House Committee's morning session in Washington on January 12, 1966, Beckwith listened intently as his close friend Gordon Lackey was intensively questioned about a number of specific events that had been reported to Committee investigators by informants. Had Lackey discussed blowing up the Greenwood headquarters of the Student Nonviolent Coordinating Committee, a project that was abandoned because FBI agents were believed to be nearby? Had he participated in a meeting at the Heidelberg Hotel in Jackson at which the White Christian Protective and Legal Defense Fund was established to raise funds for Bowers and the other Klansmen indicted in the Neshoba triple murders? Had he recruited Byron De La Beckwith into the Klan? Had he, along with Beckwith and John Winstead, painted a black stripe around a house in Greenwood because "the wrong nigger" had freshly painted it? Had he applied to the Federal Communications Commission for a citizens band radio license for use in Klan activities? Calmly and repeatedly, Lackey claimed protection under one or more amendments, as he had been instructed to do.

That afternoon, following a recess in the proceedings, Beckwith sat at the same witness table flanked by attorneys Travis Buckley, highly regarded as the Klan's premier lawyer because he personally represented Imperial Wizard Bowers, and Charles Blackwell. Although he answered cursory questions about his background, military service and employment, Beckwith refused to answer potentially incriminating questions regarding whether he knew or was recruited into the Klan by Gordon Lackey; whether he was a member of the Klan; whether he had been appointed a Kleagle; whether he had knowledge of the firebombing incident involving Laura McGhee's house in Greenwood; and whether he, Lackey and Winstead had painted a black band around the house in Greenwood. Chief Investigator Donald T. Appell asked Beckwith, "In the early morning hours of March 5, 1965, eleven quart beer bottles filled with gasoline, with rags held into them by two-inch machine bolts, were thrown at the property of Laura McGhee in Greenwood. Do you possess any knowledge of that, sir?" Beckwith leaned into the microphone to answer the question in the same manner he answered nearly all the investigator's questions after invoking the Fifth, First and Fourteenth amendments: "Sir, for the reasons previously stated, I respectfully decline to answer that question."[13]

Beckwith was in good company. Sam Bowers and two dozen other officers or members of the White Knights also invoked the protection of numerous constitutional amendments to keep from incriminating themselves. Bowers would not even answer questions about when and where he was born, his educational background, or whether he and Robert Larson, his roommate, owned Sambo Amusement Company. Although he was questioned at great length, Bowers refused to answer any of the questions posed to him. At one point, Chief Investigator Appell asked him, "As Imperial Wizard of the White Knights of the Ku Klux Klan of Mississippi, did you ever authorize the extermination or elimination of a human being?" The question hit hard. Appell continued quickly, "You seem shocked by that question. Why don't you say 'no' under oath?" Bowers quickly composed himself and gave his stock reply: "Sir, for the reasons previously stated, I respectfully decline to answer that question."[14]

The Committee's investigation revealed, among other things, the White Knights' collective paranoia. Committee investigators discovered that Bowers believed African troops were being landed in Cuba for extensive military training, and that these troops would be landed at Gulfport, Mississippi, to lead an invasion of the United States. Bowers further believed that Defense Secretary Robert McNamara would nationalize the Mississippi National Guard and turn the Southern states over to blacks, relocating whites to the North. The Imperial Wizard's claims of an imminent race war reinforced his assertion that the Klan should build up its storehouse of buried arms and ammunition. The House Committee ascertained that in Bowers's mind, he and his White Knights would be the only men to fight the invasion; if the South was to remain a white bastion, he and his men would be responsible for protecting and preserving it. He instructed his Klansmen to conduct "projects" in each province, to scatter FBI agents throughout the state and distract them.[15] For the first time, the White Knights' project tiers were laid out for public view. Project One included threatening telephone calls or personal visits by Klansmen; Project Two was a cross-burning, usually held on private property as a form of direct harassment; Project Three included beatings, burning or shooting into someone's property, or bombing; Project Four was extermination—murder. Such atrocities were generally conceived and executed by selected groups of trusted Klansmen. They worked in tandem, and their activities were not known to other members.[16]

Although common sense might have dictated calling a temporary moratorium on projects in light of the government's Klan investigations, Bowers and his men moved with calm self-assurance. A Project Three (the firebombing of NAACP leader Vernon Dahmer's home) went awry just two days before a number of members of the White Knights appeared before the House Committee. Dahmer, president of the Hattiesburg, Mississippi, NAACP branch, died of burns resulting from the bombing. The case was under investigation by federal authorities when members of the White Knights, including Imperial Wizard Bowers, were questioned by the House Committee. Like Medgar Evers, Vernon Dahmer's life had been threatened so frequently that he and his wife, Ellie, slept in shifts to keep guard. Dahmer had been refused life insurance. "I reckon he was a poor risk," his wife said in an interview. Bowers was arrested and, although never convicted, charged in connection with Dahmer's death the month following his appearance before the House Committee. During the subsequent trial, Bowers's mother contacted Dahmer's widow to explain that her son was incapable of such an act, even though the Imperial Wizard had admitted planning the attack with Delmar Dennis. Dennis immediately turned the information over to his contacts in the FBI.[17] The attack had been carefully planned and executed, following Bowers's approved procedure. His group was a "nocturnal organization," Bowers wrote, reminding his men, "We must avoid the streets, and we must avoid the daylight."[18] If there were any questions about the Imperial Wizard's proclivities for weapons and violence, they were put to rest when police searching his home on March 28 uncovered an arsenal of high-powered weapons, including a submachine gun, revolvers, ammunition, knives, machetes and Klan ephemera. Bowers also owned an impressive collection of masks and disguises, including a gorilla mask, a John F. Kennedy mask and—reflecting the Klan's latest target group—a "Jew" mask with an exaggerated, bulbous nose.[19]

When murder was not yet warranted, the White Knights took particular delight in harassing their enemies with childish tricks. Bowers taught Klansmen to use everything from roofing nails and itching powder to mad dogs and snakes to take enemies by surprise. "He liked to teach different tactics for different cases," said Delmar Dennis. "Some of it, he put in writing. For example, if you have a white, liberal educator in the community who's generally well thought of, Sam wouldn't advocate that you go out and shoot him. You would put ten pounds of roofing nails in his driveway so that when he backs out in the morning he has four flat tires before he gets to work. Or you call him every fifteen minutes all night long to wake him up—harass him with any means at your disposal, something that would be mild enough that if you got caught there wouldn't be much penalty for it, and yet you were causing a tremendous amount of anxiety and fear on the part of the victim. And a lot of that was done."

After thirty-seven days of public hearings and the testimony of almost 200 witnesses, the Committee on Un-American Activities believed it had laid bare the souls of the disparate Klan organizations across the United States. Still, Beckwith believed he might be able to shed additional light on the Klan by publishing "The Secret Report" and going public with its contents. He discussed its publication as a booklet with Elmore Greaves, who wrote a brief introduction for it, comparing it to Thomas Paine's *Common Sense* and commenting that its publication might cost Beckwith his life because of its revelations about the Ku Klux Klan. After the penetrating questioning House Committee Chief Investigator Donald Appell directed against him during the hearings, Beckwith added a preface to the report in which he counterattacked Appell, calling him a "hireling." Beckwith placed the responsibility for suppression of his report squarely on Appell's shoulders.[20] Whatever their original intent, Greaves and Beckwith eventually decided against publishing the report, and it languished.

If "The Secret Report" made its way to Bowers for review or approval, which is not only possible, but probable, it is likely that Bowers personally placed it on the back burner. Although the report did not strip away "the secrecy and hocus-pocus" or allow readers a glimpse into the "inner mysteries which are behind the white hoods and fiery crosses," as Greaves wrote in his introduction, it did set forth some incendiary theses. Beckwith posited that the civil rights struggle was a Communist plot carried out by "irresponsible malcontents" who were hell-bent on destroying the United States by first destroying states' rights—clearly drawing from materials circulated by both the Citizens' Council and the White Knights. "Any society in which the Negro is truly and independently a first class citizen," he asserted, "is a society in which savagery and cannibalism are recognized institutions." He rambled aimlessly through his report, attacking the media, claiming that blacks and whites in the South had peacefully lived together for a hundred years and comparing the work of the Ku Klux Klan to that of the early Christians.[21]

Far more important, Beckwith's report chronicled an important shift in Klan ideology which was finding increasing favor among Bowers's White Knights. The root problem, Beckwith revealed, was Jews, allusively referred to as "The Synagogue of Satan." He attacked Jews viciously as "monstrous and malignant almost beyond the grasp of human comprehension," and editorialized about the ongoing fight against Jews worldwide. "This is where Hitler failed," Beckwith wrote, adding that Hitler had given in to his hatred, executed a few hundred ghetto dwellers, and "permitted the real masters of the Synagogue of Satan to capture and destroy his party, his country and himself."

Apparently believing the fabricated conspiracy theory set forth in the *Protocols of the Learned Elders of Zion*, Beckwith propagated the myth that Jews managed an international financial cartel and had wrested control of both the Federal Reserve System and the news media. He asserted that Jews were "a supernatural aggregation of devil-worshippers" who controlled international banking, and he later referred to them as "an age-old cult" of murderous priests "whose ambitious lusts impel them to seek absolute power in ruling the entire world."[22] Beckwith's fanatical anti-Semitism would only grow during the coming decades.

Beckwith was increasingly swayed by the religious teachings of Dr. Wesley A. Swift, the charismatic minister of the Church of Jesus Christ, Christian—as opposed to Jesus Christ, Jew—which Swift founded in 1946. In his sermons, Swift interpreted Biblical scripture to support his theses that Jews were the literal offspring of Satan, and that God's "chosen people," Caucasians, were to serve as God's "battle-axe and weapons of war to destroy the powers of darkness and the forces of evil," blacks and Jews.[23] Swift's teachings provided the religious underpinnings for other racist groups, including J.B. Stoner's National States Rights Party and Robert DePugh's Minutemen. After Swift's death in October 1970, his church evolved into the group Aryan Nations.

In later years, Beckwith propounded the theory that Jews instigated even the House Committee hearings investigating the Ku Klux Klan, which he believed "only succeeded in scratching the surface" of the White Knights. Any findings the Committee uncovered, he blamed on informants.[24] Even during the hearings, the Klan could not be restrained. More than a hundred crosses burned throughout Mississippi as a protest to the hearings, during which seven Klan leaders were cited for contempt.[25] At the close of the hearings, Congressman John H. Buchanan, Jr., of Alabama said of the Klan, "Their record seems clearly one of moral bankruptcy and of staggering hypocrisy,"and Congressman Joe R. Pool of Texas said theirs was "a record of hatred, a record of double-dealing, of quarreling and fighting over spoils, of leaders deceiving followers, a record that no real American could be proud of."[26] Although there was an initial spate of publicity indicating the Committee's hearings would likely diminish the power and secrecy of the Ku Klux Klan, it is probable that those Klansmen who were still seriously engaged in acts of violence and murder, such as Beckwith's cronies in the White Knights of the Ku Klux Klan of Mississippi, only became more clandestine in their acts and more cautious about observing Bowers's "need to know" rule.

To regain some of the civil rights movement's momentum, in June 1966, James Meredith announced that he would walk more than 200 miles from Memphis to Jackson to spur black voter turnout in the state's upcoming primary election.[27] Ever since he had successfully integrated the University of Mississippi, Meredith had been a target of white hatred in the state. He was shot on the second day of his walk on Highway 51 near Hernando, Mississippi, by an irate Memphian. Other movement leaders, Dr. Martin Luther King, Jr., among them, gathered quickly to continue Meredith's "walk against fear" as a unified civil rights march. The marchers decided to canvass for voter registration in each of the towns they passed through, heightening the already palpable tension between the march's leaders and local police. While King hopscotched back and forth between the march and meetings in other cities, public participation in the march to Jackson grew.

As the march neared the hot, flat cotton country of Greenwood, tensions flared and the number of patrol guards monitoring the march was reduced from twenty officers to four. Singing spirituals and perspiring from the walk, marchers were met by Greenwood officials, who made it clear the marchers were not to pitch their tents, quite literally, on public property. As darkness fell on June 16, marchers boarded buses and rode the short distance into Greenwood proper. Beckwith's friend, Police Commissioner Buff Hammond, arrested Stokely Carmichael, executive secretary of the SNCC, along with two others, Bruce Baines and Robert Smith. They had defied orders not to erect a tent on Greenwood school grounds.[28] After several hours in lock-down, Carmichael, who was familiar in Greenwood, where SNCC had a strong presence, gave an angry, emotional speech in which he used the phrase "black power." It became a unifying theme for the remainder of the march.

The following day, King led nearly 500 marchers through downtown Greenwood to the Leflore County Courthouse. Eight blacks stood guard at the Confederate monument on the courthouse lawn—the same monument for which Beckwith's grandmother had modeled—to keep demonstrators from climbing on it, as they had in another town. Standing in the statue's shadow, King reminded the crowd that Greenwood was Beckwith's hometown, as well as the site of numerous civil rights struggles. A short time later Beckwith appeared in a pickup truck, driving repeatedly past the marchers as they left the city and headed toward Itta Bena. To Beckwith's disappointment, King had already departed for a speaking engagement in nearby Winona. The march brought the most prominent civil rights leaders right into Beckwith's backyard, and he probably wanted them to feel his presence and make them wonder what he was planning. On his own turf, Beckwith knew, he had the advantage. He could intimidate them without ever firing a shot.[29]

Although Meredith was still hospitalized, recovering from his wounds, the march seemed an ideal opportunity for Beckwith to make an appearance. He had been among the first in Greenwood to attempt to join the fray in Oxford when Meredith was finally admitted to the University of Mississippi in 1962, and Meredith believed the FBI had once investigated a report of a Beckwith plan to murder him,[30] nearly a year before Medgar Evers was assassinated. Even without Beckwith's reconnaissance attempts, driving back and forth past the marchers, the temperament in Greenwood was predictably tense. Marchers were squirted with water by a white service station attendant who was hosing down the service area, and they later passed a five-foot-tall burning cross during the march. "That don't scare me," one participant joked, " 'cause it's just a little one." Klansmen burned significantly taller crosses when they meant business.[31]

Had King's movements during the Meredith March been less erratic and better publicized, it is likely he might have met his fatal bullet earlier. While they had most often focused their hatred on targets in their home state of Mississippi, the White Knights reviled King and his ability to use the media to his advantage. King was, after all, doing a far better job than the Klan of swaying public opinion. Former Klan Titan Delmar Dennis remembered a 1965 planning session at which he was asked by Imperial Wizard Sam Bowers whether or not he could find a volunteer sniper to assassinate King as he traveled through Mississippi on a trip unrelated to the Meredith March. Bowers had learned that King would be using a highway between Philadelphia and Meridian, and planned what would have become his most ambitious Project Four. Snipers were to be placed at either end of a bridge along King's route, and would be armed and ready to fire high-powered rifles as his car approached or withdrew. Beneath the bridge, dynamite would be planted as a safeguard, in case the snipers missed their mark. Dennis reported the plan to his FBI contacts, and they made sure King changed his travel route, thwarting the White Knights' attempt on Dr. Martin Luther King, Jr.'s life.[32]

With or without prodding from Sam Bowers, Beckwith had also given King more than just a passing glance—before and after his appearance in Greenwood in June 1966. At a Klan meeting shortly after King's participation in the Meredith March, Beckwith served as a featured speaker and, while advocating violence in general terms, specifically pointed out the need to eliminate King. "Now is the time to start shooting," Beckwith told his fellow Klansmen, "starting with Martin Luther King on down." An informant within the Klan notified his FBI contacts, and the Bureau apprised King of the threat in general terms. Agents neglected to tell King that it was Beckwith who made the threat.[33]

Beckwith's threat against King's life and his escalating participation in the Klan clearly indicated to the FBI that they should continue to keep him under surveillance. A communication from J. Edgar Hoover to the Chief of the Secret Service characterized Beckwith as a "subversive, ultrarightist, racist." Beckwith's closely monitored actions, conduct and statements demonstrated, Hoover said, a "propensity for violence and antipathy toward good order and government."[34] A number of informants on the FBI payroll were reporting on Beckwith with increasing regularity. One report noted that Beckwith had given a number of members of the White Knights the impression of being "a wild man." Beckwith participated in a well-infiltrated Klan meeting at Fayette, Mississippi, and on another occasion talked with two separate Neshoba County FBI informants at a Klan meeting there. One of the informants advised that Beckwith said he was contemplating working full time for *The Southern Review,* and that at any of his appearances at Klan meetings, Beckwith continued to advocate extreme violence and infiltration of civil rights groups.[35]

Although Beckwith would be forever faithful to his oath of secrecy and deny his membership in the White Knights, his presence at secret Klan meetings and rallies was well documented by the FBI. Additionally, copies of FBI reports on Beckwith were not only passing back and forth between the FBI's field offices and headquarters, but were also being sent to the Secret Service, the Office of Naval Intelligence, the Office of Special Investigations and other agencies. Beckwith's movements were so closely monitored that when he checked into the Town and Country Motel in Foley, Alabama, agents were immediately alerted to his presence outside Mississippi. Another Mississippi informant reported on Beckwith's activities and said, "it is expected that he can cause a great deal of trouble in the state." In his continued support of the White Christian Protective and Legal Defense Fund, Beckwith submitted an ad to the Greenwood *Commonwealth* asking for local donations. Just prior to Dr. Martin Luther King, Jr.'s appearance in Greenwood, Beckwith spoke at a fund rally at the fairgrounds in Laurel (Imperial Wizard Sam Bowers' hometown) for the White Christian Protective and Legal Defense Fund.

Nearly 300 people attended the rally, although "rain and wind completely destroyed the decorations on the truck which served as the speakers platform," an informant noted. Beckwith's speech was characteristically violent, calling for the killing of communists. He "urged the small but cheering crowd to start at the top and work down killing them," and said, "the only time to be calm is when you pull the trigger." He said he was ready to do more than he had already done, and referred to himself as a "soldier." Inspired, and enjoying the crowd's undivided attention, Beckwith said that Charles Evers had "overdrawn his account in this world. He has bounced his check but it hasn't caught up with him yet."[36]

Later, in conversation with Klansmen, Beckwith told them he was still selling fertilizer, although he was making plans to be a "better worker in the Klan" than he had been in the past. Later in the month, at a lightly attended Klan meeting held in a wooded area near Monticello, Mississippi, Beckwith announced a special meeting that would be held on July 28 at the Crown Room of the King Edward Hotel in Jackson to discuss ways of building the advertising and circulation of *The Southern Review.* He said he would be working for the newspaper on a full-time basis, traveling throughout Mississippi attempting to increase circulation.[37] His stature and importance within the Klan were growing, and he believed his affiliation with the *Review* might buoy its advertising sales and popular support. It would also lay the groundwork for his impending foray into politics. Although he had not yet made an announcement, Beckwith intended to enter the political arena and believed his relationship with the newspaper would increase his visibility across the state as a political candidate.

In July of 1966, a full three years after Medgar Evers's murder, FBI agents became privy to a report that was to become the most significant and most closely guarded information about Beckwith since his arrest for Evers's murder in June of 1963. Recounting a conversation between two other men and himself, a reliable FBI informant told agents about a meeting at a lakeside clubhouse. One of the other men talked openly about participating in the planning of Medgar Evers's murder. Although the FBI's files protect the names of the informant and the other two men involved in the conversation, they carefully document the conversation itself. "[One man] stated that he and Beckwith made two or three trips to the residence in order to determine [Evers's] actions and activities and to make necessary plans. In each instance they used a white or light colored Valiant, which was also used on the night of the shooting. [The man] stated he and Beckwith were hiding in some bushes near Evers's home and shot him when he returned to his residence late one night. [The man] stated, 'They got the wrong man. Beckwith did not do the shooting.' "[38]

It might have been during those "two or three trips" to find Evers's home that the witnesses who later testified in the murder trial saw either Beckwith or his white Valiant with its distinctive whip antenna. Beckwith was identified at the bus station in Jackson by the two taxi drivers who later testified in the murder trial that Beckwith had approached them asking for directions to Evers's home. Also, several witnesses claimed during the trial to have seen Beckwith's car in the Evers neighborhood prior to the murder.

The FBI informant reported that Beckwith and the other man involved in the murder quickly left the scene of the shooting, but became separated while running back to the Valiant. Beckwith started to come out of the bushes in which they had been hiding, but saw someone coming—most likely the strolling couple, Betty Coley and Kenneth Adcock, who also testified at the murder trials—and jumped back into the brush. Beckwith then ran to his automobile and drove away from the scene, picking up his partner some distance from the bushes in which they had hidden.[39]

The conundrum was an obvious one: With only three people present during the conversation, any FBI attempt to directly question Beckwith's alleged partner in the Evers murder would immediately reveal the identity of the informant, whose continued work within the Klan for the FBI was important. FBI Assistant Director Alex Rosen noted in a memo that this particular informant had made a dozen reports offering valuable information about Klan officials, members and sympathizers. The information about Beckwith's alleged partner was so closely guarded that even District Attorney William Waller, who could have reopened the murder investigation or prosecution with what was clearly new and important evidence, was not initially notified.[40] Aside from the new evidence being clearly material evidence that would have undoubtedly reopened the Evers murder case, the participation of one or more other people in the murder would have buttressed a federal civil rights violation charge, which would have allowed the *federal* government to bring Beckwith and his partner to trial. Beckwith's earlier trials had been based on the state's murder charge.

J. Edgar Hoover quickly took a personal interest in this plot twist. He had, after all, taken credit on behalf of the FBI for having "solved" Evers's murder. In a firmly worded Airtel directed to Special Agent in Charge of the Jackson office, Roy K. Moore, Hoover wrote, "In view of the importance of this case and the importance of the information furnished by the informant, it is felt that every effort should be made to induce him to become a willing witness for the state." Hoover demanded that Moore personally interview the informant to try to strong-arm him into cooperating.[41] When agents began to pressure the informant to become a witness, he said he "loved life," and that no amount of money could make him change his mind. Although the informant refused to testify "under any circumstances," Hoover sent agents back to question him again in an attempt to wear down his resistance.[42] Again, the man refused, and the FBI was at an impasse in the case. Beckwith was blithely unaware of the tales that were circulating among agents of the FBI, and he had for the most part put the Evers murder behind him. He was already working on the draft of his announcement as a candidate for lieutenant governor of Mississippi, the state's second highest office. If there was any state in the Union in which a Klansman could be elected to high public office,

Beckwith believed, it was Mississippi. And there was, in his own mind, no more qualified individual than Byron De La Beckwith to help Mississippi reclaim its "states rights" heritage and combat the civil rights strides he believed were about to destroy the state.

On January 16, 1967, Beckwith moved into the Tanglewood Apartments at 411 Roseneath Street in Jackson, just miles from the driveway on Guynes Street where Medgar Evers had been killed. Managing his political campaign, he knew, was best handled in Jackson rather than in Greenwood. On his new mailbox, he taped a piece of paper that read:

Byron De La Beckwith, Sr.
Byron De La Beckwith, Jr.
The Southern Review

FBI agents in Jackson were tipped off to Beckwith's move by a local official of the NAACP. Tracking his movements, they went to the Wortman and Mann realty agency, which managed the apartment complex, and copied his rental application, which showed that he had moved into Apartment C after signing a six-month lease at $120 per month. Beckwith had listed *The Southern Review* as his employer since July of 1966. As the newspaper's field representative, he was being paid $500 per month, plus expenses. "Beckwith has numerous weapons stored in his apartment," an FBI memo stated.[43] Agents made note of his car, a 1966 beige four-door Chevrolet bearing 1967 Mississippi license plate number H23168, and disseminated the information to agents throughout the South.

After agents put out the word that they wanted information about Beckwith from their vast network of Klan informants, one informant told his FBI contacts that Beckwith had been mentioned by Jones County Klansmen as "a member" who would be willing to come to Jones County "to do killing for the Klan." As the FBI suspected, Beckwith's role as field representative for the *Review* also allowed him to use his position as Kleagle to recruit new members for the Klan. The informant told agents that Beckwith carried a .45 caliber pistol in a special pocket on the end of his briefcase, and said he had been traveling in the Delta soliciting members for the White Knights. He addressed a special "fellowship meeting" at Byram, Mississippi, and encouraged Klansmen to buy subscriptions to the *Review.* On a separate visit to Ripley, Mississippi, to discuss the organization of a Klan unit there, Beckwith spoke before a group of Klansmen at the Patrician Motel in nearby Ferriday, Louisiana. In and around Laurel, Mississippi, Beckwith was hawking subscriptions and introducing himself as "the man who went to jail for shooting Medgar Evers."[44]

On Valentine's Day, 1967, Beckwith announced to the press that he would run for lieutenant governor of Mississippi. Candidates for governor and lieutenant governor ran separately, so he was not affiliated with another candidate, but he made it clear he was "a candidate whose political position has already been established." In his formal announcement, Beckwith said, "I wish to express my heartfelt gratitude to the fine Christian people of Mississippi for the manner in which they have sustained and sheltered me in times past," alluding to the public support he and his defense fund had enjoyed during his murder trials. "It is as a popular candidate that I will campaign," he continued, "and it is as a popular official that I will serve. The people of Mississippi will determine their proper choice. Now is the time for all good men to come to the aid of their country. Let us all be of good heart and firm resolution to contend for what is right and remember always that with the help of Almighty God, all right things are possible."[45]

Ironically, Beckwith's former prosecutor, William Waller, was running separately for governor, and some believed Waller's dogged prosecution of Beckwith during the Evers murder trials would garner him a significant number of black votes, as a sign of appreciation. Waller had, after all, taken a particularly unpopular stand in prosecuting Beckwith twice. Former Governor Ross Barnett, who created such a stir when he visited Beckwith in the courtroom during his first murder trial, was also seeking re-election after a term out of office. When Barnett was asked whether he would depend on the support of the Ku Klux Klan in his campaign, he coyly replied, "What Klan?"[46] Beckwith was far less coy, admitting that he would accept not only Klan support, but all right wing support. It was rumored that Beckwith even approached Barnett to help finance his own campaign, allegedly asking his former ally for $20,000. Barnett reportedly laughed at Beckwith, and told him, "If I had twenty thousand dollars, I'd use it on my own campaign."[47]

Beckwith met with newsmen on February 15 after filing his qualifying papers with the Secretary of State's office, and—again true to his oath of secrecy—said he was not a member of the Klan, although he characterized it as a patriotic organization along the lines of the Daughters of the American Revolution or the Sons of Confederate Veterans. Many of Beckwith's public rallies following his entry in the race were sponsored by the Klan and its front organization, the White Christian Protective and Legal Defense Fund. Asked about the effect of the publicity surrounding his murder trials, Beckwith said, "I do not think it will hurt me," and told reporters smugly, "Everybody knows how I feel about racial matters."[48]

Mississippi blacks, at least, were vividly aware of Beckwith's position on racial matters. His entry into the race spurred many blacks to register to vote—just so they could vote against him. Charles Evers acknowledged that he expected Beckwith to rack up some votes. "That's Mississippi for you," he said jokingly, although he gave more than a passing thought to running against Beckwith for the lieutenant governor's seat. Evers gave up the idea, however, when he was unable to obtain the endorsement of Senator Robert F. Kennedy.[49] Beckwith realized that black voters had gained tremendous ground in recent years, but he denigrated their importance. "I am not concerned with the registration of Negro voters," he said. "If I can't get in on the white man's vote, then I don't deserve to get in."[50]

He capitalized on his notoriety to take subtle and not-so-subtle jabs at a few of his enemies. In an interview with Associated Press reporter James Bonney, Beckwith acknowledged he was still under indictment for murder and said he had "no intention of introducing the sordid business concerning Medgar Evers into the business of campaigning. It belongs in the province of the courts and not in a political arena." He described his former nemesis, gubernatorial candidate William Waller, as "a young and inexperienced district attorney," who, in prosecuting the murder case, was merely a pawn of Robert F. Kennedy and the FBI. Beckwith lashed out at Kennedy, saying, "If there is anyone to blame in [the Evers] case it is the venomous Bobby Kennedy who was in charge of the Justice Department."[51] Beckwith often said that a man is known more by his enemies than by his friends,[52] and as his own feeling of self-importance grew, his enemies became powerful national figures. With increasing frequency, he heaped accusations and innuendo on Kennedy—it was Robert F. Kennedy who targeted him for prosecution in the Evers murder, he believed, and Kennedy's "vendetta" would last long after his assassination.

During the campaign, however, Beckwith's supporters worried about enemies closer to home. Campaign workers for William Waller announced a fund-raising dinner to be held in Greenwood in his honor, and although it was postponed once (Waller got the mumps from one of his children and had to change the date), a spaghetti supper was held at the Elks Club on February 18. Just hours before the dinner, anonymous flyers were distributed attacking Waller for prosecuting Beckwith. As the dinner guests lined up for the buffet, a stink bomb was thrown through a window of the club, giving off what one Jackson newspaper called "a fiercely unpleasant, eye-watering gas smelling of rotten eggs." About twenty minutes later, after the disruption was resolved and another buffet line was formed, a second stink bomb was broken on the door of the club. The fire department was called, and shortly after it hosed down the door of the club, Greenwood Police Chief Curtis Lary received an anonymous phone tip that a bomb inside the club was set to detonate in five minutes. A cursory search of the premises turned up no bomb and the dinner continued, about an hour behind schedule.[53]

Waller proved graceful under pressure. He finished the dinner and gave a brief speech to those attending. He later made a statement about the disruptions and said that the people who threw the stink bombs and phoned in the bomb threat were "a dangerous minority."[54] Technically, the description was accurate, but Waller might have taken the incident more seriously if he had known Klansmen in Greenwood were probably responsible for the disruptions. The stink bombs and telephone threat were typical, time-tested methods of Klan harassment. "Harassment fulfills two important goals," Imperial Wizard Sam Bowers had written. "It provides a healthy, not-too-dangerous outlet for the Spiritual Enthusiasm of the membership and trains them to work together. If successful, it boosts morale."[55]

The stink bomb incident undoubtedly boosted Beckwith's morale, as he was always fond of seeing his enemies harassed. The Waller incident also came at a time when Beckwith might have needed a diversion. Just two days before, an editorial in *The New York Times* cast a sideways glance at Beckwith's race for office in far-off Mississippi. "His candidacy is proof of the open contempt in which the lives and opinions of Negroes are still held in parts of the South," the *Times* said, noting that his "sole claim to political preferment is that he has twice been tried though not convicted for the murder of Medgar Evers."[56] True, it was hardly enough to build a platform on. Although Beckwith outlined his qualifications and goals in general terms for reporters when he announced his candidacy, as the campaign progressed he provided a better look at his personal platform through *The Southern Review*, which became his official mouthpiece.

Referring to the "diabolical international conspiracy against states' rights and racial integrity," Beckwith outlined his views on a number of subjects for the *Review*'s readers. Most important, he addressed the issue of the burgeoning number of black voters, saying, ". . . the majority of our Mississippi Negroes—although ignorant and uneducated—are not insane. Certainly they are not in the same category of insanity with the beatniks, agitators and lunatic liberals," he said. "I am reminding the sane Negroes of Mississippi that they have a big stake themselves in preserving white rule in Mississippi. Revolution does not benefit anyone, white or black, in the long run. The sane Negro should understand that he needs protection from revolutionary agitators such as Charles Evers and Stokely Carmichael, and to receive that protection, he must have a determined and able segregationist in office to control the agitators and revolutionaries. I am telling the Negro voters in Mississippi to reject revolution and accept benevolent white rule in the interest of their own material well-being and safety."[57]

The *Review* also put the distinctive Beckwith spin on newsworthy events. On March 18, 1967, as he unloaded boxes from the back of his car, Beckwith was approached by two FBI agents, Mervin Hogan and Conrad Hassell, who attempted to interview him. The agents' subsequent report of the incident was terse: "[Beckwith] immediately invited both agents into his apartment and recorded the names of the interviewing agents on a sheet of paper. He stated he did not wish to be interviewed and the interview was then terminated."[58] Beckwith was alternately riled and amused by the incident, and he used *The Southern Review* to poke fun at the FBI. He recounted the incident, saying he invited the agents inside so he could take their photographs. "They asked me if it was my habit to take photographs of anyone who visited me," Beckwith said, "and I told them, 'Of course, not everyone—I only take pictures of those of a suspicious character, whom I catch lurking about my premises, or other interesting physiological types.' " Beckwith managed to get the agents' names, and said they were "evidently not of gentile background and of refined culture." He referred to them as race mixers and said "those who lay down with dogs get up with fleas on them," and noted that the agents "looked sort of fleabitten to me."[59]

With his name regularly in the headlines again, Beckwith revived plans to write and market the autobiography he had written while in jail. A Jackson lawyer announced he would be handling copyright matters for the book, which was now titled *Crossfire.*[60] Although Beckwith was said to have produced the manuscript in collaboration with a professional writer, the announcement was premature and the book was never published. Meanwhile, Beckwith toured the campaign trail.

As in every other city he visited, Beckwith called on a few of his fellow Klansmen in Meridian. Imperial Wizard Sam Bowers had given Beckwith the name of a Klansman in Meridian who might be helpful to *The Southern Review*—Delmar Dennis. Bowers having given Beckwith names and addresses of Klansmen in Meridian and other Mississippi towns indicated, to Dennis, at least, that Beckwith had by then deeply ingratiated himself with the Imperial Wizard. "That's how Beckwith came to my home, and he introduced himself and said, 'Sam said I should stop by and see you,' " Dennis said. "So I was his contact in Meridian." Although Dennis had moved in the company of Klansmen he knew to be killers, Beckwith's visit to his home was unnerving. "He was the the only one who ever struck any fear in me," Dennis said. "The others, I felt very comfortable around, even though I knew that they had killed and would kill again. They didn't frighten me, because I didn't think they were going to kill *me.* Beckwith was a guy who might kill anybody! I just had the feeling that if he decided in his mind that you were the enemy, that he might kill you if he had the opportunity—and not tell anybody about it, not hold a meeting, just take it upon himself to do it." As a souvenir of

Beckwith's visit, Dennis kept a copy of *The Southern Review* bearing the stamp "Compliments of Byron De La Beckwith, Candidate for Lieutenant Governor of Mississippi."

Beckwith also visited with Klansmen in Gulfport in May, and the following month visited the tiny town of Pontotoc to ask for local Klan support in his campaign. There, he handed out copies of a book entitled *We Will Survive*, which explained how to manufacture and use Molotov cocktails, land mines and booby traps. Speaking to the local Klavern, he introduced himself as the man *accused* of killing Medgar Evers. He laughingly remarked to Klansmen, "You know I didn't kill that nigger!"[61] Throughout Mississippi, he asked his fellow Klansmen for their votes in the upcoming election.

As the campaign hit full stride, Beckwith became more desperate for votes and more volatile in his public appearances. On July 7, 1967, an NBC cameraman filming mundane campaign speeches in Hernando, Mississippi, for a Huntley-Brinkley special, snapped to life when Byron De La Beckwith took the podium. "Everybody knows what my platform is," Beckwith said by way of introduction. "It's absolute white supremacy under Protestant Christian rule." He made it clear he was not courting blacks or liberals. "I'm not a one-coat cover-all candidate," he said. "I'm not trying to please everybody—I don't want the nigger vote." He talked about his travels through the state, campaigning. "What do I find in our glorious state?" he asked rhetorically. "I find a high-spirited, wide-awake courageous multitude of red-blooded white Mississippians who have already united to oppose and destroy those evil forces now operating within our sacred borders."[62] His speech was filled with "Klanspeak," and while casual listeners may not have been cued to the true meaning of his ramblings, they could not miss some of his more pointed remarks.

Claiming the federal government encouraged sex and Communism, "not to mention putting Negroes in the other corner to fraternize with your daughter," Beckwith touched momentarily on the subject of school integration. Blaming Mississippi's elected officials for school integration, Beckwith said, "The federal government did not put all these coons in your classroom with your dear children. My job is to help you get them out. We—you and I—are the government in Mississippi. Let's act like rulers instead of vassals, serfs and slaves!" Beckwith implored. "As one of our past presidents once said, 'We need to do something constructive for this country.' This is the sort of construction I'd like to see going on in Mississippi—we ought to erect a gallows here and there on which to hang a half-dozen of those grizzly anti-whites, treasoning renegades, parading around our state. It won't take many public executions of these criminals before we will have completely flushed the commode on the entire black power movement in Mississippi." Beckwith also advocated public floggings for criminals and execution for treason—all to help straighten out Mississippi and the rest of the country. "Our forefathers did not intend to smear this country with the Japanese, with the Negro or with the Eskimo," Beckwith said. "When the minority groups in America get this information straight in their heads, then they will be able to live in peace and plenty upon the earth just as long as they abide by our laws."[63] He argued that only Anglo-Saxons were capable of understanding the United States Constitution, and that only Anglo-Saxons qualified to live under it, or to rule by its authority.

Beckwith delighted in making odd juxtapositions of thought, forcing his listeners to put two-and-two together—much as when he had talked of "killing that nigger" to Klansmen, without ever mentioning Medgar Evers by name. "White folks are not going out of style," he told the crowd. "White folks are going to continue to rule America. This can be done, this will be done, and I will help you do it. All of you know how I love guns. I don't even mind niggers having guns—I want everybody to have guns. All the nigger's going to do with a gun, besides kill a few rabbits with it, is to shoot another nigger with it occasionally. Now way down South in Dixie we laughingly say in dialect, 'Dat ain't no harm in dat, is it?' "[64] Beckwith's remarks suggested that he might be becoming increasingly mentally unbalanced, and his advocacy of violence prompted the cameraman to personally deliver a copy of his film to the FBI in Jackson. Agents transcribed the tape and forwarded the transcript to J. Edgar Hoover, the Secret Service and other investigative agencies.

A woman who was at the time a close friend of Beckwith's, believes his race for lieutenant governor—and his belief that he might actually win—marked the high point in a lengthy period of self-delusion. "I think it shows how far he had departed from reality," she said, noting that she and Beckwith lost touch about that time. "I just distance myself from something I sense is going to become trouble." The voting public also distanced itself from potential trouble. In August of 1967, when the first Democratic primary returns were in, Beckwith placed fifth among six candidates. Although he managed to capture 34,675 votes across the state, he was disappointed not to have fared better. He also came in fifth in a field of six candidates in Leflore County, which hurt him deeply. He expected, at the very least, to carry his home county.

"The popularity was on the surface," said Delmar Dennis. "It wasn't real. It appeared that Beckwith was so popular that he could be elected, though he said at one point in the campaign that he didn't really think he was going to be elected. But by observing the popular reaction, and the way everybody defended him, it seemed like there were a lot of people who weren't members of the Klan who had some sympathy there. But it didn't translate into votes."

By the end of 1967, Beckwith returned to Greenwood in defeat. His trusted friend, Tom Barrentine—who served on the board of directors for the White Citizens' Legal Fund established to pay his defense costs—arranged for Beckwith to work selling boats, trailers and farm machinery for Barrentine Manufacturing Company. The FBI in Jackson and its agents in Greenwood kept Beckwith under close surveillance, and six informants regularly apprised agents of his activities, associates and whereabouts.[65] He rented an apartment in the south end of a house at 1001 Dewey Avenue, the home of an elderly couple, Mr. and Mrs. Walter Porter. Because he had no telephone, Beckwith told his friends they could call him at the Porters', but never after 8:00 P.M., when they went to bed. He acquired a new post office box, number 1172, in the post office which had been built on the George Street property, where the Yerger home had stood. And although he was Greenwood's most famous son—some might say infamous—this stature did not assure his place in the public consciousness. When he settled into his apartment and went downtown to order new stationery, the young woman who took his order apparently was unaware of his celebrity. His envelopes came back with his name misprinted *Bryon* De La Beckwith.

12

"Jewishprudence"

For five years, from 1968 through 1972, Beckwith lived an uncharacteristically quiet life in his cramped, two-room apartment. His rent—fifty dollars per month[1]—was reasonable, but to a man accustomed to the drafty, high-ceilinged rooms on George Street and the spacious backyard on West Monroe, the apartment made him feel claustrophobic. As a result, Beckwith spent as little time as possible inside. Instead, he devoted himself to his work as a salesman for Barrentine Manufacturing, traveling through Florida, Louisiana, Arkansas and parts of Georgia, Missouri and the Carolinas, selling boats and trailers. He chatted up potential customers with his distinctive drawl and exaggerated politeness. To Beckwith, selling boats was not much different from selling fertilizer or sundries; the product had a higher ticket price, but that only offered him a higher profile among the other salesmen when he had a particularly good month. The freedom to travel a wider territory was also attractive to Beckwith, as it occasionally offered him the opportunity to visit Klan units in other states. Following the House Committee investigation and the trials involving White Knights accused in the Neshoba triple murders and the Vernon Dahmer murder, the Mississippi Klan seemed effectively dismantled—on the surface. Although many of the group's leaders quickly affiliated with other extremist organizations, such as the rival United Klans of America, a core group of dedicated White Knights remained faithful to Imperial Wizard Sam Bowers.

Beckwith's appearances at Klan rallies and events were sporadic but noteworthy, and for a time the FBI continued to closely monitor his activities. In December 1967, the FBI received a call from a Florida NAACP official who said that Beckwith was staying at the Villa Rosa Motel in Winter Haven. The man, whose name was deleted from FBI records, feared Beckwith might have traveled to Florida to harm him, enticed there by some remarks the leader had recently made at a public event in a nearby county. The national office of the NAACP had earlier issued a memorandum to its chapters advising that they "should beware of Beckwith" when he visited their areas, and the official told his FBI contact that "Beckwith causes trouble wherever he goes."[2] While Beckwith was probably merely making his sales rounds for Barrentine, the FBI, as a precaution, relayed the information to the Polk County Sheriff's Office and the Winter Haven Police Department.

Although the White Knights now seemed dormant after several years of extreme violence in Mississippi, the FBI continued to pay informants who had proven themselves reliable and "invisible" within the ranks of the Klan. If any attempt was made to revitalize the White Knights, or if any individual Klansman tried to start his own extremist movement, the Bureau wanted to be apprised of such activities immediately. Although Beckwith maintained a much lower profile after his unsuccessful race for lieutenant governor in 1967, the Bureau's Jackson Division still had several informants who reported regularly on his activities. "A wealth of information has been obtained from these sources concerning Byron De La Beckwith," one FBI memo noted. "No information has been received that Byron De La Beckwith is or is contemplating again becoming active in the Klan or a related hate type organization," the memo said, its writer mistakenly assuming that the White Knights organization had been decimated. Even so, the correspondent noted, "In view of Byron De La Beckwith's potential for violence and his past acts of violence, the Jackson Division would be remiss to place the file in a closed status."[3] Beckwith might be keeping a low profile, but he was still worth watching.

Although the Jackson Division continued to maintain a file on Beckwith, for a lengthy period of time, Special Agent in Charge Roy K. Moore saw no need to file a formal report with the Bureau in Washington. Still, Beckwith continued to associate with Klansmen and members of Americans for the Preservation of the White Race (APWR), another front organization for the White Knights. APWR was chartered through the Mississippi Secretary of State's office two weeks after Medgar Evers's murder in June of 1963, and although it had lain dormant at the peak of the White Knights' activity, many Klansmen turned to the shell organization to continue the Klan's work after the organization came under intense federal scrutiny. By the spring of 1968, in fact, Klansmen had taken firm control of most chapters of APWR in Mississippi and were using the organization as an adjunct of the Klan, according to FBI files.[4]

Imperial Wizard Sam Bowers undoubtedly felt betrayed by former White Knights Delmar Dennis and Wallace Miller—trusted Klansmen who had performed double-duty as informants for the FBI and testified against him in the Neshoba triple murder case when it finally came to trial. Bowers began to rely on hard-core cell or vigilante groups, and designated their members to work on a need-to-know basis, to weed out potential informants.

"It would be surprising if he did *not* change his strategy," Delmar Dennis explained, "because what happened in the Neshoba case was devastating." The severe blow dealt the White Knights after the House Committee investigation and the prosecution of the Neshoba and Vernon Dahmer murder cases made it clear to Bowers that the Klan's survival would depend on guerilla bombing squads so small no informant could risk offering information without immediately being identified and killed by the other members. "They were no longer the predator," said former FBI Special Agent Tom Van Riper in an interview. "They were the prey."

While Beckwith appeared to be living a quiet, peaceful life in Greenwood, the Mississippi Klan's terrorist group was planning and executing a series of bombings a hundred miles to the southeast, in Meridian, Mississippi. There, the Mississippi Klan's new reign of terror began in earnest. In the Meridian area alone, eight black churches, two black homes and one white home were bombed during the first six months of 1968. Local Klansmen were among the primary suspects in the bombings.[8]

The Klan's targets had long been primarily blacks and black churches, and the small town was stunned when Temple Beth Israel was bombed and the Klan turned its hatred against local Jews, believing Jews were masterminding black revolt as part of a Communist conspiracy. The same Mississippi community, which had done little more than express quiet chagrin when its black churches were bombed, now jolted to life. Two groups, the "Committee of Concern" and the "Committee of Conscience," were established by community leaders and ministers following the temple bombings in Jackson and Meridian. Leaders of the groups loudly proclaimed their collective intention to bring a stop to the terrorism.[9] Meanwhile, the FBI learned from informants that churches, synagogues and homes were not the only targets on the Klan's agenda. Klan insiders were also circulating a hit list targeting the FBI's Roy K. Moore, Meridian Police Chief Roy Gunn, and Meridian Jewish leader Meyer Davidson. The final target on the Klan's list was a synagogue that the terrorists planned to bomb when it was filled with worshippers.[10]

The FBI was spread thinly across Mississippi monitoring the activities of individual Klansmen while also furiously investigating the rash of bombings in Meridian. Informants also continued to report on Beckwith's activities, noting his ongoing advocacy of violence in the racial struggle, but the Jackson Division's reports on him became cursory. After appearing at a Klan rally in October 1968, Beckwith chatted up a small cluster of Klansmen in which an FBI informant happened to be present. He showed the men an aerosol can marked "For Police Use Only," and explained that it was a "defense" tool. Mace in the 1960s was still a novelty, as it was not yet in wide use. Beckwith called it "nigger repellant" or "varmint tonic," and said he thought everyone should get some for protection.[11]

The remark was duly noted by the informant and placed in Beckwith's FBI file. With the entire city of Meridian paralyzed by fear, the Bureau's agents in Mississippi had much larger problems than Byron De La Beckwith peddling Mace.

The top suspects in the Meridian incidents were monitored constantly by FBI agents who attempted to link them to the bombings. What the suspects needed, ironically, was another bombing—one that could be carried out by another terrorist so that they could establish airtight alibis. If a bombing occurred at a time when none of the suspects could have been responsible, Chief Gunn and the FBI would be forced to look elsewhere for the terrorists, easing the pressure on their primary Meridian suspects.

Tall, lanky Thomas Albert Tarrants III, a twenty-one-year-old terrorist, would fit the bill handily. At six-foot-four, Tarrants's height seemed grossly exaggerated by his extreme thinness and his slight 165 pounds. His dark eyes and dark, cropped hair gave him a brooding, intense look, and few people in Mississippi knew anything about him. After leading violent demonstrations against integration at his Mobile, Alabama, high school in 1963, Tarrants contributed his talents to the activities of The John Birch Society and the National States Rights Party and he became well-versed in the religious teachings of Dr. Wesley Swift by listening to taped sermons and lectures.[12] Swift's racist, anti-Semitic doctrine affected Tarrants as strongly as it had Beckwith. More than any other hate propaganda circulating at the time, Swift's taped sermons molded Tarrants's anti-Semitic views. He placed great store in Swift's racial arguments that carried the authority of religious doctrine.

After studying the operations of clandestine groups like the Minutemen, Tarrants became fascinated by sabotage, guerilla warfare and counterinsurgency. With an inquisitive mind and a keen memory for detail, he quickly immersed himself in the world of terrorism. He learned to recognize and use military small arms from around the world—and could even cite their specifications. In the summer of 1967, when he was only twenty years old, Tarrants approached White Knights Imperial Wizard Sam Bowers, anxious to devote himself to the Klan leader's movement. Over time, Tarrants proved himself to Bowers at what was a pivotal point in the White Knights' history. He knocked on Bowers's door at Sambo Amusement Company during the lull of Klan battle in the summer of 1967, when some of the Imperial Wizard's fiercest warriors had their hands tied and were under constant surveillance by the FBI.[13] Because Tarrants was from outside Mississippi and had no history of violence there, he would be able to operate as a terrorist while more obvious suspects were being closely monitored. Unlike higher-profile Klansmen scattered across the state, Tarrants could carry out his deadly work in relative obscurity.

By the early fall of 1967, Bowers and Tarrants were firmly tethered to one another, both in spirit and in crime. They launched a plan to terrorize Mississippi's Jews, carefully selecting key black and white leaders, as well. One Klansman had a close friend employed by a demolition firm who would take more dynamite than he needed to dislodge tree stumps and rocks. The Klansman procured the remainder.[14] By the end of November, an alarming number of sites had been targeted and bombed—Jackson's Temple Beth Israel; Dean William T. Bush's home on the Tougaloo College campus; white civil rights leader Reverend Robert Kochtitzky's home; the home of Reverend Allen Johnson, a Mississippi leader of both the NAACP and the Southern Christian Leadership Conference; and the home of Temple Beth Israel's Rabbi Perry Nussbaum. Traveling together on a mission to machine-gun the home of a black man in Collins, Mississippi, Bowers and Tarrants were spotted in their car at a closed service station, where a police officer picked up the pair for questioning. It was the first time Bowers and Tarrants were publicly linked.[15]

Ironically, the car had been stolen in Memphis before Tarrants bought it, and in addition to possession of a stolen vehicle, Tarrants expected to face federal charges for possession of the submachine gun found in the car with them. Bowers was never charged in connection with the incident. The weapon had been stolen nearly a decade earlier from a National Guard Armory in Alabama.[16] Facing imprisonment for the serious charges, Tarrants decided to go underground, eventually taking up residence in a safe house in the Smoky Mountains of North Carolina. After a furtive trip to Mississippi, during which he and Bowers planned their strategy for continuing the assaults, Tarrants returned to North Carolina to wait in silence. The machine-gun and bombing attacks continued, primarily in Meridian, with other Klan terrorists carrying out Bowers's carefully laid plans. By the time Meridian's Temple Beth Israel was bombed in late May 1968, the tension in Meridian was palpable—not only among Mississippi's Jewish community, but among local law enforcement officers and FBI agents, as well.

Meyer Davidson, the prominent Jewish civic leader in Meridian, vowed to raise $80,000 in reward money. He strongly denounced the Klan, raising himself a notch or two on the hit list on which his name was already boldly written. A number of funds sprang up to assist in rebuilding efforts which quickly got underway in the wake of the bombings. A.I. Botnick, regional director of the Anti-Defamation League (ADL) of B'nai B'rith in New Orleans, drove to Meridian following the temple bombing and vowed to help raise enough money to solve the case. Chief Roy Gunn's Meridian police and the FBI worked together, using money raised by Botnick and others, to persuade two Klansmen, brothers Raymond and Alton Wayne Roberts, to inform on the Klan's top terrorists. After a series of clandestine cat-and-mouse meetings between Meridian police detective Luke Scarbrough, FBI agents Frank Watts and Jack Rucker, and the Roberts brothers, authorities were provided the name of the target, the date when the next bombing would occur, and which terrorists would be carrying it out—in exchange for almost $50,000.[17] Police planned to either capture the perpetrators or kill them.

The primary suspects turned to Tarrants, claiming they needed help in alleviating the constant police pressure and FBI harassment. For some time, Tarrants had touted Davidson as a "ripe" bombing target; there was little question in his mind that Davidson should be the next victim. Tarrants agreed to carry out the bombing, working with the Roberts brothers to ensure they had airtight alibis. Although this plan had been set, the designated terrorists changed the scenario at the last minute. Like the Roberts brothers, the intended bomber was under constant FBI surveillance, and Tarrants proposed that he be replaced on the mission to bomb Davidson's home to take some of the pressure off him, as well. His replacement was petite, brown-eyed Kathy Ainsworth, a twenty-six-year-old fifth-grade teacher who was a member of Bowers's inner circle and who had participated in previous bombings in the area.[18]

On June 29, 1968, Tarrants picked up Ainsworth at her home in Jackson (she was packing for a vacation trip to Miami) and offered to drive her on to Florida after they deposited a bomb at Meyer Davidson's home in Meridian. En route to dinner at The Captain's Table, a restaurant located on the Ross Barnett Reservoir just north of Jackson, Tarrants assured Ainsworth the bombing would go "just as smoothly as our last project together." After a leisurely dinner, Tarrants and Ainsworth drove to Meridian. They arrived just after 11:00 P.M. and called Raymond Roberts from a pay phone, then drove to a nearby truck stop, where Roberts met them several minutes later. Roberts seemed visibly disturbed by the sudden replacement of Ainsworth for the other bomber, but he rode quietly with them to survey Meyer Davidson's neighborhood. After taking Roberts back to the Holiday Inn, Tarrants set the bomb's timer for 2:00 A.M. and placed it on the front seat of the car.[19]

Just before 1:00 A.M., the two young terrorists drove slowly to within fifty feet of Davidson's driveway, and Tarrants stopped the car and placed the unwieldy Clorox box containing the bomb under his arm. It was the first bomb he hadn't constructed himself. Tarrants usually opted for a bomb with a simple length of fuse; instead, this one consisted of an electrical detonator which was activated by a mercury switch, and a clock, all wired into twenty-nine sticks of dynamite.[20] As he moved calmly toward Davidson's home, a shot rang out. Tarrants dropped the bomb and a gun battle ensued. Tarrants opened fire on officers when they yelled at him to halt, and a barrage of rifle and shotgun fire erupted. Ainsworth was shot at the base of her skull, and slumped over in the front seat. She was found dead, crouched in a fetal position with her head near the glove compartment, which held a pistol and a hand grenade. Tarrants was critically wounded after he led the police on a futile car chase through the neighborhood, Ainsworth's limp, bloody body riding alongside him.

Critically wounded, Tarrants was loaded into an ambulance with his dead partner and rushed to a nearby hospital, where one doctor predicted he might live forty-five minutes. Amazingly, Tarrants survived. After a lengthy but startling recovery, he spent eight years at Parchman Penitentiary.[21] He later successfully escaped from Parchman with the help and planning of fellow members of the White Knights, many of whose members were closely tied to the National States Rights Party, but was recaptured and imprisoned again. During his incarceration, Tarrants experienced a religious conversion, renounced his racist beliefs, and ultimately was released.[22]

Although in his book *Terror in the Night*, veteran *Los Angeles Times* reporter Jack Nelson makes a compelling argument that the Meridian police, the FBI and the ADL worked together to entrap the terrorists, Tarrants vowed in his own published memoir that Davidson was already a high-priority target whom he would have eventually attempted to bomb,[23] regardless whether the Roberts brothers had collaborated with the FBI and other officials. After the incident, Nelson recounted an interview with ADL Regional Director A.I. Botnick in New Orleans, in which Botnick admitted paying more than $36,000 to the Roberts brothers to act as informants in the case. Nelson also reported that Botnick admitted taking part not only in raising the funds, but in planning the trap, as well. "Four guys know I was in on the planning," Nelson recalled Botnick saying in an interview. "It was a trap—you know that."[24]

Inside the bullet-riddled green Buick, officers found a wealth of evidence linking Tarrants and Ainsworth to Sam Bowers and his White Knights, the National States Rights Party and other extremist organizations. When Tarrants's clothes were removed with surgical scissors at a Meridian hospital, investigators found a small notebook in one of his pockets. A handwritten entry said, in part, "Please be advised that since 23 March 1968, I, Thomas A. Tarrants have been underground and operating guerilla warfare. . . ." Among Tarrants's other belongings were two of Sam Bowers's calling cards, one of which introduced the terrorist with a handwritten note asking that he be extended every courtesy. Tarrants also carried a slip of paper naming nearly twenty prominent Southern civil rights figures, including Charles Evers and Clarksville NAACP leader Aaron Henry, who were also being considered for extermination. In the car, they also carried a can of Mace in a holster, possibly from Beckwith's supply of "nigger repellant."[25]

Ainsworth's purse, which contained students' photographs and a shopping list of cosmetics, also symbolically revealed the complete extent of her double life. It also held calling cards from Sam Bowers and L.E. Matthews, Jr., who was alleged to be the Klan's premier bomb maker and who was later elected to succeed Bowers as Imperial Wizard. Her purse also held a loaded .25 caliber Belgian pistol. Even more disturbing were the contents of her home filing cabinet. In neatly lettered folders, the school teacher carefully catalogued her racist ephemera according to categories. Also found among her papers was the weighty Minutemen guerilla warfare manual *We Will Survive,* which Beckwith touted and frequently passed out to Klansmen. The how-to book offered detailed instructions for making bombs and using firearms against "Jew-Communist" traitors.[26] Tarrants and Ainsworth were never widely linked to Beckwith,[27] and it has never been proven that the three knew each other or worked together within the ranks of the White Knights. Five pieces of circumstantial evidence, however, bind them to each other: their mutual affiliation with Sam Bowers; their shared devotion to the religious doctrine of Dr. Wesley Swift; their individual ties to the violently anti-Semitic National States Rights Party; their possession of mace at a time when it was not commonly used and was difficult to obtain; and their adherence to the guerilla warfare manual *We Will Survive*, which not only advocated violent action against Jews, but provided the necessary instruction to create bombs to achieve that end.

Ideologically, Beckwith and Tarrants obviously had a great deal in common. Both were fanatically devoted to Imperial Wizard Sam Bowers and his racist ideals for the White Knights of the Ku Klux Klan, and perhaps most important, both were capable of living by their oaths of secrecy. Both understood that they were dispensable, if necessary, for the cause. Beckwith's primary handicap was his visibility. In every other respect, though, he might have been selected as one of Bowers's primary arsonists and bombers. His long-held fascination with black powder firearms, coupled with his military training, made him an authority on explosives. He had a steady trigger finger, and as he had proven at Tarawa, was not afraid to place his life in jeopardy. In addition to possessing a vast knowledge of firearms and explosives, Beckwith had another quality which made it likely he would put that knowledge to work—zealousness. Informants within the Klan regularly provided the Jackson Division with important information about his acquisition of pistols and rifles, his willingness to provide explosives to Klansmen, and his ability to convert certain kinds of rifles into fully automatic weapons.[28] Above all, Beckwith had grown to believe that such terrorist acts were morally right and divinely ordained.

Bowers and Beckwith remained close, even as Tommy Tarrants fought for his life in a Mississippi hospital bed. Following Kathy Ainsworth's death, Bowers wrote a five-page letter to a Meridian police officer regarding the shootout. Rather than simply mailing the letter, Bowers sent it on a circuitous route. He gave it first to Beckwith, who delivered it by hand to Raymond Roberts.[29] Bowers may have done this intentionally to rattle Roberts, whom Bowers must have suspected as one of the few people who could have helped stage the ambush for Tarrants and Ainsworth. Roberts mailed the letter and the officer received it the following day.

Several months after the botched attempt on Meyer Davidson's life, an FBI informant reported that Beckwith visited Klansmen in Meridian to assuage their fears and to tell them that Bowers was planning a reorganization of the Klan following Ainsworth's death and Tarrants's wounding. He described Bowers's plan to launch "a new underground unit in Mississippi to handle guerilla-type warfare against the Jews in the state."[30] With the other reports submitted about Beckwith, this too went into his file in Jackson. Bowers however, was facing his impending jail term in the Neshoba case, so that the threat appeared, on its face, an idle one. The FBI may have believed that with Bowers and his men in jail, and with the Meridian bombers identified and stopped, the Klan in Mississippi had been decimated. In reality, their efforts had merely forced the die-hard faction of the Klan further underground.

By late February 1970, when Bowers and six others were imprisoned for their roles in the Neshoba triple murders, the Jackson Division's informants within the Klan ceased to report on Beckwith's activities. With his friends in jail at Parchman Penitentiary, Beckwith may have made a conscious decision to maintain a low profile. He was still living in the cramped apartment on Dewey Street in Greenwood, and continued to work for Barrentine Manufacturing. He traveled extensively on the job, driving a white-over-red Chevrolet pickup truck bearing the Barrentine Manufacturing Company logo and marked with the number 38 on the left front hood. In a report filed with J. Edgar Hoover, Roy K. Moore noted that "Inasmuch as there are no indications of any Klan activity by the subject within the past year, this matter is being closed within the Jackson Division."[31] It was the last formal investigative report the Jackson Division filed on Beckwith for several years.

Temporarily relieved of the FBI's constant surveillance, Beckwith spent his leisure hours reading, studying and pondering theology. The sermons of Dr. Wesley Swift—both printed and on cassette tape—continued to fascinate him. The FBI's files on Beckwith show that he occasionally hawked flyers linked to Swift's church in California, and Klan informants reported that following Swift's death in October 1970, Beckwith had grown keenly interested in his church. An informant also reportedly heard Beckwith remark that "most of the Jews in the world are living in the United States" and that he was personally ready to "get some of them."[32]

In the late 1960s, the Klan's shift toward violence against Jews was reflected in Beckwith's theology, as well. He, too, believed that Jews were propelling and financing the black civil rights movement as a step toward Communist takeover. As was the case with Bowers and other leaders of fanatically racist groups, the religious zeal and intense patriotism their members exhibited justified their terrorism. They truly believed they were carrying out God's will, and that they were acting as His instruments of war on earth. If their collective religious consciousness allowed Klansmen to believe that blacks and Jews were subhuman, what guilt could they possibly feel in exterminating such enemies of their race?

Beckwith pored over his Bible, claiming to have read it three separate times from cover to cover, hoping to unlock its secrets to apply them to his own life. Organized religion had long proven frustrating for him; his bouts with Episcopal bishops and fellow congregation members had worn him down over the years.[33] He was disillusioned because white men and women who seemed to be otherwise good Christians were slowly allowing blacks into their congregations.

Although his affiliation with the Anglican Orthodox Church had proven somewhat satisfying after his rift with the Episcopal church (at least Anglicans continued to fight to keep blacks out of their services) Beckwith was still not fulfilled in his formal religious life. When a new church, First Independent Methodist Church, organized in Greenwood, he was immediately drawn to it. The Association of Independent Methodists (AIM) set forth a list of tenets on which their congregations were founded, and Beckwith could not have been more pleased if he had drafted them himself. The church was established to "maintain integrity of the races, which is ordained of God, and to promote social separation of the races which is a rational, normal, positive principle, and is essentially constructive and moral." Member churches had been established in other parts of Mississippi, as well as in Alabama, Tennessee and Louisiana.

"We do not support the one world, one race, one religion philosophy," an explanatory brochure stated in terms that clearly delighted Beckwith. The new congregation in Greenwood brought together disgruntled Methodists, Baptists, Presbyterians and even a few stray Episcopalians—all of whom were die-hard segregationists who wanted to affiliate with a church that was independent of the National Council of Churches or the World Council of Churches. Beckwith especially admired the manner in which the individual churches were represented in the Association; each church, regardless of size, held the same equal representation at the annual meeting.[34] The Independent Methodist Church, he noted in green ink on one piece of church paperwork, was organized like the Citizens' Council.

Reverend Don Taylor preached to Sunday morning crowds of about seventy people and held Sunday evening services for approximately twenty-five of the more committed members. Beckwith immersed himself in church activities, monitoring and photographing the physical structure as it was built, offering to mow the grass occasionally—even singing in the choir and leading an adult Bible class after the congregation was ensconced in its attractive, one-story brick building on Greenwood's Medallion Drive. He seemed to be in church every time the doors were opened, involving himself in as many activities as he could juggle, again fulfilling his intense need to belong and perhaps attempting to justify his activities through religion. During 1971 he tithed $700, and by the end of 1972, he claimed to have tithed almost $1,500 to the church—approximately one-fifth of his income. Since he had helped build the church from the ground up, Beckwith even had his own key, bearing the number fifteen, and could come and go as he pleased.[35]

At about the same time, Beckwith made a job change that also helped improve his disposition. Vernon Ricks, Jr., who owned Ricks' Motor Service on Highway 82 in Greenwood, hired Beckwith as a salesman. The company sold Massey-Ferguson farm products, but carried a number of other companies' implements and equipment as well. The job change agreed with Beckwith. It put him back in contact with the farmers and planters who had been his customers when he worked for Delta Liquid Plant Food Company. The money was slightly better—one hundred dollars per week—and he was comfortable selling tractors, combines, hoes and plows.

With many of his Klan cronies in jail, Beckwith busied himself cultivating other far-right friendships and affiliations. He was drawn to Liberty Lobby because one of his old heroes, Judge Tom P. Brady of *Black Monday* fame—the man who inspired him in the wake of the 1954 U.S. Supreme Court school desegregation ruling—served on its initial Board of Policy. On its face, Liberty Lobby initially seemed a respectable conservative lobbying force in Washington, but some of its positions were outside of the conservative mainstream. As an indication of Liberty Lobby's growing popularity, in the late 1960s the circulation of its newsletter rose from 16,000 to 250,000.[36]

Like Robert Patterson of the Citizens' Council or Sam Bowers of the White Knights, Beckwith admired George Lincoln Rockwell, who had ties to Liberty Lobby organizers, as a patriot who put his ideology into practice. Rockwell had served as a Navy fighter pilot and commander in both World War II and Korea—service with which Beckwith could strongly identify—and in 1958 Rockwell adopted the swastika as his emblem in founding the American Nazi Party. *Time* magazine reported on Rockwell's platform, which included "deporting all Negroes to Africa, liquidating the Jews, and hanging all 'traitors,' e.g., Eisenhower, Truman, Chief Justice Warren." After Rockwell was assassinated in August 1967 outside a laundromat in Virginia, Beckwith and many of the White Knights studied Rockwell's lengthy manifesto, *White Power*, in which he outlined his Aryan and racist beliefs.[37]

Rockwell's book had a tremendous impact on Beckwith and other radical racists. An avid reader of racist propaganda, Beckwith came into possession of an early copy of another book widely heralded in the racist press in 1971—*None Dare Call It Conspiracy*, written by Gary Allen and published by The John Birch Society through Concord Press. Beckwith read the book and found it so illuminating, believing it offered irrefutable proof of the Jewish-Communist conspiracy, that he bought and personally gave away almost 2,000 copies. He claimed to have mailed a copy to each dues-paying member of the Mississippi Society of the Sons of the American Revolution.[38] At home on Dewey Street, he carefully pasted form letters inside the back cover of each issue, asking recipients to send him a contribution so he could continue to provide copies to the public. "This book documents in interesting detail the conspiracy which seeks to change our form of government,"[39] Beckwith warned his readers. He told acquaintances that he handed the books out without discrimination. "I give them to everybody, even bad niggers and bad Jews and sorry white folks," Beckwith chuckled.

Citing notoriously anti-Semitic sources, *None Dare Call It Conspiracy* was distributed widely between 1970 and 1972, with more than one million copies in print. Critics said the book "revives outworn and discredited anti-Jewish themes," and that it offered little more than "a range of conjecture in history, biography, world affairs, and ideology which leave most people lost in a haze of allegations."[40] Certain the book would open the public's eyes to a supposed Jewish conspiracy, Beckwith dressed in his finest double-breasted suit and had a friend photograph him in several poses cradling a stack of the books in his arms. He carried a full box in the trunk of his car and kept copies in the cab of his truck so he could pass them out when he made his sales calls. As when *Black Monday* first appeared, he became a common figure on Greenwood street corners, bowing deeply from the waist to passersby and handing out books which, most likely, many recipients graciously accepted and tossed in the trash when they got home.

The book "proved" the Jewish conspiracies to which Beckwith had subscribed through the Klan, the National States Rights Party and Swift's religious teachings. It was merely one more weapon in his arsenal of anti-Semitic beliefs. Just as the collective hatred by the Klan and other white supremacist groups shifted from blacks to Jews, so had Beckwith's hatred dramatically shifted. Immersed in the theology of Wesley Swift and the Klan doctrine of Sam Bowers—and shored up by the "proof" he found in *None Dare Call It Conspiracy*—the same salesman who had long maintained a charge account at Kantor's department store in Greenwood now reviled all Jews as the literal children of Satan.

Like others in leadership positions in the white racist movement, Beckwith began to espouse the belief that blacks weren't the real problem, but instead were merely "a Jewish promoted nuisance" and that Jews were "the real problem—worldwide and for centuries."[41] He began to pepper his speech with the complaints that "Jews and niggers" were responsible for the ills of the country, just as in the 1950s his stock-in-trade targets had been "bad niggers and sorry white folks." He believed Jews and blacks were "two of the worst things on this earth—the Jew by far the most diabolical and dangerous to all of Christendom." He also became keenly interested in Klan activities after a hiatus, and sometimes drove as many as three hundred miles to hear what a fledgling Klan group had to say about solving the South's racial problems. Although the FBI was unaware of it, Beckwith was re-entering the Klan world, and was also considering another try in the political arena, hoping to unseat a liberal incumbent in the U.S. Senate. But it was only a matter of time before Beckwith joined the ranks of active Klansmen, and gave up any hope of again running for public office. His priorities were clear. In his only documented admission of his Klan membership, Beckwith wrote that he was "as far in global (not state or county) Klan work as a fifty-six-year-old man can be, and happy at it."[42]

The more he devoted his energies to Klan work, the more vitriolic his letters grew. In 1973, in an attempt to reestablish contact with Willie, he wrote, "The goddam Jews are after me again," referring to a request that he consent to an interview for a network television report on Mississippi. Beckwith believed, however, that the reporter really only wanted to talk "about the Evers nigger that's in his coffin in Washington thank God . . . old Charles is still living I hear!!!"[43]

A decade had passed since Medgar Evers's assassination, and while Beckwith's fiery passions had not cooled, his direction had shifted. Beckwith told his former wife he had quit drinking in January and, shortly afterward, bought a dependable car on credit. The 1968 four-door Oldsmobile Ninety-Eight luxury sedan was exactly what he wanted in a car—a quiet, comfortable ride. Good shocks, no jostling. He put in a two-way radio, which he used to communicate with Ricks' Motor Service—and probably, his fellow Klansmen, as well. The car was midnight blue, with a white vinyl top, and cost him only sixty-five dollars per month after his initial down payment.[44]

That spring, in addition to working his sales rounds, Beckwith also began working to help free the Klansmen in Parchman Penitentiary who were given life sentences in the Vernon Dahmer murder case. "We had five men in—got three out—two to go!" Beckwith boasted. Once more, Byron De La Beckwith clearly felt his calling. "I have the imagination enough to think I'm important to some one, to some thing, to some cause," he wrote in the spring of 1973, in a psychologically revealing confession. By fall, his plan of attack was clear, and Beckwith was firmly entrenched among the "warriors" who planned to defeat the Jews. "I have no time to play," Beckwith said, "except with those who have a long history of actual assaults against the forces of organized Jewry and then those people's company I seek during the lull of battles—for they are nearby and we understand one another."[45]

On Wednesday afternoon, September 26, 1973, the usual lunch crowd filled the Mayflower Cafe on West Capitol Street in Jackson. It was a sticky, humid day, and the ice in customers' glasses of iced tea melted quickly in the noonday heat. Most of the diners, who had ducked inside to sit for awhile and escape the heat, were unaware of the quiet transaction taking place at one table. De La Beckwith, L.E. Matthews, Jr., and a Jackson Klansman named Gordon Clark were having lunch while carrying on a quiet conversation. Nearby, Jackson attorney Al Binder sat with an FBI agent, cautiously watching the men while they ate and talked.

Beckwith and Matthews were unaware that the previous week, Clark had talked with Special Agent Thompson Webb of the Jackson Division FBI office to tell him that Beckwith was planning a bombing in New Orleans. A.I. Botnick, the New Orleans official of the ADL who had helped plan and fund the Meridian trap for Tarrants and Ainsworth, was Beckwith's target. Clark was well-placed within the Klan and had firsthand knowledge of the plot.[46] Webb questioned Clark at length and relayed the details to Special Agent George Carter of the FBI's New Orleans office, who immediately met with officers of the Intelligence Division of the New Orleans Police Department. Clark said Beckwith did not yet have the bomb, but described his car in detail and told Webb that Beckwith carried a .45 automatic pistol on his person and usually had a .30 caliber carbine rifle in his car. During the week, Clark maintained contact with Webb, who relayed information to New Orleans. When Clark knew the final details of Beckwith's plan, and the date he was to pick up the bomb, plans were perfected to intercept Beckwith en route to Botnick's home in New Orleans.[47]

Concurrently, Binder had been approached by an informant with the same story. Binder went to the FBI in Jackson, and agents there confirmed to him that they were aware of the impending attempt on Botnick's life. An agent planned to be present at the Mayflower Cafe when Beckwith, Matthews and Clark met. Binder joined the FBI agent for lunch, and they stayed until Beckwith got in his car to leave for New Orleans.[48] At 5:30 P.M. Sergeant Bernard Windstein, Jr., of the New Orleans Police Department was notified that Beckwith was en route to New Orleans and would arrive in the city around midnight, traveling on Interstate 10 from the east, using the Twin Bridges over Lake Pontchartrain. FBI sources, providing the details to Windstein, also described in detail the bomb Beckwith was carrying and the black-painted box which contained it. A while later, agents in Jackson called again to tell New Orleans officers that Beckwith's car was bearing a license plate which had been stolen from a 1967 Oldsmobile registered to Charlene Buie in Jackson.[49]

Just after midnight on September 27—the first day of Rosh Hashanah, the holy day celebrating the beginning of the Jewish New Year—Beckwith drove into Orleans Parish, Louisiana, bearing a special New Year's gift for A.I. Botnick. In the warm, quiet, New Orleans morning, Beckwith was greeted by a welcoming committee he had not expected—armed officers of the New Orleans Police Department. During the evening, a number of police and intelligence officers were scattered along the route Beckwith was supposed to be traveling. While driving south on Interstate 10 toward New Orleans, just two miles west of the Twin Bridges over Lake Pontchartrain, Beckwith's car was sighted. Sergeant Windstein and Detective John Evans watched Beckwith's car pass, fell in behind it, followed the Oldsmobile across the bridge and turned on their blue lights. Beckwith immediately pulled onto the shoulder of the highway. It was 12:03 A.M.

Beckwith got out of his car and briskly walked back toward the officers. "Place your hands on the hood of the car," Detective Evans told Beckwith brusquely, and Beckwith did so immediately. Sergeant Windstein frisked Beckwith, finding a .45 caliber Colt automatic pistol in the waistband of Beckwith's trousers, concealed under his shirt. Detective Evans told Beckwith he was under arrest and read him his rights. When asked if he had been arrested before, Beckwith said, "Yes, I was arrested once before. They said I killed a nigger in Mississippi." In Beckwith's Oldsmobile officers found a rifle, a .50 caliber machine gun barrel, the barrel and stock of a foreign-made rifle, a wide assortment of ammunition, one .30 caliber carbine rifle with a folding stock, and, in a black-painted plywood box, a bomb made of six one-pound sticks of dynamite taped around a five-pound stick of Trojan Seismograph dynamite, along with a timing device constructed from a small white Westclox™ alarm clock. It was in the front passenger floor board, partially covered by a black clothing bag. Cryptically alluding to the bomb, Beckwith later wrote his former wife, "I'm finally convinced a wind up clock is better than an electric clock—ha! ha!"[50]

Beckwith was transported to central lockup, where he made a statement that booking officers John Evans and Dennis DeLatte thought was rather odd. "When we were leaving the booking area where John was filling out the traffic ticket," DeLatte later testified, "Mr. Beckwith stated that he liked the police. He didn't have any malice toward the police. And that he understood we had a job to do, and asked us to understand he had a job to do."[51]

Emergency Services Section officers were called to the scene near the Twin Bridges to dismantle the bomb. Windstein then examined the interior of the car, where he found on the front seat a photocopied portion of a New Orleans map, showing the route to Botnick's neighborhood near Tulane University. He initialed, timed and dated the rear of the map on one corner and tagged it as evidence.

Beckwith's Oldsmobile was towed to police headquarters, where it was further searched and inventoried. Along with his traveling clothes, officers found a steel hatchet and work gloves; a Bible; four .45 caliber automatic clips which fit Beckwith's pistol, each containing seven rounds of ammunition; a Buck knife with a six-inch steel blade; two cameras and a pair of binoculars; numerous rounds of live ammunition of different calibers; twenty copies of *None Dare Call It Conspiracy*; numerous other racist publications; three rifles; one machine gun barrel; a roll of small-gauge yellow electrical wire of the type used in the bomb's timing device and also used to attach the stolen license plate over Beckwith's own license plate; a folder of papers pertaining to Beckwith's Jefferson Davis china, which he told officers he was coming to New Orleans to sell; and the box of antique china. A medallion found in a small box in the trunk bore the legend, "The Right of the People to Bear Arms Shall Not Be Infringed."[52]

An October 2 memo from FBI Director Clarence Kelley to Attorney General Elliot Richardson described the items found in Beckwith's car, named A.I. Botnick as the target, and noted that the bomb Beckwith was carrying was "capable of destroying more than one residence." Kelley gave a quiet nod to the informant who tipped the Bureau off to the plot. "The importance of this information cannot be underestimated since Botnick lives in a highly concentrated residential area and many human lives were undoubtedly saved," Kelley wrote. "The arresting NOPD officers, exposed to extreme danger at the time of the arrest and search of the car, were obviously assisted in avoiding a catastrophe based on details furnished by the informant." In an earlier FBI teletype, the Special Agent in Charge in New Orleans noted that the information provided by the informant had been critical; it allowed officers to pinpoint Beckwith's Oldsmobile "at night on a heavily traveled, unlighted interstate highway."[53]

A federal source later remarked that the bomb intended for Botnick was "exactly like" the bomb Tommy Tarrants tried to plant at Meyer Davidson's home in Meridian, Mississippi, although Tarrants's bomb contained many more sticks of dynamite. When reporters asked Beckwith about the dynamite found in his car, he said, "I'll just say a lot of dynamite is used in the Delta to blow up stumps," but he neglected to say whether he was on a stump-hunting expedition when he drove into New Orleans at midnight.[54]

Had Beckwith been successful in planting the bomb at Botnick's home, he would have destroyed an empty house. After a series of persistent death threats, Botnick had taken his family into hiding and left New Orleans before the holiday. He had heard reports that several weeks before, Beckwith had made anti-Semitic remarks and threatened Botnick's life at a Citizens' Council of America rally in Jackson.[55] Botnick refused to talk with reporters after Beckwith's arrest, and continued to maintain a low profile during the maelstrom of publicity that followed. Even Mississippi Governor William Waller did not want to comment on Beckwith. When a reporter from *The States-Item* in New Orleans called Waller to get a statement, the governor, who had unsuccessfully prosecuted Beckwith in both Evers murder trials, said simply, "I'm glad he was in New Orleans."[56]

Beckwith was placed under state and federal bonds totaling slightly more than $150,000, and at his bond hearing on October 1, he was declared legally indigent. When asked whether he owned any valuable possessions—property, furniture, a television set—Beckwith said, "Due to the mass of ugly things on television, I have refused to own a television. I do not waste my time looking at television." Beckwith acknowledged, however, that he would accept a small television set if someone wanted to give him one. He was charged with knowingly transporting dynamite within the state without a permit. The district attorney's office declined to file an attempted aggravated arson charge. "The attempted arson charge was based on intelligence information only, and intelligence information is not competent evidence in court," Chief Assistant District Attorney John P. Volz said. Beckwith was indicted by federal grand jury in New Orleans on October 9, and three weeks after his arrest, on October 20, he was freed on $25,000 bond. A concerned "patriot"—Beckwith's description—sent his personal plane and pilot to fly Beckwith back to Greenwood.[57]

Facing another legal wrangle without funds, Beckwith knew it was time to bang his drum for contributions once more. He wrote an open letter to the Greenwood *Commonwealth*, noting that he "fell afoul of the law" in New Orleans and asking for moral and financial support "in any amount straight to me, cash, check or money order." Beckwith noted that his struggle would require "careful care, cautious planning, courage and a will to survive and do well with honor, plus money." In addition to contributions that began to trickle in from local donors, funds appeared to be forthcoming from the Louisiana Realm of the Knights of the Ku Klux Klan, whose Grand Dragon, David Duke, called Beckwith "a political prisoner" and vowed to help raise his defense purse. "This penniless victim of government illegality must be defended," Duke asserted. He later characterized Beckwith as "one of the most selfless patriots in this nation, and he should serve as an heroic example for Americans who want to stop the destruction of our school system and the destruction of our white Christian culture and civilization."[58]

A form letter with Beckwith's photo and vitae was circulated widely to drum up contributions. "Because of who I am, I have the right type of enemies," Beckwith wrote. "I am proud of my enemies. They are of every color but white, every 'creed' but Christian, they are numerous and 'in high places.' " He wrote of being accused of planning to place a bomb "in the lap" of a B'nai B'rith official, and exhibited growing paranoia. "You will discover that this plot was designed to Abolish Beckwith," he wrote. "I am still very much alive and kicking—and—with your immediate help I will outlast the Plotters."[59] Not to be outdone by Duke and his ideological brethren in Louisiana, Mississippi members of the United Klans of America said they would attempt to raise $50,000 to aid Beckwith's defense.[60]

In response to discovery motions filed by Beckwith's defense attorneys, U.S. Attorney Gerald Gallinghouse requested that the New Orleans office of the FBI supply an agent who could inform U.S. District Court Judge Jack M. Gordon, who was to hear the case, as to the identity of the informant. Special Agent Thompson Webb was dispatched to meet Judge Gordon in his chambers to identify the informant and address his credibility. Neither Beckwith nor his attorneys were present. "Further," an FBI teletype informed FBI Director Kelley and the New Orleans Division, "that there is absolutely no entrapment involved."[61] When Webb was later identified as the Jackson agent who furnished information to the FBI in New Orleans prior to Beckwith's arrest, agents in New Orleans and Jackson felt sure that if the prosecution did not subpoena Webb, Beckwith's defense attorneys would. The FBI's official posture was that if Webb was subpoenaed, he would appear, but he would stand on privilege and refuse to answer any questions. The Bureau wanted to protect Gordon Clark, the informant, at all costs. His relationships with Klan leaders had given him access few other Klansmen enjoyed. If Beckwith's original traffic arrest was "determined to be legal," an FBI file note stated, "informant's information should not be necessary."[62]

Ironically, the defense subpoenaed both Clark and L.E. Matthews, Jr. to testify that they had had an hour-and-a-half lunch with Beckwith at the Mayflower Cafe, during which time the bomb presumably could have been planted in his car. Special Agents Webb of Jackson and George Carter of New Orleans, both of whom knew the informant's identity, were also subpoenaed.[63] Jury selection took nearly four hours on Monday morning, January 14, 1974. The seated jury comprised eleven whites and one black drawn from a venire of fifty-eight people. Both alternate jurors were men, one white and one black. With the jury selected and excused, Judge Gordon heard arguments for admitting as evidence the statement Beckwith made while being booked at Central Lockup when he was arrested—that he "had a job to do."

Intelligence Division Chief Bernard Windstein, Jr., testified that FBI agents had informed his office on September 18 that Beckwith was planning a bombing attempt in New Orleans. He also testified that the map he found in Beckwith's car clearly marked a route from Interstate 10 down Claiborne Avenue to within one block of Botnick's residence, and described flashing his light into Beckwith's car and seeing the black wooden box which held the bomb.[64]

Under cross-examination, Defense Attorney Wayne Mancuso pressed Windstein to discover whether the Intelligence Division had a "mystery" source other than the FBI agent who provided the information, but Windstein stated that his only source was within the FBI. Beckwith later took the stand and testified at length about his trip to New Orleans, ostensibly to sell his grandmother's cherished Jefferson Davis china, and said he had stopped in Jackson to see friends. He denied knowing the bomb was in his car and said he knew nothing of the map found on his front seat. "I'm just as curious as you," Beckwith told Assistant U.S. Attorney Dennis Weber, "and believe me, I'm going to find out." Beckwith claimed he was ignorant of electrical theory, making it impossible for him to construct an explosive device, and said he never had "any need for such a device," and that he carried the .45 caliber pistol because he frequently traveled with large amounts of money and his life had been threatened on occasion. Beckwith's attorneys presented the argument that anyone could have planted the bomb in Beckwith's car without his knowledge.[65]

United States District Court Judge Jack M. Gordon read the indictment charging Beckwith with three counts: That he possessed a destructive device made up of six sticks of dynamite, one five-pound stick of dynamite, one alarm clock, one electrical cap, one mercury switch, and one six-volt battery, which combination of parts was wired together to constitute a bomb, which firearm was not registered to him in the National Firearms Registration and Transfer Record; that he possessed the destructive device described in the first count which was not identified by a serial number as required by law; and that he carried a .45 caliber pistol during the commission of the felony alleged in the first two counts and the pistol was not registered to him in the National Firearms Registration and Transfer Record.

"Only the guilty fleeth when no man pursueth," Beckwith confidingly told reporters while the jury was deliberating, "and I have no reason to flee." After two hours of deliberation, the jury returned with an acquittal on all three federal charges. Assistant U.S. Attorney Dennis Weber and

Judge Gordon were visibly shocked. "You have literally walked through the valley of the shadow of death," Judge Gordon told Beckwith, clearly startled that the jury had not rendered a guilty verdict. A reporter for *The New York Times* claimed the jury's verdict was easy to understand: "The only answer seems to be that Mr. Beckwith's Roman Catholic lawyer, appointed by the luck of the draw and inspired by nothing more ideologically compelling than professional challenge, handled the case more effectively than the Government lawyers did."[66]

"Well, of course, it was the result of a deep-laid plot—had to be," Beckwith told a local television reporter after his release from jail. "But as was pointed out, there are people who are in high places who know how this came about." In a thinly veiled threat, Beckwith said, "Those who plotted can suffer the consequences of the plot, and they will, I'm sure." Later, in an interview with his hometown newspaper, *The Commonwealth*, Beckwith blamed "satanic forces" for the plot. "Whoever put [the bomb] in the car accomplished what he wanted, except that he didn't destroy me or cause me to be put in jail for thirty years."[67]

Less than two weeks later, on January 31, 1974, Assistant Orleans Parish District Attorney John Volz advised that he was proceeding with the *state* charge against Beckwith for illegal transportation of explosives.[68] While Beckwith's state trial was being scheduled, the New Orleans District Attorney's Office pressed the FBI to produce its informant. In a memorandum, FBI Director Clarence Kelley noted that the District Attorney's office in New Orleans felt it would have "a strong case against Beckwith if our informant came forward and testified." Roy K. Moore, of the Jackson Division, advised on March 4 that under no circumstances should the informant be surfaced in order to testify against Beckwith in state court. Clark was, as far as the FBI was concerned, an "informant of continuing value."[69]

After several postponements, the state's trial began on May 15, 1975. If Beckwith genuinely suspected there was a plot afoot to "abolish Beckwith," his paranoid suspicions must have been confirmed when he saw the racial composition of the five-member jury seated in his state trial—"five nigger bitches," he forever after delighted in calling them. He described the legal system that sentenced him as "jewishprudence."[70] His plantation upbringing, he believed, might help him amuse and sway the jurors. "Well sir," Beckwith recounted, "those daughters of old black Joe got so tickled sitting there wiggling and giggling, yawning, stretching, picking their noses and pulling up their hose . . . that when sent out for deliberation . . . they came back in grinning—saucy-like—saying . . . 'de mudder guilty give him five years.' " Beckwith, screaming double jeopardy and failing to recognize the differences in the federal and state charges, claimed the entire scenario was "made to order for a Jewish prosecutor, an all-nigger women jury and a white man judge scared to death for his job."[71]

Clad in a brown suit, a white shirt and a brown tie, Beckwith listened intently as the prosecuting attorney, First Assistant District Attorney William Wessel, made his lengthy opening statement asserting Beckwith's guilt. The case, he said, was concerned only with whether or not Beckwith had knowingly transported an illegal explosive. Defense attorneys Travis Buckley and Harold J. Wheeler waived their opening argument, relying on "the presumption of innocence," in Wheeler's words. Glen A. Keller, assistant commander of the Emergency Services Section of the New Orleans Police Department, testified that he and his partners Robert Barrere and John Lopinto dismantled the bomb Sergeant Windstein found in Beckwith's car. He described the bomb as "very well made."[72]

The most interesting testimony came from Beckwith himself. When he was asked to list the items he had in his car, he rambled through an exhaustive litany of socks, underwear, papers, books, guns, china and other items. "Of course," Beckwith said, "I always carry a Holy Bible."[73] Although Wessel did not pick up the thread of the thought, Beckwith had established, in a single bit of testimony, the odd admixture that formed the dogma of the new Ku Klux Klan—"militant Christianity," as demonstrated by his concurrent possession of racist ephemera, guns and ammunition, a bomb and his Bible.

Beckwith elaborated on the Jefferson Davis china. Wessel asked if he still had the china in his possession. "I certainly do, sir—thank the Lord—but I would like to sell it," Beckwith said. "Do you want to buy it?" The prosecutor antagonized Beckwith in his cross-examination, trying to rile him. "Mr. Beckwith," Wessel asked deferentially, "you carry that gun because you are a small man and you need some protection from other people, or what?" Beckwith turned red. "I have a whole lot of protection," he said firmly, "but I carry that gun because I love guns. If I didn't have that gun I would have another gun, because I love guns. Just like you love good clothes."

Wessel also wanted to establish Beckwith's racist ties. "You know Sam Bowers, Jr., don't you?" Wessel asked. "Yes sir, I know him," Beckwith replied evenly. "I ran for Lieutenant Governor. I know just about everybody in Mississippi."[74] Buckley objected, and asked to make his objection without the jury present. He explained Bowers's reputed role as Imperial Wizard of the White Knights, and asked for a mistrial on the basis that Beckwith's association with Bowers might have prejudiced the all-black, five-member jury. Criminal District Court Judge Charles R. Ward, who was hearing the case, denied Buckley's motion for a mistrial.

At 9:39 P.M. on May 16, 1975, the jury unanimously convicted Beckwith of "knowingly transporting, carrying and conveying dynamite within the boundaries of the state without a license or permit." The jurors deliberated only thirty-five minutes. Defense attorneys Buckley and Wheeler indicated they would appeal the conviction, and Beckwith was freed on a $10,000 surety bond. On August 1, Judge Ward imposed the maximum sentence—a fine of $1,000 and five years imprisonment at the Louisiana State Penitentiary at Angola. He also denied the defense attorneys' motion for a new trial. Leaving the courthouse following his sentencing, Beckwith, dressed in his crisp white summer suit, offered a newspaper reporter a dollar to find out First Assistant District Attorney William Wessel's religion. "It's damn important to find out the religion of our officials in high offices," Beckwith said.[75]

Prior to the state trial, FBI Director Clarence Kelley had demanded a full report on Beckwith from Roy K. Moore. "In view of his extremist activities and obvious bent toward violence," Kelley dictated, "we should have another supplemental report to clearly indicate all of his extremist involvements since the last report six years ago." Kelley noted that the report could be delayed until the completion of the state trial against Beckwith.[76] Moore filed his report on August 22, 1975, exactly three weeks after Beckwith's sentencing. Noting that the period of report was lengthy (a formal investigative report had not been filed by the Jackson Division since October 23, 1968), Moore assured Kelley that "the Bureau has been advised of subject's activity on a continuing basis," and cited four informants who consistently provided information on Beckwith's extremist activities. The informants had continued to report on Beckwith's "verbal assaults concerning the killing of Jews, Negroes and liberal whites," and the report characterized Beckwith as "ARMED AND DANGEROUS."[77]

One informant told his Jackson FBI contact that Beckwith advocated "selected murder as a partial solution to the right wing's problem," and that he had said "he would never ask a man to do anything that he himself has not already done." The lengthy report also chronicled numerous gun purchases and trades by both Beckwith and his son, and noted that Beckwith was known to distribute papers printed by the late Dr. Wesley Swift's anti-Semitic church in California. Informants also reported to the FBI that Beckwith had attempted to lease or purchase land in Carroll County, Mississippi, but had failed. The informant said Beckwith intended to set up a firearms range there.[78]

While his case was under appeal, Beckwith attempted to resurrect the deal on the Carroll County property. With his legal battles underway, he had been unable to work out financial arrangements with the property's owner, an elderly woman named Pearl McClellan. She wanted $10,000 for seventy acres of hilly backwoods property and the frame house on it, known locally as "the old Melton place." Beckwith did not know how long his appeals would take—how long he would be free—but he knew he wanted to acquire the property before facing imprisonment. He hadn't had a permanent home since his final divorce from Willie, and his remarriages and divorces had cost him the property his Uncle Will had bequeathed him. In his mind, he may have wanted to recreate the Glen Oak Plantation of his childhood by acquiring a plot of land of his own. When he approached Mrs. McClellan again, after his sentencing, he discussed a lease-purchase arrangement in which he would make a down payment of $600, and then pay $50 per month until the total amount was paid off some fifteen years later.[79] To manage the down payment, Beckwith had to dip into his legal defense money. His lawyer, Travis Buckley, took an additional $100 to put the paperwork in order.

The four-room Melton house was built in 1909 in the small town of Cruger, in southwest Carroll County. It was an eyesore when Beckwith purchased it. The house had no running water or indoor plumbing, but Beckwith loved "roughing it." He could shoot out of any window in the house (most were already broken) and not disturb anyone; his closest neighbor was about a mile away. There were two small ponds on the property, and a gravel road across from Harmony Baptist Church led back 150 yards to the house. Beckwith moved his belongings from the small apartment on Dewey Street and set up housekeeping. While the rain made music on his tin roof, Beckwith slept on an army cot, and shuttled his water and food from Greenwood, twenty miles away. He cut his own wood every day for two fireplaces, bathed in a galvanized metal washtub and used a "slop jar" in lieu of a toilet.

The property was to be Beckwith's rallying point, a safe haven for himself and his Klan cronies.[80] There, he hoped to establish his own racist movement, where he could preach his ideas and theology to those who wanted to listen. He envisioned a retreat, where he would have a firearms range, offices, barracks, and gardens where he could grow his own food. Although he shooed off reporters and FBI agents who came around, he always enjoyed playing host to his white supremacist friends like J.B. Stoner, the chairman of the National States Rights Party in Georgia, who visited on several occasions.[81] The property gave Beckwith a sense of stability and a gravitational center. For the first time in a decade, he felt as if he had a home of his own. He piddled around the property while his appeal was underway, making minor repairs and fantasizing what it might look like in a few years.

By June 1976, with Beckwith's imprisonment virtually assured, the Jackson Division reviewed its Beckwith file and, determining that it did not meet new investigative guidelines set out by the attorney general, closed it.[82] Five months later, Beckwith received his annual Christmas card from Sam Bowers. Bowers's salutation addressed Beckwith as "my dear De La," and the card was signed, "Your friend, Sam H. Bowers, Jr."[83] Beckwith tucked it away in a drawer as a souvenir.

* * *

Facing the certainty that the Louisiana Supreme Court would uphold his conviction, Beckwith immersed himself in spiritually uplifting activities. His introduction to Christian Identity doctrine, particularly Wesley Swift's sermons, had led to his immersion in the Christian Identity Movement, as its tenets matched his personal set of beliefs and values. With roots in the nineteenth-century concept of British-Israelism, propounded in Edward Hine's 1871 book, *Identification of the British Nation with Lost Israel,* Christian Identity followers believed that the lost tribes of Israel migrated north through the Caucasus Mountains until they eventually settled in Scandinavia and the British Isles. The tribes' journey through the Caucasus Mountains made them "Caucasians." J. Gordon Melton, founder of the Institute for the Study of American Religion and author of *Encyclopedic Handbook of Cults in America,* has called Christian Identity "a religion by sociopaths, for sociopaths." Identity followers believe people of Anglo-Saxon descent are the direct biological descendants of the biblical Israelites, and as such, are God's true chosen people.[84]

Beckwith believed in the unifying value of a Christian Identity doctrine, thinking it might eventually be the key to bringing together some of the disparate, disorganized parts of the white supremacist movement. Other important figures in the white supremacist movement of the 1950s and 1960s (such as Beckwith's old friend J.B. Stoner) also increasingly realized the need to redefine the movement. The stigma associated with the Klan made it as unappealing to the general public as the dangling remains of a lynching victim. Beckwith saw splintered factions of the Klan frequently leaning toward American Nazi Party ideology, and although he was not yet ready to start his own movement, he now had the property to do so when the time was right. Christian Identity would be his vehicle.

Stoner, another violent anti-Semite, also recognized the need for racist unity. In November 1957, the United White Party was formed in Knoxville, Tennessee, by a group of disenchanted Klansmen. The following year, Stoner's fledgling National States Rights Party (NSRP) merged with the United White Party under the NSRP banner,[85] which proudly boasted Hitler's famed "SS" symbol. *Right* magazine supported the National States Rights Party during its infancy, and during the 1960s, when the Ku Klux Klan in Mississippi was at the zenith of its power, many White Knights were also linked to the NSRP.[86]

Stoner had long before proven to be cut from the same piece of cloth as Byron De La Beckwith. In 1944, Stoner filed a petition with the U.S. House of Representatives insisting on passage of a resolution recognizing that "Jews are the children of the devil, and that, consequently, they constitute a grave menace to the United States of America." He also told a reporter for *The Atlanta Constitution* that Hitler was "too moderate," and laid out his own plans to attack Jews in more modern ways—using gas, electric chairs, shooting, hanging and any other means necessary. His party's aim, Stoner said, was "to make being a Jew a crime, punishable by death."[87] He delighted in publicly referring to Dr. Martin Luther King, Jr., as "Martin Lucifer Coon." Later, in a televised commercial promoting his candidacy for the United States Senate, Stoner flatly stated, "The main reason why niggers want integration is because niggers want our white women," and followed up that thought with, "You cannot have law and order and niggers too." In a subsequent television interview, recognizing that his shock value raised public recognition of his campaign, Stoner called Atlanta Mayor Sam Massell a "Jew-gangster" and a "Christ-killer."[88]

Similar to Beckwith, Stoner's verbal assaults made him a popular "motivational" speaker for racist gatherings. Many of his NSRP members were also White Knights in the Mississippi Klan. Both Beckwith and Stoner had strong racist ties in Louisiana, which in the 1970s became a hotbed of racist activity. A dynamic young Klan leader, David Duke, was infusing new blood into what had become a dwindling Klan movement in the state. As a teenager, Duke wrote pamphlets for the local Citizens' Council. During his undergraduate days at Louisiana State University, while wearing storm trooper garb, Duke protested a speech by attorney William Kunstler. He idolized Hitler and joined the National Socialist Liberation Front, a college group supported by George Lincoln Rockwell's American Nazi Party. Duke's charisma and power as both speaker and organizer assured his quick ascent in the Knights of the Ku Klux Klan, and in 1980, while still serving as the Klan's grand wizard, he founded the wryly named National Association for the Advancement of White People.[89]

In September 1976, Beckwith, Stoner and other leading figures of the white supremacist movement gathered in New Orleans to attend the five-day World Nationalist Congress,[90] a racist convention attended by more than a thousand "delegates." Speeches and presentations centered around the Jewish-Communist conspiracy, and, according to one source in attendance, Beckwith was a featured speaker. The event included seminars, a banquet and even a parade. It was primarily a peaceful event, although David Duke and James K. Warner—who had several years earlier attempted to wrest the leadership of the American Nazi Party after George Lincoln Rockwell's assassination—were arrested for inciting to riot and failure to disperse but were released with a warning.[91]

At the time, Warner was a major player in David Duke's Louisiana faction of the Klan. His extremist New Christian Crusade Church spawned the militant Christian Defense League in 1977.[92] Warner apparently made an indelible impression on Beckwith at the World Nationalist Congress; less than a month later, in October 1976, Beckwith transferred his membership from First Independent Methodist Church in Greenwood—the church he had helped build and in whose choir he sang—to

Warner's New Christian Crusade Church in Metairie, Louisiana.[93] The transfer marked the definitive schism in Beckwith's "theological" development. After leaving the Independent Methodist Church, which was by no means mainstream, he fully adopted the dogma of the Christian Identity Movement.

Beckwith cemented his Christian Identity ties with the Reverend Buddy Tucker, pastor of Temple Memorial Baptist Church in Knoxville, Tennessee, and founder of the National Emancipation of the White Seed. Although his church was based in Tennessee, Tucker's White Seed group was headquartered in Louisiana. Beckwith had been publicly linked to Tucker as early as 1973, when the two leaders were touted as keynote speakers at the NSRP convention.[94] Dan Gayman, a leading figure in the Christian Identity Movement, was also aligned with Tucker's White Seed movement and assisted in publishing its anti-Semitic newsletter, *The Battle Ax N.E.W.S.* Beckwith frequently listened to Gayman's taped sermons, and Gayman was also affiliated with James K. Warner's New Christian Crusade Church in Metairie, Louisiana. Warner's publication, *Christian Vanguard*, regularly offered Gayman's tapes for sale. Warner also served as an officer in George Lincoln Rockwell's American Nazi Party before affiliating with Stoner's National States Rights Party. Most important, Gayman and Tucker had ties to Pastor Richard G. Butler's growing Church of Jesus Christ, Christian, in Hayden Lake, Idaho. Butler's church was the religious arm of his powerful Aryan Nations movement.Tucker's group used the Aryan Nations compound in Idaho for meetings occasionally, and Butler served on the editorial board of *The Battle Ax N.E.W.S.*, the White Seed propaganda sheet. For a brief time, Butler's Aryan Nations church affiliated with Tucker's White Seed movement, but Butler ultimately decided to form his own independent movement.[95]

Tucker's devotees were particularly colorful. In March 1975, at a three-day "Easter Conference" held at Tucker's church, speakers urged members of the congregation to start a Posse Comitatus—Latin for "power of the county." Posse members believed that no higher authority exists than the county sheriff, and they tended to be armed vigilantes and survivalists who balk at state and federal authority. Posse groups were widely publicized in the early 1980s because of their protest of the federal tax system; many members simply refused to pay federal income taxes. During the 1980s, as many as thirteen states had functioning Posse units. George Kindred, director of the Patriot's Tax Committee and the Layman Education Guild at Law in Michigan, spoke at Tucker's rally and urged local citizens to "tell officials that the penalty for violating citizens' rights or breaking the law is hanging," and to use force and violence if necessary. "I want to get rid of the niggers and Jews and I'll tell you that straight." Kindred said that some might get "suspended sentences—about two feet off the ground."[96]

On January 2, 1977, Byron De La Beckwith, still free pending his appeal, was ordained in the Gospel Ministry at Temple Memorial Baptist Church in Knoxville, Tennessee. The ordaining council was headed by Reverend Buddy Tucker and comprised assorted members of Tucker's National Emancipation of the White Seed.[97] The following month, on February 28, the Louisiana Supreme Court rejected fifteen alleged trial errors and upheld Beckwith's conviction in a 6-1 ruling. Beckwith's attorney, Travis Buckley, filed for a rehearing.[98] Meanwhile, Beckwith was planning his spring travel schedule. On April 26, while still free and awaiting word on the rehearing, the FBI was tipped off to Beckwith's attendance at a Klan event in York, Pennsylvania over the weekend of April 23–24, which he attended with a Washington, D.C., schoolteacher named Pauline Mackey. The informant indicated that Beckwith had "organized his own chapter of the Klan in Cruger," but provided no illuminating details.[99]

Former Special Agent Tom Van Riper recalled hearing rumors about Beckwith's efforts to launch a new Klan in Mississippi. "One of the agents came in one day," Van Riper said in an interview, "and he was laughing about something an informant had told him. It was about Beckwith wanting to start his own Klan. He was really proud of the things that he was doing, and felt that he could head his own organization. But that was squelched pretty quickly, though, by people above him in the Klan."

Less was known about Pauline Mackey, a spinster almost fifteen years Beckwith's senior. With her regal bearing and her refined demeanor, Mackey probably reminded Beckwith of his own faded, elegant mother. Mackey was affiliated with a number of right-wing organizations and had mailed a generous contribution to Beckwith after noticing one of his appeals in a racist periodical. He wrote and thanked her effusively, and they kept in touch by mail. She occasionally sent him additional contributions to keep his coffer full, and contributed to David Duke's faction of the Ku Klux Klan, James K. Warner's New Christian Crusade Church, Liberty Lobby and other organizations. She had, in fact, spent a few days in Warner's home while attending a "patriotic" rally in Louisiana.

The previous summer, while the nation was celebrating its bicentennial, Beckwith quit his job at Ricks' Motor Service to become an independent distributor for Sauna Oil Filters. Hoping to introduce the product to the increasing number of energy experts on Capitol Hill, Beckwith went to Washington, where he was a guest in Mackey's townhouse on Observatory Place in the fashionable Georgetown section of the city. "We went to visit some congressmen while he was here," Mackey said in an interview, explaining that Beckwith had hoped to get his distant cousin, Senator James O. Eastland, to provide introductions to government purchasing agents. Eastland refused to meet with Beckwith, but his administrative assistants cordially allowed Beckwith to show them his oil filter and discuss the product's benefits before giving him the names of several people he might contact within the Energy Research and Development Administration. After a frustrating afternoon of meeting-shuffling and cool receptions, Beckwith and Mackey returned to her townhouse to dress for dinner at a nearby restaurant. As they got out of the car they were driving, Beckwith was surrounded by a group of Secret Service agents who questioned him about his business in Washington. One of the agents asked to photograph and search Beckwith, and took from one of his coat pockets an aerosol can of Beckwith's "nigger repellant."[100] Beckwith told the agents that unless they had a warrant for his arrest, he was going to take his lady friend to dinner.

Just after 2:00 A.M. on Friday, April 29, 1977, after she and Beckwith had returned from dinner and retired to separate bedrooms, Mackey was awakened by officers pounding on her front door. "I never dreamed it would be a whole line of goofs!" she said in an interview. "They were going to break the door down if I didn't let them in. There was a whole string of them, at least half a dozen or more. And they went tromping up the steps to Byron's room, my guest room, and woke him up. And Byron collaborated—*cooperated* with them—entirely." Mackey correctly believed that an informant within the Ku Klux Klan had reported Beckwith's attendance at a local Klan meeting he attended with her the first night of his visit. She recalled that Beckwith was asked to speak at the meeting, and gave a passionate talk.

Beckwith was arrested on a fugitive warrant that he had been issued on April 26, three days earlier. Beckwith's appeal had been denied and he had failed to appear in Orleans Parish District Court to begin serving his sentence. He waived an extradition hearing in Washington and said he would voluntarily return to Louisiana to begin serving his five-year prison sentence.[101] Several of the armed officers who took Beckwith into custody at Mackey's home were black, and when he was questioned for processing at the local police department, Beckwith was handcuffed by his left hand to the "biggest negra's" desk, he recalled.

"There I was," Beckwith recounted, "me and three niggers." He found the lieutenant in charge particularly grating and cocky. "Let's get on with whatever you niggers have in mind to do," Beckwith said. The officer feigned astonishment, and turned to his fellow officers and said facetiously, "Did you know you was a nigger?" One officer told Beckwith that he, too, was a native Mississippian. "Do you know that we know how many grandchildren you have?" Beckwith recalled the officer asking him. "Where your daughter-in-law's folks live, where your son lives with his family and the people he works with, where he hunts and fishes, and all about him?" Beckwith looked at the officer with cold, clear eyes, and later wrote, "there before me sat a dead nigger—they just hadn't buried him yet!"[102]

After spending the night in jail in Washington, D.C., Beckwith was taken in a paddy wagon full of black prisoners to another prison complex to be held until authorities from Louisiana arrived to escort him back to their state. Placed in a holding cell along with several dozen black prisoners, Beckwith got into an argument with a black man who was railing against whites. "I said, look here, nigger," Beckwith remembered. "You are not looking at a piece of sorry, cowardly white trash and I'm not standing here shaking with fright at all the nigger audience you must be trying to entertain." Beckwith said he hoped, if the man threw a punch, to draw the others into the fray. Instead, Beckwith was quickly pulled out of holding and was questioned. He was later turned over to Louisiana authorities, handcuffed, and flown back to Orleans Parish Prison. En route from the local jail to the Louisiana State Prison at Angola, Beckwith suffered his greatest humiliation yet. He was handcuffed to "a little yellow-skinned perverted darkie who I was told was a queer," Beckwith later wrote.[103] On May 16, 1977, he was received and processed at the Louisiana State Penitentiary at Angola. Placed in solitary confinement, Beckwith received none of the preferential treatment he had been accorded fourteen years before in Mississippi. Separated from the other prisoners, Beckwith surveyed his cell. It would be his home for the next three years.

13

The Outskirts of Heaven

If De La Beckwith thought his prison stay in Louisiana would be even vaguely reminiscent of his earlier incarceration in Mississippi, he was grossly mistaken. Although the geographical distances and cultural differences between the two states were minimal, the decade which separated Beckwith's jail terms had brought sweeping social changes to the South. No longer was a rabid white supremacist viewed by the white public as a hero, and no longer did blacks keep their distaste for such men to themselves. In Mississippi in 1964, Beckwith was treated, as he once said, as if he had taken "a Jap admiral alive." On his arrival at the Louisiana State Penitentiary at Angola in 1977, he was among a distinct minority of white prisoners. He was reviled by black inmates who believed he was Medgar Evers's unpunished murderer, and it was widely believed Beckwith might not leave Angola alive.

"I would have been surprised if there had *not* been a price on his head," said former Angola Warden for Security, Walter Pence. At the time Beckwith was received at the prison, he was fifty-six years old, and Pence was superintendent of the building in which he was housed. "In those days, human life was pretty cheap at Angola. You could get somebody killed for a couple of cartons of cigarettes." Beckwith believed the black prisoners wanted to kill him, and further, he felt sure that any parole board would reward his murderer with leniency.[1]

For his own protection, Beckwith was separated from the other prisoners. He was placed in a protection room (not really a cell, Pence remembered) next to the prison store on the lower floor of the administration building. Beckwith's room was larger than a standard cell, and was situated near the shower stalls used by death row prisoners. When word got out among death row inmates that Beckwith was using their shower, they set to screaming every time they heard the water running. "Let them have a little recreation," Beckwith told one prison officer. "As each one finally reaches the chair, that'll cool them off." Such prison anecdotes became a staple of Beckwith's later speeches to gatherings of Klansmen and Christian Identity congregations. He was fond of recounting how little sunshine he saw while he was at Angola, and liked to joke that after showering, he would put his bare feet up in his window to let the sun sterilize them.[2]

Later, Beckwith was moved to a second-story cell near the prison doctor's office, where he spent the remainder of his imprisonment in solitary confinement. In a public statement he said he would accept a television if anyone cared to donate one, and eventually prison guards brought in an old TV set, which they placed on a fifty-five-gallon barrel. After a few days, Beckwith told them, "Take this infernal device out of my chamber! I'd rather have a live Jew or a live nigger in here than that thing!" Later, when a conservative group offered to provide another television for his cell, Beckwith graciously declined.[3]

Without a television to keep him company, Beckwith spent the majority of his time reading the Bible and writing letters. He was deeply in debt at the time of his imprisonment, having borrowed $4,000 against a paid-up life insurance policy to buy another Oldsmobile similar to the one in which he had been arrested in New Orleans. He was paying back that sum, as well as the outstanding $8,000 he owed Pearl McClellan on his "rural retreat" in Cruger. As a result, he was legally indigent.[4] Making the most constructive use of his time, Beckwith again began to lobby for financial contributions. He carefully crafted a series of solicitation letters to drum up support, and began another series of mailings. "Local patriots have earlier very generously sustained me so that I might remain a viable force in the ranks of the White Christian Right," he wrote potential donors. "However, let us realize, *my fight is and should be your fight*, being not only a regional and national matter, but also an international matter."[5]

In contrast to the quick results he had seen during the Evers murder trials, however, Beckwith seemed to be writing more and more letters, yet was receiving far fewer responses. Even contributors who had previously come to his aid with cash did not respond to his renewed pleas. Some fellow right-wingers sent cash and checks, but their donations seemed a trickle compared to the flood Beckwith received during his earlier fund drives. No matter what approach he devised—individual handwritten letters to old friends, form letters to the membership rosters of organizations to which he belonged, published letters to editors pleading for funds—Beckwith was disappointed. His public support had dwindled, and even some of his staunchest allies now seemed to be distancing themselves from him.

Another indication of his dwindling support was the dearth of visitors he received at Angola. Tucked away in solitary confinement, Beckwith probably reveled in memories of his days in jail in Jackson and Brandon, Mississippi, when local wives vied for the honor of bringing him a meal. At Angola, few such visitors came along to break up the monotony of his long days. His son visited occasionally, and Mrs. James K. Warner—

whose husband led Louisiana's militantly anti-Semitic New Christian Crusade Church, which Beckwith joined just months before his jail term began—brought gun magazines for his enjoyment. A prison chaplain also visited regularly to pray with Beckwith.[6] His most welcome visitor, however, was J.B. Stoner. Stoner had been Beckwith's guest a number of times at the "rural retreat" in Cruger, and continued his visits after Beckwith was imprisoned at Angola, making each trip at his own expense. To show his support during Beckwith's imprisonment, Stoner sent $500 to the Bank of Greenwood for deposit into Beckwith's account.[7]

Stoner's steadfast friendship meant a great deal to Beckwith during his prison term, when so many others turned their backs on him. Stoner's publication, *The Thunderbolt,* which employed the famed Hitler Youth thunderbolt symbol, was often withheld from prisoners. Still, Beckwith was able to keep his finger on the pulse of the white racist movement through other publications which passed muster as "religious" literature. Racist organizations recognized the growing importance of prisons to their "ministries." With audiences that were literally captive, groups like New Christian Crusade Church and Aryan Nations were able to swell their ranks by targeting inmates, making them feel they were an integral part of the movement, and enlisting their support when they were released from jail. Ex-convicts, once enlisted in the movement, were among its most ardent and violent supporters. Although Aryan Nations and its affiliated Church of Jesus Christ Christian launched the most successful Christian Identity prison ministry, Pastor Robert Miles's Mountain Church was also highly effective. While imprisoned at Angola, Beckwith received their publications and other Christian Identity publications which were boldly racist and anti-Semitic.[8] The Aryan Nations ministry spawned prison gangs calling themselves the Aryan Brotherhood, and Pastor Butler's workers in Hayden Lake cultivated strong relationships by mail with prisoners who were frequently recruited to the compound's halfway house in Idaho after their release.[9]

Aryan Nations, in particular, positioned its doctrine as one based not on hatred of other races, but on *love* of the Aryan race. To prisoners like Beckwith, the group's arguments made perfect sense. Many of Aryan Nations' fiercest warriors argued that they fought not from a hatred of blacks or Jews, but because they feared their race was dying—"through race-mixing, abortion, assimilation and INDIFFERENCE"[10]—one Aryan Nations pamphlet explained. "Without a pure racial body the nation will decline. To support other races who do not hold the same cultural values and goals as our own drags us down and our end will be either: (A) Pacifism, and assimilation into another brown, third-world mass on the planet, or (B) Activism, and the regeneration of the higher culture and moral standards of our ancestors." The pamphlet was written by David

C. Tate, an Aryan warrior who was later convicted of murdering a Missouri state trooper in defense of his racist ideals.

The racist tracts Beckwith regularly received—including the Aryan Nations' publications, which evolved into *The Way* and *Calling Our Nation*—were rife with conspiracy theories. With plenty of time to think about his own predicament, it became clear in Beckwith's own mind that his imprisonment was the result of Robert F. Kennedy's long-standing vendetta against him. Never mind that Kennedy had been dead since 1968. To Beckwith's thinking, the Louisiana arrest and his subsequent conviction were proof that the former attorney general's malice toward him lingered on through the organizations of the Justice Department and the FBI. And through his own special brand of circuitous logic, Beckwith *also* blamed the Louisiana arrest on a conspiracy by the ADL to help the FBI frame him for the crime, much as he believed the ADL had framed Tommy Tarrants in Meridian, Mississippi.[11]

"Are you a Jew?" Beckwith asked Lieutenant Tom R. Joseph, a correctional officer assigned to the unit where Beckwith was housed. "Not hardly," Joseph replied curtly as he pushed open the door to Beckwith's room and let another officer in with his dinner. At six-foot-two and 235 pounds, Joseph was an imposing thirty-six-year-old with dark features that hinted at his Syrian ancestry. Almost every day for the first year of Beckwith's jail term, Joseph worked the 2:00 P.M. to 10:00 P.M. shift, until he was transferred to a different camp at Angola late in 1978. Seeing him almost daily, Joseph had more contact with Beckwith than anyone else during the first year of his incarceration at Angola.

Frequently, Beckwith would stop Joseph and strike up a conversation. "He was an Old-South gentleman," Joseph remembered. "Very chosen with his words and diction, very polite toward me. He'd want to get off on some radical conversations, and normally that would be when I'd find something else to do, because he would likely go into the Bible, and that would always lead to separation of the races." Invariably, Joseph said, Beckwith wanted to talk about racial issues. "My opinion is that he was a religious man who had probably gone overboard and completely misinterpreted things, as I saw it," Joseph said. "He was overboard with religion, and it drove him into this racial thing. He could quote scripture word for word, but it all came to the same bottom line—whites are the master race. He was fanatical about religion, because he used that to prove his points about race."

Joseph also believed that Beckwith possessed charismatic qualities that could have provided leadership for the white racist movement. "A harmless little old man, that's what he looked like," Joseph said. "He was a very deceptive individual who could pass himself off as a well-educated,

Southern aristocratic type, well-off, and that's the way he'd come across. I could understand from meeting him how he could be a leader, from what he looked like and how he spoke. Look at Hitler—a small, innocent looking man in civilian clothes, but put him in a uniform at his podium in front of his microphone—I think of Beckwith along those lines. He exuded a kind of charisma, and I could understand why some people would buy his crap." The ruse was an effective one, Joseph believed. "I could see where he would be a successful salesman—he had that demeanor, and he was a successful con artist in that he'd con people into this race thing and bring them into an atmosphere of racial hatred because of his basic demeanor—a little meek, mild, mousy fellow, harmless as hell. But he had a way of talking."

Beckwith was also meticulous in his personal habits, Joseph remembered. "He spent a lot of his time writing. He had a desk in his room, and a bed. If you looked inside, it looked like a small apartment. He did an awful lot of correspondence, and if you went in his room, his writing materials were kept just so. If he wasn't in his bed it was made up neatly, military style." Much of Beckwith's writing was targeted to prospective donors, and Joseph clearly remembered one of Beckwith's written pleas for funds. "He tried to solicit me," Joseph said. Beckwith had mailed him a thick packet of racist materials—"almost as thick as a *Reader's Digest* condensed book," he said—and Joseph immediately turned the package over to his commanding officer. The only other request Beckwith made of Joseph was for baking soda. "He asked for it several times—he wanted to brush his teeth with baking soda," Joseph said. "It seemed the closest he ever came to really wanting something while he was in prison, and when you could get some from the kitchen, he was very appreciative."

Beckwith's solitary confinement, combined with his worries over the conspiracy he believed had imprisoned him, made it virtually impossible for him to forge friendships with even the white inmates at Angola. He did find a captive audience among some of the staff there. "There weren't a lot of prisoners like Beckwith," Walter Pence said with a laugh. "He was someone you wanted to keep your eye on, or he'd be running the place for you." Pence recalled Beckwith as a model prisoner—quiet, polite, and content to serve his time in solitary confinement. "He had a lot of charisma," Pence said. "Hell, there were several prison officers who fell under his spell. In fact, I transferred one officer away from the unit for that reason," Pence said. "It wasn't that the man was doing anything wrong, I just got the impression he was listening to Beckwith too much. In prison, even the officers working there have a lot of time on their hands. And you'll do a lot of things to pass the time—even listen to Beckwith."

Beckwith frequently struck up a conversation with Pence when he was walking down the hallway. "Probably if he knew I had some Jewish blood in my ancestry, he wouldn't have talked to me at all," Pence said. "He was the kind of guy, until you got to know him, that you wouldn't mind living next door to, barbecuing or having a Budweiser with. You always ended up in the same conversation, though. He didn't like blacks, and that was generally the subject of the conversation before it was over with. It seems that whatever problems he's had in his life, evidently he could trace them back to the fact that there were blacks in the world." Pence also remembered that Beckwith had a personal mannerism that was annoying. "When he talked to you, he'd rub his hands together."

A far more problematic prisoner at Angola was Paul Scheppf, who became an associate of Beckwith's. "Scheppf tried to organize a Klavern of the Klan on me in Camp C one time," Pence remembered. "He just wanted to gather him a little crew up there and kind of run things for the white boys." Pence traced Beckwith's relationship with Scheppf to a time when they were both in the Controlled Cells Reserved section of the prison. Although they were in solitary confinement, prisoners were released from their cells occasionally to walk the hallways. Scheppf was serving time for manslaughter. "He just got the idea he wanted to kill him a black," Pence said. "People were scared of him. They felt like he could back up the talk."

Like Beckwith, Scheppf was a decorated U.S. Marine. He served in Vietnam and had been a prisoner of war at Hue. He returned stateside with an intense hatred for blacks and Jews, and during his prison term was named one of three editors of the *Inter-Klan Newsletter and Survival Alert*, a publication launched to bring unity to disparate Klan organizations. Its masthead bore the legend "Death to Every Foe and Traitor," and Scheppf's co-editors were Robert Miles, the Michigan minister and Klan leader, and Louis R. Beam, a Texas Klan leader who ran his own paramilitary organization. Beam also wrote *Essays of a Klansman* and created the Klan's assassination point-system, that rewarded Aryan warriors for acts of violence and assassinations.[12]

"Scheppf gave me the impression he wasn't wrapped too tight," Pence recalled. "He could say about ten words and you'd think he was ready to throw shells in the shotgun." To Beckwith, however, Scheppf must have seemed a soul mate. He was clearly committed to the white racist cause, and additionally was a devotee of J.B. Stoner's anti-Semitic NSRP. Within five years, Scheppf was referring to Beckwith as an "old friend."[13]

Another inmate, Pete Scalise, also managed to communicate with Beckwith and become a confidant. Like Scalise, Scheppf had served in Vietnam in the Army and had been a drill instructor for several years. Scalise was known throughout Angola as "The White Knight" because of his loud and frequent claims to have inflicted as much pain as possible on "Jewniggers." Although they were imprisoned behind the thick walls of the Angola fortress, Beckwith and Scalise carried on a cautious correspondence. Through a man Scalise identified only as "Mr. Hall," the prisoners exchanged letters and ideas. Although the penitentiary offered a "farm mail" program through which inmates could communicate with each other in a manner similar to interoffice mail, Scalise and Beckwith employed an intermediary, undoubtedly to keep their correspondence from being inspected or read. It is clear from Scalise's letters that he clearly idolized Beckwith as a leader of the white racist movement and felt comfortable disclosing secrets to him.

"You have a record to be proud of," Scalise glowingly wrote Beckwith. "In White History which is truth, you will be listed as one of the great leaders in the white revolution which will surely come." Scalise explained his lifelong hatred of "niggers," and recounted murdering a black near New Orleans as his brother-in-law watched in horror. Several years later, Scalise's brother-in-law wanted to clear his conscience and made it known that he planned to go to the police and tell them of the murder. "Some hours after I killed him, I was arrested and have been here ever since," Scalise confided to Beckwith. Scalise commiserated with Beckwith, explaining that his five years in prison had taught him "real hate." He expected Beckwith's help in reestablishing on the "outside" when he was released. "I need a weapon, some transportation and a place to work from," Scalise wrote—perhaps a place like Beckwith's rural retreat in Cruger. In return, Scalise promised to serve Beckwith when he was released from prison. "One thing you don't have to worry about is me pulling the trigger to help you," Scalise wrote. "I will do so and put my life on the line for you."[14]

Scalise's apparent devotion to both the white racist movement in general, and Beckwith in particular, made him a likely candidate for the ministry Beckwith planned to launch at Cruger after his release. And like Beckwith and Scheppf, Scalise was a member of the NSRP—a link to J.B. Stoner that Beckwith undoubtedly valued. Scalise was such a strong NSRP supporter, that he had filed suit against his warden at Angola because his subscription of *The Thunderbolt* was being withheld from him.[15] Scalise's willingness to take violent action was probably refreshing to Beckwith, who filed away his letters for future reference.

As his prison term slowly crept by, Beckwith went out of his way to keep from becoming idle. Reading the Bible and racist literature helped pass some time, and Beckwith often created little projects to busy himself. Once, he made a set of cuff links from buttons he tore off his prison mattress, hooking them through the cuffs of his regulation chambray shirt as though he were still wearing a starched and monogrammed dress shirt. While jailed, he passed a painful kidney stone and underwent surgery for a hernia that had been troubling him for several years. One of his consulting physicians was Jewish, which suited Beckwith just fine. On arrival at Huey Long Hospital in Baton Rouge, Beckwith told the physician, "You are my insurance. Every patriot in Louisiana knows I am here, and why, and who will be doing the job. I have every confidence it will be well and adequately performed."[16]

Mostly, though, Beckwith's time at Angola passed slowly and uneventfully. In the spring of 1978, after eleven months in prison, he wrote an open letter to Governors Edwin Edwards of Louisiana and Cliff Finch of Mississippi, asking them to grant him a thirty-day release so he could appear before Masonic lodges in Mississippi and Louisiana to speak in his own defense. He hoped to persuade the Masonic orders to help him lobby for a new trial before an all-white, all-Christian jury. Beckwith asked the governors to allow him "to travel freely in both states or the entire Southern U.S.A. unrestricted until I am to return to Angola."[17] When editors at *Jackson* magazine lampooned Beckwith's letter as an example of "the way his mind works,"[18] he became so infuriated that he vowed to put the magazine out of business—although he had previously offered to grant the magazine an exclusive interview in exchange for three free advertisement placements. Later, after the magazine ceased publication for entirely different reasons, Beckwith circulated copies of the magazine article with a note boasting that he helped cause its demise.[19]

Behind bars, where he was unable to exert his influence on fellow Klansmen and other extremists, Beckwith's letters took on a decidedly zealous tone. In January 1978, apparently compelled by impending action to banish him from his Masonic lodge for un-Masonic conduct, Beckwith wrote a thirteen-page letter on legal paper, addressing himself to all of Masonry. His concern was that he might be expelled based on the action of the "all-nigger" jury that convicted him. His venomous hatred for the jurors was never more evident. Throughout the lengthy diatribe, he referred to them as "cannibals," "granddaughters of our folks' slaves," and—having worked up a fiery anger—"five street-walking, cotton-picking, government-fed, wall-eyed, bow-legged, snaggle-toothed tar babies."[20]

The letter is critically important, not because of Beckwith's vitriolic attacks against those who found him guilty in the Louisiana case, but because more than any other single document, it expounds on Beckwith's religious and racial beliefs and the inextricable link between the two. He writes of being "an active part" of many organizations comprised of white Christians—presumably the Klan, the Citizens' Council, the National Emancipation of the White Seed and the NSRP. "I have learned from war, history and the church that we must destroy all our enemies from within—at once—immediately—totally—completely—entirely and forever," Beckwith wrote. "As Yahveh the Ever Living God does strengthen me, I will do whatever I must—even to compelling you to act upon this great truth."[21]

Recounting the Jewish conspiracy theories that had become an integral part of his belief system, Beckwith set forth his argument that Communism was "totally, completely, entirely, 100% Jewish!" His letter was a battle cry to all of Masonry that their ranks had been infiltrated by Jews and that they should be purged. "To be Christian is to be Caucasian," Beckwith wrote. "Not Oriental—not Negroid—not Mongoloid or mixed in any way—and to hell with what Billy Graham has told you about Jesus Christ being a brown man—Billy lied." He referred to Jews as "these Luciferean children—sons of Cain—the serpent's seed, no less," and argued that his ancestors throughout Europe "were killing Jews, burning Jews, and hanging all the Jews they could lay their hands on—long—long—long before the Third Reich was ever thought of or came into being."[22]

Beckwith called the Bible "a history of the white race only," and explained to his Masonic brethren that "the covenants made were with your ancestors—and for your benefit." He also offered his own peculiar insights into the Talmud, which he described as being "filled with things that would make even a pure savage vomit, such as a Jew can have sexual intercourse with a dead relative (whether single or married) or any non-Jew child of three years or more." Finally, in closing, Beckwith made it clear he would treat with hostility any action the Masonic orders might take to renounce him, and said that he would "carry proudly the long, sharp sword of retribution which I have sold many a coat of mine to purchase," Beckwith threatened. He was so firmly convinced of his skills as a writer and a fighter that he had long before taken as his Masonic mark a crossed quill pen and a sword.[23]

A year later, on New Year's Day, 1979, Beckwith wrote another form letter targeted to Masons, addressed as well to Knights of Columbus and "all other predominantly Christian orders and societies." Looking toward the future and his eventual release from Angola, Beckwith made clear his commitment to the Christian Identity Movement and attempted to persuade his readers to become his followers. He made it clear he was starting his own religious-paramilitary group, which he had been inspired to name the Rod of Iron Christian Mission. It would be the crowning achievement of his career as a racist, and Beckwith planned to fully devote himself to its growth after his release from Angola. "I did not return from WWII with wounds of battle to be ruled by Jews, judged by the daughters of our peoples' slaves, nor to be 'bossed' about by bureaucrats!" Beckwith implored. He made an emotional appeal to his readers—"Surely your ancestors did not come here to be serfs, vassals or slaves to the monstrous whore 'Babylon the Great,' which today as always, is World Jewry!" After years of study and soul-searching—during which he had experienced not a religious evolution, but a religious reinvention—Beckwith's immersion in Christian Identity was finally complete.[24]

Clearly inspired, during his twenty-fifth month in solitary, Beckwith wrote another form letter that he distributed to conservative law firms and automobile dealers, trying to acquire a car exactly like the one in which he'd been arrested. His own car had been impounded, searched, stripped and, he asserted, destroyed. He wrote the recipients that he had "cooled down" over the matter—"down to a white-hot rage!" Not only did he ask for someone to donate a car for his use upon his release from Angola; he asked that it be "full of Ethyl (please), serviced, tag, sticker, papers too (please) here and running so I won't have to be 'bussed' out of here." He said he would accept "no substitutes, please."[25] Beckwith later admitted he was angry and was "grabbing at straws" when he sent out the letter. It was a futile attempt. Neither a conservative law firm nor an automobile dealer came to his aid.

On January 13, 1980, Beckwith was discharged early from the Louisiana State Penitentiary at Angola—for good behavior. His race hatred had not abated; his imprisonment at the hands of a black jury and a system he termed "jewishprudence" only steeled his hatred of blacks and Jews. No attempt had been made at Angola to rehabilitate Beckwith; he merely lived as quietly as possible and served his time. He had penned numerous letters to "patriots" he believed would come to his financial aid when he was released, and several opened their checkbooks to him. Pauline Mackey, with whom he had been visiting in Washington when he was arrested as a fugitive, sent donations regularly. One former U.S. Marine buddy of Beckwith's, from Louisiana, gave him $5,000. New Christian Crusade Church raised an additional $5,000 and donated it to Beckwith. For a brief time, he retreated to a "place of rest and seclusion,"[26] perhaps the Aryan Nations compound in Hayden Lake, Idaho.

He was undoubtedly still in close contact with Aryan Nations, because within months his address on the group's mailing list had correctly been changed from the Louisiana State Penitentiary at Angola to his rural route in Cruger, Mississippi.[27] Just before Thanksgiving, Beckwith received a letter from Pastor R.G. Butler on Aryan Nations letterhead, praising him as a hero of the white race and noting that his financial contributions would not be required to keep him on the list for mailings and tapes. Beckwith cherished the letter and put it away in a "fan mail" file, along with his Christmas cards from Sam Bowers and correspondence from other white supremacists like J.B. Stoner. Adjacent to his signature, Butler clearly wrote "88"—marking the eighth letter of the alphabet and signifying "Heil Hitler." When Aryan Nations' church was later bombed, Beckwith sent Butler $500 to help with the rebuilding.[28]

Beckwith's search for spiritual truth—to which he had devoted himself fully while imprisoned at Angola—shifted to more practical matters after he returned to Cruger. He had stored his few possessions on the property, and hired a bulldozer to remove three years' growth of shrubbery and underbrush around his house.[29] Having had his daily needs for food, clothing and shelter met while in prison, Beckwith was chagrined to once again be living the rough life, without electricity, running water or indoor plumbing. Further, he was a poor cook and quickly tired of his own concoctions. He was fifty-nine years old and seemed to be starting his life all over again. What he needed, Beckwith decided, was a wife.

The idea had been on his mind for several years. Five months prior to his arrest in Louisiana, in April of 1973, he contacted his former wife, Willie, when he learned her mother had died. Knowing he would be able to reach her at her mother's home in Knoxville, he sent a telegram[30] and followed it with a twenty-four-page handwritten love letter. "I want you—I need you—I must have you," he implored in his first communication with her in nearly a decade. "Will you marry me?" In another letter the following month, he pressed Willie on the matter, suggesting that they marry on September 22, their original anniversary.[31] Had she seriously considered his proposal, it would have been their fourth marriage.

For a brief time, Willie responded to his letters, but she again broke contact when he was arrested the following September, just five days after what would have been their twenty-eighth anniversary. Two years later, in the spring of 1975, (while he was still under appeal in the Louisiana case) Beckwith again wrote Willie that he hoped to remarry. Although she did not know it at the time, her former husband had approached one of her best friends, with whom she had lost contact after she fled Mississippi. "He sent me flowers," the woman, a lifelong Greenwood resident, remembered in an interview. Beckwith made his initial approach with a letter. "He told me I was such a grand lady," she recalled. "It was a very flowery letter, like someone in the 1860s had written it." She vividly remembered Beckwith's subsequent marriage proposal by mail. "I got maybe three letters, kind of in a row, then I got the flowers, and then I got a phone call." In one of the letters, which she later destroyed, Beckwith asked her to marry him. "He said he was looking for a wife, and that he would be so *honored* to have me as his wife," she recalled. "I never did say 'You're ridiculous,' or anything like that. I just thanked him and told him I really was not interested."

The following year, in the fall of 1976, perhaps to again show Willie that he was serious about finding a wife, Beckwith wrote her that he was considering marrying an older woman who had never been married—a school teacher "a year or two older" than himself.[32] His supporter from Washington, Pauline Mackey, seemed an ideal candidate for marriage. She was clearly committed to the white supremacist cause, she was a nonsmoker and never drank, and she owned a lovely town house which was far more comfortable than Beckwith's "rural retreat" in Cruger. She was, however, almost fifteen years Beckwith's senior and seemed uninterested in marriage at her advanced age.

Through Liberty Lobby, however, Mackey knew a retired nurse and vocal conservative from Signal Mountain, Tennessee, Thelma Lindsay Neff. The two women became friends at events and seminars they attended, and after their friendship was cemented, Neff occasionally stayed as Mackey's house guest in Washington. Mackey remembered planning a trip to a rally in Chattanooga, near Neff's home. "I asked her if it would be all right if Byron came, and she said 'Sure,' and she put him in the front bedroom where she had satin sheets on the bed!" Mackey recalled in an interview. Beckwith drove up from Cruger and met Mackey at Neff's modest home. Beckwith and Neff quickly became enamored of one another. "She sure took a liking to him very quickly," Mackey recalled.

Neff's first meeting with Beckwith left an indelible impression on her. "The first thing he said to me was, 'Honey, your phone's tapped!' " she recalled in an interview. She had recently written a letter to the local newspaper attacking Henry Kissinger, and she believed Jews might have bugged her telephone. "I quoted what the Rothschilds and Rockefellers were after, before anybody else even thought about One World Government," she said, "so I wrote this editorial about Kissinger, and the Jews began to call me." Like Beckwith, Thelma Neff subscribed to many of the conspiracy theories propagated by right wing publications like Liberty Lobby's *Spotlight*. "They want to get rid of the people that stand up for Christianity," she said of Jews. "They're getting ready for One World Government." Such conspiracies apparently even extended to the quiet Chattanooga suburb of Signal Mountain, where blacks and Jews have traditionally been greeted with a chilly reception. She discussed the brouhaha surrounding the arrival of an interracial couple in the clannish community. "Somebody planted them up here, we think the NAACP," she confided. "A white woman's married to a nigger. And she's got a black baby."

Having facilitated Beckwith's introduction to Neff, Mackey returned to Washington after spending several days on Signal Mountain. After his own return to Mississippi, Beckwith and Neff kept in touch. Like Mackey, Neff was more than a decade older than Beckwith. Born on May 28, 1909, she was eleven years his senior, although the age difference was not readily apparent, as, she readily volunteered in an interview, she had had a face-lift. Despite the difference in their ages, the couple had a great deal in common. They shared ultraconservative political views, strongly believed in racial separation, and cherished their family backgrounds.

Both had also been through divorces that left them disillusioned. Neff was married to Glenn Cagle in 1928, and after their divorce married William Neff in 1938. The Neffs were divorced in 1953. One early suitor, former U.S. Senator Estes Kefauver from Tennessee, sent Neff a five-word telegram—"Why did you do it?"—after one of her marriages. A prospective third husband, a physician with whom Neff was planning a winter wedding, died during an office visit with a patient.[33]

Like Beckwith, Neff fancied herself a Southern aristocrat. Her family owned land on Signal Mountain—some of the most valuable real estate in the region—and she claimed to have been crowned Miss Chattanooga during the pageant's infancy. She had been an attractive young woman, and her likeness adorned ink blotters that were distributed around the city. She fulfilled her childhood dream of becoming a nurse, served during World War II and later became a private duty nurse. A Chattanooga street was named for one of her illustrious ancestors, and her membership in the Daughters of the American Revolution matched Beckwith's long and proud affiliation with Sons of the American Revolution. Both Neff and Beckwith served on Liberty Lobby's board of policy—a distinction bestowed on those who made a financial contribution to the organization.

Their courtship began auspiciously. "As soon as he got out of Angola, that's when we started dating," she remembered. Within a year, Beckwith was professing his undying love for her. He presented her with a copy of *Line of Departure: Tarawa*, a book about the World War II battle in which he had been shot off his amphibious tractor. Beckwith wrote a syrupy inscription in his florid handwriting and signed it, "I love you, De La."[34] For numerous reasons, Beckwith found Neff an attractive potential wife. She rode the bus to Mississippi several times and helped clean up his Cruger retreat, and demonstrated that she was not afraid to get her hands dirty. More important, she owned her own home and several rental properties which assured her a regular income in addition to her Social Security benefits. Foremost, though, she was willing to commit to marriage even though she had passed her seventieth birthday.

Thelma Lindsay Neff and Byron De La Beckwith were married on June 8, 1983, in the tiny hamlet of Dunlap, Tennessee. The simple civil ceremony was notable for its lack of frills. It was the third marriage for the seventy-four-year-old bride, and the fourth marriage for the sixty-two-year-old groom. On her wedding ring finger, Thelma Beckwith began wearing a large solitaire of cubic zirconia. "I knew he was the man for me," she said. "I knew I loved him. I admire him for what he stands for." She described their early years together as "the happiest time of my life."[35]

Later the same week, to mark the twentieth anniversary of Medgar Evers's assassination, the *Jackson Daily News* ran a front-page article about

Beckwith's quiet life in the Mississippi Delta. He had not yet made the move to his new wife's home on virtually all-white Signal Mountain. Beckwith chuckled when he told friends and occasional reporters about the racial composition of his new hometown. "There's a few Jews and niggers," he would say. "But every now and then their houses burn down and they don't come back. Niggers are careless with their cigarettes, you know."[36]

Signal Mountain, and particularly Walden, the area in which the Beckwiths lived, seemed an idyllic retirement spot to Beckwith. He frequently called it "the outskirts of heaven,"[37] and he and Thelma even talked occasionally about building a larger home back in the woods on some property she owned, further off the beaten path. "He loves this mountain," Thelma Beckwith commented. Undoubtedly, he also loved living in a comfortable home with running water and electricity. The couple quickly settled into a daily routine, rising at 6:00 A.M. for coffee and retiring at sundown, unless they were entertaining company. Beckwith greatly admired his new wife's local activism. She was a well-known figure on Signal Mountain, and, like Beckwith, was an inveterate writer of letters-to-the-editor on conservative issues.

The Beckwiths became active in town meetings and even worked outdoors to help clear Mabbitt Spring, a nearby historic site. Together, with several others volunteers, the Beckwiths cut and cleared trees, removed debris, and planted flowers at the spring.[38] "It's a very pretty place, all about the history of the town of Walden," she said. "We were appointed—I was, you know—to redecorate and clean it up. It hadn't been cleaned up since 1932. So De La helped me with that." Beckwith enjoyed these projects, and enjoyed working outdoors at his new home, which had a large front yard with beautiful shade trees. Beds of brightly colored flowers were planted around their bases, and Beckwith tended them regularly. When he was not trying to sell wood stoves or water purifiers as a sideline, he spent his time working in the yard or maintaining his wife's rental properties, which included an apartment in the basement of their home on Albion Way. Each day, Beckwith would walk to the mailbox—the most decorative one on the street, as it had ornaments of hoot owls on it—to retrieve the increasing amounts of mail from associates in racist organizations with which he was still affiliated.

At Walden town meetings on Signal Mountain, De La Beckwith became a vocal participant in the proceedings. "We're real active," Thelma Beckwith said. "I suppose since De La and I have been married, we haven't missed but four or five meetings." Occasionally, Beckwith would make a foray into the local newspapers with letters about the ill effects of fluoride—another conspiracy theory propounded by followers of the Christian Identity Movement. "Since we've been married, we haven't drank any of the water," Thelma Beckwith confided. "We go out to the springs."

Christian Identity followers, in fact, believe fluoride is a "mind-bending" chemical introduced by the federal government—the Zionist Occupation Government, according to Identity followers—to make the public docile.[39] Thelma Beckwith believed fluoridation was solely responsible for Alzheimer's Disease, and she and her husband aggressively lobbied the Town of Walden's water board to persuade its members to sell back its fluoride dispensing equipment to help curb outside attempts at "mind control." When house-guests and reporters came calling, each was assured the iced tea they were being served was not made with fluoridated water. Beckwith could find only one upside in fluoride: "Currently, all the queers/perverts, and even a few innocents with AIDS, die much faster drinking fluoridated water," he asserted. "Well, if fluoride kills AIDS-infected perverts, en masse, then that to me is great—God orders the same (using stones)—or have you read your Bible lately?"[40] His diatribes about fluoride were published in the local newspapers, and Beckwith mailed copies to publications all over the country to stir up interest in the fluoride debate.

Beckwith's own health was failing, however, and no amount of outdoor activity or purified water seemed to benefit his physical condition. "I knew in the beginning he was going to be real sick," Thelma Beckwith said, "because he wasn't himself at times, and he would snap me up, and then say, 'I don't know what makes me do it.' And then twice, he just completely passed out—fell to the floor." In January 1986, Beckwith underwent experimental surgery at Vanderbilt University Medical Center. His left renal artery was removed, cleaned and replaced to relieve a ninety percent blockage to his left kidney. Beckwith's wife remembered taking advantage of his condition to ask him a question that had been nagging at her since their marriage. "When he was under the anesthetic—he was dead out—I asked him, 'Did you kill Medgar Evers?' " she recounted in an interview. His reply to her: "No, but he's dead!"

Following the surgery, from which Beckwith made a remarkable recovery, he reported every ninety days to the Vanderbilt Hypertension Clinic for checkups. When his insurance company, Mutual of Omaha, gave him a difficult time over his claim because his surgery was experimental, Beckwith said, "It must be Jew run."[41] At every turn, Beckwith felt he was being met by another arm of the Jewish conspiracy to bankrupt, imprison or kill him. Although his health improved dramatically after the surgery, his blood pressure was still uncontrollable. He underwent angioplastic surgery and an arteriogram,[42] and experienced a persistent numbness in his face. He also developed skin cancers on his ears. To make matters worse, the following year he inadvertently tripped over a chair his wife had moved into their bedroom and broke three ribs. His wife's health also declined. She developed stomach polyps or a tumor, and began seriously considering surgery herself. She also suffered a series of mishaps around the house. She fractured an ankle and an elbow, in separate incidents, and fell on her patio and bumped her head.[43]

While he and Thelma recuperated, Beckwith began his fight for restoration of the "rights and privileges" that had been denied him since his felony conviction in Louisiana—the right to vote and the right to legally own firearms. Beckwith wrote several law firms in Tennessee to check the status of his voting eligibility in Tennessee. One Chattanooga firm, Witt, Gaither & Whitaker, advised Beckwith that his Louisiana felony conviction "most likely" rendered him ineligible to vote in Tennessee. The firm also advised that following the Supreme Court's opinion in *Ballew* v. *Georgia*, courts in Louisiana consistently found that trials before five-member juries—such as the one which convicted Beckwith in the Louisiana case—were "unconstitutional," and that sentences from such juries "must be reversed." Beckwith's jubilance was impossible to hide. Although the Chattanooga firm was unable to help, it advised that he seek Louisiana counsel to help resolve his case. Beckwith was unable to find a law firm that would assist him.[44]

Although there were guns around the Beckwith house in Signal Mountain—his wife hid a pistol in the bench of her electric organ in the living room, she disclosed in an interview—as long as any gun found in the house belonged to his wife, he was not violating federal law denying felons the right to own firearms. Losing his right to vote, however, incensed Beckwith. He wrote an old friend, Charles Ellis, who was circuit court clerk in Carroll County, Mississippi. "As long as I am Circuit Clerk," Ellis assured Beckwith, "you can vote at Black Hawk. Of course, if someone contested it we might have to do different."[45] Criminals with felony convictions in another state (Beckwith was convicted in Louisiana) can legally vote in Mississippi under state law. Beckwith was unable to vote in Tennessee, however, even though that was the state in which he was residing, because state laws there clearly prohibited it. He had only one option, and he exercised it. Beckwith voted at Black Hawk in the November 1984 election.[46]

Beckwith continued to lobby to regain his rights, and in May 1986 wrote Louisiana Governor Edwin Edwards again, this time seeking a first offender pardon. "The Department of Public Safety and Corrections has recommended that you not be granted a pardon at this time," Edwards responded in a form letter. Thelma Beckwith then appealed to Governor Edwards with a letter of her own, but her appeal fell on deaf ears. "I must ask you to try to be patient," Edwards wrote.[47] Beckwith never received the pardon he believed he deserved, and concluded it was yet another example of the Jewish conspiracy against him.

Beckwith had returned to Mississippi regularly to visit his son and grandchildren, and he and his wife jointly made arrangements to sell his backwoods property in Cruger, approximately seven acres of which Beckwith had earlier given to the trustees of nearby Harmony Baptist Church. His ties to Mississippi remained strong, both in body and in spirit. Beckwith agreed to sign over his remains to the University of Mississippi Medical Center for anatomical study, and at one point in early 1984 offered his services to "literally wipe out" the narcotics trade around Greenwood at the urging of his old friend, Gordon Lackey.[48] Leaving the Mississippi Delta was difficult for Beckwith, who, except for brief periods, had never lived anywhere else. As he settled into life with his new wife on Signal Mountain, however, Beckwith found himself within the sacred boundaries of another Delta—a large triangle of land some white supremacists believed would eventually become the true white nation of biblical Israel, manifest on earth. The triangle stretched from East Tennessee to the coast of North Carolina and south into Georgia.

Although he had lost segregationist battles in the 1960s when he and his compatriots in the Citizens' Council, the Klan and other racist organizations were unable to derail the passage of civil rights laws, Beckwith hoped for a resurgence of interest in the white racist movement in this new Delta. Given the frequency of arrests and convictions for racially motivated bombings, beatings and other terrorist activities in the 1970s and early 1980s, however, the attitudes of racist groups were less palatable to the public.[49] Few among even the most conservative Southerners found crisp cotton robes and burning crosses alluring. As a result, membership in Klan organizations decreased during the 1970s and plummeted during the 1980s. Yet disparate factions of the white racist movement—from former Klansmen and Posse Comitatus members to violent young neo-Nazis and skinheads—were slowly aligning under the banner of the Christian Identity Movement. Annual gatherings at the Aryan Nations compound in Idaho, called "World Congresses," brought together leaders of extremist organizations for events ranging from sermons to target practice. Unlike the earlier World Nationalist Congress Beckwith and others attended in New Orleans in 1976, the Aryan Nations World Congresses strongly bound together their disparate racist groups with the thread of Christian Identity theology—"We will rule over those of every race *worldwide* that are not of our blood," Beckwith wrote.[50]

Safely tucked away on Signal Mountain, Beckwith found himself firmly ensconced within a surprisingly large community of Christian Identity compatriots, many of whom were involved in paramilitary and survivalist activities. Beckwith called them "a jolly band," and reveled in both their proximity and religious views. In Marietta, Georgia, just two hours south of Signal Mountain, Beckwith's old friend J.B. Stoner maintained his headquarters for the NSRP. After serving a prison term for his role in the bombing of Birmingham's Bethel Baptist Church in 1958, Stoner returned to Marietta and founded Crusade Against Corruption. "PRAISE GOD FOR AIDS," his new flyers screamed. "God is intervening in earthly affairs with AIDS to destroy His enemies and to rescue and preserve the White race." Marietta was also home to Dr. Edward Fields, a chiropractor and former associate of Stoner's who tried to usurp power of the NSRP when Stoner was jailed in 1983 for the 1958 bombing. Fields was a long-time Beckwith supporter, contributing nearly $2,000 at one point,[51] and he was also a Ku Klux Klan organizer.

In East Ridge, a suburb of Chattanooga just a few miles from Signal Mountain, John Standring led a group called the Christian Guard. Standring quickly became a close friend of the Beckwiths, and his followers attended many of the same Christian Identity church services the Beckwiths attended. Standring often told his followers, "He that hath no sword, let him sell his garment and buy one,"[52] quoting Luke 22:36 to support his argument that white Christian warriors must arm themselves. Photos of Standring, wearing fatigues and holding a high-powered rifle to his eye, adorned many of his Christian Guard flyers. Captions identified him as a "Caucasian Empire Missionary." The rifle in his hands was his not-so-subtle way of "Sending a Message from East Ridge, Tennessee." Beckwith greatly admired Standring's attempts to "shatter the hideous assaults of the anti-Christ Jew against us,"[53] and collaborated with Standring on an article they submitted to Liberty Lobby's publication, *The Spotlight.*

Less than a hundred miles from Chattanooga, in Pulaski, Tennessee, the birthplace of the original Ku Klux Klan in 1865, Klan and neo-Nazi groups annually held rallies and anniversary festivities, which the Beckwiths attended regularly. When admirers asked for photographs, the Beckwiths would smile while pictures were snapped. Thelma Beckwith enjoyed their visits to Pulaski, and she was quick to defend her husband's ties to the Ku Klux Klan. "De La acted as a *minister* to the KKs," she said in an interview. "He's not a Klan member. Never has been. But he likes what they stand for." She explained that his ministerial duties to the Klan were only one facet of his spiritual activity. "We're on the go all the time, going to big meetings," she said. "And you ought to hear De La make speeches—he has them crying one minute and laughing the next." An avid history buff, Beckwith especially enjoyed visiting Pulaski. He delighted in the town's quaint charm, and it was only minutes away from Columbia, Tennessee, where he had briefly attended Columbia Military Academy as a youth.

Perhaps the most interesting group to Beckwith, however, flourished in nearby Benton, Tennessee—just northeast of Chattanooga. It called itself the American Pistol & Rifle Association (APRA). In its flyers, APRA touted itself as an "uncompromising, freedom oriented organization." Its membership comprised "patriots, constitutionalists, survivalists and combat marksmen." Beckwith characterized the group as "more aggressive than the NRA." Beckwith's close friend, Gordon "Jack" Mohr—a prolific writer on white supremacy and Christian Identity topics—served as vice president of the national APRA organization, and Beckwith was quick to affiliate with the local chapter, even though his right to keep and bear arms had been stripped concurrent with his felony conviction. Mohr spoke to the Hiwassee Unit in Benton in August 1986, and Beckwith made a special effort to attend.[54] On the surface, the Hiwassee Unit of APRA in Benton seemed an innocuous target range, where members could hone their skills with rifles and pistols. The Benton group, however, had established ties with individuals who later joined the most frightening group of terrorists the Christian Identity Movement ever produced.

Robert Mathews, a former National Alliance activist with ties to Aryan Nations, founded a group called The Order in October 1983. Within a year, members of his group—also called the *Bruder Schweigen*, or "Silent Brotherhood"—had carried out an agenda of armed robbery, counterfeiting, bombings and murder. Counterfeit currency was printed on the grounds of the Aryan Nations compound in Hayden Lake, Idaho, and was circulated by members in faraway cities. A string of armed robberies financed the group with a sum of $4.5 million through 1984, when members of The Order murdered Denver talk show host Alan Berg. Berg's inflammatory talk show was widely known, and his propensity for riling his callers—particularly those belonging to racist groups, who frequently listened in—was equally well-known. The Order's goal, according to one member's sworn trial testimony, was "the annihilation of the Jewish race."[55] The group took its blueprint for action from a novel, *The Turner Diaries*, written under the pseudonym Andrew MacDonald by National Alliance founder Dr. William Pierce. In the novel, members of a racist group commit increasingly violent acts until they gain control of the United States and eventually the world.

While news accounts of The Order read like fiction—with real-life tales of armed robberies, shoot-outs, murders and conspiracies to overthrow the U.S. government—the secret organization might never have coalesced had it not been for a chance meeting at APRA in Benton, Tennessee. Randall Rader, a former commando leader of the Covenant, the Sword and the Arm of the Lord—CSA for short, which also stands for Confederate States of America—was a skilled survivalist and born leader who wanted to establish an "Army of God." On a survivalist outing at the APRA compound in 1981, Rader met fellow survivalists Richard Scutari, Andrew Barnhill and Ardie McBrearty. Barnhill was a longtime member of APRA, and had met some of the other men at the 200-plus-acre CSA encampment called Zarepath-Horeb in the Ozarks of Arkansas. The compound was named after the biblical sites where the Ark of the Covenant was received by the Israelites. Rader led the men into the woods on a three-day survival hike, during which they honed their skills with firearms and became close friends. Scutari, Barnhill and McBrearty looked up to Rader, who exemplified the ultimate survivalist. He once bragged of killing a dog and eating it raw. Scutari became Robert Mathews's closest advisor within The Order and led its training unit.[56]

Beckwith had no direct ties to Mathews or The Order, but his reputation was well-known by its members, as well as to members of Aryan Nations and the National Alliance. Beckwith was viewed as a hero. One member of The Order, Tom Martinez, heard Beckwith speak prior to his own involvement with Mathews's group. "I was involved with the Klan, or the National Alliance," Martinez remembered in an interview. "For sure it was before I was involved with The Order." He recalled hearing stories about Beckwith, who was revered by many of the white supremacists with whom he came in contact. "Beckwith was kind of like, not a martyr, but he was respected for what he had done, period," said Martinez.

Martinez personally knew a number of Beckwith's associates. Bob Miles, a former Klan leader and minister from Cohoctah, Michigan, allowed Martinez to stay in his home on occasion. Miles and Beckwith were friends, and Martinez remembered that Miles exhibited the same conspiracy-based paranoia for which Beckwith was widely known. "I'm sitting here with this guy who's supposed to be this terrorist," Martinez remembered, "and he comes out in his pajamas, and he's sitting there eating his Corn Flakes, and everything that came out of his mouth was 'Jew.' If the cereal was too sweet, it was because of the Jews. Or if the milk was sour, it was because the Jews had gotten to our cows."

It was another of Beckwith's friends, J. B. Stoner, whose NSRP publication, *The Thunderbolt*, published Martinez's photo with the caption, "Watch for this Arch-Traitor." Elden "Bud" Cutler, a Christian Identity follower and security chief for Aryan Nations, placed a contract on Martinez's life in 1985, after Martinez became an FBI informant and helped authorities locate Mathews and bring down The Order. Cutler was explicit in his instructions about how Martinez was to be killed. As a traitor, his head was to be severed from his body.[57] "Mathews had told me back in '84 that the Christian Identity members are more dedicated than anyone," Martinez recalled. "They were more dedicated than any of the National Alliance members and Klan members he was recruiting into

The Order. And I think they proved that when they went to jail, when a majority of them were Identity guys who wouldn't cooperate with the authorities."

The Order's leader, Robert Mathews, was killed December 8, 1984, on Whidbey Island in Washington's Puget Sound, when the house in which he had taken refuge exploded and burned.[58] Proceeds from The Order's armed robberies were allegedly secreted to fund far-flung racist organizations with ties to Beckwith.

"No one understands what's really going on in and around Tennessee," said Otis Powell, a pseudonym for a former militant Christian Identity follower who, for several years, moved within the ranks of East Tennessee's racist factions. For obvious reasons, he refused to talk about his involvement in the movement or his ties to Beckwith unless his identity was protected. He feared retribution, and acknowledged that if his identity and current whereabouts were discovered, he would not be harassed—he would be killed.

"I would be a target, right now, just by talking," said Powell. "They target anybody who threatens the movement. They also believe that if you betray them, it's not just you, it's your whole bloodline—your family. If you let out these secrets, they are not just going to kill you. They are going to *kill your family.*" Powell also described an underground network of safe houses set up to protect anyone willing to take such action. "The person who killed you would be hidden, taken underground, protected, fed and clothed—anything they ever needed or wanted would be provided through the movement. These people are not interested in going out and killing the president. They're interested in that triangle of land, the Delta, and they want to preserve it for the white race."

Through friends with ties to Signal Mountain, Powell met Beckwith, who in turn later introduced him to members of John Standring's Christian Guard. Powell describes its members as religious zealots. During his years in the movement, Powell saw firsthand the fanatical devotion of Christian Identity followers. And, although it was difficult for him to believe, eventually he learned of an even more fanatical group called the Phineas Priesthood. "I've heard it called 'the Priesthood,' " Powell said. "It *does* exist, and very, very few members of the upper echelon of the movement are in it—the brains." *The New York Times* referred to members of the Phineas Priesthood as "God's executioners."[59]

The group takes its name from the biblical book of Numbers 25, in which Phineas drove a spear through an Israelite man and a Midianite woman engaged in a biblical act of miscegenation. Phineas's act turned God's wrath away from the children of Israel, and God lifted a plague from Israel and granted Phineas an everlasting priesthood. God spoke unto Moses, "I give unto him my covenant of peace: And he shall have it, and his seed after him, even the covenant of an everlasting priesthood; because he was zealous for his God, and made an atonement for the children of Israel."[60]

Several of Beckwith's associates have recounted the story of Phineas over the years, and cite his biblical action as an example to be followed. Dr. William Pierce, the leader of the National Alliance and author of *The Turner Diaries*, which became the blueprint of action for The Order, published at least one of Beckwith's letters in his publications. In his National Alliance *Bulletin*, Pierce once advocated Phineas-type activity when he wrote, "Some may engage in individual activities, like the Pennsylvania sniper who dispatches interracial couples with his rifle. We certainly don't want to discourage that last activity. . . ."[61] Reverend Jarah Crawford, one of the ministers who ordained Beckwith in the Christian Identity Movement in 1977, elaborated on the legacy of Phineas in his book, *Last Battle Cry: Christianity's Final Conflict with Evil*. "Phineas did not deal merely with an individual's sin but with the national sin of Israel," Reverend Crawford wrote. "Zimri, the Israelite, got a spear through his body as a symbol of the sin of the whole nation. . . . It is tremendously significant that one person took matters into his own hands, the one person who has the mind of God. There was no court trial, no judge and no Supreme Court; just one man who knew the mind of God and acted upon it."[62]

Beckwith kept a copy of Crawford's book in his personal library, autographed by the author to Beckwith's wife, Thelma. Beckwith was known to recount the story of Phineas when he "preached," his wife Thelma admitted. Pressed to answer whether her husband had recounted the biblical story of Phineas ramming a spear through this couple, she hedged by saying he had spoken "on that topic some."

Richard Kelly Hoskins is the leading authority on the Phineas Priesthood, having written a voluminous "history" of the secret group. Hoskins, a stockbroker based in Lynchburg, Virginia, published *Vigilantes of Christendom* in 1990. In his book, Hoskins claimed to have studied the clandestine priesthood for twenty-five years, concurrently corresponding with prisoners who had broken the laws of the land while claiming to have upheld the laws of God.[63] According to Thelma Beckwith, they became friendly with Hoskins at Christian Identity gatherings and feasts, and the three were affiliated with Aryan Nations. Beckwith was one of the first to buy *Vigilantes*, and he called it "a wonderful, wonderful, wonderful book."[64] Just as *The Turner Diaries* provided the blueprint for action for The Order, *Vigilantes* may have provided the foundation for a resurgence of interest in the Phineas Priesthood.

Hoskins has denied knowing Beckwith, and told a reporter he could not even remember ever meeting him.[65] Thelma Beckwith, however, told a markedly different story. In an interview, she said of Hoskins, "Oh, but he's a fine person! We just love him. We go way back." She also claimed the Beckwiths and the Hoskinses "always sit together" at Identity gatherings, and are close friends. Hoskins regarded her husband so highly, she claimed, that when Beckwith sent Hoskins a check to pay for a copy of *Vigilantes of Christendom*, Hoskins returned it, uncashed, with a copy of the book.

Just as Hoskins has denied his ties to Beckwith, he has also repeatedly denied the existence of the Phineas Priesthood—even though he was able to write a lengthy history of the group. He told one reporter, "Oh, go on. There's no such organization in the world," and called his book a biblical story, "like Noah and the ark."[66] Yet in the foreword to *Vigilantes of Christendom*, Hoskins clearly stated, "It makes little difference whether you agree or disagree with the Phineas Priesthood. It is important that you know that it exists, is active, and in the near future may become a central fact in your life." Hoskins posited that historical figures such as Beowulf, Robin Hood, Captain John Smith, John Wilkes Booth and Jesse James were Phineas Priests. In more recent times, members of The Order are cited in *Vigilantes* as living examples of the Phineas Priesthood in action.[67] "As the Kamikaze is to the Japanese, as the Shiite is to Islam, as the Zionist is to the Jews, so the Phineas Priest is to Christendom," Hoskins wrote. "Regardless how the world sees them, they see themselves as the latest in a long line of God's servants stretching back into antiquity." Interestingly, in a vanity-press biography about Beckwith, author R.W. Scott noted that after the first two Evers murder trials, Beckwith declined leadership of an unnamed group "with roots traceable to antiquity," claiming he was not "intellectually or spiritually" up to that responsibility.[68] Hoskins wrote: "The thing that Phineas heroes hold in common is their dedication to the Word—the dedication to enforcing God's Law. Their ends also all read alike. Most are martyrs or are willing to be martyrs to the cause."[69]

"Beckwith, right now, is a martyr," Otis Powell said in an interview in 1993, pointing to the common belief among white supremacists that Beckwith killed Medgar Evers. "He likes being where he is. He is being a martyr for the others in the movement, because he's keeping his mouth shut. He is in—I think they call it a discipleship—because he has killed. That is the *ultimate.* There are numerous men right now who would give their lives for him, or for his family. They may not be able to keep the man out of jail, but his family will never want for anything." Powell pointed to the flood of articles about Beckwith in the racist press to support his argument. "You've seen the white supremacist newsletters—he's a national hero to these people. They will protect him."

Organizations dedicated to combating hate crimes believe the Phineas

Priesthood bears watching, although the group has not been linked thus far to any acts of violence. The fact that its members take what they perceive to be God's laws into their own hands makes tracking the movement extremely difficult. Leonard Zeskind, research director of the Center for Democratic Renewal, an Atlanta-based organization that monitors hate groups, is an expert on the Christian Identity Movement. Zeskind finds the concept of the Phineas Priesthood—propagating the concept of the self-ordained killer—particularly dangerous. "The Phineas Priesthood is definitely an Identity concept," Zeskind explained, "because it's based on Old Testament identification with the people Israel. One of the things that is interesting about it is that it glorifies the lone individual, and that is a turn in the Identity movement toward the individual killer. I think that that notion of a group of lone killers—individuals not connected to actual organizations—is something that is recent."

Like Zeskind, others believe the Phineas Priesthood exists and poses a very real danger. Former Klansman Delmar Dennis fears its members. "I was told about it by a friend in South Carolina, who had been attending several of the Identity churches and had gone to different states to their big feasts," Dennis said. "He was approached by some people at one of these meetings and had the Phineas Priesthood described to him, and he was frightened. It's almost like a one-man holy war where the Phineas Priest decides this person is the enemy of God, and it's his duty to wipe him off the face of the earth." The ramifications of such lone vigilante action continue to frighten Dennis. "If the Phineas Priesthood has individuals who just suddenly feel led by the Lord to go execute somebody, it would be hard to prevent and harder to catch him after he did it. And it would be a totally religious motivation, like the Jihad. This has devastating potential," Dennis concludes. "These people are going to commit murder in the name of God."

Richard Kelly Hoskins's newsletter, *Hoskins Report*, is circulated widely to Identity followers and radical racists. The February 4, 1991, issue carried a letter from Beckwith, written from his jail cell in Chattanooga, which mentioned his legal problems and noted that they were "capable of solution too. Phineas for President!"[70] Leonard Zeskind believed the letter revealed the possibility of Beckwith's involvement with the Phineas Priesthood. "At a minimum, Beckwith is promoting the idea of the Phineas Priesthood—he's saying that murdering people is a good thing," Zeskind said.

Prosecutors in Mississippi believed so, too. They entered Beckwith's letter to *Hoskins Report* as evidence when they made a motion to deny Beckwith bond in Mississippi, pending his third trial on the Evers murder charge. FBI Special Agent Donald Wofford, whose work for approximately six years centered around The Order, testified about the Phineas

Priesthood and its members, "who are called by God to go out and commit violent acts against people who violate their interpretation of what God's law is."[71]

Like many others who are drawn into the Christian Identity movement, Otis Powell was never strongly interested in organized religion, but the inextricable link between Christian Identity theology and its followers' paramilitary activities fascinated him. He described being invited to target shoot with a number of other men who were hard-core Identity followers. "You realize that this guy has just let you shoot $150 worth of ammunition—they'll let you shoot any gun you want to shoot—and then they'll start talking you up," Powell recalled. "They'd say, 'Well, listen to this tape,' and it would be Identity sermons. It's very planned. I went so deep, so fast," Powell said. "Looking back, it's really scary." An avid gun buff, Powell described religious gatherings at which different vendors sold arms and ammunition from the backs of their vans. "It's not a bunch of rednecks running around yelling 'nigger,' " he said. "These people have highly sophisticated weapons and are trained to use them." Weaponry, arms training and survivalist activities were the drawing card for Powell, who said he was slowly "groomed" and "indoctrinated."

"If you control someone's spirituality, they will dedicate whatever it takes to the movement—money, time, anything," Powell said. Although he felt he was indoctrinated in the theology of the movement, he balks at descriptions of Christian Identity as a cult. "The word 'cult' does it a great injustice," Powell said. "It is a very organized religion, with missionaries, finances, officers, priests, conferences—all over the country."

Powell also believed monitoring organizations (such as the ADL, the Center for Democratic Renewal and Southern Poverty Law Center) underestimate the fervor with which Christian Identity followers have adopted the movement's survivalist dogma. "Every family or group of families that I know has a water distiller that they drink from," Powell said. "They store food. Groups of families go in together and build their own bomb shelters. I've been in them, in bomb shelters, built underground. When you go in and look at them, they have any type of assault weapon that you could ever imagine, more food than you can imagine stored up, living quarters arranged, wells dug underground for water. This is a really well-organized group of people."

Far more frightening—and potentially deadly—is followers' proficiency with illegal automatic weapons. It was near Beckwith's home on Signal Mountain that Powell acquired his own arsenal of automatic weapons and participated in firearms training sessions on a large farm. "We drove down, and pulled through an iron gate onto a dirt road," Powell remembered. "The first two guards were posted with AR15 assault rifles and German shepherds, and then further down, there were two more guys. Then before you actually get into the training site, there's two more guys. And *all* of these guys had guard dogs." Powell remembered one man telling him that there was a specific outfit which provided attack-trained guard dogs which take their commands in German rather than in English.

By stockpiling weapons and ammunition, and by being trained in their use, Identity followers believe they will be able to battle the forces of Satan and establish God's kingdom on earth.[72] "It really scares me now," Powell said. "I was even told specifically what kinds of weapons I needed to buy. I needed a .223 caliber rifle. I needed a .45 caliber pistol, because if you ever had to shoot somebody, you could go to any gun show and buy a barrel for ten dollars or fifteen dollars, and throw the barrel away and still keep the gun. You can change the barrel, and there's no ballistics. I was taught how to tamper with a bullet so it could not be checked. I was taught to get high-capacity 9 mms, .223s, .308s, .45s and shotguns. Laser sights. Baffling silencers."

Powell recalled a number of occasions on which he was offered high-ticket weapons for sale. "I've walked up to vans just packed full of things, from .50 caliber machine guns that mount bipod to grenade launchers," Powell said. "You can go to any of the rallies, and any semi-automatic weapon you can think of is converted. They have the plans, or the drawings, to convert any weapon. I've seen silencers, all kinds of Class III automatic weapons, all types of chemicals you need to make explosives. I've even been offered grenades and LAWS rockets—missiles. One of their chosen weapons is a Ruger bull barrel .22 automatic, because it takes some pieces of conduit and some freeze plugs and a file to make a silencer for it. It's that simple. I've shot fully-automatic Ruger 10-22s that are fully silenced. One of the things that people don't realize is that these people have high-dollar, high-compression, custom-made pellet rifles that shoot off of air—compressed air, like a competition pellet rifle—that shoots harder than a .22 rifle, silently. And the whole purpose of having those weapons is assassination. You cannot hear it."

Powell also claimed Identity followers are particularly fond of laser sights for their high-powered rifles. "With a laser sight, you are just as accurate shooting from the hip as you are shooting from the shoulder—that's why they like them," Powell said. "Just point and pull the trigger." Given that firearms and shooting always fascinated him, Powell was drawn further into the movement because of the accessibility to automatic weapons it provided him. "My knowledge of suppressors, throw-away suppressors, explosives, improvised munitions, automatic weapons—I still own some—how to convert and baffle weapons, all came from my contacts within the movement," Powell said. "You can take a MAC 11 that you can buy at gun shows, and you can buy an eleven-dollar part at Sears, take a file, lay it on a template, and convert it to a fully automatic weapon.

And you can go to the store and buy a Ruger 10-22 and go to *any* Identity meeting, and pick up parts to make it an automatic weapon."

Still, Powell claimed, few Identity followers spend the bulk of their time shooting. "These guys may shoot a .22 rifle to keep in practice, but they don't go out and start shooting 9 mms, .223s and things like that, because the ammunition is so expensive. They have thousands of rounds of ammo, but they're saving them. I have personally seen stockpiles—people who have ten thousand rounds of ammunition per gun, for every weapon they own. And they're saving them for when the war begins."

One of Powell's most startling assertions is that he was trained not only with firearms, but was taught to use night vision goggles, as well. "When people start letting you play with a twenty-seven-thousand-dollar pair of night vision goggles, you know you're not going hunting," Powell said. "When you put them on, you lose a lot of depth perception. These are starlight goggles—they go by intensifiers of starlight," he explained. "What you see is a frosted white image. But when you look through the laser scope on your gun, you see a bright white dot on your target. They have done some maneuver training with these things, and two men wearing night vision goggles with laser scopes mounted on their rifles have been able to take out a hundred men." He also claimed that some of the Christian Identity Movement's adherents would surprise outsiders. "I will guarantee you that there are high-ranking military officials and law enforcement agents who are involved in the movement," Powell said. "I know ex–Green Berets or ex–Seals or ex–Airborne Rangers who have personally trained me."

Powell laughed at the irony of a description of the Christian Identity Movement as an "underground" operation. "You don't know how true that is," he said, referring to followers' underground stockpiles of supplies, food and munitions. "One of the things they taught us to do was take big PVC pipe, and we would make gun safes from it. They put desiccant inside the gun cases—a moisture remover that keeps the guns from rusting. The guns are wrapped up and stored in these watertight PVC containers, and then buried underground. And they're not stupid—they mark the locations on maps. But I know of at least one man who has eight to ten stashes of guns, ammunition, money, clothes, food—everything—in these containers. All he has to do is go dig them up. Below a certain depth, the ground stays at a constant temperature, and that's the depth they bury them at." Recognizing the legal charges they would face if automatic weapons were discovered by police, Identity followers are trained to bury them rather than risk being caught with them. "You're not going to bust many people in the movement on weapons charges, because they're not going to have these automatic weapons lying around," Powell said.

* * *

Admittedly, it is difficult to understand the collective psyche of the racists and survivalists who comprise the Christian Identity Movement, even with the benefit of the insights of former adherents like Otis Powell. As an individual, Byron De La Beckwith is also an enigma. Although he was examined by psychiatrists on a number of occasions—both by Dr. Roland Toms and presumably by the doctors at Whitfield—their clinical diagnoses have never been made public. Beckwith's likelihood of inherited mental instability would appear to be high, given his mother's and his Uncle Will's confinements and nervous breakdowns. It is also possible that his own alcohol abuse during his stormy marriages to his first wife, Willie, reflected an inherent tendency toward alcoholism that he might have inherited from his father.

Although no one who has not personally examined Beckwith can offer a clinical psychiatric diagnosis, his case has intrigued a number of psychiatrists—particularly those whose backgrounds include research into the psychological make up of murderers of public figures—who can point out patterns and behaviors in Beckwith's background that match existing profiles of known murderers. One such psychiatrist, Dr. Donald Lunde of the Stanford University School of Medicine, is eminently qualified to offer his observations and opinions concerning Beckwith. Lunde was one of three court-appointed psychiatrists asked to examine and evaluate Patricia Hearst during her highly publicized trial in the 1970s, and he also consulted on the Hillside Strangler, the Zodiac Killer and the Howard Hughes estate litigation cases. Based on background materials relating to Beckwith's childhood and youth, numerous letters Beckwith wrote, and detailed information about Beckwith's sex life provided by his first wife, Lunde made a number of illuminating observations about him.

Lunde pointed out in an interview that knowledge of Beckwith's impotence is crucial to understanding his potential predisposition to murder a public figure. "Common among murderers of this sort is a 'buildup state,' " Lunde said, "which can last for a few hours or a few weeks before the murder occurs. It's evident in many perpetrators of premeditated murders, and can be marked by restlessness, anxiety and even impotence." Such assassins share other traits, as well, Lunde said. "A common characteristic you see is a kind of megalomania, and among the assassins who kept diaries, what appears is a mentality of, 'I'm going to leave my mark on history, and my name will be remembered.'

"What drives them" Lunde said, "is this need to prove to all the people who ignored them early on, and treated them badly, that they really are special. In most lone-man assassination attempts, it seems particularly striking that the person does it in such a way that any reasonable person would know they're going to get caught, and there's a fair chance they're going to get killed." Lunde said that if Beckwith took such an act upon himself, or volunteered for it, that he might have been subconsciously suicidal.

Psychiatrists have posited that immersion into a violent subculture, such as the Ku Klux Klan, might increase the likelihood that an individual would commit murder. Lunde pointed out that Beckwith was a man with a strong sense of mission, and that—like Lee Harvey Oswald, who also received his firearms training in the military—Beckwith, while not predestined to murder, might have proven more destructive because of his avid interest in firearms and his military training. Lunde also believed Beckwith's ability to view his enemies as "faceless objects"—whether his enemies were the Japanese during World War II or integrationists during the civil rights era—might make their annihilation easier. "Beckwith's like a man with a cause, but without social support for it," Lunde said. "Therefore, you have to look inside Byron De La Beckwith to find out what's going on, and it probably goes back to early childhood. There is a tendency for these things—alcoholism and violence—to run in families, especially among males."

Lunde also noted that, given the times, Beckwith's father might have been a strong disciplinarian when his son was small. "And it wouldn't be unusual for Beckwith's rage to stem from some of the brutality or abuse that he may have experienced as a child, when his father was under the influence," Lunde said. "He probably has not had much affirmation in his life, or at least—this is my guess—since his mother died. He probably seldom senses that people care about him as a person. They may care, at times, that he can carry out this or that task, but they may not care about him on a personal level. And that brings up the irrationality of trying to preserve the white race. The white race, really, never did that much for Beckwith."

The psychology of criminals—and of murderers, specifically—is also of particular interest to Dr. David Abrahamsen, a respected psychoanalyst whose work has spanned more than half the century. During his lengthy career, Abrahamsen has taught at the Department of Psychiatry at the College of Physicians and Surgeons at Columbia University, Yale Law School and the New York School of Social Work at Columbia University. He consulted on the trial of David Berkowitz—the New York serial killer better known as "Son of Sam"—and wrote the definitive study of Berkowitz, based on fifty hours of personal interviews and more than 400 pages of correspondence. Abrahamsen has written widely on the psychological makeup of murderers.

In his book *The Murdering Mind,* Abrahamsen discussed political assassins and noted several common personality traits and discovered similarities in their family backgrounds. Lee Harvey Oswald, James Earl

Ray, Sirhan Sirhan and Arthur Bremer (who was convicted for the shooting of George Wallace) all had unsuccessful relationships with women, and Oswald demonstrated the same pattern of impotence and wife abuse that characterized Beckwith's multiple marriages to Willie.[72] In an interview, Abrahamsen said that hostility or domestic violence are not uncommon among men who experience impotence. "Not being able to perform sexually shows that he may himself have felt extremely inadequate," Abrahamsen posited about Beckwith. Discussing Beckwith's tendency toward violence following unsuccessful attempts to have sex with his wife, Abrahamsen said, "I think that is certainly an expression of being angry with himself, anger which he took out on his wife." Asked whether Beckwith's impotence might have stemmed from some sense of loss of control—over his wife, or more generally over his segregated way of life—Abrahamsen said, "I do believe that when this happens, there is a loss of control. That's very true. But the reason he has lost control is because he has lost control of the sexual function."

Sexual dysfunction was among several important traits Beckwith shared with Oswald, Ray, Sirhan and Bremer. Common among them were absent fathers; poor performance in school and serious problems with spelling; and they were characterized by others as "loners" who had grandiose fantasies. In reference to murderers, Abrahamsen said, "Mental disturbance is a primary factor. You see it in a very high degree, but you also see a high incidence of sexual disturbance or unsatisfactory relationships with women."

The political assassins also displayed what Abrahamsen characterized as "intense and recurrent fantasies of revenge and omnipotence which stimulated their violent impulses into action," a description that might also apply to Beckwith's vigilant need to maintain his segregated way of life. "In his case," Abrahamsen said of Beckwith, "if he has been a loner, it might be that he spent his time daydreaming of having power, wanting to have power. And his violence may have been a response to a perceived threat that his power would be taken away."

From Beckwith's earliest years as an orphan, and throughout his youth and adulthood, he wanted desperately to belong, whether to his local 4-H club or the Boy Scouts as a child, or to the Citizens' Council or the Ku Klux Klan as an adult. The South he protected during his stint in the Marine Corps soon changed beyond his recognition, as blacks demanded the basic human rights they deserved—even in Mississippi. Beckwith's struggle against the encroachment of integration of the races was both painful and futile. The very way of life he loved slowly slipped slowly from him. His friends and associates also changed slowly, and sometimes grudgingly, but for the most part, they did change. Medgar Evers's assassination—one killer's attempt to salvage the status quo just as it was beginning to crumble—gave the civil rights movement an early martyr, and, rather than thwarting black progress, helped to both inspire and achieve it.

Beckwith's use of threats and intimidation both inside and outside his home, and his ongoing advocacy of violence, marked his determination to maintain control of the world around him. In almost every case, however, Beckwith's attempts proved insufficient to maintain control. His multiple marriages to Mary Louise Williams carried him through both the most joyous and the most hate-filled years of his life, and his insatiable need to possess and control her wrecked both their lives. His immersion into the shadowy world of the Ku Klux Klan, with its secret language and symbolism and promise of black annihilation, ended in disgrace as the White Knights of the Ku Klux Klan toppled around him. Even Beckwith's pitiful attempt to inculcate himself into the world of Mississippi politics as a candidate for lieutenant governor of his beloved Mississippi proved an embarrassment, as his fellow Mississippians voted not for him, but against him.

Guided by his unorthodox religious beliefs, which fueled his racism and gave it the biblical imprimatur of scripture, Beckwith ascended to a plateau of self-delusion from which he never descended. The theological underpinnings of his racism firmly in place, even as he was under attack for the Evers murder, Beckwith called blacks "anti-Christ" and "mongrels," and accused them of voodoo and cannibalism. "If you lay down, toss your panties off and let a nigger have intercourse with you," Beckwith told one reporter, "you are going to produce mongrels forever."[73]

Like his fellow Christian Identity adherents, he believed blacks were the spawn of Satan, without souls. Medgar Evers was of little more concern to Beckwith than a snake or a mad dog—a nuisance one must eliminate to protect oneself. Mississippi's call for a new murder trial demonstrated just how dramatically the state changed in three decades. The same three decades that changed the face of Mississippi had also changed the face of Byron De La Beckwith. His racial attitudes had grown ever more vitriolic and repellant to those around him. Staring out from the front pages of newspapers the day after his arrest was the face of an angry, embittered old man. Behind him, on his front porch, a ragged Confederate flag whipped quietly in the wind. A Celtic cross dangled from a chain around his neck as he was led quietly from his home on Signal Mountain—"the outskirts of heaven"—to jail.

Epilogue

Out of Darkness

Nine months after meeting my uncle at the Hamilton County Jail in Chattanooga, Tennessee, I moved back to my hometown of Knoxville, just two hours north of where he was incarcerated, to write *Portrait of a Racist.* I visited Beckwith's home in Signal Mountain and interviewed his second wife, Thelma, on several occasions, and he and I resumed our intermittent correspondence. His first letter, mailed to my new post office box address, was marked "Knoxville, Tennessee, C.S.A." He never asked about my reasons for leaving New York and returning to the South. Aware that I had seen both Thelma and, on one occasion, his son, Beckwith probably assumed I was working on a feature article or a book, and his letters to me were alternately conciliatory and threatening. Shortly after my move, Beckwith accused me of working on behalf of "the sons and daughters of the most hideous of all Jews on earth." He enclosed several news articles, and on a separate sheet, wrote a note that said, in part, "I'm proud of my enemies—How about you?" A few months later, the salutation on one of his letters to me said, "Dear Kinsman and favorite nephew Numero Uno." By then, he had been extradited to Mississippi and his letters were usually adorned with a gold foil return address label bearing his name and the legend "Hinds County Detention Center."

At a bond hearing on November 12, 1991, my cousin, Byron De La Beckwith, Jr., appeared on his father's behalf as a witness. He characterized his father as a nonviolent man and said the first two murder trials "financially destroyed the Beckwith family." When he was cross-examined by Hinds County District Attorney Ed Peters regarding the charges in his mother's divorce cases and his father's documented propensity for violence, Beckwith said, "Did you want to mention that my mother's a total alcoholic and brought a lot of that on herself?"

"She asked to be beaten, is that what you say?" Peters asked.

"She was never beaten, sir," Beckwith replied. "There might have been charges, but my mother was never beaten, sir."

My aunt, who had by then been sober for more than a decade, and whose abuse at her former husband's hands had been well documented, said simply, "He was always his father's son."

For almost exactly two years, Beckwith was in jail awaiting trial—ten months in the Hamilton County Jail in Chattanooga, Tennessee, fighting his inevitable extradition to Mississippi, and fourteen months at the Hinds County Detention Center in Jackson. His court-appointed lawyers, first in Tennessee and then in Mississippi, sought Beckwith's release on bail, then petitioned for his release on constitutional grounds, claiming his rights to a speedy trial and due process flagrantly were being denied. Upon Beckwith's extradition to Mississippi, a trial date had been set for February 10, 1992. When Beckwith's defense attorneys requested more time to prepare the case, the trial again was postponed, until June 1.

The trial was delayed again when Beckwith's attorneys requested a change of venue, claiming that the publicity surrounding the case and local monuments to Evers would make it impossible for their client to get a fair trial in Hinds County. In August 1992, Hinds County Circuit Court Judge L. Breland Hilburn set yet another trial date of September 20, and ruled that the trial would be held in DeSoto County—where Beckwith and my aunt were married in 1945—and that the jury would be selected from Panola County, where the racial composition was similar to that of Hinds County. Almost immediately, plastic packets containing copies of Liberty Lobby's *Citizens Rule Book* littered mailboxes and driveways throughout Panola and DeSoto counties. Each packet held a photocopied note from Beckwith characterizing himself as a political prisoner.

Beckwith mailed me several of the autographed packets as souvenirs, and wrote that he believed the materials to be "so important" that he spent "$1,350 per 1,000 to mail these out," noting that it cost him an additional $740 to get them distributed by skinheads, Klansmen and others supportive of his cause. Finally, in April 1992, Beckwith's lawyers sought dismissal of the murder indictment on three separate constitutional grounds. The Hinds County Circuit Court denied the motion on August 4, 1992, and Beckwith's attorneys petitioned the state's supreme court for an interlocutory appeal. Beckwith—and the world—waited for an answer to his fate.

On December 16, 1992, the Mississippi Supreme Court ruled in a narrow four-three decision that Byron De La Beckwith must stand trial a third time for the 1963 murder of Medgar Evers. In a heated dissent, Chief Justice Roy Lee Noble called the court's decision "the worst pronouncement of law during my tenure on the Mississippi Supreme Court," and two other justices joined in his dissent. Four days later, *The Knoxville News-Sentinel* published a Sunday-edition cover story about the forthcoming publication of *Portrait of a Racist.*

My Aunt Mary and I had discussed the article at length before it appeared, as it would be the first public announcement of my work on the book, and both she and I feared the repercussions when Beckwith learned it was finished and in the hands of my editor. She and I sat up and drank coffee until the early hours of Sunday morning, when the first issues of the newspapers were delivered to a nearby gas station. After I picked up several copies, she and I sat in silence, each with our papers, reading.

For several months, she had been battling a recurrent bronchitis and a low-grade pneumonia, which refused to abate. As had been her custom during the past several years, she spent two weeks at my parents' home during the Christmas holidays. In 1989, after a serious accident impaired her ability to walk, she moved out of the apartment in which she had lived for almost a decade and lived briefly in a nursing home while she regained the use of her leg. After her recovery, she moved into a Veterans Administration domiciliary in Mountain Home, Tennessee. She held a daily job on the premises, couriering medical records between office buildings, and although she missed having an apartment of her own—she had regained her fierce independence along with her sobriety—she enjoyed the quiet surroundings and had made a number of close friends among the other veterans. None of them knew anything about her past.

On December 23, while she was still visiting with my family, her former husband was released from jail on $100,000 bond with the proviso that he remain in Mississippi and keep the court informed of his whereabouts until his trial date was set. An unidentified donor came forward with the $12,000 cash necessary to free Beckwith, and the prisoner took up residence in his son's trailer in Aberdeen, Mississippi, just in time to celebrate the holidays. My aunt was visibly upset. The news undoubtedly upset Myrlie Evers, as well, who that Christmas Eve would have celebrated the forty-first anniversary of her marriage to Medgar Evers.

My aunt's condition failed to improve, and she was quick to admit to me that she still feared her former husband, and that she had rested a lot more easily at night when she knew he was in jail. Bad dreams continued to plague her, she told me, and I had hoped that when she returned to Mountain Home after the holidays, her health might improve and her fears might be alleviated. Only two days after her return, however, she was hospitalized, and her condition grew steadily worse. Her doctors reported that she had developed a rare fungus, aspergillosis, which was growing in her lungs, and she was placed in the hospital's intensive care unit. When I made the trip to Mountain Home to visit her on January 24, 1993, she was alert and stable, and her blue eyes remained bright and clear. She held my hand tightly, and said that she was not in any pain, and that what she wanted more than anything was to get up for a walk. We talked for a while, and before I left, she pointed to her jacket, which was hanging on a wall rack in the corner of the room, and asked if I would leave five dollars in her pocket. "I just hate to be in here without any money," she said. She died two weeks later and was quietly buried in Knoxville.

I faced my uncle for the last time at his 1994 murder trial in Mississippi almost exactly a year later. The hardcover publication of *Portrait of a Racist* in January of 1994—just as Beckwith's third trial was getting under way—resulted in my being subpoenaed by the prosecution to testify against him. The timing was happenstance, and owed more to my uncle's lawyers' three years of delays and appeals than to my publisher's press schedule.

My agent at William Morris Agency called me in Knoxville to tell me he had been contacted by the Hinds County District Attorney's office, and that they very much wanted me to get in touch with them. My brief conversation with Hinds County Assistant District Attorney Bobby DeLaughter, who was shepherding the prosecution's case, was brief and to the point. "We'd like to subpoena you to testify, and we'd like to introduce some of the letters you discuss in your book as evidence," he told me. I gave his chief investigator my fax number, and I sat and watched as the subpoena scrolled out of the machine an hour later.

My flight to Jackson, Mississippi, was met by a plainclothes officer in a midnight blue Crown Victoria, who escorted me to the Hinds County District Attorney's office. I was introduced to DeLaughter, who asked me a series of questions and listened thoughtfully to my answers. Afterward, I was escorted to the downtown Holiday Inn, just blocks from the Hinds County Courthouse. I was tucked into a hotel room on a floor that housed a number of other witnesses, including Mrs. Evers, and we were under constant guard. When I was called into the courtroom, the first person I saw was my uncle, who looked at me with an aging face that seemed to register both surprise and rage.

After I had been sworn in and had taken the witness stand, my uncle's attorneys objected to my potential testimony and to the letters I had been subpoenaed to produce as evidence. During the recess, while the defense team met in a conference room to assess the potential damage of their client's own words, in his own handwriting, Myrlie Evers approached the prosecutor's table and spoke quietly to DeLaughter. He tipped his head toward me and caught my eye as he told her, "Well, you can speak to him right now. We're in recess."

Mrs. Evers stepped toward me and reached across the mahogany railing that separated us. She took my hand in hers and said, "I've read your book, and I appreciate what you've done." I looked into her eyes, but I was so moved by her gesture that I could not even speak.

My own testimony was minimal, although the defense moved for a mistrial a number of times while I was on the stand and—in their cross-examination—made me out to be a money-hungry, tell-all nephew. More important were the few facts I was asked to enter into testimony by reading from Beckwith's own letters: the bravado with which he wrote from his jail cell on November 22, 1963, "That fellow sho' done some fancy shootin', didn't he. HAW HAW HAW. I'll bet old Medgar Evers said I thought you'd get down here pretty soon boss. Ha Ha Ha." Even more telling was Beckwith's admission in one letter that he was "deep in global Klan work," despite his having given sworn testimony during the latest grand jury hearings that he was never affiliated with the Ku Klux Klan.

During a total of fifteen days of testimony, a racially mixed panel of jurors heard the voluminous evidence against my uncle. Although the murder was by then more than thirty years past, in the courtroom it was as if time had stood still. Beckwith, who occasionally showed up in a bright red sport coat with a Confederate flag pin in his lapel, was an anachronism straight out of central casting. His unrepentant racism was evident and chilling, and he was very much the same man who had faced separate hung juries thirty years earlier in that same courtroom.

What *had* changed was the evidence itself. The new jurors heard from witnesses who were unavailable during the two trials in 1964—including a total of five witnesses who said they had heard Beckwith's boasts about having committed the murder. The former Klansman and FBI informant Delmar Dennis testified that he had heard Beckwith when he appeared as a "motivational" speaker at a Ku Klux Klan rally in 1965, when Dennis was still operating undercover. "Killing that nigger gave me no more inner discomfort than our wives go through to have our babies," Dennis recounted Beckwith saying. Other witnesses told similar stories, and even without them, the weight of the evidence available during the first two trials left no reasonable doubt that Byron De La Beckwith was Medgar Evers's killer—and was proud enough of that fact to have boasted about it.

The prosecution's final witness, Mark Reiley, had guarded Beckwith during his incarceration at the Louisiana State Penitentiary at Angola, and testified that Beckwith once told him that "if he didn't have the connections he had, he would be serving time in Mississippi for getting rid of that nigger Medgar Evers." The prosecution rested on February 1, 1994, after calling thirty-eight witnesses.

The defense's case pivoted on the same alibi testimony presented in 1964 by two off-duty police officers who claimed to have seen Beckwith in Greenwood—ninety miles from Jackson—shortly after the murder. The only notable difference in the defense's case between the 1964 trials and the 1994 trial was that Beckwith did not testify in his own defense. The defense rested, and jury deliberations began during an afternoon thunderstorm on Friday, February 4. That evening, the jury retired for the night. After convening for a brief time the following morning, the jury rendered a guilty verdict.

After Judge L. Breland Hilburn sentenced Beckwith to life in prison and returned him to the Hinds County Detention Center, District Attorney Ed Peters said, simply and eloquently, "He won't be bragging about it anymore."

Afterword to the 2024 Edition

We will never know the extent to which Beckwith expected—or accepted—his guilty verdict. Whatever Beckwith's disappointments, they undoubtedly were amplified during his first several years in prison when the Mississippi Supreme Court upheld his conviction in 1997. At the same time Beckwith was mulling his fate and the remainder of his life separated from the outside world, militias throughout the United States were multiplying, and as Southern Poverty Law Center co-founder Morris Dees noted in his book *Gathering Storm: America's Militia Threat* (HarperCollins Publishers, 1996), ". . . evidence of white supremacist involvement was mounting" (p. 95). In jail at the Hinds County Detention Center, Beckwith settled into his familiar prison routine—entertaining occasional visitors who shared his affiliations and views; begging for funds to support his appeal and to pay his legal fees; and writing letters to his friends and supporters and churning the waters with his racist-religious rhetoric.

Others were writing, too. During Beckwith's incarceration, numerous books about the case—and about Medgar Evers—began to appear in print. My book may have proven to be the most legally damaging and personally hurtful for Beckwith, since its publication resulted in my being subpoenaed to testify and produce evidence at his trial. Much had been made in the press of the several letters Beckwith had written that were entered into evidence during my testimony, but to my mind the most damaging was the one in which he'd written in his distinctive cursive that he was "deep" in global Klan work, despite having sworn under oath during grand jury testimony that he'd never been a member of the Ku Klux Klan. And during the years I was conducting research and interviews for my book, not only had I found and interviewed former Klan informant Delmar Dennis, who presented damning evidence in the new trial, but I had also circled back and located one of the FBI agents to whom Dennis had regularly filed his reports during the mid-1960s, Tom Van Riper. The advance review copy of my book that landed on reporter Jerry Mitchell's desk *at* the *Clarion-Ledger* led the prosecution team to my door and also to Dennis's and Van Riper's doors as well. Both of them—as luck would have it—lived near me in East Tennessee.

While my book focused on Beckwith and attempted to help explain his history, his upbringing, and his religious mindset as they impacted his development as a racist, the next two books published—*Of Long Memory* (Addison-Wesley, 1994) by *Atlanta Journal-Constitution* reporter Adam Nossiter, and *Ghosts of Mississippi* (Little, Brown, 1995) by freelance writer Maryanne Vollers, wove the Beckwith/Evers story into the larger narrative of Mississippi's social history. Beckwith undoubtedly read these two books, although it is unlikely he read any of the others that followed during his lifetime, including Willie Morris, *The Ghosts of Medgar Evers* (Random House, 1998), or Myrlie Evers-Williams with Melinda Blau, *Watch Me Fly* (Little, Brown, 1999). Beckwith did not live to see the publication of a host of others, including Bobby DeLaughter, *Never Too Late: A Prosecutor's Story of Justice in the Medgar Evers Case* (Scribner, 2001); Myrlie Evers-Williams and Manning Marable, *The Autobiography of Medgar Evers* (Basic Civitas Books, 2005); Michael Vinson Williams, *Medgar Evers: Mississippi Martyr* (University of Arkansas Press, 2011); a book of poetry by Frank X. Walker entitled *Turn Me Loose: The Unghosting of Medgar Evers* (University of Georgia Press, 2013); Minrose Gwin, *Remembering Medgar Evers: Writing the Long Civil Rights Movement* (University of Georgia Press, 2013); or Jerry Mitchell, *Race Against Time: A Reporter Reopens the Unsolved Murder Cases of the Civil Rights Era* (Simon & Schuster, 2020).

Of the writers who penned Beckwith/Evers books, one in particular riled Beckwith. Adam Nossiter's persistence deeply unsettled Beckwith. In one of his last letters to me Beckwith had written from jail:

> I just threw the snotty-nosed, 6'4", yellow-skinned, mongrel, damned-by-God, stinking son-of-a-bitch Jew out of my comfortable chamber as he crept in with a long-time true friend of mine here. He's been writing an anti-Delay, anti-white, anti-Christian, anti-Dixie book—one mother-defiler, Adam Nossiter, who months ago had the gall to ask me to release my FIA [*sic*] FBI file to him! All of which is normal for a Jew and all who associate with Jews—for Jews [*sic*] pleasures are worse than the Jews—*so says Jesus! Who is very God, dontcha know.* Jesus is on their ass, and *me too*. I've had a file on him for several years. He slithered in Thelma's home, and that could be the end of a happy marriage—my wife letting a God-damned obvious Jew in to her home where we live!!! Shit Shit Shit.

Throughout his life, Beckwith's hatred of Jews could be specific—as in Nossiter's case—or general, as when he railed against the "Jewsmedia."

Beckwith's views on mainstream media were well documented and equally vicious, and those views likely only intensified as the longer narrative arc of television programs and films began to pay more substantial attention to his case than mere news coverage had been capable of mustering in two- and three-minute segments. First out of the gate was a 1994 HBO documentary entitled *Southern Justice: The Murder of Medgar Evers* in which a snippet of an on-camera news interview with me appeared. That snippet and the coverage of my testimony during the trial led to a lengthier interview, which was included in a documentary for the Learning Channel entitled *Shadow of the Assassin.*

Far more ambitious was director Rob Reiner's feature film *Ghosts of Mississippi,* which brought the drama of the third trial to the big screen. My own excitement about the film was probably as great as the trepidation Beckwith felt when he heard the news. To have his story told by a Jewish director who was part of the Hollywood establishment undoubtedly was an affront from which he never recovered.

I was curious about the film for a variety of reasons, not least of which was the film's casting. Since I had been interviewed and later questioned on the witness stand by Bobby DeLaughter, I wasn't certain Alec Baldwin could bring the necessary gravitas to bear in portraying DeLaughter. Likewise, I wondered whether Whoopi Goldberg could bring to the role of Myrlie Evers the quiet dignity that an actress like Diahann Carroll or Leslie Uggams might have mustered. Most curious to me—and perhaps most exciting—was the casting of James Woods as Beckwith.

Although Reiner reportedly had older actors like Jack Nicholson or Robert Duvall in mind to portray Beckwith, Woods—who was only in his forties at the time—lobbied to read for the role and convinced Reiner he was up to the challenge of playing a man who was a quarter-century older. Woods did a deep dive into the Beckwith character, watching hours of filmed interviews with Beckwith to mimic his cadence and vitriol, and reading my book to help round out his understanding of Beckwith's upbringing and his mindset. "I so admire your courage," Woods wrote me in an email he sent after the production wrapped. "In fact, I added a line to the movie, because of your book, referring to 'sissies' in one of the interviews Alec watches in the movie." I admired *his* courage in undertaking the role of such an unsympathetic character, but Woods not only captured Beckwith's essence; with prosthetics and makeup, he even looked remarkably like Beckwith. Woods's performance generated the best notices the film received, and he earned an Academy Award nomination for Best Supporting Actor.

Ghosts of Mississippi held other surprises too. I was taken aback to see my name pop up in a 1997 interview with Reiner, in which he referred to me by name and noted that he had read *Portrait of a Racist* when he was preparing for the film. I was even more surprised the following year while reading Willie Morris's book *The Ghosts of Medgar Evers: A Tale of Race, Murder, Mississippi, and Hollywood.* Morris recounted a "long and vivid scene" that was cut from the film's script. "This scene was a confrontation between Beckwith and his nephew-in-law, Reed Massengill, in a restaurant. Beckwith thinks Massengill, a writer, is interviewing him to do a glowing biography but ascertains that he is going for the truth." He quotes screenwriter Lewis Colick describing the impact of the scene. "Beckwith reveals a side of himself that makes him more multidimensional—one of those marginal men from a lost legacy with sexual problems, drinking problems. In this scene Beckwith scares Massengill to death. It shows what makes Beckwith tick. It gets into the deep darkness of him. It shows why he *hated* Medgar so much" (p. 234).

That hatred eventually burned itself out. Beckwith's death at age eighty occurred at the University of Mississippi Medical Center, where decades earlier he had accepted payment to donate his body to science. Beckwith had been transported there from his jail cell around 2 p.m. on Sunday, January 21, 2001, and he died that evening. Although no formal cause of death was given at the time, press statements issued by the hospital noted that Beckwith suffered from heart disease, high blood pressure, and "other ailments."

Loving and hating publicity as he did all during his lifetime, Beckwith undoubtedly would have chafed—and boasted—over his obituary that appeared in what he always called "The Jew York Times" two days later. He was buried on the crest of a hillside in Chattanooga Memorial Park, near his final home in Signal Mountain, Tennessee. At the graveside service, his son, Little De La, reportedly wailed "It ain't over! It ain't over!" Interred next to Beckwith is his wife, Thelma, who outlived him by six years and died in March 2007 at age ninety-seven.

Some years later, Little De La had an opportunity to speak his mind and generated his own fifteen minutes of fame with the release of the 2012 documentary *The Last White Knight.* The film had its U.S. premiere as part of the Atlanta Jewish Film Festival in early 2013, where I was in attendance. Although I had not seen my cousin since he had made a noteworthy appearance at one of my book-signing events in Jackson two decades earlier, I was struck by how much he had aged into his father's likeness. Not only did he physically resemble his father, he possessed his father's courtly demeanor and somewhat obsequious politeness. He also seemed to have inherited some of his father's boastful indiscretion. When asked by the filmmaker, Paul Saltzman, whether he was still a member of the Ku Klux Klan, he replied, "Oh, yes sir. I would say I'm an ordained Klansman till my death." He did acknowledge, however, that his sensibilities were no longer widely shared among his kin. Noting that his two adult children did not share his views, he said, "I am the last—the last—and I can tell you with my death will be the end of the Beckwith Klan era."

Later that same year, to commemorate the fiftieth anniversary of Medgar Evers's murder, I wrote a feature that was published in a Tennessee alternative newspaper. In "Remembering Medgar Evers," I recounted a story I hadn't included in my book. Once, riding the subway in New York City, where I lived and worked most of my adult life, several young black men were seated near me, and one of them wore a t-shirt with the multicolored outline of Africa and three faces silk-screened around it—Malcolm X, Dr. Martin Luther King, Jr., and Nelson Mandela. I was standing just to one side of the group, and I had my briefcase in my hand, my jacket over my arm and my tie loosened, holding the railing on the E train on my way home from work to Hell's Kitchen. I was twenty-eight years old. They were probably twenty-three, twenty-five. I leaned in toward them and nodded to the man in the shirt. "You're missing an important 'M.'" His friends looked at me quizzically, and I said, "Medgar Evers. He was assassinated before Malcolm X and Dr. King." I won't say the young man in the t-shirt got in my face, but he was visibly angry, and he started to stand up on the crowded train. One of the other men grabbed his arm as he was getting up, and said, "No, he's right. Medgar Evers. He's right." The guy in the shirt sat back down, but never broke eye contact with me. "Who are you to tell me *my* history?" he asked. The train rocked for a second as we looked at each other. "I wasn't trying to start anything," I said. "But it's not just *your* history—it's *our* history."

Several decades have passed since that incident, but it stands clear in my memory, and the times, as Bob Dylan wrote in 1963, they are a-changin'. On the upside—in my view, at least—the number of adherents to Beckwith's virulent theology of Christian Identity continues to decline, and if the Southern Poverty Law Center's data is correct, its numbers dropped 45 percent between 2017 and 2019. We can only hope. If the American political landscape during that same time period taught us anything, however, it was that what were once "subterranean" or less apparent racist ideologies might rise to the surface and bleed into the mainstream in unexpected ways. A timely example was the violent spectacle we witnessed at the Unite the Right rally in Charlottesville, Virginia, in August 2017. The calendar may have moved forward since 1963, but the pendulum of racist sentiment in many respects seems to keep swinging backward, despite Dylan's entreaty " . . . come senators, congressmen, please heed the call. . . . There's a battle outside and it's raging."

Katherine Stewart's excellent book *The Power Worshippers: Inside the Dangerous Rise of Religious Nationalism* (Bloomsbury Publishing, 2022) outlines vividly how parts and pieces of Beckwith's own theology have been toned down but continue to percolate in what today is known more commonly as "dominion" theology—Christian nation mythologizers who insist public officials should be steered by a "biblical worldview." Stewart presciently writes: "Perhaps the most obvious paradox of Christian nationalism is that it preaches love but everywhere practices intolerance, even hate." Having spent time among religious nationalists over the years, she notes that ". . . they seek to punish those who are different. It is not enough for them to assert that they alone are religiously righteous; they want everyone else to conform to their ideas of righteousness." Local school boards, city councils across the nation, state governor's mansions, and now the U.S. Congress are increasingly populated with adherents to religious nationalism, their agenda sustained and supported by an almost unceasing supply of cash provided by conservative religious groups and wealthy individuals.

And while the days of Alabama Governor George Wallace standing in the schoolhouse door to prevent segregation may be past, our nation faces new and perhaps more potent threats from our elected officials. A late 2022 poll, conducted by Politico and publicized by MoveOn.org, indicated that a vast majority of Republican voters believe the United States to be "a Christian nation" and advocate officially ending the separation of church and state. "This ideology, called 'Christian nationalism,' is the belief that the U.S. was founded as a white, Christian nation and that there is no separation between church and state. Living under a white supremacist Christian theocracy could allow Congress and the courts to consider extremist interpretations of the Bible and other religious texts in writing laws and deciding cases. And it could even allow politicians to outlaw other religions and mandate that children be religiously indoctrinated in public schools."

Although that might sound farfetched, Congresswoman Lauren Boebert was videotaped in a public appearance in June 2022 saying, "The church is supposed to direct the government. The government is not supposed to direct the church—that is not how our founding fathers intended it. And I'm tired of this separation of church and state junk that's not in the Constitution."

I do not have an advanced degree in history, nor am I a social scientist or philosopher. But I reflect on the content and character of President John F. Kennedy's civil rights address to the nation televised on the night Medgar Evers was assassinated, in which Kennedy said, " . . . this nation, for all its hopes, and all its boasts, will not be fully free until all its citizens are free." And I think of President Donald J. Trump's remarks at the Ellipse on January 6, 2021, the day hundreds of armed insurrectionists stormed and breached the U.S. Capitol. Following both those speeches, on both those days, people died who were simply doing their jobs.

I think of the voter poll tax Medgar Evers fought against, and his efforts to register black voters in Mississippi, and I reflect on the gerrymandering and redistricting taking place around the United States, and today's concerted political efforts to suppress voters of color. "At this inflection point," President Joe Biden told congregants at Ebenezer Baptist Church in January 2023, "we know there's a lot of work that has to continue on economic justice, voting rights and protecting our democracy, and I'm remembering that our job is to redeem the soul of America." Those aspirations were as vivid in 2023 as they were in 1963 or 1983.

I compare the roots of Beckwith's Christian Identity theology, and its necessity to twist and reinterpret scripture to its own ends, to the once nascent and now widespread religious nationalism that has crept into city councils, county commissions, and even Congressional prayer breakfasts. And I think of the growth and consolidation of power of the evangelical "religious right" in the United States, and its continued exertion of power over the Republican Party, its intentions, and its candidates.

I think of the elder Klansmen who began dying off in the 1980s and 1990s, replaced during those years by skinheads and neo-Nazis and members of Aryan Nations and The Order who perpetuated the Klan's ideology and activities. And I'm reminded of the quiet growth in the interim of the armed militias, the Oath Keepers, and the Proud Boys. And I think of *The Turner Diaries*, required reading for white supremacists, militia members, and conspiracy theorists of the 1980s, and of that book's embrace by members of all the groups that have sprung up since that time. And I am reminded of the frightening parallels between the book's fictional recounting of an armed attack on the U.S. Capitol, which was no less than a blueprint for the January 6, 2021, armed insurrection against our democracy.

I think of the thousands of lynchings that took place throughout the early twentieth century, when white-mob mentality ruled, particularly in Mississippi. I think of Emmett Till, the teenager who was beaten, mutilated, shot in the head, and whose body was bound with rusty barbed wire to part of a cotton gin and then dumped into the Tallahatchie River in 1955. I think of the 1998 death of James Byrd, Jr., who was offered a ride by three white men in Texas who drove him to a remote country road, beat him and spray-painted his face, urinated and defecated on him, and chained him by his ankles to their truck. They dragged him along an asphalt road until he was decapitated when his head hit a culvert, then drove the body another mile and a half to dump his torso in front of a black church before they attended a cookout. I think of Ahmaud Arbery, jogging through a suburban neighborhood in Georgia in 2020, chased down by three white men in a truck, who was shot and killed simply for jogging in the "wrong" neighborhood. And I think of a Minneapolis police officer with his knee on George Floyd's neck for more than nine minutes that same year.

Today, six decades later, I'm still haunted by the image of Medgar Evers, shot in the back in his own driveway under darkness of night. Just as I am haunted by the image of Breonna Taylor, shot by police six times, in the darkness of her own apartment, in the middle of the night.

The times, they are a-changin'.

Acknowledgments 2024

Today, three decades after this book's initial publication and sixty years after Medgar Evers's assassination, I'm thankful that this updated edition of *Portrait of a Racist* gives me an opportunity to acknowledge some of the people whose gracious contributions to its success came not during the research and writing, but after its initial publication.

I've been fortunate to serve as a speaker to a broad range of audiences at civic groups, high schools, and colleges around the United States, and I'm thankful to all of them for their invitations, their attention, and their feedback about the book. One engagement in particular was truly life changing for me. During the summer of 1995, a year after the book's initial release, I spent orientation week with the incoming freshman class of Centenary College of Louisiana. The college's Women's Endowment Quorum purchased copies of *Portrait* for each incoming freshman and their faculty advisors, and we spent the week working together in small groups, breakout sessions, and large-group discussions before they ended the week with a carnival and placed me in a dunk tank. I want to thank Dr. Dana Kress for extending the invitation and making me feel so welcome; Dr. Kenneth Schwab, former president of Centenary College, for hosting me as President's Convocation speaker for the installation of that class at the end of its orientation; and Dr. Dorothy Bird Gwin for her encouragement during that visit and for her friendship following that remarkable week.

All authors owe a debt to the journalists, columnists, and reviewers who cover the release of new books, and *Portrait* garnered more than its share of press coverage when it first appeared because of the timeliness of its release, the overwhelming interest in the third trial of Byron De La Beckwith, and his ultimate conviction so many years after the murder of Medgar Evers. Although there are far too many journalists to acknowledge individually, I particularly want to thank Dr. David Garrow, who has been a longtime vocal supporter of this book and its value; the late Henry Hampton, visionary creator of the "Eyes on the Prize" documentaries, who reviewed *Portrait of a Racist* for *The New York Times Book Review*; and the authors whose books about the Evers murder and Beckwith's trial helped bring context and enduring relevance to this important story—Adam Nossiter, author of *Of Long Memory* (1994); Maryanne Vollers, author of *Ghosts of Mississippi* (1995), the late Willie Morris, author of *The Ghosts of Medgar Evers* (1998), and Jerry Mitchell, author of *Race Against Time* (2020).

There are others whose contributions have assured Medgar Evers and Byron De La Beckwith a place not just in history, but also in our popular culture. Film director Rob Reiner, whose *Ghosts of Mississippi* brought the Evers assassination and Beckwith's final trial to the big screen, deserves thanks for bringing this story to a much wider audience with passion and sensitivity. I'm personally appreciative that he acknowledged both me and my book in an interview with *Los Angeles Daily News*. I'd also like to acknowledge screenwriter Lewis Colick, whose early script drafts included a tense confrontation scene between Beckwith and me, and which I regret was cut from later drafts of the script. And most of all, I want to thank James Woods for his passionate pursuit of the role of Byron De La Beckwith and the chilling accuracy he brought to bear in his Oscar-nominated performance, as well as his kind acknowledgment in his emails to me that he used *Portrait of a Racist* to help deepen his understanding of Beckwith.

At the Mississippi Department of Archives & History, Director of Collections Nan Prince and Acquisitions & Collections Coordinator Laura Anne Heller proved not only very helpful but congenial, and I'm appreciative of their efforts on my behalf.

I'm especially grateful to the artist Sanders McNeal, whose courtroom sketches of the third Beckwith trial captured the action on the witness stand as it happened, and who graciously allowed me to publish one of her sketches herein for the first time in three decades. I would also like to thank Bruce Plante, former editorial cartoonist at the *Chattanooga Times*, for allowing me to reproduce his important and chilling work.

At the Betsey B. Creekmore Special Collections and University Archives, University of Tennessee, Knoxville, I am grateful to the many librarians and archivists who helped catalog and process—and who maintain—my research materials for this book. Hundreds of Beckwith's letters and photographs are available for study, and a number of them are reproduced in this edition for the first time. Special thanks to Assistant Dean and Director Jennifer Beals and Digital Specialist Kyle Hovious.

At the University of Tennessee Press, I'm indebted to Director Scot Danforth for encouraging me to revisit this book with fresh eyes all these years after its initial publication. The members of his team have been wonderful advocates for the book, and I'm indebted in particular to Business Manager Lisa Davis, Marketing Manager Tom Post, Production Coordinator Stephanie Thompson, and Copyediting Coordinator Jonathan Boggs.

Three informal readers of this book's "new" ending were particularly helpful at a critical juncture. My sister, Leslie Cutshaw, my cousin Judy Valliant, and my dear friend, Cathy Irwin, offered comments and observations that helped me immensely as I worked to place this story in the context of the three decades that have followed Beckwith's final trial.

I'm fortunate to have a core group of friends, scattered geographically but always close, to help keep me grounded. For their enduring friendship I want to thank my longtime best friend, Scott Morelock, and my dear friends Richard Taddei, David Preaus, Mike Stengel, and Sasha Chuprina. And for unwittingly playing a role in this new, expanded publication of *Portrait of a Racist*, I'd like to thank Lynne Sullivan. I owe you a drink.

Appendix

UNITED STATES GOVERNMENT

Memorandum

TO: W. C. SULLIVAN

FROM: D. J. BRENNAN

SUBJECT: MEDGAR EVERS
NATIONAL ASSOCIATION FOR THE ADVANCEMENT OF COLORED PEOPLE (NAACP) FIELD SECRETARY
JACKSON, MISSISSIPPI
CIVIL RIGHTS

Morning newspapers and radio broadcasts have reported the shooting of Medgar Evers, NAACP Field Secretary, Jackson, Mississippi, on the late evening of June 11, 1963, or early morning of June 12, 1963.

████████ Staff Director, Commission on Civil Rights (CCR), on the morning of June 12, 1963, telephonically contacted the Liaison Agent to advise that in his opinion the shooting of Evers could be the spark that will set off the biggest and most violent racial demonstration this country has known.
████████ described Evers as a very tolerant, courageous and level-headed Negro leader whom the CCR considered the most reliable Negro in the Jackson, Mississippi, area.

████████ stated that he realized that there was no Federal violation involved and that in all probability the FBI could not enter the case. However, he felt he wanted to convey to the Director his concern over the shooting and to alert the Bureau to the possibility of the problems that might flow from this incident. ████████ was advised that at the request of the Department, the Bureau is following this matter closely and keeping the Department apprised of all developments but that we are not actively engaged in investigating this shooting. ████████ indicated he appreciates the Bureau's position in this matter. He stated he expects to advise Burke Marshall, Assistant Attorney General for Civil Rights, of his concern resulting from the shooting of Evers.

ACTION:

For information.

1 - Mr. Belmont
1 - Mr. Sullivan
1 - Mr. McGowan
1 - Liaison
1 - Mr. [redacted]

CITY OF JACKSON
MISSISSIPPI

ALLEN C. THOMPSON
MAYOR

June 13, 1963

Mr. J. Edgar Hoover, Director
Federal Bureau of Investigation
Washington, D.C.

Attention: FBI Laboratory

Re: Unknown Subject
Medgar Evers, Victim
Murder

At about 12:40 A.M. on 6-12-63 Unknown subject shot and killed Medgar Evers, Field Secretary, NAACP at Jackson, Mississippi. Evers had just arrived at his home and had gotten out of his car when the shot was fired. He was killed with one bullet which entered his back, passed through his body and continued through a living room window in his residence, passed through an inner wall into the kitchen where it was found. It is estimated the bullet was fired from a point about 200 feet away from the victim.

Later on the same date a 1917 Model Eddystone 30.06 rifle, Serial No. 105 2682 with a 6 x 32 Power "Golden Hawn", United Binoculars Chicago 20, Manufactured in Japan, telescopic sight Serial No. 69431 was found in a clump of honeysuckle vines at the Southeast corner of Joe's Truck Stop parking lot in the vicinity of the residence of Evers. The rifle was examined for latent fingerprints by Captain Ralph Hargrove, Identification Office, and one latent print was located on the right side of the front of the telescopic sight which was photographed and lifted. It was determined there was one empty cartridge case in the chamber of the rifle and six rounds of live ammunition bearing markings 30.06 Super Speed Sprg. in the magazine. The bullet, rifle, with the telescopic sight, the lift of the latent fingerprint, and a photograph of the latent print, the live ammunition and the empty cartridge case are being delivered to the laboratory by hand.

The laboratory is requested to search the latent fingerprint through the Single Fingerprint File. It is also requested that the rifle be searched through the National Stolen Property File. A ballistic examination is requested on the rifle to determine whether the bullet found in the rsidence of Medgar Evers was fired from this weapon.

It is further requested that an examination be conducted on the ammunition to determine make, calibre, manufacturer, and whether it is identical with the bullet found in Evers residence

The laboratory is requested to determine the make and calibre of weapon from which fired, type of bullet, and if possible the manufacturer.

Also determine if there are sufficient markings for ballistics comparison. It is also requested that the bullet be searched through the National Unidentified Ammunition File.

It is also requested that any other logical examination deemed advisable be conducted.

The above evidence has not been examined by any other examiner, other than the latent fingerprint examination.

Please return the bullet after examination.

Respectfully yours,

W. D. Rayfield
Chief of Police

M. B. Pierce
Chief of Detectives

PLAIN TEXT

TELEGRAM URGENT - COLLECT

MR. W. D. RAYFIELD
CHIEF OF POLICE
ATTENTION: MR. M. B. PIERCE
CHIEF OF DETECTIVES
JACKSON, MISSISSIPPI

MEDGAR EVERS MURDER CASE. RE OUR TELEGRAM 6-14-63.
LATENT FINGERPRINT FROM TELESCOPIC SIGHT OF RIFLE NOT IDENTIFIED IN OUR SINGLE FINGERPRINT FILE.

HOOVER

1 - Mr. Rosen
1 - [redacted], Room 2710, JB

UNITED STATES GOVERNMENT

Memorandum

TO: Mr. Belmont

FROM: A. Rosen

SUBJECT: UNKNOWN SUBJECT;
KILLING OF MEDGAR EVERS
JACKSON, MISSISSIPPI, 6-12-63
RACIAL MATTERS

The latent fingerprint, which the police developed on the telescopic sight of the Eddystone rifle believed to have been used in the killing of Evers, has not been identified in our single fingerprint file; however, we are continuing to search this print against the fingerprints of various suspects furnished by the Jackson, Mississippi, Police Department and by our New Orleans Office.

We are continuing the detailed check of records of Army depots and distributors of the Eddystone rifle in an effort to identify the owner of the weapon although the serial number of the rifle.

The Jackson, Mississippi, Police Department has extended its neighborhood investigation in the vicinity of the scene of the killing to additional residential areas. The Police Department is presently attempting to identify an unknown white male who made inquiry of two taxi drivers on the night of 6-9-63 as to the location of Evers' home and reportedly stated that it was important that he find where Evers lived in the next couple of days.

The Police Department is also attempting to identify the 1963 white Valiant automobile with a long whiplash antenna observed in the vicinity of Evers' home on 6-7-63 and again observed on a parking lot of a drive-in restaurant in the vicinity of the crime scene earlier on the night of the shooting.

1 - Mr. Mohr
1 - Mr. Conrad
1 - Mr. DeLoach
1 - Mr. Evans
1 - Mr. Trotter

The Attorney General   June 20, 1963

Director, FBI

UNKNOWN SUBJECT;
MEDGAR EVERS - VICTIM
RACIAL MATTERS

1 - Mr. Belmont
1 - Mr. Rosen
1 - Mr. Malley
1 - Mr. McGowan
1 - [redacted]
1 - Mr. Mohr
1 - Mr. DeLoach
1 - Mr. Evans

The Jackson, Mississippi, Police Department is continuing a most intensive investigation and we are rendering every assistance possible to the police.

No logical suspect has been developed as of the present time. Every effort is being made to trace the rifle which was found near the crime scene and in this connection, records of various arsenals, other Government installations and numerous private concerns dealing in such firearms have been checked.

We are also vigorously pursuing every possibility of tracing the telescopic sight with which the suspect rifle was equipped. The United Binoculars Company in Chicago, Illinois, is the sole distributor of this type of telescopic sight. It has been determined from the records of this company that similar sights have been shipped to 171 customers, including business establishments as well as private individuals. We are tracing each sight which has been sold by the distributor and active investigation in this regard is presently being conducted b y 42 of our field offices.

The Jackson Police Department has advised that the latent fingerprint which was developed on the telescopic sight has been compared with the fingerprints of 337 [redacted] and [redacted] without effecting an identification.

All aspects of this investigation are being handled on a top priority basis.

1 - The Deputy Attorney General

1 - Mr. Burke Marshall
Asisstant Attorney General

FEDERAL BUREAU OF INVESTIGATION

Date 6/26/63

JOHN W. GOZA, ████████████████████ ████████, Mississippi, was advised that he did not have to make a statement; that any statement made by him could be used against him in a court of law; no threats or promises were made to him in obtaining a statement; and he was advised of his right to first consult an attorney before making a statement. He declined to furnish a signed statement, but did furnish the following information:

Mr. GOZA stated he operates Durk's Tackle Shop, Grenada, Mississippi, and has operated this tackle shop for many years. He said the tackle shop has been at its present location for about 6½ years.

He said at this tackle shop, he sells guns, fishing equipment, and old coins. He said that in the latter part of 1962, he purchased 4 rifle scopes from the United Binocular Company, Chicago, Illinois. He said one was for a .22 rifle. Two were 4 power scopes for high powered rifles, and one was a 6 power scope.

He said that several months ago, ████████ an ████████ at ██████ Tennessee, who is also a gun collector, traded him a 30.06 rifle and a 243 Savage Rifle for a .16 gauge shotgun. He said he later traded the guns back to ██████. He said that between trades, when he had possession of the rifles, ████████████████, Mississippi, put two rifle scopes on the rifles. He said he recalls that the 6 power scope went on the 243 Savage Rifle and the 4 power scope went on the 30.06 rifle. He vaguely recalls that ██████ did not want the scopes and the scopes were removed at his tackle shop. He said there was no difficulty experienced in removing the scopes. He said he put the scopes in a cabinet and thinks possibly in the cabinet where the pistols are kept.

At this point in the interview, Mr. GOZA stated he realized he was being questioned concerning the killing of a Negro at Jackson, Mississippi.

He said on June 8, 1963, he went to ████████, Arkansas, to the ██████████ operated by ████████.

On 6/21/63 at ████████ Mississippi File # ME 44-1067 by SA ██████████.:cjs Date dictated 6/24/63

He said the trip was made in his car, a 1959 Oldsmobile Station Wagon, which bore a Mississippi license plate. He said he made this trip by himself.

██

At this point in the interview, Mr. GOZA stated, "Wait a minute, I'll tell you what I think you want to know". He then said that about May or June,

1963, BYRON DE LA BECKWITH of Greenwood, Mississippi, a specialty salesman, who sells candy, etc., and who is an ex-Marine, was in his store about 8:00 p.m. at Grenada, Mississippi. He said BECKWITH traded him 2 old .45 pistols and some shotgun shells and he is sure that he let BECKWITH have one of the rifle telescopes which he received from the United Binocular Company, Chicago, Illinois. He said he remembered this deal when interviewed by FBI Agents on June 20, 1963, but did not want to mention BECKWITH's name as he is a friend and he did not want to get BECKWITH in trouble. He said he is sure he traded BECKWITH a rifle scope but does not recall if it was a 4 power or a 6 power scope. He said he could have traded BECKWITH both a 6 power and a 4 power scope.

Mr. GOZA said he realized he had been questioned in the past about the murder case at Jackson, Mississippi, involving a Negro who was killed and he thought possibly the scope he had sold to BECKWITH might be the scope which was found on the rifle and for this reason he did not want to get BECKWITH involved in any trouble.

At this point Mr. GOZA said he had a terrific headache, that he wanted a drink, and that he had rather not discuss the matter anymore.

As the Agent was leaving, Mr. BECKWITH stated, "I think you have what you are looking for."

INVESTIGATION BY FBI TO TRACE RIFLE

On June 13, 1963, the Boston Division advised that ██████████ Security Officer, Springfield Armory, Springfield, Massachusetts, advised that armory maintains no record of serial numbers of rifles manufactured there. ████ suggested a check be made at Letterkenny Ordnance Depot, Attention MISMA, Chambersburg, Pennsylvania.

On June 13, 1963, the Bureau instructed the Springfield Division to contact the Rock Island Arsenal, Rock Island, Illinois, to determine if any record of the rifle recovered by the Jackson Police Department was maintained.

On June 13, 1963, a local gun smith at Jackson advised the Jackson Police Department that surplus army weapons, including guns similar to the rifle located by the Jackson Police Department, had been advertised for sale by Hunters Lodge, 200 South Union Street, Alexandria, Virginia, and some surplus weapons had been purchased by residents of the Jackson, Mississippi, area. On the same date, a doctor in Jackson, who is a member of the American Rifle Association, advised the Jackson Police Department that the American Rifle Association purchased a large quantity of 1917 Model Eddystone Rifles which were made available to members of the association for $8.00 apiece. This doctor stated that the Director of Civilian Marksmanship, American Rifle Association, 1600 Rhode Island Avenue, Washington, D. C., would be in a position to check the records of that organization under the serial number of the rifle recovered by the Jackson Police Department to determine whether the weapon was sold by that association. The Richmond and Washington Field Divisions were requested to check the above-mentioned organizations to determine whether the Eddystone Rifle was sold by either organization and the identity of the person to whom sold.

On June 13, 1936, the Springfield Division advised that small arms specialists, Rock Island Arsenal, Rock Island, Illinois, advised that the rifle recovered by the Jackson Police Department is a military rifle manufactured by Eddystone Manufacturing Company, Philadelphia, Pennsylvania, a subsidiary of Baldwin Locomotive Works, Philadelphia, for the U. S. Army during World War I. Over two million of these rifles were manufactured with the termination date November 9, 1918. After World War I these rifles were sold as surplus at camps and army depots and veterans clubs throughout the United States, and after World War II were either sold or given to lend-lease countries throughout the world, including China and India. These rifles were thought to be sold by Sears and Roebuck Company, Chicago, Illinois. Rock Island Arsenal authorities felt it is almost impossible to locate records for the sale of the rifle; however, records may be located at Major Items and Small Arms Section, U. S. Army Depot, Anniston, Alabama, and Major Items Supply Management Agency (MISMA), Letterkenny Arsenal, Chambersburg, Pennsylvania.

The Philadelphia Division advised on June 13, 1963, that ██████████████ Base Security Officer, Letterkenny Ordnance Depot, checked the records of the MISMA, which is the central record of all small arms sold or disposed of by the Army since 1950, but no record was located of the weapon recovered by the Jackson Police Department.

The Springfield Division advised on June 13, 1963, that all gun sales records of the Property Disposal Unit, Rock Island Arsenal, Rock Island, Illinois, had been reviewed, and no record of any Eddystone weapon was located. Rock Island Arsenal authorities advised that prior to 1956, the property disposal offices were not permitted to sell or dispose of weapons in any way, but the weapons were disposed of by Army Ordnance Depots throughout the United States, which installations routinely destroyed such records of sales when three years old. Rock Island Arsenal authorities advised that MISMA, Letterkenny Arsenal, Chambersburg, Pennsylvania, should have the records of all small arms records disposed of by the U. S. Army for any reason since the inception of the Arms Central File System in approximately 1948. Long-time experienced employees of the Rock Island Arsenal advised that U. S. Model 1917 Enfield rifles were manufactured during World War I by Winchester, Remington, and Eddystone Arsenal located Eddystone, Pennsylvania, with a total of about two million rifles being produced prior to termination of contract November 9, 1918.

On June 13, 1963, the Philadelphia Division advised that ██████████, Base Security Officer, Letterkenny Ordnance Department, checked the records of MISMA without locating any record of an Eddystone Springfield Rifle. Inquiry Baldwin Company and Eddystone Manufacturing Company revealed that rifles were never manufactured by either company.

██████████ Former Supervisor, Remington Arms Co., Eddystone, Pennsylvania, plant, advised rifles for military made from 1916 to 1918 in plant owned by Baldwin at Eddystone. During that period, no corporate connection between Remington and Baldwin, and records are probably located Remington Arms Co., Bridgeport, Connecticut.

The Washington Field Office advised on June 13, 1963, that ██████████, Government Equipment Sales Division, National Rifle Association, 1600 Rhode Island Avenue Northwest, Washington, D. C., had advised on that date that no record of 30.06 caliber 1917 Model Eddystone Rifle, Serial No. 1052682, had been located has having been sold through the National Rifle Association.

Washington Field advised there was no association in Washington known as the American Rifle Association; however, ██████████ had advised that the name of the magazine published by the National Rifle Association is "American Rifleman."

On June 14, 1963, the Chicago Division advised that ██████████, Sears Roebuck and Company, 925 South Homan, Chicago, Illinois, advised on June 13 and 14, 1963, that he is the purchaser of guns for 750 stores and 11 mail order plants owned and operated by Sears Roebuck and Company. ██████████ advised he has purchased rifles, including the Eddystone 30.06 Model 1917, from ██████████, Inter-Armco, Ltd., 10 Prince Street, Alexandria, Virginia. ██████████ also advised that Golden State Arms,

386 West Green Street, Pasadena, California, is also a large supplier of military surplus guns.

On June 14, 1963, the New Haven Division advised that Lieutenant Remington Arms Company, Bridgeport, Connecticut, advised on that date that no records of firearms are maintained at Remington Arms Company, Bridgeport. Lieutenant ascertained that all records of military rifles manufactured during World War I at the Ilion Plant of Remington Arms Company have been destroyed. Copies of records of manufacture were turned over at U. S. Government direction to the Rochester Ordnance, Rochester, New York.

On June 14, 1963, Assistant Chief of Police, M. B. PIERCE, Jackson, Mississippi Police Department, advised that information has been received by his department from , Memphis, Tennessee, to the effect that Klein's, 227 West Washington Street, Chicago, Illinois sells .30-06 rifles with pre-mounted Japanese made telescopic sights. According to the information received from Klein's is reported to be a mail order firm.

On June 14, 1963, the Richmond Division advised that , the Vice-President of Interanco, 10 Prince Street, Alexandria, Virginia, had advised that Hunters Lodge is a retail outlet for Interanco. Potomac Arms Corporation is also an affiliate of Interanco and trades as Ye Old Hunter. Hunters Lodge is primarily a mail order business while Ye Old Hunter deals mainly with over the counter sales. According to , the rifle recovered by the Jackson Police Department is an Enfield rifle and several years ago, a large number of these rifles were sold to National Gun Traders, 251 South West 22nd Avenue, Miami, Florida, by the Canadian Government.

The Buffalo Division advised on June 14, 1963, that Major , New York Procurement District, United States Army, Rochester Regional Office, Rochester, New York, had advised on that date that the Rochester Ordnance District was abolished in 1958 and records were forwarded to the United States Army Records Center, 9700 Page Boulevard, St. Louis, Missouri.

On June 14, 1963, the Birmingham Division advised that all sales records at the Anniston Army Depot, Anniston, Alabama prior to July 1, 1960 have been destroyed. Birmingham advised that since 1948 to present date, Form 001172 had been prepared on each sale of firearms when released from military responsibility and this form then forwarded to MISMA Letterkenny Chalmersburg, Pennsylvania.

The Los Angeles Division advised on June 14, 1963, that , Golden State Arms, Pasadena, California, advised on that date that his company bought basic mechanisms of various firearms including .30-06 model rifles from the Government of Viet Nam as surplus. Golden State shipped material to Mace Corporation, a subsidiary, who installed stocks for Springfield rifle barrels. made available records which were examined but no record located of instant rifle.

On June 15, 1963, the Miami Division advised that ████████████████████, National Gun Traders, advised on that date he could not recall purchase of large number of Enfield rifles from any firm in Canada or from Canadian Government. Stated serial numbers of all guns are recorded without regard to make, type or caliber or date of purchase and a search of records would require extensive review of records. He further stated that his company does not handle the Golden Hawk telescopic sight. ██████ also advised that all guns sold are reported by serial number to the Dade County Department of Public Safety and the Miami Police Department. The serial number of the rifle recovered by the Jackson Police Department was checked through the records of the Miami Police Department and the Dade County Department of Public Safety with negative results.

The Springfield Division advised on June 15, 1963, that the Deputy Commanding Officer, Rock Island Arsenal, Rock Island, Illinois, had informed that all records of gun sales for the Army Depot previously maintained at the Rock Island Arsenal were forwarded to MISMA Letterkenny Arsenal Chalmersburg, Pennsylvania, on the inception of Misma.

The St. Louis Division advised on June 15, 1963 that a search of the personnel records, MTRC, St. Louis, Missouri for the Rochester Ordnance District, had developed no information concerning the rifle recovered by the Jackson Police Department, the manufacturer or ownership of the rifle.

The Philadelphia Division advised on June 15, 1963, that all available records at MISMA Letterkenny Army Depot, Chalmersburg, Pennsylvania had been checked on the rifle recovered by the Jackson Police Department with negative results.

On June 15, 1963, the Chicago Division advised that records of Klein's Sporting Goods, Chicago, Illinois, had been checked on that date but no record of the rifle recovered by the Jackson Police Department was located.

The St. Louis Division advised on June 17, 1963 that an extensive search of all records of the Military Personnel Records Center, St. Louis, Missouri, for the Rochester Ordnance District and World War I records, failed to locate any information concerning instant rifle.

The Miami Division advised on June 19, 1963 that ████████, National Gun Traders, Miami, Florida, had stated that approximately 1500 Model 1917 Enfield rifles had been purchased during the past eight years from Numrich Arms Company, W. Hurley, New York and Golden State Arms Company, 386 West Green Street, Pasadena, California.

On June 21, 1963, the New York Division advised that ████████████████, Retail Sales, Numrich Arms Company, W. Hurley, New York, advised that a search of records on all Enfield rifles, failed to reveal any rifle sold with the serial number 1052682.

████████, Numrich Arms Company, stated his invoices revealed a shipment of 400 Enfield rifle barrel receivers shipped June 13,

1960 to the National Gun Traders, Miami, Florida, but these were parts of rifles and no serial numbers were recorded at Numrich Arms.

Assistant Chief of Police, M. B. PIERCE, Jackson, Mississippi, Police Department, advised on June 23, 1963 that THORN MC INTYRE Greenwood, Mississippi, telephone number GL 3-7743, telephonically contacted Captain RALPH HARGROVE, Identification Officer of the Jackson Police Department on June 14, 1963. Mr. MC INTYRE informed that he had traded a 1917 Enfield rifle about three years ago to De La BECKWITH, 306 George Street, Greenwood, Mississippi.

On June 24, 1963, the Memphis Division advised that INNES T. MC INTYRE, III, Route 2, Itta Bena, Mississippi has informed that he observed an advertisement in the classified advertisement section of the American Rifle Magazine, issued during the Spring of 1959, offering Enfield .30-06 rifles for sale. A check of the back issues of the American Rifle Magazine in MC INTYRE's possession disclosed an advertisement in the issues of April and May, 1959, by the International Firearms, 22 Kingman Street, St. Albans, Vermont, offering .30-06 U.S. Enfield rifles for sale. MC INTYRE stated he feels almost certain this is the company from which he bought instant rifle during the Spring of 1959.

MC INTYRE advised that about Christmas, three years ago, he exchanged the rifle he had purchased with BECKWITH for a similar rifle which had a bad barrel. MC INTYRE said at the time, the rifle he traded BECKWITH had standard sights.

According to MC INTYRE, BECKWITH told him he wanted a gun of this model in shooting condition and nothing was said about changing sights. MC INTYRE said he has not seen the gun he traded to BECKWITH since the date of the trade. He stated that he has no serial numbers for the gun he traded BECKWITH and stated that from pictures appearing in the newspapers of the weapon recovered by the Jackson Police Department, the gun seems almost identical except for sights. MC INTYRE advised that no mention was made by BECKWITH regarding ammunition for the gun, but that ammunition for this weapon is generally commercially available in the Greenwood area. MC INTYRE stated that he has seen BECKWITH several times since the trade, but no mention has been made of the gun. MC INTYRE further advised that he has fired target practice with BECKWITH on occasions and described him as a better than average shot. MC INTYRE advised that he has not seen BECKWITH's gun collection and could furnish no details about it.

UNITED STATES GOVERNMENT

Memorandum

TO : Mr. Tolson DATE: June 22, 1963

FROM : A. H. Belmont

SUBJECT: UNKNOWN SUBJECT;
MEDGAR EVERS - VICTIM
RACIAL MATTERS

In response to the Attorney General's discussion with Mr. Rosen wherein the Attorney General pointed out the potential weakness of a prosecution of subject Beckwith in Federal Court, I called Assistant Attorney General Burke Marshall at 4:00 p.m. today and advised him that we feel it is up to the Department to make a decision as to the course of action to be taken against Beckwith. I said there are two alternatives, either we go ahead as the Department indicated earlier today and have the complaint and warrant issued with FBI Agents picking Beckwith up in which case we would take him to Jackson, arraign him and then make it very clear that we will cooperate 100 per cent with local authorities in the matter of testimony, evidence and investigation; or the information should be turned over to the local police for handling by them. In the latter instance, there is the possibility that the subject will not be arrested promptly, that he may flee and, of course, the Department of Justice would get little credit in the whole matter.

I told Mr. Marshall that from a practical standpoint our opinion is that we should go ahead as originally planned, but reiterated that this was a decision for the Department. Mr. Marshall said he would talk to the Attorney General and would call me back.

Mr. Marshall called back at 4:10 p.m. and advised that the Department feels that the first course of action is preferable. He asked that the Attorney General be notified when we locate Beckwith as the Attorney General wants to call the Mayor of Jackson before we make the arrest to let him know what is happening and to make it clear that full cooperation will be given local authorities. I told Mr. Marshall this was not possible, that once the warrant is issued our Agents will have to pick up Beckwith as soon as they see him otherwise we may be chasing him over the countryside at 100 miles an hour. I stated that we can and will notify the Attorney General as soon as we pick Beckwith up on the warrant so that the Attorney General can take such action as he desires. I pointed out, however, that we are going to contact the Chief of Police at Jackson immediately after the arrest to notify him of the arrest and that we are bringing Beckwith to Jackson for arraignment, and, thereafter, he will be available to local authorities and we will give the police full cooperation in the matter of testimony, evidence and investigation so that we can make it clear that we are cooperating. In addition, publicity in this matter will clearly state that we are taking these steps for the benefit of local authorities. Mr. Marshall was in full agreement of this position. He said that he would notify the Attorney General when the warrant was issued and that he was instructing the U. S. Attorney to go ahead with the complaint and warrant and he would leave it up to us to notify the Attorney General when the arrest was made. I told him we would do this.

1 - Mr. Mohr
1 - Mr. DeLoach
1 - Mr. Evans

Memorandum to Mr. Tolson
RE: UNKNOWN SUBJECT;
MEDGAR EVERS - VICTIM

UNITED STATES GOVERNMENT

Memorandum

TO : Mr. McGowan DATE: 6/24/63

FROM : A. Rosen

SUBJECT: BYRON DE LA BECKWITH;
MEDGAR EVERS - VICTIM
RACIAL MATTER

For record purposes, this will reflect that on Saturday morning, June 22, 1963, at 8:00 a.m., we started discussions and negotiations for obtaining a complaint charging Beckwith with a Federal violation in this case.

It is recalled I communicated with Assistant Attorney General Burke Marshall, when I reached him in his office first thing in the morning, at which time I told him I desired to talk with him immediately concerning a very important matter. He told me he had stepped out of his office and that Dr. King was presently with him. I told him I wanted to see him alone and he said I should meet him immediately in his office. Messrs. Belmont, McGowan, [redacted] and myself proceeded to Marshall's office. I went in, the others being with me waited in an anteroom in Marshall's office. I was greeted by Mr. Norman of the Civil Rights Division who advised me that Marshall had left for the White House. Norman was expecting me and indicated Marshall would appreciate it if I would talk with John Doar. I asked for John Doar and he had slipped out and was unavailable. I advised Norman I would be in my office and would expect a call from Doar as soon as he was located. Shortly thereafter John Doar called me and I asked him to come to my office.

Doar arrived and present in my office were Messrs. Belmont, McGowan and [redacted]. I initially presented the case, the facts which had been developed, and the possibility of proceeding under Section 241, Title 18, as the only one which appeared to be most likely. Considerable discussion was had concerning the weaknesses of the Federal Statute: (1) the fact that there were no co-conspirators identified, and (2) the question of clearly establishing a right guaranteed under the Constitution was difficult.

During our discussion I received a number of calls from Mr. Marshall. Doar was able to talk with Marshall and explained our preliminary discussion to him and I also talked with Marshall while he was at the White House in conference with the President. It is noted that we had reached him through the President's secretary and that obviously Marshall had been called out of the meeting which was presently under way with the President. It is noted considerable publicity was given to the meeting which the President had that day with groups interested in the integration problem.

Doar departed after these preliminary discussions and indicated that a conference would be had concerning the Department's position as to authorization of any filing of a complaint.

In the interim, John Murphy of the Civil Rights Division was called in, he having been conferred with telephonically by John Doar concerning the filing of a complaint, and he drafted a so-called proposed complaint to be filed with the U.S. Commissioner at Jackson, Mississippi. This proposed complaint was brought to our attention in the afternoon by Murphy and several inaccuracies were corrected. It was then expected that the complaint would be given to the U. S. Attorney at Jackson, Mississippi, Robert E. Hauberg. His view was to be obtained. In the meantime numerous telephone calls had been made by me to SAC Maynor at Jackson, Mississippi, for the purpose of attempting to locate U. S. Attorney Hauberg who had departed his home and whose car was observed on the street downtown but he could not be located. After several hours he was located and he was put in touch with John Doar of the Department. He was given the language of the complaint and apparently a question was raised as to whether the complaint was not defective in that probable cause was not clearly shown. This created additional discussions in the Department. Marshall advised me they were concerned about this and so did Doar and that they would have to talk to the Attorney General about it.

In the meantime the Attorney General, who had been at his office and also at the White House, was now at his residence at McLean, Virginia. The Attorney General, having been advised by Marshall of the Bureau's position, called and I had a telephonic discussion with him of some 25-30 minutes. I went over the details which had been developed in our investigation. He was familiar with the mutilated bullet, the gun and sight, as well as the latent fingerprint. He continued to express concern over the weakness of the case and indicated that he realized there would be considerable public appeal insofar as the arrest of subject in this case was concerned but that somewhere along the line the Government might be tested if we had to go to trial. He understood there were no co-conspirators identified and indicated the obvious weaknesses in the case which had previously been gone over in detail with Doar and Marshall in our preliminary discussions leading up to the position which the Department had indicated it would take when Marshall earlier said he thought we ought to proceed. It is recalled I had previously indicated to Marshall, when he asked my opinion, that I had agreed with John Doar's views that there were certain weaknesses in the case but that I felt that there was a compelling over-all consideration which had to be considered. I indicated to Marshall this was no ordinary case; that based upon facts which had been developed, the Government had a grave responsibility to fulfil an obligation which it had assumed.

It was indicated that as a practical matter, circumstantial evidence in this case indicated Beckwith had commited the offense. It was also realized that if the Federal Government didn't precipitate some affirmative action at this time, chances are nothing would be done. Bearing this in mind, it was indicated if the Government did initiate some affirmative action, it was reasonable to expect that some of the pieces would fall in line and the State would be in a position to proceed with the more enormous offense - namely murder, against Beckwith. It was also indicated that it would appear that the Government would defer any action which it might take so that the State might proceed with the more grave offense. Having reiterated this to Doar and to Marshall, I also pointed this out to the Attorney General.

It appeared he was desirous of getting a firm assurance from the Bureau that this was what we wanted the Attorney General to do when, as a matter of fact, the responsibility for making the decision was the Department's.

The above situation was called to the attention of Mr. Belmont and he, in turn, was able to reach Mr. Tolson and the Director and discuss the matter with them. As indicated in subsequent memoranda prepared by Mr. Belmont, he reiterated the Bureau's position to Mr. Marshall and the alternatives were presented: (1) that we would proceed upon the conspiracy complaint and take the prisoner to Jackson, Mississippi, where he subsequently would be made available to the Jackson, Mississippi, authorities; or (2) we could turn the whole matter over to the Jackson authorities now for handling. Marshall chose the former position, namely, that we would proceed Federally against him.

Having obtained this final view, it became necessary to work out arrangements with SAC Maynor at Jackson and SAC Dissly at Memphis concerning the apprehension of the subject and his handling in Jackson. It is noted that we had a number of considerations in connection with our activity because of the untrustworthiness and unavailability of certain of the Commissioners and it was finally agreed to get a complaint filed before the U. S. Commissioner at Hattiesburg, Mississippi. This was done.

At 4:45 Mississippi time (6:45 D. C. time), the complaint was filed before U. S. Commissioner Margaret Estes by Special Agent Edgar C. Fortenberry. At 6:22, the above information was given to both the Jackson and Memphis offices. The subject was subsequently located through the assistance of his cousin, Yerger Morehead of Greenwood, Mississippi.

It is recalled Agents were surveilling the home of Beckwith and apparently this became known to people in the area because a Mr. Morehead contacted the Agents, identified himself and indicated subject had been in touch with him; that he was fearful of returning home because he thought he was being sought by the FBI and the police. He was informed at that time that a warrant was in existence for his arrest by the Federal Government. Subsequent developments indicated Morehead had been in touch with Beckwith again and that Beckwith had asked that a suit of clothes be picked up at his home. Morehead told the Agents about this and also related to them the fact that Beckwith's attorney, Mr. Lott, would have Beckwith available at his office for surrender later on. This surrender was effected. He was taken into custody and transported to Jackson, Mississippi.

During the discussions Marshall asked me whether the Bureau would have any objection to State authorities going along with the FBI at the time Beckwith is arrested. I advised him we could not do this because the Jackson authorities had no authority to make such an arrest and that the police would add nothing to our position in the matter and as a matter of fact it would detract from the very thing which the Federal Government was trying to bring about - namely, affirmative, independent action on its part for the assistance of the State. Marshall said he was merely raising this question because it might be brought up by the Attorney General in discussions. He said he realized our position very clearly.

UNITED STATES GOVERNMENT

Memorandum

TO : Mr. Rosen DATE: June 24, 1963

FROM : C. A. Evans

SUBJECT: BYRON DE LA BECKWITH;
MEDGAR EVERS - VICTIM
RACIAL MATTER

For record purposes, it is noted that I placed a telephone call at 1:10 a.m., Washington time, on June 23, 1963, to Mayor Allen Thompson of Jackson, Mississippi, and reached him at about 1:20 a.m.

The Mayor was informed that I was calling him at the suggestion of Attorney General Kennedy. He was informed that as he knew, the FBI had been cooperating with the Jackson Police Department since June 12, 1963, relative to the slaying of Medgar Evers. I told the Mayor that only a few minutes ago Byron De La Beckwith had been taken into custody by FBI Agents at Greenwood, Mississippi; that he was being brought to Jackson, and after arraignment would be immediately available to the local authorities.

The Mayor was also informed that the Attorney General had asked me to call him so the Mayor would be assured the action taken in arresting subject was in furtherance of our cooperation with the authorities at Jackson; that the more serious offense constituting a violation of state law was recognized; and that the FBI would continue to cooperate with the police in this case. It was stressed our fingerprint and laboratory experts, as well as our investigating Agents, will be available to testify in state proceedings and that we are continuing our all-out investigation to assist the Jackson Police in all ways possible.

I also told the Mayor that our Agents in Jackson were immediately contacting the Chief of Police there to furnish him full details, but that we wanted the Mayor to be alerted to the action that had just been taken.

Mayor Thompson expressed his appreciation for our cooperation and assistance. He thanked me for calling him to advise him of the developments and said that since the FBI was getting in touch with the Chief of Police, he saw no need for any immediate action on his part.

1:01 p.m. June 25, 1963

MEMORANDUM FOR MR. TOLSON
MR. BELMONT
MR. ROSEN
MR. DE LOACH

While discussing another matter, the Attorney General advised me he had just talked to Burke Marshall and learned the lawyer for Beckwith is going to go to court to find the basis for our arrest. The Attorney General stated we can always reindict and they are going to dismiss the Federal case.

I told the Attorney General I thought this was good. I also advised him the State is going to send Beckwith to a mental institution for examination and that he had previously been in an institution in Mississippi. I stated it is obvious the defense is going to be insanity.

The Attorney General stated that at least we know we got the right person. I assured him this was true; that two witnesses identified the car; that Beckwith asked a taxicab driver Ever's address; all this in addition to the fingerprint, gun and sight on the gun.

Very truly your,

John Edgar Hoover
Director

UNITED STATES GOVERNMENT

Memorandum

TO : Mr. Belmont DATE: October 1, 1963

FROM : A. Rosen

SUBJECT: BYRON DE LA BECKWITH, AKA;
MEDGAR EVERS - VICTIM
CIVIL RIGHTS; RACIAL MATTERS

With reference to the evidence available to local authorities at Jackson, Mississippi, in connection with the prosecution of Beckwith, the following information is set forth for your information. It has previously been covered in memoranda submitted heretofore.

There is no eyewitness to the Evers shooting and Beckwith has made no admission to this crime. The local case against Beckwith is a circumstantial one. The circumstantial evidence includes the following.

On 6/12/63, the date Evers was shot and killed, the Jackson Police Department recovered a 30.06 Eddystone rifle located in a clump of vines on a vacant lot in the rear of Joe's Drive In in Jackson which is approximately 250 feet from the Evers' residence. According to local authorities, the spot where the rifle was found is in a direct line with the spot where Evers was probably standing when shot. This rifle had attached thereto a telescopic sight. The rifle and sight were processed by local authorities who lifted a latent fingerprint off the sight. After being exhibited to numerous gunsmiths in the general area in an effort to identify the owner, local authorities turned over the rifle and sight to the New Orleans Office with the request it would be submitted to the FBI Laboratory for ballistic examination. New Orleans had the gun delivered to the Laboratory by Agent courier for immediate handling. The actual lift containing the above latent fingerprint accompanied the rifle and sight.

No latent fingerprints were developed by the Laboratory since numerous unknown individuals had handled the rifle and sight. The murder bullet recovered at the crime scene was badly mutilated and did not bear sufficient microscopic marks to make identification. Despite this fact, the Laboratory was able to determine that the bullet had been fired from a gun having the same type of rifling as the above weapon While this examination could not establish that the murder bullet was fired from the above rifle, the examination was of circumstantial value to the case.

During the investigation to trace the sight, we talked to John Goza, a gunsmith of Grenada, Mississippi, who furnished information which resulted in Byron de la Beckwith, Greenwood, Mississippi, being considered a suspect. Beckwith was contacted 6/21/63 but refused to talk with our Agents.

Beckwith's name was then immediately called to the attention of the

Identification Division, at which time a search of our fingerprint files was instituted. A fingerprint card submitted in connection with Beckwith's previous military service was located. Arrangements were immediately made to have the latent fingerprint developed by local authorities compared with Beckwith's fingerprints. This comparison established that the latent fingerprint was identical to Beckwith's right index finger.

Through very extensive investigation by the FBI, the telescopic sight was traced from United Binoculars, Chicago, Illinois, to John Goza who stated he sold the sight to Beckwith. Following Beckwith's arrest by FBI Agents on 6/22/63, we continued to conduct an extensive investigation in an effort to develop additional evidence. We were successful in tracing the rifle from a Montreal, Canada, firearms company to Innes McIntyre of Itta Bena, Mississippi, who stated he sold the rifle to Beckwith. Our investigation in tracing the rifle and sight involved 48 field divisions and one legat. Subsequent to Beckwith's arrest, we also interviewed Beckwith's employer and contacted five oil companies in an effort to locate any purchase record indicating Beckwith was in Jackson, Mississippi, on 6/12/63. It is noted that Beckwith was in possession of credit cards of these companies when arrested. Investigation along this line developed nothing of pertinence.

At the time of his arrest, Beckwith was driving a 1962 white Valiant with a whip antenna. Investigation by local authorities located two witnesses at Joe's Drive In who stated they observed a similar automobile on the drive in parking lot several hours before the shooting. This automobile was occupied by a white male. These witnesses viewed Beckwith in a lineup following his arrest but neither was able to make an identification. Upon viewing Beckwith's automobile, neither could positively state the car was identical to the automobile observed on the parking lot on the night of 6/11/63.

At the local preliminary hearing in this matter on 6/25/63, Captain Ralph Hargrove of the Jackson Police Department testified that the latent fingerprint developed by him on the sight was identical with the right index finger of Beckwith. Local newspapers further quoted Hargrove as stating that the latent fingerprint could not have been placed on the sight over 12 hours prior to the time he developed it. Our latent fingerprint examiner has not testified to date concerning this matter but will undoubtedly be used during Beckwith's trial. With regard to Captain Hargrove's testimony, according to the Identification Division, there is no technical method of determining the age of latent fingerprints.

A local grand jury at Jackson indicted Beckwith for the Evers murder on 7/2/63. The Mississippi State Supreme Court is expected to decide on 10/14/63 whether Beckwith must submit to mental examination before being tried.

ACTION:

We are continuing to follow local prosecution in this matter.

UNITED STATES GOVERNMENT

Memorandum

TO : Assistant Attorney General
CIVIL RIGHTS DIVISION

DATE: 10-17-63

FROM : Director, FBI

SUBJECT: BYRON DE LA BECKWITH
MEDGAR EVERS - VICTIM
CIVIL RIGHTS - RM

Reference is made to ______________ memorandum dated ______________ (your file ______________).

There is enclosed one copy of a letterhead memorandum dated 10-15-63 at Memphis.

A. ❑ This covers the preliminary investigation and no further action concerning a full investigation will be taken by this Bureau unless the Department so directs.

B. ❑ The investigation is continuing and you will be furnished copies of reports as they are received.

C. ❑ The investigation requested by you has now been completed. Unless advised to the contrary no further inquiries will be made by this Bureau.

D. ❑ Pursuant to instructions issued by the Department, no investigation will be conducted in this matter unless specifically directed by the Department.

EXX❑ Please advise whether you desire any further investigation.

F. ❑ This is submitted for your information and you will be advised of further developments.

G. ❑ This is submitted for your information and no further investigation will be conducted unless specifically requested by the Department.

H. ❑ This covers the receipt of a complaint and no further action will be taken by this Bureau unless the Department so directs. Information in the attached was previously furnished to Mr. Barrett of your Division and he advised that he desired no further action be taken until the Department has opportunity to review these matters for appropriate determination. No further action will be taken nor dissemination made pending receipt of advice from the Department.

UNITED STATES GOVERNMENT

Memorandum

TO : Mr. Mohr DATE: February 5, 1964

FROM : C. D. DeLoach

SUBJECT: BYRON DE LA BECKWITH TRIAL
PRESS INQUIRY
FEBRUARY 5, 1964

████████ ████████████ correspondent, called my office today and talked to Leinbaugh. He said that he had just received an inquiry from their representative in Jackson, Mississippi, wanting to know if it was possible that Lee Harvey Oswald could be involved in the slaying of Medgar Evers. ██████ said that supposedly defense attorneys had claimed some time this morning that Oswald was implicated in the slaying of Medgar Evers. ██████ had no other details and a quick check made at that time failed to reveal that we had been advised of such a rumor.

After checking, ██████ was contacted and told that the FBI could make no comment regarding his query. He fully understood and appreciated the Bureau's position.

A check was made of our files on Oswald and he was working for the William B. Reily and Company, Inc., New Orleans, Louisiana, from May 10 through July 19, 1963. Medgar Evers was shot at about 12:30 a.m. on the morning of June 12, 1963. On the pertinent dates our investigation reveals that Oswald left his place of employment at 5:30 p.m., June 11, 1963, and that he reported at 8:56 a.m. on the morning of June 12, 1963.

The above is for information.

1 - Mr. Belmont
1 - Mr. Sullivan
1 - Mr. Rosen
1 - Mr. Jones

September 13, 1965

BYRON DE LA BECKWITH

Byron De la Beckwith, a white male America, was born November 9, 1920, at Sacramento, California. He has a high school education and served in the United States Marine Corps from January 5, 1942 to January 4, 1946 receiving an honorable discharge. Beckwith is currently a resident of Greenwood, Mississippi, residing in a trailer at 410 West Park Avenue. He is employed as a salesman by the Delta Liquid Plant Food Company, Incorporated, of Greenville, Mississippi.

Beckwith was arrested on June 22, 1963 for the murder of Medgar Evers, National Association of the Advancement of Colored People (NAACP), Field Secretary, Jackson, Mississippi, who was slain June 12, 1963. Beckwith was subsequently tried on two occasions in Circuit Court, Jackson, Mississippi, and on each occasion the jury was unable to reach a verdict. Beckwith was released on bond.

"Delay" Beckwith was sworn into the White Knights of the Ku Klux Klan in Greenwood, Mississippi, following his release from jail on bond where he was tried for the murder of Medgar Evers. The White Knights of the Ku Klux Klan of Mississippi is reported to have paid the salary, car note, home note, and law fees for Beckwith while he was held in jail.

Beckwith was allegedly appointed a Kleagle at Large in the White Knights of the Ku Klux Klan of Mississippi in about August, 1965.

UNITED STATES DEPARTMENT OF JUSTICE

FEDERAL BUREAU OF INVESTIGATION

Jackson, Mississippi
June 19, 1966

BYRON DE LA BECKWITH
MEDGAR EVERS - VICTIM
CIVIL RIGHTS - RACIAL MATTERS

On June 17, 1966, Mr. William Waller, Hinds County District Attorney, Jackson, Mississippi, advised that no new developments have taken place in this case since last contacted by the FBI. He advised that the indictment against Byron De La Beckwith is still outstanding and he does not contemplate dismissing the indictment in the near future.

Mr. Waller stated that he does not plan any further prosecutive action on the murder charge in the foreseeable future until additional evidence, if any, comes to his attention.

This document contains neither recommendations nor conclusions of the FBI. It is the property of the FBI and it loaned to your agency; it and its contents are not to be distributed outside your agency.

F B I

Date: 7/13/66

Transmit the following in ______________________________

(Type in plaintext or code)

Via AIRTEL ______________ AIRMAIL

(Priority)

TO: DIRECTOR, FBI (157-901)

FROM: SAC, JACKSON (157-44)

BYRON DE LA BECKWITH, aka;
MEDGAR EVERS - VICTIM
CR - RM

Re Jackson airtel and LHM dated 6/19/66 and report of SA [redacted] dated 7/16/63 at Memphis.

Enclosed herewith are original and seven copies of an LHM suitable for dissemination. One copy of the LHM is being furnished to USA's at Jackson and Oxford, Mississippi, for their information.

The information contained in the LHM was furnished by [redacted] to SA [redacted]. According to the source, the statements made by [redacted] were made in his presence, as well as in the presence of [redacted]. The source cautioned that his name must not be mentioned and that [redacted] should not be directly questioned since only the above mentioned three individuals were present during this conversation.

Inasmuch as two Mississippi [redacted] members verified in June, 1963, that [redacted] was in their company during the night in question and returning to the [redacted] about 1:00 a.m. on June 12, 1963, no further action being taken by the Jackson Office.

Jackson indices discloses no record identifiable for [redacted] and [redacted].

No dissemination is being made to WILLIAM WALLER, Hinds County District Attorney, Jackson, Mississippi, pending Bureau advice.

The Bureau will be kept informed of any new developments in this case.

UNITED STATES DEPARTMENT OF JUSTICE

FEDERAL BUREAU OF INVESTIGATION

Jackson, Mississippi
July 13, 1966

BYRON DE LA BECKWITH;
MEDGAR EVERS - VICTIM
CIVIL RIGHTS - RACIAL MATTERS

A source of the Jackson Office of the FBI, who has furnished reliable information in the past, advised on May 28, 1966, that a conversation was had between ██████ now of ██████, Mississippi, and ██████ at a clubhouse located on a lake near ██████ in the vicinity of ██████, Mississippi. This club was operated by ██████ and the conversation took place sometime prior to when Byron De La Beckwith was first tried.

At this time, ██████ talked about being involved in the shooting of Medgar Evers, stating that Beckwith had obtained the gun used to kill Evers from a man in ██████, Mississippi. ██████ stated that he and Beckwith made two or three trips to the residence of Evers in order to determine his actions and activities and to make necessary plans. In each instance, they used a white or light colored Valiant, which was also used on the night of the shooting. ██████ stated he and Beckwith were hiding in some bushes near Evers' home and shot him when he returned to his residence late one night. ██████ stated, "They got the wrong man, Beckwith did not do the shooting."

The source stated that Beckwith and ██████ left the scene of the shooting as soon as they could but became separated while running back to their automobile. Beckwith started to come out of some bushes in which he and ██████ had been hiding, saw someone coming and jumped back into the concealing brush. Beckwith then went to his automobile and drove away from the scene, picking up ██████ some distance from the area as ██████ had remained concealed in the bushes. The source stated that according to ██████ he, ██████, had to sneak out of a ██████ and was almost caught when he returned.

Investigation previously conducted in this case disclosed that ██████ was an ██████ member of the ██████ Mississippi ██████ and that ██████ along with other members of his ██████ attended ██████ at ██████ Mississippi, from June 9, 1963, to June 23, 1963.

██████ Mississippi, advised in June, 1963, that on June 11, 1963, he was at ██████ ██████ Mississippi, but left the ██████ with other ██████, whose names he did not recall, and went to ██████ for "a night on the town." He stated while at he did not go anywhere near Jackson, Mississippi.

In June, 1963, , Mississippi, advised he recalled on the evening of June 11, 1963, seeing leave the area at about 7:00 p.m. with and in Mercury Monterey. said he did recall that was present for at 5:30 a.m. on June 12, 1963. He said there was no way of knowing what time actually returned to the that night.

In June, 1963, Mississippi, advised that on Tuesday Night, June 11, 1963, he, and others went away from the at approximately 7:00 p.m. until after midnight. He stated they went out in 1956 or 1957 Mercury. He said, he, and were together during the entire evening, and after leaving the they drove to about five miles south of and from there they went to the where they remained until returning to the sometime between midnight and 1:00 a.m. He said they definitely did not go to Jackson, Mississippi, that night.

Mississippi, advised in June, 1963, that on June 11, 1963, he, and left in 1958 Mercury Monterey, and during the night they visited the the and they returned to the at approximately 1:00 a.m. the following morning. stated he was certain that was with them during the entire evening and that they did not go to Jackson, Mississippi, during this period.

This document contains neither recommendations nor conclusions of the FBI. It is the property of the FBI and is loaned to your agency; it and its contents are not to be distributed outside your agency.

AIRTEL

TO: SAC, Jackson PERSONAL ATTENTION (44-37)

FROM: Director, FBI (157-901)

BYRON DE LA BECKWITH, AKA
MEDGAR EVERS - VICTIM
CR - RM

Reurairtel 7/19/66.

It is stated that the informant in this matter has advised he will not testify but it is not clear whether this is based upon a specific statement with regard to this particular information or whether this is based upon some general statement made in the past.

In view of the importance of this case and the importance of the information furnished by the informant, it is felt that every effort should be made to induce him to become a willing witness for the state. The SAC should personally interview for the purpose of determining whether he can be induced to testify for the state.

NOTE: Medgar Evers, Negro leader, Jackson, Mississippi, was murdered 6/12/63. Byron De La Beckwith was arrested by FBI Agents on Federal Civil Rights charges which were later dismissed in favor of State prosecution. Beckwith stood trial twice on state murder charges which resulted in a hung jury each time. The indictment is still outstanding. has now advised the Jackson Office that on

F B I

Date: 7/27/66

Transmit the following in ______________________
(Type in plaintext or code)

Via AIRTEL ______________________
(Priority)

TO: DIRECTOR, FBI (157-901)

FROM: SAC, JACKSON (157-44)

BYRON DE LA BECKWITH, aka
MEDGAR EVERS - VICTIM
CR - RM

ReJNairtel 7/19/66 and Bureau airtel 7/21/66, captioned matter.

Jackson airtel of reference was in error in that it referred to ████████ when in fact it should have read ████████ Appropriate error scored.

In accord with the Bureau's instructions contained in referenced airtel, ████████ was contacted on Tuesday, 7/26/66. He states he has never been nor is he now desirous to testify in any court case. He stated to be most frank he "loves life," and that there is not sufficient money available to change his mind.

In view of the foregoing, the Jackson Office can only suggest as an alternative that we endeavour through ████████ who initially introduced BECKWITH to ████████ to have him on some other occasion introduce BECKWITH to someone who may be willing to testify and perhaps BECKWITH will make the same admission before this person and ████████ who has already agreed to testify in other proceedings.

Notes

PROLOGUE: PORTRAIT OF A RACIST

1. JCL 12/18/90, p. A1; CNFP 12/18/90, p. B2; CT 12/18/90, p. A1; JCL 12/17/90, p. A9.
2. CT 12/19/90, p. A9; Thelma Beckwith interview 5/24/91. When the author later tried to confirm Mrs. Beckwith's participation in the Miss Chattanooga contest, officials said their records did not "go back that far."
3. Beckwith letter to Mary Louise Williams, 4/25/75, author's collection.
4. Copy of Beckwith's ordination certificate, author's collection. Beckwith was ordained in the Kingdom ministry of the Christian Identity Movement on 1/2/77, just four months before he was imprisoned at the Louisiana State Penitentiary at Angola. The head of the ordaining council was Dewey H. "Buddy" Tucker, a notorious anti-Semite and head of a racist group called the National Emancipation of the White Seed. Increasingly, references to the Klan, neo-Nazi and survivalist right movements are including background information on Christian Identity Movement theology. Some of the best include: J. Gordon Melton's *Encyclopedic Handbook of Cults in America*, published by Garland Publishing, 1986; Leonard Zeskind's *The "Christian Identity" Movement*, published by The Division of Church and Society of the National Council of Churches of Christ in the U.S.A., 1987; ADL Facts, *The "Identity Churches": A Theology of Hate*, published by the Anti-Defamation League of B'nai B'rith, Spring 1983; James Coates's *Armed and Dangerous: The Rise of the Survivalist Right*, Hill and Wang, 1987 (Chapter 3); and Stephen Singular's *Talked to Death: The Life and Murder of Alan Berg*, Beech Tree Books, William Morrow, New York, 1987 (Chapter 4). By far the best sources of information about Identity, however, come from newsletters and flyers distributed by members of the movement, particularly those published by Aryan Nations.
5. JCL/JDN 7/26/87, p. A1; GC 7/26/87, p. A-1; Beckwith letter to the author, 8/14/87, author's collection.
6. Charles Ramberg letter to editor, JDN 8/9/87, included in Beckwith letter to the author, 8/14/87, author's collection.
7. JCL 10/1/89, p. A1; NYT 10/26/89, p. B-9; WP 10/26/89, p. A-20; CT 11/3/89, p. A-1; JCL 11/26/89, "Perspective" section; *Time* 12/25/89, p. 35; NMDJ 11/4/89; KNS 11/5/89, p. B-4. Although Beckwith stated unequivocally on numerous occasions that he would name Evers's murderer in his own book, his sanctioned biography, R.W. Scott's *Glory in Conflict* puts forth the argument that Lee Harvey Oswald might have been the killer. Interestingly, on February 5, 1964, the head of FBI's Crime Records division, Cartha "Deke" DeLoach, received a call from a Scripps-Howard correspondent who inquired whether Beckwith's defense attorneys had in fact implicated Oswald in the murder, as he had been informed. Although the FBI would not respond to the reporter's inquiry, DeLoach did check the Bureau's files on Oswald, and found that Oswald had left his job at William B. Reily and Co. in New Orleans at 5:30 P.M. on June 11, and clocked back in the following day at 8:56 A.M., giving him a tighter alibi than Beckwith.
8. McIlhaney, p. 38; Dennis interview 1/29/91.
9. JCL 5/2/90, p. A-1; "Who Killed Medgar Evers?" segment transcript, "PrimeTime Live," 6/14/90, pp. 5-6; JCL 6/19/90,

p. A-1; *Newsweek* 7/23/90, p. 24; *Black Enterprise* 10/90, p. 17; CT 12/10/90, p. B-3.
10. Thelma Beckwith interviews 2/8/91 and 5/24/91; CT 12/19/90, p. A-1; CNFP 12/19/90, p. A-1; NYT 12/19/90, p.A-18.
11. Beckwith letter to the author, 4/22/86, author's collection.
12. Beckwith letters to the author, 10/21/86 and 12/23/87, author's collection.
13. JDN 11/15/55, p. 2 ; GMS 1/27/56, p. 2; CA 3/17/57, section V, p. 3.
14. CNFP 10/23/86, p. A7; Beckwith "open letter" to Signal Mountain water board, 10/24/86, author's collection.
15. Beckwith letters to the author, 4/22/86 and 10/21/86, author's collection.
16. Flynn, pp. 188 and 259; *Extremism on the Right*, pp. 51-4.
17. Racist tracts and Identity pamphlets, author's collection.
18. Beckwith letters to the author, 10/21/86, 12/30/86 and 10/31/87, author's collection; Copy of Bowers card to Beckwith, 12/22/76, author's collection.
19. Copy of Butler letter to Beckwith, 11/20/80, author's collection; Oakley, p. 5; Chalmers, pp. 344, 352; *The White Beret*, April-May 1991, p. 6; NOTP 1/20/74, p. 3.
20. Scott, R.W., p. 174.
21. Hoskins, p. 353; Thelma Beckwith interviews 2/8/91 and 5/24/91.
22. Beckwith letters to the author, 4/22/86, 4/9/87 and 10/31/87, author's collection.
23. Beckwith letter to the author, 5/18/86, author's collection.
24. Beckwith attempted a half dozen times to get a biography written and published. In jail in 1964, he began a series of essays he hoped would become his autobiography, and his title was an attempt to answer the rhetorical question: What are the integrationists trying to get? Beckwith's answer, and the book's title, according to trial testimony, was *My Ass, Your Goat and the Republic.* In 1967, during his campaign for Lieutenant Governor of Mississippi, a lawyer in Jackson announced he was handling copyright matters for a forthcoming Beckwith memoir titled *Crossfire*, which never materialized. Later, Beckwith collaborated briefly with Mrs. James M. Hooper of Sidon, Mississippi, on a memoir tentatively entitled *When in Rome, Act Like White Folks*, which was never completed. Beckwith later turned over his notes to B.J. Hanks, an acquaintance in Grenada, Mississippi, who wrote a fictionalized account of Beckwith's life story entitled *The Segregationist*, which was never published. In the late 1980s, after attempting unsuccessfully to collaborate with Massengill, Beckwith turned to John Grandt, but quickly abandoned any hope of them producing a book together. Beckwith's sanctioned biography, *Glory in Conflict*, was written and privately printed by R.W. Scott of Camden, Arkansas, in 1991.
25. Beckwith letter to the author, 4/22/86, author's collection.
26. Thelma Beckwith telephoned the author at 10:00 P.M. on 12/17/90. She cried intermittently during the half-hour conversation and offered the author an acre of land on Signal Mountain if he could find a publisher for Beckwith's book. She said she suspected something was afoot before the police came to arrest Beckwith on the new murder indictment and explained, "I'm psychic, you know."

1 TANGLED BRANCHES

1. CDS 11/10/20, p. 4; Kenkel, p. 218; Byron De La Beckwith's birth certificate shows that he was born at Mater Misericordiae Hospital in Sacramento on November 9, 1920, at 1:00 P.M. The baby was delivered by Dr. G.N. Drysdale, and Beckwith's father was thirty-seven and his mother was thirty-three when their only child was born. Susie Yerger Beckwith had two bachelor brothers, Will and Shall, which increased the family pressure to carry on the Yerger name in whatever way possible. Her sister, Sallie, had in fact named her only son Yerger Morehead, to keep the family name alive.
2. Although for the past twenty years or so Beckwith has signed his name as Byron De La Beckwith VI, he is in fact only the third to bear the name. From the time of his first marriage through the late 1960s, in fact, Beckwith consistently signed his name Byron De La Beckwith III. The author's genealogical research in Lake County, Ohio, where Beckwith's grandfather was born, proves incontestably that Beckwith's great-grandfather was Russell Beckwith, who died of consumption in Grant County, Wisconsin, on November 8, 1857.
3. Extensive genealogical information about Beckwith's lineage was obtained from a number of sources, including: LCHS; CCA; International Genealogical Index; Family History Department, Church of Jesus Christ of Latter-Day Saints, Salt Lake City, UT; and Dolores Beckwith Carruth Papers, Sacramento, CA. See also Lambert and McComish, pp. 569-71; *The Lodi (CA) Sentinel*, 5/6/04, p. 1; *Painesville (OH)*

Telegraph, 3/11/1880, p. 3 and 11/24/1881, p. 3. National Archives Microfilm Publication M841, *Record of Appointment of Postmasters, 1832-September 30, 1971*, shows that B.D. Beckwith was appointed Lodi's postmaster on 11/27/1874 and served until 11/21/1881.
4. McComish and Lambert, p. 569.
5. Beck and Williams, p. 282; *Scientific American* 6/2/06, pp. 457-8.
6. Marriage license for Byron D. Beckwith and Mary Bray, 2/15/1882; Death Certificate for Mary Oliver Beckwith, 7/18/1888, Vol. 3, p. 19; both on file at the San Joaquin County, CA, Recorder's Office.
7. Colusa County, CA, Record of Deaths, January to September, 1904; Byron D. Beckwith Probate File #1130, Colusa County, CA; all, CCA. See also CDS 5/2/04, p. 1; CDS 5/3/04, p. 1; LS 5/6/04, p. 1; Untitled, undated newspaper clipping, probably from CDS circa 1900, author's collection; McComish pp. 228-32, p. 570; B. De La Beckwith, Administrator, etcetera of *Byron D. Beckwith, Deceased, Appellant*, v. *Willard M. Sheldon et. al.*, Respondents, Supreme Court of California in Bank, 10/13/08. Most of the details of the litigation are taken from legal synopses of the court cases, although several local histories also are illuminating and offer additional information. Especially helpful were McComish and Lambert's *History of Colusa and Glenn County* (published in 1918) and Green's *Colusa County, California*, published by Elliott and Moore in 1880.
8. McComish and Lambert, p. 570; *Beckwith* v. *Sheldon et. al.*, Supreme Court of California, 12/10/14.
9. Hoover, pp. 48-9; McComish and Lambert, pp. 166, 228, 272, 570; R.W. Scott, p. 22.
10. McComish and Lambert, pp. 267-71.
11. Many years later, when Sallie Green died at the age of 92, it was Byron D. Beckwith who provided the details for her death certificate. Certificate of Death, Colusa County, California, Local Registered No. 40, 6/3/25, CCA.
12. McComish and Lambert, pp. 569-71 and 271-3; Scott, R.W., p. 22.
13. National Archives Microfilm Publication M841, *Record of Appointment of Postmasters, 1832-September 30, 1971* shows that Byron De La Beckwith was appointed Colusa's postmaster on 9/30/10 and served until 3/23/14. See also Thirteenth Census of the United States: 1910 Population, Colusa Township, CA, CCA; McComish and Lambert, pp. 164-7, pp. 272-3 and p. 570; Scott, R.W., p. 23.
14. Frey, pp. 43-5; UPI reports, 10/18/78 show that President Jimmy Carter signed a bill posthumously restoring full citizenship to Davis, the Confederacy's only president, who died in 1889. Carter said the amnesty bill "officially completes the long process of reconciliation that has reunited our people following the tragic conflict between the states." Letters written by Varina Howell Davis just two or three years prior to her death in 1906 indicate she might not have felt as warmly about the United Daughters of the Confederacy as Susan Yerger thought. One letter spoke of "the niggardliness" of the UDC and their disposition of furnishings at Beauvoir, and another noted that the association running Beauvoir as a Confederate veteran's home, unbeknownst to Mrs. Davis, sold the home's furnishings for two thousand dollars. The letters, highlights of which were published in an R.M. Smythe & Co. auction catalog, were sold at auction in 1991.
15. Sinclair, Mary Craig, pp. 17 and 61.
16. Ibid., pp. 131-41; Upton Sinclair, *American Outpost*, p. 263; Hanks, p. 37; R.W. Scott p. 23; Beck and Williams, pp. 402-4, 476.
17. Sinclair, Mary Craig, p. 13. The Morgan branch of the family later proved important to Beckwith, because it was through his distant ancestor William Morgan that he was eligible for membership in the Sons of the American Revolution. Copy of Beckwith's membership certificate, Sons of the American Revolution, dated 1/29/54, author's collection.
18. *Newsweek*, 7/8/63, pp. 22-3; *Time*, 7/5/63, pp. 15-6.
19. Wyatt-Brown, pp. 216-220; Wilson and Ferris, pp. 1553-5.
20. *Ladies Home Journal*, June 1903, p. 8; Wyatt-Brown p. 202; Scott, Anne F., pp. 25-7.
21. Wilson and Ferris, p. 1553; Wyatt-Brown, pp. 238-9. Wyatt-Brown's chapter nine, "Women in a Man's World: Role and Self-Image," is particularly illuminating regarding the Southern view of spinsterhood, widowhood and barrenness.
22. *Confederate Veteran* 12/13, p. 574; NOTP 12/4/77, Section 3, p. 5. Leflore died August 21, 1865 and Malmaison was destroyed by fire on March 31, 1842. Raines, p. 238, sets forth the popular (but unfounded) legend that Leflore died on his front porch while the Union flags were waved above him.
23. Extensive genealogical information about

Yerger's lineage was obtained from a number of sources, including: MDAH; International Genealogical Index; Family History Department, Church of Jesus Christ of Latter-Day Saints, Salt Lake City, UT. See also Lambert and McComish, pp. 569-71. Official Confederate military records on file at MDAH show that L.P. Yerger was a member of the Twenty-Eighth Regiment of the Mississippi Cavalry, Confederate States of America, and that he served as a Private in Company D of that Regiment. International Genealogical Index records and Carroll County, MS, marriage records show that L.P. Yerger and Susie F. Southworth were married December 10, 1879.
24. *Southern Enterprise* (Greenville, S.C.) April 1868, noted in Clark and Kirwan, p. 42-3. Dates of the original founding of the Ku Klux Klan vary from source to source. Many histories of the Klan note that the first meeting was held in December of 1865. The author has used the date offered in William Garrott Brown's *The Lower South in American History*, originally published in 1902, because his chapter "The Ku Klux Movement," which cites the 1866 date, was taken from the recollections of an original member of Nathan Bedford Forrest's group.
25. Wyatt-Brown, pp. 88-9; Cavan, p. 89; Davis, Gardner and Gardner, pp. 84-6.
26. Scott, R.W., p. 23.
27. Ibid., p. 23; GC 2/2/12; GE 2/2/12.
28. Hoover, Rensch and Rensch, pp. 47-50.
29. McComish and Lambert, pp. 86, 165-67.
30. Ibid., p. 165.
31. Ibid., pp. 165, 240, 250; Carter, p. 8; Anne F. Scott, pp. 144-9; Report, SA [deleted] Memphis to USA Oxford, MS and USA Jackson, MS, BUfile 157-901-348, 7/16/63. In the FBI's files on Beckwith, his former guardian, Yerger Morehead, provided details about Beckwith's early life, including information that his mother had been "in a private mental institution in California on one or more occasion."
32. *Confederate Veteran* 6/11, p. 303 and 12/13, pp. 572-4; GC 10/27/53, p. 4; Foster, p. 46. Foster's *Ghosts of the Confederacy* deserves special mention for its sensitive look at how white Southerners adjusted to and interpreted their defeat in the Civil War.
33. Cooper and Terrill, pp. 598-9.
34. McComish and Lambert, p. 166; *Beckwith* v. *Sheldon et. al.*, Supreme Court of California, 12/10/14.
35. Notice of Completion of Work filed filed by Byron D. Beckwith 3/20/18, Colusa County, CA, Recorder's Office, CCA. See also Carter, p. 168; McComish p. 171, 569-71. The Beckwith house was a landmark in Colusa. It stood until the late 1980s, when it was demolished to make way for a new Court House addition. Local preservationists tried—but failed—to save it.
36. McComish and Lambert, p. 571.
37. *Current Biography* 1962; Scott, R.W., p. 23.
38. Birmingham, pp. 245-48.
39. Wyatt-Brown, pp. 235-42.
40. Scott, R.W., p. 23.
41. Death certificate, Sallie Morgan Green, Colusa County, California, Local Registered No. 40, 6/3/25. Dr. George W. Desrosier attributed Sallie Green's death at age ninety-two to chronic myocarditis, chronic bronchitis, bronchial asthma and senility, CCA.
42. *Thomas Rutledge, Executor*, vs. *Byron D. Beckwith*, Superior Court Complaint #6143, Colusa County, CA. Filed 7/22/26, CCA.
43. *Byron D. Beckwith* vs. *A.H. Quatman, et. al.*, Superior Court Complaint #5703, Colusa County, CA. Filed 7/15/24, CCA. The case was dismissed in October 1926, two months after Beckwith's death.
44. Death Certificate for Byron DeLay [sic] Beckwith, Placer County, California, 8/10/26. City or town of death is listed as "near Lincoln," and there are no state index or local registration numbers; Bills filed by Drs. Rathbun, Thomas and Williams, In the Matter of the Estate of Byron D. Beckwith, Superior Court, Colusa County, California, Probate File No. 2038, 1926, CCA.
45. Scott, R.W., pp. 21-4; McComish and Lambert, p. 569; CDS 8/10/26, p. 1; CH 8/10/26, p. 1; Death Certificate for Byron DeLay [sic] Beckwith, Placer County, California, August 10, 1926.
46. MMFR; Sullivan Brothers' records on the Beckwith funeral and burial exist, but strangely, no information about arrangements was noted on the forms; County Clerk's Office, Placer County, California, has the coroner's register through 1903 only; Placer County Coroner's Office, California, "was created in the 1950s or 1960s, and the function per se didn't exist until then," an official told the author. There are no coroner's records for the years prior to the agency's creation.
47. Byron De La Beckwith is buried in Colusa Cemetery in Grave 7, Lot 56, Section K. Susie Yerger purchased only one plot.

48. The numerous examples of claims against Beckwith's estate are documented in detail in his probate file; In the Matter of the Estate of Byron D. Beckwith, Superior Court, Colusa County, California, Probate File No. 2038, 1926, CCA.
49. In the Matter of the Estate of Byron D. Beckwith, Superior Court, Colusa County, California, Probate File No. 2038, 1926; Colusa County, CA, Book 3 of Wills, page 144, CCA.
50. In the Matter of the Estate of Byron D. Beckwith, Superior Court, Colusa County, California, Probate File No. 2038, 1926; Thirteenth Census of the United States: 1910 Population, Colusa Township, CA; Fourteenth Census of the United States: 1920 Population, Colusa Township, CA; all, CCA. See also Cartmell listings from Polk's City Directory of Oakland/ Berkeley/Alameda, CA, 1928.
51. Petition dated 10/29/26, to be heard 11/ 8/26 at 10:00 A.M.; Colusa County, California, Homesteads Book F, p. 54, CCA.
52. Scott, R.W., p. 24.
53. Carter, p. 168; Scott, R.W., p. 25.
54. Scott, R.W., p. 24.
55. Beckwith letter to the author, 11/10/92, author's collection.
56. Hanks, p. 39; Scott, R.W., p. 28.

2 RETURN TO GLEN OAK PLANTATION

1. Wyatt-Brown, pp. 240.
2. Scott, R.W., p. 31.
3. Scott, Anne F., pp. 97-101; Hanks, pp. 33-9.
4. Hanks, p. 33-4; Scott, R.W., pp. 24-6 and 48-50.
5. *Time* 7/5/63, pp. 15-16; *Newsweek* 7/8/63, pp. 22-3; Scott, R.W., p. 25.
6. *Confederate Veteran* 7/32, p. 272; Report, SA [deleted] Memphis to USA Oxford, MS and USA Jackson, MS, 6/27/63, BUfile 157-901-317, p. 42; Hanks pp. 39-40.
7. Scott, R.W., p. 30; Hanks, p. 37.
8. Death certificate for Susie Southworth Beckwith, Mississippi State File #4223; Scott, R.W., p. 35.
9. Scott, R.W., pp. 30, 35, 177; Hanks, p. 40; *Time* 7/5/63, pp. 15-6.
10. Will Yerger ephemera, author's collection.
11. Ibid.
12. Beckwith letter to the author, 5/4/86, author's collection.
13. *Saturday Evening Post* 4/27/07, pp. 3-5; Loewen & Sallis, pp. 192-3; Clark & Kirwan, pp. 122-23.
14. JDN 5/12/57, p. D-1.
15. Eaton, p. 445; Woodward pp. 394-5; Loewen & Sallis, pp. 238-9; Clark & Kirwan, p. 123; A. Wigfall Green, p. 101-5. In 1991, during an interview visit to the Beckwiths' home on Signal Mountain, Thelma Beckwith loaned the author several books from Byron De La Beckwith's personal library, including Theodore Bilbo's *Take Your Choice*, American Nazi Party founder George Lincoln Rockwell's *White Power*, and a number of Christian Identity and Klan books and pamphlets.
16. Scott, R.W., p. 37.
17. Laurence McMillin's *The Schoolmaker: Sawney Webb and the Bell Buckle Story*, published by The University of North Carolina Press, is a compelling account of the evolution of The Webb School and the work of its distinguished founder.
18. 1936-37 and 1937-38 rollbooks for The Webb School; letter to the author from Dorothy Elkins, The Webb School, 2/11/92, author's collection; Scott, R.W., pp. 38-9.
19. Laurence McMillin, pp. xvi and xix.
20. Letter to the author from Dorothy Elkins, The Webb School, 2/11/92; letter to the author from Mariemma Grimes, Columbia Academy, 2/25/92; undated article from The Webb School's alumni newsletter, circa 1945; all, author's collection.
21. Columbia Military Academy catalog, circa 1939-40; Peebles interview. Peebles notes that walking the bullring was a disciplinary measure and not necessarily an intentionally humiliating experience. He acknowledges, however, that the other cadets knew you were in trouble if you were made to walk the bullring.
22. Letters to the author from Mariemma Grimes, Columbia Academy, 2/25/92 and 3/6/92, author's collection. Beckwith's grades were not forwarded to Greenwood High School, indicating that his guardian had not requested an official transfer. Although Beckwith was unsuccessful at The Webb School and Columbia Military Academy, both institutions figured prominently in Beckwith's life for decades. As late as the 1970s, Beckwith's personal stationery listed these institutions on his letterhead.
23. Letter to the author from Robbie Woodard, Greenwood High School, 2/11/92, author's collection; Mr. and Mrs. Jack Galey, former classmates of Beckwith's, provided a reunion program which listed class members' birthdates, from which the age calculations were made.

24. Aldridge, p. 9; Scott, R.W., p. 176.
25. Ibid., pp. 31, 44, 36, 40, 44.
26. Ibid., pp. 41, 52, 54-5.
27. Ibid. pp. 45, 49.
28. Now Mississippi State University. According to a letter to the author from the Mississippi State University registrar, official university records indicate that Beckwith withdrew shortly after the fall 1940 term began, without completing any academic work. See also, Hanks, p. 48; CT 12/19/90, p. A9.
29. Scott, R.W., p.41.
30. Report, SA [deleted] Memphis to USA Oxford, MS and USA Jackson, MS, 6/27/63, BUfile 157-901-317, p. 42-3.
31. Hanks, pp. 50-7; Scott, R.W., p. 44.

3 IDENTIFYING THE ENEMY

1. Marines were nicknamed "leathernecks" because of the leather collar lining that was once part of their uniforms.
2. Report, SA [deleted] Memphis to USA Oxford, MS and USA Jackson, MS, BUfile 157-901-317, p. 42, 6/27/63.
3. Scott, R.W., p. 47.
4. Russ, p. 56; Scott, R.W., p. 44.
5. Moïse Papers; Robert McAfee Brown, p. 18.
6. Russ, pp. 44-5.
7. Willard, pp. 95-7.
8. Ibid., p. 123.
9. Hanks, pp. 50-7. Many of the specifics of Beckwith's travels are documented in Hanks's fictional manuscript, which was based in part on Beckwith's letters to his uncles during the war. The chronology of his travels is documented in an undated alumni newsletter from The Webb School, circa 1945, which details his journeys as a Marine.
10. Baldwin, pp. 238-9.
11. Russ, p. 13.
12. Ibid., pp. 12-5.
13. Ibid., p. 25.
14. Moore Papers; Baldwin, p. 240; Rooney, pp. 12-3.
15. Rooney, p. 13.
16. Sherrod, p. 52; Willard, p. 213; Russ, p. 43.
17. Baldwin, p. 241-2; Sherrod, p. 58; Rooney, p. 15-23.
18. Ibid., p. 245; Moïse Papers; Sherrod, photo cutline.
19. Moore Papers; Muster Roll of Officers and Enlisted Men of the U.S. Marine Corps, 2d Amph. Tr. Bn., Div. Ser. Trs., 2d Mar. Div., FMF, In the Field, 11/1/43 to 11/30/43 Inclusive. The official muster roll incorrectly lists Beckwith's wound as a "gunshot wound in chest," when he was, in fact, shot in the left thigh. The chest wound information was erroneously reported in *Time*, 7/5/63, pp. 15-16, and the inaccuracy has been widely re-reported since 1963.
20. Scott, R.W., pp. 45-6; Russ, pp. 72-3.
21. Moore Papers; Sherrod, p. 175. Robert Sherrod, a Time-Life correspondent, traveled with the Marines to Tarawa and wrote a matchless account of the battle. In his book's casualty listings, however, he misspelled Beckwith's name as "Bryon," although Beckwith's rank is correctly listed as corporal.
22. Beckwith letter to Mary Williams Beckwith, 8/22/63, author's collection.
23. Rooney, p. 48.
24. Baldwin, p. 246.

4 MISALLIANCE

1. WAVES was a U.S. Navy acronym for Women Accepted for Voluntary Emergency Service. The term was discontinued after World War II.
2. Quotes from Beckwith's first wife, Willie, were culled from an extensive series of taped and videotaped interviews spanning more than five years. Because she legally reassumed her maiden name when she left Mississippi, her interviews are listed in the bibliography under the name Mary Louise Williams.
3. Beckwith's own account of his war travels and his recovery following the Tarawa invasion appear in an undated alumni newsletter from The Webb School, circa 1945; Muster Roll of Officers and Enlisted Men of the U.S. Marine Corps, 2d Amphib. Tr. Bn., Div. Ser. Tra., 2d Mar. Div., FMP, In The Field. From 1 November to 30 November 1943, Inclusive, Sheet No. 11. The muster roll supports Beckwith's account that he was evacuated and had surgery aboard USS *Solace*, although the document mistakenly states that he received "gunshot wounds in chest" and makes no mention of his debilitating thigh wound. In an interview with Edward J. Moore, one of Beckwith's cronies from the 2d Amphibian Tractor Battalion, who was also severely wounded during the initial assault on Tarawa, Moore said he remembers that both he and Beckwith were placed aboard USS *Middleton* for evacuation to Pearl Harbor. Moore's recollection is that they were then

transferred to USS *Solace* for stateside transport to San Diego.
4. Mary Louise Williams's birth certificate shows that she was born at 12:35 A.M. on 5/13/23. The baby was delivered at the parents' home in Knoxville, Tennessee, by Dr. L.O. Blalock. At the time, her father, Jesse Williams, was twenty-six and her mother, Hattie McGill Williams, was twenty-four. Mary was their fourth child, their first girl.
5. Scott, R.W., p. 30.
6. Hanks, pp. 71, 77.
7. Report, SA [deleted] Memphis to USA Oxford, MS and USA Jackson, MS, BUfile 157-901-317, p. 42, 6/27/63. According to the report of the special agent who examined Beckwith's Marine Corps file and summarized it for this report, Beckwith "advised the examiner that his father and mother were both deceased and that there was no mental disease in the family history." Beckwith must have been convinced Willie would marry him. The same FBI report notes that on 5/21/45, Beckwith underwent a physical examination at Cherry Point as an application requirement for a $1,000 life insurance policy through National Service Life Insurance. He made the policy payable to his wife, although he and Willie were not married until late the following September, four months later.
8. Undated alumni newsletter, The Webb School, circa 1945.
9. De Soto County, Mississippi, Marriage Record 40, P. 322, 9/22/45. The newlyweds spent five days on their honeymoon at the Peabody Hotel in Memphis. Guest registers are discarded after seven years, according to hotel management, so there is no permanent record of their stay.
10. *Mary Louise Long* v. *Hugh Long*, Court of Juvenile and Domestic Relations of Knox County, Tennessee, (Fourth Circuit), Vol. 13, 10/31/40, Rule Docket Page 328, No. 6815; *Mary Louise Williams Duck* v. *Henry Milton Duck*, et. al., Court of Juvenile and Domestic Relations of Knox County, Tennessee, (Fourth Circuit), Vol. 17, 9/2/43, Rule Docket P. 165, No. 8734; both, KCA.
11. Scott, R.W., p. 48. Scott's account mistakenly stated that Beckwith's job was with Delta Airlines, and asserted that Delta later became Chicago & Southern Airlines. Beckwith was employed by Chicago & Southern Airlines. Davies, pp. 253-4, explained that Chicago & Southern merged with Delta Airlines in May 1953 and continued to use the more widely recognized Delta Airlines brand name.
12. In addition to a number of the interviews conducted for this book, additional sources point to mental problems in Beckwith's family. While jailed for the Evers murder, Beckwith wrote a tribute to his Uncle Will, which he intended to include as part of his memoirs, tentatively titled *My Ass, Your Goat and the Republic.* Beckwith acknowledged that his Uncle Will had suffered several nervous breakdowns. FBI Airtel, SAC, New Orleans to Director, FBI, 7/18/63, BUfile 157-901-342, notified J. Edgar Hoover that Beckwith's cousin and former guardian, Yerger Morehead, testified as a witness for District Attorney William Waller, prosecutor in the Evers murder trials, to support his motion for a sanity hearing for Beckwith. Morehead stated that Beckwith's mental condition had changed after he returned from military service, and also testified that his Uncle Will had at one time been committed to Mississippi State Hospital at Whitfield. FBI Report, SA [Deleted], Memphis to USA, Oxford, Mississippi and USA, Jackson, Mississippi, 7/16/63, BUfile 157-901-348; On page 78 of the report, one of the FBI's sources reported that "the Yerger side of Beckwith's family had mental trouble," and specifically named Beckwith's mother and his Uncle Will; On pages 82-6, the results of the FBI's questioning of Beckwith's cousin, Yerger Morehead, are presented in detail. Morehead stated that "there is inherited mental trouble in Beckwith's family," and pointed specifically to Beckwith's mother and his Uncle Will. In one of her many interviews with the author, Willie Beckwith remembered a conversation she once had with F.M. Southworth, Uncle Holmes's nephew, who told her that Uncle Will needed to be at Whitfield [the state mental hospital] and confirmed that Susie Beckwith had in fact been institutionalized in California before her return to Mississippi. See also *Time* 7/5/63, pp. 15-6; *Newsweek* 7/8/63, pp. 22-3; *The Saturday Evening Post* 3/14/64, pp. 77-81.
13. Although the Beckwiths saw Mamie every weekday during the extended time they lived in the big house, Willie believes they never knew her last name. And although Annie continued to baby-sit for them after their move to the house on West Monroe, and often worked for them during the next eight or nine years, Willie has no recollection of her last name, either. "It's funny," she said, "that we could know

someone so well, and trust them with our children, and never know their last names."

14. *Time* 7/5/63, p. 15. Beckwith always complained about the press brouhaha over the decayed condition of the house, and claimed the media chose to overlook that it was to be purchased by the federal government as the site of a new Greenwood post office. While that might explain why Beckwith did not pursue repairs on the property after his Uncle Will died in 1962, it does not accommodate for the family's persistent unwillingness to maintain the house during the prior twenty years. See also Scott, R.W., p. 79.

15. *Congressional Record - Senate* 6/29/45, pp. 6992-4.

16. Copy of Beckwith's vitae circa 1987, author's collection. While pursuing a pardon from Governor Edwin Edwards of Louisiana in the firearms case for which he was convicted, Beckwith typed out a four-page vitae listing his past and present activities and affiliations. In addition to listing his membership in National Muzzle Loading Association and National Reloading Association (among other firearms groups ranging from the National Rifle Association to the obscure, survivalist American Pistol & Rifle Association in Benton, Tennessee), Beckwith listed among his chief hobbies "antique and modern arms" and called himself "a hand loader with special likes for antique/black powder arms and shooting."

17. FBI fingerprint record, file number 541 216 E, showed that Beckwith was fingerprinted 1/5/42 at Jackson, Mississippi, when he enlisted in the Marine Corps, and was again fingerprinted 3/18/46 in New Orleans, Louisiana, concurrent with his application for a job with the Federal Communications Commission. These records were later incorporated into Beckwith's full FBI file, BUfile 157-901, following the Evers murder.

18. Scott, R.W., p. 47-8.

19. Byron De La Beckwith, Jr.'s birth certificate shows that he was born at Greenwood Leflore Hospital at 12:18 P.M. on 9/9/46. At the time, De La and Willie were twenty-five and twenty-three years old, respectively.

20. *Mary Louise Long* v. *Hugh Long*, Court of Juvenile and Domestic Relations of Knox County, Tennessee, (Fourth Circuit), vol. 13, 10/31/40, Rule Docket Page 328, No. 6815; *Mary Louise Williams Duck* v. *Henry Milton Duck*, et. al., Court of Juvenile and Domestic Relations of Knox County, Tennessee, (Fourth Circuit), vol. 17, 9/2/43, Rule Docket P. 165, No. 8734; both, KCA.

21. JCL 11/3/91, pp. 1, 13.

22. Because Beckwith had suffered a 30 percent disability at Tarawa, he was eligible for a veteran's disability pension. Willie remembered that it was "maybe $40 or $50 a month—not more than that," during their marriage.

23. Beckwith even noted in many of his letters from jail during the Evers trials that he had "the red ass" for a number of reasons—money was not flowing into the defense fund fast enough, his lawyers were not keeping him apprised of their pre-trial progress, or Willie and Little De La were not visiting as frequently as he wished. It was an expression he coined and used often. In another letter to Willie, Beckwith mentioned that he was going to write to Jimmy Hogue, their pharmacist in Greenwood, and have him send a supply of condoms to the jail, so that he and Willie could more fully enjoy their conjugal visits.

24. Innumerable people interviewed by the author, both on the record and off the record, said that Greenwood residents laughed at Beckwith behind his back. Most attributed the ridicule to his embellished mannerisms and outlandish courtesy, although some who knew him during the throes of the civil rights controversies claim he was more reviled than ridiculed because of his incessant segregation talk.

25. FBI Report, SA [Deleted], Memphis to USA, Oxford, Mississippi and USA, Jackson, Mississippi, 7/16/63, BUfile 157-901-348, pp. 64-6.

26. Although Mississippi Circuit Judge Tom Brady made the term "Black Monday" famous, it was actually coined by Mississippi Congressman John Bell Williams, who used the term to refer to the day the decision was handed down.

27. Raines, p. 298; Luce, p. 17.

28. Raines, p. 297.

29. McMillen, pp. 16-7; Martin, John Bartlow, p. 2; Raines, p. 298. After the Citizens' Council was established, it garnered a number of nicknames, among them the "country club klan" and the "white-collar klan."

30. Vander Zanden, p. 30; McMillen, p. 16.

31. McMillen, p. 11.

32. *The Saturday Evening Post* 3/14/64, p. 79; McMillen, p. 17.

33. Brady, p. 64.

34. Dr. James Silver's Presidential Address before the Southern Historical

Association, Asheville, NC, 11/7/63, Civil Rights Collection, MS-334, Box 1, Folder 16, HLSC; In a jab to Brady, Silver called *Black Monday* "hastily written and scholastically barren" in his address. See also Brady, p. 78. Brady lists Bilbo's *Take Your Choice* in his book's bibliography.
35. Luce, p. 45 and pp. 30-2.
36. Cagin and Dray, p. 54; Luce, p. 32.

5 SEPARATE AND UNEQUAL LIVES

1. Evers, Mrs. Medgar with Peters, William, pp. 72-4; Eagles, p. 70; *Ebony*, 9/63, p. 145. Although a wealth of source materials on Medgar Evers exists, the author has relied primarily on books by Evers's wife and brother, along with cited magazine articles, for background information on his life and work.
2. Evers, Mrs. Medgar with Peters, William, pp. 14-20; Evers, Charles, pp. 22-4, 30, 34, 41, 73; *Playboy*, 10/71, p. 86; Mendelsohn p. 65.
3. *Ebony*, 9/63, p. 145; Evers, Charles, p. 88; Myrlie Evers interview transcript, p. 8. Medgar Evers later used his editorial skills to help launch *Mississippi Free Press*, a weekly tabloid that was printed by famed newspaperwoman Mrs. Hazel Brannon Smith, who published several several small Mississippi weeklies. The *Free Press* became the voice of the civil rights movement in Mississippi. See Cagin and Dray, p. 174.
4. Mendelsohn, p. 65-6; Evers, Charles, pp. 92-96. Charles Evers's biographical account differed. He asserted that both he and his brother were allowed to vote in the 1947 county election.
5. Evers, Mrs. Medgar with Peters, William, pp. 90-6; *Playboy*, 10/71, p. 90; Evers. Charles, pp. 74-5 and 114-5; *Ebony*, 9/63, pp. 143-4; Weisbrot, p. 93. In her account, Mrs. Evers offered a far broader interpretation of her husband's Mau Mau leanings. She also explained that when hospital officials required an official name for her son's birth certificate, she slipped in the first name "Darrell" without her husband's knowledge.
6. Williams, pp. 46-7; *Ebony*, 9/63, p. 145; Myrlie Evers interview transcript, p. 13.
7. *Southern School News*, Vol. 1, 4/55, p. 3, cited in Vander Zanden.
8. Evers, Mrs. Medgar with Peters, William, pp. 100-3; Evers, Charles, p. 41; *Ebony*, 9/63, p. 145; *Playboy*, 10/71, p. 88; JDN, 1/22/54, p. 1; Vander Zanden, p. 363.
9. Beckwith letter dated 3/19/57, submitted for publication, cited in Hanks, p. 297.
10. Brady, p. 64.
11. Vander Zanden, p. 351.
12. Peltason, p. 42.
13. Humphrey, p. 32.
14. Peltason, p. 46. Cited from a transcript of Eisenhower's 9/3/57 news conference.
15. Burk, p. 23; Luce, p. 10; *Reader's Digest*, 9/54, p. 51, 55; Peltason, p. 46, cited from a transcript of Eisenhower's 9/5/56 news conference.
16. Loewen and Sallis, p. 254; "Intimidation, Reprisal and Violence in the South's Racial Crisis," p. 13, Southern Regional Council Literature, Box 4/5, Civil Rights Collection, HLSC. This 1959 report, listing a state-by-state accounting of racial violence from 1/55 through 1/59, was published jointly by the Southeastern Office, American Friends Service Committee, the Department of Racial and Cultural Relations, National Council of the Churches of Christ in the United States of America, and Southern Regional Council.
17. Black, p. 60.
18. *Southern School News*, 1/55, p. 3, cited in Vander Zanden, p. 324.
19. Letter from Beckwith addressed to "Distributors of Philip Morris Tobacco Products in Mississippi and Other States," 7/3/56, author's collection.
20. Vander Zanden, p. 326; Luce, pp. 88-9.
21. *Time*, 7/5/63, p. 16.
22. Copy of Beckwith vitae, 1/25/87; Copy of letter to Beckwith from A.H. Richter, Secretary and Recorder, Greenwood Lodge No. 135, F.&A.M., 1/31/78, chronologically outlining Beckwith's Masonic Degrees and Orders; Copy of Beckwith letter to Col. Francis E. Davis, Chamberlain Hunt Academy, 11/28/63; all, author's collection.
23. Copy of certificate, National Society of the Sons of the American Revolution, National #77603, State #304, date of admission 1/29/54 by virtue of descent from William Morgan, author's collection.
24. *The Saturday Evening Post*, 3/14/64, p. 79; Copy of letter to Beckwith from Dr. James B. Butler dated 8/19/57. Butler, President of the Mississippi Society, Sons of the American Revolution, credited Beckwith with the resolution, which was adopted at the 67th Congress held at Salt Lake City, May 26–, 1957. The resolution stated, "All men are not created equal," and set forth the argument that those propounding human equality were actually propagandists for communism.

25. *Newsweek* 7/8/63, p. 23; *Time* 7/5/63, p. 16.
26. Hanks, pp. 129-32.
27. Copy of letter from Beckwith to Rt. Rev. Duncan M. Gray dated 11/58, author's collection. According to records on file at Church of the Nativity in Greenwood, Beckwith was confirmed on 11/15/34. The presenting rector was The Rev. Warren Botkin, and the confirming bishop was Rt. Rev. William Mercer Green.
28. Hanks, p. 127.
29. Episcopal Society for Cultural and Racial Unity flyer titled "Statement of Purpose," Braden Papers, MS-425, HLSC.
30. FBI Report, SA [deleted], New Orleans to USA Jackson, MS and USA Oxford, MS, BUfile 157-901-330, 7/12/63, pp. 64-69.
31. *Southern School News,* 2/56, p. 15, cited in Vander Zanden, p. 350; CA 8/4/57, section V, p. 3.
32. Loewen and Sallis, p. 257.
33. Beckwith letter to Governor J.P. Coleman, dated 5/16/56, cited in JCL 11/3/91, p. 1, 13. Jerry Mitchell, the *Clarion-Ledger* reporter who broke a number of important stories about the misdeeds of the Sovereignty Commission and subsequently helped reopen the murder case against Beckwith, credited Jackson civil rights activist Ken Lawrence with uncovering Beckwith's application letter to Coleman.
34. JDN 11/15/55, p. 2 ; Hanks, p. 299.
35. Hanks, p. 126.
36. JDN 5/22/57, p. 3.
37. See Smith's autobiography, *Congressman from Mississippi,* pp. 105-6, for a more complete account of Smith's meeting with and reminiscences of Beckwith.
38. GMS 1/27/56, p. 2.
39. See JDN 5/17/57, p. 5, in which two of Beckwith's letters appear. The first began, "Every time you print one of my letters in your paper you make my heart swell with pride...." The second letter simply congratulated the newspaper on its fine editorials.
40. Beckwith letter to Dr. H. Reed Carroll dated 9/21/57, author's collection.
41. Greenwood Leflore Hospital records show that Willie Beckwith was hospitalized on the following occasions for the reasons cited: 1/2/57 through 1/5/57 for acute alcoholism; 9/2/57 through 9/6/57 for a D&C, biopsy of cervix, and cauterization of cervix; 11/5/57 through 11/9/57 for a hiatus hernia; 10/14/59 through 10/20/59 for acute bronchitis; 4/15/60 through 4/22/60 for a fracture of fibula talar ligament of left ankle, and a cast was applied; 8/23/62 through 8/28/62 for functional uterine bleeding, right unguinal hernia; 12/9/62 through 12/12/62 for acute pyelitis and cystitis with hematuria; 6/17/63 through 6/29/63 (the time period during which Beckwith was arrested and charged with the Evers murder) for acute pyelitis with secondary cystitis; 7/12/63 through 7/16/63 for a laceration and large hematoma of right side of forehead, chest contusion, and back strain as a result of an auto accident; 7/27/63 through 7/29/63 for acute alcoholism; 9/29/63 through 10/1/63 for acute alcoholism; 5/24/64 through 6/3/64 for anterior/posterior vaginal repair, D&C, biopsy and cauterization of cervix; and 7/23/65 through 8/2/65 for acute alcoholism.
42. Although Beckwith never formally addressed his alcoholism through a program like Alcoholics Anonymous, he admitted or alluded to his alcoholism on a number of occasions. The earliest was his 1957 letter to Dr. H. Reed Carroll, cited previously. In a letter to his wife dated 11/2/63, Beckwith acknowledged a report on alcoholism she sent him while he was jailed during his murder trials and said, "The shoe fits me too I am sure." FBI Report, SA [Deleted], Memphis to Bureau, et. al., 7/12/63, BUfile 157-901-330, page 83, notes that the headmaster at Chamberlain Hunt Academy, where the Beckwiths' son attended school, was questioned by the FBI and revealed that Beckwith had admitted to him "that his wife was an alcoholic," and that "he, himself, had been an alcoholic at one time." In a letter to Willie dated 4/19/73, Beckwith sought a reconciliation and wrote that alcohol had wrecked their lives, and that drinking had always adversely affected him.
43. FBI Report, SA [Deleted], Memphis to USA, Oxford, Mississippi and USA, Jackson, Mississippi, 7/16/63, BUfile 157-901-348, pp. 52, 78; FBI Memorandum, A. Rosen to Mr. Belmont, 6/25/63, BUfile 157-901-225, p. 3.
44. FBI Airtel, SAC, New Orleans to Director, FBI, 7/18/63, BUfile 157-901-342, pp. 1-3; *Mrs. Mary Louise Williams Beckwith* vs. *Byron De La Beckwith,* Chancery Court of Leflore County, Mississippi, October 1960, Term, Complaint #12,795.
45. *Mrs. Mary Louise Williams Beckwith* vs. *Byron De La Beckwith,* Chancery Court of Leflore County, Mississippi, October 1960, Term, Complainant #12,882, Final Decree, Minute Book 44, P. 181. The Beckwiths' first divorce was granted on

10/11/60; Copy of letter from Norman C. Brewer, Willie Beckwith's attorney, to Superintendent, Chamberlain Hunt Academy, 12/16/60, author's collection.
46. Marriage Record A-10, page 272, Leflore County, Mississippi, 2/14/61; Declaration of Intention in Holy Matrimony, required by Canon 17, Section 3 of the Episcopal Church. The couple signed the declaration, along with Jones S. Hamilton, rector of Church of the Nativity, who performed the ceremony on Valentine's Day evening.
47. FBI Teletype, SAC, New Orleans to Director, FBI, 6/25/63, BUfile 157-901-279, pp. 5-6.
48. Undated clipping from the University of Mississippi student newspaper, circa 1962.
49. Will Book 8, page 483, Will Records of Leflore County; Land Deed Record 135, Leflore County, filed 11/29/61. In November 1961, Beckwith deeded more than 100 acres of land to his wife—land his Uncle Will had left him—because of his "natural love and affection" for her. She used proceeds from the sale of the land to buy the house on Montgomery Street, and since the land had been in her name the new home was also purchased in her name.
50. GC 12/23/61, p. 5.
51. FBI Airtel, SAC, New Orleans to Director, FBI, 7/18/63, BUfile 157-901-342, p. 2; A judgment by Justice of the Peace C.C. Williamson of Leflore County found Beckwith guilty of threatening his wife. He was placed under a Peace Bond. *Mrs. Mary Louise Williams Beckwith* vs. *Byron De La Beckwith*, Chancery Court of Leflore County, Mississippi, October 1962, Term, Complainant #13,565, Minute Book 49, p. 127. The Beckwiths' first divorce was granted on 10/9/62.
52. Certificate of Marriage, Dade County, Georgia, 10/30/62, James V. Jenkins, Probate Judge, officiating; author's collection.
53. In a 1/23/63 letter to Beckwith from a fellow member of the SAR Board of Governors, Dr. James B. Butler, Butler wrote that he had met Dr. Toms previously, but had not had an opportunity to form a friendship with him. This letter was obviously in response to a letter Beckwith had written Butler inquiring about Dr. Toms.
54. FBI Report, SA [Deleted], Memphis to USA, Oxford, Mississippi and USA, Jackson, Mississippi, 7/16/63, BUfile 157-901-348, p. 79. An informant reported to the FBI that "some rumor had arisen to the effect that the police had told Beckwith on that occasion to stay away from the University of Mississippi." See also Scott, R.W., p. 61.
55. Namorato, pp. 130-1; Loewen and Sallis, pp. 264-5; Powledge, pp. 437-41; Dr. James Silver's Presidential Address before the Southern Historical Association, Asheville, NC, 11/7/63, Civil Rights Collection, MS-334, Box 1, Folder 16, HLSC.
56. Meredith, pp. 226, 310; On 1/19/63, De La and C.E. Holmes of the SAR drafted a resolution adopted by the Mississippi Society, Sons of the American Revolution, which protested federal interference into state affairs and the forced enrollment of James Meredith in the University of Mississippi, under force of arms.
57. FBI Report, SA [Deleted], Memphis to USA, Oxford, Mississippi and USA, Jackson, Mississippi, 7/16/63, BUfile 157-901-348, p. 27; FBI Memorandum, A. Rosen to Mr. Belmont, 6/26/63, BUfile 157-901-258, p. 3.
58. FBI Report, SA [Deleted], Memphis to USA, Oxford, Mississippi and USA, Jackson, Mississippi, 7/16/63, BUfile 157-901-348, p. 70; *Time*, 7/5/63, p. 16; Hanks, p. 4; FBI Report, SA [Deleted], Memphis to USA, Oxford, Mississippi and USA, Jackson, Mississippi, 7/16/63, BUfile 157-901-348, p. 104. For additional corroboration that Beckwith was on very friendly terms with the police, and rode in their patrol cars following his two murder trials, see also Sutherland, p. 177; Belfrage, p. 128; Letter from SNCC worker Bill Hodes to his parents dated 7/22/64, Posey Papers, MS-334, Box 3, Folders 3 and 4, HLSC.
59. Reporter's Transcript, *State of Mississippi* v. *Byron De La Beckwith*, Circuit Court of the First Judicial District of Hinds County, Mississippi, No. 17,824, 1/31/64, vol. 4, p. 881; Scott, R.W., p. 155.
60. Loewen and Sallis, pp. 265-6; Voter Education Project News Release, 3/31/63, Braden Papers, MS-425, Box 3, File: Mississippi 1963, HLSC.
61. "Survey: Current Field Work, Spring, 1963, Student Nonviolent Coordinating Committee, Record Group 1, Box 8, Folder 128, SNCC; Carawan Tapes 22 and 24, Greenwood, MS; both, HREC.
62. Carawan Tapes 22 and 24, Greenwood, MS, HREC.
63. Salter, p. 84; Carson, pp. 80-1; Press Release, Southern Conference Educational Fund, Inc., 3/13/63, MS-425, Braden Papers Box 3, File: Mississippi 1963, MS-425, HLSC; Carawan Tape 22, Greenwood, MS, HREC.
64. Carson, pp. 80-1. See also Press Release,

Southern Conference Educational Fund, Inc., 3/13/63, MS-425, Braden Papers Box 3, File: Mississippi 1963, MS-425; Voter Education Project News Release, 3/31/63, Braden Papers, MS-425, Box 3, File: Mississippi 1963; both, HLSC.
65. Eagles, pp. 78-9; Carawan Tape 25, Greenwood, MS, HREC.
66. FBI Teletype, SAC, Memphis to Director, FBI, 6/26/63, BUfile 157-901-253, p. 1; Scott, R.W., p. 159.
67. FBI Report, SA [Deleted], Memphis to USA, Oxford, Mississippi and USA, Jackson, Mississippi, 7/16/63, BUfile 157-901-348, pp. 70, 83.
68. Ibid., p. 58; FBI Teletype, SAC, New Orleans to Director, FBI, 6/25/63, BUfile 157-901-279, p. 1.
69. Interview with Mrs. Betty W. Carter, 1979, Vol. 150, pp. 40-1, MOHP; AJC 3/3/91, pp. M1, M4; Reporter's Transcript, *State of Mississippi* v. *Byron De La Beckwith*, Circuit Court of the First Judicial District of Hinds County, Mississippi, No. 17,824, 1/31/64, vol. 2, p. 467.
70. Copies of Beckwith flyers distributed between 1959 and 1963, author's collection; *Time* 7/5/63, p. 16.
71. Mendelsohn, pp. 82-3; Hanks, p. 314.
72. Copies of Beckwith flyers distributed between 1959 and 1963, author's collection.

6 THE RISING TIDE OF DISCONTENT

1. Mendelsohn, p. 68.
2. Juan Williams, p. 219.
3. Branch, p. 815; Mendelsohn, p. 68.
4. Dittmer, p.66; Mendelsohn, p. 69; Salter, pp. 119-20; Juan Williams, p. 219-20; Evers, Mrs. Medgar with Peters, William, pp. 266-9; Eagles, p. 66-7.
5. Hampton and Fayer, pp. 150-1; Salter, pp. 95, 139; Kunstler, p. 205; Evers, Mrs. Medgar with Peters, William, pp. 273-6; Juan Williams, p. 220; Moody, pp. 264-73; Wilkins, p. 287; *The New York Times Magazine*, 5/17/92, p. 60. Salter's *Jackson, Mississippi: An America Chronicle of Struggle and Schism*, is a peerless account of the Jackson movement and its inner workings.
6. Juan Williams, p. 220; Wilkins, p. 288.
7. *The Saturday Evening Post* 3/14/64, p. 79; Juan Williams, p. 221; Evers, Mrs. Medgar with Peters, William, pp. 282-4. Although she may not have known it at the time, Lena Horne had also been a target of Citizens' Council criticism. When the NAACP's 1957 Christmas Seal campaign was underway, the solicitation letter was signed by Horne. The Citizens' Council circulated copies of the letter with an arrow marking her signature and noting, "Married to a white man." See Luce, p. 52.
8. GC 6/12/63, p. 1; Myrlie Evers interview transcript, pp. 39-40.
9. Herbers remembered being invited to dinner by Cliff Sessions, who succeeded Herbers as UPI Bureau Chief in Jackson. "Cliff and his wife were living in an apartment building on North State Street, and he decided that he would have Medgar Evers and his wife to dinner, which was just unheard of, because of course the apartment house was segregated. So my wife and I went, and we had a lovely dinner party and sat around and talked—at great risk. He and Myrlie were both extraordinary. They were not in any way self-serving. You find that even Martin Luther King was self-serving in so many ways, but never Medgar Evers."
10. FBI Report, SA [deleted] New Orleans to USA Jackson, MS and USA Oxford, MS, BUfile 157-901-330, pp. 64-69, 7/12/63.
11. Ibid., pp. 64-69. John Book worked all day with Beckwith on Monday, 6/10/63, and was later questioned on several separate occasions by FBI agents working on the Evers murder case.
12. Ibid.; Officers of the Jackson Police Department interviewed Beckwith's employer and obtained Beckwith's handwritten work reports covering the week of the Evers murder. These reports were included in FBI Report, SA [deleted] New Orleans to USA Jackson, MS and USA Oxford, MS, BUfile 157-901-330, 7/12/63, pp. 64-9; KNS 7/18/63, p. 1; FBI Teletype, SAC, New Orleans to Director, 157-901, 6/26/63; FBI Memorandum, FBI Director J. Edgar Hoover to Attorney General Robert F. Kennedy, BUfile 157-901-263, 6/27/63.
13. FBI Teletype, SAC, New Orleans to Director and SAC, Memphis, 157-1163, 6/25/63; FBI Memorandum, FBI Director J. Edgar Hoover to Attorney General Robert F. Kennedy, BUfile 157-901-263, 6/27/63; FBI Report, SA [deleted] New Orleans to USA Jackson, MS and USA Oxford, MS, BUfile 157-901-330, pp. 97, 101-2, 7/12/63; Raines, pp. 271-2; Evers, Mrs. Medgar with Peters, William, pp. 288-9.
14. FBI Memorandum, A. Rosen to Mr. Belmont, BUfile 157-101-258, 6/26/63; FBI Teletype, SAC, New Orleans to Director, BUfile 157-901, 6/26/63; FBI

Report, SA [deleted] New Orleans to USA Jackson, MS and USA Oxford, MS, BUfile 157-901-330, p. 98, 104, 7/12/63; Evers, Mrs. Medgar with Peters, William, p. 334.
15. FBI Report, SA [deleted] New Orleans to USA Jackson, MS and USA Oxford, MS, BUfile 157-901-330, pp. 64-69 7/12/63.
16. Branch, pp. 822-4
17. National network news broadcasts for 6/11/63, The Museum of Television & Radio, New York City.
18. Branch, pp. 823-5; Garrow, pp. 268-69.
19. President John F. Kennedy's 6/11/63, civil rights speech, Museum of Television and Radio, New York City; *U.S. News & World Report* 6/24/63, pp. 79-80; NYT 6/12/63, p. 20.
20. Evers, Mrs. Medgar with Peters, William, p. 299; *State of Mississippi* v. *Byron De La Beckwith*, Circuit Court, First Judicial District of Hinds County, Mississippi, No. 17,824, p. 6.
21. Evers, Charles, p. 121; MFP 6/13/64, p. 4; FBI Report, SA [deleted] New Orleans to USA Jackson, MS and USA Oxford, MS, BUfile 157-901-330, p. 100, 7/12/63. The FBI files also reveal that Evers apparently "had some sort of premonition of some disaster befalling him," and that he told Current he was "hurrying to bring various insurance policies up to date."
22. Evers, Mrs. Medgar with Peters, William, pp. 298-9; "PrimeTime Live," 6/14/90, pp. 5-6; *Newsweek*, 7/23/90, p. 24; NYT 12/19/90, p. A-18; MFP, 6/13/64, p. 4; Mendelsohn, p. 72; *The Independent Magazine*, 8/24/91, p. 29; *The New York Times Magazine*, 5/17/92, p. 84.
23. Mendelsohn, p. 72.
24. Salter, p. 24; Evers, Mrs. Medgar with Peters, William, p. 302; GC 6/12/63, p. 1; Myrlie Evers interview transcript, pp. 32-3. Most newspapers picked up wire service reports of the murder, which mentioned that Evers dropped T-shirts when he was shot. The author defers to Mrs. Evers's book, which described the shirts as sweatshirts.
25. *State of Mississippi* v. *Byron De La Beckwith*, Circuit Court, First Judicial District of Hinds County, Mississippi, No. 17,824, p. 7.
26. Ibid., pp. 42-9.
27. Ibid., p. 16.
28. FBI Teletype, SAC, Chicago to Director, FBI, 7/23/63, BUfile 157-901-344, p. 1.
29. Evers, Mrs. Medgar with Peters, William, p. 306; *State of Mississippi* v. *Byron De La Beckwith*, Circuit Court, First Judicial District of Hinds County, Mississippi, No. 17,824, p. 42; Raines, p. 272.
30. *State of Mississippi* v. *Byron De La Beckwith*, Circuit Court, First Judicial District of Hinds County, Mississippi, No. 17,824, pp. 25-8.
31. At the time, Jackson did not have its own FBI office, and a number of agents from other cities, particularly Memphis and New Orleans, were in the Mississippi capitol working on another FBI case that involved Medgar Evers: "Desegregation of Jackson, Miss., Business Establishments and Public Facilities," as the FBI named it.
32. FBI Memorandum, A. Rosen to Mr. Belmont, BUfile 157-901-12, 6/12/63.
33. FBI Teletype, SAC, New Orleans to Director, FBI, BUfile 157-901-20, 6/13/63; FBI Report, SA [deleted] New Orleans to USA Jackson, MS and USA Oxford, MS, BUfile 157-901-330, p. 104, 7/12/63.
34. Interview with Honorable Charles Evers, 1973, Vol. 7, pp. 21-4, MOHP.

7 THE LONE SUSPECT

1. NYT 6/13/63, p. 1; Moody, pp. 277-80; Salter, pp. 185-92; Evers, Mrs. Medgar with Peters, William, p. 308.
2. Moody, pp. 278; NYT 6/13/63, p. 13; Copy of letter from President John F. Kennedy to Mrs. Medgar Evers, 6/13/63, JFKL; NYT 6/16/63, pp. 1, 58; CDD 6/13/63, p. 31.
3. MFP, 6/13/64, p. 4; Evers, Mrs. Medgar with Peters, William, p. 306.
4. *State of Mississippi* v. *Byron De La Beckwith*, Circuit Court, First Judicial District of Hinds County, Mississippi, No. 17,824 (first murder trial), p. 167.
5. Ibid., p. 177
6. FBI Memorandum, A. Rosen to Mr. Belmont, BUfile 157-901-61, 6/12/63.
7. Mendelsohn, p. 74; Chain Letter, Swisshelm Papers, Box 1, Folder 7, HLSC.
8. Meredith, p. 305. Also cited in James Silver's *Running Scared*, p. 90.
9. Moody, p. 278; Evers, Mrs. Medgar with Peters, William, pp. 287-90, 297-8; Salter, p. 182.
10. Salter, pp. 192-3; NYT 6/13/63, p. 12.
11. NYT 6/15/63, pp. 1, 9.
12. Sorensen, p. 496; FBI Memorandum, D.J. Brennan to W.C. Sullivan, BUfile 157-901-67, 6/12/63.
13. Branch, p. 829; Garrow, p. 269; Evers, Mrs. Medgar with Peters, William, p. 232.
14. GC 6/12/63, p. 1
15. "Where is the Voice Coming From?," *The New Yorker*, 7/6/63, pp. 24–5; Welty, pp. 603–7.
16. GC 6/12/63, p. 1. In a large bundle of

clippings Beckwith once sent the author to photocopy as background material, he included a dog-eared, faded original of the *Commonwealth* clipping he had saved.
17. Beckwith's work report for 6/12/63, included in FBI Report, SA [deleted] New Orleans to USA Jackson, MS and USA Oxford, MS, BUfile 157-901-330, pp. 64–69, 7/12/63.
18. FBI Memorandum, A. Rosen to Mr. Belmont, BUfile 157-901-123, 6/13/63.
19. Evers, Mrs. Medgar with Peters, William, p. 235.
20. Letter, W.D. Rayfield and M.B. Pierce, Jackson Police Department to J. Edgar Hoover, FBI Director, Washington, BUfile 157-901-79, 6/13/63.
21. Telegram, J. Edgar Hoover, FBI Director, Washington to W.D. Rayfield and M.B. Pierce, Jackson Police Department, 157-901-78, 6/14/63; FBI Teletype, J. Edgar Hoover, FBI Director, Washington to SAC, New Orleans, 157-901-69, 6/14/63; FBI Teletype, FBI Director J. Edgar Hoover to SAC, Boston, 157-901-6, 6/12/63; FBI Teletype, FBI Director J. Edgar Hoover to SAC, New Orleans, 157-901-7, 6/13/63.
22. FBI Teletype, Director FBI to SAC, New Orleans, BUfile 157-901-27, 6/12/63; FBI Report, SA [deleted], Memphis to USA Oxford, MS and USA Jackson, MS, BUfile 157-901-348, 7/16/63.
23. Telegram, Director FBI to W.D. Rayfield, Chief of Police, Jackson, BUfile 157-901-35, 6/14/63; FBI Memorandum, S.F. Latona to Mr. Trotter, BUfile 157-901-38,
6/14/63.
24. Moody, p. 339.
25. NYT 6/15/63, p. 9.
26. Salter, p. 209; Kunstler, p. 207; Branch, pp. 826-8; Mendelsohn, pp. 77-80.
27. NYT 6/16/63, p. 1; Moody, pp. 281-2; Kunstler, pp. 206-10; Hampton and Fayer, pp. 155-6; Evers, Mrs. Medgar with Peters, William, pp. 316-22.
28. John Doar interview transcript, Sound Roll 1143, p. 8; Williams, p. 225; NYT 6/16/63, p. 1.
29. UPI wire report, 6/17/63; CDD 6/18/63, p. 4; Clipping, BUfile 157-901-90; NYT 6/18/63, p. 23.
30. *LIFE* 6/28/63; NYT 6/20/63, p. 18; De Toledano, p. 196.
31. Martin, Ralph G., pp. 454-5.
32. Evers, Mrs. Medgar with Peters, William, pp. 326-7.
33. Greenwood Leflore Hospital records show that Beckwith's wife was admitted to the hospital on 6/17/63 and remained there under the care of Dr. H. Reed Carroll until she was released on 6/29. When her husband was arrested for Evers's murder while she was hospitalized, many newspapers erroneously reported she had been admitted for alcoholism. While she had been admitted to treat her alcoholism on a number of occasions, she claims this particular stay was due to a urinary tract infection. Her hospital records support her claim. FBI Report, SA [Deleted], Memphis to USA, Oxford, Mississippi and USA, Jackson, Mississippi, 7/16/63, BUfile 157-901-348, p. 24, cites Dr. Carroll's recollection of Beckwith's visit on 6/19/63, the day Evers was buried at Arlington National Cemetery.
34. FBI Memorandum, Director, FBI to The Attorney General, BUfile 157-901-105, 6/20/63; Radiogram, SAC, New Orleans to Director and [38 SACs], BUfile 157-901-172, 6/21/63.
35. FBI Teletype, SAC, Chicago to Director, FBI, 7/4/63, BUfile 157-901-306, p. 4.
36. McMillen, p. 360.
37. *LOOK* 4/30/57, pp. 59, 68; "Intimidation, Reprisal and Violence in the South's Racial Crisis," pp. 3, 27, Southern Regional Council Literature, Box 4/5, Civil Rights Collection, HLSC; *Activities of the Ku Klux Klan in the United States*, Part 4, p. 2936, Hearings Before the Committee on Un-American Activities, House of Representatives, Eighty-Ninth Congress, Second Session.
38. Dennis Interview 4/23/92; Silver, *Mississippi: The Closed Society*, pp. 29-30.
39. Meredith, p. 305; Silver, *Running Scared*, p. 90; NYT 6/15/63, p. 9; Moody, p. 339; Powledge, p. 190.
40. FBI Letterhead Memorandum, Director, FBI to Assistant Attorney General, Civil Rights Division, BUfile 157-901-371, 10/17/63, pp. 1-2.
41. Ibid., pp. 2-3.
42. Villano and Astor, pp. 90-4. Anthony Villano's co-author, Gerald Astor, told the author that reputed New York mafioso Gregory Scarpa was "Julio" in Villano's account in *Brick Agent*. The author's repeated attempts to interview Scarpa in 1992 and 1993 proved futile, as Scarpa was under indictment for both a New York State weapons charge and a federal murder conspiracy indictment.
43. Gentry, pp. 566-7.
44. FBI Report, SA [deleted] Chicago to SAC, Memphis, BUfile 157-901-265, 6/18/63, pp. 4-5; CDD 6/19/63, p. 13.
45. FBI Report, SA [deleted] Memphis to

USA Oxford, MS and USA Jackson, MS, BUfile 157-901-317, 6/26/63, pp. 25-6.
46. Ibid.
47. FBI Memorandum, C.L. McGowan to Mr. Rosen, BUfile 157-901-203, 6/22/63.
48. Ibid.
49. FBI Memorandum, A. Rosen to Mr. McGowan, BUfile 157-901-270, 6/24/63.
50. FBI Memorandum, A.H. Belmont to Mr. Tolson, BUfile 157-901-226, 6/22/63.
51. FBI Memorandum, C.L. McGowan to Mr. Rosen, FBI, BUfile 157-901-188, 6/21/63. The memo noted that "De La Beckwith was described as a radical member of the White Citizens' Council."
52. FBI Report, SA [deleted] Memphis to USA Oxford, MS and USA Jackson, MS, BUfile 157-901-317, 6/27/63, p. 34. The chain of events from the time of the morning's search for Beckwith through his arrest and transport to Jackson is taken from the same lengthy report.
53. FBI Report, SA [deleted] Memphis to USA Oxford, MS and USA Jackson, MS, BUfile 157-901-317, 6/26/63, p 30.
54. NYT 2/8/64, p. 10; FBI Report, SA [deleted] Memphis to USA Oxford, MS and USA Jackson, MS, BUfile 157-901-317, 6/26/63, pp. 31-3.
55. FBI Report, SA [deleted] Memphis to USA Oxford, MS and USA Jackson, MS, BUfile 157-901-317, 6/26/63, pp. 34-5; FBI Memorandum, C.A. Evans to Mr. Rosen, BUfile 157-901-271, 6/24/63.
56. FBI Teletype, SAC, New Orleans to Director, FBI and SAC, Memphis, BUfile 157-901-183, 6/23/63.
57. FBI Teletype, SAC, New Orleans to Director, FBI, BUfile 157-901-177, 6/24/63; FBI Letterhead Memorandum, SAC, New Orleans to Director, FBI, BUfile 157-901-330, 7/25/63, pp. 51–2.
58. FBI Teletype, SAC, New Orleans to Director, FBI and SAC, Memphis, BUfile 157-901-183, 6/23/63.
59. FBI Teletype, SAC, New Orleans to Director, FBI, BUfile 157-901-177, 6/24/63.
60. FBI Memorandum, M.A. Jones to Mr. DeLoach, BUfile 157-901-246, 6/24/63.
61. FBI Memorandum, C.D. DeLoach to Mr. Mohr, BUfile 157-901-269, 6/24/63.
62. FBI Press Coverage, BUfile 157-901-214, 6/25/63.
63. FBI Memorandum, J. Edgar Hoover to Mssrs. Tolson, Belmont, Rosen and DeLoach, BUfile 157-901-256, 6/25/63.
64. FBI Memorandum, A. Rosen to Mr. Belmont, BUfile 157-901-286, 6/26/63.

8 "SUCH IS THE FATE OF A PATRIOT"

1. "Meet the Press" transcript, vol. 7, No. 24, 6/23/63, produced by Lawrence E. Spivak, guest, Honorable Robert F. Kennedy, Attorney General of the United States, SIMPD.
2. Jack Galey interview; Sampson and business leader quotes, *Time* 7/5/63, pp. 15-6; Note to Beckwith from S.H. Montgomery of Greenwood, 2/10/64.
3. White Citizens' Legal Fund ephemera, author's collection.
4. CT 6/25/63, p. 1; GC 6/24/63, p. 1.
5. KNS 7/11/63, p. 16; CA 7/10/63, p. 19.
6. "Evers Fund" chain letter, Swisshelm Papers, MS-334, Box 1, Folder 7, HLSC; NYT 1/11/64, p. 24.
7. *The New Yorker* 8/31/63, p. 21; *Ebony* 3/65, p. 28; *Jet* 6/30/66, pp. 46-7; Branch, pp. 828-30; CDD 6/25/63, pp. 1-2, 5; CDD 6/26/63, p. 2; NYT 6/15/63, p. 9; Evers, Mrs. Medgar with Peters, William, pp. 342-3.
8. Undated letter to Barnett from Jack Kendrick asking Barnett's "thoughtful consideration," and asking the governor to forward fifty dollars to Beckwith; 8/3/63 letter from Barnett to Kendrick stating, in part, "I appreciate your kind remarks, as well as your donation to the defense of Mr. Beckwith," noting that he was forwarding the check to Hardy Lott in Greenwood to be placed in Beckwith's defense fund; and 8/5/63 letter from Hardy Lott to Kendrick noting that his client was unable to reply, but wished to send his thanks. Author's collection.
9. Letter from Beckwith to B. D. Beckwith, Jr. dated 7/15/63; Letter from Beckwith to Mary Williams Beckwith dated 7/1/63; both, author's collection.
10. Letters from Beckwith to Mary Williams Beckwith dated 8/15/63 and 8/22/63, author's collection.
11. Letters to Beckwith dated 9/17/63, author's collection; CA 10/28/63, p. 1.
12. Miscellaneous letters from Beckwith to Mary Williams Beckwith dated 8/63 and 9/63; Beckwith letter to Jesse R. Williams, Jr.; all, author's collection. In his letter to Williams, his brother-in-law, Beckwith displayed his jovial good humor, signing himself "Your Brother (in-law, out-law etc. Ha! Ha!")
13. Copies of letters from Beckwith to Sampson, James Jarman, Bill Ramsey and Guy Futral asking for help in finding a job for his wife, 12/4/63; Letter from

Beckwith to "Compatriot McEwan," SAR, Chicago, et. al, 10/31/63 and notation in letter from Beckwith to Jesse R. Williams, Jr., 12/2/63, that he had written 32 SAR chapters and had his boss, Dewitt Walcott, mimeograph 300 more for mailing; Letter from Beckwith to Viola Sanders, Commander, USN WAVES, 11/10/63; all, author's collection. Favorite photo, JCL 1/28/64, p. 1; Letter from Beckwith to Mary Williams Beckwith, 11/13/63, author's collection.

14. Copy of Beckwith's solicitation flyer and handwritten note, FBI Airtel, SAC, Chicago to Director, FBI and SAC, New Orleans, 7/24/63, BUfile 157-901-347, pp. 1-2.

15. Copy of Beckwith's letter to Intercontinental Arms, FBI Airtel, SAC, Los Angeles to Director, FBI, 4/9/64, BUfile 157-901-472, enclosure pp. 1-10.

16. Copy of Beckwith's letter to Minox Camera Company, FBI Memorandum, SAC, New York to Director, FBI, 12/6/63, BUfile 157-901-389.

17. FBI Report, SA [Deleted], New Orleans to Bureau, et. al., 10/4/64, BUfile 157-901-368, pp. 1-17; FBI Airtel, SAC, WFO to Director, FBI, 1/29/64, BUfile 157-901-416, p. 1; FBI Teletype, FBI, New Orleans to Director, 1/28/64, BUfile 157-901-413, pp. 1-3. The Teletype, p. 3, also noted that Waller had a psychologist examining Beckwith's letters and hoped "to be able to introduce evidence based on psychologist's review of these letters showing mental condition of Beckwith." Reporter's Transcript, *State of Mississippi* v. *Byron De La Beckwith*, Circuit Court of the First Judicial District of Hinds County, Mississippi, No. 17,824, 1/31/64, p. 918. Also NYT, 2/7/64, p. 28; *The Nation*, 2/24/64, p. 180.

18. The subject of this interview submitted to three hours of taped questioning on the condition that none of the quotations or information be attributed by name.

19. Letters from Beckwith to Jesse R. Williams, Jr., 11/6/63 and 12/11/63; Letter from Beckwith to B. D. Beckwith Jr., 3/1/64; all, author's collection.

20. FBI Airtel, SAC, New Orleans to Director, FBI, 7/18/63, BUfile 157-901-342, pp. 1-3; FBI Report, SA [Deleted], Memphis to USA, Oxford, Mississippi and USA, Jackson, Mississippi, 7/16/63, BUfile 157-901-348, pp. 52, 78, 82-6; FBI Report, SA [Deleted], Memphis to Bureau, et. al., 7/12/63, BUfile 157-901-330, p. 73; KNS 7/18/63, p. 1.

21. Ibid.

22. FBI Report, SA [Deleted], Memphis to USA, Oxford, Mississippi and USA, Jackson, Mississippi, 7/16/63, BUfile 157-901-348, pp. 85-6.

23. Evers, Mrs. Medgar with Peters, William, p. 335.

24. Hanks, p. 156; KNS 7/26/63, p. 4; KJ 7/26/63, p. 10.

25. Beckwith letter to Mary Williams Beckwith, 8/15/63, author's collection.

26. KNS 8/10/63, p. 1; CA 8/2/63, p. 1; JDN 11/18/63, p. 1; GC 11/19/63, p. 1; JDN 11/19/63, p. 1.

27. Letter from Beckwith to Jesse R. Williams, Jr., 8/13/63; Letter from Beckwith to Mary Williams Beckwith, 8/14/63; both, author's collection.

28. *Newsweek* 12/16/63, p. 29.

29. Corroborated in letters from Beckwith to Mary Williams Beckwith, 9/27/63, 10/4/63 and 11/20/63, author's collection. Beckwith's relative freedom is also mentioned in Williams, p. 224; Evers, Mrs. Medgar with Peters, William, pp. 354-5; Scott, R.W., pp. 77-8.

30. Letters from Beckwith to Mary Williams Beckwith, 9/20/63, 10/1/63, 1/10/64, 2/8/64; all, author's collection.

31. Reply to Beckwith from Martin Cooley of The Devin-Adair Company, New York, author's collection.

32. JDN 11/13/63, p.10.

33. Letter from Beckwith to Mary Williams Beckwith, 11/14/63, author's collection.

34. Letter from Beckwith to Mary Williams Beckwith, 9/20/63; Letter from Beckwith to Jesse R. Williams, Jr., 9/24/63; Letter from Beckwith to Colonel Francis E. Davis, 11/28/63; all, author's collection. In the initiation ceremony of the White Knights of the Ku Klux Klan of Mississippi, initiates take an oath of allegiance in which they vow total secrecy. Beckwith has never publicly admitted his membership in the White Knights of the Ku Klux Klan of Mississippi.

35. *The Present-Day Ku Klux Klan Movement*, Report by the Committee on Un-American Activities, 12/11/67, pp. 29-31, 44-7; Several exceptional books have been written about the murders of Goodman, Schwerner and Chaney and the ensuing investigation. Among the best are *Three Lives for Mississippi* by William Bradford Huie and *We Are Not Afraid* by Seth Cagin and Philip Dray.

36. During his run for Lieutenant Governor, Beckwith even called on Dennis at his home in Meridian. He had been given Dennis's name by Imperial Wizard Sam Bowers as someone who might be helpful to

The Southern Review in Meridian. Along with Elmore Greaves, Beckwith was part owner of the tabloid, which was the mouthpiece of the White Knights and which, Dennis asserted, Bowers controlled. As a souvenir of Beckwith's visit, Dennis kept a copy of *The Southern Review* bearing a "Compliments of De La Beckwith" stamp.
37. KNS 1/13/66, p. B-3; FBI Report, SA [Deleted], Jackson to Bureau, et. al., 1/10/66, BUfile 44-31489-13, p. 7.
38. Beckwith's jail writings were being compiled to form a book, which he tentatively titled, *My Ass, Your Goat and the Republic.*
39. Letters from Beckwith to Mary Williams Beckwith, 11/22/63 and 11/27/63, author's collection.
40. Letter from Beckwith to Mary Williams Beckwith, 11/22/63 and 11/23/63, author's collection.
41. Letter to Beckwith from a man in Etlel, Louisiana, 10/30/64, author's collection.
42. CL 11/13/63, p. 1; KNS 2/3/64, p. 11.
43. Letter from Beckwith to Mary Williams Beckwith, 9/21/63, author's collection.
44. *Newsweek* 12/16/63, p. 29.
45. Letter from Beckwith to Mary Williams Beckwith, 11/29/63, author's collection. Beckwith claimed to have read the Bible several times in its entirety, and said he had used his time in jail to brush up on his Biblical knowledge.
46. Letter from Beckwith to Mary Williams Beckwith, 8/21/63, author's collection.
47. Letter from Beckwith to Mary Williams Beckwith, 1/10/64, author's collection.
48. Letters from Beckwith to Mary Williams Beckwith, 1/17/64 and 1/23/64, author's collection.

9 "MY ASS, YOUR GOAT AND THE REPUBLIC"

1. NYT 1/30/64, p. 15.
2. CA 1/28/64, p. 1.
3. NYP 1/28/64, p. 5.
4. NYT 1/30/64, p. 15; NYT 1/28/64, p. 22; JCL 1/28/64, p. 8; NYP 1/28/64, p. 5.
5. Hanks, p. 189.
6. NYT 1/28/64, p. 22; CA 1/28/64, p. 1; JCL 1/28/64, p. 1; NYT 1/31/64, p. 12; NYT 1/29/64, p. 18; GC 1/29/64, p. 2; KNS 1/31/64, p. 3. According to an Associated Press wire report released 1/30/64, the final jury included Darth H. Cumberland, J.D. Entrekin, W.C. Hudspeth, Charles B. Jones, J.M. Moss, Billy J. Morton, Charles O. Patrick, F.E. Plummer, Cecil S. Selman, Bruce H. Thompson, J.B. Thompson and William A. Weeks. The alternate juror was Arnold W. West.
7. GC 1/29/64, p. 1.
8. Ibid.
9. Copy of an unmarked newspaper clipping from Beckwith's files, author's collection.
10. Bryant and Milan were acquitted in the Emmett Till case. They later sold their story to journalist William Bradford Huie, who reported their admissions of the killing in a celebrated article in *LOOK* 1/24/56, pp. 46-50.
11. KJ 2/1/64, p. 3; Evers, Mrs. Medgar with Peters, William, pp. 351-4; Friedman, pp. 139-40.
12. Reporter's Transcript, *State of Mississippi* v. *Byron De La Beckwith*, Circuit Court of the First Judicial District of Hinds County, Mississippi, Number 17,824, 1/31/64. Evers Testimony, pp. 3-12.
13. Ibid., pp. 12-9.
14. Ibid., pp. 28-96.
15. Evers, Mrs. Medgar with Peters, William, p. 307.
16. NYT 1/31/64, p. 12; MPS 2/3/64, p.4; KJ 2/1/64, p.3; Scott, R.W., p. 119.
17. *Time* 2/14/64, p. 20; *The Nation* 2/24/64, p. 180. Beckwith recounts the cigar incident in detail in R.W. Scott's authorized biography, *Glory in Conflict*, pp. 119-20, in a brief essay entitled "No More Cigars, Please!" Beckwith claims he placed cigars in Waller's pocket to "shame and ridicule him and belittle him."
18. UPI wire report, 2/6/64.
19. Reporter's Transcript, *State of Mississippi* v. *Byron De La Beckwith*, Circuit Court of the First Judicial District of Hinds County, Mississippi, Number 17,824, 1/31/64. Coley Testimony, pp. 134-48; Adcock Testimony, pp. 148-160.
20. Ibid., pp. 160-93.
21. Ibid., pp. 193-221.
22. FBI Report, SA [Deleted], Memphis to USA, Oxford, Mississippi and USA, Jackson, Mississippi, 7/16/63, BUfile 157-901-348, Synopsis pp. 1-2; FBI Memorandum and addenda, SAC, New Orleans to Director, FBI, 7/25/63, BUfile 157-901-350, pp. 40-1.
23. FBI Memorandum, A. Rosen to Mr. Belmont, BUfile 157-901-286, 6/26/63.
24. FBI Memorandum, A. Rosen to Mr. Belmont, 10/1/64, BUfile 157-901-369, p. 3: "We were successful in tracing the rifle from a Montreal, Canada, firearms company to Inness [sic] McIntyre of Itta Bena, Mississippi, who stated he sold the rifle to Beckwith. Our investigation in

tracing the rifle and sight involved 48 field divisions and one legat."

25. Reporter's Transcript, *State of Mississippi* v. *Byron De La Beckwith*, Circuit Court of the First Judicial District of Hinds County, Mississippi, No. 17,824, 1/31/64. Finley Testimony, pp. 221-8; Poppleton Testimony, pp. 230-79.

26. FBI Memorandum, A. Rosen to Mr. Belmont, 10/1/64, BUfile 157-901-369, p. 3, stated: "During the investigation to trace the sight, we talked to John Goza, a gunsmith of Grenada, Mississippi, who furnished information which resulted in Byron De La Beckwith, Greenwood, Mississippi, being considered a suspect. Beckwith was contacted 6/21/63 but refused to talk with our agents. Beckwith's name was then immediately called to the attention of the Identification Division, at which time a search of our fingerprint files was instituted."

27. Letter from Beckwith to Mary Williams Beckwith, 9/20/63, author's collection.

28. Reporter's Transcript, *State of Mississippi* v. *Byron De La Beckwith*, Circuit Court of the First Judicial District of Hinds County, Mississippi, No. 17,824, 1/31/64. Goza Testimony, pp. 282-98.

29. Ibid., pp. 316-93.

30. Ibid., pp. 394-427.

31. FBI Memorandum, A. Rosen to Mr. Belmont, 10/1/64, BUfile 157-901-369, p. 3.

32. Reporter's Transcript, *State of Mississippi* v. *Byron De La Beckwith*, Circuit Court of the First Judicial District of Hinds County, Mississippi, No. 17,824, 1/31/64. Speight Testimony, pp. 427-47.

33. Ibid., pp. 448-459.

34. Ibid., pp. 585-600.

35. Ibid. Walcott Testimony, pp. 462-85; Bratley Testimony, pp. 632-7.

36. Ibid., pp. 638-49.

37. Ibid., pp. 649-71.

38. Ibid. Sumrall Testimony, pp. 671-81; Haven Testimony, pp. 681-93.

39. Ibid. Roy Adkins Testimony, pp. 693-701; Windale Stringer Testimony, pp. 702-11; Conner Testimony, pp. 741-51.

40. Ibid., pp. 752-803.

41. Ibid., pp. 803-25.

42. Ibid. Book Testimony, pp. 825-8; McCoy, Sr., Testimony, pp. 829-31; McCoy, Jr., Testimony, pp. 831-2.

43. Ibid. Jones Testimony, pp. 832-53; Cresswell Testimony, pp. 853-64; Holley Testimony, pp. 864-75.

44. Scott, R.W., p. 258.

45. KNS 2/6/64, p. 2; CA 1/6/64, p. 1.

46. Reporter's Transcript, *State of Mississippi* v. *Byron De La Beckwith*, Circuit Court of the First Judicial District of Hinds County, Mississippi, No. 17,824, 1/31/64. Beckwith Testimony, pp. 876-953.

47. *Time* 2/14/64, p. 21; *The Saturday Evening Post* 3/14/64, p. 80; KNS 2/6/64, pp. 1-2.

48. NYT 2/8/64, p. 1.

49. Reporter's Transcript, *State of Mississippi* v. *Byron De La Beckwith*, Circuit Court of the First Judicial District of Hinds County, Mississippi, No. 17,824, 1/31/64. Beckwith Testimony, pp. 916-7. The same letter appeared in CA 3/17/57, section V, p. 3.

50. Reporter's Transcript, *State of Mississippi* v. *Byron De La Beckwith*, Circuit Court of the First Judicial District of Hinds County, Mississippi, No. 17,824, January 31, 1964. Beckwith Testimony, pp. 918-20. Some reporters covering the trial quoted Beckwith's letter as stating, "For the next 15 years, we here in Mississippi are going to have to do a lot of shooting to protect our wives, our children and ourselves from bad niggers and sorry white folks," but the official trial transcript does not bear that out. See NYT 2/7/64, p. 28; *The Nation* 2/24/64, p. 180.

51. Even as the *Outdoor Life* letter was being introduced into evidence, another query letter to Field & Stream was being handed over to the FBI by the magazine's editors. Written on January 26—just one day before jury selection began—Beckwith offered the same article for sale. In a handwritten note below his signature, Beckwith had even offered a possible title for the piece, "After Sundown." See FBI SPECIAL, SAC, New York to M.H. Jones, Crime Research Section, 2/5/64, BUfile 157-901-436, pp. 2-3. Although Waller asked about *Outdoor Life*, Beckwith later in the trial proceedings referred to the letter he had written *Field & Stream.* The blunder went unnoticed. At the time, Waller was unaware Beckwith had queried another magazine trying to sell the same article.

52. FBI SPECIAL, SAC, New York to M.H. Jones, Crime Research Section, 2/5/64, BUfile 157-901-436, pp. 2-3.

53. Waller cited 150 letters which Beckwith had purportedly written since his arrest. To his wife alone, Beckwith wrote more than 200 letters during his incarceration, and claimed during his trial testimony that he wrote "about five to 20 letters a day," making Waller's estimate highly conservative. See Reporter's Transcript, *State of Mississippi* v. *Byron De La Beckwith*, Circuit Court of the First Judicial District

of Hinds County, Mississippi, No. 17,824, January 31, 1964, p. 929.
54. *The Nation* 2/24/64, p. 180.
55. NYT 2/7/64, p. 28; *The Saturday Evening Post* 3/14/64, p. 81.
56. NYT 2/7/64, p. 28; KNS 2/6/64, p. 1; KNS 2/7/64, p. 2.
57. NYT 2/7/64, p. 28; KNS 2/7/64, p. 2.
58. NYT 2/8/64, p. 10.
59. Cagin and Dray, pp. 175-6. Russel Moore died in 1987. The Enfield rifle identified as the murder weapon in the Evers case was later found in Judge Moore's home. In a weird plot twist, Moore had apparently taken the rifle as a souvenir after the case passed to the files. Moore was the father-in-law of Assistant District Attorney Bobby DeLaughter, who pursued the reopening of the murder case against Beckwith and spearheaded the fourteen-month investigation which resulted in Beckwith's December 1990 arrest.
60. NYT 2/7/64, p. 28; NYT 2/8/64, p. 1; Silver, *Mississippi: The Closed Society*, p. 239; Evers, Mrs. Medgar with Peters, William, pp. 367-8. In an interview for the celebrated public television series "Eyes on the Prize," Myrlie Evers claimed it was while she was on the witness stand that former Governor Ross Barnett made his appearance at the Beckwith trial. (See also Williams, p. 224) In her book, *For Us, The Living*, however, she stated that Barnett made his appearance in the courtroom after the jury had retired. Many accounts inaccurately state that Barnett visited before the jury retired, implying that his presence swayed the jurors. Although it does make a better story, unfortunately it is not accurate.
61. *The Saturday Evening Post* 3/14/64, p. 77.
62. KNS 2/7/64, p. 1; CA 2/8/64, p. 1; *Time* 2/14/64, p. 20; NYT 2/8/64, p. 1; *The Saturday Evening Post* 3/14/64, p. 81. Note that some sources reported the split to be an even six-six. The author has deferred to *The New York Times* report which cited a court bailiff as its source. See also Evers, Mrs. Medgar with Peters, William, p. 368.
63. Undated BN clipping, author's collection.
64. *SCLC Newsletter* 2/64, p. 4.
65. CA 2/8/64, p. 2; Evers, Mrs. Medgar with Peters, William, p. 368; Silver, *Mississippi: The Closed Society*, p. 239.
66. KNS 2/8/64, p. 12.

10 AND TEN CROSSES BURNED

1. CA 2/8/64, p. 1; KNS 2/8/64, p. 1.
2. GC 2/10/64, p 1; JCL 7/31/64, p. 10; CA 8/1/64, p. 18; FBI Memorandum, A. Rosen to Mr. Belmont, 8/6/64, BUfile 157-901-485.
3. Letters from Beckwith to Mary Williams Beckwith, 2/7/64, 2/8/64, 2/22/64, author's collection.
4. Letter from Beckwith to Mary Williams Beckwith, 4/11/64, author's collection.
5. Copy of Sovereignty Commission document 1-77-3, "Assisting Honorable Stanney [sic] Sanders, Defense Attorney for Byron De La Beckwith, charged with murdering Medgar Evers, c/m, in checking the background of prospective jurors," 4/9/64, author's collection; JCL 10/1/89, p. 1; JCL 10/3/89, p. 1; JCL 11/3/91, p. 1; NYT 10/25/89, p. A19; *Washington Journalism Review* 10/91, p. 38.
6. Letter from Beckwith to Mary Williams Beckwith, 2/28/64, author's collection; NYT 4/8/64, p. 30.
7. According to an Associated Press wire report released 4/12/64, the final jury in Beckwith's second trial included N.A. Newman, L.C. Hammond, John T. Hester, Benjamin Barnes, J.T. Reynolds, Ronald C. Cox, Charles L. Fosster, Robert L. Hollimon, Charles S. Corder, John T. Offenhiser, G.H. Owens and William B. Boling. No alternate juror was named in the report. In *The New York Times*, reporter John Herbers noted that the jury selected to hear the case was unusual in that it contained seven college graduates, two of whom were originally from the North.
8. NYT 4/7/64, p. 19.
9. NYT 4/14/64, p. 34.
10. NYT 4/12/64, p. 42; MFP 4/25/64, p. 1.
11. CA 4/15/64, p. 1.
12. CA 4/17/64, p. 1.
13. NYT 4/17/64, p. 18; CA, 4/17/64, p. 1.
14. NYT 4/18/64, p. 1.
15. Hanks, p. 361. In one of her interviews for this book, Willie Beckwith confirmed that her husband had been given a gun to protect himself en route to Greenwood. "He said they gave him a machine gun in the car, in case something happened," she said. "But now, I don't know if that's true or not."
16. Belfrage, p. 128; GC 4/17/64, p. 1; NYT 4/18/64, p. 1.
17. GC 4/17/64, p. 1.
18. GC 4/17/64, p. 1; NYT 4/18/64, p. 1; *The New Republic*, 5/23/64, pp. 9-10.

19. Letters from Beckwith to Mary Williams Beckwith, 7/12/63, 9/8/63 and 9/10/63, author's collection.
20. McIlhany, p. 215; Cagin and Dray, pp. 37, 450. Akin was later indicted—and acquitted—in the federal case against the Klan members accused of depriving Andrew Goodman, James Chaney and Michael Schwerner of their civil rights by murdering and burying them in an earthen dam in Neshoba County, Mississippi. Akin died soon afterward, and his friends believed harassment by the FBI and the stress of the trial brought on the heart attack that killed him.
21. Letters from Beckwith to Mary Williams Beckwith, 7/1/63 and 9/15/63, author's collection.
22. Lackey Interview.
23. MPS 4/20/64, p. 9.
24. MFP 4/25/64, p. 4. The complete text of Charles Evers's statement read: "The Beckwith trial was not a litigation involving the family of Medgar Evers vs. Beckwith nor the NAACP against Beckwith. It was a lawsuit with the state of Mississippi as the plaintiff and Beckwith as the defendant. If the action of former Governor Barnett, in shaking Beckwith's hand in open court, the public recognition given Beckwith by the Supreme Commander of the Oxford Invasion, General Walker, in visiting Beckwith in jail and in open court and the hero's welcome by a standing ovation of many people when Beckwith entered the courtroom had any influence upon the outcome of the trial in Beckwith's favor, then it was the state of Mississippi, solely, that was denied a fair and impartial trial as guaranteed by law. Such actions as I have referred to was [sic] sufficient to warrant a mistrial, without mentioning others. If the state of Mississippi did get a raw deal in this trial, then the people of Mississippi were recipients of same. However, the indecisive action of a jury representing a cross-section of the people, shows clearly that all the people were not misled one way or another by the tactics which may have been promoted by some to do so. This is encouraging, and shows progress toward the goal of justice in Mississippi. To all citizens, Negro and White, who are sympathetic to the cause of real justice in Mississippi, may I make a personal plea, please do not resort to violence in any form against Beckwith or anyone else, because Medgar nor I would want you to do so, but instead keep moving in a non-violent way for justice and equality for all Mississippians regardless to race, creed, or color without malice or hatred in our hearts."
25. *Playboy* 10/71, p. 186; Evers, Charles, p. 114; "Good Morning, America," 10/15/92.
26. Enclosure with a letter from Beckwith to the author, 5/9/86, author's collection.
27. DDT 2/21/66, p. 1; "The Continuing Crisis: An Assessment of New Racial Tensions in the South," Report issued by The Southern Regional Council and The American Jewish Committee, 5/66, pp. 16-7, 40, SRC Civil Rights Literature, Box 4, Civil Rights Collection, HLSC.
28. FBI Report, SA [Deleted], Jackson to Bureau, et. al., 7/29/65, BUfile 157-3744-1. An FBI informant advised that "Gordon Mims Lackey made the statement that he, Lackey, swore 'Delay' Beckwith into the Klan in the trailer of Lackey following the trial of Beckwith at Jackson, Mississippi, where he was tried for the murder of Medgar Evers. [Informant] advised that the WKKKKOM is reported to have paid the salary, car note, home note and law fees for Beckwith while he was being held in jail. The statewide cross-burning which occurred after Beckwith was 'acquitted' after his second trial was a celebration by the Klan of this 'acquittal.' " See also KNS 1/13/66, p. B-3.
29. Letter from Beckwith to Mary Williams Beckwith, 9/20/63; Letter from Beckwith to Jesse R. Williams, Jr., 9/24/63; Letter from Beckwith to Col. Francis E. Davis, 11/28/63; Beckwith ephemera; all, author's collection. In the initiation ceremony of the White Knights of the Ku Klux Klan of Mississippi, initiates take an oath of allegiance in which they vow total secrecy. Beckwith has never publicly admitted his Klan membership.
30. Text of the Oath of Allegiance to the White Knights of the Ku Klux Klan of Mississippi is taken from the WKKKKOM initiation ceremony.
31. *The Present-Day Ku Klux Klan Movement,* Report by the Committee on Un-American Activities, House of Representatives, Ninetieth Congress, First Session, 12/11/67, pp. 25, 30, 44.
32. Cagin and Dray, pp. 245-7; McIlhany, pp. 30-1, 39 and 52; Wade, p. 334; *New South* Fall 1968, p. 51; *Reader's Digest* 9/70, p. 196; *Newsweek* 4/11/66, p. 40.
33. Letter from Beckwith to Mary Williams Beckwith, 4/11/64, author's collection.
34. Whitehead p. 158; CA 4/25/64, p. 1. Former Klan Province Titan and FBI informant Delmar Dennis remembered that Imperial Wizard Sam Bowers personally

sanctioned the cross-burning in support of Beckwith. "I heard Sam talk about it," Dennis said. "They wanted to burn one on every courthouse lawn simultaneously, to make a point, in 82 counties. He thought that it would shake the state to its foundation." Although crosses were not burned in every county, the display got Bowers's point across and created the impression that the Klan possessed tremendous strength throughout the state.
35. Lipset and Raab, p. 328-9; *New South* Fall 1968, p. 54.
36. "Executive Lecture of March 1, 1964," p. 1; "My Fellow American" recruiting brochure; both, author's collection. See Appendices 1.7 and 1.2.
37. *The Present-Day Ku Klux Klan Movement*, Report by the Committee on Un-American Activities, House of Representatives, Ninetieth Congress, First Session, 12/11/67, pp. 44-5. See also Scott, R.W., p. 175; Tarrants, pp. 41 and 59.
38. Ibid., pp. 96-8.
39. "Executive Lecture of March 1, 1964," p. 4, author's collection; *The Present-Day Ku Klux Klan Movement*, Report by the Committee on Un-American Activities, House of Representatives, Ninetieth Congress, First Session, 12/11/67, p. 45.
40. McIlhany, pp. 40-1; *Christianity Today* 9/22/78, p. 13; *The Present-Day Ku Klux Klan Movement*, Report by the Committee on Un-American Activities, House of Representatives, Ninetieth Congress, First Session, December 11, 1967, p. 65.
41. *The Present-Day Ku Klux Klan Movement*, Report by the Committee on Un-American Activities, House of Representatives, Ninetieth Congress, First Session, 12/11/67, pp. 98 and 111.
42. "Imperial Executive Order," 5/3/64, cited in *The Present-Day Ku Klux Klan Movement*, Report by the Committee on Un-American Activities, House of Representatives, Ninetieth Congress, First Session, 12/11/67, p. 98.
43. *The Present-Day Ku Klux Klan Movement*, Report by the Committee on Un-American Activities, House of Representatives, Ninetieth Congress, First Session, 12/11/67, pp. 102-3.
44. Ibid., p. 46; Von Hoffman, p. 45.
45. Ibid., pp. 29-31 and 44-7; The film "Mississippi Burning" was a fictionalized account of the celebrated murders and the subsequent federal investigation of the case.
46. "Executive Lecture of March 1, 1964," p. 3, author's collection.
47. *The Present-Day Ku Klux Klan Movement*, Report by the Committee on Un-American Activities, House of Representatives, Ninetieth Congress, First Session, 12/11/67, p. 98.
48. Ibid., p. 46; McIlhany, p. 30.
49. Von Hoffman, p. 5.
50. Dennis Interview, 1/29/91.
51. Posey Papers, MS-334, Jane E. Hodes File 10, Box 3, HLSC.
52. "The Continuing Crisis: An Assessment of New Racial Tensions in the South," Report issued by The Southern Regional Council and The American Jewish Committee, 5/66, pp. 16-7, 40, SRC Civil Rights Literature, Box 4, Civil Rights Collection, HLSC.
53. Although Freedom Summer activities garner only the briefest mention here, many fascinating chronicles of that summer have been written by scholars, lawyers and former volunteers. Among the best are Von Hoffman's *Mississippi Notebook*; Belfrage's *Freedom Summer*; Sutherland's *Letters from Mississippi*; McAdam's *Freedom Summer*; and Holt's *The Summer That Didn't End*. See bibliography for publication information.
54. MFP 4/11/64, p. 3; Von Hoffman, p. 12.
55. Holt, pp. 281-5; Friedman, p. 30.
56. Posey Papers, MS-334, Jane E. Hodes File 10, Box 3, HLSC.
57. *The New Republic* 5/23/64, pp. 9-10; Belfrage, p. 128; Posey Papers, MS-334, Jane E. Hodes File 10, Box 3, HLSC; Sutherland, p. 177; "Law Enforcement in Mississippi," a special report issued by the Southern Regional Council, 7/14/64, p. 18, MS-334, Box 1, Folder 7, HLSC.
58. FBI Teletype, SAC New Orleans to Director, 5/4/64, BUfile 157-901-477, p. 1; FBI Memorandum, SAC New Orleans to Director, 6/4/64, BUfile 157-901-480.
59. FBI Memorandum, SAC Memphis to Director, 6/9/64, BUfile 157-901-481, p. 2; FBI Airtel, Director to SACs, Memphis and New Orleans, 6/12/64, BUfile 157-901-481, p. 3.
60. Carson, pp. 108-9 and 123-9; "Overview of the Freedom Schools," HREC Archives, RG1, Box 8, Folder 128, SNCC.
61. Holt, p. 12; Eagles, p. 82.
62. FBI Letter, Director to Honorable Walter W. Jenkins, Special Assistant to the President, 7/13/64, BUfile 157-6-54-15, p. 2.
63. Ibid., pp. 5-6.
64. Holt, p. 12.
65. Belfrage, pp. 130-1; Von Hoffman, pp. 106-9; Holt, pp. 217-8.
66. Holt, pp. 241-4.

67. *Activities of Ku Klux Klan Organizations in the United States,* Part 3, p. 2700. Hearings Before the Committee on Un-American Activities, House of Representatives, Eighty-Ninth Congress, Second Session. U.S. Government Printing Office, 1966; KJ 1/13/66, p. 11.
68. Letter from Beckwith to Mary Louise Williams, 11/16/76, author's collection.
69. Greenwood Leflore Hospital Record #93362, 6/3/64, author's collection.
70. JCL 9/10/64, p. 1; JDN 9/10/64, p. 4.
71. "Constitution of the White Knights of the Sovereign Realm of Mississippi," p. 23, author's collection.
72. See Scott, R.W., p. 269. Beckwith's sanctioned biography refers to Delmar Dennis as a "stooge and informer" and as a "pitiful example who admittedly took a solemn oath and violated it."
73. Also see McIlhany, p. 38.
74. FBI Airtel, SAC, Jackson to Director, 9/13/65, BUfile 157-3744-1, p. 12; FBI Report, SA [Deleted], Jackson to Bureau, Secret Service, et. al., 2/3/66, BUfile 157-3744-2, p. 3.
75. *Byron De La Beckwith* v. *Mary Louise Williams Beckwith,* No. 14,710, Chancery Court of Leflore County, Mississippi, 9/21/65, Minute Book 56, pp. 549-50.
76. *In the Matter of the Guardianship of Byron De La Beckwith, Jr., A Minor.* Chancery Court of Leflore County, Mississippi, 9/12/67.
77. Letter from Mildred Merck to Frances Williams, 10/25/65, author's collection.
78. *Ex Parte Mrs. Mary Louise Williams Beckwith.* Decree Changing Name, Chancery Court of Leflore County Mississippi, 2/18/66.

11 A PERIOD OF SELF-DELUSION

1. Leflore County, Mississippi, Veterans Service Record Book 17, Page 181, filed 10/13/66. Records show that Byron De La Beckwith, Jr., was released from active duty on 4/17/66, with a reserve duty obligation until 8/30/71.
2. FBI Report, SAC, Jackson to Bureau, et. al., 2/3/66, BUfile 157-3744-2, p. 1.
3. FBI Airtel, Director to SAC, Jackson, 11/10/65, BUfile 44-31489-2; FBI Report, Jackson to Bureau, 11/17/65, BUfile 44-31489-3, pp. 3-11.
4. Weisbrot, pp. 149-53; "The Continuing Crisis: An Assessment of New Racial Tensions in the South," Report issued by The Southern Regional Council and The American Jewish Committee, 5/66, p. 17, SRC Civil Rights Literature, Box 4, Civil Rights Collection, HLSC; FBI Airtel, Director to SAC, Jackson, 11/10/65, BUfile 44-31489-2; FBI Airtel, SAC, Jackson to Director, FBI, 11/17/65, BUfile 44-31489-4.
5. FBI Airtel, Director, FBI to SAC, Jackson, 11/19/65, BUfile 44-31489-5; FBI Airtel, Director, FBI to SAC, Jackson, 11/30/65, BUfile 44-31489-6; FBI Airtel, Director, FBI to SAC, Jackson, 12/6/65, BUfile 44-31489-7; FBI Report, SA [Deleted], Jackson to Bureau, 12/9/65, BUfile 44-31489-8, pp. C and 4.
6. FBI Report, SA [Deleted], Jackson to Bureau, 1/10/66, BUfile 44-31489-13.
7. *Activities of Ku Klux Klan Organizations in the United States, Part 3,* Hearings Before the Committee on Un-American Activities, House of Representatives, Eighty-Ninth Congress, Second Session, January 4-7, 11-14, 18, and 28, 1966, p. 2698.
8. Braden Papers, MS-425, Box 3, File HUAC, HLSC.
9. Beckwith vitae, 1/25/87, author's collection.
10. Beckwith letter to the author, 4/22/86, author's collection; NYT 2/15/67, p. 25.
11. *The Present-Day Ku Klux Klan Movement,* Report by the Committee on Un-American Activities, House of Representatives, Ninetieth Congress, First Session, 12/11/67, p. 47. Also "Articles of Formation, "The White Christian Protective and Legal Defense Fund; "Rules and Procedure for the Placing and Collection of Jars," The White Christian Protective and Legal Defense Fund; Initial solicitation letter and related Fund correspondence and ephemera; all, author's collection.
12. "My Fellow American" recruiting brochure, author's collection.
13. *Activities of Ku Klux Klan Organizations in the United States, Part 3,* Hearings Before the Committee on Un-American Activities, House of Representatives, Eighty-Ninth Congress, Second Session, January 4-7, 11-14, 18, and 28, 1966, pp. 2698-2701; KJ 1/13/66, p. 11; KNS 1/13/66, p. B-3.
14. *The Present-Day Ku Klux Klan Movement,* Report by the Committee on Un-American Activities, House of Representatives, Ninetieth Congress, First Session, 12/11/67, p. 46; *Activities of Ku Klux Klan Organizations in the United States, Part 4,* Hearings Before the Committee on Un-American Activities, House of Representatives, Eighty-Ninth Congress,

Second Session, February 1-4 and 7-11, 1966, p. 2925-8.
15. *Activities of Ku Klux Klan Organizations in the United States, Part 3,* Hearings Before the Committee on Un-American Activities, House of Representatives, Eighty-Ninth Congress, Second Session, January 4-7, 11-14, 18, and 28, 1966, p. 2775; *Activities of Ku Klux Klan Organizations in the United States, Part 4,* Hearings Before the Committee on Un-American Activities, House of Representatives, Eighty-Ninth Congress, Second Session, February 1-4 and 7-11, 1966, p. 2907.
16. *Activities of Ku Klux Klan Organizations in the United States, Part 3,* Hearings Before the Committee on Un-American Activities, House of Representatives, Eighty-Ninth Congress, Second Session, January 4-7, 11-14, 18, and 28, 1966, p. 2666; *The Present-Day Ku Klux Klan Movement,* Report by the Committee on Un-American Activities, House of Representatives, Ninetieth Congress, First Session, 12/11/67, p. 64.
17. Ellie J. Dahmer interview, pp. 25 and 32; McIlhany, p. 9.
18. *The Present-Day Ku Klux Klan Movement,* Report by the Committee on Un-American Activities, House of Representatives, Ninetieth Congress, First Session, 12/11/67, pp. 172-3.
19. Wade, p. 343-4; *The Present-Day Ku Klux Klan Movement,* Report by the Committee on Un-American Activities, House of Representatives, Ninetieth Congress, First Session, 12/11/67, pp. 103-4.
20. From the preface to "The Secret Report" by Byron De La Beckwith, author's collection.
21. "The Secret Report," pp. 1, 7, 15-19, author's collection.
22. Ibid., pp. 21-7.
23. Wade, p. 399; Zeskind, p. 14; ADL Facts, Spring 1983, Vol. 28, No. 1, *The "Identity Churches": A Theology of Hate,* p. 6; Undated sermon delivered by Dr. Wesley A. Swift, Church of Jesus Christ, Christian, Hollywood, California.
24. Beckwith letter to the author, 4/22/86, author's collection.
25. "The Continuing Crisis: An Assessment of New Racial Tensions in the South," Report issued by The Southern Regional Council and The American Jewish Committee, 5/66, p. 34, SRC Civil Rights Literature, Box 4, Civil Rights Collection, HLSC.
26. *The Present-Day Ku Klux Klan Movement,* Report by the Committee on Un-American Activities, House of Representatives, Ninetieth Congress, First Session, 12/11/67, p. 142.
27. Garrow, p. 473.
28. CA 6/17/66, p. 19; Garrow, p. 481.
29. Garrow, p. 482; CA 6/18/66, p. 4.
30. Meredith, p. 310.
31. CA 6/19/66, p. 18.
32. Delmar Dennis interview; McIlhany, pp. 53-4.
33. FBI Airtel, SAC, Jackson to Director, 7/19/66, BUfile 157-901-502, pp. 2-3.
34. FBI Blind Memorandum, Director to Chief, United States Secret Service, 7/29/65, BUfile 157-3744-1, p. 10.
35. FBI Report, SA [Deleted], Jackson to Bureau, Secret Service, et. al., 8/30/66, BUfile 157-3744-3, p. P; FBI Report, SA [Deleted], Jackson to Bureau, Secret Service, et. al., 2/3/66, BUfile 157-3744-2.
36. FBI Report, SA [Deleted], Jackson to Bureau, Secret Service, et. al., 8/30/66, BUfile 157-3744-3, pp. 3-6.
37. Ibid.
38. FBI Letterhead Memorandum, 7/13/66, BUfile 157-901-503, pp. 1-3.
39. Ibid.
40. FBI Airtel, SAC, Jackson to Director, FBI, 7/13/66, BUfile 157-901-503.
41. FBI Airtel, Director to SAC, Jackson, Personal Attention, 7/21/66, BUfile 157-901-502; Van Riper interview.
42. FBI Airtel, SAC, Jackson to Director, FBI, 7/27/66, BUfile 157-901-505; FBI Airtel, Director, FBI to SAC, Jackson, 8/1/66, BUfile 157-901-505.
43. FBI Letterhead Memorandum, 1/31/67, BUfile 157-3744-4, pp. 1-2.
44. FBI Report, SA [Deleted], Jackson to Bureau, Secret Service, et. al., 4/21/67, BUfile 157-3744-5, pp. 3-5.
45. JDN 2/14/67, p. 1.
46. JDN 2/16/67, pp. 2, 16.
47. FBI Report, SA [Deleted], Jackson to Bureau, Secret Service, et. al., 4/21/67, BUfile 157-3744-5, p. 8.
48. JCL 2/16/67, p. 6; FBI Report, SA [Deleted], Jackson to Bureau, Secret Service, et. al., 10/23/68, BUfile 157-3744-13.
49. JDN 2/14/67, p. 1.
50. JCL 2/16/67, p. 6.
51. JCL 2/15/67, p. 1.
52. Beckwith letter to the author, 5/8/92, author's collection.
53. JCL 2/17/67, p. C-8; JCL 2/19/67, p. A-18.
54. JCL 2/20/67, p. 12.
55. *The Present-Day Ku Klux Klan Movement,* Report by the Committee on Un-

American Activities, House of Representatives, Ninetieth Congress, First Session, 12/11/67, p. 98, 172.
56. NYT 2/16/67, p. 38.
57. Undated, unmarked clipping from *The Southern Review*, circa 1967, author's collection.
58. FBI Report, SA [Deleted], Jackson to Bureau, Secret Service, et. al., 4/21/67, BUfile 157-3744-5, p. 5.
59. *The Southern Review* 4/1/67, p. 1, cited in FBI Report, SA [Deleted], Jackson to Bureau, Secret Service, et. al., 4/21/67, BUfile 157-3744-5, p. 6.
60. JCL 2/17/67, p. C-8.
61. FBI Report, SA [Deleted], Jackson to Bureau, Secret Service, et. al., 10/23/68, BUfile 157-3744-13, p. 12.
62. FBI Letterhead Memorandum and Attachment, 7/12/67, BUfile 157-3744-6, pp. 1-2.
63. Ibid., pp. 4-5.
64. Ibid., p. 7.
65. FBI Memorandum, SAC, Jackson to Director, 4/2/68, BUfile 157-3744-12; FBI Report, SA [Deleted], Jackson to Bureau, Secret Service, et. al., 10/23/68, BUfile 157-3744-13.

12 "JEWISHPRUDENCE"

1. Letter from Beckwith to Mary Louise Williams, 4/19/73, author's collection.
2. FBI Teletype, Tampa to Director and New Orleans, Urgent 12/3/67, BUfile 157-3744-10; FBI Letterhead Memorandum, Tampa, Florida, 12/6/67, BUfile 157-3744-11.
3. FBI Memorandum, SAC, Jackson to Director, FBI, 4/2/68, BUfile 157-3744-12, pp. 1-2.
4. FBI Report, SA [Deleted], Jackson to Bureau, Secret Service, et. al., 10/23/68, BUfile 157-3744-13, p. 15.
5. Ibid., p. 18; Nelson, pp. 151, 159, 200.
6. Turner, p. 58; Raines, pp. 355-60.
7. *Playboy* 10/71, p. 80.
8. Tarrants, p. 3; Nelson, pp. 53-4, 115.
9. Nelson, pp. 44, 115.
10. Whitehead, p. 290.
11. FBI Report, SA [Deleted], Jackson to Bureau, Secret Service, et. al., 10/23/68, BUfile 157-3744-13, p. 2; Copy of Beckwith letter to Associate Editor Fred Blahut of *The Spotlight*, 4/1/87, pp. 6-8, author's collection.
12. Tarrants, pp. 33-41.
13. Nelson, pp. 24-9.
14. Ibid, p. 169.
15. Tarrants, pp. 56-9.
16. *New South*, Fall 1968, p. 44.
17. Nelson, pp. 150, 198.
18. Tarrants, pp. 4-5.
19. Ibid., pp. 5-7; *New South*, Fall 1968, p. 46.
20. Tarrants, p. 7.
21. Whitehead, pp. 294-5; Tarrants, p. 124.
22. Sims, p. 164. Tarrants's memoir, *The Conversion of a Klansman*, is the fullest account of his religious conversion and its profound impact on his life.
23. Tarrants, pp. 125-6.
24. AJC 9/30/73, p. 2-A; Nelson, p. 219.
25. Turner, p. 56; *New South*, Fall 1968, pp. 41-57; Nelson, p. 186.
26. Whitehead, p. 297; *New South*, Fall 1968, p. 42; FBI Report, SA [Deleted], Jackson to Bureau, Secret Service, et. al., 10/23/68, BUfile 157-3744-13, p. 12.
27. See NYT 1/21/74, p. 10 and *The Spotlight* 8/24/87, p. 30.
28. FBI Report, SA [Deleted], Jackson to Bureau, Secret Service, et. al., 10/23/68, BUfile 157-3744-13, pp. 13-4.
29. Nelson, p. 190.
30. FBI Report, SA [Deleted], Jackson to Bureau, Secret Service, et. al., 10/23/68, BUfile 157-3744-13, pp. 13-4.
31. FBI Memorandum, SAC Jackson to Director, FBI 10/21/70, BUfile 157-3744-14, pp. 1-2.
32. Social Security Death Index records for Wesley Swift; FBI Report, Jackson to Bureau, et. al., 8/22/75, BUfile 157-3744-58, p. 4.
33. Letter from Beckwith to Mary Louise Williams, 4/19/73, author's collection; Scott, R.W., p. 174.
34. The Association of Independent Methodists brochures: "Purposes! Why Organized! Organizational Structure!" and "A.I.M. for the 70's;" [sic] author's collection.
35. Miscellaneous First Independent Methodist Church programs and Association of Independent Methodists ephemera, author's collection; Letters from Beckwith to Mary Louise Williams, 5/5/73 and 5/27/73, author's collection.
36. Mintz, pp. 5-6, 71, 77-8; Ridgeway, pp. 64-5.
37. *Time* 8/17/62, p. 19; Ridgeway, p. 68; Rockwell, pp. 431-4.
38. Letter from Beckwith to Mary Louise Williams, 5/5/73, author's collection.
39. Beckwith form letter addressed to "Dear Friend," pasted in copies of *None Dare Call It Conspiracy*, author's collection.
40. Forster and Epstein, pp. 287-90; Mintz, p. 148; Filler, p. 232.

41. Beckwith letter to author, 3/27/87, author's collection.
42. Press announcement regarding Beckwith's candidacy for Congress, marked "First Draft" but never released, author's collection; Letters from Beckwith to Mary Louise Williams, 5/5/73 and 11/16/76, author's collection.
43. Letter from Beckwith to Mary Louise Williams, 5/5/73, author's collection.
44. Ibid.
45. Letters from Beckwith to Mary Louise Williams, 4/19/73 and 11/16/76, author's collection.
46. FBI Teletype, New Orleans to Director, Attention: Intelligence Division; Jackson, 9/27/73, BUfile 157-3744-18; FBI Letterhead Memorandum, 10/30/73, BUfile 157-3744-26, p. 4; In a 5/13/82 letter to Beckwith, J.B. Stoner named Gordon Clark as the informant; copy, author's collection. Clark died in March 1982 in Jackson.
47. FBI Teletype, Jackson to Director, Attn: Intelligence Division, 9/28/73, BUfile 157-3744-23, pp. 2-3; New Orleans Police Department Report, Arrest of Byron De La Beckwith, Item I-22796-73, 10/9/73, pp. 2-3.
48. Nelson, pp. 249-50.
49. New Orleans Police Department Report, Arrest of Byron De La Beckwith, Item I-22796-73, 10/9/73, pp. 2, 13.
50. FBI Teletype, New Orleans to Director, Attention: Intelligence Division; Jackson, 9/27/73, BUfile 157-3744-18; FBI Memorandum, Director, FBI to Attorney General, 10/2/73, BUfile 157-3744-17, pp. 1-2; New Orleans Police Department Report, Arrest of Byron De La Beckwith, Item I-22796-73, 10/9/73, pp. 3-6; FBI Letterhead Memorandum, 10/30/73, BUfile 157-3744-26, p. 2; Letter from Beckwith to Mary Louise Williams, 2/17/75, author's collection.
51. Reporter's Transcript, *State of Louisiana* v. *Byron De La Beckwith*, Criminal District Court, Parish of Orleans, Case No. 238-459, May 15-16, 1975, p. 252; FBI Teletype, New Orleans to Director, Attn: Intelligence Division, 9/27/73, BUfile 157-3744-19.
52. New Orleans Police Department Report, Arrest of Byron De La Beckwith, Item I-22796-73, 10/9/73, pp. 4-16.
53. FBI Memorandum, Director, FBI to Attorney General, 10/2/73, BUfile 157-3744-17, pp. 1-2; FBI Letterhead Memorandum, 10/30/73, BUfile 157-3744-26, p. 2; FBI Teletype, New Orleans to Director, Attention: Intelligence Division; Jackson, 9/27/73, BUfile 157-3744-18, p. 4.
54. NYP 9/29/73, pp. 2, 8; Sims, p. 160. NOTP 9/28/73, p. 1.
55. NOTP 9/28/73, p. 1; NYT 9/28/73, p. 35; AJC 9/30/73, p. 2-A.
56. NOSI 9/27/73, pp. 1, 3.
57. NOTP 10/2/73, p. 1; NOTP 10/10/73, p. 24; NYT 10/21/73, p. 48; FBI Teletype, New Orleans to Director, Attn: Intelligence Division, 10/10/73, BUfile 157-3744-21; Copy of Beckwith letter to Associate Editor Fred Blahut of *The Spotlight*, 4/1/87, pp. 4-5, author's collection.
58. NOTP 10/7/73, Section One, p. 42; NOTP 10/11/73, Section Two, p. 8; NYT 10/12/73, p. 13; NOTP 1/20/74, Section One, p. 3.
59. Copy of Beckwith letter, "Dear Christian Patriots—one and all," circa 11/73, author's collection; Beckwith letter to author 9/3/86, author's collection.
60. FBI Report, Jackson to Bureau, et. al., 8/22/75, BUfile 157-3744-58, pp. 8-9.
61. FBI Teletype, Jackson to Director and New Orleans, 11/20/73, BUfile 157-3744-27, p. 1.
62. FBI Informative Note, 11/23/73, preceding BUfile 157-3744-28.
63. FBI Informative Note, [No Citation Information], 1/16/74, preceding BUfile 157-3744-32.
64. NOTP 1/15/74, Section One, p. 6; NOSI 1/15/74, p. 1.
65. NOTP 1/18/74, Section One, p. 6; NOTP 1/20/74, p. 1.
66. NOTP 1/15/75, p. 6; FBI Informative Note, 1/19/74, preceding BUfile 157-3744-31; NOTP 1/20/74, Section One, p. 3; NYT 1/21/74, p. 10.
67. NYT 1/21/74, p. 10; GC 1/21/74, p. 1.
68. Reporter's Transcript, *State of Louisiana* v. *Byron De La Beckwith*, Criminal District Court, Parish of Orleans, Case No. 238-459, 5/15-1675, p. 99.
69. FBI Memorandum, Director, FBI to Assistant Attorney General, Criminal Division, 3/6/74, BUfile 157-3744-35; FBI Urgent Teletype, SAC, New Orleans to Director, FBI, 11/12/74, BUfile 157-3744-41, p. 3.
70. Beckwith letter to author 8/6/86; Copy of letter from Beckwith to "All of Masonry," 1/15/78, p. 1; both, author's collection.
71. Copy of Beckwith letter to Associate Editor Fred Blahut of *The Spotlight*, 4/1/87, p. 6, author's collection.
72. Reporter's Transcript, *State of Louisiana* v. *Byron De La Beckwith*, Criminal District

Court, Parish of Orleans, Case No. 238-459, 5/15-1675, p. 183.
73. Ibid., p. 439.
74. Ibid., pp. 480, 484, 493; NOTP 5/17/75, p. 1.
75. JCL 3/1/77, p. 14; FBI Teletype, New Orleans to Director, FBI, and Jackson, 5/17/75, BUfile 157-3744-50; FBI Airtel, SAC, New Orleans to Director, FBI, 8/13/75, BUfile 157-3744-57; NOTP 8/2/75, p. 4; GC 8/4/75, p. 1. The jurors were five black women, and Beckwith expected a verdict of guilty. See Scott, R.W., p. 208: "It was no surprise to Beckwith when the quintet of acquiescent darkies came frolicking down from the jury room with a crudely scribbled verdict of guilty."
76. FBI Letter, Director, FBI to SAC, Jackson, 11/26/74, BUfile 157-3744-43, pp. 1-2.
77. FBI Report, Jackson to Bureau, et. al., 8/22/75, BUfile 157-3744-58, pp. Cover-6.
78. Ibid.
79. Letter from Beckwith to Mary Louise Williams, 4/25/75, author's collection; Scott, R.W., p. 175.
80. Letters from Beckwith to Mary Louise Williams, 12/28/74 and 2/1/75, author's collection.
81. Scott, R.W., p. 175.
82. FBI Memorandum, SAC, Jackson to Director, FBI, 6/24/76, BUfile 157-3744-64.
83. Copy of Christmas card from Sam H. Bowers, Jr. to Beckwith, postmarked 12/22/76, author's collection.
84. CTR 7/20/86, Section 5, pp. 1, 6; Melton, pp. 53-61.
85. Tarrants, p. 40.
86. Nelson, p. 119.
87. *Activities of Ku Klux Klan Organizations in the United States, Part 5,* Hearings Before the Committee on Un-American Activities, House of Representatives, Eighty-Ninth Congress, Second Session, February 14, 15, 21, 23 and 24, 1966; September 29, July 28, August 24, and October 6, 1965; and January 28, 1966, pp. 3809-10. The HCUA document reprints the AC article, dated 7/5/46, without page citation; *Hate Groups in America: A Record of Bigotry and Violence,* a publication of The Anti-Defamation League of B'nai B'rith, p. 37.
88. Sims, p. 164; Raines, p. 322; *America* 9/9/72, p. 153; Forster and Epstein, p. 301.
89. Zatarain, pp. 110-7.
90. Letter from Beckwith to Mary Louise Williams, 11/16/76 author's collection; AJC 3/3/91, p. M4.
91. Zatarain, pp. 229-31; Turner, p. 113.
92. *Extremism on the Right,* a publication of The Anti-Defamation League of B'nai B'rith, pp. 168-70; *Hate Groups in America: A Record of Bigotry and Violence,* a publication of The Anti-Defamation League of B'nai B'rith, p. 46.
93. Copy of letter to Beckwith from Reverend Kern Wickware, First Independent Methodist Church, 10/11/76, author's collection.
94. Sims, p. 163.
95. *The Battle Ax N.E.W.S.,* 10/76, p. 10; ADL Facts, Spring 1983, Vol. 28, No. 1, *The "Identity Churches": A Theology of Hate,* pp. 9-10; *Hate Groups in America: A Record of Bigotry and Violence,* a publication of The Anti-Defamation League of B'nai B'rith, p. 46; Flynn and Gerhardt, p. 54; Singular, p. 49.
96. KNS 3/31/75, p. 12.
97. Copy of Beckwith's original ordination certificate, 1/2/77, author's collection.
98. *State of Louisiana* v. *Byron De La Beckwith,* Supreme Court of Louisiana, 2/28/77 (Rehearing denied 4/22/77); NOTP 3/1/77, p. 3; CA 3/1/77, p. 3.
99. FBI Memorandum, SAC, New Orleans to Director, FBI, 4/26/77, BUfile 157-3744-72, pp. 1-2.
100. Copy of Beckwith letter to Associate Editor Fred Blahut of *The Spotlight,* 4/1/87, pp. 6-8, author's collection.
101. WP 4/30/77, p. C-2; NOTP 4/30/77, p. 6.
102. Copy of Beckwith letter to Associate Editor Fred Blahut of *The Spotlight,* 4/1/87, pp. 8-10, author's collection.
103. Ibid., pp. 11-3.

13 THE OUTSKIRTS OF HEAVEN

1. Scott, R.W., pp. 213-4.
2. Copy of Beckwith letter to Fred Blahut, Associate Editor of *The Spotlight,* 4/1/87, p. 13, author's collection; recounted by Thelma Neff Beckwith in a 5/24/91 interview.
3. Copy of Beckwith letter to Fred Blahut, Associate Editor of of *The Spotlight,* 4/1/87, p. 14, author's collection; Scott, R.W., p. 216.
4. Letter from Beckwith to Mary Louise Williams, 11/16/76, author's collection; Scott, R.W., p. 193.
5. Copy of Beckwith letter to "Those of you who have known me from my youth," circa 1987, author's collection.
6. Scott, R.W., pp. 213-5; JCL 12/18/90, p. 9-A.

7. Copy of letter to Bank of Greenwood from J.B. Stoner, 5/1/79, author's collection; Scott, R.W., pp. 175.
8. *Extremism Targets the Prisons: An ADL Special Report*, a publication of The Anti-Defamation League of B'nai B'rith, pp. 1-9; Coates, pp. 221-2; Singular, pp. 51-2; *Hate Groups in America: A Record of Bigotry and Violence*, a publication of The Anti-Defamation League of B'nai B'rith, pp. 55-9; copy of *The Councilor*, 12/30/78, addressed to Beckwith at Angola, author's collection.
9. Martinez with Guinther, p. 140.
10. Aryan Nations pamphlet "Love or Hate? White Racism: Where Does it Come From?"
11. Scott, R.W., pp. 51, 204-5.
12. *Aryan Nations* newsletter, 4/83, pp. 9-12; *Inter-Klan Newsletter*, circa May 1983, p. 2; Dees, p. 7; ADL Special Report, May 1985, *Propaganda of the Deed": The Far Right's Desperate 'Revolution'*, p. 10; Ridgeway, pp. 87-9.
13. *Aryan Nations* newsletter, 4/83, p. 12.
14. Copies of letters from Pete Scalise to Beckwith, 6/2/78 and 6/3/78, author's collection.
15. Ibid.
16. Scott, R.W., pp. 215-6 and 225.
17. GC 4/7/78, p. 4.
18. *Jackson* 6/78, p. 8.
19. Enclosure in Beckwith letter to the author, 1/29/87, author's collection.
20. Copy of letter from Beckwith to "All of Masonry," 1/15/78, p. 1, author's collection.
21. Ibid., p. 1.
22. Ibid., p. 2.
23. Ibid., pp. 5-6 and 11; copy of letter to Beckwith from A.H. Richter, Secretary and Recorder, Greenwood Lodge No. 135, F.&A.M., 1/31/78, author's collection.
24. Copy of letter from Beckwith to "Dear Able Servants of our King," 1/1/79, author's collection.
25. Copy of Beckwith letter to "Any 'Conservative' Law Firm in Louisiana anxious to take up my claim: Also, Concerned Auto Dealers," circa 1979, author's collection.
26. Letters from Beckwith to the author, 6/30/92 [notation on Issue 137 of *The CDL Report*] and 11/24/92, author's collection; Scott, R.W., p. 226.
27. Copy of Aryan Nations mailing list circa 1982 with date of 6/24/80 noted beneath Beckwith's listing.
28. Oakley, p. 5; Flynn and Gerhardt, p. 336; Beckwith letter to the author, 6/30/92, author's collection.
29. Scott, R.W., p. 175.
30. Western Union Telegram from Beckwith to Mary Louise Williams, 4/19/73, author's collection.
31. Letters from Beckwith to his former wife, 4/19/73 and 5/13/73, author's collection.
32. Letters from Beckwith to his former wife, 4/25/75 and 11/16/76, author's collection.
33.JCL 2/2/92, p. 1A, 11A.
34. Copy of the title page of Thelma Neff Beckwith's copy of *Line of Departure: Tarawa*, dated 11/27/81.
35. Sequatchie County, Tennessee, Marriage Record Book 10, P. 372.;JCL 2/2/92, p. 1, 11A ; CNFP 1/8/91, p. A6.
36. CT 12/19/90, p. A9.
37. Copy of letter from Beckwith addressed "An open letter to the Town of Walden's Water Board," 10/24/86, author's collection; CT 12/19/90, p. A9.
38. CNFP 7/21/85, p. K8.
39. Martinez with Guinther, p. 54.
40. Copy of letter from Beckwith addressed "An open letter to the Town of Walden's Water Board," 10/24/86, author's collection.
41. Copy of Beckwith letter to Associate Editor Fred Blahut of *The Spotlight*, 4/1/87, p. 2, author's collection; Letter from Beckwith to the author, 5/4/86, author's collection.
42. Copy of Thelma Beckwith Affidavit C filed in the Criminal Court of Hamilton County Tennessee, Division II, Record on Appeal No. 185562, 1/10/91.
43. Beckwith letters to the author, 8/6/86, 10/21/86 and 12/23/87, author's collection.
44. Copy of letter to Beckwith from Hugh J. Moore, Jr., Witt, Gaither & Whitaker, 9/6/84; copy of letter to Beckwith from John R. Rarick, Rarick and Brumfield, 12/23/85; Beckwith letter to the author, 10/21/86; all, author's collection.
45. Copy of letter to Beckwith from Carroll County Circuit Court Clerk Charles Ellis, 3/6/86, author's collection.
46. JCL 6/9/91, pp. 1, 17A.
47. Copy of letter to Beckwith from Edwin W. Edwards, 5/27/86; copy of letter to Thelma Beckwith from Edwin W. Edwards, 7/1/86; both, author's collection.
48. Copy of University of Mississippi Medical Center Authorization for Anatomical Gift signed by Byron De La Beckwith, 12/8/83; copy of Beckwith letter to Hon. Webb Franklin, 2/14/84; both, author's collection.
49. *The KKK and the Neo-Nazis: A 1984 Status Report*, a publication of The Anti-

Defamation League of B'nai B'rith, 11/84, p. 8.
50. Beckwith letter to the author, 1/29/87, author's collection.
51. Beckwith letters to the author, 10/21/86 and 6/30/92; Crusade Against Corruption flyer; all, author's collection.
52. Christian Guard Dispatch No. 77, "The Inevitability of Conflict," circa 1986, author's collection.
53. Beckwith letter to the author, 10/21/86; United Nationalist Party flyer; both, author's collection.
54. Flyers from APRA to Beckwith, one postmarked 4/15/86; Beckwith letters to the author, 4/22/86 and 9/3/86; all, author's collection.
55. *Newsweek* 9/19/88, p. 21; *"Propaganda of the Deed": The Far Right's Desperate Revolution,* ADL Special Report, 5/85, p. 1; *Extremism on the Right,* a publication of The Anti-Defamation League of B'nai B'rith, pp. 51-4; *Hate Groups in America: A Record of Bigotry and Violence,* a publication of The Anti-Defamation League of B'nai B'rith, p. 43.
56. Coates, p. 152; Flynn and Gerhardt, pp. 139-40, 188, 258-9, 307; *Extremism on the Right,* a publication of The Anti-Defamation League of B'nai B'rith, p. 126.
57. Martinez with Guinther, p. 196; *Hate Groups in America: A Record of Bigotry and Violence,* a publication of The Anti-Defamation League of B'nai B'rith, pp. 42-3.
58. *Harper's* 7/86, pp. 53-62; *Extremism on the Right,* a publication of The Anti-Defamation League of B'nai B'rith, p. 52.
59. NYT 10/30/91, p. A18.
60. See Numbers 25:6-14.
61. Martinez with Guinther, pp. 33-4.
62. Crawford, p. 395.
63. Hoskins, p. vi.
64. Beckwith letter to the author, 6/30/92, author's collection.
65. LNDA 11/1/91, p. A3.
66. AJC 11/3/91, p. A16.
67. Hoskins, pp. v, 63, 77, 232-3, and 244.
68. Ibid., p. vi; Scott, R.W., p. 174.
69. Hoskins, p. 65.
70. *Hoskins Report* 2/4/91, p. 4.
71. *State of Mississippi* vs. *Byron De La Beckwith,* Circuit Court of the First Judicial District of Hinds County, Mississippi, #90-3-945 [CR] [C], 11/12/91, p. 68.
72. Abrahamsen, pp. 20–1; McMillan, p. 257, 265–6.
73. "Who Killed Medgar Evers?" segment transcript, "PrimeTime Live," 6/14/90, p. 4; *The Independent* 10/16/91, p. X.

Bibliography

SELECTED BOOKS

Abernathy, Ralph David. *And the Walls Came Tumbling Down.* Harper & Row, 1989.

Abrahamsen, David. *The Murdering Mind.* Harper & Row, 1973.

Ahmann, Matthew H., ed. *The New Negro.* Fides Publishers, 1961.

Aldridge, Minter, ed. *The Deltonian 1940.* Published by the Greenwood High School Senior Class, 1940.

Allen, Gary with Abraham, Larry. *None Dare Call It Conspiracy.* Concord Press, 1971.

Allport, Gordon W. *The Nature of Prejudice.* Doubleday Anchor Books, 1958.

Amann, William Frayne, ed. *Personnel of the Civil War.* Thomas Yoseloff, 1961.

Ashmore, Harry S. *The Negro and the Schools.* The University of North Carolina Press, 1954.

Baker, Ray Stannard. *Following the Color Line: American Negro Citizenship in the Progressive Era.* Harper Torchbooks, 1964.

Baldwin, Hanson W. *Battles Lost and Won: Great Campaigns of World War II.* Harper & Row, 1966.

Beck, Warren A. and Williams, David A. *California: A History of the Golden State.* Doubleday & Co., Inc., 1972.

Belfrage, Sally. *Freedom Summer.* Fawcett Crest, 1966.

Bell, Daniel, ed. *The Radical Right.* Anchor Books, 1964.

Benedict, Ruth. *Race: Science and Politics.* The Viking Press, 1964.

Berman, Daniel M. *It Is So Ordered: The Supreme Court Rules on School Segregation.* W.W. Norton & Co., Inc., 1966.

Bickel, Alexander M. *The Supreme Court and the Idea of Progress.* Harper Torchbooks, 1970.

Bilbo, Theodore G. *Take Your Choice: Separation or Mongrelization.* Historical Review Press U.S.A., 1980.

Birmingham, Stephen. *California Rich.* Simon and Schuster, 1980.

Black, Earl. *Southern Governors and Civil Rights: Racial Segregation as a Campaign Issue in the Second Reconstruction.* Harvard University Press, 1976.

Brady, Tom P. *Black Monday: Segregation or Amalgamation . . . America Has Its Choice.* Citizens Councils of America, 1955.

Branch, Taylor. *Parting the Waters: America in the King Years 1954–63.* Simon and Schuster, 1988.

Broderick, Francis L. and Meier, August, eds. *Negro Protest Thought in the Twentieth Century.* The Bobbs-Merrill Company, Inc., 1965.

Brough, R. Clayton. *The Lost Tribes: History, Doctrine, Prophecies, and Theories About Israel's Lost Ten Tribes.* Horizon Publishers, 1979.

Brown, Robert McAfee. *Religion and Violence: A Primer for White Americans.* The Westminster Press, 1973.

Brown, William Garrott. *The Lower South in American History.* Greenwood Press, Publishers, 1969. (Reprint of a 1902 Macmillan Co. edition.)

Burk, Robert Fredrick. *The Eisenhower Administration and Black Civil Rights.* The University of Tennessee Press/Knoxville, 1984.

Cagin, Seth and Dray, Philip. *We Are Not Afraid: The Story of Goodman, Schwerner, and Chaney and the Civil Rights Campaign for Mississippi.* Macmillan Publishing Company, 1988.

Campbell, Will D. *Race and the Renewal of the Church.* The Westminster Press, 1962.

Carmer, Carl. *Stars Fell on Alabama.* The Literary Guild, 1934.

Carson, Clayborne. *In Struggle: SNCC and the Black Awakening of the 1960s.* Harvard University Press, 1982.

Carter, Jane Foster. *If The Walls Could Talk.* The Heritage Preservation Committee/City of Colusa, California, 1988.

Cash, W.J. *The Mind of the South.* Alfred A. Knopf, 1941.

Cavan, Ruth Shonle. *The American Family.* Thomas Y. Crowell Co., 1969.

Chalmers, David M. *Hooded Americanism: The History of the Ku Klux Klan.* Duke University Press, 1987.

Clark, Thomas D. and Kirwan, Albert D. *The South Since Appomattox: A Century of Regional Change.* Oxford University Press, 1967.

Coates, James. *Armed and Dangerous: The Rise of the Survivalist Right.* Hill and Wang, 1987.

Cooper, William J. and Terrill, Thomas E. *The American South: A History.* Alfred A. Knopf, 1990.

Crain, Robert L. *The Politics of School Desegregation.* Anchor Books, 1969.

Crawford, Jarah B. *Last Battle Cry: Christianity's Final Conflict with Evil.* Jann Publishing, 1986.

Davies, R.E.G. *A History of the World's Airlines.* Oxford University Press, 1964.

Davis, Allison; Gardner, Burleigh B.; and Gardner, Mary R. *Deep South: A Social Anthropological Study of Caste and Class.* University of Chicago Press, 1941.

Davis, Lenwood G. and Sims-Wood, Janet L. *The Ku Klux Klan: A Bibliography.* Greenwood Press, 1984.

Dees, Morris, with Fiffer, Steve. *A Season for Justice: The Life and Times of Civil Rights Lawyer Morris Dees.* Charles Scribner's Sons, 1991.

———. *Hate on Trial: The Case Against America's Most Dangerous Neo-Nazi.* Villard Books, 1993.

De Haan, Richard W. *Israel and the Nations in Prophecy.* Zondervan Books, 1968.

Dennis, Delmar Daniel. *To Stand Alone: Inside the KKK for the FBI.* Covenant House Books, 1991.

De Toledano, Ralph. *RFK: The Man Who Would Be President.* G.P. Putnam's Sons, 1967.

Dunn, L.C. and Dobzhansky, T.H. *Heredity, Race and Society.* Pelican Books, 1946.

Eagles, Charles W., ed. *The Civil Rights Movement in America.* University Press of Mississippi, 1986.

Eaton, Clement. *A History of the Old South: The Emergence of a Reluctant Nation.* Macmillan Publishing Co., Inc., 1975.

Ellul, Jacques. *Violence: Reflections from a Christian Perspective.* The Seabury Press, 1969.

Evers, Charles, with Halsell, Grace. *Evers.* The World Publishing Company, 1971.

Evers, Mrs. Medgar, with Peters, William. *For Us, The Living.* Doubleday, 1967.

Finch, Phillip. *God, Guts, and Guns: A Close Look at the Radical Right.* Seaview/Putnam, 1983.

Fisher, William H. *The Invisible Empire: A Bibliography of the Ku Klux Klan.* The Scarecrow Press, Inc., 1980.

Flynn, Kevin and Gerhardt, Gary. *The Silent Brotherhood: Inside America's Racist Underground.* The Free Press, 1989.

Forster, Arnold and Epstein, Benjamin R. *The New Anti-Semitism.* McGraw-Hill, 1974.

Foster, Gaines M. *Ghosts of the Confederacy: Defeat, the Lost Cause, and the Emergence of the New South 1865 to 1913.* Oxford University Press, 1987.

Fredrickson, George M. *White Supremacy: A Comparative Study in American and South African History.* Oxford University Press, 1981.

Frey, Herman S. *Jefferson Davis.* Frey Enterprises, 1977.

Friedman, Leon, ed. *Southern Justice.* Pantheon Books, 1965.

Garrow, David J. *Bearing the Cross: Martin Luther King, Jr., and the Southern Christian Leadership Conference.* William Morrow, 1986.

Gayer, M.H. *The Heritage of the Anglo Saxon Race.* Destiny Publishers, 1941.

Gentry, Curt. *J. Edgar Hoover: The Man and the Secrets.* W.W. Norton & Co., Inc., 1991.

Green, A. Wigfall. *The Man Bilbo.* Louisiana State University Press, 1963.

Green, Will S. *Colusa County, California.* Elliott and Moore, San Francisco, 1880.
Hampton, Henry and Fayer, Steve. *Voices of Freedom: An Oral History of the Civil Rights Movement from the 1950s through the 1980s.* Bantam Books, 1990.
Hanks, B.J. *The Segregationist.* Unpublished manuscript. Author's collection.
Haselden, Kyle. *The Racial Problem in Christian Perspective.* Harper Torchbooks, 1964.
Herskovits, Melville J. *The American Negro: A Study in Racial Crossing.* Indiana University Press, 1968.
———. *The Myth of the Negro Past.* Beacon Press, 1964.
Holt, Len. *The Summer That Didn't End.* William Morrow & Co., 1965.
Hoover, Mildred Brooke; Rensch, Hero Eugene; and Rensch, Ethel Grace. *Historic Spots in California.* Stanford University Press, 1966.
Horn, Stanley F. *Invisible Empire: The Story of the Ku Klux Klan 1866–1871.* John E. Edwards, Publisher, 1969.
Hoskins, Richard Kelly. *Vigilantes of Christendom: The Story of the Phineas Priesthood.* The Virginia Publishing Company, 1990.
Humphrey, Hubert H., ed. *Integration vs. Segregation.* Thomas Y. Crowell Co., 1964.
Jacoway, Elizabeth and Colburn, David R., eds. *Southern Businessmen and Desegregation.* Louisiana State University Press, 1982.
Johnston, Erle. *I Rolled with Ross: A Political Portrait.* Moran Publishing Corporation, 1980.
———. *Mississippi's Defiant Years: 1953–1973.* Lake Harbor Publishers, 1990.
Katz, William Loren. *The Invisible Empire: The Ku Klux Klan Impact on History.* Open Hand Publishing Inc., 1986.
Kenkel, William F. *The Family in Perspective.* Goodyear Publishing Co., Inc., 1977.
Kilpatrick, James Jackson. *The Southern Case for School Segregation.* The Crowell-Collier Press, 1962.
Kunstler, William M. *Deep in My Heart.* William Morrow & Co., 1966.
Lipset, Seymour Martin and Raab, Earl. *The Politics of Unreason: Right-Wing Extremism in America, 1790–1970.* Harper Torchbook, 1973.
Lunde, Donald T. *Murder and Madness.* San Francisco Book Company, Inc., 1976.
Martin, John Bartlow. *The Deep South Says "Never."* Ballantine Books, 1957.
Martin, Ralph G. *A Hero for Our Time.* Macmillan, 1983.
Martinez, Thomas with Guinther, John. *Brotherhood of Murder.* McGraw-Hill, 1988.
Mays, Benjamin E. *Seeking to Be Christian in Race Relations.* Friendship Press, Inc., 1957.
McAdam, Doug. *Freedom Summer.* Oxford University Press, 1988.
McComish, Charles David and Lambert, Rebecca T. *History of Colusa and Glenn Counties, California, with Biographical Sketches.* Historic Record Company, 1918.
McCuen, Gary E. *The Religious Right.* Gary E. McCuen Publications, Inc., 1989.
McIlhaney, William H. II. *Klandestine: The Untold Story of Delmar Dennis and His Role in the FBI's War Against the Ku Klux Klan.* Arlington House, 1975.
McMillan, Priscilla Johnson. *Marina and Lee.* Harper & Row, 1977.
McMillin, Laurence. *The Schoolmaker: Sawney Webb and the Bell Buckle Story.* The University of North Carolina Press, 1971.
McMillen, Neil R. *The Citizens' Council: Organized Resistance to the Second Reconstruction, 1954–64.* University of Illinois Press, 1971.
Melton, J. Gordon. *Encyclopedic Handbook of Cults in America.* Garland Publishing Inc., 1986.
Mendelsohn, Jack. *The Martyrs: Sixteen Who Gave Their Lives for Racial Justice.* Harper & Row, 1966.
Meredith, James. *Three Years in Mississippi.* Indiana University Press, 1966.
Mintz, Frank P. *The Liberty Lobby and the American Right: Race, Conspiracy, and Culture.* Contributions in Political Science, Number 121, Greenwood Press, 1985.
Moody, Anne. *Coming of Age in Mississippi.* Dell Publishing Co., 1974.
Namorato, Michael V., ed. *Have We Overcome? Race Relations Since Brown.* University Press of Mississippi, 1979.
Nash, Gary B. and Weiss, Richard. *The Great Fear: Race in the Mind of America.* Holt, Rinehart and Winston, Inc., 1970.
Nelson, Jack. *Terror in the Night: The Klan's Campaign Against the Jews.* Simon & Schuster, 1993.
Oakley, Andy. *88: An Undercover News Reporter's Expose of American Nazis and the Ku Klux Klan.* P.O. Publishing Company, 1987.
Overstreet, Harry A. and Overstreet, Bonaro W. *The Strange Tactics of Extremism.* W.W. Norton & Co., Inc., 1964.

Patai, Raphael and Wing, Jennifer Patai. *The Myth of the Jewish Race.* Charles Scribner's Sons, 1975.

Peltason, J.W. *58 Lonely Men: Southern Federal Judges and School Desegregation.* Harcourt, Brace & World, Inc., 1961.

Perlmutter, Nathan and Perlmutter, Ruth Ann. *The Real Anti-Semitism in Ameria.* Arbor House, 1982.

Polenberg, Richard. *One Nation Divisible: Class, Race, and Ethnicity in the United States Since 1938.* The Viking Press, 1980.

Powledge, Fred. *Free at Last? The Civil Rights Movement and the People Who Made It.* Little, Brown and Company, 1991.

Quarles, Benjamin. *The Negro in the Making of America.* Collier Books, 1969.

Raines, Howell. *My Soul is Rested: Movement Days in the Deep South Remembered.* G.P. Putnam's Sons, 1977.

Rand, Howard R. *The Covenant People.* Destiny Publishers, 1972.

Record, Wilson. *Race and Radicalism: The NAACP and the Communist Party in Conflict.* Cornell University Press, 1964.

Ridgeway, James. *Blood in the Face: The Ku Klux Klan, Aryan Nations, Nazi Skinheads, and the Rise of a New White Culture.* Thunder's Mouth Press, 1990.

Rockwell, George Lincoln. *White Power.* New Christian Crusade Church, 1972.

Rowland, Dunbar. *Military History of Mississippi 1803–1898.* The Reprint Company, Publishers, 1978.

Rose, Peter I. *They & We: Racial and Ethnic Relations in the United States.* Random House, 1965.

Rosenberg, Alfred. *Race and Race History.* Harper Torchbooks, 1970.

Rowe, Gary Thomas, Jr. *My Undercover Years with the Ku Klux Klan.* Bantam Books, 1976.

Russ, Martin. *Line of Departure: Tarawa.* Doubleday & Co., 1975.

Salter, John R., Jr. *Jackson, Mississippi: An American Chronicle of Struggle and Schism.* Exposition Press, 1979.

Sanders, Ronald. *Lost Tribes and Promised Lands: The Origins of American Racism.* Little, Brown and Company, 1978.

Scott, Anne Firor. *The Southern Lady: From Pedestal to Politics 1830–1930.* The University of Chicago Press, 1970.

Scott, R.W. *Glory in Conflict; A Saga of Byron De La Beckwith.* Camark Press, 1991.

Silberman, Charles E. *Crisis in Black and White.* Vintage Books, 1964.

Silver, James W. *Mississippi: The Closed Society.* Harcourt, Brace & World, Inc., 1964.

———. *Running Scared: Silver in Mississippi.* University Press of Mississippi, 1984.

Sims, Patsy. *The Klan.* Stein & Day, 1978.

Sinclair, Mary Craig. *Southern Belle.* Sinclair Press, 1962.

Sinclair, Upton. *American Outpost.* Farrar & Rinehart, 1932.

———. *The Autobiography of Upton Sinclair.* Harcourt, Brace & World, Inc., 1962.

Singular, Stephen: *Talked to Death: The Life and Murder of Alan Berg.* Beech Tree Books, 1987.

Sitkoff, Harvard. *The Struggle for Black Equality 1954–1980.* Hill and Wang, 1987.

Smith, Frank E. *Congressman from Mississippi.* Pantheon Books, 1964.

Smith, Lillian. *Now is the Time.* The Viking Press, 1955.

Sorensen, Theodore C. *Kennedy.* Harper & Row, Publishers, 1965.

Stang, Alan. *It's Very Simple: The True Story of Civil Rights.* Western Islands, 1965.

Steffgen, Kent H. *The Bondage of the Free.* Vanguard Books, 1966.

Sugarman, Tracy. *Stranger at the Gates: A Summer in Mississippi.* Hill and Wang, 1966.

Tarrants, Thomas A. III. *The Conversion of a Klansman: The Story of a Former Ku Klux Klan Terrorist.* Doubleday & Company, Inc., 1979.

Thernstrom, Stephan, ed. *Prejudice: A Series of Selections from the Harvard Encyclopedia of American Ethnic Groups.* The Belknap Press of Harvard University Press, 1982.

Thompson, Jerry. *My Life in the Klan.* Rutledge Hill Press, 1988.

Topp, Mildred Spurrier. *Smile Please.* Houghton Mifflin Company, 1948.

Turner, William W. *Power on the Right.* Ramparts Press, 1971.

Villano, Anthony with Astor, Gerald. *Brick Agent: Inside the Mafia for the FBI.* Quadrangle/ The New York Times Book Company, 1977.

Von Hoffman, Nicholas. *Mississippi Notebook.* David White Company, 1964.

Wade, Wyn Craig. *The Fiery Cross: The Ku Klux Klan in America.* Touchstone, 1988.

Watson, Peter, ed. *Psychology and Race.* Aldine Publishing Company, 1973.

Watters, Pat and Cleghorn, Reese. *Climbing Jacob's Ladder: The Arrival of Negroes in Southern Politics.* Harcourt, Brace & World, Inc., 1967.

Weisbrot, Robert. *Freedom Bound: A History of America's Civil Rights Movement.* W.W. Norton & Co., 1990.

Welty, Eudora. *The Collected Stories of Eudora Welty.* Harcourt Brace Jovanovich, Publishers, 1980.

Wertham, Fredric. *The Show of Violence.* Doubleday & Co., Inc., 1949.

Whitehead, Don. *Attack on Terror: The FBI Against the Ku Klux Klan in Mississippi.* Funk & Wagnalls, 1970.

Widney, Joseph P. *Race Life of the Aryan Peoples.* Funk & Wagnalls, 1907.

Wilkins, Roy, with Mathews, Tom. *Standing Fast: The Autobiography of Roy Wilkins.* The Viking Press, 1982.

Willard, W. Wyeth. *The Leathernecks Come Through.* Fleming H. Revell Co., 1944.

Williams, Juan. *Eyes on the Prize: America's Civil Rights Years, 1954–1965.* Viking Penguin Inc., 1987.

Willie, Charles V., Kramer, Bernard S., and Brown, Bertram S., eds. *Racism and Mental Health.* University of Pittsburgh Press, 1977.

Wilson, Charles Reagan and Ferris, William, coeds. *Encyclopedia of Southern Culture.* The University of North Carolina Press, 1989.

Woodward, C. Vann. *A History of the South, Vol. IX, Origins of the New South 1877–1913.* Louisiana State University Press, 1951.

———. *The Strange Career of Jim Crow.* Oxford University Press, 1966.

Wyatt-Brown, Bertram. *Southern Honor: Ethics & Behavior in the Old South.* Oxford University Press, 1982.

Young, Whitney M., Jr. *Beyond Racism: Building an Open Society.* McGraw Hill Book Company, 1969.

Zatarain, Michael. *David Duke: Evolution of a Klansman.* Pelican Publishing Company, 1990.

Zeskind, Leonard. *The 'Christian Identity' Movement: Analyzing Its Theological Rationalization for Racist and Anti-Semitic Violence.* Division of Church and Society of the National Council of the Churches of Christ in the U.S.A., 1987.

NEWSPAPERS

AC	Atlanta Constitution (Atlanta, GA)
AJ	Atlanta Journal (Atlanta, GA)
AJC	Atlanta Journal-Constitution (Atlanta, GA)
BN	Birmingham News (Birmingham, AL)
CA	The Commercial Appeal (Memphis, TN)
CDD	Chicago Daily Defender (Chicago, IL)
CH	The Colusa Herald (Colusa, CA)
CJ	The Courier-Journal (Louisville, KY)
CNFP	Chattanooga News-Free Press (Chattanooga, TN)
CDS	The Colusa Daily Sun (Colusa, CA)
CS	The Sun (Colusa, CA)
CT	The Chattanooga Times (Chattanooga, TN)
CTR	Chicago Tribune (Chicago, IL)
DP	The Daily Progress (Charlottesville, VA)
ENT	The Enterprise (Greenwood, MS)
GC	The Commonwealth (Greenwood, MS)
GMS	The Morning Star (Greenwood, MS)
HP	The Houston Post (Houston, TX)
JCL	The Clarion-Ledger (Jackson, MS)
JDN	Jackson Daily News (Jackson, MS)
KJ	The Knoxville Journal (Knoxville, TN)
KNS	The Knoxville News-Sentinel (Knoxville, TN)
LAT	Los Angeles Times (Los Angeles, CA)
LNDA	The News & Daily Advance (Lynchburg, VA)
LS	The Lodi Sentinel (Lodi, CA)
MFP	Mississippi Free Press (Jackson, MS)
MPS	Memphis Press-Scimitar (Memphis, TN)

MS Meridian Star (Meridian, MS)
NB The Nasvhille Banner (Nashville, TN)
ND Newsday (New York, NY)
NMDJ Northeast Mississippi Daily Journal (Tupelo, MS)
NOTP The Times-Picayune (New Orleans, LA)
NOSI The States-Item (New Orleans, LA)
NT The Tennessean (Nashville, TN)
NYN Daily News (New York, NY)
NYP New York Post (New York, NY)
NYT The New York Times (New York, NY)
RNL Richmond News Leader (Richmond, VA)
SB The Sacramento Bee (Sacramento, CA)
WP The Washington Post (Washington, D.C.)
WSJ The Wall Street Journal (New York, NY)
WSN Washington Star-News (Washington, D.C.)

SELECT PERIODICALS, PAMPHLETS AND FLYERS

Attention Goy! "We Have Accomplished Our Goal", a publication of Aryan Nations, Hayden Lake, ID.

The Battle Ax N.E.W.S., a publication of National Emancipation of the White Seed, Dandridge, TN and Humansville, MO.

Calling Our Nation, a publication of Aryan Nations, Hayden Lake, ID.

The CDL Report, a publication of the New Christian Crusade Church, Metarie, LA.

The Citizen, official journal of the Citizens' Councils of America, Jackson, MS.

Citizens Informer, a publication of Tri-State Informer, St. Louis, MO.

Citizens Rule Book, a publication of Liberty Lobby, Washington, D.C.

Communism is Dead: A Media Myth, a publication of Kingdom Restoration Ministries, Smithville, OK.

The Councilor, Shreveport, LA.

Freedman, Ben. *The Hidden Tyranny*, a publication of New Christian Crusade Church.

Hoskins Report, a publication of Richard Kelly Hoskins, Lynchburg, VA.

Inter-Klan Newsletter & Survival Alert, a joint Klan publication, Hayden Lake, ID.

Kingdom Chronicle, a publication of Stone Kingdom Ministries, Asheville, NC.

The Klan Ledger, a publication of the White Knights of the Ku Klux Klan of Mississippi.

Love or Hate—White Racism: Where Does It Come From?, a publication of Aryan Nations, Hayden Lake, ID.

Mohr, Brig. Gen. Jack. Editor of *The Christian Patriot Crusader* and author of the pamphlets *The Birthright or The Right to Govern, Christian Patriot's Defense League Citizen's Emergency Defense System, Satan's Kids*, and *Are You a True American?*

Praise God for AIDS, a publication of Crusade Against Corruption, Marietta, GA.

The Southern National Newsletter, a publication of the Southern National Party, Memphis, TN.

The Southern Review, a publication of the Southern National Party, Jackson, MS.

The Spotlight, a publication of Liberty Lobby, Washington, D.C.

Swift, Dr. Wesley A. *Behold! I Make All Things New*, a sermon.

The Thunderbolt, a publication of National States Rights Party, Marietta, GA.

Truth at Last, published by Dr. Ed Fields, Marietta, GA.

The Way, a publication of Aryan Nations, Hayden Lake, ID.

The Watchdog, published in Slidell, LA.

The White Beret, a publication of the White Knights of the Ku Klux Klan, Catoosa, OK.

White Paper on the ADL: An Official Report, a publication of Liberty Lobby, Washington, D.C.

The White Patriot, a publication of The Knights of the Ku Klux Klan, Harrison, AR.

Why Dixie Must Be Free!, a publication of the Southern National Party, Memphis, TN.

Winrod, Gordon. *Vindication*, Our Savior's Church, Gainesville, MO.

Woods, John S. *Jews Are of Their Father, the Devil.*

PAPERS AND ARCHIVAL COLLECTIONS

ADL	Research and Evaluation Department, Anti-Defamation League of B'nai B'rith, New York, NY
CAA	Columbia Academy Archives, Columbia, TN
CCA	Colusa County Arcives, Colusa, CA
CDR	Center for Democratic Renewal, Atlanta, GA and Kansas City, MO
CRPB	Civil Rights Project, Blackside, Inc., Boston, MA
DBCP	Dolores Beckwith Carruth Papers, Sacramento, CA
DDDP	Delmar Daniel Dennis Papers, Sevierville, TN
EJMP	Edward J. Moore Papers, San Diego, CA
ETHC	East Tennessee Historical Center, Knoxville, TN
HLSC	Hoskins Library Special Collections, University of Tennessee, Knoxville, TN
HREC	Highlander Research and Education Center Archives, New Market, TN
HRWP	Hazen R. Williams Papers, Lenoir City, TN
JDWL	John Davis Williams Library/Archives and Special Collections, University of Mississippi, University, MS
JEGP	Jack and Emma Galey Papers, Greenwood, MS
JFKL	John F. Kennedy Library, Columbia Point, Boston, MA
JRWP	Jesse R. Williams, Jr., Papers, Knoxville, TN
jtp	Julia Tucker Papers, Knoxville, TN
KCA	Knox County Archives, Knoxville, TN
KCNSC	King Center for Nonviolent Social Change, Atlanta, GA
LCHS	Lake County Historical Society, Mentor, OH
LDS	Family History Department, Church of Jesus Christ of Latter-Day Saints, Salt Lake City, UT
MDAH	Mississippi Department of Archives and History, Jackson, MS
MMFR	McNary-Moore Funeral Service Records, Colusa, CA
MOHP	Mississippi Oral History Program, University of Southern Mississippi, Hattiesburg, MS
MWBP	Martha Williams Bryant Papers, Knoxville, TN
NCCJ	National Conference of Christians and Jews, Inc., Knoxville, TN
NMP	Norman Moise Papers, Houston, TX
RWFP	Ruby Williams Flanigan Papers, Knoxville, TN
SIMPD	Smithsonian Institution/Motion Picture Division, Washington, D.C.
TNBP	Thelma Neff Beckwith Papers, Signal Mountain, TN
TVRP	Tom Van Riper Papers, Oak Ridge, TN
TWSA	The Webb School Archives, Bell Buckle, TN
ZPCL	Zumwalt Papers/Colusa County Free Library, Colusa, CA

THESES

Luce, Phillip Abbott. *The Mississippi White Citizens Council: 1954–1959.* Unpublished M.A. thesis, The Ohio State University, 1960.

Vander Zanden, James Wilfrid. *The Southern White Resistance Movement to Integration.* Unpublished Ph.D. thesis, The University of North Carolina, 1958.

INTERVIEWS

Abrahamsen, David. Massengill, 6/30/93, New York, NY

Barnett, Ross R. Neil McMillen, 5/8/71, Vol. 26, MOHP

Barnett, Ross R. John Dittmer and John Jones, 2/11/81, OH82-01, MDAH

Barnett, Ross R. Kenneth McCarty, 8/2/82, Vol. 26, MOHP

Beckwith, Byron De La. Thomas Atwine, 7/67, Jackson, MS

Beckwith, Byron De La. Paula C. Wade, 11/3/89, Signal Mountain, TN

Beckwith, Byron De La. Massengill, 1/30/91, Hamilton County Jail, Chattanooga, TN

Beckwith, Thelma. Massengill, 1/21/91, Signal Mountain, TN

Beckwith, Thelma. Massengill, 2/8/91, Signal Mountain, TN

Beckwith, Thelma. Massengill, 5/24/91, Signal Mountain, TN

Beckwith, Thelma. Massengill, 6/10/91, Signal Mountain, TN
Beckwith, Thelma. Don Williams, 1/5/93, Signal Mountain, TN
Carruth, Dolores Beckwith. Massengill, 10/13/92, Sacramento, CA
Carter, Betty W. Orley B. Caudill, 8/17/77, Vol. 150, MOHP
Clegg, Hugh H. Michael Garvey and Orley B. Caudill, 10/1-2/75, Vol. 99, MOHP
Cobb, James C. Massengill, 3/17/92, Knoxville, TN
Coleman, J.P. Orley B. Caudill, 11/12/81, Vol. 203, MOHP
Dahmer, Ellie J. Orley B. Caudill, 7/2/74, Vol. 281, MOHP
DeJong, Raymond L. Massengill, 3/25/92, Alton, IA
Dennis, Delmar. Massengill, 1/29/91, Sevierville, TN
Dennis, Delmar. Massengill, 2/2/91, Sevierville, TN
Dennis, Delmar. Massengill, 5/20/91, Sevierville, TN
Dennis, Delmar. Massengill, 8/28/91, Sevierville, TN
Dennis, Delmar. Massengill, 4/23/92, Sevierville, TN
Doar, John. Blackside, 11/15/85, New York, NY
Ellis, Rod. Massengill, 10/7/92, Columbus, OH
Evers, Charles. Robert Smith, 12/3/71, Vol. 7, MOHP
Evers, Charles. John Jones, 2/10/81, OH81-14, MDAH
Evers, Charles. Eric Norden, *Playboy* 10/71, pp. 77+
Evers, Myrlie. Blackside, 11/27/85, Los Angeles, CA
Galey, Emma Day. Massengill, 2/28/92, Greenwood, MS
Galey, Jack. Massengill, 2/28/92, Greenwood, MS
Gray, Duncan M. Jr. Massengill, 5/9/92, Jackson, MS
Hauberg, Robert E. John Jones, 10/12/79, OH80-05, MDAH
Henry, Aaron. Neil McMillen and George Burson, 5/1/72, Vol. 33, MOHP
Herbers, John. Massengill, 12/12/91, Bethesda, MD
Horne, Lena. Massengill, 2/20/91, New York, NY
Johnson, Eloise Duggins. Massengill, 3/16/92, Franklin, TN
Johnston, Erle. Orley B. Caudill, 7/16 and 30/80, Vol. 276, MOHP
Jones, Ervin B. Massengill, 3/18/92, Okmulgee, OK
Jones, Maureen. Massengill, 1/9/92, Knoxville, TN
Jones, Willard. Massengill, 1/9/92, Knoxville, TN
Joseph, Tom R. Massengill, 1/14/93, Angie, LA
Lackey, Gordon. Adam Nossiter, 12/14/92, Greenwood, MS
Lunde, Donald T. Massengill, 2/28/92, Palo Alto, CA
Lunde, Donald T. Massengill, 3/6/92, Palo Alto, CA
Mackey, Pauline L. Massengill, 1/6/92, Washington, D.C.
Martinez, Tom. Massengill, 12/31/91, Undisclosed Location
Martinez, Tom. Massengill, 1/26/93, Undisclosed Location
Meredith, James. Neil McMillen, 12/19/72, Vol. 280, MOHP
Moise, Norman. Massengill, 6/15/92, Houston, TX
Moore, Edward J. Massengill, 5/28/92, San Diego, CA
Peebles, James ("Mac"). Massengill, 3/11/92, Columbia, TN
Pence, Walter. Massengill, 1/13/93, Bogalusa, LA
Powell, Otis. Massengill, 1/4/93, Undisclosed Location
Pruitt, Charles. Massengill, 2/5/93, Millington, TN
Simmons, William J. Orley B. Caudill, 6/26/79, Vol. 372, MOHP
Smith, Frank E. Massengill, 1/10/92, Jackson, MS
Stoner, J.B. David Garrow, 9/7/79, Marietta, GA
Tucker, Julia. Massengill, 6/5/92, Knoxville, TN
Van Riper, Tom. Massengill, 10/17/92, Oak Ridge, TN
Williams, Mary Louise. Massengill, 4/3/88, Knoxville, TN
Williams, Mary Louise. Massengill, 8/24/89, Knoxville, TN
Williams, Mary Louise. Massengill, 9/2/89, Knoxville, TN
Williams, Mary Louise. Massengill, 8/18/90, Knoxville, TN
Williams, Mary Louise. Massengill, 1/26/91, Knoxville, TN
Williams, Mary Louise. Massengill, 1/28/91, Johnson City, TN
Williams, Mary Louise. Massengill, 1/2/92, Knoxville, TN
Williams, Mary Louise. Massengill, 3/11/92, Knoxville, TN
Williams, Mary Louise. Massengill, 7/7/92, Knoxville, TN
Zeskind, Leonard. Massengill, 5/30/91, Kansas City, MO

GOVERNMENT PUBLICATIONS AND DOCUMENTS

Department of Commerce and Labor, Bureau of the Census. *Twelfth Census of the United States: 1900-Population.* Colusa Township, Colusa County, California.

Department of Commerce and Labor, Bureau of the Census. *Thirteenth Census of the United States: 1910-Population.* Colusa Township, Colusa County, California.

Department of Commerce and Labor, Bureau of the Census. *Fourteenth Census of the United States: 1920-Population.* Colusa Township, Colusa County, California.

Congressional Record—Senate, June 29, 1945.

U.S. Department of Justice, Federal Bureau of Investigation File 157-901, "Byron De La Beckwith, Medgar Evers-Victim, CR; RM."

U.S. Department of Justice, Federal Bureau of Investigation File 157-31489, "Byron De La Beckwith, Destruction of Public Notice, Federal Examiners Office, Leflore County, Mississippi."

U.S. Department of Justice, Federal Bureau of Investigation File 157-3744, "Byron De La Beckwith, aka 'Delay,' 'Dela.' "

Voting in Mississippi. A Report of the United States Commission on Civil Rights, 1965.

Activities of Ku Klux Klan Organizations in the United States (Parts 1–5). Hearings Before the Committee on Un-American Activities, House of Representatives, Eighty-Ninth Congress, Second Session. U.S. Government Printing Office, 1966.

The Present-Day Ku Klux Klan Movement. Report by the Committee on Un-American Activities, House of Representatives, Ninetieth Congress, First Session. U.S. Government Printing Office, 1967.

COURT CASES

Byron D. Beckwith, Plantiff, v. *Willard M. Sheldon, et al., Defendants,* Lis Pendens, Superior Court, Colusa County, California, February 4, 1904.

In the Matter of the Estate of Byron D. Beckwith, Superior Court, Colusa County, California, Probate File No. 1130, 1904.

B. De La Beckwith, Administrator, etc. of Byron D. Beckwith, Deceased, Appellant, v. *Willard M. Sheldon et al., Respondents,* Supreme Court of California in Bank, October 13, 1908.

Beckwith v. *Sheldon et al.,* Superior Court of California, Opinion of Court on Motion to Strike Out, Case No. 2857, March 6, 1909.

Beckwith v. *Sheldon et al.,* Supreme Court of California, April 16, 1913.

Beckwith v. *Sheldon et al.,* Supreme Court of California, December 10, 1914.

Byron D. Beckwith v. *Henry William Von Dorsten, et. al.,* Superior Court, Colusa County, California, December 31, 1919.

Jesse G. Boydstun, Receiver of the First National Bank of Colusa v. *Byron D. Beckwith,* Superior Court, Colusa County, California, November 16, 1923.

Byron De La Beckwith, also known as B.D. Beckwith v. *The Reclamation Board of the State of California, et al.,* Superior Court, Colusa County, California, January 24, 1925.

B. De La Beckwith, Administrator of the Estate of Byron D. Beckwith, Deceased, v. *Willard M. Sheldon et al.,* Supreme Court of California, July 16, 1925.

Sacramento & San Joaquin Drainage Dist. v. *Superior Court in and for the County of Colusa, Ernest Weyand, Judge Thereof, Percy King, Judge Presiding Therein and Byron De La Beckwith,* Supreme Court of California, July 16, 1925.

Thomas Rutledge, as the Executor of the Last Will of Sallie Morgan Green, Deceased v. *Byron D. Beckwith,* Superior Court, Colusa County, California, July 17, 1926.

Byron D. Beckwith v. *A.H. Quatman, et al.,* Superior Court, Colusa County, California, October 6, 1926.

In the Matter of the Estate of Byron D. Beckwith, Superior Court, Colusa County, California, Probate File No. 2038, 1926.

F.S. Jones v. Edward C. Barrell, Jr., and H.C. Stovall, Executors of the Last Will and Testament of Byron D. Beckwith, Deceased; Susie Y. Beckwith; et. al., Superior Court, Colusa County, California, October 16, 1928.

Mary Louise Long v. *Hugh Long,* Court of Juvenile and Domestic Relations of Knox County, Tennessee, October 31, 1940.

Mary Louise Williams Duck v. *Henry Milton Duck, et. al.*, Court of Juvenile and Domestic Relations of Knox County, Tennessee, September 2, 1943.

Mrs. Mary Louise Williams Beckwith v. *Byron De La Beckwith*, Chancery Court of Leflore County, Mississippi, Complainant Nos. 12,795 and 12,882, filed June 23, 1960. Decree rendered October 11, 1960, Minute Book 44, p. 181.

Mrs. Mary Louise Williams Beckwith v. *Byron De La Beckwith*, Chancery Court of Leflore County, Mississippi, Complainant No. 13,565, filed September 31, 1962. Decree rendered October 9, 1962, Minute Book 49, p. 127.

In the Matter of the Guardianship of Byron De La Beckwith, Jr., a Minor, by Mrs. Mary Louise Williams Beckwith, Guardian, Chancery Court of Leflore County, Mississippi, No. 13,531, filed October 9, 1962.

Jaquith v. *Beckwith*, No. 42,939, Supreme Court of Mississippi, November 12, 1963.

State of Mississippi v. *Byron De La Beckwith*, Circuit Court of the First Judicial District of Hinds County, Mississippi, No. 17,824, January 31, 1964.

Byron De La Beckwith v. *Mary Louise Williams Beckwith*, Chancery Court of Leflore County, Mississippi, Complainant No. 14,710, filed August 20, 1965. Decree rendered September 21, 1965, Minute Book 56, p. 549.

Ex Parte Mrs. Mary Louise Williams Beckwith, Decree Changing Name, Chancery Court of Leflore County, Mississippi, February 18, 1966, Minute Book 57, p. 456.

In the Matter of the Guardianship of Byron De La Beckwith, Jr., A Minor, Chancery Court of Leflore County, Mississippi, September 12, 1967.

United States of America v. *Byron De La Beckwith*, United States District Court for the Eastern District of Louisiana, Magistrate's Docket 73M, Case No. 320, September 27, 1973.

State of Louisiana v. *Byron De La Beckwith*, Criminal District Court, Parish of Orleans, Section A, Case 238-459, April 22, 1974.

State of Louisiana v. *Byron De La Beckwith*, Criminal District Court, Parish of Orleans, Section A, Case 238-459, November 15, 1974.

State of Louisiana v. *Byron De La Beckwith*, Criminal District Court, Parish of Orleans, Section A, Case 238-459, December 6, 1974.

State of Louisiana v. *Byron De La Beckwith and James McGhee, Jr.*, No. 55,816, Supreme Court of Louisiana, January 23, 1975.

State of Louisiana v. *Byron De La Beckwith*, Criminal District Court, Parish of Orleans, Section A, Case 238-459, April 21, 1975.

State of Louisiana v. *Byron De La Beckwith*, Criminal District Court, Parish of Orleans, Section A, Case 238-459, May 15–16, 1975.

State of Louisiana v. *Byron De La Beckwith*, Criminal District Court, Parish of Orleans, Section A, Case 238-459, August 1, 1975.

State of Louisiana v. *Byron De La Beckwith*, No. 58,586, Supreme Court of Louisiana, February 28, 1977. (Rehearing denied April 22, 1977.)

State of Tennessee ex rel Byron De La Beckwith v. *H.Q. Evatt, Sheriff*, Criminal Court of Hamilton County, Tennessee, Division II, No. 185562, January 14, 1991.

State of Tennessee ex rel Byron De La Beckwith, Appellee, v. *H.Q. Evatt, Sheriff, Appellant*, Court of Criminal Appeals of Tennessee at Knoxville, No. 03c01-9104-CR-00043 Hamilton County, May 17, 1991.

State of Mississippi v. *Byron De La Beckwith*, No. 90-3-495 [CR] [C], Circuit Court of the First Judicial District of Hinds County, Mississippi, November 12, 1991.

Byron De La Beckwith v. *State of Mississippi*, No. 91-IA-1207, Supreme Court of Mississippi, December 16, 1992.

Index

Zeskind, Leonard, 305